PENGUIN BOOKS

THE PENGUIN HISTORY OF MODERN RUSSIA

Robert Service is Professor of Russian History at Oxford University and a Fellow of St Antony's College. His other books include *Lenin: A Biography* and a textbook on the Russian Revolution as well as *Russia: Experiment with a People*, *From 1991 to the Present*. He has also published *Stalin: A Biography* and *Comrades: A World History of Communism*. He writes and broadcasts frequently on Russia and is a Fellow of the British Academy.

ROBERT SERVICE

The Penguin History of Modern Russia

FROM TSARISM TO THE TWENTY-FIRST CENTURY

THIRD EDITION

PENGUIN BOOKS

To Adele, with love

PENGUIN BOOKS

Published by the Penguin Group
Penguin Books Ltd, 80 Strand, London WC2R 0RL, England
Penguin Group (USA) Inc., 375 Hudson Street, New York, New York 10014, USA
Penguin Group (Canada), 90 Eglinton Avenue East, Suite 700, Toronto, Ontario, Canada M4P 2Y3
(a division of Pearson Penguin Canada Inc.)
Penguin Ireland, 25 St Stephen's Green, Dublin 2, Ireland (a division of Penguin Books Ltd)
Penguin Group (Australia), 250 Camberwell Road,
Camberwell, Victoria 3124, Australia (a division of Pearson Australia Group Pty Ltd)
Penguin Books India Pvt Ltd, 11 Community Centre,
Panchsheel Park, New Delhi – 110 017, India
Penguin Group (NZ), 67 Apollo Drive, Rosedale, North Shore 0632, New Zealand
(a division of Pearson New Zealand Ltd)
Penguin Books (South Africa) (Pty) Ltd, 24 Sturdee Avenue,
Rosebank, Johannesburg 2196, South Africa

Penguin Books Ltd, Registered Offices: 80 Strand, London WC2R 0RL, England

www.penguin.com

First published by Allen Lane 1997
Published in Penguin Books as *A History of Twentieth-Century Russia* 1998
Second edition published as *A History of Modern Russia*, with revisions 2003
Third edition published under the current title with further revisions 2009
3

Maps by Nigel Andrews

The moral right of the author has been asserted

Printed in England by Clays Ltd, St Ives plc

978-0-141-03797-4

www.greenpenguin.co.uk

Contents

PART ONE

PART TWO

PART THREE

PART FOUR

Acknowledgements

These are unusual times to be studying Russia even by Russian standards. Archives have been opened and contacts with Russian writers are no longer difficult. Important documentary collections have been published. The need exists for the newer items of information to be incorporated in a general description and analysis.

In picking up this task, I have been very fortunate to have assistance from the following scholars who read preliminary drafts: Francesco Benvenuti, Archie Brown, Bob Davies, Peter Duncan, Israel Getzler, Geoffrey Hosking, László Péter, Silvio Pons, Martyn Rady, Arfon Rees and Karen Schönwälder. Their comments have led to a very large number of improvements, and each of them kindly helped further by replying to my follow-up queries. Also to be thanked are members of the press study group at SSEES and others in London who have alerted me to interesting materials in Russian newspapers and journals: John Channon, Norman Davies, Peter Duncan, Julian Graffy, Jane Henderson, Geoffrey Hosking, Lindsey Hughes, John Klier, Maria Lenn, John Morrison, Rudolf Muhs, Judith Shapiro and Faith Wigzell.

Nor should I omit to acknowledge the value of discussions over several years with the historians Gennadi Bordyugov, Vladimir Buldakov, Oleg Khlevnyuk, Vladimir Kozlov and Andrei Sakharov. Quite apart from their professional expertise, each of them have shared insights and intuitions about Russian history foreclosed to any foreigner.

While writing some of the chapters, I had access to the Russian Centre for the Conservation and Study of Documents of Recent History (RTsKhIDNI), to the State Archive of the Russian Federation

(GARF) and to the Special Archive (OA). In the first two of these three archives I found useful materials in conditions that reflected the recent political changes which have occurred in Russia, and I shall always remember the occasion in September 1991 when Bob Davies and I walked into the Russian Centre for the Conservation and Study of Documents of Recent History as it was being 'unsealed' after the abortive August 1991 coup. Equally, I shall not quickly forget the experience shared two years later with Rudolf Muhs in the Special Archive, an institution which gave us material to read in the morning whose existence it denied in the afternoon. But in general the libraries and archives in Moscow have been as helpful as the SSEES Library in London – and this is saying a lot because John Screen, Lesley Pitman and Ursula Phillips could not have done more to facilitate the research on the book.

My greatest debt is to my wife Adele Biagi, who examined the early drafts and nudged me away from the temptation to take too particularist a viewpoint on Russia. It has also been a pleasure to talk about Russian history with our daughters and sons – Emma, Owain, Hugo and Francesca – as they have been growing up. They read some of the chapters, and their suggestions led to several useful revisions. Russia is a source of changing but perennial fascination – and it is a fascination which I hope this book will do its bit to spread.

January 1997

It is five years since this book appeared and much has changed in Russian politics, economy and society. The second edition takes the account into the twenty-first century. Most chapters have undergone minor revision and some recent works have been added to the bibliography. Chapter 27 has been entirely re-written. The Introduction has been overhauled to sharpen the focus on historiographical debate – and here I was helped by comments from Adele Biagi, Archie Brown, Bob Davies, Richard Evans and David Priestland. The main lines of argument in the first edition have been repaired but not replaced.

November 2002

The events of the past few years have shaken the kaleidoscope of Russian affairs. In bringing the story and the analysis up to date I have kept the book's basic line of analysis and have been fortunate in being able to talk this over with Archie Brown, Paul Chaisty and Alex Pravda in the Russian and Eurasian Studies Centre at St Antony's College in Oxford, with Katya Andreyev at Christ Church, Oxford, with Nick Stargardt at Magdalen College, Oxford and with Robert Conquest, Paul Gregory, Amir Weiner, Norman Naimark and Yuri Slezkine while I was working on research projects at the Hoover Institution in Stanford University. I am indebted to the detailed advice given by Archie Brown about the introduction and by Paul Chaisty and Hugo Service about the chapters on the past two decades. Above all, my wife Adele Biagi has given inestimable assistance by going through the entire book yet again and suggesting ways of improving on the previous edition: I am grateful to her for her patience and insight.

Robert Service
February 2009

A Note on Transliteration

The transliterations in this book are a simplified version of the system used by the US Library of Congress. The first difference consists in the dropping of both the diacritical mark and the so-called soft *i*. Thus whereas the Library of Congress system has *Sokol'nikov* and *Krestinskii*, this book has *Sokolnikov* and *Krestinski*. Secondly, the *yo* sound which appears in words such as *Gorbachyov* is given as an *ë*, as in *Gorbachëv*. Thirdly, the *yeh* sound is rendered as *ye* when it occurs at the beginning of proper nouns such as *Yeltsin*.

These differences are intended to make the text less exotic in appearance. By and large, I have kept to the Russian version of proper names. But some look so odd in English that I have Anglicized them: thus *Alexander* rather than *Aleksandr*. Finally there are several non-Russian names in the text. In the case of Polish, Hungarian and Czech leaders, for example, their names are given in their native version; and the names of Ukrainian leaders are transliterated without the simplification used for Russians. This is inconsistent, but it helps to give a sense of the variety of countries involved in Russian history. A further inconsistency lies in my use of Russian-language names for most places in the USSR: thus Kharkov, not Kharkiv. Until all of us become more accustomed to place-names according to their post-Soviet official nomenclature this seems a decent workable compromise.

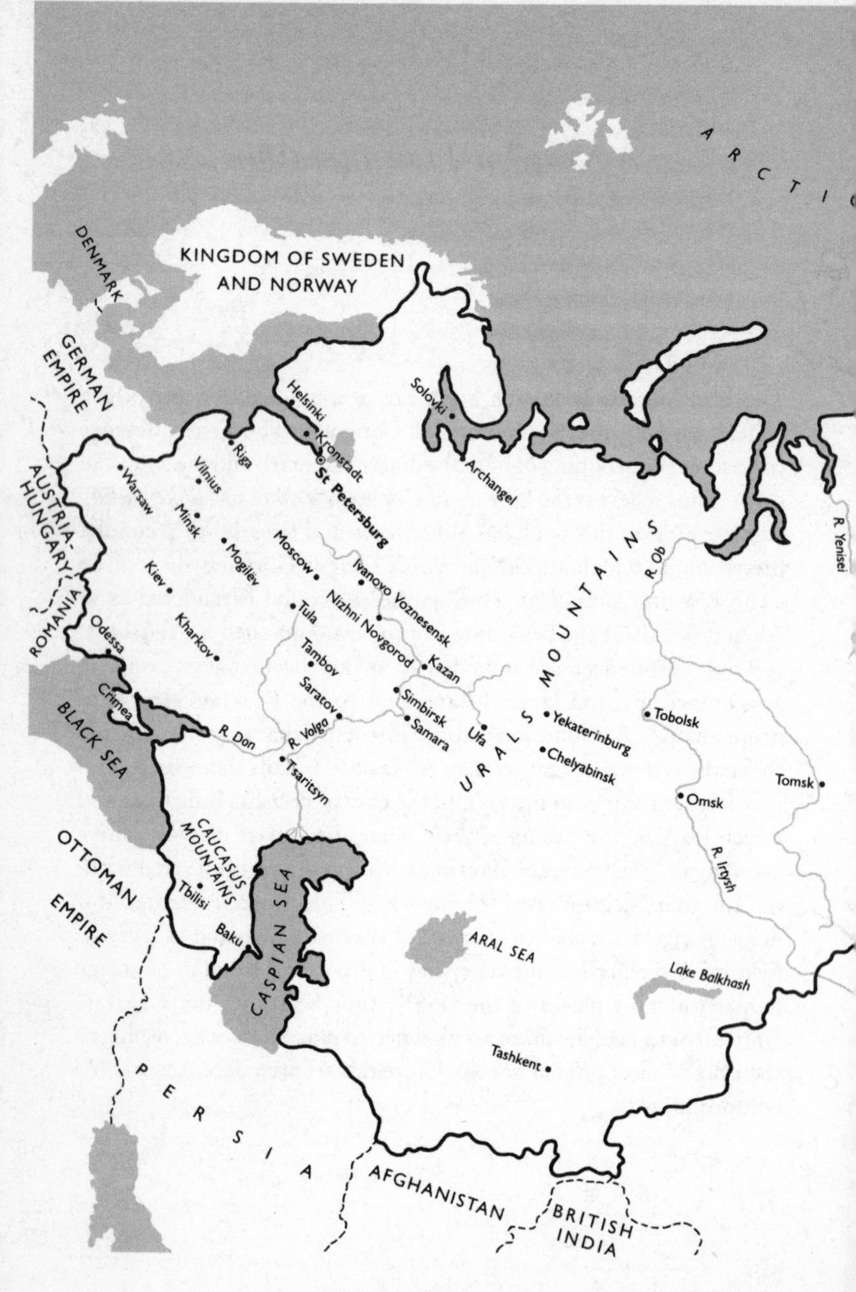
ARCTIC
KINGDOM OF SWEDEN AND NORWAY
DENMARK
GERMAN EMPIRE
AUSTRIA-HUNGARY
ROMANIA
Helsinki
Kronstadt
St Petersburg
Riga
Vilnius
Warsaw
Minsk
Mogilev
Kiev
Kharkov
Odessa
Crimea
BLACK SEA
Moscow
Ivanovo Voznesensk
Nizhni Novgorod
Tula
Tambov
Saratov
Kazan
Simbirsk
Samara
Ufa
R. Don
R. Volga
Tsaritsyn
Solovki
Archangel
URALS MOUNTAINS
Yekaterinburg
Chelyabinsk
R. Ob
R. Yenisei
Tobolsk
Omsk
Tomsk
R. Irtysh
CAUCASUS MOUNTAINS
Tbilisi
Baku
CASPIAN SEA
ARAL SEA
Lake Balkhash
Tashkent
OTTOMAN EMPIRE
PERSIA
AFGHANISTAN
BRITISH INDIA

1 *The Russian Empire in 1900*

ARCTIC
NORWAY
Oslo
SWEDEN
DENMARK
GERMANY
Stockholm
FINLAND
Helsinki
Tallinn
ESTONIA
LATVIA
Riga
LITHUANIA
Kaunas
CZECHOSLOVAKIA
Warsaw
POLAND
Minsk
BELORUSSIAN SSR
Kronstadt
Leningrad (Petrograd)
Solovki
Archangel
Vorkuta
RUSSIAN SOVIET FEDERAL
Moscow
Smolensk
ROMANIA
Kiev
UKRAINIAN SSR
Kharkov
Dnepropetrovsk
Orël
Kursk
Tula
Ryazan
Ivanovo Voznesensk
Nizhni Novgorod
Kazan
Molotov (Perm)
Magnitogorsk
Chelyabinsk
Sverdlovsk (Yekaterinburg)
Ufa
Ulyanovsk (Simbirsk)
Kuibyshev (Samara)
Orenburg
Saratov
Odessa
Shakhty
BLACK SEA
Rostov
Crimea (RSFSR)
Astrakhan
Stalingrad (Tsaritsyn)
Grozny
TURKEY
Tbilisi
Yerevan
Nakhichevan (Azerbaijan)
Nagorny Karabakh
Baku
CASPIAN SEA
KAZAKH SOVIET SOCIALIST REPUBLIC
(Until 1936: Kazakh ASSR of RSFSR)
ARAL SEA
UZBEK SSR
TURKMEN SSR
Lake Balkhash
Alma Ata
Tashkent
KIRGIZ SSR
TADJIK SSR
Omsk
Tomsk
Novosibirsk
AFGHANISTAN
BRITISH INDIA
IRAN
1. GEORGIAN SSR
2. ARMENIAN SSR
3. AZERBAIJAN SSR
(Until 1936: Georgia, Armenia and Azerbaijan formed the Transcaucasian Socialist Federal Soviet Republic)
TADJIK SSR
(Until 1929: part of Uzbek SSR)
KIRGIZ SSR
(Until 1936: part of RSFSR)

2 *The Soviet Union, 1924–1936*

3 *The Soviet Union and Eastern Europe after 1945*

ARCTIC
NORWAY
SWEDEN
DENMARK
FEDERAL REPUBLIC OF GERMANY
Kaliningrad Province (RSFSR)
FINLAND
ESTONIA
LATVIA
LITHUANIA
POLAND
BELARUS
SLOVAKIA
HUNGARY
ROMANIA
MOLDOVA
UKRAINE
RUSSIAN
BLACK SEA
TURKEY
1
2
3
Nakhichevan
Nagorny Karabakh
1. GEORGIA
2. ARMENIA
3. AZERBAIJAN
CASPIAN SEA
KAZAKHSTAN
ARAL SEA
Lake Balkhash
UZBEKISTAN
TURKMENISTAN
KYRGYSTAN
TAJIKESTAN
PEOPLE'S
IRAN
AFGHANISTAN
PAKISTAN

4 *The Commonwealth of Independent States in 1997*

ARCTI
Murmansk
KARELIYA
Petrozavodsk
Archangel
St Petersburg
Kaliningrad
Province
(RSFSR)
KOMI
Yaroslavl
Nizhni Novgorod
Moscow
Voronezh
Perm
Kazan
Saratov
Samara
Chelyabinsk
Ufa
Yekaterinburg
BLACK SEA
Rostov
Volgograd
Orenburg
Stavropol
Krasnodar
Astrakhan
Omsk
Novosibirsk
Kemerovo
Grozny
CASPIAN SEA
ARAL SEA
Lake Balkhash
1. DAGESTAN
2. CHECHNYA
3. INGUSHETIYA
4. NORTH OSETIYA
5. KABARDINO-BALKARIYA
6. KALMYKIYA
7. MORDOVIYA
8. CHUVASHIYA
9. MARII EL
10. TATARSTAN
11. UDMURTIYA
12. BASHKORTOSTAN

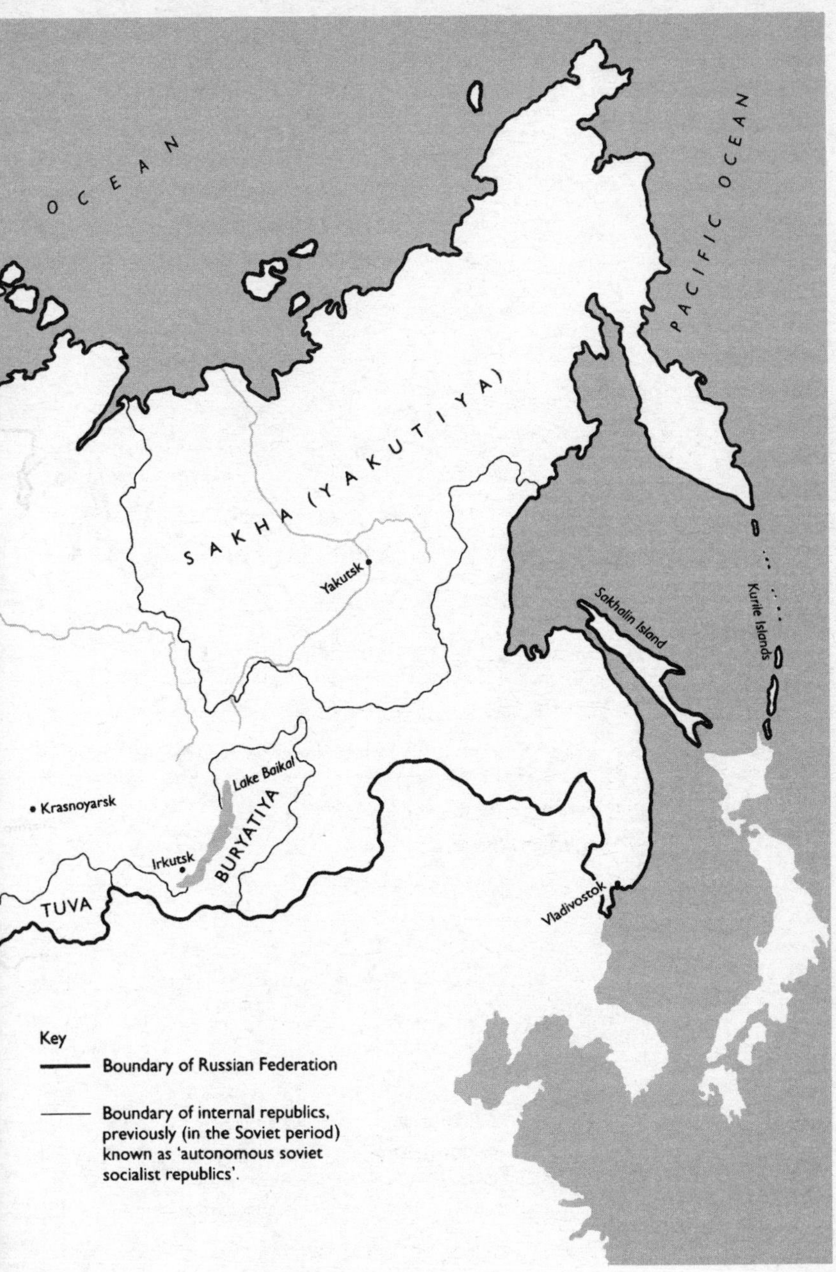
OCEAN
PACIFIC OCEAN
SAKHA (YAKUTIYA)
Yakutsk
Sakhalin Island
Kurile Islands
Lake Baikal
Krasnoyarsk
BURYATIYA
Irkutsk
TUVA
Vladivostok
Key
Boundary of Russian Federation
Boundary of internal republics, previously (in the Soviet period) known as 'autonomous soviet socialist republics'.

5 The Russian Federation 1997

Introduction

The centrepiece of this history of contemporary Russia is the period of communist government. The weight of the Soviet years continues to lie heavily on the country. Before 1917 the Russian Empire was ruled by the tsars of the Romanov dynasty. Nicholas II was overthrown in the February Revolution, and the ensuing Provisional Government of liberals and socialists lasted merely a few months. Vladimir Lenin and his communist party organized the October Revolution in 1917 and established the world's first communist state, which survived until the USSR's abolition at the end of 1991. A new compound of politics, society, economics and culture prevailed in the intervening years. The USSR was a highly centralized, one-party dictatorship. It enforced a single official ideology; it imposed severe restrictions on national, religious and cultural self-expression. Its economy was predominantly state-owned. This Soviet compound served as model for the many communist states created elsewhere.

The phases of the recent Russian past have passed with breathtaking rapidity. After the October Revolution a Civil War broke out across Russia and its former empire. Having won the military struggle, the communists themselves came close to being overthrown by popular rebellions. Lenin introduced a New Economic Policy in 1921 which made temporary concessions, especially to the peasantry; but at the end of the same decade Iosif Stalin, who was emerging as the leading party figure after Lenin's death in 1924, hurled the country into a campaign for forced-rate industrialization and forcible agricultural collectivization. The Great Terror followed in the late 1930s. Then came the Second World War. After Germany's defeat in 1945, Stalin brought Eastern Europe under Soviet dominion and undertook post-war reconstruction with his own brutal methods. Only after his death in 1953 could the party leadership under Nikita Khrushchëv begin to reform the Soviet order. But Khrushchëv's rule produced such political instability and resentment that in 1964 he was ousted by his colleagues.

His successor Leonid Brezhnev presided over a phase, and a lengthy phase at that, of uneasy stabilization. When he died in 1982, the struggle over the desirability of reform was resumed. Mikhail Gorbachëv became communist party leader in 1985 and introduced radical reforms of policies and institutions. A drastic transformation resulted. In 1989, after Gorbachëv had indicated that he would not use his armed forces to maintain Soviet political control in Eastern Europe, the communist regimes there fell in quick succession. Russia's 'outer empire' crumbled. At home, too, Gorbachëv's measures undermined the status quo. Most of his central party and governmental associates were disconcerted by his reforms. In August 1991 some of them made a bungled attempt to stop the process through a *coup d'état*. Gorbachëv returned briefly to power, but was constrained to abandon his own Soviet communist party and accept the dissolution of the USSR.

Russia and other Soviet republics gained their independence at the start of 1992, and Boris Yeltsin as Russian president proclaimed the de-communization of political and economic life as his strategic aim. Several fundamental difficulties endured. The economy's decline sharply accelerated. The manufacturing sector collapsed. Social and administrative dislocation became acute. Criminality became an epidemic. In October 1993, when Yeltsin faced stalemate in his contest with leading opponents, he ordered the storming of the Russian White House and their arrest. Although he introduced a fresh constitution in December, strong challenges to his policies of reform remained. Communism had not been just an ideology, a party and a state; it had been consolidated as an entire social order, and the attitudes, techniques and objective interests within society were resistant to rapid dissolution. The path towards democracy and the market economy was strewn with obstacles. Yeltsin's successors

Vladimir Putin and Dmitri Medvedev busied themselves with orderly central power at the expense of the constitution and legality. They also cultivated respect for Soviet achievements, calling for an end to denigration of the USSR. Political and business elites benefited hugely from the profits made in energy exports. The Kremlin's ruling group ruthlessly eliminated opposition. Authoritarian rule was re-imposed.

This turbulent history led to differing interpretations. Journalists and former diplomats published the initial accounts. Some were vehemently anti-Soviet, others were equally passionate on the other side of the debate – and still others avoided taking political sides and concentrated on depicting the bizarre aspects of life in the USSR. Few foreigners produced works of sophisticated analysis before the Second World War. It was Russian refugees and deportees who provided the works of lasting value. The Western focus on Soviet affairs was sharpened after 1945 when the USSR emerged as a world power. Research institutes were created in the USA, Western Europe and Japan; books and articles appeared in a publishing torrent. Debate was always lively, often polemical. Such discussions were severely curtailed for decades in Moscow by a regime seeking to impose doctrinal uniformity; but from the late 1980s Soviet writers too were permitted to publish the results of their thinking.

Official communist propagandists from 1917 through to the mid-1980s claimed there was nothing seriously wrong with the Soviet Union and that a perfectly functioning socialist order was within attainable range.[1] Such boasts were challenged from the start. Otto Bauer, an Austrian Marxist, regarded the USSR as a barbarous state. He accepted, though, that the Bolsheviks had produced as much socialism as was possible in so backward a country.[2] Yuli Martov, Karl Kautsky, Bertrand Russell and Fëdor Dan retorted that Leninism, being based on dictatorship and bureaucracy, was a fundamental distortion of any worthwhile version of socialism.[3] By the end of the 1920s Lev Trotski was making similar points about bureaucratic degeneration, albeit with the proviso that it was Stalin's misapplication of Leninism rather than Leninism itself that was the crucible for the distorting process.[4] Other writers, especially Ivan

Ilin and, in later decades, Alexander Solzhenitsyn, denounced Leninism as an import entirely alien to traditional Russian virtues and customs.[5] This school of thought was challenged by the religious philosopher and socialist Nikolai Berdyaev who depicted the USSR as a reincarnation of Russian intellectual extremism. Berdyaev argued that the regime of Lenin and Stalin had reinforced the traditions of political repression, ideological intolerance and a passive, resentful society.[6]

René Fülöp-Miller's rejoinder was that all this underestimated the cultural effervescence after the October Revolution.[7] But Nikolai Trubetskoi, who fled Russia after the communist seizure of power, offered yet another interpretation. He stressed that Russian history had always followed a path which was neither 'European' nor 'Asian' but a mixture of the two. From such ideas came the so-called Eurasianist school of thought. Trubetskoi and his fellow thinkers regarded a strong ruler and a centralized administrative order as vital to the country's well-being. They suggested that several basic features of Soviet life – the clan-like groups in politics, the pitiless suppression of opposition and the culture of unthinking obedience – were simply a continuation of ages-old tradition.[8] Nikolai Ustryalov, a conservative émigré, concurred that the communists were not as revolutionary as they seemed, and he celebrated Lenin's re-establishment of a unitary state in the former Russian Empire. He and fellow analysts at the 'Change of Landmarks' journal insisted that communism in power was not merely traditionalism with a new red neckscarf. Ustryalov regarded the communists as essentially the economic modernizers needed by society. He predicted that the interests of Russia as a great power would mean steadily more to them than the tenets of their Marxism.[9]

After the Second World War the Eurasianism of Trubetskoi underwent further development by Lev Gumilëv, who praised the Mongol contribution to Russian political and cultural achievements.[10] E. H. Carr and Barrington Moore in the 1950s steered clear of any such idea and instead resumed and strengthened Ustryalov's stress on state-building. They depicted Lenin and Stalin first and foremost as authoritarian modernizers. While not expressly condoning state terror, Carr and Moore treated communist rule as the sole effective modality for Russia to compete with the economy and culture of the West.[11]

This strand of interpretation appeared downright insipid to Franz Neumann, who in the late 1930s categorized the USSR as a 'totalitarian' order. Merle Fainsod and Leonard Schapiro picked up this concept after the Second World War.[12] They suggested that the USSR and Nazi Germany had invented a form of state order wherein all power was exercised at the political centre and the governing group monopolized control over the means of coercion and public communication and intervened deeply in the economy. Such an order retained a willingness to use force against its citizens as a normal method of rule. Writers of this persuasion contended that the outcome was the total subjection of the entire society to the demands of the supreme ruling group. Individual citizens were completely defenceless. The ruling group, accordingly, had made itself invulnerable to reactions in the broader state and society. In Stalin's USSR and Hitler's Germany such a group was dominated by its dictator. But the system could be totalitarian even if a single dictator was lacking. Fainsod and Schapiro insisted that the main aspects of the Soviet order remained intact after Stalin's death in 1953.

Viewing things from a somewhat different angle, the Yugoslav former communist Milovan Djilas suggested that a new class had come into existence with its own interests and authority. Accordingly the USSR, far from moving towards a classless condition, had administrative elites capable of passing on their privileges from generation to generation.[13] While not repudiating Djilas's analysis, Daniel Bell argued that trends in contemporary industrial society were already pushing the Soviet leadership into slackening its authoritarianism – and Bell noted that Western capitalist societies were adopting many measures of state economic regulation and welfare provision favoured in the USSR. In this fashion, it was said, a convergence of Soviet and Western types of society was occurring.[14]

There was a grain of validity in the official Soviet claim that advances were made in popular welfare, even though several of them failed to take place until many decades after 1917. Yet Martov and others possessed greater weight through their counter-claim that Lenin distorted socialist ideas and introduced policies that ruined the lives of millions of people; and, as Solzhenitsyn later emphasized, many features of Soviet ideology originated outside Russia. Berdyaev for his part was convincing in his suggestion that the USSR reproduced pre-revolutionary ideological and social traditions. Trubetskoi was justified in pointing to the impact of Russia's long encounter with Asia. So, too, was Ustryalov in asserting that the policies of communist leaders were increasingly motivated by considerations of the interests of the USSR as a Great Power. As Carr and Moore insisted, these leaders were also authoritarian modernizers. There was plausibility, too, in Djilas's case that the Soviet administrative élites were turning into a distinct social class in the USSR; and Bell's point was persuasive that modern industrial society was producing social and economic pressures which could not entirely be dispelled by the Kremlin leadership. And Fainsod and Schapiro were overwhelmingly right to underline the unprecedented oppressiveness of the Soviet order in its struggle for complete control of state and society.

This book incorporates the chief insights from the diverse interpretations; but one interpretation – the totalitarianist one – seems to me to take the measure of the USSR better than the others. There are difficulties with totalitarianism as an analytical model. A comparison of Stalin's USSR and Hitler's Germany reveals differences as well as similarities. In Nazi Germany many traditions of a civil society survived. The economy remained largely a capitalist one and state ownership was never dominant. The churches continued to function; priests were arrested only if they criticized Nazism. Private associations and clubs were allowed to survive so long as they offered no direct challenge to Hitler's government. The contrast with the Soviet Union was that Hitler could count on support or at least acquiescence from most of Germany's inhabitants, whereas Stalin had reason to distrust a dangerously large number of those over whom he ruled. State terror was a dominant presence in both the USSR and the Third Reich. But whereas most German families lived lives undisrupted by Nazism in many ways until the middle of the

Second World War, Russians and other peoples of the Soviet Union were subjected to an attack on their values and aspirations. Hitler was a totalitarianist and so was Stalin. One had a much harder job than the other in regimenting his citizens.

The USSR for most years of its existence contained few features of a civil society, market economics, open religious observance or private clubs. This was true not only in the 1930s and 1940s but also, to a very large extent, in subsequent decades.[15] The Soviet compound was unrivalled, outside the communist world, in the scope of its practical intrusiveness. The ingredients included a one-party state, dictatorship, administrative hyper-centralism, a state-dominated economy, restricted national self-expression, legal nihilism and a monopolistic ideology. Central power was exercised with sustained callousness. It penetrated and dominated politics, economics, administration and culture; it assaulted religion; it inhibited the expression of nationhood. Such ingredients were stronger in some phases than in others. But even during the 1920s and 1970s, when the compound was at its weakest, communist rulers were deeply intrusive and repressive. What is more, the compound was patented by communism in the USSR and reproduced after the Second World War in Eastern Europe, China and eventually in Cuba and countries in Africa.

Unfortunately most works categorizing the USSR as totalitarian contained gross exaggerations. The concept worked best when applied to politics. Nevertheless the Soviet leadership never totally controlled its own state – and the state never totally controlled society. From the 1970s several writers in Western Europe and the USA complained that current writings were focused on Kremlin politicians and their policies to the neglect of lower administrative levels, of 'the localities' and of broad social groups. 'History from below' was offered as a corrective. This revisionism, as it became known, started up fitfully in the 1950s when David Granick and Joseph Berliner studied the Soviet industrial managers of the post-war period;[16] and it raced forward in the 1970s. Ronald Suny investigated the south Caucasus in 1917–1918.[17] The present author examined local party committees under the early Soviet regime.[18] Diane

Koenker and Steve Smith chronicled workers in the October Revolution.[19] Francesco Benvenuti looked at the political leadership of the Red Army, Orlando Figes looked at peasants in the Civil War and Richard Stites highlighted experimental and utopian trends throughout society.[20] The 1930s, too, were scrutinized. R. W. Davies examined the dilemmas of policy-makers in Stalin's Kremlin; Moshe Lewin pointed to the turbulent conditions which brought chaos to state administration.[21] Francesco Benvenuti, Donald Filtzer and Lewis Siegelbaum researched the industrial labour force before the Second World War.[22] An unknown USSR was hauled into the daylight as the chronic difficulties of governing the USSR were disclosed.

Initially this kind of scholarship existed only in the West; it was rejected in the USSR until radical political reforms began in the late 1980s and enabled Russian historians to join in the discussions.[23] But revisionism's success in shining a lamp on neglected areas of the Soviet past could not disguise its failure to supply a general alternative to the totalitarianist model it cogently criticized. There were anyhow serious divisions within revisionist writing. Sheila Fitzpatrick urged that social factors should take precedence over political ones in historical explanation. She and others attributed little importance to dictatorship and terror and for many years suggested that Stalin's regime rested on strong popular approval.[24] Stephen Kotkin proposed that Stalin built a new civilization and inculcated its new values in Soviet citizens.[25] Such interpretations were contentious. Stephen Cohen, Moshe Lewin and R. W. Davies agreed with Fitzpatrick that Lenin's revolutionary strategy in the last years of his life broke with his violent inclinations in earlier years; but they objected to the gentle treatment of Stalin and his deeds.[26] Objections also continued to be widely made to any downplaying of terror's importance in the building of Stalinism.

A parallel controversy sprang up about what kind of USSR existed in the decades after Stalin's death. Jerry Hough investigated the authority and functions of the provincial party secretaries; and Gordon Skilling and Franklyn Griffiths as well as Hough contended that something like the economic and social interest groups that influenced politics in the West also functioned in the communist countries.[27] Moshe Lewin argued that the Stalinist mode of industrialization proved unable to resist the influence of long-term trends in advanced industrial society. Universal schooling gave people a better understanding of public life and a higher set of personal aspirations.[28] T. H. Rigby maintained that informal organizational links had characterized the Soviet state since its inception and that patronage networks had become strong at every level.[29] The effect of such writings was to counteract the notion that no important change happened – or could happen – without being instigated by the men in the Kremlin. Disputes among the commentators were less about the trends themselves than about their significance. Archie Brown denied that institutional and interest groupings had autonomy from the Politburo; but he insisted that drastic reform was possible if a dynamic reformer were to become party leader.[30] The diagnoses of recent politics in the USSR were quite as fiercely disputed as those being offered for pre-war history.

General accounts of the Soviet period fell away, at least outside the bickerings among Western communist grouplets, as the concentration on specific phases grew. The general trend was towards compartmentalizing research. Politics, economics and sociology were studied in sealed boxes. History, moreover, became disjoined from contemporary studies.

Supporters of the totalitarianist case took a bleak view of those writings which held back from condemning the Soviet order. Martin Malia and Richard Pipes castigated what they saw as a complete lapse of moral and historical perspective.[31] The debates among historians produced sharp polemics. Often more heat than light was generated. What was ignored by the protagonists on both sides was that several innovative studies in the totalitarianist tradition, particularly the early monographs of Merle Fainsod and Robert Conquest, had stressed that cracks had always existed in the USSR's monolith. They had drawn attention to the ceaseless dissension about policy in the midst of the Kremlin leadership. They had emphasized too that whole sectors of society and the economy in the Soviet Union proved resistant to official policy.[32] The history and scope of totalitarianism acquire fresh nuances. Archie Brown argued that whereas the concept was an apt description of Stalin's USSR, it lost its applicability when Khrushchëv's reforms were introduced, and the state remained extremely authoritarian but was no longer totalitarian.[33] Geoffrey Hosking stressed that pre-revolutionary attitudes of faith, nationhood and intellectual autonomy survived across the Soviet decades, even to some degree under Stalin, and functioned as an impediment to the Politburo's commands.[34]

The theory of totalitarianism, even in these looser applications, falls short of explaining the range and depth of resistance, non-compliance and apathy towards the demands of the state. The USSR was regulated to an exceptional degree in some ways while eluding central political control in others. Behind the façade of party congresses and Red Square parades there was greater disobedience to official authority than in most liberal-democratic countries even though the Soviet leadership could wield a panoply of dictatorial instruments. Informal and mainly illegal practices pervaded existence in the USSR. Clientelist politics and fraudulent economic management were ubiquitous and local agendas were pursued to the detriment of Kremlin policies. Officials in each institution systematically supplied misinformation to superior levels of authority. People in general withheld active co-operation with the authorities. Lack of conscientiousness was customary at the workplace – in factory, farm and office. A profound scepticism was widespread. Such phenomena had existed in the Russian Empire for centuries. But far from fading, they were strengthened under communism and were constant ingredients in the Soviet compound so long as the USSR lasted.

The core of my analysis is that these same features should not be regarded as wrenches flung into the machinery of state and society. They did not obstruct the camshafts, pulleys and engine. Quite the opposite: they were the lubricating oil essential for the machinery to function. Without them, as even Stalin accepted by the end of the 1930s, everything would have clattered to a standstill.

Thus the Soviet compound in reality combined the official with the unofficial, unplanned and illicit. This dualism was a fundamental feature of the entire course of the USSR's history. So if we are to use totalitarianism in description and analysis, the term needs to undergo fundamental redefinition. The unofficial, unplanned and illicit features of existence in the Soviet Union were not 'lapses' or 'aberrations' from the essence of totalitarianist state and society: they were integral elements of totalitarianism. The conventional definition of totalitarianism is focused exclusively on the effective and ruthless imposition of the Kremlin's commands; this is counterposed to the operation of liberal democracies. What is missing is an awareness that such democracies are by and large characterized by popular consent, obedience and order. It was not the same in the USSR, where every individual or group below the level of the central political leadership engaged in behaviour inimical to officially approved purposes. The result was a high degree of disorder from the viewpoint of the authorities – and it was much higher than in the countries of advanced capitalism. The process was predictable. Soviet rulers treated their people badly. The people reacted by defending their immediate interests in the only ways they could.

Even so, the communist rulers achieved a lot of what they wanted. They were unremovable from power and could always quell revolts and disturbances and suppress dissent. Only if they fell out irrevocably among themselves would leaders face a fundamental threat to their rule. Or indeed if, as happened in the late 1980s, they opted for policies that undermined the foundations of the Soviet order.

Alternative terms such as 'mono-organizational society', 'bureaucratic centralism' (or, for the period after Stalin, 'bureaucratic pluralism') are altogether too bland. They fail to encapsulate the reality of the USSR, red in tooth and claw with its dictatorial party and security police, its labour camps and monopolistic ideology. Thus totalitarianism, suitably re-designated as involving insubordination and chaos as well as harshly imposed hierarchy, is the most suitable concept to characterize the USSR. The system of power, moreover, stood in place for seven decades. Undoubtedly the regimes of Lenin, Stalin, Khrushchëv and Brezhnev had their own distinctive features. Yet the differences were less significant than the likenesses and this book postulates that the entire period of communist rule had a basic unity. Political dictatorship, administrative centralism, judicial arbitrariness, cramped national and religious self-expression, ideological uniformity and massive state economic intervention were durable ingredients of the Soviet compound. They were put into the crucible by Lenin and his party within a couple of years of the October Revolution; Gorbachëv's Politburo started to remove them only two or three years before the whole USSR was dissolved. The list of ingredients was constant from beginning to end.

Across the years, though, the central political leadership found that these same ingredients produced solvents which modified the original compound. The process was dynamic. Thus the consolidation of a one-party state had the unintended effect of encouraging individuals to join the party for the perks of membership. Quite apart from careerism, there was the difficulty that Marxism-Leninism was ambiguous in many fundamental ways. Nor could even a one-ideology state terminate disputes about ideas if central party leaders were among the participants in controversy. Furthermore, leaders in the localities as well as at the centre protected their personal interests by appointing friends and associates to posts within their administrative fiefdoms. Clientelism was rife. So, too, were attempts by officials in each locality to combine to dull the edge of demands made upon them by the central leadership; and the absence of the rule of law, together with the ban on free elections, gave rise to a culture of corruption.

Mendacious reporting to higher administrative authority was a conventional procedure. Accounts were fiddled; regulations on working practices were neglected. There were persistent grounds for worry, too, on the national question. Many peoples of the USSR enhanced their feelings of distinctness and some of them aspired to national independence. Official measures to de-nationalize society had the effect of strengthening nationalism.

The Soviet central authorities repeatedly turned to measures intended to re-activate the compound's elements. This sometimes led to purges of the party, mostly involving mere expulsion from the ranks but in the 1930s and the 1940s being accompanied by terror. Throughout the years after the October Revolution, furthermore, institutions were established to inspect and control other institutions. A central determination existed to set quantitative objectives to be attained by local government and party bodies in economic and political affairs. The Kremlin leaders resorted to exhortations, instructions and outright threats and gave preferential promotion in public life to those showing implicit obedience to them. Intrusive political campaigns were a standard feature; and exaggerated rhetoric was employed as the regime, centrally and locally, tried to impose its wishes within the structure of the compound created in the first few years after the October Revolution.

The efforts at re-activation prompted individuals, institutions and nations to adopt measures of self-defence. People strove after a quiet life. Evasiveness and downright disruption were pervasive at every lower level. This in turn impelled the central leadership to strengthen its intrusiveness. Over the seven decades after 1917 the USSR experienced a cycle of activation, disruption and re-activation. There was an ineluctable logic to the process so long as the leadership aimed to preserve the compound of the Soviet order.

Consequently the rulers of the USSR never exercised a completely unrestrained authority. The jailers of the Leninist system of power were also its prisoners. But what jailers, what prisoners! Lenin, Stalin, Khrushchëv and Gorbachëv have gripped the world's imagination. Even losers in the struggles of Soviet politics, such as Trotski and Bukharin, have acquired an enduring reputation. And although a succession of Soviet central leaders fell short of their ambition in utterly dominating their societies, each leader wielded enormous power. The political system was centralized and authoritarian. It was also oligarchic: just a few individuals made the principal decisions – and Stalin turned it into a personal despotism. So that the particularities of character were bound to have a deep effect on public life. The USSR would not have come into being without Lenin's intolerant confidence; and it would not have collapsed when and how it did without Gorbachëv's naïve audacity.

The idiosyncratic ideas of leaders, too, left their mark. Lenin's thinking about dictatorship, industrialization and nationality had a formative influence on the nature of the Soviet state; Stalin's grotesque enthusiasm for terror was no less momentous. Such figures shaped history, moreover, not only by their ideas but also by their actions. Stalin made a calamitous blunder in denying that Hitler was poised to invade the USSR in mid-1941; Khrushchëv's insistence in 1956 in breaking the official silence about the horrors of the 1930s brought enduring benefit to his country.

These were not the sole unpredictable factors that channelled the course of development. The factional struggles of the 1920s were complex processes, and it was not a foregone conclusion that Stalin would defeat Trotski. The political culture, the institutional interests and the course of events in Russia and the rest of the world worked to Stalin's advantage. In addition, no communist in 1917 anticipated the measure of savagery of the Civil War. State and society were brutalized by this experience to an extent that made it easier for Stalin to impose forcible agricultural collectivization. Nor did Stalin and his generals foresee the scale of barbarity and destruction on the Eastern front in the Second World War. And, having industrialized their country in the 1930s, Soviet leaders did not understand that the nature of industrialism changes from generation to generation. In the 1980s they were taken aback when the advanced capitalist states of the West achieved a rapid diffusion of computerized technology throughout the civilian sectors of their economies. Contingency was a major factor in the history of twentieth-century Russia.

Even as dominant a ruler as Stalin, however, eventually had to have an eye for the internal necessities of the system. The compound of the Soviet order was continuously imperilled, to a greater or less degree, by popular dissatisfaction. Stabilizing ingredients had to be introduced to preserve the compound, and an effort was needed to win the support from a large section of society for the maintenance of the status quo. Rewards had to be used as well as punishments.

The attempt at stabilization started soon after 1917 with the introduction of a tariff of privileges for the officials of party and government. Before the October Revolution there had been a tension in Leninist thought between hierarchical methods and egalitarian goals; but as soon as the communists actually held power, the choice was persistently made in favour of hierarchy. Officialdom did not have it entirely its own way. Far from it: in the late 1930s the life of a politician or an administrator became a cheap commodity. But the general tendency to give high remuneration to this stratum of the population was strengthened. The young promotees who stepped into dead men's shoes were also occupying their homes and using their special shops and special hospitals. Social equality had become the goal for an ever receding future, and Marxist professions of egalitarianism sounded ever more hollow: from Stalin to Gorbachëv they were little more than ritual incantations.

None the less the central political leaders also ensured that the tariff was not confined to officials but was extended lower into society. As early as the 1920s, those people who enrolled as ordinary party members were given enhanced opportunities for promotion at work and for leisure-time facilities. In most phases of the Soviet era there was positive discrimination in favour of the offspring of the working class and the peasantry. It was from among such beneficiaries of the regime that its strongest support came.

Yet the nature of official policies meant that not everyone could live a cosseted life. Huge sacrifices were exacted from ordinary people at times of crisis. The basic amenities of existence were unavailable to them during the Civil War, the First Five-Year Plan and the Second World War. Life was extremely harsh for Soviet citizens in those and other phases. But at other times the regime took care not to push its demands dangerously hard. Labour discipline was notoriously slack by the standards of modern industry elsewhere. Quality of workmanship was low, punctuality poor. In addition, there was more or less full employment in the USSR from the early 1930s; and a safety-net of minimal welfare benefits was erected even for the most disadvantaged members of society from the late 1950s. It was not a comfortable existence for most people, but the provision of a predictable level of food, clothing and housing helped to reconcile them to life under the Soviet order.

Even so, revolts occurred at the end of the Civil War and at the end of the 1920s, and urban disturbances took place sporadically in the mid-1960s, the 1970s and the late 1980s. But, on the whole, rebellion was rare. This infrequency resulted not only from the state's ruthless violence but also from its provision of primitive social security. There was a tacit contract between the regime and society which endured to the end of the communist era, a contract which has proved difficult for the country's subsequent government to tear up.

Russians and other peoples of the USSR had always had ideas of social justice and been suspicious of their rulers, and the Soviet regime's repressiveness fortified this attitude. They also noted the communist party's failure, from one generation to another, to fulfil its promises. The USSR never became a land of plenty for most of its citizens, and the material and social benefits bestowed by communism could not camouflage the unfairnesses that pervaded society. In time, moreover, a country of peasants was turned into an industrial, urban society. As in other countries, the inhabitants of the towns directed an ever greater cynicism at politicians. The increasing contact with Western countries added to the contempt felt for an ideology which had never been accepted in its entirety by most citizens. Russia, which was hard enough to tame in 1917–1918, had become still less easy to hold in subjection by the late 1980s.

The rulers anyway faced problems which were not simply the consequence of 1917. The heritage of the more distant past also bore down upon them. Russia's size, climate and ethnic diversity greatly complicated the tasks of government. It also lagged behind its chief competitors in industrial and technological capacity; it was threatened by states to the West and the East and its frontiers were the longest in the world. Arbitrary state power was a dominant feature in public life. Official respect for legality was negligible and the political and administrative hierarchy was over-centralized. Russia, furthermore, had an administration which barely reached the lower social classes on a day-to-day basis. Most people were preoccupied by local affairs and were unresponsive to appeals to patriotism. Education was not widely spread; civic integration and inter-class tolerance were minimal. The potential for inter-ethnic conflict, too, was growing. Social relationships were extremely harsh, often violent.

Lenin and the communists came to power expecting to solve most of these problems quickly. Their October Revolution was meant to facilitate revolution throughout Europe and to re-set the agenda of politics, economics and culture around the globe. To their consternation, revolution did not break out across Europe and the central party leaders increasingly had to concentrate on problems inherited from the tsars.

In reality the behaviour of Lenin and his successors often aggravated rather than resolved the problems. Their theories even before the October Revolution had an inclination towards arbitrary, intolerant and violent modes of rule. While proclaiming the goal of a society devoid of oppression, they swiftly became oppressors to an unprecedented degree of intensity. Soviet communists, unconsciously or not, fortified the country's traditional political postures: the resort to police-state procedures, ideological persecution and anti-individualism derived as much from tsarist political and social precedents as from Marxism-Leninism. What is more, the concern that Russia might lose its status as a Great Power was as important to Stalin and his successors as to the Romanov dynasty. The appeal to Russian national pride became a regular feature of governmental pronouncements. Office-holders thought of themselves as Marxist-Leninists; but increasingly they behaved as if Russia's interests should have precedence over aspirations to worldwide revolution.

Russia, of course, was not the entire USSR and not all Soviet citizens were Russians. Furthermore, it was party policy throughout the USSR's history to transmute existing national identities into a sense of belonging to a supranational 'Soviet people'. This was part of a general endeavour by the state to eradicate any organizations or groupings independent of its control. The central politicians could not afford to let Russian national self-assertiveness get out of hand.

But what on earth was Russia? And what was Russia's part in the Soviet Union? These are questions which are much less easy to answer than they superficially appear. The borders of the Russian republic within the USSR were altered several times after 1917. Nearly every redefinition involved a loss of territory to the USSR's other republics. The status of ethnic Russians, too, changed under several political leaderships. Whereas Lenin was wary of Russian national self-assertiveness, Stalin sought to control and exploit it for his political purposes; and the Soviet communist leadership after Stalin's death, despite coming to rely politically upon the Russians more than upon other nationalities in the Soviet Union, never gave them outright mastery. Nor was Russian culture allowed to develop without restriction: the Orthodox Church, peasant traditions and a free-thinking intelligentsia were aspects of Mother Russia which no General Secretary until the accession of Gorbachëv was willing to foster. Russian national identity was perennially manipulated by official interventions.

For some witnesses the Soviet era was an assault on everything fundamentally Russian. For others, Russia under Stalin and Brezhnev attained its destiny as the dominant republic within the USSR. For yet others neither tsarism nor communism embodied any positive essence of Russianness. The chances are that Russian history will remain politically sensitive. This is not simply a case of public figures whipping up debate. Russians in general are interested in discussions of Nicholas II, Lenin, Stalin and Gorbachëv; and the past and the present are enmeshed in every public debate.

Russia is under the spotlight in this book. But the history of Russia is inseparable from the history of the Russian Empire, the Soviet Union and the Commonwealth of Independent States. It would be artificial to deal exclusively with Russian themes in those many cases in which these themes are knotted together with the situation in adjacent areas. My rule of thumb has been to omit from the account those events and situations that had little impact upon 'Russia' and affected only the non-Russian areas of the Russian Empire, the Soviet Union and the Commonwealth of Independent States. On the other hand, the chapters are not designed as an account of the Russian Empire, the Soviet Union and the Commonwealth of Independent States with the 'Russian factor' being addressed only glancingly. For the general history of this huge area of Europe and Asia can be understood only when Russia's history is thrown into relief.

In still broader terms, the plan is to treat Soviet history as a unitary period and to explain the inner strengths and strains of the USSR. Recently it has become fashionable to assert that communism in

Russia could easily have been eradicated at any moment in its seventy years of existence. This is just as exaggerated a notion as the earlier conventional notion that the regime was impervious to any kind of domestic or foreign pressure.

But what kind of regime was the USSR? Continuities with the tsarist years are examined in the following chapters; so, too, are the surviving elements of the communist order in post-Soviet Russia. The shifting nature of Russian national identity is also highlighted. And an account is offered not only of the central political leadership but also of the entire regime as well as of the rest of society. This means that the focus is not confined to leading 'personalities' or to 'history from below'. Instead the purpose is to give an analysis of the complex interaction between rulers and ruled, an interaction that changed in nature over the decades. Not only politics but also economics, sociology and culture are examined. For it is an organizing principle of the book that we can unravel Russia's mysteries only by taking a panoramic viewpoint.

Greater attention is given to politics than to anything else. This is deliberate. The Soviet economic, social and cultural order in Russia is incomprehensible without sustained attention to political developments. The policies and ideas of the party leadership counted greatly; it also mattered which leader was paramount at any given moment. Politics penetrated nearly all areas of Soviet society in some fashion or other; and even though the purposes of the leadership were frequently and systematically thwarted, they never lost their deep impact on society.

Russia has had an extraordinary history since 1900. Its transformation has been massive: from autocratic monarchy through communism to an elected president and parliament; from capitalist development through a centrally owned, planned economy to wild market economics; from a largely agrarian and uneducated society to urban industrialism and literacy. Russia has undergone revolutions, civil war and mass terror; its wars against foreign states have involved defence, liberation and conquest. In 1900 no one foresaw these abrupt turns of fortune. Now nobody can be sure what the twenty-first century has in store. Yet few Russians want to repeat the experience of their parents and grandparents: they yearn for peaceful, gradual change. Among the factors that will affect their progress will be an ability to see the past through spectacles unblurred by mythology and unimpeded by obstacles to public debate and access to official documents. The prospects are not wholly encouraging. Official Russian policies since the start of the twenty-first century have unfortunately been aimed at inhibiting open-ended research and debate.

Winston Churchill described Russia as a 'riddle wrapped in a mystery inside an enigma'. As many obscurities are being dispelled, we have never been in a better position to take the measure of a country whose history after 1917 turned the world upside down. For seven decades Soviet communism offered itself as a model of social organization; and even in transition from communism Russia has kept its intriguing interest. It has been a delusion of the age, after the dissolution of the USSR, to assume that capitalism has all the answers ready-made to the problems faced by our troubled world. Communism is the young god that failed; capitalism, an older deity, has yet to succeed for most of the world's people most of the time.

I

And Russia? (1900–1914)

No imperial power before the First World War was more reviled in Europe than the Russian Empire. Generations of democrats hated the Romanov dynasty. Neither Kaiser Wilhelm II of Germany nor Emperor Franz Joseph of Austria-Hungary rivalled Russia's Emperor Nicholas II in notoriety. Repression of Russian parties and trade unions was severe. In 1905 Nicholas reluctantly conceded a parliament (or *Duma*) after months of revolutionary turmoil; but the First Duma, which met in 1906, proved unable to stand hard against the monarchy. Manipulating the new Basic Law to his advantage, the Emperor dispersed the Second Duma and redrew the electoral rules so as to obtain a more compliant Third Duma.

Yet the Russian Empire had weaknesses. Although in 1812 its troops chased Napoleon's troops back into France, its subsequent embroilments were less impressive. In 1854–6, confronting British and French expeditionary forces in Crimea, it failed to drive them into the Black Sea. Russian pride was retrieved to some extent by victory over the Turks in the war of 1877–8. But there was no room for complacency; for the Ottoman Empire was generally recognized as being in a condition of irreversible decline. Successive Romanov emperors, whose dynasty had ruled Russia since 1613, saw that much needed to be done to secure their frontiers. And two powers were thought extremely menacing: Germany and Austria-Hungary. They were expected to take military and economic advantage of Ottoman decline; and, in particular, Berlin's plan to construct a railway from the Mediterranean seaboard to Baghdad was regarded with trepidation in St Petersburg.

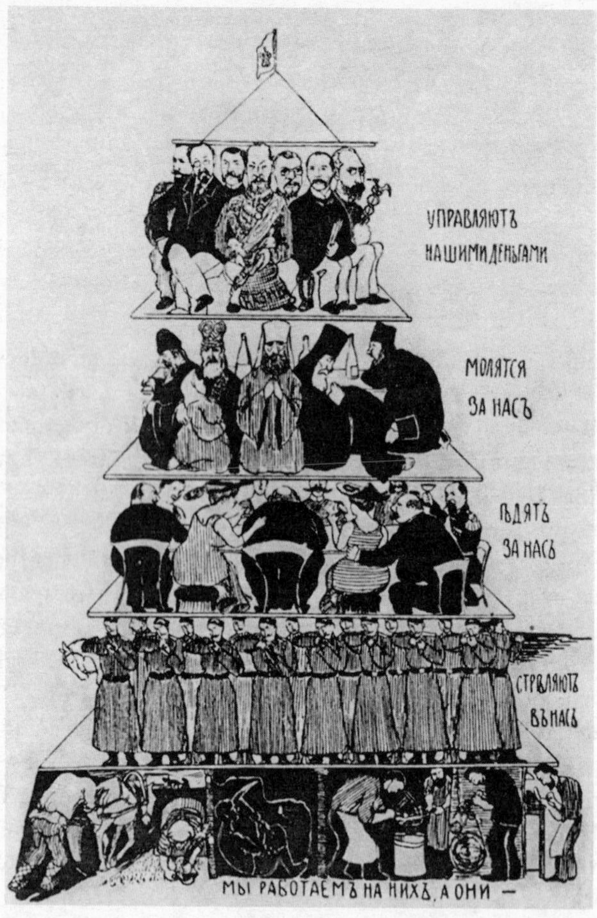

An anonymous picture of the structure of Russian Imperial society circulated before 1917. The workers at the bottom declare how the other layers of people relate to them. From top to bottom, the statements are as follows:

'They dispose of our money.'
'They pray on our behalf.'
'They eat on our behalf.'
'They shoot at us.'
'We work for them while they . . .'

Nicholas II's problems did not exist solely in the west. The Russian Empire, covering a sixth of the world's earth surface, was a continent unto itself. Its boundaries stretched from the Baltic and Black Seas to the Pacific Ocean. In the late nineteenth century, the government in St Petersburg – which was then the Russian capital – joined in the international scramble to expand imperial possessions in Asia and, in 1896, compelled Beijing to grant a profitable railway concession to Russia in northern China. But Japan's rising power gave cause for concern. In January 1904 Nicholas ill-advisedly decided to declare war on her: the result was humiliating defeat both on land and at sea. Japanese military power remained a menace to Russia for the ensuing four decades.

Japan ended this particular war in 1906 through the treaty of Portsmouth on terms generous to Nicholas II. Central Europe, however, remained dangerous and Russia had to cultivate a friendship with France in order to counterbalance the Germans. A Franco-Russian security agreement had been signed in 1893, and this was followed in 1907 by an Entente involving both France and Britain. Meanwhile conciliatory gestures continued to be made to Germany. For Russia, while being a rival of Germany, also benefited from trade with her. Grain, timber and dairy products were exported to Germany; and German finance and industry were important for the growth of manufacturing in St Petersburg. Russia had reason to avoid any closer alliance with Britain and France. Britain competed with Russia for influence in Persia and Afghanistan, and France made occasional demands infringing Russian interests in the Near East. Yet Russia's financial well-being depended more heavily upon France and Britain than upon Germany; and in the longer run the rivalry with Germany and Austria-Hungary would be hard to restrict to the modalities of diplomacy.

Russia's very vastness was more a problem than an advantage. Only Britain with her overseas domains had a larger empire; but Britain could lose India without herself being invaded: the same was not true of Russia and her land-based empire. Russia had prospective enemies to the west, south and east.

The link between industrialization and military effectiveness had been recognized by Peter the Great, who reigned from 1689 to 1725 and set up armaments works in Tula and elsewhere. But Peter's fervour for industrial growth resulted more from a wish to improve his armies' fighting capacity than to achieve general industrialization. In any case, his keenness to establish factories was not emulated by his immediate successors. Even so, railways had started to be built in the 1830s, and in the 1880s and 1890s governmental policy became favourable again to rapid industrialization. Sergei Witte, Minister of Finances, zealously promoted the case for factories, mines and banks as the Russian Empire pursued its capitalist economic development. Nicholas II gave him his support at home, and Witte relayed his own message to the world's financiers that the profit margins in Russia were huge and the workers obedient.[1]

And so manufacturing and mining output rose by an annual rate of eight per cent in the last decade of the nineteenth century and of six per cent between 1907 and the outbreak of the Great War. Fifty thousand kilometres of rail-track had been laid by 1914, including the Trans-Siberian line which linked Moscow to Vladivostok on the edge of the Pacific Ocean. State contracts were vital for this purpose. The armaments factories were sustained by the government's determination to become secure against Germany and Austria-Hungary in the west and Japan in the east. Investment from abroad was also crucial. Nearly half the value of Russian securities excluding mortgage bonds was held by foreigners.[2] Metallurgical development was especially dynamic. So, too, was the exploitation of the empire's natural resources. Alfred Nobel turned the Baku oilfields into the world's second largest producer after Texas. Timber was also a major export; and coal, iron and gold were extracted intensively.

Russia's domestic industrialists and bankers, too, were highly active. In the Moscow region in particular there was a growing number of large textile plants. At the same time there was an increased output of consumer goods. Clothing, which was manufactured mainly for the home market, was easily Russia's largest industry and, in combination with food-processing, amounted to half of the empire's industrial output (while metal-working and mining enterprises contributed about a seventh).[3] Not only armaments and railways but also shoes, furniture and butter were vital elements in the Russian Empire's economic transformation. Her industry was by no means neglectful of the market for goods of popular consumption.

Although industry led the advance, agriculture was not motionless. Grain harvests increased by an annual average of roughly two per cent from the beginning of the 1880s through to 1913. This change was not smooth and there were several set-backs. The worst was the great famine which afflicted Russia's Volga region in 1891–2, and droughts remained an intermittent problem across the empire. Yet the general situation was moderately positive. For example, cereal production per capita rose by thirty-five per cent between 1890 and 1913. The Russian Empire's exports of wheat and rye made her the world's greatest grain exporter, and roughly 11.5 million tons of cereals were sold abroad each year in the half-decade before the Great War. In the villages, moreover, there was a growing willingness to experiment with new crops: the acreage of sugar-beet was expanded by two fifths between 1905 and 1914.[4] There was success with the attempt to expand the production of potatoes and dairy products in the Baltic region, and areas of 'Russian' central Asia were given over to cotton-growing.

This diversification of crops was facilitated by the use of factory-produced equipment. Such machinery was found mainly on the large landed estates where the hired hands were the principal section of the labour-force; but peasants, too, bought metal ploughs, corrugated-iron roofs and wire fences as well as leather shoes, nails and greatcoats whenever they could afford it.

Attitudes, however, were altering only very slowly. Peasants, while making money from the expanded market for their products, kept to traditional notions and customs. In Russia the main rural institution was the village land commune. This body meted out justice according to the local understandings about economic and social fairness. In some areas this involved the periodic redistribution of land among the households of the commune; but even where land was held fixedly, peasants continued to comply with the decisions of the commune. A degree of egalitarianism existed. There was also a tradition of mutual responsibility, a tradition that had been fortified by the Emancipation Edict of 1861 which levied taxes from the village commune as a whole rather than from particular households or individuals. Peasants were accustomed to acting collectively and to taking decisions among themselves about life in the village.[5]

But this did not mean that the peasantry's conditions were wholly equalized. A handful of households in a commune would typically be better off than the rest; and the affluent peasants became known as *kulaki* (which in Russian means 'fists'). They lent money, they hired labour; they rented and bought land. Poorer households, especially those which lacked an adult male and had to get by with youngsters doing the work, tended to decline into penury. Life was nasty, brutish and short for most peasants.

So long as the peasantry complied with the state's demands for taxes and conscripts, there was little governmental interference in rural affairs. Until the mid-nineteenth century, most peasants had been bonded to the noble owners of landed estates. Emperor Alexander II saw this to have been an important reason for the Russian Empire's débâcle in the Crimean War of 1854–6, and in 1861 he issued an Emancipation Edict freeing peasants from their bondage. The terms of their liberation were ungenerous to them. On average, peasants were left with thirteen per cent less land to cultivate than before the Edict.[6] Consequently despite being pleased to be relieved of the gentry's domineering administration of the villages, the peasantry was discontented. There was a belief among peasants that the Emperor ought to transfer all land, including their former masters' fields and woods, to them and that they themselves should appropriate this land whenever the opportunity might arise.

The Emancipation Edict, by removing the gentry's automatic authority over the peasantry, had to be accompanied by several reforms in local government, the judiciary, education and military training. Elective representative bodies known as the *zemstva* were set up in the localities to carry out administrative functions. Local courts, too, were established; and provision for popular education was increased: by the turn of the century it was reckoned that about a quarter of the rural population was literate – and in the largest cities the proportion was three quarters.[7] The armed forces reduced the term of service from twenty-five years to six years at the most. Still the peasants were unsatisfied. They were annoyed that they had to pay for the land they received through the Emancipation Edict. They resented also that they, unlike the nobility, were liable to corporal punishment for misdemeanours. They remained a class apart.

Alexander II also insisted that they should have permission from their communes before taking up work in towns; for he and his ministers were fearful about the rapid creation of an unruly urban 'proletariat' such as existed in other countries. But this brake on industrial growth was insubstantial. In order to meet their fiscal obligations, communes found it convenient to allow able-bodied young men to seek jobs in factories and mines and remit some of their wages to the family they left behind them in the village. By 1913 there were about 2.4 million workers in large-scale industry.[8] The figure for the urban working class reached nearly eleven million when hired labourers in small-scale industry, building, transport, communications and domestic service were included. There were also about 4.5 million wage-labourers in agriculture. Thus the urban and rural working class quadrupled in the half-century after the Emancipation Edict.[9]

Change occurred, too, amidst the middle and upper classes. Owners of large estates in the more fertile regions adopted Western agricultural techniques and some of them made fortunes out of wheat, potatoes and sugar-beet. Elsewhere they increasingly sold or rented their land at prices kept high by the peasantry's land-hunger. The gentry took employment in the expanding state bureaucracy and joined banks and industrial companies. With the increase in the urban population there was a rise in the number of shopkeepers, clerks and providers of other products and services. The cities of the Russian Empire teemed with a new life that was bursting through the surface of the age-old customs.

The monarchy tried to hold on to its prerogatives by ensuring that the middle and upper classes should lack organizations independent from the government. There were a few exceptions. The Imperial Economic Society debated the great issues of industrialization. The

Imperial Academy, too, managed to elude excessive official restriction, and several great figures won international acclaim. The chemist Mendeleev and the behavioural biologist Pavlov were outstanding examples. But the various professional associations were subjected to constant surveillance and intimidation, and could never press their case in the Emperor's presence. The industrialists and bankers, too, were nervous and their organizations were confined to local activities; and tsarism kept them weak by favouring some at the expense of others. Imperial Russia put obstacles in the way of autonomous civic activity.

And so the transformation of society was in its early stages before the Great War and the bulk of economic relationships in the Russian Empire were of a traditional kind: shopkeepers, domestic servants, carriage-drivers and waiters lived as they had done for decades. The *khodoki* – those peasants who travelled vast distances to do seasonal work in other regions – were a mass phenomenon in central and northern Russia.

Even those factories which used the most up-to-date, imported machinery continued to rely heavily upon manual labour. Living conditions in the industrial districts were atrocious. Moscow textile-factory owners had a paternalist attitude to their work-force; but most of them failed to supply their workers with adequate housing, education and other amenities. Russian workers lived in squalor and were poorly paid by the standards of contemporary industrial capitalism. Like the peasants, they felt excluded from the rest of society. A chasm of sentiment separated them from their employers, their foremen and the police. They were forbidden to form trade unions; they were subordinated to an arbitrarily-applied code of labour discipline at their places of work. The Ministry of Internal Affairs in the late nineteenth century showed sympathy with their plight. But the interests of the owners were usually given official protection against the demands of the workers.

The established working class which had existed in Moscow, St Petersburg and Tula grew rapidly under Nicholas II. But the precariousness of their conditions encouraged workers to maintain their ties with the countryside. Relatives cultivated the communal allotments of land for them; and, in the event of strikes, workers could last out by returning to the villages. This was a system of mutual assistance. Peasant households expected the workers not only to help them financially but also to come back to help with the harvest.

The linkage between countryside and town helped to sustain traditional ideas. Religious belief was prevalent across the empire, and Christmas, Easter and the great festivals were celebrated with gusto by Russians and other Christian nationalities. The priest was a central figure, accompanying the peasants into the fields to bless the sowing and pray for a good crop. But pagan vestiges, too, survived in the peasant world-view and the ill-educated, poorly-paid parish priest rarely counteracted the prejudices of his parishioners. Both the Russian peasant and the Russian worker could be crude in the extreme. Heavy drinking was common. Syphilis was widespread. Fists and knives were used to settle disagreements. And the peasantry ferociously enforced its own forms of order. It was not uncommon for miscreants to undergo vicious beating and mutilation. The sophistication of St Petersburg salons was not matched in the grubby, ill-kempt villages.

Thus the Russian Empire was deeply fissured between the government and the tsar's subjects; between the capital and the provinces; between the educated and the uneducated; between Western and Russian ideas; between the rich and the poor; between privilege and oppression; between contemporary fashion and centuries-old custom. Most people (and ninety per cent of the Emperor's subjects had been born and bred in the countryside)[10] felt that a chasm divided them from the world inhabited by the ruling élites.

Ostensibly the Russian nation was the pre-eminent beneficiary of the empire; but national consciousness among Russians was only patchily developed and local traditions and loyalties retained much influence. This was evident in a number of ways. One example is the way that migrants, as they moved into the towns for work, tended to stay together with people from the same area. The man from Saratov found the man from Arkhangelsk almost as alien as someone from Poland or even Portugal. Remarkable differences of dialect and accent prevailed. Despite the current economic transformation, furthermore, most Russians did not move to the nearest town: many did not even visit the neighbouring village. The lifestyles of Russian peasant communities were so strongly rooted in particular localities that when peasants migrated to areas of non-Russian population they sometimes abandoned these lifestyles and identified themselves with their new neighbours.

There had nevertheless been times when the peasants had rallied to the government's side. Patriotic sentiments were roused by the Napoleonic invasion in 1812 and the Russo-Turkish war of 1877–8;[11] and a deep dislike of foreign traders, mercenaries and advisers had existed in previous centuries.[12] The general processes of industrialization and education, too, had an effect on popular sentiments. Russians were moving to towns; they were becoming literate; they could travel from one part of the country to another; they had chances of changing their type of occupation. As they met and talked and worked together, they started to feel that they had much in common with each other.

Yet national consciousness was not a dominant sentiment among Russians. Except at times of war, most of them at the beginning of the twentieth century were motivated by Christian belief, peasant customs, village loyalties and reverence for the tsar rather than by feelings of Russian nationhood. Christianity itself was a divisive phenomenon. The Russian Orthodox Church had been torn apart by a reform in ritual imposed by Patriarch Nikon from 1653. Those who refused to accept Nikon's dispensations fled to the south, the south-east and the north and became known as the Old Believers. Other sects also sprang up among Russians. Some of these were strange in the extreme, such as the *Khlysty* who practised castration of their adherents. Others were pacifists; notable among them were the Dukhobors. There was also a growth of foreign Christian denominations such as the Baptists. What was common to such sects was their disenchantment not only with the Russian Orthodox Church but also with the government in St Petersburg.

This situation limited the Russian Orthodox Church's ability to act as the unifying promoter of Russian national values. Compelled to act as a spiritual arm of the tsarist state, the Church conducted a campaign of harassment against the Russian sects. The kind of intellectual effervescence characteristic of 'national' churches in other countries was discouraged in Russia. The tsar and his ecclesiastical hierarchy wanted an obedient, obscurantist traditionalism from the Russian Orthodox Church, and had the authority to secure just that.

Nor did a clear sense of national purpose emanate from the intelligentsia even though the leading cultural figures in the nineteenth century explored how best the human and natural resources of Russia might be organized. The poems of Alexander Pushkin; the novels of Lev Tolstoy, Fëdor Dostoevski and Ivan Turgenev; the paintings of Ivan Repin; the music of Modest Musorgski and Pëtr Chaikovski: all such works stressed that Russia had a great potential which had yet to be effectively tapped. Among creative artists, the musicians were exceptional in displaying allegiance to the monarchy. Most of the intellectuals in their various ways hated tsarism and this attitude was shared by students, teachers, doctors, lawyers and other professional groups.[13] It was a commonplace amidst the intelligentsia that the autocratic monarchy was stifling the development of the Russian national spirit.

And yet the intellectuals were remote from agreeing what they meant by Russianness. Indeed many of them abhorred the discourse of national distinctiveness. While criticizing the imperial nature of the state, they disliked the thought of breaking it up into several nation-states; instead they pondered how to create a multinational state which would deny privileges to any particular nation. Anti-nationalism was especially characteristic of the socialists; but several leading liberals, too, refused to invoke ideas of Russian nationalism.

It was left to far-right public figures, including some bishops of the Russian Orthodox Church, to argue for the interests of ethnic Russians at the expense of the other peoples of the Russian Empire. Several monarchist organizations came into existence after 1905 which sought to promote this case. The most influential of them was the Union of the Russian People, which had the undisguised support of Nicholas and his family.[14] Such organizations called for the unconditional restoration of autocracy. They lauded the tsar, the Russian Orthodox Church and 'the simple people'. They hated the Jews, whom they blamed for all the recent disturbances in the empire. They helped to form gangs, usually known as the Black Hundreds, which carried out bloody pogroms against Jewish communities in the western borderlands. By stirring up a xenophobic hysteria, they aimed to reunite the tsar and the Russian people.

After his initial declaration of sympathy for the Union of the Russian people, Nicholas took a more measured public stance. He left it to the Union to do what it could. But he was a tsar. He was far too austere to become a rabble-rouser, and his wish to be respected by fellow monarchs abroad was undiminished. Nothing done by Nicholas had an entirely clear purpose or consistent implementation.

Among Nicholas's inhibitions was the fact that he could not feel confident about the loyalty of his Russian subjects. The Imperial state oppressed Russian peasants, soldiers and workers as well as their non-Russian counterparts. What is more, the Russians constituted only forty-four per cent of the Imperial population in the two decades before 1917.[15] The empire was a patchwork quilt of nationalities, and the Russians were inferior to several of the other nations in educational and occupational accomplishment. Nicholas II's German, Jewish and Polish subjects had a much higher average level of literacy than his Russian ones;[16] and Germans from the Baltic region held a disproportionately large number of high posts in the armed forces and the bureaucracy. Moreover, the Poles, Finns, Armenians, Georgians had a clearer sense of nationhood than Russians: their resentment of imperial interference was strong. It would not have made sense to alienate such nationalities from the regime more than was necessary.[17]

Thus the tsarist state in the nineteenth century was primarily a supranational state; it was not one of those several nation-states that had simply acquired an empire. Loyalty to the tsar and his dynasty was the supreme requirement made by the Russian Empire.

Not that the tsars were averse to brutal repression. The Polish Revolt of 1863 had been savagely quelled; and in the North Caucasus, which had been conquered only in the 1820s, the rebel leader Shamil raised a Muslim banner of revolt against tsarism and was not defeated until 1859. The autonomy granted to Finnish administration and education was trimmed on the instructions of Emperor Nicholas II. The Uniate Church in Ukraine and Belorussia; the Armenian and Georgian Orthodox Churches; the Lutheran Churches among Estonians and Latvians; the Catholic Church in Lithuania and 'Russian' Poland: all resented the official interference in their practices of worship and became crucibles of anti-tsarist discontent. Meanwhile most Jews were constrained to live within the Pale of Settlement in the empire's western borderlands – and Nicholas crudely believed them to be responsible for subverting the entire empire.

In his more reflective moments, however, he recognized that the regime's security was endangered less by the 'national question' than by the 'labour question' – and most factory workers were ethnic Russians. The illegal labour movement had come to life intermittently in the 1890s, but strikes were more the exception than the rule. Peasant disturbances also occurred. Until after the turn of the century, however, tsarism was strongly in place. Rumblings against the monarchy were only intermittent. Liberals, being forbidden to form a political party, held grand banquets to celebrate anniversaries of past events that had embarrassed the monarchy. Peasants whose harvests were twice ruined by bad weather after 1900 were intensely discontented. Workers, too, were disgruntled. The government, acting on the advice of Moscow police chief Sergei Zubatov, had allowed the setting up of politically-controlled local trade unions; and this gave rise to a legal labour movement determined to take on the authorities.

On Sunday, 9 January 1905 a revolutionary emergency occurred when a peaceful procession of demonstrators, led by Father Georgi Gapon, was fired upon outside the Winter Palace in St Petersburg. Innocent civilians, including women and children, were slaughtered. The event became known as Bloody Sunday. Immediately across the Russian Empire there were strikes and marches in protest. Poland and Georgia became ungovernable over the following weeks. In Russia there was revulsion against the Emperor among factory workers, and their demonstrations were initially given approval by industrialists.

As the press began to criticize the authorities, Nicholas II set up an enquiry into the reasons for popular discontent. The news from the Far East brought further discredit to the monarchy. In February 1905 Russian land forces were crushed at Mukden; in May the Baltic fleet was annihilated in the battle of Tsushima. The myth of the regime's invincibility was dissipated and the illegal political parties emerged from clandestinity. The two largest of them were the Russian Social-Democratic Labour Party and the Party of Socialist-Revolutionaries. The former were Marxists who wanted the urban working class to lead the struggle against the monarchy; the latter were agrarian socialists who, while also trying to appeal to workers, put greater faith in the revolutionary potential of the peasantry. Both sought the overthrow of the Romanov dynasty. Liberals, too, organized themselves by establishing the Constitutional-Democratic Party in October 1905. On all sides the autocracy was under siege.

Workers formed strike committees; peasants began to make illegal use of the gentry's timber and pastures and to take over arable land. A mutiny took place in the Black Sea fleet and the battleship *Potëmkin* steamed off towards Romania. Troops returning from the Far East rebelled along the Trans-Siberian railway. In September 1905 the St Petersburg Marxists founded a Soviet (or Council) of Workers' Deputies. It was elected by local factory workers and employees and became an organ of revolutionary local self-government. Nicholas II at last took the advice from Sergei Witte to issue an October Manifesto which promised 'civil liberty on principles of true inviolability of person, freedom of conscience, speech, assembly and association'. There would also be an elected Duma and adult males in all classes of the population would be enfranchised. Without the Duma, no law could be put into effect. It seemed that autocracy was announcing its demise.

The Manifesto drew off the steam of the urban middle-class hostility and permitted Nicholas II to suppress open rebellion. Many liberals urged that the Emperor should be supported. The Petersburg Soviet leaders – including its young deputy chairman Lev Trotski –

were arrested. An armed uprising was attempted by the Moscow Soviet under the Social-Democrats and Socialist-Revolutionaries in December 1905. But the rising was quelled. Loyal military units were then deployed elsewhere against other organizations and social groups in revolt. And, as order was restored in the towns and on the railways, Nicholas II published a Basic Law and ordered elections for the State Duma. By then he had introduced qualifications to his apparent willingness to give up autocratic authority. In particular, he could appoint the government of his unrestricted choice; the Duma could be dissolved at his whim; and he could rule by emergency decree. Not only Social-Democrats and Socialist-Revolutionaries but also the Constitutional-Democrats (or Kadets) denounced these manoeuvres.

The peasantry had not been much slower to move against the authorities than the workers: most rural districts in European Russia were categorized as 'disorderly' in summer 1905.[18] Illegal sawing of timber and pasturing of livestock on landlords' land took place. Threats were made on gentry who lived in the countryside. Often a cockerel with its neck slit would be laid on the doorstep of their houses to warn them to get out of the locality. The Russian peasant households organized their activities within their communes – and frequently it was the better-off households which took the leading role in the expression of the peasantry's demands. In 1905–6 the countryside across the empire was in revolt. Only the fact that Nicholas II could continue to rely upon a large number of the regiments which had not been sent to the Far East saved him his throne. It was a very close-run thing.

And so the First State Duma met in April 1906. The largest group of deputies within it was constituted by peasants belonging to no party. Contrary to Nicholas II's expectation, however, these same deputies stoutly demanded the transfer of the land from the gentry. He reacted by dissolving the Duma. The party with the greatest number of places in the Duma was the Constitutional-Democratic Party and its leaders were so angered by the Duma's dispersal that they decamped to the Finnish town of Vyborg and called upon their fellow subjects to withhold taxes and conscripts until a fuller parliamentary order was established. Nicholas faced them down and held a further set of elections. To his annoyance, the Second Duma, too, which assembled in March 1907, turned out to be a radical assembly. Consequently Nicholas turned to his Minister of Internal Affairs, Pëtr Stolypin, to form a government and to rewrite the electoral rules so as to produce a Third Duma which would increase the importance of the gentry at the expense of the peasantry.

Stolypin was a reforming conservative. He saw the necessity of agrarian reform, and perceived the peasant land commune as the cardinal obstacle to the economy's efficiency and society's stability. He therefore resolved to dissolve the commune by encouraging 'strong and sober' peasant households to set themselves up as independent farming families. When the Second Duma had opposed him for his failure to grant the land itself to the peasantry, Stolypin had used the emergency powers of Article 87 of the Basic Law to push through his measures. When Russian peasants subsequently showed themselves deeply attached to their communes, he used a degree of compulsion to get his way. Nevertheless his success was very limited. By 1916 only a tenth of the households in the European parts of the empire had broken away from the commune to set up consolidated farms – and such farms in an area of great fertility such as west-bank Ukraine were on average only fifteen acres each.[19]

It was also recognized by Stolypin that the Imperial government would work better if co-operation were forthcoming from the Duma. To this end he sought agreements with Alexander Guchkov and the so-called Octobrist Party (which, unlike the Kadets, had welcomed the October Manifesto). Guchkov's Octobrists were monarchist conservatives who thought roughly along the same lines as Stolypin, but insisted that all legislation should be vetted by the Duma.[20] At the same time Stolypin wanted to strengthen a popular sense of civic responsibility; he therefore persuaded the Emperor to increase the peasantry's weight in the elections to the zemstva. Peasants, he argued, had to have a stake in public life. The political, social and cultural integration of society was vital and Stolypin became convinced that Russian nationalists were right in arguing that Russia should be treated as the heartland of the tsarist empire. Further curtailments were made on the already narrow autonomy of Poles, Finns and other nations of the Russian Empire; and Stolypin strengthened the existing emphasis on Russian-language schooling and administration.

At court, however, he was regarded as a self-interested politician bent upon undermining the powers of the Emperor. Eventually Nicholas, too, saw things in this light, and he steadily withdrew his favour from Stolypin. In September 1911, Stolypin was assassinated by the Socialist-Revolutionary Dmitri Bogrov in Kiev. There were rumours that the *Okhrana*, the political police of the Ministry for the Interior, had facilitated Bogrov's proximity to the premier – and even that the Emperor may have connived in this. Whatever the truth of the matter, the Emperor resumed policies involving the minimum of co-operation with the State Duma. Intelligent conservatism passed away with the death of Pëtr Stolypin.

Yet it was no longer possible for tsarism to rule the country in quite the old fashion. In the eighteenth century it had been exclusively the nobility which had knowledge of general political affairs. The possession of this knowledge served to distance the upper classes from the rest of society. At home the families of the aristocracy took to speaking French among themselves; they imbibed European learning and adopted European tastes. A line of exceptional noblemen – from Alexander Radishchev in the 1780s through to an anti-tsarist conspiracy known as the Decembrists in 1825 – questioned the whole basis of the old regime's legitimacy. But vigorous suppression did not eliminate the problem of dissent. Some of the greatest exponents of Russian literature and intellectual thought – including Alexander Herzen, Nikolai Chernyshevski, Ivan Turgenev and Lev Tolstoy – made it their life's work to call for a drastic change in conditions.

Permanent opposition had taken organized form from the 1860s despite the prohibition on the formation of political parties, on the holding of political meetings and on public demands for political freedom. Most of the rebels were believers in agrarian socialism. Called the *narodniki* (or populists), they argued that the egalitarian and collectivist spirit of the peasant land commune should be applied to the whole society. At first they had gathered in little secret circles. But by 1876 they had founded a substantial party, Land and Freedom, which conducted propaganda among intellectuals and workers as well as among peasants, and also carried out acts of terror upon officials. When Land and Freedom fell apart, a group of terrorists calling themselves People's Will was formed. It succeeded in assassinating Emperor Alexander II in 1881. Political repression was intensified; but as quickly as one group might be arrested another would be formed. Not only narodniki but also Marxists and liberals founded tenacious organizations in the 1890s.

The culture of opposition was not confined to the revolutionary activists. In the nineteenth century there was a remarkable expansion of education: secondary schools and universities proliferated and students were remarkably antagonistic to the regime. The methods of instruction and discipline grated upon young people. Nor did their unease disappear in adulthood. The tsarist order was regarded by them as a humiliating peculiarity that Russia should quickly remove.

Their feelings were strengthened by journalists and creative writers who informed public opinion with a freedom that increased after 1905.[21] Previously, most legal newspapers had been conservative or very cautiously liberal; afterwards they spanned a range of thought from proto-fascist on the far right to Bolshevik on the far left. Although the Okhrana closed publications that openly advocated sedition, the excitement of opinion against the authorities was constant. Not only newspapers but also trade unions, sickness-insurance groups and even Sunday schools were instruments of agitation. The regime stipulated that trade unions should be locally based and that their leaderships should be drawn from the working class. But this served to give workers an experience of collective self-organization. By thrusting people on to their own resources, tsarism built up the antidote to itself. The rationale of the old monarchy was further undermined.

Even so, the Okhrana was very efficient at its tasks. The revolutionary leaders had been suppressed in 1907; their various organizations in the Russian Empire were penetrated by police informers, and the arrest of second-rank activists continued. Contact between the *émigrés* and their followers was patchy.

The repression secured more time for the dynasty; it also strengthened the determination of the revolutionaries to avoid any dilution of their ideas. At the turn of the century it had been the Marxists who had been most popular with political intellectuals. A party had been formed, the Russian Social-Democratic Labour Party, in 1898. But it quickly dissolved into factionalism, especially among the *émigrés*. One of the factions, the Bolsheviks (or Majoritarians), was led by Vladimir Lenin. His booklet of 1902, *What Is To Be Done?*, described the need for the party to act as the vanguard of the working class. He laid down that party members should be disciplined in organization and loyal in doctrine. The party in his opinion should be highly centralized. His theories and his divisive activity disrupted the Second Party Congress in 1903. And Lenin compounded his controversial reputation in 1905 by proposing that the projected overthrow of the Romanov monarchy should be followed by a 'provisional revolutionary democratic dictatorship of the proletariat and the peasantry' – and he anticipated the use of terror in order to establish the dictatorship.[22]

These specifications alarmed his opponents – the so-called Mensheviks (or Minoritarians) – in the Russian Social-Democratic Labour Party who had always contended that Russia should undergo a 'bourgeois' revolution and complete her development of a capitalist economy before undertaking the 'transition to socialism'. They denounced the projected dictatorship as having nothing in common with genuinely socialist politics. And they wanted a more loosely-organized party than the Bolsheviks had devised.

The other great revolutionary party was the Party of Socialist-Revolutionaries, which inherited the traditions of the narodniki of the nineteenth century. Their leading theorist was Viktor Chernov. Unlike the narodniki, the Socialist-Revolutionaries did not think that Russia could move straight into socialism without a capitalist stage of economic development. But whereas the Marxists, be they Bolsheviks or Mensheviks, saw the urban workers as the great revolutionary class, the Socialist-Revolutionaries held the peasantry in higher regard and believed that peasants embodied, however residually, the egalitarian and communal values at the heart of socialism. But the Socialist-Revolutionaries recruited among the working class, and in many cities, were rivals to the Russian Social-Democratic Party. In many ways there were differing emphases rather than totally sharp distinctions between Marxists and Socialist-Revolutionaries in their ideas at lower organizational levels of their respective parties; and they suffered equally at the hands of the Okhrana.

The events of 1905–6 had already shown that if ever the people were allowed free elections, it would be these three parties that would vie for victory. The Kadets recognized the limitations of their own popularity and responded by adopting a policy of radical agrarian reform. They proposed to transfer the land of the gentry to the peasantry with suitable monetary compensation for the gentry. But this would never be sufficient to outmatch the appeal of the Socialist-Revolutionaries, Mensheviks and Bolsheviks unless that franchise was formulated in such a way as to give advantage to the middle classes.

Truly this was already a creaky structure of power. Matters were not helped by the fact that the Emperor was not respected. He was a monarch whose capacity for hard work was not matched by outstanding intelligence. He had no clear vision for Russia's future and wore himself out with day-to-day political administration. He found contentment only in the company of his family and was thought to be hen-pecked by his spouse Alexandra. In fact he was more independent from her than the rumours suggested, but the rumours were believed. Furthermore, he surrounded himself with advisers who included a variety of mystics and quacks. His favouritism towards the Siberian 'holy man' Grigori Rasputin became notorious. Rasputin had an uncanny ability to staunch the bleeding of the haemophiliac heir to the throne, Aleksei; but, protected by the Imperial couple, Rasputin gambled and wenched and intrigued in St Petersburg. The Romanovs sank further into infamy.

It was not that Nicholas entirely isolated himself from the people. He attended religious ceremonies; he met groups of peasants. In

1913 the tercentenary of the Romanov dynasty was celebrated with acclaim, and the Emperor was filmed for the benefit of cinema-goers. But he seems to have had a horror of his urban subjects: intellectuals, politicians and workers were distrusted by him.[23] Nicholas was out of joint with his times.

Yet the immediate danger to the regime had receded. The empire's subjects settled back into acceptance that the Okhrana and the armed forces were too strong to be challenged. Peasant disturbances were few. Stolypin had been ruthless ordering the execution of 2796 peasant rebel leaders after field courts-martial.[24] The hangman's noose was known as 'Stolypin's necktie'. Student demonstrations ceased. National resistance in the non-Russian regions virtually disappeared. Professional associations behaved circumspectly so as to avoid being closed down by the authorities. The labour movement, too, was disrupted by police intervention. Strikes ceased for a while. But as the economy experienced an upturn and mass unemployment fell, workers regained their militant confidence. Sporadic industrial conflicts returned, and a single event could spark off trouble across the empire.

This eventually occurred in April 1912 when police fired upon striking miners in the gold-fields near the river Lena in Siberia. Demonstrations took place in sympathy elsewhere. A second upsurge of opposition took place in June 1914 in St Petersburg. Wages and living conditions were a basic cause of grievance; so, too, was the resentment against the current political restrictions.[25]

The recurrence of strikes and demonstrations was an index of the liability of the tsarist political and economic order to intense strain. The Emperor, however, chose to strengthen his monarchical powers rather than seek a deal with the elected deputies in the State Duma. Not only he but also his government and his provincial governors could act without reference to legal procedures. The Duma could be and was dispersed by him without consultation; electoral rules were redrawn on his orders. Opponents could be sentenced to 'administrative exile' by the Ministry of Internal Affairs without reference to the courts – and this could involve banishment to the harshest regions of Siberia. In 1912, 2.3 million people lived under martial law and 63.3 million under 'reinforced protection'; provincial governors increasingly issued their own regulations and enforced them by administrative order.[26] The 'police state' of the Romanovs was very far from complete and there were signs that civil society could make further advances at the state's expense. Yet in many aspects there was little end to the arbitrary governance.

Nicholas would have made things easier for himself if he had allowed himself to be restrained constitutionally by the State Duma. Then the upper and middle classes, through their political parties, would have incurred the hostility that was aimed at the Emperor. Oppressive rule could have been reduced at a stroke. The decadence and idiocy of Nicholas's court would have ceased to invite critical scrutiny; and by constitutionalizing his position, he might even have saved his dynasty from destruction. As things stood, some kind of revolutionary clash was practically inevitable. Even the Octobrists were unsympathetic to their sovereign after his humiliation of Stolypin.

But Nicholas also had reason to doubt that the Duma would have been any better at solving the difficulties of the Russian Empire. Whoever was to rule Russia would face enormous tasks in transforming its economic, cultural and administrative arrangements if it was not to fall victim to rival Great Powers. The growth in industrial capacity was encouraging; the creation of an indigenous base of research and development was less so. Agriculture was changing only at a slow pace. And the social consequences of the transformation in town and countryside were tremendous. Even the economic successes caused problems. High expectations were generated by the increased knowledge about the West among not only the intelligentsia but also the workers. The alienated segment of society grew in number and hostility.

Yet the empire suffered as much from traditionalism as from modernity. For example, the possession of land in the village commune or the ability to return to the village for assistance was a powerful factor in enabling Russian workers to go on strike. Russian and Ukrainian peasants identified more with their village than with any imperial, dynastic or national idea. Furthermore, those inhabitants of the empire who had developed a national consciousness, such as the Poles, were deeply discontented at their treatment and would always cause trouble. The religious variety of the empire only added to the regime's problems, problems which were likely to increase as urbanization and education proceeded.

Yet if the empire was ever to fall apart, it would not even be clear to which area Russia might easily be confined. Russians lived everywhere in the Russian Empire. Large pockets of them existed in Baku, in Ukraine and in the Baltic provinces. Migrations of land-hungry Russian peasants had been encouraged by Stolypin, to Siberia and to Russia's possessions in central Asia. No strict notion of 'Russia' was readily to hand, and the St Petersburg authorities had always inhibited investigation of this matter. The Russian-ruled region of Poland was described as 'the Vistula provinces'; 'Ukraine', 'Latvia' and 'Estonia' did not appear as such on official maps. So where was Russia? This sprawling giant of a country was as big or as small as anyone liked to think of it as being. Few Russians would deny that it included Siberia. But westwards was it to include Ukraine and Belorussia? National demography and geography were extremely ill-defined, and the vagueness might in the wrong circumstances lead to violence.

After the turn of the century it was getting ever likelier that the wrong circumstances would occur. Social strife was continual. National resentments among the non-Russians were on the rise. Political opposition remained strident and determined. The monarchy was ever more widely regarded as an oppressive, obsolescent institution which failed to correspond to the country's needs. Nicholas II had nearly been overthown in 1905. He had recovered his position, but the basic tensions in state and society had not been alleviated.

2

The Fall of the Romanovs (1914–1917)

Yet it was not the internal but the external affairs of the empire that provided the definitive test of the dynasty. Clashes of interest with Japan, the United Kingdom and even France were settled peacefully; but rivalry with Austria-Hungary and Germany became ever more acute. In 1906 a diplomatic dispute between Germany and France over Morocco resulted in a French triumph that was acquired with Russian assistance. In the Balkans, the Russians themselves looked for France's help. The snag was that neither Paris nor St Petersburg relished a war with Austria-Hungary and Germany. Consequently the Russian government, despite much huffing and puffing, did not go to war when the Austrians annexed Bosnia and Herzegovina in 1908. The existence of a Duma and of a broad press meant that newspaper readers appreciated that a diplomatic defeat had been administered to Nicholas II. Tsarism, which had paraded itself as the protector of Serbs and other Slavs, looked weak and ineffectual. It looked as if the monarchy was failing the country.[1]

The diplomatic rivalries intensified. The British and the Germans did not abandon friendly relations with each other; but the Anglo-German naval race narrowed the options in Britain. Meanwhile Russia looked on nervously lest Germany might take advantage of the crumbling condition of the Ottoman Empire. Exports of Russian and Ukrainian grain from Odessa through the Straits of the Dardanelles were important to the empire's balance of trade. In 1912 Bulgaria, Serbia and Greece declared war on the Ottoman Empire. In this instance Russia refused to back Serbian efforts to obtain access to a sea-port and a crisis in Russo-Austrian relations was avoided. Unfortunately this sensible decision was seen in Russia as yet another sign of Nicholas II's weakness of will. Then a second Balkan war broke out in 1913. This time it occurred between Serbia and Bulgaria, the joint victors over the Turks. As a result Serbia obtained greater territory in Macedonia and appeared even more menacing to Austrian interests.

Russia's relations worsened with Austria-Hungary and Germany even though Serbia had not been acting at Russian instigation. And on 28 June 1914 a fateful event occurred. This was the assassination of the heir to the Habsburg throne, Archduke Franz Ferdinand, by the Serbian nationalist Gavrilo Princip in Sarajevo, capital of recently-annexed Bosnia. Austria demanded humiliating concessions from the Serbian government, which it blamed for the Archduke's death. Russia took Serbia's side, and Germany supported Austria. Austria stood by her ultimatum and declared war on Serbia. Russia announced a general mobilization of her armies. Then Germany declared war on Russia and France. Britain showed solidarity with France and Russia by declaring war on Germany and Austria-Hungary.

Nobody had anticipated exactly this denouement. No one as yet had definite ideas about war aims. Nor was there much understanding that the fighting might drag on for years and bring down dynasties and whole social orders. The calculation in Russian ruling circles was that a short, victorious war would bind Imperial society more closely together. A few long-sighted politicians such as Pëtr Durnovo could see that war against Germany would lead to intolerable strains and might initiate the regime's downfall. But such thoughts were not given a hearing in mid-1914. The Emperor's sense of dynastic and imperial honour predominated.[2] He might anyway have run into trouble if he had not taken up the challenge in the Balkans. The Octobrists and Kadets would have made a fuss in the Duma; even many socialists, whose Second International had opposed general war in Europe, felt that German pretensions should be resisted.

In the event their pressure did not need to be exerted: Nicholas II leapt into the darkness of the Great War without anyone pushing him. The decisions of the European powers had consequences of massive significance. The Great War produced the situation in Russia, Austria and Germany that shattered the Romanov, Habsburg and Hohenzollern monarchies. It also made possible the Bolshevik seizure of power in October 1917. Except for the Great War, Lenin would have remained an *émigré* theorist scribbling in Swiss libraries; and even if Nicholas II had been deposed in a peacetime transfer of power, the inception of a communist order would hardly have been likely. The first three years of this military conflict, however, caused an economic and political disorder so huge that Nicholas II had to abdicate in February 1917. The subsequent Provisional Government proved no less unequal to its tasks, and Lenin became the country's ruler within months of tsarism's overthrow.

But let us return to 1914. As massive military struggle commenced, the Russian steamroller moved effortlessly into East Prussia in mid-August. Victory over Germany was identified as the crucial war aim. Even so, Austria-Hungary was also a redoubtable enemy and the Russians had to mount an attack on the southern sector of what was becoming known in the rest of Europe as the Eastern front. Not since the Napoleonic wars had so many countries been directly involved in military conflict.

Yet the Russians were quickly encircled by German forces. At the Battle of Tannenberg 100,000 Russian prisoners-of-war were taken, and the Germans advanced into Russian-ruled Poland.[3] On the Western front, too, Belgium and north-eastern France were overrun by German forces. But the Allies – Russia, France and the United Kingdom – regrouped and the lines were held. Static warfare ensued with two great systems of trenches cutting north to south across Europe. By the end of 1916, the Russian Imperial Army had conscripted fourteen million men, mainly peasants. Russian industrial expansion was substantial; so, too, was the size of Russia's factory and mining work-force, rising by roughly forty per cent in the first three years of the Great War.[4] All classes of the population supported Russian entry into the war and sought victory over Germany and Austria-Hungary. A surge of patriotic feeling was suddenly available to the government.

The Emperor was determined to gain the greatest advantage from the war. Negotiating with the Western Allies in early 1915, his Foreign Minister Sazonov laid down that the Straits of the Dardanelles should be incorporated into the Russian Empire when the Central Powers were defeated. Secret treaties were signed with Britain and France in accordance with these demands. Russian war aims were not simply defensive but expansionist.

All this had to be kept strictly confidential; otherwise the Fourth State Duma might not have rung loud with support for the war when it voted financial credits to the government in January 1915. Only the socialist parties had sections that repudiated the war as an 'imperialist' conflict. Yet it was not long before popular antagonism to the monarchy reappeared. The scandalous behaviour of Rasputin, the favourite 'holy man' of Nicholas and Alexandra, brought still greater opprobrium on the court. Rasputin was assassinated by a disgusted monarchist, Prince Yusupov, in 1916. But Alexandra's German ancestry continued to feed rumours that there was treachery in high places. Nicholas II did not help his cause by dutifully deciding to stay at military headquarters at Mogilëv for the duration of the war. Thereby he cut himself off from information about the situation in the capital. The government's conduct of affairs induced Milyukov, the Kadet party leader, to put the question in the State Duma: 'Is this folly or is it treason?'[5]

Sharp dilemmas none the less awaited any conceivable wartime administration in Petrograd (the new name for the capital after St Petersburg was judged to be too German-sounding). Food supplies were a difficulty from the start; the task of equipping and provisioning the soldiers and horses of the Imperial armed forces was prodigious. The government showed no lack of will. In the winter of 1915–16 it introduced fixed prices for its grain purchases and disbarred sellers from refusing to sell to it. Nor had Nicholas II entirely run out of luck. Weather conditions in 1916 were favourable and agricultural output was only ten per cent below the record annual level attained in 1909–13.[6] And the German naval blockade of the Black Sea had the benefit of preventing the export of foodstuffs and releasing a greater potential quantity of grain for domestic consumption.

All this, however, was outweighed by a set of severe disadvantages for the Russian Empire's economy after 1914. Sufficient foodstuffs regularly reached the forces at the Eastern front; but the government was less successful in keeping the state warehouses stocked for sale to urban civilians. Among the problems were the peasantry's commercial interests. Peasants were affected by the rapid depreciation of the currency and by the shortage of industrial goods available during the war; they therefore had little incentive to sell grain to the towns. Certainly there was massive industrial growth: by 1916 output in large enterprises was between sixteen and twenty-two per cent higher than in 1913.[7] But the increase resulted almost exclusively from factories producing armaments and other military supplies. About four fifths of industrial capital investment was directed towards this sector, and the production of goods for the agricultural sector practically ceased.[8]

No remedy was in sight so long as the country was at war and military exigencies had to dominate industrial policy. Not even the huge state loans raised from the empire's banks and private investors, from Russia's allies and from American finance-houses were sufficient to bail out the Imperial economy.[9] The government was compelled to accelerate the emission of paper roubles to deal with the budgetary pressures. Rapid inflation became unavoidable.

Transport was another difficulty. The railway network had barely been adequate for the country's uses in peacetime; the wartime needs of the armed forces nearly crippled it.[10] Grain shipments to the towns were increasingly unreliable. Industrialists complained about delays in the delivery of coal and iron from the Don Basin to Petrograd and Moscow. Financiers, too, grew nervous. In 1916 the banks started to exert a squeeze on credit. Each sector of the economy – agriculture, trade, industry, finance, transport – had problems which aggravated the problems in the other sectors. Nor was it human error that was mainly to blame. Not enough Russian factories, mines, roads, railways, banks, schools and farms had attained the level of development achieved by the world' s other leading powers. A protracted war against Germany – the greatest such power on the European continent – unavoidably generated immense strains.

Nicholas II characteristically fumbled the poor hand he had been dealt. Above all, he continued to treat liberal leaders of the State Duma with disdain; he rejected their very moderate demand for a 'government of public confidence' even though it was only by introducing some liberals to his cabinet that he could hope to have them on his side if ever his government reached the point of revolutionary crisis.

The tsar, a devoted husband and father, was more adept at ordering repression than at mustering political support. The Marxist deputies to the Duma, including both Mensheviks and Bolsheviks, were arrested in November 1914 on the grounds of their opposition to the war effort; and the Okhrana broke up the major strikes which occurred across the country in late 1915 and late 1916. The socialist parties survived only in depleted local groups: most Bolshevik, Menshevik and Socialist-Revolutionary leaders were in Siberian exile or Swiss emigration or had withdrawn from political activity. The state's sole compromise with the labour movement came with its granting of permission to workers to join their employers in electing War-Industry Committees. These bodies were supposed to flush out the blockages in industrial output. But the existence of the Committees allowed work-forces to discuss their grievances as well as any proposals for the raising of productivity – and this gave the labour movement a chance to escape the government's tight grip.[11]

Furthermore, Nicholas II's very acknowledgement of the necessity of the War-Industry Committees counted against him. Traditionally the emperors had invoked the assistance of 'society' only when the state authorities despaired of solving their difficulties by themselves. But the German government was intent upon the dismemberment of the Russian Empire. This was a life-or-death combat for Russia, and the Emperor perceived that his administration could not cope by itself.

The War-Industry Committees were not his only compromise. In 1915 he allowed the municipal councils and the provincial zemstva to establish a central body known as *Zemgor*. The aim was to enhance the co-ordination of the country's administration. Zemgor was also authorized to supplement the inadequate medical facilities near the front. But neither Zemgor under Prince Georgi Lvov nor the War-Industry Committees under the Octobrist leader Alexander Guchkov were given much scope for initiative. Frustrated by this, opposition politicians in the State Duma, the War-Industry Committees and Zemgor started to discuss the possibilities of joint action against Nicholas – and often they met in the seclusion of freemason lodges. Thus co-operation grew among the leading figures: Guchkov the Octobrist, Milyukov the Kadet, Lvov of Zemgor and Kerenski the Socialist-Revolutionary. Something drastic, they agreed, had to be done about the monarchy.

Yet timidity gripped all except Guchkov, who sounded out opinion among the generals about some sort of palace *coup d'état*; but in the winter of 1916–17 he still could obtain no promise of active participation. His sole source of consolation was that the commanders at Mogilëv tipped him the wink that they would not intervene to save the monarchy. Indeed nobody was even willing to denounce him to the Okhrana: opinion in the highest public circles had turned irretrievably against Nicholas II.

This did not happen in an ambience of pessimism about Russian victory over the Central Powers. On the contrary, it had been in 1916 that General Brusilov invented effective tactics for breaking through the defences of the enemy.[12] Although the Central Powers rallied and counter-attacked, the image of German invincibility was impaired. The hopeful mood of the generals was shared by industrialists. They, too, felt that they had surmounted their wartime difficulties as well as anyone could have expected of them. The early shortages of equipment experienced by the armed forces had been overcome; and the leaders of Russian industry, commerce and finance considered that the removal of Nicholas II would facilitate a decisive increase in economic and administrative efficiency. Such public figures had not personally suffered in the war; many of them had actually experienced an improvement either in their careers or in their bank accounts. But they had become convinced that they and their country would do better without being bound by the dictates of Nicholas II.

The Emperor was resented even more bitterly by those members of the upper and middle classes who had not done well out of the war. There was an uncomfortably large number of them. The Okhrana's files bulged with reports on disaffection. By 1916 even the Council of the United Gentry, a traditional bastion of tsarism, was reconsidering its loyalty to the sovereign.[13]

The background to this was economic. There were bankruptcies and other financial embarrassments among industrialists who had failed to win governmental contracts. This happened most notably in the Moscow region (whereas Petrograd's large businesses gained a great deal from the war). But small and medium-sized firms across the empire experienced trouble; their output steadily declined after 1914 and many of them went into liquidation.[14] Plenty of businessmen had grounds for objection to the sleazy co-operation between ministers and the magnates of industry and finance. Many owners of rural estates, too, were hard pressed: in their case the difficulty was the dual impact of the depreciation of the currency and the shortage of farm labourers caused by military conscription;[15] and large commercial enterprises were discomfited by the introduction of state regulation of the grain trade. But the discontent did not lead to rebellions, only to grumbles.

The peasantry, too, was passive. Villages faced several painful problems: the conscription of their young males; the unavailability of manufactured goods; inadequate prices for grain and hay; the requisitioning of horses. There was destitution in several regions.[16] Even so, the Russian Empire's vast economy was highly variegated, and some sections of the peasantry did rather well financially during the war. They could buy or rent land more cheaply from landlords. They could eat their produce, feed it to their livestock or sell it to neighbours. They could illicitly distil it into vodka. Nothing, however, could compensate for the loss of sons buried at the front.

Those peasants who moved actively against the monarchy were soldiers in the Petrograd garrison, who resented the poor food and the severe military discipline and were growing reluctant to carry out orders to suppress disorder among other sections of society. Matters came to a head with the resumption of industrial conflict in February 1917. Wages for workers in the Petrograd armaments plants probably rose slightly faster than inflation in 1914–15; but thereafter they failed to keep pace – and the pay-rates in the capital were the highest in the country. It is reckoned that such workers by 1917 were being paid in real terms between fifteen and twenty per cent less than before the war.[17] Wages in any case do not tell the whole story. Throughout the empire there was a deficit in consumer products. Bread had to be queued for, and its availability was unreliable. Housing and sanitation fell into disrepair. All urban amenities declined in quality as the population of the towns swelled with rural migrants searching for factory work and with refugees fleeing the German occupation.

Nicholas II was surprisingly complacent about the labour movement. Having survived several industrial disturbances in the past dozen years, he was unruffled by the outbreak of a strike on 22 February 1917 at the gigantic Putilov armaments plant. Next day the women textile labourers demonstrated in the capital's central thoroughfares. The queuing for bread, amidst all their other problems, had become too much for them. They called on the male labour-force of the metallurgical plants to show solidarity. By 24 February there was virtually a general strike in Petrograd.

On 26 February, at last sensing the seriousness of the situation, Nicholas prorogued the State Duma. As it happened, the revolutionary activists were counselling against a strike since the Okhrana had so easily and ruthlessly suppressed trouble in the factories in December 1916. But the popular mood was implacable. Army commanders reported that troops sent out to quell the demonstrations were instead handing over their rifles to the protesters or simply joining them. This convinced the local revolutionaries – Bolsheviks, Mensheviks and Socialist-Revolutionaries – that the monarchy could be overthrown, and they resumed the task of agitating and organizing for such an end. The capital had become a maelstrom of revolt; and by closing down the Duma, the Emperor had effectively thrust conservatives and liberals, too, into a posture of outright opposition.

The Emperor was given dispiriting counsel by those whom he consulted. The Duma speaker, the Octobrist Mikhail Rodzyanko, who fancied his chances of becoming prime minister by mediating among the Duma's politicians, urged Nicholas to agree that his position was hopeless. The Emperor would indeed have faced difficulties even if he had summoned regiments from the Eastern front; for the high command stayed very reluctant to get involved in politics. It is true that the monarchy's troubles were as yet located in a single city. Yet this limitation was only temporary; for Petrograd was the capital: as soon as news of the events spread to the provinces there was bound to be further popular commotion. Antipathy to the regime was fiercer than in 1905–6 or mid-1914. The capital's factories were at a standstill. The streets were full of rebellious soldiers and workers. Support for the regime was infinitesimal, and the reports of strikes, mutinies and demonstrations were becoming ever more frantic.

Abruptly on 2 March, while travelling by train from Mogilëv to Petrograd, the Emperor abdicated. At first he had tried to transfer his powers to his sickly, adolescent son Aleksei. Then he offered the throne to his liberally-inclined uncle, Grand Duke Mikhail. Such an outcome commended itself to Milyukov and the right wing of the Kadets. But Milyukov was no more in touch with current realities in Petrograd than the Emperor. Appearing on the balcony of the Tauride Palace, he was jeered for proposing the installation of a constitutional monarchy.[18]

Nicholas's final measure as sovereign was to abdicate. State authority was assumed by an unofficial committee created by prominent figures in the State Duma after the Duma had been prorogued in February. The formation of the Provisional Government was announced on 3 March. Milyukov, an Anglophile and a professor of Russian history, became Minister of Foreign Affairs, and the War Ministry was occupied by the ebullient Guchkov. But the greatest influence was held by men at the centre and the left of Russian liberalism. This was signalled by the selection of Lvov, who had led Zemgor, as Minister-Chairman of the Provisional Government. It was also evident in Lvov's invitation to Kerenski, a Socialist-Revolutionary, to head the Ministry of Justice. Lvov and most of his colleagues, while celebrating the removal of the Romanovs, argued that government and 'people' could at last co-operate to mutual advantage.

Under direct pressure from the socialist leaders of the anti-Romanov demonstrations in Petrograd, the cabinet announced a series of radical reforms. Universal and unconditional civil freedoms were promulgated: freedoms of opinion, faith, association, assembly and the press. Religious and social privileges were abolished. In addition, elections were promised for a Constituent Assembly and all adults over twenty-one years of age, including women, were to have the vote. These measures immediately made wartime Russia freer than any other country even at peace.

Although they had not secured the post of Minister-Chairman for their leader Milyukov, the Kadets were the mainstay of the first Provisional Government.[19] Before 1917 they had tried to present themselves as standing above class and sectional aspirations. In particular, they had aspired to resolve the 'agrarian question' by handing over the gentry-owned estates to the peasantry and compensating landlords in cash. But in 1917 they argued that only the Constituent Assembly had the right to decide so fundamental a question and that, anyway, no basic reform should be attempted during the war lest peasant soldiers might desert the Eastern front to get their share of the redistributed land. It is true that the Provisional Government initially condoned the bargaining between striking workers and their employers over wages and conditions; but rapidly the need to maintain armaments production took precedence in the minds of ministers and any industrial stoppage incurred official disapproval.

And so the Kadets, as they observed a society riven between the wealthy élites and the millions of workers and peasants, chose to make common cause with the interests of wealth. Nor did they see much wrong with the expansionist war aims secretly agreed by Nicholas II with Britain and France in 1915. Thus the Provisional Government was not pursuing a strictly defensive policy which would maintain the willingness of soldiers to die for their country and of workers to work uncomplainingly in deteriorating conditions. The Kadets were taking a grave risk with the political dominance they had recently been donated.

They overlooked the fact that they had benefited from the February

Revolution without having played much part in it. The heroes on the streets had been Petrograd's workers and garrison soldiers, who believed that Russia should disown any expansionist pretensions in the war. The Mensheviks and Socialist-Revolutionaries shared this feeling and elaborated a policy of 'revolutionary defencism'. For them, the defence of Russia and her borderlands was the indispensable means of protecting the civic freedoms granted by the Provisional Government. Mensheviks and Socialist-Revolutionaries had great political authority. Even before Nicholas II had abdicated, they had helped to create the Petrograd Soviet of Workers' and Soldiers' Deputies and established themselves in its leading posts. And they obtained dominance in the soviets which were established in other cities. Without the consent of the Mensheviks and Socialist-Revolutionaries, the Provisional Government could never have been formed.

Lvov had been given his opportunity because Mensheviks and Socialist-Revolutionaries, recognizing that workers were a tiny minority of the population, made the judgement that any campaign for the immediate establishment of socialism would lead to civil war. They had always contended that Russia remained at much too low a level of industrialization and popular education for a socialist administration to be installed. On his return from Siberian exile, the Menshevik Irakli Tsereteli gave powerful expression to such opinions in the Petrograd Soviet. Mensheviks and Socialist-Revolutionaries concurred that, for the foreseeable future, the country needed a 'bourgeois government' led by the Kadets. Socialists should therefore offer conditional support to Prince Lvov. Even several leading Bolshevik leaders in Petrograd were of a similar mind.

At the same time neither Mensheviks nor Socialist-Revolutionaries renounced their struggle on behalf of the working class; and, through the Petrograd Soviet, they wielded so large an influence that ministers referred to the existence of 'dual power'. The cabinet could not have been created without the sanction of the Soviet, and the Soviet acted as if it had the right to give instructions to its own supporters – mainly workers and soldiers – which then became mandatory for the entire local population. Order No. 1, issued by the Petrograd

Soviet on 1 March, abolished the code of military discipline in the Petrograd garrison and enjoined troops to subject themselves to the authority of the Soviet.[20] This was the most famous of the early derogations from the Provisional Government's capacity to govern. Other such orders introduced the eight-hour day and various improvements in factory working conditions. Lvov and fellow ministers could do nothing but wring their hands and trust that things would eventually settle down.

Of this there was no likelihood. The crisis in the economy and administration traced a line of ineluctable logic so long as Russia remained at war. Milyukov understood this better than most ministers; but on 18 April he displayed a wilful stupidity unusual even in a professor of Russian history by sending a telegram to Paris and London in which he explicitly affirmed the cabinet's commitment to the secret treaties signed with the Allies in 1915. The contents of the telegram were bound to infuriate all Russian socialist opinion if ever they became publicly revealed. Just such a revelation duly happened. The personnel of Petrograd telegraph offices were Menshevik supporters to a man and instantly informed on Milyukov to the Petrograd Soviet. The Mensheviks, Socialist-Revolutionaries and Bolsheviks organized a street demonstration against the Provisional Government on 20 April. Against this assertion of the Petrograd Soviet's strength, the Provisional Government offered no resistance, and Milyukov and Guchkov resigned.

After such a trial of strength, Lvov despaired of keeping a liberal-led cabinet in office. His solution was to persuade the Mensheviks and Socialist-Revolutionaries to take up portfolios in government. Both parties had huge memberships in mid-1917. The Mensheviks had 200,000 members and the Socialist-Revolutionaries claimed to have recruited a full million.[21] On 5 May, a second cabinet was created. The Socialist-Revolutionary Alexander Kerenski was promoted to the War Ministry; and the Mensheviks Irakli Tsereteli and Mikhail Skobelev and the Socialist-Revolutionary leader Viktor Chernov became ministers for the first time.

Their inclination had once been to let the Kadet ministers stew in their own juice; but they now agreed to join them in the pot in an attempt to take Russian politics off the boil. They did not do this without exacting substantial concessions. Skobelev's Ministry of Labour pressed for workers to have the right to impartial arbitration in cases of dispute.[22] Firmer state regulation of industry was also ordered as part of a governmental campaign against financial corruption. And Chernov as Minister of Agriculture allowed peasants to take advantage of the rule that any land that had fallen into disuse in wartime could be taken over by elective 'land committees' and re-allocated for cultivation.[23] There was also a modification of governmental policy on the non-Russian regions. Tsereteli, Minister of Posts and Telegraphs, went outside his specific cabinet brief by insisting that broader autonomy for self-government should be offered to Ukraine.[24]

These adjustments in policy might have worked reasonably well for the liberals and the more moderate socialists if peace had reigned. But society and economy continued to be dislocated by the war. Class antagonisms lost none of their volatility, and the situation in factory, garrison and village was a powder-keg that might be ignited at any time.

Workers in most places desisted from outright violence. But there were exceptions. Unpopular foremen in several Petrograd factories were tied up in sacks and paraded around their works in wheelbarrows.[25] Some victims were then thrown into the icy river Neva. Violence occurred also in the Baltic fleet, where several unpopular officers were lynched. Such was the fate of Admiral Nepenin in Helsinki. The dissatisfaction with the old disciplinary code made the sailors indiscriminate in this instance; for Nepenin was far from being the most authoritarian of the Imperial Navy's commanders. Most crews, at any rate, did not resort to these extreme methods. In both the Imperial Army and Navy the tendency was for the men to restrict themselves to humiliating their officers by behaviour of symbolic importance. Epaulettes were torn off. Saluting ceased and the lower ranks indicated their determination to scrutinize and discuss instructions from above.

The defiant mood acquired organizational form. Workers set up factory-workshop committees, and analogous bodies were established by soldiers and sailors in military units. The committees were at first held regularly accountable to open mass meetings. A neologism entered Russian vocabulary: *mitingovanie*. If a committee failed to respond to its electors' requests, an open meeting could be held and the committee membership could straightaway be changed.

The example set by workers, soldiers and sailors was picked up by other groups in society. The zeal to discuss, complain, demand and decide was ubiquitous. People relished their long-denied chance to voice their opinions without fear of the Okhrana, and engaged in passionate debate on public policy and private needs. Indeed politics embraced so large an area that the boundary disappeared between the public and private. Passengers on the trains of the Trans-Siberian railway to Vladivostok elected carriage councils ('soviet'!). They did this not out of ideological fanaticism but from the consideration that the train would need to pick up and distribute food on the journey. Each carriage needed to ensure it received its fair share. Thus the practical requirements of subsistence were in themselves a stimulus to popular participation.

The country's cultural customs also had their effect. The village land communes of Russia and Ukraine had traditionally enabled peasants to speak their mind on questions of local importance. This practice had been transmitted to those many industrial workers who hired themselves to factories not as individuals but as members of work-groups (*arteli*); and soldiers and sailors operated in small units under their terms of service. The apparent 'modernity' of politics in 1917 had a past which stretched back over centuries.

The various sectional groups became more assertive after perceiving the cabinet to be tardy in holding elections to a Constituent Assembly. In the absence of an elected government, it was every group for itself. Employers regarded 'wheel-barrowing' as the beginning of a Red Terror. They were over-reacting. But there was realism in their claim that the militance of the workers was having a deleterious impact on the economy. Strikes undoubtedly lowered productivity. Even more alarming to owners in Petrograd, from May 1917 onwards, were the instances of factory-workshop committees instituting 'workers' control' over the management of enterprises.[26] This was direct action; it was no longer merely forceful lobbying: managers were not allowed to do anything that might incur the disapproval of their work-force. Such a turnabout had its rural equivalent. Already in March there were cases of peasants seizing gentry-owned land in Penza province. Illegal pasturing and timber-felling also became frequent.[27]

The middle classes, dismayed by what they saw as the cabinet's indulgence of 'the masses', contributed to the embitterment of social relations. They, too, had an abundance of representative bodies. The most aggressive was the Petrograd Society of Factory and Works Owners, which had encouraged a series of lock-outs in the capital in summer 1917.[28] Nor was the atmosphere lightened by the comment of the Moscow industrialist P. P. Ryabushinski that only 'the bony hand of hunger' would compel workers to come to their senses. Even the owners of rural estates were bestirring themselves as their Union of Landowners campaigned against peasant demands in the countryside.

Yet not only did few gentry owners live on their estates but also none of them dared to attempt the sort of open challenge to 'the masses' delivered by the capital's industrialists. Instead they tried to recruit the richer peasants into the Union of Landowners.[29] In reality it would have made little difference if they had succeeded in expanding their membership in this fashion. For the influence of any given class or group depended on its ability to assemble cohesive strength in numbers in a given locality. Not even the Petrograd industrialists maintained their solidarity for very long; and this is not to mention the chaotic rivalries across the country among the industrialists, financiers and large landowners. Demoralization was setting in by midsummer. Savings were expatriated to western Europe; the competition for armaments-production contracts slackened; the families of the rich were sent south by fathers who worried for their safety.

Their concern had been induced by the somersault in social relations since February 1917, a concern that was also the product of the collapse of the coercive institutions of tsarism; for the personnel of the Okhrana and the local police had been arrested or had fled in fear of vengeance at the hands of those whom they had once persecuted. The provincial governors appointed by Nicholas II were at first replaced by 'commissars' appointed by the Provisional Government. But these commissars, too, were unable to carry out their job. What usually happened was that locally-formed committees of public safety persuaded them to stand down in favour of their recommended candidate.[30]

The main units of local self-assertion were the villages, the towns and the provinces of the Empire. But in some places the units were still larger. This was the case in several non-Russian regions. In Kiev a Ukrainian Central *Rada* (or Council) was formed under the leadership of socialists of various types; and, at the All-Ukrainian National Congress in April, the Rada was instructed to press for Ukraine to be accorded broad powers of self-government. The same idea was pursued by the Finns, whose most influential party, the social-democrats, called for the *Sejm* (parliament) to be allowed to administer Finland. Similar pressure was exerted from Estonia – which had been combined into a single administrative unit by the Provisional Government itself – and Latvia. In the Transcaucasus the Provisional Government established a Special Transcaucasian Committee; but the Committee operated under constant challenge from the socialist parties and soviets established by the major local nationalities: the Georgians, Armenians and Azeris.[31]

Among these various bodies, from Helsinki in the north to Tbilisi in the south, there was agreement that their respective national aspirations should be contained within the boundaries of a vast multinational state. Autonomy, not secession, was demanded. The country was no longer officially described as the Russian Empire, and even many anti-Russian nationalist leaders were reluctant to demand independence in case this might leave them defenceless against invasion by the Central Powers.

The peoples in the non-Russian regions were typically motivated less by national than by social and economic matters.[32] The demand for bread and social welfare was general, and increasingly there was support for the slogan of peace. Furthermore, peasants were the huge majority of the population in these regions and nearly all of them favoured parties which promised to transfer the agricultural land into their keeping. Georgians, Estonians and Ukrainians were united by such aspirations (and, of course, the Russian workers, peasants and soldiers shared them too). The problem for the Provisional Government was that the Rada, the Sejm and other national organs of self-government among the non-Russians were beginning to constitute a tier of unofficial regional opposition to policies announced in Petrograd.

Thus the centralized administrative structure, shaken in the February Revolution, was already tottering by spring 1917. The Provisional Government had assumed power promising to restore and enhance the fortunes of state. Within months it had become evident that the Romanov dynasty's collapse would produce yet further disintegration. The times were a-changing, and hopes and fears changed with them.

PART ONE

'"Lenin has died."
"England has given official recognition to the USSR."
"100,000 workers have joined the Russian Communist Party."'
Boris Yefimov's 1924 drawing of a foreign capitalist pondering the latest news as his delight turns to anger and finally to fear.

3

Conflicts and Crises (1917)

Disputes intensified after the February Revolution about the future of the old Russian Empire. Hardly any politicians, generals or businessmen advocated a return of the monarchy; it was widely taken for granted that the state would become a republic. Yet the precise constitutional form to be chosen by the republic was contentious. The Kadets wished to retain a unitary administration and opposed any subdivision of the empire into a federation of nationally-based territorial units. Their aim was to rule through the traditional network of provinces.[1] In contrast, the Mensheviks and Socialist-Revolutionaries wanted to accede to the national aspirations of the non-Russian population. In particular, they intended to grant regional self-government to Ukraine, which had been merely a collection of provinces in the tsarist period. When the Kadets argued that this would ultimately bring about the disintegration of the state, the Mensheviks and the Socialist-Revolutionaries replied that it offered the sole way to prevent separatist movements from breaking up the state.

The Kadets played for time, stipulating that any regional reorganization would have to await decision by the Constituent Assembly. But popular opinion was shifting against them on many other policies. In particular, the liberal ministers were regarded as having expansionist war aims even after the resignation of Milyukov, the arch-expansionist, from the cabinet.

Yet the Kadets in the Provisional Government, despite being faced by problems with the non-Russians, felt inhibited about making a patriotic appeal exclusively to the Russians. Liberal ministers were understandably wary lest they might irritate the internationalist sensibility of the Mensheviks and the Socialist-Revolutionaries. In any case, Russian nationalism was not very attractive to most Russians, who could see for themselves that their non-Russian fellow citizens were as keen as they were to defend the country. There was a general feeling that ordinary folk of all nationalities were oppressed by the same material difficulties. Not having been very nationalistic before the Great War, Russians did not suddenly become so in 1917. On the whole, they responded most positively to slogans which had a direct bearing on their everyday lives: workers' control, land, bread, peace and freedom. And they assumed that what was good for their locality was good for the entire society.

Yet although the Russians did not act together as a nation, Russian workers, peasants and soldiers caused difficulties for the cabinet. It was in the industrial cities where the soviets, trade unions and factory-workshop committees were concentrated; and since Russians constituted a disproportionately large segment of factory workers, they were to the fore in helping to form these bodies. Furthermore, such bodies were instruments of political mobilization; they were also dedicated to the country's rapid cultural development.[2] And they established their internal hierarchies. In early June, for example, soviets from all over the country sent representatives to Petrograd to the First All-Russia Congress of Workers' and Soldiers' Deputies. This Congress elected a Central Executive Committee to co-ordinate all soviets across the country. A potential alternative framework of administration was being constructed.

Meanwhile the Provisional Government depended on its marriage of convenience with socialists. Liberal ministers gritted their teeth because they recognized that the Mensheviks and Socialist-Revolutionaries alone could preserve them in power. They had to hope that eventually they would be in a position to annul the marriage and rule without socialist interference. This was always a bit of a gamble, being based on the premiss that no trouble would arise from the other large socialist party which was consolidating itself after the February Revolution: the Bolsheviks. Initially the gamble did not seem a very long shot. The Bolsheviks were a minority in the Petrograd Soviet; there were even those among them who were willing to contemplate giving conditional support to the Provisional Government. Perhaps the Bolsheviks, too, could be embraced in the marital arrangement.

But all this was set to change. On 3 April, Lenin came back to Russia via Germany in a train put at his disposal by the German government. He returned to a party divided on strategy, and he quickly found that there were plenty of Bolsheviks eager to support a policy of vigorous opposition to the cabinet. The February Revolution had disappointed all Bolsheviks. Against their expectations, the monarchy's overthrow had not been followed by a 'provisional revolutionary democratic dictatorship of the proletariat and peasantry'; and the Bolsheviks had failed to gain control over the Petrograd Soviet.

For some weeks they had been in disarray. Several of their leaders – including Lev Kamenev and Iosif Stalin – favoured some co-operation with the Mensheviks; but Lenin put a stop to this. When Kamenev boarded his train on its way to Petrograd, Lenin expostulated: 'What have you been writing in *Pravda*? We've seen a few copies and called you all sorts of names!'[3] Despite not having been in Russia for ten years and having had flimsy contact with fellow Bolsheviks since 1914, he articulated a strategy that successfully expressed the anger of those who detested the Provisional Government. On 4 April he presented his *April Theses* to comrades in the Tauride Palace. Lenin's central thought involved a reconstruction of Bolshevism. He called upon the party to build up majorities in the soviets and other mass organizations and then to expedite the transfer of power to them. Implicitly he was urging the overthrow of the Provisional Government and the inception of a socialist order.[4]

His audience was stunned: no Bolshevik had previously suggested that the 'transition to socialism' might be inaugurated instantly after the monarchy's removal. The party's conventional notion had been that Russia would still require an epoch of capitalist economic development. Yet the Bolsheviks had also always stressed that the bourgeoisie could not be trusted to establish political democracy and that a temporary 'democratic dictatorship' should be set up by socialists. Essentially Lenin was now striking out the qualification that socialist rule should be temporary.[5]

The ideas of the *April Theses* were accepted by the Seventh Party Conference at the end of the month; and his party cut its remaining links with the Mensheviks. Without Lenin, the crystallization of a far-left opposition to the Provisional Government would have taken longer. But while he chopped away at his party's formal doctrines, undoubtedly he was working with the grain of its impatience and militancy. All Bolshevik leaders had always hated Nicholas II and liberals with equal venom. Few were squeamish about the methods that might be used to achieve the party's ends. Dictatorship was thought desirable, terror unobjectionable. Bolsheviks wanted to reduce the schedule for the eventual attainment of communism. Their lives had been dedicated to revolutionary aims. Hardly any veteran Bolshevik had evaded prison and Siberian exile before 1917; and, while operating in the clandestine conditions, each had had to put up with much material distress. Lenin's return gave them the leadership they wanted.

Those who disliked his project either joined the Menshevik party or abandoned political involvement altogether.[6] The Bolshevik party anticipated socialist revolution across Europe as well as in Russia. The word went forth from Petrograd that when the Bolsheviks took power, great changes would immediately be set in motion. By midsummer 1917 they had worked out slogans of broad appeal: peace; bread; all power to the soviets; workers' control; land to the peasants; and national self-determination.

The Bolshevik party adhered to democratic procedures only to the extent that its underlying political purpose was being served; and the circumstances after the February Revolution fulfilled this condition. In May and June the Bolsheviks increased their representation at the expense of the Mensheviks and Socialist-Revolutionaries in many factory committees and some soviets. The party is said to have expanded its membership to 300,000 by the end of the year. Apparently about three fifths of Bolsheviks were of working-class background.[7] Such was the expansive revolutionary spirit among them that the Bolshevik leaders were carried away by it at least to some extent. And unlike the Mensheviks and Socialist-Revolutionaries, the Bolsheviks had neither any governmental responsibility nor many administrative burdens in the soviets. They had the time to conduct inflammatory propaganda, and they used it.

Intellectuals of middle-class origins were prominent in the party's higher echelons; the return of the *émigrés* – including Trotski, who worked alongside the Bolsheviks from summer 1917 after years of antagonism to Lenin – reinforced the phenomenon. Their skills in writing articles and proclamations and in keeping records were essential to party bodies. Yet the fact that practices of electivity and accountability pervaded the party impeded Bolshevik intellectuals from doing just as they pleased. At any rate, Bolsheviks were united by their wish for power and for socialism regardless of class origins. From Lenin downwards there was a veritable rage to engage in revolutionary action.[8] Lenin revelled in his party's mood. At the First All-Russia Congress of Soviets in June 1917, the Menshevik Irakli Tsereteli commented that no party existed that would wish to take power alone. Lenin, from the floor, corrected him: 'There is!'[9]

Liberal ministers, however, were almost as worried about the Mensheviks and Socialist-Revolutionaries as about the Bolsheviks. In late June, when the Provisional Government decided to recognize the Ukrainian Rada as the organ of regional government in Kiev, the Kadets walked out of the cabinet.[10] This could not have happened at a worse time. A Russian military offensive had been started on the Eastern front's southern sector: Prince Lvov and Alexander Kerenski, his War Minister, wanted to prove Russia's continuing usefulness to her Allies and to gain support at home by means of military success. But German reinforcements were rushed to the Austro-Hungarian lines and Russian forces had to retreat deep into Ukraine. And in those very same days the Bolsheviks were making mischief in Petrograd. They had tried to hold their own separate demonstration against the cabinet earlier in June – and only a last-minute intervention by the First All-Russia Congress of Soviets stopped them. The inhabitants of Petrograd were gripped by the uncertainty of the situation.

The Bolshevik Central Committee drew encouragement from the crisis, and planned to hold yet another armed demonstration in the capital on 3 July. Evidently if things went his way, Lenin might opt to turn the crisis into an opportunity to seize power.[11] The Provisional Government quickly issued a banning order. Unnerved by this display of political will, the Bolshevik Central Committee urged the assembled workers and troops, who had sailors from the Kronstadt naval garrison among them, to disperse. By then Lenin had absented himself from the scene, and was spending his time at a dacha at Neivola in the Finnish countryside. But the crowd wanted its demonstration. The sailors from the Kronstadt naval garrison were prominent among the more unruly elements, but local workers and soldiers were also determined to march through the central streets of Petrograd. The Provisional Government ordered reliable troops to break up the demonstration by firing on it. Dozens of people were killed.

Ministers held the Bolshevik Central Committee responsible for the clashes even though it had refrained from participating in the demonstration. Ministry of Internal Affairs officials claimed that the Bolsheviks had received money from the German government. Lenin and Zinoviev managed to flee into hiding in Finland, but Trotski, Kamenev and Alexandra Kollontai were caught and imprisoned. In Petrograd, if not in most other cities, the Bolshevik party reverted to being a clandestine party.

These complications were too much for Prince Lvov, who resigned in favour of his War Minister, Kerenski. Russia's ruin was ineluctable, according to Lvov, unless her socialists agreed to take prime responsibility for the affairs of state. Certainly Kerenski was already a master of the arts of twentieth-century political communication. He wore his patriotism on his sleeve. He was a brilliant orator, receiving standing ovations from his audiences and especially from women who were enraptured by his charm. He had a picture designed of himself and printed on tens of thousands of postcards; he had newsreels made of his major public appearances. Kerenski was temperamental, but he was also energetic and tenacious. He had carefully kept contact with all the parties willing to lend support to the Provisional Government, and had avoided favouritism towards his own Party of Socialist-Revolutionaries. Kerenski believed he had positioned himself so as to be able to save Russia from political disintegration and military defeat.

His elevation had been meteoric since the February Revolution. Born in 1881 in Simbirsk, he was just thirty-six years old when he succeeded Prince Lvov. By training he was a lawyer and had specialized in the defence of arrested revolutionaries. He also was acquainted with many leading figures in Russian public life through membership of the main Freemasons' lodge in Petrograd; but he had no experience in administration. And he was thrust into power at a time of the greatest crisis for the country since the Napoleonic invasion of 1812.

His delight at being invited to replace Prince Lvov was followed by weeks of difficulty even in putting a cabinet together. The rationale of his assumption of power was that socialists ought to take a majority of ministerial portfolios; but Tsereteli, the leading Menshevik minister under Lvov, stood down in order to devote his attention to the business of the soviets. Most Kadets, too, rejected Kerenski's overtures to join him. Not until 25 July could he announce the establishment of a Second Coalition. It is true that he had managed to ensure that ten out of the seventeen ministers, including himself, were socialists. Even the Socialist-Revolutionary leader Chernov agreed to stay on as Minister of Agriculture. Moreover, three Kadets were persuaded to ignore their party's official policy and join the cabinet. Nevertheless Kerenski was exhausted even before his premiership began, and already he was sustaining himself by recourse to morphine and cocaine.

He focused his cabinet's attention on the political and economic emergencies in Russia. Diplomatic discussions with the Allies were not abandoned, but there was no serious planning of further offensives on the Eastern front. Nor did Kerenski place obstacles in the way of Mensheviks and Socialist-Revolutionaries who sought to bring the war to an end by convoking a conference of socialist parties from all combatant countries in Stockholm.[12] In fact the conference was prevented from taking place by the intransigence of the Allied governments, which stopped British and French delegates from attending. It had been a doomed effort from the start, as Lenin was pleased to note.

The Mensheviks and Socialist-Revolutionaries retorted that there was no greater plausibility in Lenin's plan to bring the military struggle to a halt by means of a 'European socialist revolution'; they contended that the Bolsheviks overlooked the will and the capacity of both the Allies and the Central Powers to fight it out to the war's bitter end. In the interim Kerenski had two priorities. First, he wanted to reimpose the government's authority in the towns and at the front; second, he aimed to secure a more regular supply of food from the countryside. He signalled his firmness by appointing General Lavr Kornilov, an advocate of stern measures against unruly soviets, as Supreme Commander of Russian armed forces. He also refused – at least initially – to accede to the peasants' demands for increased prices for their products. A complete state monopoly on the grain trade had been announced in March and comprehensive food rationing in April. Kerenski gave an assurance that his cabinet would bring a new efficiency to the task of guaranteeing the availability of bread for urban consumption.

But he could not keep his promises. Foreign financial support became harder to obtain; and although a 'Liberty Loan' was raised at home, this still had to be supplemented by an accelerated emission of banknotes by the Ministry of Finances.[13] An accelerated rate of inflation was the inevitable result. It was of little comfort to Kerenski that the harvest of 1917 was only three per cent lower than the total for 1916.[14] Peasants continued to refuse to release their stocks until there was a stable currency and an abundance of industrial products. On 27 August the cabinet reluctantly licensed a doubling of prices offered for wheat. But little improvement in food supplies followed. In October, the state was obtaining only fifty-six per cent of the grain procured in the same month in the previous year, and Petrograd held stocks sufficient only to sustain three days of rations.[15]

The military situation was equally discouraging. After repelling the Russian offensive in June, the German commanders drew up plans for an offensive of their own on the northern sector of the Eastern front. Russia's prospects were grim. Her soldiers had become ill-disciplined and had begun to ask whether the war was worth fighting, especially when they suspected that the Provisional Government might still be pursuing expansionist aims. They were agitated, too, by talk that a comprehensive expropriation of the landed gentry's estates was imminent. Desertions occurred on a massive scale. The German advance met with the weakest resistance since the start of the war. Riga was lost by the Russians on 22 August. No natural obstacle lay in the five hundred kilometres separating the German army and the Russian capital. The Provisional Government could no longer be confident of avoiding military defeat and territorial dismemberment.

The fortunes of war and revolution were tightly interwoven; Kerenski's chances of surviving as Minister-Chairman depended in practice upon the performance of Allied armies on the Western front. Were the British and French to lose the battles of the summer, the Germans would immediately overrun Russia. The obverse side of this was the possibility that if the Allies were quickly to defeat Germany, they would relieve the Provisional Government's position because Russia would gain prestige and security as a victor power. Unfortunately for the Provisional Government, the Central Powers were nowhere near to military collapse in summer and autumn 1917.

Trepidation about the situation led to a rightward shift in opinion among the middle and upper social classes. Their leading figures were annoyed by Kerenski's manoeuvres to maintain support among the Mensheviks and Socialist-Revolutionaries; they had come to regard even the Kadets as hopelessly weak and inept. The problem for middle-class opinion was that the other anti-socialist organizations were weaker still. The Union of the Russian People had virtually ceased activity and its leaders had gone into hiding. Their close association with the monarchy before the February Revolution left them discredited. While most citizens endorsed political freedom and national tolerance there was no chance that the traditional political right would make a comeback – and citizen Nikolai

Romanov said nothing that might encourage monarchists: he and his family lived as unobtrusively as they could in sleepy Tobolsk in western Siberia from July 1917.[16]

Even the Russian Orthodox Church, freed at last from the constraints of tsarism, resisted the temptation to play the nationalist card. Bishops and priests dedicated their energies to internal debates on spirituality and organization. When an Assembly (*Sobor*) was held in August, politics were largely avoided. Months of discussions followed. Only in November did the Assembly feel ready to elect a Patriarch for the first time since 1700. The choice fell upon Metropolitan Tikhon, who had lived abroad for much of his life and was untainted by association with tsarism.[17]

And so it fell to elements in the army to take up the cause of the political right. Most Russian military commanders were steadily losing any respect they had for Kerenski. Initially Kornilov and Kerenski had got on well together, and had agreed on the need for greater governmental control over the soviets and for the reintroduction of capital punishment for military desertion. Both called for the restoration of 'order'. But Kerenski was soon irked by Kornilov, who allowed himself to be greeted ecstatically by right-wing political sympathizers on his visits from the Eastern front. Kerenski, having summoned Kornilov to Petrograd to stiffen the Provisional Government's authority, changed his mind and countermanded the transfer of any troops. On 27 August, Kornilov decided that this was a sign of the cabinet's ultimate abandonment of the programme of necessary action already agreed with him. He pressed onwards to Petrograd in open mutiny.[18]

Kerenski stood down the Second Coalition and governed through a small inner group of trusted ministers. The emergency was made even more acute by the bad news from the Eastern front, where Riga had fallen to the Germans only five days before. Kerenski had no choice but to turn for assistance to the very Petrograd Soviet which he had lately been trying to bring to heel. The response was immediate and positive. Bolsheviks as well as Mensheviks and Socialist-Revolutionaries went out to confront Kornilov's troops and persuade them to abandon their mission to Petrograd. The efforts of this united front of socialist activists were crowned with success. The troops halted their own trains from moving further towards Petrograd and General Kornilov was put under arrest. His mutiny had ended in fiasco.

Meanwhile popular discontent increased as conditions in the country worsened. Soldiers wanted peace, peasants wanted land, workers wanted job security and higher real wages. Not only the working class but also the large number of 'middling' people faced a winter of hunger. Shopkeepers, carriage-drivers and providers of various other services shared the fear that bread and potatoes might soon become unobtainable; and their small businesses were disrupted by the general economic chaos.[19] Moreover, the urban cost of living rose sharply: the price index more than doubled between March and October.[20] The wage-rises negotiated after Nicholas II's abdication did not keep pace with inflation. Unemployment, too,was becoming widespread; and there was no state welfare for those thrown out of work. All workers in factories, mines and other enterprises felt the adverse effects of a collapsing economy. They formed a united front against their employers.

Kerenski could not begin to satisfy these desires except if he withdrew from the war. And yet if he were indeed to withdraw from the war, he would be castigated by all parties – including the Bolsheviks – for betraying Russia's vital interests. As it was, he was being subjected to Lenin's wholly unfair accusation of plotting to hand over Petrograd to the Germans.[21] Nor did Kerenski stand much chance of surviving in power once the elections to the Constituent Assembly were held. Again Lenin made charges of malpractice. Kerenski, he claimed, was deliberately delaying the elections. In fact a huge administrative task, especially in wartime, was entailed in the accurate compilation of voters' rolls. Nevertheless Kerenski's prospects were far from good once the process had been completed.

Already the Provisional Government was confronted by direct social disruption. Peasants in each village put aside their mutual rivalries. The wealthier among them joined with the poor against the gentry landlords. Their activity took the form of illegally using arable land, grabbing crops and equipment, cutting timber and grazing livestock. But already in March there were three cases of outright seizure of land owned by gentry. In July, 237 such cases were reported. Admittedly there were only 116 cases in October;[22] but this was not a sign that the peasants were calming down. A truer index of their mood was their increasing willingness to attack landowners and burn their houses and farming property. Whereas there had been only five destructive raids of this sort in July, there were 144 in October.[23] After the harvest had been taken in, the peasantry was delivering a final warning to both the government and the landed gentry that obstruction of peasant aspirations would no longer be tolerated.

Simultaneously the slogan of 'workers' control' gained in appeal to the working class. In most cases this meant that elective committees of workers claimed the right to monitor and regulate managerial decisions on finance, production and employment. In a few cases the committees completely removed their managers and foremen and took over the enterprises. Such a step was taken most often in Ukraine and the Urals, where owners had always been uncompromising towards the labour movement. Miners in the Don Basin, for example, went as far as taking their managers captive, releasing them only after Kerenski sent in army units. But even the less extreme versions of 'workers' control' involved a massive interference with capitalist practices. In July it was in force in 378 enterprises. By October it had been spread to 573 and involved two fifths of the industrial working class.[24]

The sailors and soldiers, too, were self-assertive. First they elected their committees in the garrisons, but quickly after the February Revolution committees were also set up by troops at the front. Commands by officers were subject to scrutiny and challenge with increasing intensity. The hierarchy of military command was no longer fully functional, especially after the Kornilov mutiny in August. Furthermore, troops caused a problem not only collectively but also as individuals. The combined effect of the unpopularity of the June offensive and the news that land was being seized in the villages induced tens of thousands of conscripts to desert. Peasants-in-uniform wanted their share of the redistributed property of the gentry. Leaping into railway carriages with their rifles over their shoulders, they added to the disorder of transport and public governance.[25]

In trying to deal with such a crisis, the Provisional Government lacked the aura of legitimacy that a popular election might have conferred upon it. Ministers since February 1917 had perforce relied upon persuasion to control the populace. For the disbanding of the tsarist police limited Kerenski's scope for repression. So, too, did the unwillingness of the army garrisons to give unstinted obedience to the Provisional Government's orders.

Kerenski for some weeks after the Kornilov mutiny ruled by means of a temporary five-man Directory consisting of himself, the two armed service chiefs, the obscure Menshevik A. M. Nikitin and the recent Minister for Foreign Affairs M. I. Tereshchenko. But this was an embarrassing mode of rule for a government claiming to be democratic and Kerenski badly needed to widen the political base of the government. On 14 September he therefore agreed to the convocation of a 'Democratic Conference' of all parties and organizations to the left of the Kadets; and Kerenski himself agreed to address the opening session. But the Conference turned into a shambles. The Bolsheviks attended only in order to declare their disgust with Kerenski. Quite apart from their opposition, the Conference remained too divided to be able to supply a consensus of support for Kerenski.[26]

Kerenski put on a show of his old confidence; he resolved to reassert governmental authority and started to send troops to acquire food supplies from the countryside by force. This stiffening of measures enabled him to persuade six Kadets into a Third Coalition on 27 September. Only seven out of the seventeen ministers were socialists, and anyway these socialists had policies hardly different from those of the liberals. The Provisional Government in its latest manifestation would neither offer radical social and economic reforms nor concentrate its diplomacy in quest of a peaceful end to the Great War.

The Democratic Conference proposed to lend a representative, consultative semblance to the Third Coalition by selecting a

Provisional Council of the Russian Republic. This Council would include not only socialists but also liberals and would function as a quasi-parliamentary assembly until such time as the Constituent Assembly met. Formed on 14 October, it became known as the Pre-Parliament. To the Pre-Parliament's frustration, however, Kerenski refused to limit his freedom of decision by making himself accountable to it. And the Pre-Parliament could not steel itself to stand up to him.[27] Kerenski could and did ignore it whenever he liked. The long-winded debates in the Pre-Parliament simply brought its main participating parties – Kadets, Mensheviks and Socialist-Revolutionaries – into deeper disrepute. Neither Kerenski nor the Pre-Parliament possessed the slightest popular respect.

Lenin, from his place of hiding in Helsinki, saw this disarray as a splendid opportunity for the Bolsheviks. Less words, more action! For Bolsheviks, the course of Russian politics since the February Revolution vindicated the party's argument that two lines of development alone were possible: 'bourgeois' or 'proletarian'. They declared that the Mensheviks and Socialist-Revolutionaries had become agents of the bourgeoisie by dint of collaborating with liberal ministers and the magnates of capitalism.

By September Lenin was urging his party to seize power immediately (and he busily composed a treatise on *The State and Revolution* to justify his strategy). The Central Committee, convening in his absence, rejected his advice. Its members saw more clearly than their impatient leader that popular support even in Petrograd was insufficient for an uprising.[28] But the revulsion of society against the Provisional Government was growing sharply. First the factory-workshop committees and the trade unions and then, increasingly, the city soviets began to acquire Bolshevik-led leaderships. In Kronstadt the soviet was the local government in all but name, and the Volga city of Tsaritsyn declared its independence from the rest of Russia in midsummer. By 31 August the Petrograd Soviet was voting for the Bolshevik party's resolutions. The Moscow Soviet followed suit a few days later. Through September and October the urban soviets of northern, central and south-eastern Russia went over to the Bolsheviks.

Disguised as a Lutheran Pastor, Lenin hastened back to Petrograd. On 10 October 1917 he cajoled his Central Committee colleagues into ratifying the policy of a rapid seizure of power. The Central Committee met again on 16 October with representatives of other major Bolshevik bodies in attendance.[29] Lenin again got his way strategically. In the ensuing days Trotski and other colleagues amended his wishes on schedule, insisting that the projected uprising in Petrograd should be timed to coincide with the opening of the Second All-Russia Congress of Soviets of Workers' and Soldiers' Deputies. Thus the uprising would appear not as a *coup d'état* by a single party but as a transfer of 'all power to the soviets'.

Lenin was infuriated by the re-scheduling: he saw no need for the slightest delay. From his hiding-place in the capital's outskirts, he bombarded his colleagues with arguments that unless a workers' insurrection took place immediately, a right-wing military dictatorship would be installed. It is doubtful that he believed his own rhetoric; for no army general was as yet in any position to try to overthrow Kerenski and tame the soviets. Almost certainly Lenin guessed that the Kerenski cabinet was on the brink of collapse and that a broad socialist coalition would soon be formed. Such an outcome would not meet Lenin's approval. Even if he were to be invited to join such an administration, his participation would unavoidably involve him in compromises on basic issues. Lenin did not fancy sharing power with Mensheviks and Socialist-Revolutionaries whom he accused of betraying the revolution.[30]

Since July, Yuli Martov and the left-wing faction of the Menshevik party had been calling for the Kerenski cabinet to be replaced with an all-socialist coalition committed to radical social reform;[31] and the left-wingers among the Socialist-Revolutionaries broke entirely with their party and formed a separate Party of Left Socialist-Revolutionaries in October. With these groups Lenin was willing to deal. But not with the rump of the Menshevik and Socialist-Revolutionary Parties: they had supped with the capitalist Devil and deserved to be thrust into outer darkness.

The situation favoured Lenin, and he knew it. For just a few months the workers and soldiers and peasants held Russia's fate in their hands. The Imperial family was under house arrest. Courtiers, bishops and aristocrats were staying out of the public eye. The generals were still too shocked by the Kornilov fiasco to know what to do. The middle classes were sunk in despair. The shopkeepers and other elements in the urban lower middle class had a thorough dislike for the Provisional Government. Thus the main danger for the Bolsheviks was not 'bourgeois counter-revolution' but working-class apathy. Even Lenin's supporters in the Bolshevik central leadership warned him that the Petrograd workers were far from likely to turn out to participate in an insurrection – and perhaps this was yet another reason for Lenin's impatience. If not now, when?

Yet it was also a crucial advantage for Lenin that the political and administrative system was in an advanced condition of disintegration. Peasants in most villages across the former Russian Empire governed themselves. The military conscripts intimidated their officers. The workers, even if they were loath to take to the streets, wished to impose their control over the factories and mines. Kerenski had lost authority over all these great social groups.

While central power was breaking down in Petrograd, moreover, it had virtually collapsed in the rest of Russia. And in the non-Russian regions, local self-government was already a reality. The Finnish Sejm and the Ukrainian Rada disdained to obey the Provisional Government. In the Transcaucasus, Georgians and Armenians and Azeris created bodies to challenge the Special Transcaucasian Committee appointed by the cabinet in Petrograd.[32] An alternative government existed in the soviets in practically every region, province, city and town of Russia. Soviets were not omnipotent organizations. But they were stronger than any of their institutional rivals. They had formal hierarchies stretching from Petrograd to the localities; they had personnel who wanted a clean break with the old regime of Nicholas II and the new regime of Lvov and Kerenski. They could also see no prospect of improvement in political, social and economic conditions until the Provisional Government was removed.

Kamenev and Zinoviev had been so appalled by Lenin's *démarche* that they informed the press of his plan for a seizure of power; they contended that the sole possible result would be a civil war that would damage the interests of the working class. But Trotski, Sverdlov, Stalin and Dzierżyński – in Lenin's continued absence – steadied the nerve of the Bolshevik central leadership as plans were laid for armed action. Trotski came into his own when co-ordinating the Military-Revolutionary Committee of the Petrograd Soviet. This body's influence over the capital's garrison soldiers made it a perfect instrument to organize the armed measures for Kerenski's removal. Garrison troops, Red Guards and Bolshevik party activists were being readied for revolution in Russia, Europe and the world.

4

The October Revolution (1917–1918)

The Provisional Government of Alexander Kerenski was overthrown in Petrograd on 25 October 1917. The Bolsheviks, operating through the Military-Revolutionary Committee of the City Soviet, seized power in a series of decisive actions. The post and telegraph offices and the railway stations were taken and the army garrisons were put under rebel control. By the end of the day the Winter Palace had fallen to the insurgents. On Lenin's proposal, the Second Congress of Soviets of Workers' and Soldiers' Deputies ratified the transfer of authority to the soviets. A government led by him was quickly formed. He called for an immediate end to the Great War and for working people across Europe to establish their own socialist administrations. Fundamental reforms were promulgated in Russia. Land was to be transferred to the peasants; workers' control was to be imposed in the factories; the right of national self-determination, including secession, was to be accorded to the non-Russian peoples. Opponents of the seizure of power were threatened with ruthless retaliation.

Bolsheviks pinpointed capitalism as the cause of the Great War and predicted further global struggles until such time as the capitalist order was brought to an end. According to this prognosis, capitalism predestined workers in general to political and economic misery also in peacetime.

Such thoughts did not originate with Bolshevism; on the contrary, they had been shared by fellow socialist parties in the Russian Empire, including the Mensheviks and Socialist-Revolutionaries, and in the rest of Europe. The Socialist International had repeatedly expressed this consensus at its Congresses before 1914. Each of its parties thought it was time for the old world to be swept away and for socialism to be inaugurated. The awesome consequences of the Great War confirmed them in their belief. Other ideas, too, were held by Bolsheviks which were socialist commonplaces. For example, most of the world's socialists subscribed strongly to the notion that central economic planning was crucial to the creation of a fairer society. They contended that social utility rather than private profit ought to guide decisions in public affairs. Not only far-left socialists but also the German Social-Democratic Party and the British Labour Party took such a standpoint.

It was the specific proposals of the Bolshevik party for the new world order that caused revulsion among fellow socialists. Lenin advocated dictatorship, class-based discrimination and ideological imposition. The definition of socialism had always been disputed among socialists, but nearly all of them took it as axiomatic that socialism would involve universal-suffrage democracy. Lenin's ideas were therefore at variance with basic aspects of conventional socialist thought.

The Mensheviks and Socialist-Revolutionaries drew attention to this, but their words were not always understood by socialists in the rest of Europe who did not yet have much information about Bolshevik attitudes. There persisted a hope in Western socialist parties that the divisions between the Mensheviks and the Bolsheviks might yet be overcome and that they might reunite to form a single party again. And so the mixture of contrast and similarity between Bolshevism and other variants of socialist thought baffled a large number of contemporary observers, and the confusion was made worse by the terminology. The Bolsheviks said they wanted to introduce socialism to Russia and to assist in the making of a 'European socialist revolution'; but they also wanted to create something called communism. Did this mean that socialism and communism were one and the same thing?

Lenin had given a lengthy answer to the question in *The State and Revolution*, which he wrote in summer 1917 and which appeared in 1918. His contention was that the passage from capitalism to communism required an intermediate stage called the 'dictatorship of the proletariat'. This dictatorship would inaugurate the construction of socialism. Mass political participation would be facilitated and an unprecedentedly high level of social and material welfare would be provided. Once the resistance of the former ruling classes had been broken, furthermore, the need for repressive agencies would disappear. Dictatorship would steadily become obsolete and the state would start to wither away. Then a further phase – communism – would begin. Society would be run according to the principle: from each according to his ability, to each according to his need. Under communism there would be no political or national oppression, no economic exploitation. Humanity would have reached its ultimate stage of development.[1]

Most other socialists in Russia and elsewhere, including Marxists, forecast that Lenin's ideas would lead not to a self-terminating dictatorship but to an extremely oppressive, perpetual dictatorship.[2] They were furious with Lenin not only out of horror at his ideas but also because he brought them too into disrepute in their own countries. Liberals, conservatives and the far right had no interest in the niceties of the polemics between Bolsheviks and other socialists. For them, Bolshevik policies were simply proof of the inherently oppressive orientation of socialism in general. 'Bolshevism' was a useful stick of propaganda with which to beat the socialist movements in their own countries.

In 1917, however, such discussions seemed very abstract; for few of Lenin's critics gave him any chance of staying in power. Lenin himself could hardly believe his good fortune. Whenever things looked bleak, he convinced himself that his regime – like the Paris Commune of 1871 – would offer a paradigm for later generations of socialists to emulate. The Bolsheviks might be tossed out of power at any time. While governing the country, they 'sat on their suitcases' lest they suddenly had to flee into hiding. Surely the luck of the Bolsheviks would soon run out? The governments, diplomats and journalists of western and central Europe were less interested in events in Petrograd than in the shifting fortunes of their own respective armies. Information about the Bolsheviks was scanty, and it took months for Lenin to become a personage whose policies were known in any detail outside Russia.

For the events of 25 October had taken most people by surprise even in Petrograd. Most workers, shop-owners and civil servants went about their customary business. The trams ran; the streets were clear of trouble and there were no demonstrations. Shops had their usual customers. Newspapers appeared normally. It had been a quiet autumnal day and the weather was mild.

Only in the central districts had anything unusual been happening. The Military-Revolutionary Committee of the Petrograd Soviet as well as the Red Guards, under Trotski's guidance, were hard at work organizing the siege of the Winter Palace, where Kerenski and several of his ministers were trapped, and in securing the occupation of other key strategic points: the post and telegraph offices, the railway stations, and the garrisons. The battleship *Aurora* from the Baltic Sea fleet was brought up the river Neva to turn its guns towards the Winter Palace. Kerenski could see that he lacked the forces to save the Provisional Government. Exploiting the chaos, he got into an official limousine which was allowed through the ranks of the besiegers. Lenin had meanwhile come out of hiding. Taking a tram from the city's outskirts, he arrived at Bolshevik headquarters at the Smolny Institute, where he harassed his party colleagues into intensifying efforts to take power before the Second Congress of Soviets opened later in the day

The reason for Lenin's continuing impatience must surely have stemmed from his anticipation that the Bolsheviks would not have a clear majority at the Congress of Soviets – and indeed they gained only 300 out of 670 elected delegates.[3] He could not drive his policies through the Congress without some compromise with other parties. It is true that many Mensheviks and Socialist-Revolutionaries had lately accepted that an exclusively socialist coalition, including the Bolsheviks, should be formed. But Lenin could think of nothing worse than the sharing of power with the Mensheviks and Socialist Revolutionaries. The Congress of Soviets might foist a coalition upon him. His counter-measure was to get the Military-Revolutionary Committee to grab power hours in advance of the Congress on the assumption that this would probably annoy the Mensheviks and Socialist-Revolutionaries enough to dissuade them from joining a coalition with the Bolsheviks.

The ploy worked. As the Congress assembled in the Smolny Institute, the fug of cigarette smoke grew denser. Workers and soldiers sympathetic to the Bolsheviks filled the main hall. The appearance of Trotski and Lenin was greeted with a cheering roar. The Mensheviks and Socialist-Revolutionaries were disgusted, and denounced what they described as a Bolshevik party *coup d'état*. The Menshevik Yuli Martov declared that most of the Bolshevik delegates to the Congress had been elected on the understanding that a general socialist coalition would come to power, and his words were given a respectful hearing. Yet tempers ran high among other Mensheviks and Socialist-Revolutionaries present. In an act of stupendous folly, they stormed out of the hall.[4]

Their exodus meant that the Bolsheviks, who had the largest delegation, became the party with a clear-cut majority. Lenin and Trotski proceeded to form their own government. Trotski suggested that it should be called the Council of People's Commissars (or, as it was in its Russian acronym, *Sovnarkom*). Thus he contrived to avoid the bourgeois connotations of words such as 'ministers' and 'cabinets'. Lenin would not be Prime Minister or Premier, but merely Chairman, and Trotski would serve as People's Commissar for Foreign Affairs. The Second Congress of Soviets had not been abandoned by all the foes of the Bolsheviks: the Left Socialist-Revolutionaries had remained inside the Institute. Lenin and Trotski invited them to join Sovnarkom, but were turned down. The Left Socialist-Revolutionaries were waiting to see whether the Bolshevik-led administration would survive; and they, too, aspired to the establishment of a general socialist coalition.

Lenin and Trotski set their faces against such a coalition; but they were opposed by colleagues in the Bolshevik Central Committee who also wanted to negotiate with the Mensheviks and Socialist-Revolutionaries to this end. Furthermore, the central executive body of the Railwaymen's Union threatened to go on strike until a coalition of all socialist parties had been set up, and the political position of

Lenin and Trotski was weakened further when news arrived that a Cossack contingent loyal to Kerenski was moving on Petrograd.

But things then swung back in favour of Lenin and Trotski. The Mensheviks and Socialist-Revolutionaries no more wished to sit in a government including Lenin and Trotski than Lenin and Trotski wanted them as colleagues. The negotiations broke down, and Lenin unperturbedly maintained an all-Bolshevik Sovnarkom. Three Bolsheviks resigned from Sovnarkom, thinking this would compel Lenin to back down.[5] But to no avail. The rail strike petered out, and the Cossacks of General Krasnov were defeated by Sovnarkom's soldiers on the Pulkovo Heights outside the capital. The Bolshevik leaders who had stood by Lenin were delighted. Victory, both military and political, was anticipated by Lenin and Trotski not only in Russia but also across Europe. Trotski as People's Commissar for Foreign Affairs expected simply to publish the secret wartime treaties of the Allies and then to 'shut up shop'.[6] For he thought that the Red revolutions abroad would end the need for international diplomacy altogether.

Trotski met the Allied diplomats, mainly with the intention of keeping the regime's future options open. The burden of energy, however, fell elsewhere. Sovnarkom was the government of a state which was still coming into being. Its coercive powers were patchy in Petrograd, non-existent in the provinces. The Red Guards were ill-trained and not too well disciplined. The garrisons were as reluctant to fight other Russians as they had been to take on the Germans. Public announcements were the most effective weapons in Sovnarkom's arsenal. On 25 October, Lenin wrote a proclamation justifying the 'victorious uprising' by reference to 'the will of the huge majority of workers, soldiers and peasants'. His sketch of future measures included the bringing of 'an immediate democratic peace to all the peoples'. In Russia the Constituent Assembly would be convoked. Food supplies would be secured for the towns and workers' control over industrial establishments instituted. 'Democratization of the army' would be achieved. The lands of gentry, crown and church would be transferred 'to the disposal of the peasant committees'.[7]

Two momentous documents were signed by Lenin on 26 October.

The Decree on Peace made a plea to governments and to 'all the warring peoples' to bring about a 'just, democratic peace'. There should be no annexations, no indemnities, no enclosure of small nationalities in larger states against their will. Lenin usually eschewed what he considered as moralistic language, but he now described the Great War as 'the greatest crime against humanity':[8] probably he was trying to use terminology congruent with the terminology of President Woodrow Wilson. But above all he wanted to rally the hundreds of millions of Europe's workers and soldiers to the banner of socialist revolution; he never doubted that, without revolutions, no worthwhile peace could be achieved.

The Decree on Land, edited and signed by him on the same day, summoned the peasants to undertake radical agrarian reform. Expropriation of estates was to take place without compensation of their owners. The land and equipment seized from gentry, crown and church was to 'belong to the entire people'. Lenin stressed that 'rank-and-file' peasants should be allowed to keep their property intact. The appeal was therefore directed at the poor and the less-than-rich. This brief preamble was followed by clauses which had not been written by him but purloined from the Party of Socialist-Revolutionaries, which had collated 242 'instructions' set out by peasant committees themselves in summer 1917. Lenin's decree repeated them verbatim. Land was to become an 'all-people's legacy'; it could no longer be bought, sold, rented or mortgaged. Sovnarkom's main stipulation was that the large estates should not be broken up but handed over to the state. Yet peasants were to decide most practicalities for themselves as the land passed into their hands.[9]

Other decrees briskly followed. The eight-hour day, which had been introduced under the Provisional Government, was confirmed on 29 October, and a code on workers' control in factories and mines was issued on 14 November. This was not yet a comprehensive design for the transformation of the economy's urban sector; and, while industry was at least mentioned in those early weeks of power, Lenin was slow to announce measures on commerce, finance and taxation. His main advice to the party's supporters outside Petrograd was to 'introduce the strictest control over production and account-keeping' and to arrest those who attempted sabotage.[10]

Frequently Sovnarkom and the Bolshevik Central Committee declared that the new administration intended to facilitate mass political participation. A revolution for and by the people was anticipated. Workers, peasants, soldiers and sailors were to take direct action. 'Soviet power' was to be established on their own initiative. But Lenin's will to summon the people to liberate themselves was accompanied by a determination to impose central state authority. On 26 October he had issued a Decree on the Press, which enabled him to close down any newspapers publishing materials inimical to the decisions of the Second Congress of Soviets of Workers' and Soldiers' Deputies.[11] Repressive measures were given emphasis. Lenin pointed out that the authorities lacked a special agency to deal with sabotage and counter-revolutionary activity; and on 7 December, Sovnarkom at his instigation formed the so-called Extraordinary Commission (or *Cheka*). Its task of eliminating opposition to the October Revolution was kept vague and extensive: no inhibition was to deter this forerunner of the dreaded NKVD and KGB.[12]

Nor did Lenin forget that the tsars had ruled not a nation-state but an empire. Following up his early announcement on national self-determination, he offered complete independence to Finland and confirmed the Provisional Government's similar proposal for German-occupied Poland. This was done in the hope that Soviet revolutionary republics would quickly be established by the Finns and the Poles, leading to their voluntary reabsorption in the same multinational state as Russia. Lenin believed that eventually this state would cover the continent.[13] His objective was the construction of a pan-European socialist state. Meanwhile Lenin and his colleague Iosif Stalin, People's Commissar for Nationalities, aimed to retain the remainder of the former empire intact; and on 3 November they jointly published a Declaration of the Rights of the Peoples of Russia, confirming the abolition of all national and ethnic privileges and calling for the formation of a 'voluntary and honourable union'. The right of secession was confirmed for the various nations involved.[14]

The Allied ambassadors in Petrograd did not know whether to laugh or cry. How could such upstarts pretend to a role in global politics? Was it not true that Lenin had spent more time in Swiss libraries than Russian factories? Was he not an impractical intellectual who would drown in a pool of practical difficulties once he actually wielded power? And were not his colleagues just as ineffectual?

It was true that not only the party's central figures but also its provincial leaders were entirely inexperienced in government. Marx's *Das Kapital* was their primer, which was studied by several of them in the prison cells of Nicholas II. Few of them had professional employment in private or governmental bodies before 1917. An oddity was Lev Krasin, a veteran Bolshevik still working for the Siemens Company at the time of the October Revolution. He was later to be appointed People's Commissar for Foreign Trade. The rest of them were different. Most leading members of the party had spent their adult life on the run from the Okhrana. They had organized small revolutionary groups, issued proclamations and joined in strikes and demonstrations. They had studied and written socialist theory. Public life, out in the gaze of society, was a new experience for them as their days of political obscurity and untestable theorizing came to an end.

Lenin was the fastest at adjusting to the change. Until 1917 he had been an obscure Russian emigrant living mainly in Switzerland. Insofar as he had a reputation in Europe, it was not flattering; for he was known as a trouble-maker who had brought schism to the Marxists of the Russian Empire. Even many Bolsheviks were annoyed by him. His supporters were constantly asking him to spend less time on polemics and more time on making a real revolution, and alleged that his head was made giddy with all that Alpine air.

But, for Lenin, there were great questions at stake in almost any small matter. He had been involved in an unending line of controversies since becoming a revolutionary as a student at Kazan University. Born in the provincial town of Simbirsk in 1870, his real name was Vladimir Ulyanov. 'Lenin' was a pseudonym assumed years after he became a political activist. His background was a mixture of Jewish, German and Kalmyk as well as Russian elements. In the empire of the Romanovs this was not a unique combination. Nor was his father wholly unusual as a man of humble social origins in rising to the rank of province schools inspector (which automatically conferred hereditary nobility upon him and his heirs). This was a period of rapid educational expansion. The Ulyanovs were characteristic beneficiaries of the reforms which followed the Emancipation Edict.

The most extraordinary thing about the family, indeed, was the participation of Vladimir's older brother Alexander in a conspiracy to assassinate Emperor Alexander III in 1887. The attempt failed, but Alexander Ulyanov was found out and hanged. A family which had dutifully made the best of the cultural opportunities available suddenly became subject to the police's intense suspicion.

Lenin shared his brother's rebelliousness, and was expelled from Kazan University as a student trouble-maker. He proceeded to take a first-class honours degree as an external student at St Petersburg University in 1891; but it was Marxism that enthralled him. He joined intellectual dissenters first in Samara and then in St Petersburg. The police caught him, and he was exiled to Siberia. There he wrote a book on the development of capitalism in Russia, which was published legally in 1899. He was released in 1900, and went into emigration in the following year. Young as he was, he had pretty definite notions about what his party – the Russian Social-Democratic Workers' Party – needed organizationally. *What Is To Be Done?*, printed in Russian in Munich in 1902, asserted the case for discipline, hierarchy and centralism; and it provoked the criticism that such a book owed more to the terrorists of Russian agrarian socialism than to conventional contemporary Marxism.

In 1903 the dispute over the booklet led the *émigrés* to set up separate factions, the Bolsheviks and Mensheviks, in the Russian Social-Democratic Workers' Party. As Bolshevik leader he never lost the common touch. He personally met comrades arriving off the trains from Russia; and he volunteered to help fellow party member Nikolai Valentinov with his part-time job to trundle a customer's belongings by handcart from one side of Geneva to another.[15]

Doubtless he liked subordinate admirers better than rivals; all colleagues who rivalled his intellectual stature eventually walked out on him. Nor was his abrasiveness to everyone's taste. An acquaintance likened him to 'a schoolteacher from Småland about to lay into the priest with whom he had fallen out'.[16] But when Lenin returned to Russia in the near-revolution of 1905–6, he showed that he could temper his fractiousness with tactical flexibility, even to the point of collaborating again with the Mensheviks.

The Okhrana's offensive against the revolutionaries drove him back to Switzerland in 1907, and for the next decade he resumed his schismatic, doctrinaire ways. Acolytes like Lev Kamenev, Iosif Stalin and Grigori Zinoviev were attracted to him; but even Stalin called his disputations about epistemology in 1908–9 a storm in a tea-cup. Moreover, Lenin struggled against the foundation of a legal workers' newspaper in St Petersburg. Spurning the chance to influence the labour movement in Russia on a daily basis, he preferred to engage in polemics in the journals of Marxist political and economic theory.[17]

His political prospects had not looked bright before the Great War. He could exert influence over Bolsheviks in face-to-face sessions, but his dominance evaporated whenever they returned to clandestine activity in Russia; and his call in 1914 for the military defeat of his native country lost him further support in his faction. But he held out for his opinions: 'And so this is my fate. One campaign of struggle after another – against political idiocies, vulgarities, opportunism, etc.'[18] The self-inflicted loneliness of his campaigns cultivated in him an inner strength which served him handsomely when the Romanov dynasty fell in February 1917. He was also older than any other leading Bolshevik, being aged forty-seven years while Central Committee members on average were eleven years younger.[19] He was cleverer than all of them, including even Trotski. And while lacking any outward vanity, he was convinced that he was a man of destiny and that his tutelage of the Bolsheviks was essential for the inception of the socialist order.[20]

His rise to prominence was effected with minimal technological resources. The central party newspaper *Pravda* carried no photographs and had a print-run that did not usually exceed 90,000.[21]

Such few cinemas as Russia possessed had shown newsreels not of Lenin but of Alexander Kerenski. Nevertheless he adapted well to the open political environment. His ability to rouse a crowd was such that adversaries recorded that he could make the hairs stand on the back of their necks with excitement. He also contrived to identify himself with ordinary working people by giving up his Homburg in favour of a workman's cap. Lenin and the Bolsheviks were becoming synonyms in the minds of those Russians who followed contemporary politics.[22]

The mass media became freely available to him after the October Revolution. The Decree on Land had a large impact on opinion amidst the peasantry, and became popularly known as Lenin's Decree.[23] But Bolsheviks were extremely small in number; and most of the very few village 'soviets' were really communes under a different name.[24] Moreover, the usual way for the peasantry to hear that the October Revolution had occurred in Petrograd was not through *Pravda* but from the accounts of soldiers who had left the Eastern front and the city garrison to return to their families and get a share of the land that was about to be redistributed. In the towns the profile of the Bolshevik party was much higher. Already having won majorities in dozens of urban soviets before the Provisional Government's overthrow, Bolsheviks spread their rule across central, northern and south-eastern Russia; and their success was repeated in major industrial centres in the borderlands. Baku in Azerbaijan and Kharkov in Ukraine were notable examples.[25]

For the most part, the Bolsheviks came to power locally by means of local resources. Sovnarkom sent auxiliary armed units to assist the transfer of authority in Moscow; but elsewhere this was typically unnecessary. In Ivanovo the Mensheviks and Socialist-Revolutionaries put up little resistance, and the Bolsheviks celebrated Sovnarkom's establishment with a rendition of the *Internationale*. In Saratov there was fighting, but it lasted less than a day. On assuming power, the Bolsheviks were joyful and expectant: 'Our commune is the start of the worldwide commune. We as leaders take full responsibility and fear nothing.'[26]

And yet the October Revolution was not yet secure. The political base of the Sovnarkom was exceedingly narrow: it did not include the Mensheviks, the Socialist-Revolutionaries or even the Left Socialist-Revolutionaries; it failed to embrace all Bolsheviks after the walk-out of the three People's Commissars. Yet Lenin, backed by Trotski and Sverdlov, did not flinch. Indeed he seemed to grow in confidence as difficulties increased. The man was an irrepressible leader. Without compunction he gave unrestrained authority to the Extraordinary Commission and their chairman, Felix Dzierżyński. Initially Dzierżyński refrained from executing politicians hostile to Bolshevism; his victims were mainly fraudsters and other criminals. But the sword of the Revolution was being sharpened for arbitrary use at the regime's demand. Lenin had no intention of casually losing the power he had won for his party.

Steadily the Bolshevik central leaders who had walked out on him and Trotski returned to their posts; and in mid-December the Left Socialist-Revolutionaries, cheered by the Decree on Land and convinced that their political duty lay with the October Revolution, agreed to become partners of the Bolsheviks in Sovnarkom. As Left Socialist-Revolutionaries entered the People's Commissariats, a two-party coalition was put in place.

Yet the question remained: what was to happen about the Constituent Assembly? Lenin had suggested to Sverdlov in the course of the October seizure of power in the capital that the elections should not go ahead.[27] But Bolshevik party propaganda had played heavily upon the necessity of a democratically-chosen government. Lenin himself had jibed that Kerenski would find endless pretexts to postpone the elections and that, under the Bolsheviks, the overwhelming majority of society would rally to their cause.[28] And so Lenin's last-minute doubts about the Constituent Assembly were ignored. The final polling arrangements were made by November and were put to use in the first more or less free parliamentary elections in the country's history. (They were to remain the only such elections in Russia until 1993.) To the horror of Sverdlov, who had dissuaded Lenin from banning the elections, the Bolsheviks gained only a quarter of the votes cast while the Socialist-Revolutionaries obtained thirty-seven per cent.[29]

The Sovnarkom coalition reacted ruthlessly: if the people failed to perceive where their best interests lay, then they had to be protected against themselves. The Constituent Assembly met on 5 January 1918 in the Tauride Palace. The Socialist-Revolutionary Viktor Chernov made a ringing denunciation of Bolshevism and asserted his own party's commitment to parliamentary democracy, peace and the transfer of land to the peasants. But he had more words than guns. The custodian of the building, the anarchist Zheleznyakov, abruptly announced: 'The guard is tired!' The deputies to the Assembly were told to leave and a demonstration held in support of the elections was fired upon by troops loyal to Sovnarkom. The doors of the Constituent Assembly were closed, never to be reopened.

The handful of garrison soldiers, Red Guards and off-duty sailors who applied this violence could crush opposition in the capital, but were less impressive elsewhere. Contingents were sent from Petrograd and Moscow to Ukraine where the local government, the Rada, refused to accept the writ of Sovnarkom. Tens of thousands of armed fighters reached Kiev. The struggle was scrappy, and it took until late January 1918 before Kiev was occupied by the Bolshevik-led forces.

All this was gleefully noted by the German and Austrian high commands. Negotiations were held at Brest-Litovsk, the town nearest the trenches of the Eastern front's northern sector on 14 November, and a truce was soon agreed. The Soviet government expected this to produce an interlude for socialist revolutions to break out in central Europe. Confident that the 'imperialist war' was about to end, Lenin and his colleagues issued orders for the Russian armies to be demobilized. To a large extent they were merely giving retrospective sanction to desertions. Ludendorff and Hindenburg at any rate were delighted; for it was German policy to seek Russia's dissolution as a military power by political means. Inadvertently the Bolsheviks had performed this function brilliantly. Now the Bolsheviks, too, had to pay a price: in December 1917 the German negotiators at Brest-Litovsk delivered an ultimatum to the effect that Sovnarkom should allow national self-determination to the borderlands and cease to claim sovereignty over them.

Around New Year 1918 Lenin asked his colleagues whether it was really possible to fight the Germans.[30] Trotski saw the deserted Russian trenches every time he travelled to and from Brest-Litovsk. A Russian army no longer existed to repel attack. In this situation, as Trotski contended, Sovnarkom could not fulfil its commitment to waging a 'revolutionary war'. And yet Trotski also argued against signing a separate peace with the Central Powers, a peace that was intolerable not only to the Bolsheviks but also to all other Russian political parties. His recommendation was that Bolsheviks should drag out the negotiations, using them as an opportunity to issue calls to revolution which would be reported in Berlin as well as in Petrograd.

Despite his professional inexperience, Trotski proved a match for Richard von Kühlmann and Otto von Czernin who parleyed on behalf of the Central Powers. His tactic of 'neither war nor peace' was so bizarre in the world history of diplomacy that his interlocutors did not immediately know how to reply. But in January 1918 the Central Powers gave their ultimatum that, unless a separate peace was quickly signed on the Eastern front, Russia would be overrun. Lenin counselled Sovnarkom that the coalition had no choice but to accept the German terms, and that procrastination would provoke either an immediate invasion or a worsening of the terms of the ultimatum. All the Left Socialist-Revolutionaries rejected his advice. Successive meetings of the Bolshevik Central Committee, too, turned it down. As the ill-tempered deliberations proceeded, Trotski's policy of neither war nor peace was temporarily adopted. But eventually a choice would have to be made between war and peace.

Lenin concentrated upon persuading fellow leading Bolsheviks. On 8 January he offered his 'Theses on a Separate and Annexationist Peace' to the party's faction at the Third Congress of Soviets of Workers', Soldiers' and Cossacks' Deputies. Only fifteen out of sixty-three listeners voted for him.[31] But Lenin was fired up for the struggle. He secured Trotski's private consent that he would support Lenin if and when it came to a straight choice between war and peace; and he tempted the vacillators with the thought that a peace on the Eastern front would enable the Bolsheviks to 'strangle' the

Russian bourgeoisie and prepare better for an eventual revolutionary war in Europe.[32]

Steadily Lenin gained ground in the Central Committee. Sverdlov, Stalin, Kamenev and Zinoviev backed him strongly, and Bukharin and the Left Communists, as they were becoming known, began to wilt in the heat of Lenin's assault. At the Central Committee he circulated a questionnaire on contingency planning. Bukharin conceded that there were imaginable situations when he would not object in principle to the signature of a separate peace. Sverdlov's Secretariat plied the local party committees with a version of the debate that was biased in Lenin's favour. There was also a distinct lack of impartiality in the Secretariat's arrangements for the selection of delegates to a Seventh Party Congress which would definitively decide between war and peace.[33] And as Lenin had warned, the Germans were not fooled by Trotski's delaying tactics. On 18 February they advanced from Riga and took Dvinsk, only six hundred kilometres from Petrograd. That evening, at last, a shaken Central Committee adopted Lenin's policy of bowing to the German terms.

The vote had gone seven to five for Lenin because Trotski had joined his side. But then Trotski had second thoughts and again voted against Lenin. Germany and Austria-Hungary, however, increased their demands. The Soviet government had previously been asked to relinquish claims of sovereignty over the area presently occupied by the German and Austrian armies. Now Lenin and his colleagues were required to forgo all Ukraine, Belorussia and the entire south Baltic region to the eastern edge of the Estonian lands. Sovnarkom would lose all the western borderlands.

Sverdlov took the news to the Central Committee on 23 February that the Germans were giving them until seven o'clock the next morning to announce compliance. Momentarily Stalin suggested that their bluff should be called. But Lenin furiously threatened to withdraw from Sovnarkom and campaign in the country for a separate peace: 'These terms must be signed. If you do not sign them, you are signing the death warrant for Soviet power within three weeks!'[34] Trotski found a way to climb down by declaring a preference for revolutionary war but postulating that it could not be fought by a divided party. He therefore abstained in the vote in the Central Committee, and victory was handed to Lenin. The Treaty of Brest-Litovsk was signed on 3 March. Cannily Lenin, Russia's pre-eminent advocate of a separate peace, declined to attend the official ceremony and entrusted this task instead to Central Committee member Grigori Sokolnikov.

Opinion in the rest of the party had also been moving in Lenin's favour; and at the Party Congress, which lasted three days from 6 March, his arguments and Sverdlov's organizational manipulations paid off: the delegates approved the signature of 'the obscene peace'. But at a price. Disgusted Left Communists, with Bukharin at their head, resigned from both Sovnarkom and the Bolshevik Central Committee. The Left Socialist-Revolutionaries were no less horrified, and pulled their representatives out of Sovnarkom. Not even Lenin was totally confident that the separate peace with the Central Powers would hold. On 10 March the seat of government was moved from Petrograd to Moscow, which had not been the Russian capital for two centuries, just in case the German armies decided to occupy the entire Baltic region. Nor was it inconceivable that Moscow, too, might become a target for the Germans.

In fact it was in Germany's interest to abide by the terms of the treaty so as to be able to concentrate her best military divisions on the Western front.[35] Ludendorff needed to finish off the war against Britain and France before the USA could bring her formidable military and industrial power in full on their side. Only then would Germany have the opportunity to turn on Russia. The Bolsheviks had to keep on hoping that socialist revolution would occur in Berlin before any such contingency might arise.

In the meantime Sovnarkom faced enormous difficulties. By the stroke of a pen Russia had been disjoined from Ukraine, Belorussia and the Baltic region. Half the grain, coal, iron and human population of the former Russian Empire was lost to the rulers in Petrograd and Moscow. There would have been an economic crisis even without the Treaty of Brest-Litovsk. The harvest of summer 1917 was only thirteen per cent below the average for the half-decade before the Great War; but this was 13.3 million metric tons of grain short of the country's requirements.[36] Ukraine, southern Russia and the Volga region usually enjoyed good enough harvests with which to feed themselves and sell the remainder in the rest of the Russian Empire. These three regions had a shortfall in 1917–18, and possessed no surplus to 'export' to other parts. The Treaty of Brest-Litovsk made a bad situation worse.

In addition, such peasant households as had surplus stocks of wheat and rye continued to refuse to sell them. The state, which maintained its monopoly on the grain trade, tried to barter with them. But to little avail. The warehouses of agricultural equipment had been nearly emptied. Industrial output in general was tumbling. In 1918 the output of large and medium-sized factories fell to a third of what it had been in 1913.[37] The multiple difficulties with transport, with finance and investment and with the unavailability of raw materials continued. Enterprises closed down also because of the 'class struggle' advocated by the Bolsheviks. Owners retired from production and commerce. Inflation continued to shoot up. In January 1918 a military-style system was introduced on the railways so as to restore efficiency. The banks had been nationalized in the previous December and many large metallurgical and textile plants were state owned by the spring.[38]

Even so, the decrees to assert control by government and by people were unable to restore the economy. The increased state ownership and regulation were, if anything, counter-productive to the restoration of the economy. The Bolshevik party was menaced by a gathering emergency of production, transportation and distribution which the Provisional Government had failed to resolve. Lenin had blamed all problems on ministerial incompetence and bourgeois greed and corruption. His own attempt to reconstruct the economy was proving to be even more ineffectual.

Within a couple of years the party's opponents were to claim that Sovnarkom could have rectified the situation by boosting investment in consumer-oriented industrial output and by dismantling the state grain-trade monopoly. Yet they were not saying this in 1917–18. At the time there was a recognition that the difficulties were largely beyond the capacity of any government to resolve. All of them were adamantly committed to the prosecution of the war against the Central Powers. The necessity to arm, clothe and feed the armed forces was therefore paramount. A free market in grain would have wrecked the war effort. The Bolsheviks alone were willing, just about willing, to sign a separate peace with the Germans and Austrians. But they set their face determinedly against economic privatization. What the liberal administration of Prince Lvov had nationalized they were not going to restore to the conditions of an unregulated market.

For they were a far-left political party, and proud of their ideas and traditions: they renamed themselves as the 'Russian Communist Party (Bolsheviks)' expressly in order to demarcate themselves from other types of socialism.[39] Ideological impatience infused their thinking. Lenin was more cautious than most Bolsheviks on industrial and agrarian policies, and yet he never seriously contemplated denationalization. If he had done, he would not have got far with his party. Victory in the Brest-Litovsk controversy had already stretched the party to breaking-point. Any further compromise with Bolshevik revolutionary principles would have caused an unmendable split. As it was, the Treaty threatened its own disaster. A country which already could not properly feed and arm itself had lost crucial regions of population and production. Could the October Revolution survive?

5

New World, Old World

Bolshevik leaders had assumed that people who supported them in 1917 would never turn against them and that the party's popularity would trace an unwavering, upward line on the graph. In the Central Committee before the October Revolution, only Kamenev and Zinoviev had dissented from this naïve futurology – and their scepticism had incurred Lenin's wrath. Certainly there were excuses for misjudging the potential backing for the party. The Bolsheviks had not yet got their message through to millions of fellow citizens, and it was not unreasonable for them to expect to reinforce their influence once their reforms and their propaganda had had their desired effect. Lenin and his associates could also point out that the Constituent Assembly results had underplayed the popularity of the Sovnarkom coalition because the candidate lists did not differentiate between the Left Socialist-Revolutionaries and the Socialist-Revolutionaries.

Nor had it been senseless to anticipate socialist revolution in central and western Europe. Bread riots had led to upheaval in Russia in February 1917. There were already reports of urban discontent in Germany and Austria and disturbances had taken place in the Kiel naval garrison. The Bolsheviks were right to suspect that the governments of both the Central Powers and the Allies were censoring newspapers so as to hide the growth of anti-war sentiment.

When all due allowance is made, however, the Bolsheviks had not acquired a governmental mandate from the Constituent Assembly elections; and their popularity, which had been rising in the last months of 1917, declined drastically in 1918. It was also clear that most persons in the former Russian Empire who voted for the party had objectives very different from those of Lenin and Trotski. The Constituent Assembly polls had given eighty-five per cent of the vote to socialists of one kind or another.[1] But the Bolsheviks were a single socialist party whereas the working class wanted a coalition government of all socialist parties and not just the Bolsheviks or an alliance restricted to Bolsheviks and Left Socialist-Revolutionaries. Workers in general did not demand dictatorship, terror, censorship or the violent dispersal of the Constituent Assembly. Nor did most of the soldiers and peasants who sided with the Bolshevik party know about the intention to involve them in a 'revolutionary war' if revolutions failed to occur elsewhere.[2]

This discrepancy was not accidental. The public agenda of Bolshevism had not been characterized by frankness; and sympathizers with the Bolshevik party, including most rank-and-file party members, had little idea of the basic assumptions and principles of the Central Committee. Yet this was not the whole story. For the Central Committee, while fooling its party and its electoral supporters, also deluded itself that the October Revolution would be crowned with easily-won success. They believed that their contingency plan for revolutionary war was unlikely to need to be implemented. When they replaced 'land nationalization' as a policy with 'land socialization', they felt that the peasantry would eventually see that nationalization was in its basic interest.[3]

Also of importance was the need for the Bolshevik leaders to simplify their policies to render them comprehensible to their own party and to society. Open politics had been hobbled in the tsarist period, and the public issues most readily understood by ordinary men and women after the February Revolution were those which were of direct significance for their families, factories and localities. Whereas they immediately perceived the implications of the crises in Russian high politics over Milyukov's telegram in April and the Kornilov mutiny in August, their grasp of the less sensational issues of war, politics and economics was less sure. Consequently it was vital for the Bolsheviks to concentrate on uncomplicated slogans and posters that would attract people to their party's side.[4] This was a difficult task; for the universal political euphoria at the downfall of the Romanov dynasty gave way to widespread apathy amidst the working class about the soviets and other mass organizations in subsequent months.

A further problem was that the Bolsheviks were not agreed among themselves. There had been a serious split in the Central Committee over the composition of the government in November 1917, and another in March 1918 over the question of war and peace. At a time when the party's need was to indoctrinate society, it had yet to determine its own policies. Even Lenin was probing his way. Society, the Russian Communist Party and its central leaders were finding out about each other and about themselves.

The party's difficulties were especially severe in the borderlands, where Lenin's regime was regarded as illegitimate. Practically the entire vote for the Bolsheviks in the Constituent Assembly had come from Russian cities or from industrial cities outside Russia that had a large working class embracing a goodly proportion of ethnic Russians. Only in the Latvian and Estonian areas, where hatred of the Germans was greater than worry about Russians, did the Bolsheviks have success with a non-Russian electorate.[5] In the Transcaucasus, the Mensheviks of Georgia got together with Armenian and Azeri politicians to form a Transcaucasian Commissariat. A *Sejm*, or parliament, was set up in February 1918. But already there were divisions, especially between the Armenians and Azeris; and an alliance between the Bolsheviks and Armenian nationalists in Baku led to a massacre of the Muslim Azeris. The Ottoman army intervened on the Azeri side in spring.[6] By May 1918 three independent states had been set up: Georgia, Azerbaijan and Armenia. The communists had been ousted even from Baku, and the entire Transcaucasus was lost to them.

Lenin and Stalin, as they continued to deliberate on this, recognized that their 'Declaration of the Rights of the Peoples of Russia', issued on 3 November 1917, had gone unnoticed by most of the non-Russian population.[7] Over the ensuing weeks they altered their public commitment to the goal of a unitary state, and Lenin on 5 December published a Manifesto to the Ukrainian People which expressed the idea that the future government of Russia and Ukraine should be based on federal principles. In his subsequent Declaration of the Rights of the Toiling and Exploited People, which he wrote for presentation to the Constituent Assembly, he generalized this expectation by calling for a 'free union of nations as a federation of Soviet republics'.[8] After dispersing the Constituent Assembly, he came to the Third Congress of Soviets in late January and proclaimed the formation of the Russian Socialist Federal Soviet Republic (RSFSR).[9]

The 'Russian' in the title was not *Russkaya* but *Rossiiskaya*. This was deliberate. The former had an ethnic dimension; the latter connoted the country which was inhabited by many nations of which the Russians were merely one, albeit the largest one. Lenin wanted to emphasize that all the peoples and territories of the former Russian Empire were being welcomed into the RSFSR on equal terms in a federal system. He was also indicating his acceptance – in marked contrast with Nicholas II – that there were areas of the old empire that were not 'Russia'. Russians were not to enjoy any privileges under Soviet rule.

The Treaty of Brest-Litovsk in March 1918 foreclosed the possibility to test this policy in the borderlands on Russia's south-west, west and north-west. The Ukrainian, Belorussian, Lithuanian, Latvian and Estonian provinces of the former Russian Empire joined Poland under German military control. A puppet government of 'Hetman' Pavlo Skoropadskyi was installed in Kiev. Communist party leaders, some of whom attempted to organize a partisan movement, were chased out of Ukraine. In each of the lands occupied by the Germans a balance was struck between the enforcement of Berlin's wishes and the encouragement of local national sentiment. Political, administrative and economic ties were broken with Moscow and Petrograd, and the Russian Communist Party's task of reincorporating the lost territory was made the harder. There were problems even in areas where neither the Central Powers nor the Allies were active. The Muslim peoples of central Asia, most of whom dwelt outside cities, had little communication with Russia; and within Russia, by the river Volga and in the southern Urals, the Tatars and Bashkirs had yet to be persuaded that Sovnarkom would not rule the country primarily for the benefit of the Russians.

By the middle of 1918 the triple effect of the October Revolution, the Constituent Assembly's dispersal and the Treaty of Brest-Litovsk had been to trap the Bolsheviks in a Russian enclave. This was infuriating for them. Apart from Bukharin, Russians were not the leading figures in the Central Committee: Trotski, Kamenev, Zinoviev and Sverdlov were Jews; Stalin was a Georgian, Dzierżyński a Pole; Lenin was only partly an ethnic Russian. They had seized power in Petrograd so as to remake the politics of all Europe, and at home they had intended to transform the Russian Empire into a multi-national socialist state of free and equal nations. This remained their dream. But until the Red Army could impose itself on the borderlands the dream would not come near to reality. The Bolsheviks' efforts in the meantime would perforce be concentrated in an area inhabited predominantly by Russians.

But how would these efforts be organized? Like his communist leaders, Lenin asserted that socialism should be built not only through a strongly centralized state but also by dint of the initiative and enthusiasm of the 'masses'. He liked to quote Goethe's dictum: 'Theory is grey but life is green.' Yakov Sverdlov, the Central Committee Secretary, had two other reasons for encouraging local initiative: the lack of sufficient personnel and the paucity of information about conditions in the provinces. To a party activist he wrote: 'You understand, comrade, that it is difficult to give you instructions any more concrete than "All Power to the Soviets!"' Sovnarkom decrees did not lay down a detailed legal framework. Law meant infinitely less to Lenin, a former lawyer, than the cause of the Revolution. Sovnarkom was offering only broad guidelines for action to workers, soldiers and peasants. The aim was to inform, energize, excite and activate 'the masses'. It did not matter if mistakes were made. The only way to avoid a blunder was to avoid doing anything.

The effect of the Decree on Land was particularly cheering for the Bolshevik party. Many peasants had been diffident about seizing whole estates before the October Revolution. They wanted to have at least a semblance of governmental permission before so precipitate a step. Lenin's words released them from their fears. The gentry's houses and agricultural equipment were grabbed in a rising number of incidents and peasants shared them among themselves.[10]

Not every region experienced this commotion. In central Asia the old social structure was preserved and property was left with its owners. In Ukraine the proximity of the Eastern front had discouraged peasants from a hasty movement against landowners in case the Central Powers broke through and restored the old social order – and this fear was realized with the Brest-Litovsk Treaty. But elsewhere the peasantry sensed that their historic opportunity had arrived. There was solidarity among established households of each village. Where the peasant land commune existed, as in most parts of Russia and Ukraine, its practices were reinforced. In thirty-nine Russian provinces only four per cent of households stayed outside the communal framework. Kulaks were pulled back into it; many of them needed little persuasion since they, too, wanted a share of the land of the dispossessed gentry. The peasants in Russia's central agricultural region gained control over an area a quarter larger than before 1917; and in Ukraine the area was bigger by three quarters.[11]

Many a household divided itself into several households so as to increase its members' claim to land. The unintended consequence was that sons had a say in communal affairs whereas previously the father would have spoken on their behalf. As young men were conscripted, furthermore, women began to thrust themselves forward when decisions were taken: gradually the revolutions in the villages were affecting rural relationships.[12] But the main feature was the peasantry's wish to arrange its life without outside interference. Liberated from indebtedness to the landlord and from oppression by the land captains, peasants savoured their chance to realize their ancient aspirations.

Among the other beneficiaries of this transformation were the soldiers and sailors of Russian armed forces. Sovnarkom had authorized their demobilization in the winter of 1917–18. This gave *post factum* sanction to a mass flight from the trenches and garrisons that had been occurring since midsummer. Most of the conscripts were peasants who, with rifles slung over their shoulders, jumped on trains and horse-carts and returned to their native villages. Their arrival gave urgency to the process of land reform, especially in places where little had hitherto been known about the Bolsheviks and their Land Decree. Those military units which were not demobilized had much internal democracy. Election of officers was commonplace and soldiers' committees supervised the activities of the structure of higher command. Many such units were supporters of the Bolsheviks in the Constituent Assembly elections and fought in the early campaigns to consolidate the October Revolution in Moscow and Ukraine.

They demanded and received good rations, disdaining discipline as a relic of the tsarist regime. Several units were little better than a rabble of boozy ne'er-do-wells who had no homes to return to. Those which were well led and had high morale were treasured by the Bolshevik party. The outstanding ones were typically non-Russian. Without the Latvian Riflemen the regime might well have collapsed; and Lenin was in no position to quibble when the Latvians insisted on consulting with each other before deciding whether to comply with his orders.

Workers, too, relished their new status. Palaces, mansions and large town houses were seized from the rich and turned into flats for indigent working-class families.[13] The expropriations took place at the instigation of the local soviets or even the factory-workshop committees and trade union branches. The authorities also gave priority to their industrial labour-force in food supplies. A class-based rationing system was introduced. Furthermore, truculent behaviour by foremen vanished after the October Revolution. The chief concern of the working class was to avoid any closure of their enterprise. Most remaining owners of enterprises fled south determined to take their financial assets with them before Sovnarkom's economic measures brought ruin upon them. But factory-workshop committees unlocked closed premises and sent telegrams informing Sovnarkom that they had 'nationalized' their factories and mines. The state was gaining enterprises at a faster rate than that approved by official policy.

The movement for 'workers' control' continued. Factory-workshop committees in central and south-eastern Russia followed their counterparts in Petrograd in instituting a tight supervision of the management.[14] Most committees contented themselves with the supervising of existing managers; but in some places the committees contravened the code on workers' control, sacked the managers and took full charge. There was also a movement called Proletarian Culture (*Proletkult*) which sought to facilitate educational and cultural self-development by workers. Lenin often worried that both 'workers' control' and Proletkult might prove difficult for the party to regulate. Already in 1918 he was seeking to limit the rights of the workers in their factories and in the 1920s he moved against Proletkult. Even so, the working class kept many gains made by it before and during the October Revolution.

These fundamental changes in politics and economics demoralized the middle and upper social classes. Only a few diehards tried to form counter-revolutionary associations: the Main Council of the Landowners' Union still operated and some Imperial Army officers banded together to form a 'Right Centre'.[15] General Kornilov escaped from house arrest outside Petrograd. After several weeks of travel in disguise, he reached southern Russia, where he joined General Alekseev in calling for the formation of a Volunteer Army to bring about the overthrow of the Soviet government. Yet such persons were exceptional. Most industrialists, landlords and officers tried to avoid trouble while hoping for a victory for counter-revolutionary forces. Many went into hiding; others were so desperate that they hurriedly emigrated. They took boats across the Black Sea, trains to Finland and haycarts into Poland. Panic was setting in. About three million people fled the country in the first years after the October Revolution.[16]

Their exodus caused no regret among the Bolsheviks. The Constitution of the RSFSR, introduced in July 1918, defined the state unequivocally as 'a dictatorship of the urban and rural proletariat and the poorest'. The right to vote was withdrawn from all citizens who hired labour in pursuit of profit, who derived their income from financial investments or who were engaged in private business.

Quickly they became known as 'the deprived ones' (*lishentsy*). In the main, the discrimination against them was based upon economic criteria. The Constitution stressed that this 'republic of soviets of workers', soldiers' and peasants' deputies' had been established so as to effect the 'transition' to a socialist society. There was a formal specification that 'he who does not work shall not eat'. Other disenfranchised groups included any surviving members of the Romanov dynasty, former members of the Okhrana and the clergy of all denominations.[17] Lenin wanted it to be clearly understood that the RSFSR was going to be a class dictatorship.

Nevertheless there was less of a transformation than at first met the eye; this revolutionary society remained a highly traditional one in many ways. Several workers who had helped to take the Winter Palace on 25 October 1917 had simultaneously helped themselves to the bottles of the Romanov cellars. (Their carousing gave new meaning to calls for a replenishment of the revolutionary spirit.) Vandalism and thuggishness were not uncommon in other places. Traditional working-class behaviour was prominent, warts and all. Sensing that the usual constraints on them had been removed, factory labourers, horsecab-drivers and domestic servants behaved everywhere in a fashion that had once been confined to the poor districts of the towns and cities. Bolsheviks and Left Socialist-Revolutionaries, who had begun by admiring such displays of belligerence, began to understand the negative implications.

At any rate the fact that most workers had voted for socialist parties in elections to the soviets and the Constituent Assembly did not signify that they themselves were committed socialists. After the October Revolution they consulted their sectional interests to an even greater extent than before. Their collectivism was expressed in a factory work-force deciding how to improve its particular conditions without a thought for the 'general proletarian cause'. Warehouse stocks were ransacked for items which could be put on sale by workers in groups or as individuals. A conscientious attitude to work in the factories and mines had never been a notable virtue of the unskilled and semi-skilled sections of the Russian working class, and the reports of slackness were plentiful. Such a phenomenon was understandable in circumstances of urban economic collapse. Workers were unable to rely on the state for their welfare and looked after themselves as best they could.

Many, too, fell back on to the safety net of the countryside. They were returning to their native villages to find food, to obtain a share of the expropriated land or to sell industrial products. Their customary connections with the rural life were being reinforced.

This same rural life was in vital ways resistant to the kind of revolution desired by the communists: the Russian village organized itself along centuries-old peasant precepts. Peasants were fair, or could be made to be fair, in their dealings with other peasants so long as they belonged to the same village. But rivalries between villages were often violent; and the elders of a given commune seldom agreed to any land passing into the hands of 'outsiders' or even of agricultural wage-labourers who had worked for years within the village.[18] Furthermore, the peasantry maintained its own ancient order. There was no lightening of the harsh punishment of infringers of tradition. The peasants wanted a revolution that complied with their interests: they wanted their land and their commune; they desired to regulate their affairs without urban interference.

The peasantry already had grounds for resenting Sovnarkom on this score. The February 1918 Decree on the Separation of Church from State had disturbed the Russian Orthodox believers, and they and the various Christian sects were annoyed by the atheistic propaganda emitted from Moscow. At a more materialist level, peasants were also irritated at not being offered a good price for their agricultural produce. Their pleasure in the Decree on Land did not induce them to show gratitude by parting willingly with grain unless they received a decent payment. Each household's pursuance of its narrow financial interests cast a blight over the working of the entire economy. The food-supplies crisis would become steadily more acute until the peasantry's attitude could somehow be overcome.

Furthermore, the more or less egalitarian redistribution of land did not bring about an agrarian revolution that might have boosted production. The salient change was social rather than economic. This was the process known as 'middle-peasantization'. As landholdings were equalized, so the number of peasant households classifiable as rich and poor was reduced. The middling category of peasants (*serednyaki*) – vaguely-defined though the category remains – constituted the vast bulk of the peasantry in the Russian provinces.[19] This shift in land tenure, however, was not usually accompanied by a sharing of implements and livestock so that peasants who lacked either a plough or a cow were consequently reduced to renting out their additional patches of soil to a richer household which already had the wherewithal. There was little sign of rapid progress to a more sophisticated agriculture for Russia. Apart from the expropriation of the gentry, the rural sector of the economy survived substantially unaltered from before the Great War.

To most communists this appeared as a reason to redouble their revolutionary endeavour. Such problems as existed, they imagined, were outweighed by the solutions already being realized. Fervour had to be given further stimulation. Workers, soldiers and peasants needed to be mobilized by Russian Communist Party activists: the message of socialist reconstruction had to be relayed to all corners of the country so that Bolshevism might be understood by everyone.

One of the obstacles was technical. Communication by post and telegraph between cities was woeful; and even when metropolitan newspapers reached the provinces it was not unknown for people to use their pages not for their information but as cigarette-wrappers. Moreover, the villages were virtually cut off from the rest of the country save for the visits made by workers and soldiers (who anyway tended not to return to the cities). The structures of administration were falling apart. Policies enunciated by Sovnarkom were not enforced by the lower soviets if local Bolsheviks objected. Trade unions and factory-workshop committees in the localities snubbed their own supreme bodies. Inside the party the lack of respect for hierarchy was just as remarkable: the Central Committee was asked for assistance, but usually on the terms acceptable to the regional and city party committees.[20] The country lacked all system of order.

The problem was not merely administrative but also political: Bolsheviks were in dispute about the nature of their party's project for revolutionary transformation. Disagreements erupted about matters that had received little attention before October 1917 when the party had been preoccupied with the seizing of power. It was chiefly the pace of change that was controversial. About basic objectives there was consensus; Bolsheviks agreed that the next epoch in politics and economics around the world would involve the following elements: the dictatorship of the proletariat; the state's ownership and direction of the entire economy; the gathering together of society into large organizational units; and the dissemination of Marxism. At the centre Lenin urged a cautious pace of industrial nationalization and agricultural collectivization whereas Bukharin advocated the more or less immediate implementation of such objectives.[21]

The friction between Lenin and Bukharin seemed of little significance to most citizens. For although Lenin was a moderate in internal debates among Bolsheviks on the economy, he was an extremist by the standards of the other Russian political parties. Lenin, no less than Bukharin, preached class war against the bourgeoisie; and, for that matter, Lenin was the hard Old Man of Bolshevism on political questions: it was he who had invented the Cheka and destroyed the Constituent Assembly. Consequently it was the common immoderacy of the party that impressed most people.

The communist party therefore had to engage in a propaganda campaign to win supporters and to keep those it already had. Newspaper articles and speeches at factory gates had helped to prepare for the seizure of power. Something more substantial was needed to consolidate the regime. Plans were laid to establish a central party school, whose students would supplement the handful of thousands of activists who had belonged to the communist party before the February Revolution of 1917.[22] Discussions were also held about the contents of the new party programme. Yet the communist leaders had not learned how to dispense with Marxist jargon. When the final version was settled in 1919, the language would have foxed all except intellectuals already acquainted with the works of Marx, Engels and Lenin.[23] Neither the school nor the programme solved the questions of mass communication.

The Bolshevik central leadership sought to improve the situation in various ways. Posters portraying the entire Central Committee were commissioned. Statues were erected to the heroes of Bolshevism, including Marx and Engels (and even rebels from ancient Rome such as Brutus and Spartacus).[24] Busts of Lenin started to be produced, and his colleague Zinoviev wrote the first biography of him in 1918.[25] The leadership appreciated, too, the potential of cinema. A short film was made of Lenin showing him shyly pottering around the grounds of the Kremlin with his personal assistant V. D. Bonch-Bruevich. Lenin also agreed to make a gramophone recording of some of his speeches. Few cinemas were in fact operating any longer; but propaganda was also conducted by so-called agit-trains and even agit-steamships. These were vehicles painted with rousing pictures and slogans and occupied by some of the party's finest orators, who gave 'agitational' speeches to the crowds that gathered at each stop on the journey.

The party aimed to monopolize public debate and shut down all Kadet and many Menshevik and Socialist-Revolutionary newspapers; and the freedom of these parties to campaign openly for their policies was wrecked by the dispersal of the Constituent Assembly as well as by the overruling of elections to the soviets that did not yield a communist party majority.[26] Nevertheless the battle of ideas was not entirely ended. The Bolsheviks had secured privileged conditions to engage its adversaries in polemics, resorting to force whenever it wished, but the clandestine groups of the Mensheviks and Socialist-Revolutionaries continued to operate among the workers and agitate for the replacement of the communists in power.

The communist party had to compete, too, against its coalition partners in 1917–18. The Left Socialist-Revolutionaries largely succeeded in prohibiting the use of force to acquire peasant-owned grain stocks even though several towns were on the verge of famine; they also issued denunciations of the Treaty of Brest-Litovsk. Unlike the Mensheviks and Socialist-Revolutionaries, moreover, they managed to keep their printing presses running even after the party formally withdrew from the governmental coalition in March 1918.[27] The Orthodox Church, too, confronted the communists. Tikhon, the Moscow bishop, had been elected Patriarch in November 1917.

There had been no Patriarch since 1700; and when the Decree on the Separation of Church from State forbade the teaching of religion in schools and disbarred the Church from owning property, Tikhon anathematized those who propounded atheism.[28] The Church relayed this message through its priests to every parish in the country.

Force gave the communists an unrivalled advantage in countering the anti-Bolshevik current of opinion. But force by itself was not sufficient. The enlistment of help from the intelligentsia was an urgent objective for the Bolsheviks. The problem was that most poets, painters, musicians and educators were not sympathetic to Bolshevism. The People's Commissariat of Enlightenment, led by Anatoli Lunacharski, made efforts to attract them into its activities. It was axiomatic for the Bolsheviks that 'modern communism' was constructible only when the foundations of a highly educated and industrialized society had been laid. The 'proletarian dictatorship' and the 'nationalization of the means of production' were two vital means of achieving the party's ends. A third was 'cultural revolution'.

The teachers behaved more or less as the communists wanted. They had to co-operate with Sovnarkom if they wanted to be paid and obtain food rations; and in any case they shared the party's zeal for universal literacy and numeracy. But artistic intellectuals were a matter of greater concern. They had caused perennial difficulties for the tsars by their commentaries upon political life and had acted as a collective conscience for the Russian nation; and the Bolshevik party worried lest they might start again to fulfil this role in the Soviet state. Official policy towards artists and writers was therefore double sided. On the one hand, intellectuals were subjected to the threat of censorship embodied in the Decree on the Press; on the other, the party appealed to them to lend their support to the revolutionary regime – and material benefits were offered to those willing to comply.

Some responded positively. The operatic bass Fëdr Shalyapin sang his repertoire to packed theatres at cheap seat-prices. The Jewish painter Marc Chagall was given a large studio in Vitebsk where he taught workers to paint. Even the poet Sergei Yesenin believed the best of the Russian Communist Party, declaring that the intelligentsia was like 'a bird in a cage, fluttering desperately to avoid a calloused, gentle hand that wanted only to take it out and let it fly free'.[29] It would be hard to imagine a statement of more naïve trust in the party's tolerance. Yesenin's friend and fellow poet Alexander Blok harboured no such illusions; but even Blok felt no hostility to the October Revolution as such. His great poem, *The Twelve*, caught the chaotic spirit of the times through the image of a dozen ill-disciplined revolutionaries tramping the streets of Petrograd, talking about politics and sex and engaging in occasional acts of thuggery, and Blok was caught between admiration and repulsion for them.

Most intellectuals in the arts and scholarship were more hostile even than Blok to the Bolsheviks and saw the Decree on the Press as a preliminary step towards a comprehensive cultural clampdown. But there were few heroes amidst the intelligentsia. The times precluded the composition of lengthy works castigating Bolshevism: novels are not written in revolutions. Material circumstances, too, had an influence. Intellectuals could not live by ideas alone. Most of them were worse off than workers, who were given larger food rations by Sovnarkom. Increasingly the official authorities tried to suborn the intelligentsia by giving bread and money in return for newspaper articles, posters and revolutionary hymns. Hunger, more than direct censorship, pulled the intellectuals into political line.[30] And so a tacit truce was coming into effect. The regime obtained the educative tracts it desired while the intellectuals waited to see what would happen next.

The intelligentsia of the arts, science and scholarship was not alone in being courted by the Bolsheviks. Also indispensable to the maintenance of communist rule was the expertise of engineers, managers and administrators. The dictatorship of the proletariat, as Lenin continued to emphasize, could not dispense with 'bourgeois' specialists until a generation of working-class socialist specialists had been trained to replace them.[31]

More than that: Lenin suggested that Russian industry was so backward that its small and medium-size enterprises should be exempted from nationalization and aggregated into large capitalist syndicates responsible for each great sector of industry, syndicates which would introduce up-to-date technology and operational efficiency. Capitalism still had a role to play in the country's economic development; socialism could not instantly be created. But the Soviet authorities would be able to direct this process for the benefit of socialism since they already owned the banks and large factories and controlled commerce at home and abroad.[32] Sovnarkom would preside over a mixed economy wherein the dominant influence would be exerted by socialist institutions and policies. Capitalism, once it had ceased to be useful, would be eradicated.

Lenin's term for this particular type of mixed economy was 'state capitalism', and in April 1918 he encouraged the iron and steel magnate V. P. Meshcherski to submit a project for joint ownership between the government and Meshcherski's fellow entrepreneurs.[33] This pro-capitalist initiative caused an outcry on the Bolshevik party's Left. Brest-Litovsk had been one doctrinal concession too many for them, and Lenin lacked the political authority to insist on accepting Meshcherski's project. It is anyway open to query whether Lenin and Meshcherski could have worked together for very long to mutual advantage. Lenin hated the bourgeoisie, depriving it of civic rights after the October Revolution. When it looked as if the Germans were going to overrun Petrograd in January, he had recommended the shooting on the spot of the party's class enemies.[34] Meshcherski was a rare industrialist who briefly considered political cohabitation with Lenin to be feasible.

There was anyway full agreement between Lenin and the Left Communists that the party had to strengthen its appeal to the workers. All Bolshevik leaders looked forward to a time when their own endeavours in basic education and political propaganda would have re-educated the entire working class. But in the interim they had to be satisfied by the promotion of outstanding representatives of the 'proletariat' to administrative posts within the expanding Soviet state institutions. Talented, loyal workers were invited to become rulers in their own dictatorship.

A rising proportion of the civilian state administration by 1918–19 claimed working-class origins. Here the Petrograd metal-workers were prominent, who supplied thousands of volunteers for service in local government. In the People's Commissariat of Internal Affairs the removal of tsarist personnel had been started under the Provisional Government and the process continued under Sovnarkom throughout the agencies of administration. Social background counted heavily as a qualification for promotion; but there was also a need for the promotees to be comfortable with paper-work. Soviets at central and local levels discovered how difficult it was to find enough such people.[35] The 'localities' asked the 'centre' to provide competent personnel; the 'centre' made the same request of the 'localities'. But demography told against the hopes of Bolshevism. There were over three million industrial workers in 1917, and the number tumbled to 2.4 million by the following autumn. A predominantly 'proletarian' administration was impossible.

Furthermore, the official percentages were misleading. As small and medium-size businesses went bankrupt, their owners had to secure alternative employment. Jobs for them were unavailable in the economy's shrinking private sector; but desk jobs in an ever-swelling administration were plentiful: all it took was a willingness to pretend to be of working-class background. Many 'petit-bourgeois elements', as the Russian Communist Party designated them, infiltrated the institutions of state after the October Revolution.

Meanwhile many members of the urban working class proved troublesome. The violence used by Sovnarkom was a shock to popular opinion, and the labour-forces of Petrograd metal and textile plants, which had once supported the Bolsheviks, led the resistance. With some assistance from the Menshevik activists, they elected representatives to an Assembly of Plenipotentiaries in Petrograd in spring 1918.[36] The Assembly bore similarities to the Petrograd Soviet after the February Revolution inasmuch as it was a sectional organization whereby workers aimed to obtain civic freedoms and larger food rations. But the Assembly operated in a hostile environment. The workers were tired, hungry and disunited. Among them were many who still sympathized with several Bolshevik policies. The communists were ruthless. In May a demonstration by Assembly supporters at the nearby industrial town of Kolpino was suppressed by armed troops. The message could not have been blunter that the 'dictatorship of the proletariat' would be defended by any means against the demands of the proletariat itself.

So that the question arose: how new was the world being built by Lenin and Sovnarkom? The RSFSR had facets reminiscent of the tsarist order at its worst. Central state power was being asserted in an authoritarian fashion. Ideological intolerance was being asserted and organized dissent suppressed. Elective principles were being trampled under foot. The tendency for individuals to take decisions without consultation even with the rest of their committees was on the rise.

Lenin in *The State and Revolution* had stated that his government would combine a vigorous centralism with a vigorous local autonomy.[37] The balance was already tilted in favour of a centralism so severe that the communists quickly became notorious for authoritarian excesses; and, in the light of Lenin's casualness about the restraints of democratic procedure throughout 1917, this was hardly surprising. The Bolsheviks wanted action and practical results. As proponents of efficient 'account-keeping and supervision' they presented themselves as the enemies of bureaucratic abuse. Yet their own behaviour exacerbated the problems they denounced. There was an increase in the number of administrators, whose power over individuals rose as the existing restraints were demolished. In addition, the Soviet state intruded into economic and social affairs to a greater depth than attempted by the Romanov Emperors – and the increased functions assumed by the state gave increased opportunities to deploy power arbitrarily.

A cycle of action and reaction was observable. As Sovnarkom failed to obtain its desired political and economic results, Lenin and his colleagues assumed that the cause was the weakness of hierarchical supervision. They therefore invented new supervisory institutions. More and more paperwork was demanded as proof of compliance. At the same time officials were licensed to do whatever they felt necessary to secure the centrally-established targets. And, moreover, new laws, decrees, regulations, commands and instructions cascaded from higher to lower organs of authority even though law in general was held in official disrespect. The unsurprising consequence of these contradictory phenomena continued to surprise the Russian Communist Party's leadership: a rise in bureaucratic inefficiency and abuse.

Herein lay grounds for a popular disgruntlement with the communists which would have existed even if the party had not applied force against dissenters and if there had been no fundamental crisis in economic and international relations. Citizens were being made to feel that they had no inalienable rights. The state could grant favours, and it could just as easily take them away. Even local officialdom developed an uncooperative attitude towards Moscow. As the central political authorities kept on demanding ever greater effort from them, so administrators in the localities were learning to be furtive. They protected themselves in various ways. In particular, they gave jobs to friends and associates: clientalism was becoming a political habit. They also formed local groups of officials in various important institutions so that a locality could present a common front to the capital. They were not averse to misreporting local reality so as to acquire favour from the central political leadership.

Thus many of the elements of the later Soviet compound had already been put in place by Lenin's Russian Communist Party. But not all of them. At least through to mid-1918 the republic was not yet a one-party, one-ideology state; and the chaos in all institutions as well as the breakdown in communications, transport and material supplies was a drastic impediment to a centralized system of power. The Soviet order was extremely disorderly for a great deal of the time.

Yet the movement towards a centralized, ideocratic dictatorship of a single party had been started. Neither Lenin nor his leading comrades had expressly intended this; they had few clearly-elaborated policies and were forever fumbling and improvising. Constantly they found international, political, economic, social and cultural difficulties to be less tractable than they had assumed. And constantly they dipped into their rag-bag of authoritarian concepts to work out measures to help them to survive in power. Yet their survival would surely have been impossible if they had not operated in a society so little capable of resisting them. The collapse of the urban sector of the economy; the breakdown of administration, transport and communication; the preoccupation of organizations, groups and individuals with local concerns; the widespread physical exhaustion after years of war; the divisions among the opposition: all such phenomena gave the Bolsheviks their chance – and the Bolsheviks had the guile and harshness to know how to seize it.

And they felt that their ruthless measures were being applied in the service of a supreme good. Bolsheviks in the capital and the provinces believed that the iniquities of the old regime in Russia and the world were about to be eliminated. The decrees of Sovnarkom were formulated to offer unparalleled hope to Russian workers and peasants, to non-Russians in the former Russian Empire, to the industrialized societies of Europe and North America, to the world's colonial peoples. The Russian Communist Party had its supporters at home. Local revolutionary achievements were not negligible in urban and rural Russia. The party was inclined to believe that all obstacles in its path would soon be cast down. It surely would win any civil war. It would surely retake the borderlands. It would surely foster revolution abroad. The agenda of 1917 had not yet been proved unrealistic in the judgement of the Bolshevik leadership.

6

Civil Wars (1918–1921)

Civil war had been a recurrent theme in statements by Lenin and Trotski before the October Revolution. Whenever workers' rights were being infringed, the Bolshevik leaders sang out that the bourgeoisie had started a civil war. What others might dub industrial conflict acquired a broader connotation. After 1917, too, Lenin and Trotski used class struggle and civil war as interchangeable terms, treating expropriations of factories and landed estates as part of the same great process as the military suppression of counter-revolution.

Increasingly the Bolshevik Central Committee used the term in a more conventional way to signify a series of battles between two sets of armies. Yet the military challenge was still expected by Sovnarkom to be easily surmountable; Lenin and his Central Committee, remembering the rapid defeat of the Kornilov mutiny, assumed that they would quickly win any serious conflict. One substantial campaign had been waged when Bolshevik-led forces invaded Ukraine in December 1917; but otherwise the tale had been of scrappy engagements since the October Revolution. A skirmish with a Cossack contingent in the Don region in late January 1918 resulted in a Soviet victory that was celebrated by Lenin over the next four months as marking the end of civil war.[1] The Bolsheviks began to build a Workers' and Peasants' Red Army from February; but their intention was not merely to fight internal armed enemies: Lenin wanted a vast force to be prepared in time to be sent to the aid of the anticipated uprising of the Berlin working class.[2]

As he discovered in May 1918, this assumption was erroneous. The Socialist-Revolutionary leadership fled to Samara on the river

Volga to establish a Committee of Members of the Constituent Assembly (or *Komuch*), which laid claim to be the legitimate government of Russia. A socialist Volga confronted socialist Moscow and Petrograd, and fighting could not permanently be forestalled. Komuch as yet had a weaker military capacity even than Sovnarkom. But this was not the case with other Russian opponents of the communists. Generals Alekseev and Kornilov had escaped to southern Russia where they were gathering a Volunteer Army for action against the Bolsheviks. In mid-Siberia a contingent of Imperial officers was being formed under Admiral Kolchak, who had commanded the Black Sea fleet. General Yudenich invited other volunteers to his banner in the north-west. The forces of Alekseev, Kornilov, Kolchak and Yudenich soon became known as the White armies.

The German forces remained the dominant military power in the western borderlands of the former Russian Empire, and were invited by Lenin to help the Bolsheviks in northern Russia (even though, ultimately, Sovnarkom's declared eventual purpose was to overthrow Kaiser Wilhelm II).[3] For the Brest-Litovsk Treaty angered the British into dispatching an expeditionary contingent to Archangel and Murmansk, purportedly to defend Allied military equipment on Russian soil. Other threats, too, were realized. The French landed a naval garrison in Odessa on the Black Sea. The Turks were on the move on the frontiers of the 'Russian' Transcaucasus. Japanese forces occupied territory in the Far East, and the American contingent was not far behind them. Russia had been reduced to a size roughly the same as medieval Muscovy. Seemingly it would not be long before a foreign power reached Moscow and overthrew the Bolsheviks.

In the capital the Bolshevik Central Committee members put on a brave face. The Left Socialist-Revolutionaries agitated against them, continuing to put the case against official communist policies. Even leading supporters of Lenin in the Brest-Litovsk controversy began to ask whether the treaty with the Central Powers had brought any benefit. G. Sokolnikov, who had signed the treaty on Lenin's behalf, declared that it was not worth the paper it was printed on.[4]

The military situation of the Bolsheviks deteriorated in the same weeks. A legion of Czech and Slovak prisoners-of-war was being conveyed along the Trans-Siberian railway to the Far East for further shipment to Europe in compliance with an earlier agreement with the Allies. These troops intended to join the struggle against the Central Powers on the Western front. But there had always been distrust between the Czechoslovak Legion's leaders and the Bolsheviks. Trotski, who became People's Commissar for Military Affairs in March 1918, dealt with them abrasively. Then the Chelyabinsk Soviet unilaterally tried to disarm the units of the Legion as their train passed through the town.[5] The Legion resisted this action, and travelled back to the Urals and the Volga to pick up the rest of its units. By the end of May it had reached Samara, crushing the Bolshevik local administrations on the way. Komuch persuaded it to forget about the Western front and join in the common effort to overthrow Sovnarkom.

In central Russia there was panic. Although there were only fifteen thousand Czechs and Slovaks, they might well prove more than a match for the nascent Red Army. Sovnarkom and the Cheka could not guarantee security even in Moscow. The Left Socialist-Revolutionary Central Committee was planning an insurrection against Bolshevism. Its other tactic was to wreck the relationship between the Soviet and German governments by assassinating Count Mirbach, Germany's ambassador to Moscow. Yakov Blyumkin, a Left Socialist-Revolutionary member of the Cheka, procured documents sanctioning a visit to the embassy. On 6 July he met Mirbach in the embassy and killed him.

Lenin, fearing that Berlin might rip up the Treaty of Brest-Litovsk, visited the embassy to express his condolences. Having carried out this distasteful errand, he instructed the Latvian Riflemen to arrest the Left Socialist-Revolutionaries. Their preliminary duty was to liberate Dzierżyński from the hands of the Left Socialist-Revolutionaries who had taken him hostage.[6] The Russian Socialist Federal Soviet Republic was clearly not yet a properly-functioning police state if this could happen to the Cheka's chairman. The Latvians succeeded in releasing Dzierżyński and suppressing the Left Socialist-Revolutionaries; and the Fifth Congress of Soviets, which was taking place at the time, passed all the resolutions tendered by the Bolsheviks. Already on 9 May a Food-Supplies Dictatorship had been proclaimed, and armed requisitioning of grain was turned from an intermittent local practice into a general system. The removal of the Left Socialist-Revolutionaries from the Congress eliminated the last vestige of opposition to the new policy.

While Lenin, Sverdlov and a shaken Dzierżyński imposed their authority in Moscow, Trotski rushed to the Volga where the Czechoslovak Legion took Kazan on 7 August 1918. Komuch was poised to re-enter central Russia. Trotski's adaptiveness to the role of People's Commissar for Military Affairs was impressive. Not all the orators of 1917 had managed an effective transition to the wielding of power; but Trotski, having dazzled his diplomatic adversaries at Brest-Litovsk, was turning his talents with equal success towards the Red Army.

Temperamentally he was as hard as a diamond. Like Lenin, he came from a comfortable family and had been a brilliant student. Trotski's real name was Lev Davydovich Bronshtein. He was a Jew from southern Ukraine, whose farming father sent him to secondary school in Odessa. His flair for writing and for foreign languages revealed itself early; but so, too, did a restlessness with the kind of society in which he had been brought up. He drew close to the clandestine populist groups which approved of terrorism. But by late adolescence he was a Marxist and by 1900 he was in Siberian exile. He made a dramatic escape by sleigh a couple of years later, joining Lenin in London and working with him on the *émigré* Marxist journal, *Iskra*. At the Second Party Congress in 1903, however, Trotski denounced Lenin for provoking the split between Bolsheviks and Mensheviks.

In organization, Trotski had agreed with Menshevik criticisms of Leninist organizational ideas, which he predicted would result in a dictator placing himself in authority over the Central Committee. He meant this satirically, and was not to know that Stalin would one day realize the prophecy; but his hostility to Bolshevik divisiveness was sincere at the time. Trotski was already a distinctive figure among Marxists. While opposing the Bolsheviks on organizational questions, he stood close to them on strategy. His theory of revolution in Russia squeezed the schedule for the introduction of socialism to a shorter span of time than even Lenin would accept: in 1905 Trotski was calling for the installation of a 'workers' government'.

It was in September of the same year that he distinguished himself as the firebrand deputy chairman of the Petersburg Soviet. Within the Russian Social-Democratic Workers' Party he refused to show allegiance to either the Bolsheviks or the Mensheviks; and, after returning abroad in 1907, he tried to unify the factions. Unfortunately Trotski was arrogant even when doing his best to reunify the party. Both the Bolsheviks and the Mensheviks thought Trotski was a windbag whose personal ambition mattered more to him than his radical political strategy. Yet they could not deny his talents. Trotski was a master of Russian literary prose, being incapable of writing an inelegant paragraph. His knowledge of the history of European politics and diplomacy was extensive. In 1912 he had covered the war in the Balkans as a correspondent for the *Kiev Thought* newspaper and therefore had an early insight into military affairs.

Trotski returned from North America in May 1917 and was horrified to find the Mensheviks collaborating with the Provisional Government. Needing to belong to a party if he was to have any influence, he accepted Lenin's invitation to join the Bolsheviks. His fluency of tongue and pen were a great asset. He was a handsome fellow, a few inches taller than the average Russian, and he had quick reflexes in dangerous situations. It was he who had saved the Socialist-Revolutionary leader Viktor Chernov, despite their political differences, from being torn apart by a mob in midsummer 1917.[7] Trotski himself spent weeks in prison after the 'July Days', but turned his detention to effect by writing *Pravda* articles that coruscated with contempt for the Provisional Government. On his release in late August, he had revelled in being the Bolshevik party's spokesman in the Petrograd Soviet.

His brilliance had been proved before 1918. What took everyone aback was his organizational capacity and ruthlessness as he transformed the Red Army into a fighting force. He ordered deserters to be shot on the spot, and did not give a damn if some of them were communist party activists; and in this fashion he endeared himself to Imperial Army officers whom he encouraged to join the Reds. He sped from unit to unit, rousing the troops with his revolutionary zeal. The hauteur of spirit which made him so annoying to his rival politicians was an asset in situations where hierarchical respect was crucial. His flair, too, paid dividends. He organized a competition to design a Red Army cap and tunic; he had his own railway carriage equipped with its own map room and printing press. He also had an eye for young talent, bringing on his protégés without regard for the length of time they had belonged to the Bolshevik party.

The Red Army's first task was to retake Kazan. Lenin still suspected Trotski of being weak minded, and wrote urging him not to worry if historic buildings were damaged. Trotski needed no urging. On 10 September the city was recaptured for the communists. Trotski was the hero of the hour. Lenin was delighted, and turned his attention to Red Army commanders whom he suspected of reluctance to press home their advantage. From Moscow he sent telegrams emphasizing the need to clear the Volga region of the Komuch forces.[8]

The Red Army overran Komuch's base in Samara on 7 October, and the Czechoslovak Legion retreated to the Urals and then to mid-Siberia before regrouping under the command of Admiral Kolchak, who initially recognized Komuch as Russia's legitimate government. His loyalty lasted only a few days. On 17 November Kolchak's officers organized a coup against the Socialist-Revolutionary administration, arresting several ministers. Kolchak was proclaimed 'Supreme Ruler' and the Party of Socialist-Revolutionaries never again played a leading role upon the Russian national stage. Kolchak's blood was up. He moved westwards from Omsk into the Urals, capturing the provincial centre of Perm in late December. The Red Army, the soviets and the party crumbled in his path. The Reds briefly counter-attacked and succeeded in taking Ufa, to the south of Perm; but Kolchak's central group of forces were not deflected from their drive on Moscow.

The last months of 1918 were momentous on the Western front

in the Great War. The Allies had seen off the German summer offensive in France, and military disarray ensued for the Central Powers. On 9 November, Kaiser Wilhelm II abdicated. The German army had been defeated; and, for the Russian Communist Party, this meant that the Treaty of Brest-Litovsk could be disregarded as obsolete. First and foremost, Lenin sought links with German far-left socialists and gave encouragement to the formation of a German Communist Party. Revolutionary opportunities beckoned. Within days of the German military defeat, Red forces were aiding local Bolsheviks to set up Soviet republics in Estonia, Latvia, Lithuania and Ukraine.

In Russia, violence intensified not only on the war fronts but also in civilian politics as Lenin widened the Cheka's scope to suppress rival political parties. The Socialist-Revolutionaries and Mensheviks were excluded from the soviets in June 1918 on the grounds of being associated with 'counter-revolutionary' organizations, and the Left Socialist-Revolutionaries were arrested in large numbers. Many Kadets were already in prison. Lenin, Trotski and Dzierżyński believed that over-killing was better than running the risk of being overthrown. And so, as the anti-Bolshevik forces approached the Urals in the summer, the communist central leadership considered what to do with the Romanovs, who had been held in Yekaterinburg for some months. They opted to murder not only the former Emperor but also his entire family, including his son and daughters. On 17 July the deed was done. Lenin and Sverdlov claimed that the responsibility lay with the Bolsheviks of the Urals region, but the circumstantial evidence strongly points to the Central Committee having inspired the decision.[9]

On 30 August Lenin himself got it literally in the neck. As he addressed a meeting of workers at the Mikhelson Factory in Moscow, shots were fired at him. His chauffeur Stepan Gil bundled him into the official limousine and drove him away. A woman standing nearby, Fanya Kaplan, was arrested. It is doubtful that she carried out the shooting since she was almost blind;[10] but she was a sympathizer with the Socialist-Revolutionaries and may well have been involved in the plot in some form or other. Be that as it may, she was executed as the principal malefactor while Lenin convalesced at the government's new sanatorium at the Gorki estate, thirty-five kilometres from the capital.

The attempt on Lenin's life was answered with the promulgation of a Red Terror. In some cities, prisoners were shot out of hand, including 1300 prisoners in Petrograd alone. Fire would be met by fire: Dzierżyński's Cheka had previously killed on an informal basis and not very often; now their executions became a general phenomenon. Lenin, as he recovered from his wounds, wrote the booklet *Proletarian Revolution and the Renegade K. Kautsky*, in which he advocated dictatorship and terror.[11] His confidential telegram to Bolshevik leaders in Penza on 11 August had contained the instruction: 'Hang no fewer than a hundred well-known kulaks, rich-bags and blood-suckers (and make sure that the hanging takes place in full view of the people).'[12] Another such telegram went to Petrograd in October 1919 at the time of an offensive by General Yudenich: 'If the attack is begun, is it impossible to mobilize another 20,000 Petrograd workers plus 10,000 workers of the bourgeoisie, set up cannons behind them, shoot a few hundred of them and obtain a real mass impact upon Yudenich?'[13]

Terror was to be based on the criterion of class. Martyn Latsis, a Cheka functionary, was in favour of exterminating the entire middle class; and even Lenin made remarks to this effect.[14] The purpose was to terrify all hostile social groups. Lenin intended that even the regime's supporters should be intimidated. His recommendation to the Penza communists had made this explicit: 'Do it so that for hundreds of kilometres around the people might see, might tremble!'[15] According to official records, 12,733 prisoners were killed by the Cheka in 1918–20; but other estimates put the figure as high as 300,000.[16] Other prisoners were held either in prison or in the concentration camps that were sanctioned by official decrees in September 1918 and April 1919.[17]

The premisses of Bolshevik policy were worked out quickly. The Food-Supplies Dictatorship which had been established in May 1918 was consolidated. The territory under Soviet control was divided into provinces and sub-divided into districts, and quotas of grain were assigned to each of them for delivery to the government. This system of apportionment (or *razvërstka*) was based upon the statistical evidence available, but Sovnarkom admitted that much guesswork was involved; and in practice the People's Commissariat of Food Supplies grabbed grain wherever it could find it – and peasant households were often left starving. Sovnarkom had hoped to keep most peasants on its side. In June 1918 Lenin had decreed the establishment of 'committees of the village poor' (*kombedy*), which were meant to report the richer peasant families hoarding grain to the authorities;[18] and in return they were to receive a hand-out from the requisitioned stocks. In reality the peasantry resented the entire scheme. Clashes with the urban squads were widespread and the kombedy fell into disrepute.

By December the kombedy had to be abolished by Lenin, who also strove to prevent his local party comrades from forcing peasants to give up the land they had taken since 1917 and enter collective farms.[19] Upon re-conquering Ukraine, communist leaders accompanying the Red Army independently introduced a policy of collectivization which it took the Central Committee months to reverse.[20] Yet peasants were battered even by Lenin; for the state procurement of grain nearly quadrupled between the fiscal years 1917–18 and 1918–19.

And yet the increase was never enough to feed the towns after the Red Army's requirements had been met. Less than a third of the urban diet in the Civil War came from state-provided rations: the rest had to be obtained from the so-called sack-men who travelled from the villages and sold produce on street corners in defiance of the Cheka.[21] The black market was an integral part of the wartime economy. So, too, was the determination of the workers to eke out their rations by selling hand-made or even stolen goods on the side. Monetary wages became virtually worthless as the currency depreciated to 0.006 per cent of its pre-war value by 1921.[22] Sheer physical survival was everyone's aim. Industrial production formally recorded in the official statistics declined precipitately: large-scale enterprises in 1921 produced a fifth of the total recorded for 1913.[23] Key armaments plants and textile factories were the main enterprises kept going. Nevertheless the Reds took on the Whites primarily with inherited military supplies; and labour discipline in the factories and mines, despite the introduction of ever more severe legislation, was poor.

Meanwhile peasant households in the villages had to endure immense exactions of grain-stocks, conscripts and labour power. Villages tried to seal themselves off from the towns and hoard their stores. Wherever possible, peasants kept back their cereal and vegetable crops for trade with peasants from nearby villages or for wages in kind in return for work done by the many workers who were leaving the towns. The rural economic sector survived the Civil War in better shape than the urban sector;[24] but the reason for this was not the government's competence but the peasantry's ability to frustrate the government's intentions.

The Bolsheviks recognized the patchiness of their military, political and economic control over town and countryside. Their leaders in Moscow and the provinces aspired to a centralized party, a centralized government, a centralized army, a centralized security force. Discipline, hierarchy and decisive action were their common aims. Lenin, Trotski, Dzierżyński, Sverdlov, Kamenev, Zinoviev and Bukharin were generally in agreement: their disputes affected mainly matters of secondary importance. For instance, Bukharin and Kamenev disliked the licence given to the Cheka to execute in secret.[25] Yet neither of them had a conscience about executions carried out after peremptory trials. What is more, no communist leader objected to the predominant economic orientation adopted since mid-1918. A strengthened campaign of industrial nationalization had occurred, and by 1919 all large factories and mines were owned by government. Grain requisitioning, too, was uncontroversial among the Bolsheviks. The Russian Communist Party became more militaristic in methods. Their members grew from about 300,000 in late 1917 to 625,000 in early 1921, and most of these Bolsheviks, old and new, fought in the Red Army.[26]

The intensification of military hostilities softened the disagreements between Lenin and the Left Communists. It is not hard to see why. There was a surge of measures to bring the entire economy into the state's control in the early months of the Civil War, and little reason remained for the Left Communists to cavil at Lenin's industrial and agricultural policy. The utopian spirit prevailed throughout the communist party. Russia, according to the party's leaders, was on the verge of creating a socialist society. At such a time the need for political authoritarianism was an article of faith. Soviets, trade unions and factory-workshop committees were instructed to reinforce centralism at the expense of electivity and consultation. Power in Moscow was the priority; and, as Sverdlov explained, this was unachievable unless a single institution controlled the state at each level. Everyone agreed that only the Russian Communist Party should and could fulfil this role. The party alone had the reliable personnel, the ideology and the *esprit de corps*.[27]

There was no objection to this at the party's lower levels. Provincial communist leaders had always been centralizers in theory, and their present sense of political isolation and military danger in their localities convinced them in practice that a fundamental overhaul of the political and administrative machinery was essential: they wanted greater central intervention because they needed the help. In the economy, too, their inclination had always been to nationalize. Local practicality reinforced this inclination. Every province which had serious shortfalls in supplies, whether in grain or coal or oil or machinery, sought Moscow's assistance.[28] Lenin had always taken it for granted that the guidance of the party was vital to the October Revolution's consolidation. Now he and his leading administrators, including Sverdlov, opted to give institutional form to this. The party was to become the supreme state institution in all but name.[29]

There was a reshuffling of arrangements in the capital. The Central Committee could meet only infrequently because most of its members were political commissars on the fronts or in cities outside Moscow. From January 1919 two inner subcommittees were introduced, the Politburo and the Orgburo. The Politburo was to decide the great questions of politics, economics, war and international relations; the Orgburo, serviced by an expanded Secretariat, was to handle internal party administration. Sovnarkom's authority was permanently reduced in favour of the Politburo, which was chaired by Lenin and immediately began to give rulings on everything from military strategy against Kolchak to prices of shoes and eggs in Saratov. The Politburo became an unofficial government cabinet.

Its founding members were Lenin, Trotski, Stalin, Kamenev and Nikolai Krestinski. On the whole, this was an effective body even though Trotski and Stalin usually had to be consulted by telegram. Lenin was good at coaxing his team to co-operate with each other. In the case of Trotski and Stalin he had his hands full. Stalin bridled at having to take instructions from Trotski as People's Commissar for Military Affairs. They hated each other, but there was also a political edge to their clash. Stalin disliked the practice of employing Imperial Army officers, and he encouraged other Bolsheviks to complain about it. Thus was born a Military Opposition in the party. Trotski retorted that the Red Army could not function without experienced officers – and Lenin supported the policy at the Eighth Party Congress in March 1919.[30] Trotski was anyway not wholly traditional in his military preferences. He attached a political commissar to each officer; he also took the families of many officers hostage to ensure loyalty. Proud of his ruthlessness, he published a book in 1920, *Terrorism and Communism*, which eulogized mass terror.

Admiral Kolchak's advance into the Urals in winter 1918–19 prevented Trotski from attending the Eighth Party Congress. Lenin had been so worried that he put out feelers to the Allies to see whether they might broker a halt to the Civil War if the communists forswore sovereignty over the parts of the country not presently occupied by the Reds.[31] This was not defeatism but a temporary ploy. His thoughts were still directed at the 'European socialist revolution'. A rising of far-left German socialists, the Spartakists, occurred in Berlin in January 1919; it was suppressed, but successful insurrections took place in March in Munich and Budapest. In the same month Lenin summoned communist and other far-left parties from around the world to the First Congress of the Communist International (or Comintern) in Moscow.

Kolchak was defeated by the Reds in April 1919. Perm was back in their hands in July, Omsk in November. Kolchak himself was captured and executed in the following year. The Volunteer Army in southern Russia which had been founded by the anti-Bolshevik Generals Alekseev and Kornilov was taken over by General Denikin, who moved his forces into Ukraine in summer. Denikin seized Kharkov in late June and Kiev and Odessa in August. Orël, only 350 kilometres from the capital, fell to him in mid-October. His strategy was expressed in a Moscow Directive ordering a rapid advance into central Russia. Yet the Red Army had been able to regroup after seeing off Kolchak. A devastating counter-attack against the Whites was organized which, by mid-December, resulted in the capture of Kiev and the re-establishment of a Ukrainian Soviet Republic. Luck was again on the side of the Reds; for it was only in October that General Yudenich had crossed the Estonian frontier in the direction of Petrograd. There was no co-ordination between him and Denikin. By the middle of November, Yudenich's army was retreating in tatters to Estonia. The Civil War in Russia, including Siberia, and Ukraine had been won by the Reds.

This outcome of the war between the Reds and the Whites determined the result of most of the many armed conflicts elsewhere in the former Russian Empire. In the Transcaucasus, the Georgians contended against the Armenians; the Armenians also fought the Azeris. And each state in the region had internal strife. For example, battles and massacres occurred in Georgia between Georgians and Abkhazians.[32] Consequently the armed struggle in the lands of the Romanov dynasty was never merely a 'Russian' Civil War. Indeed it was not just one Civil War at all: there were dozens of civil wars after 1917, wars in which the Red Army was able to intervene after its defeat of Kolchak, Denikin and Yudenich.

The communists aimed to make their task easier by offering various concessions to non-Russians. This policy had already been implemented in the RSFSR itself. Lenin established a People's Commissariat for Nationalities (*Narkomnats*), headed by Stalin, to realize the official commitment to native-language schools and to cultural autonomy. Stalin and his subordinates did not merely allow non-Russians to exercise their freedom: they actively propelled them in this direction. Politically-compliant representatives of these nationalities were introduced to Narkomnats. Propaganda was prepared in each of their languages. Enquiries were put in hand to ascertain the boundaries of the territories inhabited mainly by these nationalities.[33] The Russian Communist Party bent over backwards to appease non-Russians – and towards the end of the Civil War the Russian Cossacks in the North Caucasus were ejected from their farms in favour of the local Chechens, whose land had been seized by the tsars and given to the Cossacks in the nineteenth century.

Both Lenin and Stalin, moreover, committed themselves to introducing a federal mode of rule once the Civil War had ended. From 1918, as proof of their intent, they started to set up internal 'autonomous' republics in the RSFSR wherever the Russians constituted a minority of the population. The first plan to set up a Tatar-Bashkir Republic within the RSFSR collapsed in some measure because Tatars and Bashkirs refused to collaborate with each other. There were also difficulties because ethnic Russians, too, lived among them, and the major towns had a Russian majority: not all Russians, by any means, felt that non-Russians should receive such apparent indulgence. Representations were made to Moscow that Russians were being done down. But the communists persisted and founded both a Tatar Republic and a Bashkir Republic.[34] As Soviet-occupied territory was expanded, so the number of autonomous republics rose.

Certain outlying regions had experienced years of independent statehood in the course of the Civil War, a statehood that in most cases was unprecedented for them. It would therefore have been difficult to incorporate them without further ado into the RSFSR. Ukrainians in particular did not take kindly to their resubjugation to Russian rule. Consequently Ukraine, once reoccupied by the Red Army, was proclaimed as a Soviet republic in its own right. This device was repeated elsewhere. By the time of the completed conquest of the Transcaucasus in March 1921, Soviet republics had been founded also in Belorussia, Azerbaijan, Armenia and Georgia. And the RSFSR had bilateral relations with each of them.

This had much cartographic importance. In January 1918, when the creation of the RSFSR had been announced, the assumption had been that each piece of land conquered by Soviet forces would be incorporated in the RSFSR through a federal arrangement of some kind. But the pressing need of the Bolsheviks to win support in the non-Russian borderlands had led to the creation of several Soviet republics. The RSFSR was easily the largest, the most powerful and the most prestigious; but formally it was only one Soviet republic among all the others. Quite what constitutional settlement there would be at the end of the Civil War had not yet been decided. But one thing had been resolved: namely that there was a place called 'Russia' which would occupy a defined territory on the map, a territory which was considerably smaller than the former Russian Empire. The RSFSR was the state that governed this Russia and the vast majority of its population consisted of Russians.

Yet a distinct ethnically-based sense of Russian statehood could not develop. For the boundaries of the RSFSR were not set exclusively by considerations of national and ethnic geography. In particular, there was no Soviet republic in central Asia on the model of the Ukrainian Soviet Republic. Instead the lands of the Kazakhs, Kirgiz, Tajiks and Uzbeks belonged to 'the Turkestani Region' and were included in the RSFSR. A so-called 'Kirgiz (Kazakh) Republic' was at last established in 1920, but only as an autonomous republic within the RSFSR.[35]

At any rate, the fundamental reality was that the entire RSFSR was subjected to highly centralized authority and that both the RSFSR and all other Soviet republics were ruled by the Politburo. This was done in several ways. The most effective was the stipulation in the Party Rules drawn up in March 1919 that the communist organizations in the various Soviet republics were to be regarded merely as regional organizations of the Russian Communist Party.[36] Thus the central party bodies of the Ukrainian Bolsheviks in Kiev were strictly subordinated to the Central Committee in Moscow. Party centralism was to prevail. Lenin and his colleagues also drew up a confidential instruction to republican governments to the effect that republican people's commissariats were to act as mere regional branches of Sovnarkom.[37] In addition, the new Soviet republics on the RSFSR's borders were disallowed from having ties with any other republic except the RSFSR.[38] The aim was not to reinforce the RSFSR but to consolidate the Politburo's capacity to control all the republics, including the RSFSR, from Moscow.

Yet enough concessions were being made to the sensitivities of non-Russians to make the Civil War easier for the Reds than for the Whites in the non-Russian regions. Jews in particular were terrified by the anti-Semitic mayhem perpetrated by the Whites.[39] Yet the advantage held by the Reds was helpful without being decisive. Invading troops misbehaved in all the armies. The Reds frequently committed butchery against religious leaders. Twenty-eight bishops and thousands of priests of the Russian Orthodox Church were killed; and the other Christian sects as well as Islam and Judaism were also subjected to a campaign of terror. Lenin's policy was to introduce atheism by persuasion; but he, too, instigated the mass murder of clerics.[40] For most people, religious belief was entwined with their national or ethnic identity. The rampaging of the Red Army – and especially its cavalrymen – undid much of the good done for Sovnarkom's cause by the People's Commissariat for Nationalities.

Nevertheless the Whites had lost. The dispirited Denikin, as he retreated to Crimea, resigned his command to General Vrangel; Yudenich and his forces faded into inactivity. The Whites were in a hopeless position. Vrangel belatedly appreciated the damage done to their campaigns by their refusal to leave the peasants with the land taken by them since the October Revolution. Kolchak had given farms to landlords at the peasantry's expense even in places where the landlords had not owned estates.[41] By announcing their faith in 'Russia One and Indivisible', the Whites alienated those non-Russian nationalities who recognized the slogan as thinly disguised Russian imperialism. By hanging trade unionists, they made workers think twice before turning against the Russian Communist Party.

Kolchak, Denikin and Yudenich had rested their hopes in a military knock-out blow, and refused to fight a 'political' war. They were contemptuous of the Kadets who organized the civilian administration for them.[42] Lip service was given by the White commanders to the ultimate goal of re-convoking a representative assembly of some kind; but their officers were hostile to this: their fundamental aim was a right-wing military dictatorship. Kolchak and Denikin came within striking range of Moscow; Yudenich reached the outskirts of Petrograd. It would therefore be wrong to dismiss their calculations out of hand. But they had the odds stacked against them. The Reds always held an area with a hugely greater availability of conscripts and military equipment;[43] they also were based at the heart of the country's network of telegraph, railways and administration. The Reds had high morale and felt certain that they were making a new, better world and that science and social justice were on their side.

Indisputably, luck was with them. The Germans lost the Great War and stopped interfering in Russian affairs; the Allies donated money and guns to the Whites, but never seriously undertook the conquest of Russia themselves. The peoples of the West were in any event ill-disposed to fighting in eastern Europe once Germany had been defeated. Many Western socialists argued that the Bolshevik party should be given the chance to soften its dictatorial rule, and there were plenty of industrialists, especially in the United Kingdom, who wished to resume commercial links with Russia.[44] In January 1920 the Supreme Allied Council lifted the economic blockade on the RSFSR. The Whites were left to fend for themselves.

The Bolsheviks had won, and felt that their ideas had helped them to this end. They had become comfortable with the one-party, one-ideology state as the basis of their power. They legalized and reinforced arbitrary rule and had no intention of holding free elections. Dictatorship and terror appealed to them as modes of solving problems. They were convinced that Bolshevism was the sole authentic form of socialism. This internal party consensus contained its own disagreements. A group known as the Democratic Centralists sprang up in 1919 and contended that too few officials were taking too many decisions at both central and local levels of the party, that the party was run inefficiently, that the central party bodies too rarely consulted opinion in the local committees. Another Bolshevik group, the Workers' Opposition, emerged in 1920; its complaint was that the aspirations of the factory labourers were being flouted. Workers' Oppositionist leader Alexander Shlyapnikov urged that power should be shared among the party, the soviets and the trade unions and that ordinary workers and peasants should have influence over decisions on economic affairs.

Neither the Democratic Centralists nor the Workers' Opposition wished to stop the harassment of the other political parties or to end the requisitioning of grain. Their factional disagreements with the Central Committee took second place in their minds to the need for loyalty to the party. While they may have thought of themselves as the conscience of the Revolution, they, too, had given up part of the more idealistic heritage of 1917. At any rate their factions were numerically tiny: they could not hope to beat the Central Committee for votes at the yearly Party Congresses.

A military-style approach to party organization and to politics in general had become customary in the Civil War. Orders replaced consultation. Having served in the Red Army, most Bolshevik officials had acquired the habits of command. Another novelty was the 'cleansing' of the party. The Russian word for this, *chistka*, is usually translated as purge; and the first purge in May 1918 was confined to the expulsion of 'idlers, hooligans, adventurers, drunkards and thieves' from the party's ranks. By mid-1919 there were 150,000 party members: half the total claimed twelve months previously. The willingness to exclude people in order to maintain purity of membership can be traced back to Lenin's wrangles with the Mensheviks in 1903. But practicality as well as ideology was at work; for the one-party state was attracting recruits to the party who were not even committed socialists. Periodic cleansings of the ranks were vital to raise the degree of political dependability.

The political leadership at central and local levels distrusted the various state institutions, and repeatedly called for 'the most severe discipline'. In 1920 a Central Control Commission was established to eradicate abuses in the party. But the party was not the only institution presenting problems of control. The People's Commissariats gave even greater cause of concern to the Kremlin leadership, and a Workers' and Peasants' Inspectorate was established in the same year to investigate the reliability and efficiency of the various civilian state bodies in their day-to-day work.

Of all bodies, it was the party that underwent the largest change. Yet the habit of criticizing the leadership remained; and, while the official who counted for most in local party committees was the committee secretary,[45] discussion with other committee members was still the norm. Furthermore, the Politburo, Orgburo and Secretariat lacked the accurate, up-to-date information which would have enabled them to intervene with confidence in local disputes. The Red Army, too, was resistant at its lower levels to tight detailed control. Ill-discipline among soldiers was notorious. There are thought to have been a million deserters and conscription defaulters by the end of 1919.[46] Indisputably the Soviet state as a whole increased its internal co-ordination in the Civil War; but chaos remained in all institutions. And the proliferation of bodies such as the Workers' and Peasants' Inspectorate had the effect of enlarging the bureaucracy without increasing its efficiency.

This sprawling state ruled a disgruntled society, and there was much to give rise to resentment. The food rations were poor. Disease and malnutrition killed eight million people in 1918–20.[47] Political parties other than the Bolsheviks were persecuted or suppressed. 'Barrier detachments' were arresting persons carrying food for the black market.[48] The workers were angry about such conditions and called for an end to the Bolshevik monopoly of political power. Strikes took place in Petrograd, Moscow, Tula and elsewhere during the Civil War; they became especially intense once the danger from the Whites had been eliminated. The women, girls, boys and residual skilled men in the Russian work-force had just enough energy left to make protest. Mutinies broke out in army garrisons, and by mid-1920 there were hints that the loyalty of the pro-Bolshevik sailors of the Kronstadt naval garrison might be fading.

Peasants clashed with the food-supplies commissars across the country. According to official figures, 344 rebellions are reported as having broken out by mid-1919.[49] In 1920, severe trouble was reported from the Volga provinces, especially Tambov, from Ukraine, Siberia and the North Caucasus. The villages were in revolt. They hated the conscription of their menfolk, the requisitioning of foodstuffs, the infringements of customary peasant law, the ban on private trade with the towns and the compulsion of households to supply free labour to the authorities for the felling of timber and the clearing of roads.[50] The Bolshevik party assumed that the answer was to intensify repression. Industry and agriculture, too, were to be brought more firmly under the state's control. Trotski proposed that Red Army soldiers, instead of being demobilized, should be transferred into labour armies; Lenin was firmly attached to the policy of requisitioning foodstuffs through a centrally-assigned set of quotas: the economic programme of the Civil War was to be maintained in peacetime.

The other way out of the emergency for the Russian Communist Party was socialist revolution in Europe. During 1919 they had continued to probe opportunities to link up with the Hungarian Soviet Republic until its collapse in August. The Bavarian Soviet Republic had been overturned in May. Yet the cities of northern Italy, too, were in ferment: as one door closed, another was thought to be opening. The party's optimism was all the more striking since Red rule in the borderlands of Russia remained under threat. Conflicts with the Poles took place in the course of the year, and erupted into full-scale war when Józef Piłsudski invaded Ukraine and took Kiev in May 1920. The Red Army gathered support at this conjuncture from Russians in general. The arthritic former Imperial commander Alexander Brusilov came out of retirement to urge his former subordinates to fulfil their patriotic duty by seeing off the Poles; and, by July, Piłsudski's army was fleeing westwards.

Lenin spotted his chance to carry revolution into central Europe. The Red Army was instructed to plunge into Poland and then into Germany. To his colleagues Lenin confided: 'My personal opinion is that for this purpose it is necessary to sovietize Hungary and perhaps Czechia and Romania too.'[51] Italian communists in Moscow for the Second Congress of Comintern were told to pack their bags and go home to help organize a revolution. In fact the other Politburo members were doubtful about Lenin's judgement; they especially questioned whether the Polish working class would rise to welcome the Red Army as its liberator. But Lenin had his way and the Reds hastened across eastern Poland. A pitched battle occurred by the river Vistula, short of Warsaw, in mid-August. The Reds were defeated. The dream of taking revolution to other countries on the point of a bayonet was dispelled.

The débâcle in Poland concentrated minds upon the difficulties at home. Even before the Polish-Soviet War there had been attempts to modify economic policies. The most notable was Trotski's proposal to the Central Committee in February 1920 that, in certain provinces and with certain restrictions, grain requisitioning should be replaced with a tax-in-kind that would be fixed at a lower level of procurement. He was turned down after a heated debate in which Lenin denounced him as an advocate of *laissez-faire* capitalism.[52]

Such disputes demonstrated how hard it was to promote any change of policy; for Trotski's proposal seemed bold only within a milieu which viscerally detested capitalism. Lenin, too, suffered as he had made Trotski suffer. When a Soviet republic was set up in Azerbaijan in April 1920, Lenin proposed that foreign concessionnaires should be invited to restore the Baku oilfields to production. Since 1918 he had seen 'concessions' as vital to economic recovery, but his suggestion now caused outrage among Bolshevik leaders in the Transcaucasus. If Baku oil were to be exploited again by the Alfred Nobel Company, hardly any non-private industry would be left in Baku.[53] Lenin also urged, at the Eighth Congress of Soviets in December 1920, that richer peasant households should be materially rewarded for any additional gains in agricultural productivity rather than be persecuted as kulaks. The Congress was horrified and most of Lenin's scheme was rejected.[54] The party leadership at the centre and the localities was determined to maintain existing economic policy.

And so it came about that the great controversy in the Bolshevik party in the winter of 1920–21 was not about grain requisitioning or about the return of foreign companies but about the trade unions. In November, Trotski had proposed that the unions should be turned into agencies of the state. Strikes would be banned; wage increases would be forgone. The Workers' Opposition criticized this as yet another sign of the bureaucratization of the October Revolution. Others in the party, including Lenin, simply felt that Trotski's project was unrealizable at a time of turmoil in the country. Ferocious debate broke out within the party. But as Bolshevik leaders haggled over Marxist doctrine on the labour movement, the Soviet economy moved towards catastrophe and a growing number of peasants, workers, soldiers and sailors rebelled against the victors of the Civil War.

7
The New Economic Policy (1921–1928)

The basic compound of the Soviet order had been invented by Lenin and his fellow communist leaders within a couple of years of the October Revolution. There had been created a centralized, one-ideology dictatorship of a single party which permitted no challenge to its monopoly of power. The Bolshevik party itself was strictly organized; the security police were experts at persecution and there was systematic subordination of constitutional and legal propriety to political convenience. The regime had also expropriated great segments of the economy. Industry, banking, transport and foreign trade were already nationalized and agriculture and domestic trade were subject to heavy state regulation. All these elements were to remain intact in ensuing decades.

The Civil War had added to the pressures which resulted in the creation of the compound. On taking power in 1917, the communist leaders had not possessed a preparatory blueprint. Nevertheless they had come with assumptions and inclinations which predisposed them towards a high degree of state economic dominance, administrative arbitrariness, ideological intolerance and political violence. They also lived for struggle. They wanted action; they could barely contain their impatience. And they were outnumbered by enemies at home and abroad. They had always expected the party to be 'the vanguard' of the Revolution. Leadership was a key virtue for them. If they wanted to prevail as the country's rulers, the communists would have been pushed into introducing some kind of party-run state even in the absence of a civil war – and, of course, the way that the

October Revolution had occurred made a civil war virtually certain.

This in turn meant that once the Civil War was over, the party-state was unlikely to be dismantled by the Russian Communist Party. The party-state was at the core of the Soviet compound. Without the party-state, it would not be long before all the other elements in the compound underwent dissolution.

Even as things stood, not all the elements were as yet sustainable – at least, not in their entirety – in the harsh conditions of 1920–21. Popular discontent could no longer simply be suppressed. Even among those segments in society which had preferred the Reds to the Whites in the Civil War there were many people unwilling to tolerate a prolongation of wartime policies. Administrative disorder was increasing. Whole nations and whole regions were supervised only patchily from Moscow. The technical facilities for control were in a ruinous state: transport and communications were becoming a shambles. Most industrial enterprises had ceased production: factory output in 1920 was recorded as being eighty-six per cent lower than in 1913. Agriculture, too, had been reduced to a shabby condition. The grain harvest of 1920 was only about three fifths of the annual average for the half-decade before the Great War.[1]

By the start of 1921, strategical choice could no longer be avoided. Lenin, having had conversations while visiting peasants, at last recognized the enormity of the emergency. For him, the ultimate alarm bell was sounded by the rural revolt in Tambov province. The last great peasant risings in Russia had occurred in the seventeenth and eighteenth centuries under the leaderships of Razin, Bolotnikov and Pugachëv. Ancient Russia now confronted the Bolsheviks in struggle. Lenin foresaw that force alone would not be enough to quell the peasants, and he decided that in order to sustain the political dictatorship he had to offer economic relaxations.

In his opinion, the peasantry had to be placated by the replacement of grain requisitioning with a tax in kind. Knowing that this would evoke intense opposition in his party, he initially limited the discussion to the Politburo. On 8 February 1921 he convinced its members of the need for urgent measures and a resolution was passed calling for a partial re-legalization of 'local economic exchange' in grain.[2] Such fussiness of language was necessary to avoid offending the ideological sensibilities among fellow Bolsheviks. But the underlying purpose was unmistakable: the Politburo intended to restore private commercial activity. In addition, the tax-in-kind was to be set at a much lower level than the grain-requisitioning quotas and would secure only the minimum of the state's requirements on behalf of civilian consumers. These measures were the core of what quickly became known as the New Economic Policy (or NEP).

Some such gamble was essential for the regime to survive. The Politburo permitted a press campaign to commend the NEP's merits to the rest of the party. Having had his fingers burnt in the Brest-Litovsk controversy, Lenin for some weeks distanced himself from the policy by getting obscure party officials to put his case; and the commission established by the Politburo to elaborate the details was headed not by himself but by Kamenev.[3]

But thereafter Lenin, supported by Trotski and Kamenev, canvassed for the NEP. It was of assistance to him that the party had exhausted itself in the winter's dispute about the trade unions. A desire for unity had emerged before the opening of the Tenth Party Congress on 15 March 1921, a desire stiffened by news of the outbreak of a mutiny by the naval garrison on Kronstadt island. The sailors demanded multi-party democracy and an end to grain requisitioning. Petrograd was affected by discontent and strikes broke out in its major factories. Those many Congress delegates who had not accepted Lenin's arguments were at last persuaded of the argument for economic reform. Lenin anyway stressed that he did not advocate political reform. Indeed he asserted that the other parties should be suppressed and that even internal factions among the Bolsheviks should be banned. The retreat in economics was to be accompanied by an offensive in politics.

Congress delegates from all factions, including the Workers' Opposition, volunteered to join the Red Army units ordered to quell the Kronstadt mutineers. Mikhail Tukhachevski, a commander who had recently returned from the Polish front, clad his soldiers in white camouflage to cross the iced-over Gulf of Finland undetected. In the meantime a depleted Party Congress ungratefully condemned the Workers' Opposition as an 'anarcho-syndicalist deviation' from the principles of Bolshevism.

Lenin had got his way at the Congress in securing an end to grain requisitioning. And yet there was trouble ahead. The NEP would remain ineffective if confined to a legalization of private trade in foodstuffs. Other economic sectors, too, needed to be removed from the state's monopolistic ownership and control. Peasants would refrain from selling their crops in the towns until they could buy industrial goods with their profits; but large-scale state-owned factories could not quickly produce the shoes, nails, hand-ploughs and spades that were wanted by the peasantry. Rapid economic recovery depended upon a reversion of workshops and small manufacturing firms to their previous owners. There was no technical impediment to this. But politically it would be hard to impose on local communist officials who already at the Party Congress had indicated their distaste for any further compromises with the principle of private profit.[4]

Lenin had to come into the open to persuade these officials to soften their stance. Indefatigably he tried to attract Western capitalists to Soviet Russia. On 16 March, after months of negotiation, an Anglo-Soviet Trade treaty was signed; and Soviet commercial delegations were established in several other European countries by the end of the year. Lenin also continued to push for the sale of 'concessions' in the oil industry in Baku and Grozny. The Red Army's defeat in the war in Poland convinced him that temporary co-operation with international capitalism would better facilitate economic reconstruction than the pursuit of 'European socialist revolution'. If Lenin needed proof, it was supplied by the German communists. In the last fortnight of March 1921, encouraged by Zinoviev and Bukharin, they tried to seize power in Berlin. The German government easily suppressed this botched 'March Action'; and Lenin roundly upbraided his comrades for their adventurism.

By then Lenin was no longer looking only to foreign concessionaires for help with economic recovery. In April he argued in favour of expanding the NEP beyond its original limits; and he achieved his ends when the Tenth Party Conference in May 1921 agreed to re-legalize private small-scale manufacturing. Soon afterwards peasants obtained permission to trade not only locally but anywhere in the country. Commercial middlemen, too, were allowed to operate again. Private retail shops were reopened. Rationing was abolished in November 1921, and everyone was expected to buy food from personal income. In August 1921, state enterprises had been reorganized into large 'trusts' responsible for each great manufacturing and mining subsector; they were instructed that raw materials had to be bought and workers to be paid without subsidy from the central state budget. In March 1922, moreover, Lenin persuaded the Eleventh Party Congress to allow peasant households to hire labour and rent land.

Thus a reintroduction of capitalist practices took place and 'War Communism', as the pre-1921 economic measures were designated, was ended. A lot of Bolsheviks felt that the October Revolution was being betrayed. Tempers became so frayed that the Tenth Conference proceedings were kept secret.[5] Not since the Brest-Litovsk controversy had Lenin had to endure such invective. But he fought back, purportedly shouting at his critics: 'Please don't try teaching me what to include and what to leave out of Marxism: eggs don't teach their hens how to lay!'[6]

He might not have succeeded at the Conference if his critics had not appreciated the party's need for unity until the rebellions in the country had been suppressed; and Lenin sternly warned about the adverse effects of factionalism. Throughout 1921–2 there persisted an armed threat to the regime. The Kronstadt mutiny was put down; its organizers were shot and thousands of ordinary sailors, most of whom had supported the Bolsheviks in 1917, were dispatched to the Ukhta labour camp in the Russian north.[7] The rural revolts, too, were crushed. Red Army commander Tukhachevski, after defeating the Kronstadters, was sent to quell the Tambov peasant uprising in mid-1921.[8] Insurrections in the rest of the Volga region, in Ukraine, Siberia and the North Caucasus were treated similarly. The Politburo also smashed the industrial strikes. The message went forth from the Kremlin that the economic reforms were not a sign of weakened political resolve.

Not only real but also potential trouble-makers were dealt with severely. Those members of the Socialist-Revolutionary Party's Central Committee who were still at liberty were rounded up. In summer 1922 they were paraded in Soviet Russia's first great show-trial and given lengthy prison sentences. There was a proposal by Lenin to do the same to the Menshevik Organizational Committee, and he was annoyed at being overruled by the Politburo.[9] But the lesson was administered that the Bolshevik party, having won the Civil War, would share its power with no other party.

Nor were there to be illusions about national self-determination. It is true that Finland, Estonia, Latvia and Lithuania had gained independence and that provinces had been lost to Poland, Romania and Turkey. Yet by March 1921, when Georgia was re-conquered, the Red Army had largely restored the boundaries of the Russian Empire. Russian nationalists applauded this. It would not be long, they surmised, before the Bolsheviks accommodated themselves to Russia's geo-political interests and abandoned their communist ideas. Red Army commanders, some of whom had served as officers in the Imperial Army, were delighted that Russian military, political and economic power had risen again over two continents. In the People's Commissariats, too, many long-serving bureaucrats felt a similar pride. The *émigré* liberal Professor Nikolai Trubetskoi founded a 'Change of Landmarks' group that celebrated the NEP as the beginning of the end of the Bolshevik revolutionary project.

The Bolsheviks responded that they had made the October Revolution expressly to establish a multinational state wherein each national or ethnic group would be free from oppression by any other. They refused to accept that they were imperialists even though many nations were held involuntarily under their rule. They were able to delude themselves in this fashion for two main reasons. The first was that they undoubtedly wanted to abolish the old empires around the world. In this sense they really were anti-imperialists. Secondly, the central Bolshevik leadership had no conscious desire to give privileges to the Russian nation. Most of them were appalled by the evidence that Russian nationalist sentiment existed at the lower levels of the Soviet state and even the communist party. And so by being anti-nationalist, Lenin and his colleagues assumed that they were automatically anti-imperialist.

But how, then, were they going to resolve their very complex problems of multi-national governance in peacetime? Probably most leading Bolsheviks saw the plurality of independent Soviet republics as having been useful to gain popularity during the Civil War but as being likely to reinforce nationalist tendencies in the future.[10] There was consensus in the party that a centralized state order was vital; no one was proposing that any of the republican governments or communist parties should have the right to disobey the Bolshevik leadership in the Kremlin. But how to achieve this? Stalin, who headed the People's Commissariat for Nationalities, wished to deprive the Soviet republics of even their formal independence by turning them into autonomous republics within the RSFSR on the Bashkirian model. His so-called federalism would therefore involve the simple expedient of incorporating Ukraine, Belorussia, Armenia, Azerbaijan and Georgia into an enlarged RSFSR, and he had been working along these lines since mid-1920.[11]

Lenin thought Stalin's project smacked of Russian imperial dominance; and his counter-proposal was to federate the RSFSR on equal terms with the other Soviet republics in a Union of Soviet Socialist Republics.[12] In summer 1922 their disagreements became acrimonious. Yet it must be noted that the ground separating Lenin and Stalin was narrow. Neither aimed to disband the system of authoritarian rule through a highly centralized, unitary communist party run from Moscow. While castigating the United Kingdom's retention of India with her empire, the Politburo had no scruples about annexing states which had gained their independence from Russia between 1917 and 1921.

In any case Lenin and Stalin themselves faced common opposition in the localities. Their adversaries fell into two main groups. The first group demanded a slackening of the Kremlin's grip on republican political bodies.[13] Even so, none of these persons demanded a complete release. They wished to remain part of a common Soviet state and understood that they depended upon the Red Army for their survival in government. The other group of adversaries felt that official policy was not too strict but too indulgent towards the non-Russian republics. Both Lenin and Stalin wished to keep the promises made since the October Revolution that native-language schools, theatres and printing presses would be fostered. Stalin in 1921 was accused of 'artificially implanting' national consciousness; the charge was that, if the Belorussians had not been told they were Belorussians, nobody would have been any the wiser.[14]

This debate was of great importance (and the reason why it remains little noticed is that Stalin suppressed discussion of it in the 1930s when he did not wish to appear indulgent to the non-Russians). Stalin's self-defence was that his priority was to disseminate not nationalist but socialist ideas. His argument was primarily pragmatic. He pointed out that all verbal communication had to occur in a comprehensible language and that most of the people inhabiting the Soviet-held lands bordering Russia did not speak Russian. A campaign of compulsory Russification would therefore cause more political harm than good.

Nor did Stalin fail to mention that the vast majority of the population was constituted by peasants, who had a traditional culture which had yet to be permeated by urban ideas.[15] If Marxism was to succeed in the Soviet Union, the peasantry had to be incorporated into a culture that was not restricted to a particular village. Whatever else they were, peasants inhabiting the Belorussian region were not Russians. It behoved the communist party to enhance their awareness of their own national culture – or at least such aspects of their national culture that did not clash blatantly with Bolshevik ideology. Thus would more and more people be brought into the ambit of the Soviet political system. Bolshevism affirmed that society had to be activated, mobilized, indoctrinated. For this reason, in contrast with other modern multinational states which had discouraged national consciousness, Politburo members fostered it. They did so because they worried lest there should be further national revolts against Bolshevism; but they also calculated that, by avoiding being seen as imperial oppressors, they would eventually win over all their national and ethnic groups to principles of international fraternity. The central party leaders had not ceased being militant internationalists.

A few leading Bolsheviks resented this as being a cynical approach. Practically all these critics were post-1917 recruits to the party, and prominent among them was a young Tatar named Mirza Said Sultan-Galiev. As a functionary in the People's Commissariat for Nationalities, he had impugned any action that seemed to favour Russians at the expense of the other national and ethnic groups.[16] Matters came to a head in 1923 when Sultan-Galiev advocated the desirability of a pan-Turkic socialist state uniting the Muslim peoples of the former Russian and Ottoman Empires. Sultan-Galiev was arrested for promoting a scheme that would have broken up the Soviet state. This first arrest of a senior communist leader by the communist authorities was a sign of the acute importance they attached to the 'national question'.

Yet Politburo members remained worried about the potential appeal of pan-Turkism, and sought to accentuate the differences among Muslims by marking out separate administrative regions for the Uzbeks, Tajiks and Kazakhs. Stimulation was given for their paths of cultural development to diverge. This was not the sole method whereby the Bolsheviks tried to divide and rule: they also bought the acquiescence of majority nationalities in each Soviet republic at the expense of the local minorities. Romanians, Greeks, Poles and Jews in Ukraine did not receive as much favourable attention as Ukrainians. And if the attempt to rule the nations by dividing them among themselves ever became ineffectual, the Cheka – which was known from 1923 as the United Main Political Administration (or by its Russian acronym OGPU) – arrested troublesome groups and individuals. In the last resort the Red Army, too, was used. A Georgian insurrection against the Soviet regime in 1924 was ferociously suppressed.[17]

Nations picked up whatever scraps the Bolshevik leadership was willing to toss from its table. These scraps were far from insubstantial. Native-language schooling flourished as never before in Russian history (and the Soviet authorities provided the Laz people, which numbered only 635 persons, with not only a school building but even an alphabet).[18] Ukraine had not been an administrative-territorial unit before 1917; in formal terms it had been only a collection of provinces subject to the tsar. In the 1920s the Politburo sanctioned the return to Kiev from abroad of the nationalist historian Mihaylo Hrushevskyi, who made no secret of his nationalism.

At the same time the Bolshevik central leadership wanted to give stiff ideological competition to Hrushevskyi and his counterparts in other Soviet republics. The difficulty was that the party's rank-and-file membership even in the non-Russian regions consisted overwhelmingly of Russians. Steps were taken to train and promote cadres of the local nationality. This was the policy known as *korenizatsiya* (or 'the planting down of roots'). Initially it could not be done, especially in central Asia but in other places too, without appeals being made to young men and women who were not necessarily of working-class background. Many potential recruits would have to be drawn from the local traditional élites. The hope was that the People's Commissariat of Enlightenment and the Party Central Committee's Agitation and Propaganda Department would succeed in nudging the promotees towards feeling that their national and cultural aspirations were compatible with Bolshevik revolutionary aims.

Confidential discussions to settle the state's constitutional structure proceeded. In September 1922 Lenin, despite still convalescing from a major stroke, won his struggle against Stalin's proposal for the RSFSR to engorge the other Soviet republics. Instead all these republics, including the RSFSR, were to join a federation to be called the Union of Soviet Socialist Republics (or USSR). This meant that Russia – in the form of the RSFSR – was for the first time given its own boundaries within the larger state it belonged to. At the time this hardly mattered in any practical way to most Russians; it was only in the late 1980s, when Boris Yeltsin campaigned for the Russian presidency before the USSR's disintegration, that the possible implications of delineating 'Russia' as a cartographic entity became evident. Under the NEP, however, the Bolsheviks anticipated not disintegration but, if anything, expansion. And so the decision on the USSR Constitution was ratified in principle by the First All-Union Congress of Soviets on 31 December 1922, and the central government newspaper *Izvestiya* hailed the events as 'a New Year's gift to the workers and peasants of the world'.[19]

In the communist party across the country only the Georgian leadership made strong objection. They had lobbied Lenin for several months, claiming that Stalin had ridden roughshod over Georgian national sensitivities. They particularly resented the plan to insert Georgia into the USSR not as a Soviet republic but as a part of a Transcaucasian Federation. In their estimation, this was a trick whereby Stalin could emasculate Lenin's somewhat gentler attitude to Georgians as a people. They demanded that Georgia should enter the USSR on the same terms as Ukraine. But Lenin and the Politburo accepted Stalin's advice in this specific matter. The formation of a Transcaucasian Federation would enable the curtailment of unpleasantries meted out to their respective ethnic minorities by the Armenian, Azerbaijani and Georgian Soviet republics: there was abundant evidence that the Georgians, sinned against by Stalin, were not blameless in their treatment of non-Georgians.[20]

The Transcaucasian Federation would also diminish Turkey's temptation to interfere in Muslim-inhabited areas on the side of Azerbaijan against Armenia. Continuing nervousness about the Turks induced central party leaders to award Nagorny Karabakh to 'Muslim' Azerbaijan despite the fact that the local population were Armenian Christians.[21]

Azeri-inhabited Nakhichevan, too, was given to Azerbaijan even though Nakhichevan lay enclosed within Armenia and did not abutt upon Azerbaijani territory. The central party leadership's measures were therefore not untainted by considerations of expediency, and Armenians had little cause to celebrate the territorial settlement. Cossack farmers in the North Caucasus were even less contented. The Politburo took the decision to secure the acquiescence of the non-Russian peoples of that region by returning land to them that had been taken from them in the previous century by the tsarist authorities. Thousands of Cossack settlers were rounded up and deported to other regions held by the Soviet authorities in April

1921.[22] National deportations were to become a basic aspect of governmental policy in the 1930s and 1940s, but the precedent had been set under Lenin.

Yet there was a degree of justification in the party's claim that its treatment of the national and ethnic minorities put many European governments to shame; and prominent Bolshevik C. G. Rakovsky argued that many peoples in eastern and central Europe would relish the degree of autonomy accorded in the USSR.[23] Nevertheless several leading party figures were fearful of the long-term risks involved. The administrative demarcation of territory according to national and ethnic demography laid down internal boundaries that could become guidelines for nationalism. The opportunities for linguistic and cultural self-expression, too, allowed the different peoples to develop their respective national identities. Only ruthless interventions from Moscow stopped these chickens of official policy coming home to roost before the late 1980s. Lenin thought he was helping to resolve the national question; in fact he inadvertently aggravated it.

The nation with the greatest potential to upset Bolshevik policy were the Russians themselves. According to the census published in 1927 they amounted to nearly three fifths of the population,[24] and it could not be discounted that one day they might prove susceptible to nationalist ideas. Under the NEP they were therefore the nationality most tightly restricted in their cultural self-expression. Classic Russian nineteenth-century writers who had disseminated anti-socialist notions lost official approval; and Fëdor Dostoevski, who had inspired thinkers as diverse as Nietzsche and Freud, was no longer published. Russian military heroes such as Mikhail Kutuzov, the victor over Napoleon, were depicted as crude imperialists. Allegedly no emperor, patriarch or army general had ever done a good deed in his life. Non-Bolshevik variants of Russian socialist thought were equally subjected to denigration, and Menshevik and Socialist-Revolutionary policies were denounced as hostile to the requirements of working people. Traditions of Russian thought which were uncongenial to Bolshevism were systematically ridiculed.

The Russian Orthodox Church especially alarmed the Bolsheviks.

A survey of Russian peasants in the mid-1920s suggested that fifty-five per cent were active Christian worshippers. This was almost certainly a large underestimate; and there can be no denying that the Russian Orthodox Church constituted part and parcel of the Russian identity in the minds of most ethnic Russians. In 1922 Lenin arranged for the execution of several bishops on the pretext that they refused to sell their treasures to help famine relief in the Volga region. Anti-religious persecution did not cease with the introduction of the NEP, and Lenin's language in Politburo discussions of Christianity was vicious, intemperate and cynical.[25]

Yet generally the Bolsheviks became more restrained in the mid-1920s. The OGPU was instructed to concentrate its efforts on demoralizing and splitting the Church by indirect methods rather than by physical assault. This policy took the form of suborning priests, spreading disinformation and infiltrating agents; and when Patriarch Tikhon died in 1925, the Church was prevented by the Soviet authorities from electing a successor to him. Metropolitan Sergei, who was transferred from Nizhni Novgorod to Moscow, was allowed to style himself only as Acting Patriarch. Meanwhile Trotski had observed the rise of a 'Living Church' reform movement in the Church that despised the official ecclesiastical hierarchy and preached that socialism was Christianity in its modern form. The adherents of this movement were reconcilable to Soviet rule so long as they could practise their faith. Trotski urged that favourable conditions should be afforded to 'Living Church' congregations in order that a wedge could be driven down the middle of the Russian Orthodox Church.[26]

Other Christian denominations were handled less brusquely. Certain sects, such as the Old Believers, were notable for their farming expertise and the central party leadership did not want to harm their contribution to the economy as a result of clashes over religion.[27] Non-Russian Christian organizations were also treated with caution. For instance, the harassment of the Georgian and Armenian Orthodox Churches diminished over the decade. Islam was left at peace even more than Christianity (although there was certainly interference with religious schools and law-courts). The Politburo saw that, while secularism was gaining ground among urban Russians, Muslims remained deeply attached – in towns as in the villages – to their faith. In desperation the party tried to propagate Marxism in Azerbaijan and central Asia through the medium of excerpts from the Koran that emphasized communal, egalitarian values. Yet the positive results for the party were negligible: 'the idiocy of religion' was nowhere near as easy to eradicate as the communists had imagined.

They had a nerve in being so condescending. Leading Bolshevik cadres themselves were intense believers in a faith of a certain kind. The works of Karl Marx and Friedrich Engels were like prophetic works in the Bible for most of them; and Lenin as well as Marx and Engels were beatified. Marxism was an ersatz religion for the communist party.

Real religious belief was mocked in books and journals of the state-subsidized League of the Militant Godless. Citizens who engaged in public worship lost preferment in Soviet state employment; and priests had been disenfranchised under the terms of successive constitutions since 1918. In local practice, however, a more relaxed attitude was permitted. Otherwise the middle strata of the Azerbaijani government would have had to be sacked. Even in Russia there was the same problem. Officials in Smolensk province decided that since a disavowal of God did not appear in the party rules, it should not be a criterion for party membership.[28] Such pragmatism, as with other aspects of the NEP, stemmed from a sense of short-term weakness. But this did not signify any loss of medium-term confidence: both the central and local party leadership continued to assume that religious observance was a relic of old 'superstitions' that would not endure.

Not only priests but also all potentially hostile groups in society were denied civic rights. The last remaining industrialists, bankers and great landlords had fled when Vrangel's Volunteer Army departed the Crimean peninsula, paying with their last roubles to take the last available ferries across the Black Sea or to hide in haycarts as they were trundled over the land frontier with Poland.

As the 'big and middle bourgeoisie' vanished into the emigration or into obscurity in Russia, the Politburo picked on whichever suspected 'class enemies' remained. Novelists, painters and poets were prominent victims. The cultural intelligentsia had always contained restless, awkward seekers after new concepts and new theories. The Bolshevik leaders discerned the intelligentsia's potential as a shaper of public opinion, and for every paragraph that Lenin wrote castigating priests he wrote a dozen denouncing secular intellectuals. The most famous representatives of Russian high culture were held under surveillance by the OGPU and the Politburo routinely discussed which of them could be granted an exit visa or special medical facilities:[29] the nearest equivalent would be a post-war British cabinet deciding whether George Orwell could visit France or Evelyn Waugh have a gall-bladder operation.

In summer 1922 the Soviet authorities deported dozens of outstanding Russian writers and scholars. These included a philosopher of world importance, Nikolai Berdyaev, who was interrogated by Dzierżyński. Berdyaev complained that he, too, was a socialist, but one with a more individualist outlook than Dzierżyński. His assertion was rejected; for the Bolsheviks treated non-Bolshevik varieties of socialism as an acute threat to the regime. The deportations taught the intelligentsia that no overt criticisms of the regime would be tolerated; and in June 1922 the Politburo drove home the lesson by reintroducing pre-publication censorship through the agency of a Main Administration for Affairs of Literature and Publishing Houses (which became known as *Glavlit* and which lasted until its abolition by Gorbachëv). The aim was to insulate Soviet society from the bacillus of ideas alien to Bolshevism.[30]

The dilemma for Politburo members was that they badly needed the help of intellectuals in effecting the cultural transformation essential for the creation of a socialist society. Scarcely any writers of distinction were Bolsheviks or even sympathizers with the party. An exception was the Futurist poet Vladimir Mayakovski. Not all central party leaders regarded him as a boon to Bolshevism. Lenin remarked: 'I don't belong to the admirers of his poetic talent, although I quite admit my own incompetence in this area.'[31] A warmer welcome was given to the novelist Maksim Gorki even though he had often denounced Leninism and called Lenin a misanthrope before 1917. Gorki, however, had come to believe that atrocities committed in the Civil War had been as much the fault of ordinary citizens in general and of the Soviet state in particular; and he began to soften his comments on the Bolsheviks. Even so, he continued to prefer to live in his villa in Sorrento in Italy to the dacha he would obtain if he returned home.

Trotski and Zinoviev persuaded the Twelfth Party Conference in 1922 that as long as writer-Bolsheviks were so few, the regime would have to make do with 'fellow travellers'.[32] Writers and artists who at least agreed with some of the party's objectives were to be cosseted. Thousands of roubles were thrown at the feet of those who consented to toe the political line; and Mayakovski, taking pity on the plight of his friends who opposed Marxism-Leninism, discreetly left his banknotes on their sofas. But acts of personal charity did not alter the general situation. Large print-runs, royalties and fame were given to approved authors while poverty and obscurity awaited those who refused to collaborate.

Dissentient thought continued to be cramped under the NEP. The authorities did not always need to ban books from publication: frequently it was enough to suggest that an author should seek another publisher, knowing that Gosizdat, the state publishers, owned practically all the printing-presses and had reduced most private publishers to inactivity. Nevertheless the arts in the 1920s could not have their critical edge entirely blunted if the state also wished to avoid alienating the 'fellow travellers'. Furthermore, the state could not totally predetermine which writer or painter would acquire a popular following. Sergei Yesenin, a poet and guitar-player who infuriated many Bolshevik leaders because of his Bohemian lifestyle, outmatched Mayakovski in appeal. Whereas Mayakovski wrote eulogies for the factory, twentieth-century machinery and Marxism-Leninism, Yesenin composed nostalgic rhapsodies to the virtues of the peasantry while indulging in the urban vices of cigar-smoking and night-clubbing.

Neither Yesenin nor Mayakovski, however, was comfortable in his role for very long. Indeed both succumbed to a fatal depression:

Yesenin killed himself in 1925, Mayakovski in 1930. Yet several of their friends continued to work productively. Isaak Babel composed his masterly short stories about the Red Cavalry in the Polish-Soviet War. Ilf and Petrov wrote *The Twelve Chairs* poking fun at the NEP's *nouveaux riches* as well as at the leather-clad commissars who strutted out of the Red Army into civilian administrative posts after the Civil War. Their satirical bent pleased a Politburo which wished to eradicate bureaucratic habits among state officials; but other writers were less lucky. Yevgeni Zamyatin wrote a dystopian novel, *We*, which implicitly attacked the regimentative orientation of Bolshevism. The novel's hero did not even have a name but rather a letter and number, D-503, and the story of his pitiful struggle against the ruler – the baldheaded Benefactor – was a plea for the right of the individual to live his or her life without oppressive interference by the state.

Zamyatin's work lay unpublished in the USSR; it could be printed only abroad. The grand theorizings of Russian intellectuals about the meaning of life disappeared from published literature. Painting had its mystical explorers in persons such as Marc Chagall (who, until his emigration to western Europe in 1922, went on producing canvasses of Jewish fiddlers, cobblers and rabbis in the poverty-stricken towns and villages around Vitebsk). Practically no great symphonies, operas or ballets were written. The October Revolution and the Civil War were awesome experiences from which most intellectuals recoiled in shock. Many entered a mental black hole where they tried to rethink their notions about the world. It was a process which would last several years; most of the superb poetry of Osip Mandelshtam, Boris Pasternak and Anna Akhmatova came to maturity only in the 1930s.

Central party leaders endeavoured to increase popular respect for those works of literature that conformed to their Marxist vision. They used the negative method of suppression, seizing the presses of hostile political parties and cultural groups and even eliminating those many publications which took a non-political stance. Apolitical light-heartedness virtually disappeared from the organs of public communication.[33] Party leaders also supplied their own propaganda for Bolshevism through *Pravda* and other newspapers. Posters were produced abundantly. Statues and monuments, too, were commissioned, and there were processions, concerts and speeches on May Day and the October Revolution anniversary.

The regime gave priority to 'mass mobilization'. Campaigns were made to recruit workers into the Russian Communist Party, the trade unions and the communist youth organization known as the *Komsomol*. Special attention was paid to increasing the number of Bolsheviks by means of a 'Lenin Enrolment' in 1924 and an 'October Enrolment' in 1927. As a result the membership rose from 625,000 in 1921 to 1,678,000 at the end of the decade;[34] and by that time, too, ten million workers belonged to trade unions.[35] A large subsidy was given to the expansion of popular education. Recreational facilities also underwent improvement. Sports clubs were opened in all cities and national teams were formed for football, gymnastics and athletics (in 1912 the Olympic squad had been so neglected that the ferry-boat to Stockholm left without many of its members). Whereas tsarism had struggled to prevent people from belonging to organizations, Bolshevism gave them intense encouragement to join.

The Bolshevik leaders were learning from recent precedents of the German Social-Democratic Party before the Great War and the Italian fascists in the 1920s. Governments of all industrial countries were experimenting with novel techniques of persuasion. Cinemas and radio stations were drawn into the service of the state; and rulers made use of youth movements such as the Boy Scouts. All this was emulated in the USSR. The Bolsheviks had the additional advantage that the practical constraints on their freedom of action were smaller even than in Italy where a degree of autonomy from state control was preserved by several non-fascist organizations, especially by the Catholic Church, after Mussolini's seizure of power in 1922.

Yet most Soviet citizens had scant knowledge of Marxism-Leninism in general and the party's current policies. Bolshevik propagandists acknowledged their lack of success,[36] and felt that a prerequisite for any basic improvement was the attainment of universal literacy. Teachers inherited from the Imperial regime were induced to return to their jobs. When the Red Cavalry rode across the borderlands in the Polish-Soviet War, commissars tied flash-cards to the backs of the cavalrymen at the front of the file and got the rest to recite the Cyrillic alphabet. This kind of commitment produced a rise in literacy from two in five males between the ages of nine and forty-nine years in 1897 to slightly over seven out of ten in 1927.[37] The exhilaration of learning, common to working-class people in other societies undergoing industrialization, was evident in day-schools and night classes across the country.

Despite all the problems, the Soviet regime retained a vision of political, economic and cultural betterment. Many former army conscripts and would-be university students responded enthusiastically. Many of their parents, too, could remember the social oppressiveness of the pre-revolutionary tsarist regime and gave a welcome to the Bolshevik party's projects for literacy, numeracy, cultural awareness and administrative facility.

This positive reception could be found not only among rank-and-file communists but also more broadly amidst the working class and the peasantry. And experiments with new sorts of living and working were not uncommon. Apartment blocks in many cities were run by committees elected by their inhabitants, and several factories subsidized cultural evenings for their workers. A Moscow orchestra declared itself a democratic collective and played without a conductor. At the end of the Civil War, painters and poets resumed their normal activity and tried to produce works that could be understood not only by the educated few but by the whole society. The Bolshevik central leaders often wished that their supporters in the professions and in the arts would show less interest in experimentation and expend more energy on the basic academic education and industrial and administrative training of the working class. But the utopian mood was not dispelled: the NEP did not put an end to social and cultural innovation.[38]

For politically ambitious youngsters, furthermore, there were courses leading on to higher education. The new Sverdlov University in Moscow was the pinnacle of a system of 'agitation and propaganda' which at lower levels involved not only party schools but also special 'workers' faculties' (*rabfaki*). Committed to dictatorship of the proletariat, the Politburo wished to put a working-class communist generation in place before the current veteran revolutionaries retired. (Few of them would in fact reach retirement age, because of Stalin's Great Terror in the 1930s.) Workers and peasants were encouraged, too, to write for newspapers; this initiative, which came mainly from Bukharin, was meant to highlight the many petty abuses of power while strengthening the contact between the party and the working class. Bukharin had a zest for educational progress. He gathered around himself a group of young socialist intellectuals and established an Institute of Red Professors. In 1920 he had shown the way for his protégés by co-authoring a textbook with Yevgeni Preobrazhenski, *The ABC of Communism.*

Thus the tenets of Bolshevism were disseminated to everyone willing to read them.[39] The Soviet proletariat was advertised as the vanguard of world socialism, as the embodiment of the great social virtues, as the class destined to remake history for all time. Posters depicted factory labourers wielding hammers and looking out to a horizon suffused by a red dawn. On everything from newspaper mastheads to household crockery the slogan was repeated: 'Workers of the world, unite!'

Bolshevik leaders, unlike tsars, strove to identify themselves with ordinary people. Lenin and head of state Mikhail Kalinin were renowned for having the common touch. As it happens, Kalinin – who came from a family of poor peasants in Tver province – had an eye for young middle-class ballerinas. But such information did not appear in *Pravda*: central party leaders tried to present themselves as ordinary blokes with unflamboyant tastes. This was very obvious even in the way they clothed themselves. Perhaps it was Stalin who best expressed the party's mood in the 1920s by wearing a simple, grey tunic: he thereby managed to look not only non-bourgeois but also a modest but militant member of a political collective. The etiquette and material tastes of the pre-revolutionary rich were repudiated. Any interest in fine clothes, furniture or interior décor was treated as downright reactionary. A roughness of comportment, speech and dress was fostered.

In fact these leaders were emphasizing what appealed to them in working-class culture and discarding the rest. Much as they extolled the virtues of the industrial worker, they also wanted to reform him or her. Ever since 1902, when Lenin had written his booklet *What Is To Be Done?*, Bolshevik theory had stressed that the working class would not become socialist by its own devices. The party had to explain and indoctrinate and guide.

The authorities emphasized the need not only for literacy and numeracy but also for punctuality, conscientiousness at work and personal hygiene. The desirability of individual self-improvement was stressed; but so, too, was the goal of getting citizens to subordinate their personal interests to those of the general good as defined by the party. A transformation in social attitudes was deemed crucial. This would involve breaking people's adherence to the way they thought and acted not only in public life but also within the intimacy of the family, where attitudes of a 'reactionary' nature were inculcated and consolidated. Official spokesmen urged wives to refuse to give automatic obedience to husbands, and children were encouraged to challenge the authority of their fathers and mothers. Communal kitchens and factory cafeterias were established so that domestic chores might not get in the way of fulfilment of public duties. Divorce and abortion were available on demand.[40]

Social inhibitions indeed became looser in the 1920s. Yet the Great War and the Civil War played a more decisive role in this process than Bolshevik propaganda. For the popular suspicion of the regime remained acute. A particular source of grievance was the fact that it took until the late 1920s for average wages to be raised to the average amount paid before 1914. This was unimpressive to a generation of the working class which had felt exploited by their employers under Nicholas II. Strikes were frequent under the NEP. The exact number of workers who laid down tools is as yet unascertained, but undoubtedly it was more than the 20,100 claimed by governmental statisticians for 1927.[41]

Not that the Politburo was greatly disconcerted by the labour movement. Conflicts tended to be small in scale and short in duration; the raging conflicts of 1920–21 did not recur. The long-standing policy of favouring skilled workers for promotion to administrative posts in politics and industry had the effect of removing many of those who might have made the labour movement more troublesome; and although wages were no higher than before 1914, the state had at least increased rudimentary provision for health care and unemployment benefit.[42] Above all, the party and the trade unions had offices in all factories and were usually able to see off trouble before it got out of hand; and the resolution of disputes was facilitated by arbitration commissions located in the workplace. The OGPU, too, inserted itself into the process. Once a strike had been brought to an end, the Chekists would advise the management about whom to sack in due course so that industrial conflict might not recur. Sometimes strike leaders were quietly arrested.

Obviously the party leaders could not be complacent about the situation. They could never be entirely sure that a little outbreak of discontent in some factory or other would not explode into a protest movement such as had overwhelmed the monarchy in February 1917. Through the 1920s the Politburo was fumbling for ways to understand the working class in whose name it ruled the USSR.

Workers were not the only group to cause perplexity: the whole society baffled the authorities. The NEP had reintroduced a degree of capitalism; but it was a capitalism different from any previous capitalism in Russia or the external world. Bankers, big industrialists, stockbrokers and landlords were a thing of the past. Foreign entrepreneurs were few, and those few kept out of public view. The main beneficiaries of the NEP in the towns did not conform to the stereotype of a traditional high bourgeoisie; they were more like British spivs after 1945. As a group they were called 'nepmen' and were quintessentially traders in scarce goods. They trudged into the villages and bought up vegetables, ceramic pots and knitted scarves. They went round urban workshops and did deals to obtain chairs, buckles, nails and hand tools. And they sold these products wherever there were markets.

It was officially recognized that if the market was to function, there had to be rules. Legal procedures ceased to be mocked as blatantly as in the Civil War. A Procuracy was established in 1922 and among its purposes was the supervision of private commercial transactions. More generally, people were encouraged to assert their rights by recourse to the courts.[43]

But arbitrary rule remained the norm in practice. The local authorities harassed the traders, small-scale manufacturers and stallholders: frequently there were closures of perfectly legal enterprises and arrests of their owners.[44] Lenin had anyway insisted that the Civil Code should enable the authorities to use sanctions including even terror.[45] This had the predictable effect of inducing the nepmen to enjoy their profits while they could. The dishonest, fur-coated rouble millionaire with a bejewelled woman of ill-repute on either arm was not an excessive caricature of reality in the 1920s. Yet if many nepmen had criminal links, the fault was not entirely theirs; for the regime imposed commercial conditions which compelled all traders to be furtive. Without the nepmen, the gaps in the supply of products would not have been plugged; with them, however, the Bolsheviks were able to claim that capitalist entrepreneurship was an occupation for speculators, sharpsters and pimps.

Yet the Bolshevik belief that the middle class was striving to grab back the economic position it had occupied before 1917 was untrue not only of the higher bourgeoisie but also of lower members of the old middle class. The Russian Empire's shopkeepers and small businessmen for the most part did not become nepmen. Instead they used their accomplishments in literacy and numeracy to enter state administrative employment. As in the Civil War, they found that with a little redecoration of their accounts of themselves they could get jobs which secured them food and shelter.

The civil bureaucracy included some famous adversaries of the communist party. Among them were several economists, including the former Menshevik Vladimir Groman in the State Planning Commission and ex-Socialist-Revolutionary Nikolai Kondratev in the People's Commissariat of Agriculture. But such figures with their civic dutifulness were untypical of bureaucrats in general. The grubby, unhelpful state offices became grubbier and even less helpful. Citizens got accustomed to queuing for hours with their petitions. Venality was endemic below the central and middling rungs of the ladder of power. Even in the party, as in Smolensk province in 1928, there was the occasional financial scandal. A pattern of evasiveness had not ceased its growth after the Civil War, and it affected the workers as much as the bureaucrats. In the factories and mines the labour force resisted any further encroachment on their rights at work. Although by law the capacity to hire and fire was within the gift of management, factory committees and local trade union bodies still counted for something in their own enterprises.[46]

Older workers noted that infringements which once would have incurred a foreman's fine resulted merely in a ticking off. The workers sensed their worth to a party which had promulgated a proletarian dictatorship; they also knew the value of their skills to enterprises which were short of them. One task for the authorities was to inhibit the work-force from moving from job to job. Other jobs and enterprises were nearly always available at least for skilled labour (although unemployment in general grew in the 1920s). Managers were commencing to bribe their best men and women to stay by conceding higher wages.[47]

All these factors reduced the likelihood of the working class revolting against 'Soviet power'. The mixture of blandishment, manipulation and coercion meant few labourers were keen to join the scanty, scattered groups of anti-Bolshevik socialists – be they Mensheviks, Socialist-Revolutionaries or disillusioned former Bolsheviks – who tried to stir them into organized resistance. Nor is it surprising that the peasants were not minded to challenge 'Soviet power'. The peasantry had not forgotten the force used by the party to obtain food-supplies, labour and conscripts in the Civil War. They also remembered that the NEP, too, had been introduced by means of unremitting violence. The Red Army, including cavalry units, had been deployed not only to suppress revolts but also to force peasants to increase the sown area in 1921–2. A deep rancour was still felt towards the town authorities, but it was the rancour of political resignation, not of rebellious intent.

In any case, not everything went badly for the peasantry. The total fiscal burden as a proportion of the income of the average peasant household differed little from the normal ratio before the

Great War; and their standard of living recovered after the Civil War. Certainly the pattern of the grain trade changed in the 1920s. This was mainly the result of the fall in prices for cereals on the world market. Consequently most of the wheat which had gone to the West under Nicholas II stayed in the country. A large amount of any harvest was not sold to the towns, for peasant households could often get better deals in other villages. Alternatively they could feed up their livestock or just hoard their stocks and wait for a further raising of prices. The villages were theirs again, as briefly they had been in 1917–18. Rural soviets were installed by visiting urban officialdom, but their significance consisted mainly in the creation of an additional layer of administrative corruption. Moscow's political campaigns went barely noticed. Peasants continued to have a hard, short and brutish life; but at least it was their own style of life, not a style inflicted upon them by Emperor, landlord or commissar.

This was a phenomenon regretted by the Bolsheviks, who managed to establish only 17,500 party groups in the countryside by 1927[48] – one for every 1200 square kilometres. It was bad enough that workers preferred Charlie Chaplin and Mary Pickford to Soviet propaganda films.[49] Worse still was the fact that few peasants even knew what a cinema was or cared to find out. The USSR was a predominantly agrarian country with poor facilities in transport, communication and administration. As a result, it was virtually as 'under-governed' as the Russian Empire.

Such a structure of power was precarious and the Soviet regime reinforced its endeavour to interpose the state into the affairs of society. The stress on 'accountancy and supervision' had not originated in Russia with the Bolsheviks: it had been a feature of the tsarist administrative tradition. But Leninist theory gave huge reinforcement to it. Surveillance, both open and covert, was a large-scale activity. Contemporary bureaucracies in all industrial countries were collecting an ever larger amount of information on their societies, but the trend was hyper-developed in the USSR. Vast surveys were conducted on economic and social life: even the acquisition of a job as a navvy entailed the completion of a detailed questionnaire. For example, Matvei Dementevich Popkov's work-book shows that he was born in 1894 to Russian parents. He had only a primary-school education. Popkov joined the Builders' Union in 1920 but refrained from entering the communist party. He had had military experience, probably in the Civil War.

The distrust felt by the central party leadership for both its society and even its own state continued to grow. Control organs such as the Workers' and Peasants' Inspectorate and the Party Central Control Commission had their authority increased. Investigators were empowered to enter any governmental institution so as to question functionaries and examine financial accounts.[50]

And yet who was to control the controllers? The Bolshevik leaders assumed that things would be fine so long as public institutions, especially the control organs, drew their personnel mainly from Bolsheviks and pro-Bolshevik workers. But how were the leaders to know who among such persons were genuinely reliable? Under the NEP the system known as the *nomenklatura* was introduced. Since mid-1918, if not earlier, the central party bodies had made the main appointments to Sovnarkom, the Red Army, the Cheka and the trade unions. In 1923 this system was formalized by the composition of a list of about 5,500 designated party and governmental posts – the nomenklatura – whose holders could be appointed only by the central party bodies. The Secretariat's Files-and-Distribution Department (*Uchraspred*) compiled a file-index on all high-ranking functionaries so that sensible appointments might be made.[51]

And provincial party secretaries, whose posts belonged to this central nomenklatura, were instructed to draw up local nomenklaturas for lower party and governmental posts in analogous fashion. The internal regulation of the one-party state was tightened. The graded system of nomenklaturas was meant to ensure that the policies of the Politburo were carried out by functionaries whom it could trust; and this system endured, with recurrent modifications, through to the late 1980s.

This same system, although it increased central control, had inherent difficulties. Candidates for jobs knew in advance that overt political loyalty and class origins counted for more than technical expertise. But this induced people to lie about their background. Over-writing and over-claiming became a way of life. The state reacted by appointing emissaries to check the accuracy of reports coming to Moscow. Yet this only strengthened the incentive to lie. And so the state sent out yet more investigative commissions. The party itself was not immune to the culture of falsehood. Fiddling and fudging pervaded the operation of lower Bolshevik bodies. Each local leader formed a group of political clients who owed him allegiance, right or wrong.[52] There was also a reinforcement of the practice whereby local functionaries could gather together in a locality and quietly ignore the capital's demands. Although the party was more dynamic than the rest of the Soviet state, its other characteristics gave cause for concern in the Kremlin.

The NEP had saved the regime from destruction; but it had induced its own grave instabilities into the compound of the Soviet order. The principle of private profit clashed in important economic sectors with central planning objectives. Nepmen, clerics, better-off peasants, professional experts and artists were quietly beginning to assert themselves. Under the NEP there was also a resurgence of nationalist, regionalist and religious aspirations; and the arts and sciences, too, offered cultural visions at variance with Bolshevism. Soviet society under the New Economic Policy was a mass of contradictions and unpredictabilities, dead ends and opportunities, aspirations and discontents.

8

Leninism and its Discontents

It would have been possible for these instabilities to persist well into the 1930s if the Politburo had been more favourably disposed to the NEP. Admittedly Lenin came to believe that the NEP, which had started as an economic retreat, offered space for a general advance. He argued that the policy would enable the communists to raise the country's educational level, improve its administration, renovate its economy and spread the doctrines of communism. But not even Lenin saw the NEP as permanently acceptable.[1]

And there was huge tension between what the communist party wanted for society and what the various social groups – classes, nationalities, organizations, churches and families – wanted for themselves. Most Bolshevik leaders had never liked the NEP, regarding it at best as an excrescent boil on the body politic and at worst a malignant cancer. They detested the reintroduction of capitalism and feared the rise of a new urban and rural bourgeoisie. They resented the corrupt, inefficient administration they headed; they disliked such national, religious and cultural concessions as they had had to make. They were embarrassed that they had not yet eliminated the poverty in Soviet towns and villages. They yearned to accelerate educational expansion and indoctrinate the working class with their ideas. They wanted a society wholly industrialized and equipped with technological dynamism. They desired to match the military preparedness of capitalist powers.

What is more, Lenin's NEP had always disconcerted many central and local party leaders. His chief early opponent behind the scenes was Trotski. The disagreement between them related not to the basic immediate need for the NEP but to its scope and duration. Lenin wanted large-scale industry, banking and foreign trade to remain in Sovnarkom's hands and ensured that this was achieved. This was not enough for Trotski, who urged that there should be an increase in the proportion of investment in industry and that the State Planning Commission (*Gosplan*) should draw up a single 'plan' for all sectors of the economy; and although he did not expressly demand a debate on the timing of the eventual phasing out of the NEP, his impatience with the policy evoked sympathy even among those communists who were suspicious of Trotski's personal ambitions.

Lenin secretly arranged for Stalin and other associates to face down Trotski at the Eleventh Party Congress in March 1922.[2] Yet Lenin himself was ailing; and the Central Committee, on the advice of Molotov and Bukharin, insisted that he should reduce his political activity. In the winter of 1921–2 he was residing at a sanatorium in Gorki, thirty-five kilometres from the capital, while he recuperated from chronic severe headaches and insomnia. In May 1922, however, he suffered a major stroke and his influence upon politics diminished as his colleagues began to run the party and government without him.

He continued to read *Pravda*; he also ordered the fitting of a direct telephone line to the Kremlin.[3] Stalin, too, kept him informed about events by coming out to visit him. With Lenin's approval, Stalin had become Party General Secretary after the Eleventh Congress and knew better than anyone what was happening in the Politburo, Orgburo and the Secretariat. Lenin looked forward to Stalin's visits, ordering that a bottle of wine should be opened for him.[4] And yet the friendliness did not last long. The constitutional question about what kind of federation should be created out of the RSFSR and the other Soviet republics flared up in summer 1922, and found Lenin and Stalin at odds. Stalin also infuriated Lenin by countenancing the abolition of the state monopoly over foreign trade as well as by running the central party apparatus in an authoritarian manner. Now perceiving Trotski as the lesser of two evils, Lenin turned to him for help in reversing the movement of policy in a Politburo controlled by Stalin, Kamenev and Zinoviev.

On foreign trade Trotski won the Central Committee discussion in mid-December 1922, as Lenin remarked, 'without having to fire a shot'.[5] Lenin also began to have success in his controversy with Stalin over the USSR Constitution. But his own ill-health made it highly likely that his campaign might not be brought to a successful conclusion before he died. In late December 1922, despairing of his own medical recovery, he dictated a series of confidential documents that became known as his political testament. The intention was that the materials would be presented to the next Party Congress, enabling it to incorporate his ideas in strategic policies.

He had always behaved as if his own presence was vital to the cause of the October Revolution; his testament highlighted this when he drew pen-portraits of six leading Bolsheviks: Stalin, Kamenev, Zinoviev, Pyatakov, Bukharin and Trotski. Not one of them – not even his newly-found ally Trotski – emerged without severe criticism.[6] The implication was plain: no other colleague by himelf was fit to become supreme leader. Lenin sensed that Bolshevism's fate depended to a considerable extent on whether Stalin and Trotski would work harmoniously together. Hoping that a collective leadership would remain in place after his own demise, he argued that an influx of ordinary factory-workers to the Party Central Committee, the Party Central Control Commission and the Workers' and Peasants' Inspectorate would prevent a split in the Politburo and eradicate bureaucracy in both the party and the state as a whole.

In January 1923 Lenin dictated an addendum to his testament, to the effect that Stalin was too crude to be retained as the Party General Secretary.[7] Lenin had learned that Stalin had covered up an incident in which Sergo Ordzhonikidze had beaten up a Georgian Bolshevik who opposed the line taken by Stalin and Ordzhonikidze on the USSR Constitution. Lenin had also discovered from his wife Nadezhda Krupskaya that Stalin had subjected her to verbal abuse on hearing that she had broken the regime of Lenin's medical treatment by speaking to him about politics.

Yet Lenin's health had to hold out if he was to bring down the General Secretary. On 5 March 1923 he wrote to Stalin that unless an apology was offered to Krupskaya, he would break personal relations with him.[8] It was all too late. On 6 March, Lenin suffered another major stroke. This time he lost the use of the right side of his body and could neither speak nor read. In subsequent months he made little recovery and was confined to a wheel-chair as he struggled to recover his health. His wife Nadezhda and sister Maria nursed him attentively; but the end could not long be delayed. On 21 January 1924 his head throbbed unbearably, and his temperature shot up. At 6.50 p.m. he let out a great sigh, his body shuddered and then all was silence. The leader of the October Revolution, the Bolshevik party and the Communist International was dead.

There was no disruption of politics since the Politburo had long been preparing itself for Lenin's death. Since Trotski was recuperating from illness in Abkhazia at the time, it was Stalin who headed the funeral commission. Instead of burying him, the Politburo ordered that Lenin should be embalmed and put on display in a mausoleum to be built on Red Square. Stalin claimed that this corresponded to the demands of ordinary workers; but the real motive seems to have been a wish to exploit the traditional belief of the Russian Orthodox Church that the remains of truly holy men did not putrefy (even though the Church did not go as far as displaying the corpses in glass cabinets[9]). A secular cult of Saint Vladimir of the October Revolution was being organized. Krupskaya, despite being disgusted, was powerless to oppose it.

The NEP had increased popular affection for Lenin; and the members of the Politburo were hoping to benefit from his reputation by identifying themselves closely with him and his policies. Arrangements were made for factory hooters to be sounded and for all traffic to be halted at the time of his funeral. Despite the bitter cold, a great crowd turned out for the speeches delivered by Lenin's colleagues on Red Square. The display of reverence for him became mandatory and any past disagreements with him were discreetly overlooked. Bukharin, Dzierżyński, Kamenev, Preobrazhenski, Stalin, Trotski and Zinoviev had each clashed with him in the past. None of them was merely his cipher. As his body was being laid out under glass, a competition took place as to who should be recognized as the authentic heir to his political legacy.

Oaths were sworn to his memory and picture-books of his exploits appeared in large print-runs. An Institute of the Brain was founded where 30,000 slices were made of his cerebral tissue by researchers seeking the origins of his 'genius'. His main works were published under Kamenev's editorship while rarer pieces of Leniniana were prepared for a series of volumes entitled the Lenin Collection.[10] Petrograd was renamed Leningrad in his honour. On a more practical level, Stalin insisted that homage to Lenin should be rendered by means of a mass enrolment of workers into the ranks of the Russian Communist Party, which in 1925 renamed itself the All-Union Communist Party (Bolsheviks).

But what was Leninism? Lenin had eschewed giving a definition, affirming that Marxism required perpetual adjustment to changing circumstances. But his successors needed to explain what essential ideology they propounded in his name. The principal rivals – Trotski, Zinoviev, Bukharin, Kamenev and Stalin – produced speeches, articles and booklets for this purpose in 1924. A new term emerged: Marxism-Leninism. (There were still clumsier neologisms such as Marksovo-Engelso-Leninism; but Marxism-Leninism was clumsy enough: it was as if Mohammed had chosen to nominate his doctrines as Christianity-Islam.) The contenders for the succession announced their commitment to every idea associated with Lenin: the dictatorship of the proletariat; violence as the midwife of revolutionary transformation; hierarchy, discipline and centralism; concessions to peasants and oppressed nationalities; the incontrovertibility of Marxism; and the inevitability of world revolution.

Each Bolshevik leader believed in the one-party state, the one-ideology state, in legalized arbitrary rule and in terror as acceptable methods of governance, in administrative ultra-centralism, in philosophical amoralism. Neither Lenin nor any of the others used this terminology, but their words and deeds demonstrated their commitment. The speculation that if only Lenin had survived, a humanitarian order would have been established is hard to square with this gamut of agreed principles of Bolshevism.

The differences with Lenin's *oeuvre* touched only on secondary matters. Trotski wished to expand state planning, accelerate industrialization and instigate revolution in Europe. Zinoviev objected to the indulgence shown to richer peasants. Kamenev agreed with Zinoviev, and continued to try to moderate the regime's authoritarian excesses. Bukharin aspired to the creation of a distinctly 'proletarian' culture (whereas Lenin wanted cultural policy to be focused on traditional goals such as literacy and numeracy).[11] Intellectual and personal factors were entangled because several Politburo members were engaged in a struggle to show who was the fittest to don Lenin's mantle. Although Zinoviev and Kamenev had joined hands with Stalin to prevent Trotski from succeeding Lenin, by summer 1923 they were also worrying about Stalin; and they conferred with Bukharin and even Stalin's associates Ordzhonikidze and Voroshilov in the north Caucasian spa of Kislovodsk as to how best to reduce Stalin's powers.

They might eventually have achieved their purpose had Trotski not picked that moment to challenge the wisdom of the Politburo's handling of the economy. Fear of Trotski continued to be greater than annoyance with Stalin; and Kamenev, Zinoviev and Bukharin put aside their differences with Stalin in order to repel Trotski's attack.

Economically it appeared that the NEP had succeeded beyond everyone's expectations. Agricultural output in 1922 had risen enough for the Politburo to resume the export of grain. As trade between town and countryside increased, output recovered. By 1923, cereal production had increased by twenty-three per cent over the total recorded for 1920. Domestic industrial recovery also gathered pace: in the same three years output from factories rose by 184 per cent.[12] The snag was that, as Trotski memorably put it, a 'scissors' crisis' divided the economy's urban and rural sectors. For by 1923, the retail prices of industrial goods were three times greater than they had been in relation to agricultural goods back in 1913. The state's pricing policy had turned the terms of trade against the peasantry, which responded by refraining from bringing its wheat, potatoes and milk to the towns. The two scissor blades of the economy had opened and the NEP was put at risk.

The fault lay not with market pressures but with the decisions of politicians, and Trotski teased the ascendant central leadership for its incompetence. Many on the left of the communist party welcomed Trotski's decision to speak his mind. In October 1923 Preobrazhenski and others signed a Platform of the Forty-Six criticizing the Politburo and demanding an increase in central state economic planning and internal party democracy. They were not a monolithic group: most of them insisted on appending their own reservations about the document.[13] Trotski made arguments similar to those of the Platform in *The New Course*, published in December. It was his contention that the stifling of democracy in the party had led to a bureaucratization of party life. Debate and administration had become inflexible. The erroneous decisions on the prices of industrial goods were supposedly one of the results.

Zinoviev, Stalin, Kamenev and Bukharin counter-attacked. They rebutted the charge of mismanagement and authoritarianism and argued that Trotski had been an anti-Leninist since the Second Party Congress in 1903. Trotski's proposal for more rapid industrialization, they declared, would involve a fiscal bias against the peasantry. At the Thirteenth Party Conference in January 1924 they accused him of wishing to destroy Lenin's NEP. 'Trotskyism' overnight became a heresy. By the mid-1920s, moreover, Bukharin had concluded that further steps in the 'transition to socialism' in Russia were unachievable by mainly violent means. The October Revolution and Civil War had been necessary 'revolutionary' phases, but the party ought presently to devote itself to an 'evolutionary' phase. The objective, according to Bukharin, should be civil peace and a gradual 'growing into socialism'. He was enraptured by the NEP, urging that the Bolshevik philosophical and political antagonism to private profit should temporarily be abandoned. To the peasantry Bukharin declared: 'Enrich yourselves!'

This imperative clashed so blatantly with the party's basic ideology that Bukharin had to retract his words; and it was Stalin who supplied a doctrine capable of competing with the Left's criticisms. In December 1924 he announced that it was a perfectly respectable tenet of Leninism that the party could complete the building of 'Socialism in One Country'. This was a misinterpretation of Lenin;

but it was a clever political move at the time. Trotski's appeal to Bolshevik functionaries in the party, the Komsomol, the armed forces and the security police derived in part from his urgent will to industrialize the USSR and create a socialist society. Stalin's doctrinal contribution reflected his long-held opinion that Europe was not yet 'pregnant with socialist revolution'; and he maintained that Trotski's insistence on the need for fraternal revolutions in the West underestimated the Soviet Union's indigenous revolutionary potential. Stalin, by talking up the achievability of socialism without Trotskyist policies, was offering an encouraging alternative.

As Stalin began to add an ideological dimension to his bureaucratic authority, he was also contriving to clear his name of the taint applied to it by the deceased Lenin. At the Twelfth Party Congress in April 1923 Stalin leant on Kamenev and Zinoviev, who still preferred Stalin to Trotski, to restrict knowledge of Lenin's political testament to the leaders of provincial delegations.

He worked hard to win the confidence of such leaders and their fellow committee-men, putting aside time at Congresses and in his Secretariat office to converse with them. Yet abrasiveness, too, remained part of his style when he attacked oppositionists. His language was sarcastic, repetitious and aggressive; his arguments were uncompromising and schematic. At the Party Conference in January 1924 it had been he who had lined up the speakers for the assault upon Trotski, Preobrazhenski and the so-called Left Opposition. Stalin's ability to run the Secretariat was well attested; the surprise for his rivals, inside and outside the Left Opposition, was his talent at marshalling the entire party. He personified the practicality of those Bolsheviks who had not gone into emigration before 1917; and his recent military experience increased his image as a no-nonsense leader.

Stalin stressed that the party was the institutional cornerstone of the October Revolution. This had been Lenin's attitude in practice, but not in his theoretical works. Stalin gave a series of lectures in 1924 on *The Foundations of Leninism* that gave expression to this.[14] As General Secretary he derived advantage from the absolutizing of the communist party's authority and prestige. Yet this served to aggravate again the worries of Kamenev and Zinoviev. Kamenev was Moscow Soviet chairman and Zinoviev headed both the Comintern and the Bolshevik party organization of Leningrad. They were unreconciled to seeing Stalin as their equal, and continued to despise his intellectual capacity. The rumour that Stalin had plagiarized material from F. A. Ksenofontov in order to complete *The Foundations of Leninism* was grist to the mill of their condescension.[15] Now that Trotski had been pulled off his pedestal, Stalin had exhausted his usefulness to them; it was time to jettison him.

The struggle intensified in the ascendant party leadership about the nature of the NEP. Bukharin and Zinoviev, despite advocating measures at home that were substantially to the right of Trotski's, were adventuristic in foreign affairs. Not only had they prompted the abortive March Action in Berlin in 1921, but also Zinoviev had compounded the blunder by impelling the Communist Party of Germany to make a further ill-judged attempt to seize power in November 1923. This attitude sat uncomfortably alongside Stalin's wish to concentrate on the building of socialism in the USSR.

The issues were not clear cut. Bukharin and Zinoviev, while itching to instigate revolution in Berlin, wanted to negotiate with Western capitalist powers. After signing the trade treaties with the United Kingdom and other countries in 1921, the Politburo aimed to insert itself in European diplomacy on a normal basis. The first opportunity came with the Genoa Conference in March 1922. Under Lenin's guidance, the Soviet negotiators were not too ambitious. Lenin had given up hoping for diplomatic recognition by the Allies as long as the French government demanded the de-annulment of the loans to Russia made by French investors before the October Revolution. People's Commissar for Foreign Affairs Georgi Chicherin was instructed to seek a separate deal with Germany. And so the two pariah powers after the Great War got together. They agreed, at the Italian resort of Rapallo, to grant diplomatic recognition to each other and to boost mutual trade; and, in a secret arrangement, the Soviet authorities were to help Germany to obviate the Treaty of Versailles's restrictions on German military reconstruction by setting up armaments factories and military training facilities in the USSR.[16]

The Rapallo Treaty fitted with Lenin's notion that economic reconstruction required foreign participation. But German generals proved more willing partners than German industrialists. Lenin's scheme for 'concessions' to be used to attract capital from abroad was a miserable failure. Only roughly a hundred agreements were in operation before the end of 1927.[17] Insofar as Europe and North America contributed to the Soviet Union's economic regeneration, it occurred largely through international trade. But the slump in the price of grain on the world market meant that revenues had to be obtained mainly by sales of oil, timber and gold; and in the financial year 1926–7 the USSR's exports were merely a third in volume of what they had been in 1913.[18]

Bukharin by the mid-1920s had come over to Stalin's opinion that capitalism was not yet on the verge of revolutionary upheaval. The intellectual and political complications of the discussion were considerable. Trotski, despite castigating Stalin's ideas about 'Socialism in One Country', recognized the stabilization of capitalism as a medium-term fact of life.[19] In criticizing the March Action of 1921 and the Berlin insurrection of November 1923, he was scoffing at the Politburo's incompetence rather than its zeal to spread revolution; and his ridicule was focused upon Zinoviev, whom he described as trying to compensate for his opposition to Lenin's seizure of power in Russia in October 1917 with an ultra-revolutionary strategy for Germany in the 1920s. Bukharin and Stalin replied to Trotski that their own quiescence in foreign policy by 1924 had yielded an improvement in the USSR's security. A Soviet-Chinese treaty was signed in the same year and relations with Japan remained peaceful. The Labour Party won the British elections and gave *de jure* recognition to the Soviet government.

This bolstered the Politburo's case for concentrating upon economic recovery. A further adjustment of the NEP seemed desirable in order to boost agricultural output, and Gosplan and the various People's Commissariats were ordered to draft appropriate legislation. After a wide-ranging discussion, it was decided in April 1925 to lower the burden of the food tax, to diminish fiscal discrimination against better-off peasants, and to legalize hired labour and the leasing of land.

Yet the Politburo's unity was under strain. Zinoviev and Kamenev asserted that excessive compromise had been made with the aspirations of the peasantry. Bukharin stepped forward with a defiant riposte. At the Fourteenth Party Congress in December 1925 he declared: 'We shall move forward at a snail's pace, but none the less we shall be building socialism, and we shall build it.' Throughout the year Trotski had watched bemused as Zinoviev and Kamenev built up the case against official party policy. Zinoviev had a firm organizational base in Leningrad and assumed he was too strong for Stalin; but the Politburo majority were on the side of Stalin and Bukharin, and in 1926 Stalin's associate Sergei Kirov was appointed to the party first secretaryship in Leningrad. Zinoviev and his Leningrad Opposition saw the writing on the wall. Overtures were made by Zinoviev to his arch-enemy Trotski, and from the summer a United Opposition – led by Trotski, Zinoviev and Kamenev – confronted the ascendant party leadership.

The United Opposition maintained that Stalin and Bukharin had surrendered entirely to the peasantry. This was not very plausible. In August 1925 Gosplan took a major step towards comprehensive state planning by issuing its 'control figures for the national economy'. At the Fourteenth Congress in December, moreover, industrial capital goods were made the priority for longer-term state investment. The Central Committee repeated the point in April 1926, making a general call for 'the reinforcement of the planning principle and the introduction of planning discipline'.[20] Two campaigns were inaugurated in industry. First came a 'Regime of Economy', then a 'Rationalization of Production'. Both campaigns were a means of putting pressure upon factories to cut out inefficient methods and to raise levels of productivity.

The USSR's industrialization was never far from the Politburo's thoughts. The United Opposition, for its part, was constantly on the defensive. Stalin sliced away at their power-bases as the Secretariat replaced opponents with loyalists at all levels of the party's hierarchy;

Bukharin had a merry time reviling his leading critics in books and articles. The United Opposition's access to the public media was continually reduced. Prolific writers such as Trotski, Radek, Preobrazhenski, Kamenev and Zinoviev had their material rejected for publication in *Pravda*. Claques were organized at Party Congresses to interrupt their speeches. In January 1925 Trotski was removed as People's Commissar for Military Affairs, and in December he lost his Politburo seat. Zinoviev was sacked as Leningrad Soviet chairman in January 1926 and in July was ousted from the Politburo with Kamenev. In October 1926 the leadership of the Executive Committee of the Comintern passed from Zinoviev to Dmitri Manuilski.

The United Opposition leaders fell back on their experience as clandestine party activists against the Romanov monarchy. They produced programmes, theses and appeals on primitive printing devices, keeping an eye open for potential OGPU informers. They also arranged unexpected mass meetings where they could communicate their ideas to workers. They talked to sympathizers in the Comintern. They would not go gently into oblivion.

Yet although the Left Opposition, the Leningrad Opposition and the United Opposition exposed the absence of internal party democracy, their words had a hollow ring. Trotski and Zinoviev had treated Bolshevik dissidents with disdain until they, too, fell out with the Politburo. Their invective against authoritarianism and bureaucracy seemed self-serving to the Workers' Opposition, which refused to co-operate with them. In any case, no communist party critic of the Politburo – from Shlyapnikov through to Trotski – called for the introduction of general democracy. The critics wanted elections and open discussion in the party and, to some extent, in the soviets and the trade unions. But none favoured permitting the Mensheviks, Socialist-Revolutionaries and Kadets to re-enter politics. The All-Union Communist Party's monopoly, while having no sanction even from the USSR Constitution, was an unchallenged tenet; and oppositionists went out of their way to affirm their obedience to the party. Even Trotski, that remarkable individualist, demurred at being thought disloyal.

Such self-abnegation did him no good: Stalin was out to get the

United Opposition and the OGPU smashed their printing facilities and broke up their meetings. Stalin's wish to settle accounts with Trotski and Zinoviev was reinforced by the débâcles in international relations. In May 1927 a massacre of thousands of Chinese communists was perpetrated by Chiang Kai-shek in Shanghai. The Soviet Politburo had pushed the Chinese Communist Party into alliance with Chiang, and Trotski did not fail to point out that foreign policy was unsafe in the hands of the existing Politburo.

This time Stalin had his way: in November 1927 the Central Committee expelled Trotski, Kamenev and Zinoviev from the party. Hundreds of their followers were treated similarly. Kamenev and Zinoviev were so demoralized that they petitioned in January 1928 for re-admittance to the party. They recanted their opinions, which they now described as anti-Leninist. In return Stalin re-admitted them to the party in June. Trotski refused to recant. He and thirty unrepentant oppositionists, including Preobrazhenski, were sent into internal exile. Trotski found himself isolated in Alma-Ata, 3000 kilometres from Moscow. He was not physically abused, and took his family, secretaries and personal library with him; he was also allowed to write to his associates elsewhere in the USSR. But the activity of the United Opposition was in tatters, and Pyatakov and V. A. Antonov-Ovseenko were so impressed by Stalin's industrializing drive that they decided to break with Trotski on the same terms as Kamenev and Zinoviev.

Victory for Stalin and Bukharin was completed by the winter of 1927–8. The NEP had apparently been secured for several more years and the Politburo seemed to be made up of nine men who gave no sign of serious divisions among themselves. Their record of achievement, furthermore, was substantial. The statistics are controversial, but there seems little doubt that the output of both industry and agriculture was roughly what it had been in the last year before the Great War. Economic recovery had more or less been achieved.[21]

And the skewing of official policy since 1925 had led to a re-attainment of the late tsarist period's proportion of industrial production reinvested in factories and mines. The NEP was showing itself able not merely to restore industry but also to develop it further.

The engineering sub-sector, which was almost wholly state-owned, had already been expanded beyond its pre-war capacity. But private small-scale and handicrafts output also increased: by 1926–7 it was only slightly less than in 1913. Later computations have suggested that an annual growth of six per cent in production from Soviet factories and mines was possible within the parameters of the NEP.[22] The villages, too, displayed renewed liveliness. Agriculture was undergoing diversification. Under Nicholas II about ninety per cent of the sown area was given over to cereal crops; by the end of the 1920s the percentage had fallen to eighty-two. Emphasis was placed, too, upon sugar beet, potatoes and cotton; and horse-drawn equipment was also on the increase.[23]

The Politburo could take satisfaction inasmuch as this was achieved in the teeth of hostility from the capitalist world. Direct foreign investment, which had been crucial to the pre-revolutionary economy, had vanished: the Soviet authorities had to pay punctiliously for every piece of machinery they brought into the country. Even if they had not refused to honour the loans contracted by Nicholas II and the Provisional Government, the October Revolution would always have stood as a disincentive to foreign banks and industrial companies to return to Russia.

The central party leadership did not recognize its own successes as such, but brooded upon the patchiness of economic advance. It was also jolted by difficulties which were of its own making. In 1926 the party's leaders had introduced large surcharges on goods carried by rail for private commerce; they had also imposed a tax on super-profits accruing to nepmen. Article No. 107 had been added to the USSR Criminal Code, specifying three years' imprisonment for price rises found to be 'evil-intentioned'.[24] In the tax year 1926–7 the state aimed to maximize revenues for industrial investment by reducing by six per cent the prices it paid for agricultural produce. In the case of grain, the reduction was by 20–25 per cent.[25] Simultaneously the state sought to show goodwill to agriculture by lowering the prices for goods produced by state-owned enterprises. The effect was disastrous. Nepmen became more elusive to the tax-collecting agencies than previously. Peasants refused to release their stocks to the state procurement bodies – and even the lowered industrial prices failed to entice them since factory goods were in exceedingly short supply after their prices had been lowered and they had been bought up by middlemen.

These measures were fatal for the policy inaugurated by Lenin in 1921. By the last three months of 1927 there was a drastic shortage of food for the towns as state purchases of grain dropped to a half of the amount obtained in the same period in the previous year. Among the reasons for the mismanagement was the ascendant party leaders' ignorance of market economics. Another was their wish to be seen to have a strategy different from the United Opposition's. Trotski was calling for the raising of industrial prices, and so the Politburo obtusely lowered them. Such particularities had an influence on the situation.

Nevertheless they were not in themselves sufficient to induce the NEP's abandonment. Although there was a collapse in the amount of grain marketed to the state, no serious crop shortage existed in the country: indeed the harvests of 1926–7 were only five per cent down on the best harvest recorded before the First World War. But whereas Bukharin was willing to raise the prices offered by the state for agricultural produce, Stalin was hostile to such compromise. Stalin's attitude was reinforced by the basic difficulties experienced by the party earlier in the decade. The national and religious resurgence; the administrative malaise; poverty, ill-health and illiteracy; urban unemployment; military insecurity; problems in industrial production; the spread of political apathy; the isolation of the party from most sections of society: all these difficulties prepared the ground for Stalin to decide that the moment was overdue for a break with the NEP.

The alliance of Stalin and Bukharin had been the cardinal political relationship in the defeat of successive challenges to the ascendant party leadership. With help from Zinoviev and Kamenev, Stalin and Bukharin had defeated Trotski and the Left Opposition. Together they had proceeded to crush the United Opposition of Trotski, Zinoviev and Kamenev. They seemed a formidable, unbreakable duumvirate. But disagreements on food-supplies policy started to divide them. And whatever was done about this policy would inevitably deeply affect all other policies. The USSR was entering another political maelstrom.

PART TWO

'Vaterland.'

A Pravda *cartoon (1938) by Boris Yefimov alleging that the communist leaders put on show trial are like pigs being fed from the trough of Nazism.*

9

The First Five-Year Plan (1928–1932)

From 1928 Stalin and his associates undertook a series of actions that drastically rearranged and reinforced the compound of the Soviet order. Lenin's basic elements were maintained: the single-party state, the single official ideology, the manipulation of legality and the state's economic dominance. In this basic respect Stalin's group was justified in claiming to be championing the Leninist cause.

Yet certain other elements were greatly altered and these became the object of dispute. Compromises with national and cultural aspirations had existed since 1917, and there had been relaxations of religious policy from the early 1920s: Stalin brusquely reversed this approach. Moreover, he crudified politics and hyper-centralized administrative institutions. Yet this was still a compound bearing the handiwork of Lenin's communist party – and in economics, indeed, he strengthened the state's existing dominance: legal private enterprise above the level of highly-restricted individual production and commerce practically ceased. Stalin's enemies in the party contended that a rupture with Leninism had occurred and that a new system of Stalinism had been established. Official spokesmen, inveterate liars though they were, were nearer to the truth in this matter when they talked of the development of 'Marxism-Leninism-Stalinism'. Such a term asserted continuity while affirming that Stalin had changed the balance and composition of the elements of the Soviet compound.

The fracturing of the NEP began not in Moscow but in the provinces – and at the time there were few signs that anything was afoot. Nor did it start with foreign policy or factional struggles or industrializing schemes. The origins can be traced to a journey to the Urals and Siberia taken by Stalin in January 1928. He was travelling there on behalf of the Central Committee in order to identify what could be done about the fall-off in grain shipments to the towns. None of his colleagues had any idea of his true intentions.

Once he was beyond the scrutiny of his central party colleagues, Stalin brashly issued fresh instructions for the collection of cereal crops in the region. In many ways he was re-instituting the methods of War Communism as peasants were called to village gatherings and ordered to deliver their stocks of grain to the state authorities. The policy of grain requisitioning was replicated later in 1928 across the USSR. Anastas Mikoyan, Andrei Andreev, Andrei Zhdanov, Stanislav Kosior and Stalin's newly-discovered supporter in mid-Siberia, Sergei Syrtsov, were instructed to lead campaigns in the major agricultural regions. Over the next two years the New Economic Policy was piece by piece destroyed. In agriculture it was replaced by a system of collective farms. In industry it gave way to a Five-Year Plan which assigned both credit and production targets to factories, mines and construction sites. Private commercial firms vanished. Force was applied extensively. Kulaks were repressed, managers were persecuted, wages were lowered.

Planning as a concept acquired a great vogue around the world. The instability of capitalism after the Great War had an impact upon the attitudes of many people in the West, especially when the foundations of the global financial system were shaken by the Great Depression in autumn 1929. Mass unemployment afflicted all capitalist countries. There was a slump in trade and production across Europe. Bankrupt financiers leapt out of the windows of New York skyscrapers.

Central state direction of economic development gained in favour as politicians and journalists reported that the Soviet Union was avoiding the financial catastrophe that was engulfing the Western economies. Outside the global communist movement there continued to be abhorrence for the USSR; but the use of authoritarian measures to effect an exit from crisis acquired broader respectability. Dictatorship was not uncommon in inter-war Europe. Benito Mussolini, an ex-socialist, had seized power in Rome in 1922 for his National Fascist Party, and right-wing dictatorships were established in countries such as Poland, Romania and Yugoslavia. In Germany, too, democracy was under threat in the 1920s from a Nazi party which – like the German Communist Party – did not disguise its contempt for due legal process. Confidence in the old – and not so old – ways of conducting politics was widely being eroded.

Yet Stalin, while talking of the virtues of planning, did not have detailed projects in mind when changing policy in 1928–32. If he had a Grand Plan, he kept it strictly to himself. Nevertheless he was not behaving at random: his activities occurred within the framework of his prejudices and ambition; and there was an internal logic to the step-by-step choices that he made.

Stalin attracted much support from fellow communist leaders. The use of force on 'kulaks' was welcomed as an end of ideological compromise: Stalin seemed to be fulfilling the commitments of the October Revolution and ending the frustrations of the NEP. In particular, several central politicians warmed to his initiative: Central Committee Secretaries Vyacheslav Molotov and Lazar Kaganovich; Supreme Council of the National Economy Chairman Valeryan Kuibyshev; and Workers' and Peasants' Inspectorate Chairman Sergo Ordzhonikidze. Their enthusiasm for Stalin was replicated in many local party bodies. Favour was also shown by low-level functionaries in the OGPU, the Workers' and Peasants' Inspectorate, the Komsomol and the Russian Association of Proletarian Writers. Personnel in those institutions with an interest in increasing their control over society were in the forefront of his supporters. In Stalin they found a Politburo leader who gave them the opportunity they had been seeking.

Certain economists, too, backed his case. S. G. Strumilin argued that it did not matter if the setting of economic targets was not based on the normal extrapolation of statistics; his demand was always for the party to aim at achieving the impossible. This 'teleological' school of economic planning signified a determination to make the data fit any desired objective. Supporters such as Strumilin treated Stalin's programme like a priceless photographic film waiting to be exposed to the light by their eager professional chemistry.

Stalin's actions appalled his ally Nikolai Bukharin. The NEP had entered a critical phase by the winter of 1927–8; but whereas Bukharin wished to assure peasants that the party aimed to foster their immediate interests, Stalin had lost patience. Ostensibly Bukharin was in a strong position. The list of communist party luminaries who supported the NEP was impressive: Aleksei Rykov, Lenin's successor as Chairman of Sovnarkom; Mikhail Tomski, Chairman of the Central Council of Trade Unions; Nikolai Uglanov, Moscow City Party First Secretary. The fact that Bukharin, Rykov and Tomski also belonged to the Politburo meant that they could press their opinions at the summit of the political system. Moreover, they had privileged access to the media of public communication. Through the pages of *Pravda*, which Bukharin edited, they affirmed to their readers that the NEP had not been abandoned.

Stalin dared not contradict this. The NEP was closely associated with the name of Lenin, and Stalin always saw the point of identifying his policies as a continuation of Lenin's intentions. Even in later years, when the NEP had been completely jettisoned, Stalin went on claiming that his new measures were merely an incremental development of the NEP.

His sensitivity had been acute upon his return from the Urals and Siberia; for he knew that he could not yet count on being able to convince the central party leadership that his requisitioning campaign should be extended to the rest of the country. In January 1928 he had already been contemplating the rapid collectivization of Soviet agriculture as the sole means of preventing the recurrent crises in food supplies.[1] But he was still unclear how he might achieve this; and his need at the time was to withstand criticisms by Bukharin and his friends. The Politburo met in April 1928 to discuss the results of the requisitioning campaign. Bukharin was unsettled by the violence; but he, too, was reticent in public. Having just seen off the United Opposition, he did not wish to reveal any divisions in the ascendant party leadership. Thus although the Politburo condemned 'excesses' of local grain-seizing authorities, the resolution did not appear in the newspapers and did not mention the main culprit, Stalin, by name.

For some weeks it seemed to many who were not privy to the balance of authority in the Politburo that Bukharin was getting the upper hand. The July 1928 Central Committee plenum debated the party's attitude to the agrarian crisis, and Bukharin proposed that conciliatory measures were overdue. The plenum decided to raise prices paid by governmental agencies for grain. The hope was to revive the willingness of rural inhabitants to trade their surpluses of wheat and other cereal crops. The restoration of voluntary trade between countryside and town seemed to have become the central party's goal yet again. But the plenum's decision had little impact on the availability of food supplies and tensions in the Politburo did not abate. In September a frantic Bukharin published 'Notes of an Economist', an article which summarized the arguments for the party to abide by the NEP. The impression was given that official policy had reverted to its earlier position and that the emergency situation would shortly be brought to an end.[2]

In reality, Stalin and Bukharin were barely on speaking terms and Stalin had in no way become reconciled to rehabilitating the NEP. Bukharin was accustomed to standing up for his opinions. As a young Marxist in 1915, he had argued against Lenin on socialist political strategy. In 1918 he had led the Left Communists against signing the Treaty of Brest-Litovsk. In 1920–21 he had criticized not only Trotski but also Lenin in the 'trade union controversy'; and he had held his ground when Lenin had subsequently continued to attack his views on philosophy and culture.

He was intellectually inquisitive and rejected the conventional Bolshevik assumption that only Marxists could contribute to knowledge about history and politics. He lectured at the Institute of Red Professors, and brought on a group of young Bolshevik philosophers as his protégés. His mind had a cultural sophistication; he loved poetry and novels and was a talented painter in oils: he would always come back from his summertime trips to the mountains with freshly-finished canvases. He also liked a bit of levity in his life: he did cartwheels on a Paris pavement in order to impress a new wife.[3] Bukharin identified himself with the country's youth, often wearing the red necktie sported by teenage adherents of the Komsomol. Born in 1888 to a schoolmaster's family, he was nearly a decade younger than Stalin. As Lenin once remarked, he was 'the golden boy' of the Bolshevik party. Even oppositionists found it hard to dislike him.

Bukharin was no saint. In the 1920s he had shown his nasty side in internal party polemics about the NEP. In the universities, moreover, he imperturbably ruined the career of many non-communist academics. But he also had more than his fair share of naïvety. In particular, he had been taken in by Stalin's gruff charm. They appeared to get on famously together, and Bukharin did much to make Stalin respectable again after the brouhaha over Lenin's testament. By 1928 it was too late for Bukharin to admit to Kamenev and Zinoviev that they had been right – however belatedly, even in their case – about Stalin's personal degeneracy.

This was not a politician who had the insight or skills to defeat Stalin. By the last months of 1928 the spat between them was resumed when the results of Bukharin's defence of the NEP became apparent. The increase in prices offered by the state for agricultural produce failed to induce the peasantry to return to the market on the desired scale. At the Central Committee plenum in November, Stalin went back on to the offensive and demanded a comprehensive policy of requisitioning. From the Urals and Siberia there also came a proposal that the grain supplies should be seized mainly from the kulaks. This would be done, it was suggested, by local authorities calling a meeting of all peasants within a given locality and invoking them to indicate which of the richer households were hoarding grain. The poorer households were simultaneously to be enabled to have a share of the cereal stocks discovered during the campaign. This process, which became known as 'the Urals-Siberian method', was applied across the USSR from the winter of 1928–9.[4]

Every action by Stalin put Bukharin at a disadvantage; for the struggle between them was not confined to the problem of grain supplies. In March 1928, at Stalin's instigation, it had been announced that a counter-revolutionary plot had been discovered among the technical staff at the Shakhty coal-mine in the Don Basin. The trial was a judicial travesty. Stalin took a close, direct part in decisions about the engineers.[5] His ulterior purpose was easy to guess. He was grasping the opportunity to use Shakhty as a means of intimidating every economist, manager or even party official who objected to the raising of tempos of industrial growth. This was a feature of his *modus operandi*. Although his own basic thinking was unoriginal, he could quickly evaluate and utilize the ideas of others: Stalin knew what he liked when he saw it, and his supporters quickly learned the kind of thing that appealed to him.

It ought to be noted that he also added his own little flourishes. The Shakhty engineers were physically abused by the OGPU, forced to memorize false self-incriminations and paraded in a show-trial in May and June 1928. Five of the accused were shot; most of the rest were sentenced to lengthy terms of imprisonment. The Shakhty trial stirred up industrial policy as crudely as Stalin's visit to the Urals and Siberia had done to agricultural policy. Experts in Gosplan were harassed into planning for breakneck economic growth; and factory and mining managers were intimidated into trying to put all Gosplan's projects into effect. Otherwise they faced being sacked and even arrested.

A campaign of industrialization was being undertaken that went beyond the ambitions of the defeated United Opposition. By mid-summer 1928, Stalin was telling the central party leadership that industry's growth required that a 'tribute' should be exacted from agriculture. Factories were to be built with the revenues from the countryside. Yet most of the expansion, he declared, would be financed not by rural taxation but by a further massive campaign of rationalization of industrial production. Thus the 'optimal' version of the Plan sanctioned by the Fifth USSR Congress of Soviets in May 1929 anticipated a rise by only thirty-two per cent in the number of workers and employees in industry whereas labour productivity was expected to rise by 110 per cent. Stalin was supported robustly by Molotov, Kuibyshev and Ordzhonikidze in the press and at party gatherings. Their prognosis was outlandish (although it may possibly have been intended sincerely); but it allowed them to predict that the average real wages of the working class would rise by seventy per cent.[6]

This placed Bukharin in the unenviable position of arguing against an economic policy purporting to guarantee an improvement in the standard of living of the urban poor. Stalin's belligerence increased. At the joint meeting of the Central Committee and the Central Control Commission in January 1929 he upbraided Bukharin for his objections and accused him of factionalism. The last Politburo leader to be found guilty of this, Trotski, was deported from the country in the same month. Bukharin was placed in serious political danger as the charge was levelled that he and Rykov and Tomski headed a Right Deviation from the principles of Marxism-Leninism.

'Deviation' was a significant term, implying that Bukharin's group was too ill-organized to merit being called an Opposition.[7] But Bukharin did not give up. At the next Central Committee meeting, in April 1929, he attacked the pace of industrialization being imposed by Stalin; he also castigated the resumption of violent requisitioning of agricultural produce. Stalin counter-attacked immediately: 'None of your côterie is a Marxist: they're fraudsters. Not one of you has got an understanding of Lenin.' Bukharin retorted: 'What, are you the only one with such an understanding?'[8] But the mood of the majority of Central Committee members was against the 'Rightists', and the industrial quotas and the grain seizures were approved. Across the country the active supporters of Bukharin, few as they were, were dismissed from their posts. In Moscow, Nikolai Uglanov was replaced by Molotov as City Party Committee secretary. The NEP became virtually irretrievable.

Stalin was roused by the response to his reorientation of policy. The Urals Regional Committee, for instance, commissioned the making of a ceremonial sword: on one side of the blade was inscribed 'Chop the Right Deviation', on the other 'Chop the Left Deviation'; and on the butt were the words: 'Beat Every Conciliator'. This was the language Stalin liked to hear. His career would be ruined unless the Five-Year Plan was successful, and he was determined that there should be no shilly-shallying. Stalin put the matter vividly in 1931:

'To lower the tempos means to lag behind. And laggards are beaten. But we don't want to be beaten. No, we don't want it! The history of old Russia consisted, amongst other things, in her being beaten continually for her backwardness. She was beaten by the Mongol khans. She was beaten by the Turkish beys. She was beaten by the Swedish feudal lords. She was beaten by the Polish-Lithuanian nobles. She was beaten by the Anglo-French capitalists. She was beaten by the Japanese barons. She was beaten by all of them for her backwardness.'[9]

The economic transformation, in Stalin's opinion, could not be accomplished unless the USSR stayed clear of military entanglements abroad. His Five-Year Plan was premised on the Kremlin's need to purchase up-to-date machinery from these powers. It would obviously be difficult to induce foreign governments and business companies to enter into commercial deals if there remained any suspicion that the Red Army might be about to try again to spread revolution on the points of its bayonets.

The ascendant party leaders assumed that Soviet grain exports would pay for the machinery imports; but there was a further slump in global cereal prices in 1929: the result was that although over twice as much grain was shipped abroad in 1930 than in 1926–7, the revenue from such sales rose by only six per cent.[10] Since gold exports were not enough to bridge the gap, short-term credits had to be raised to finance the Five-Year Plan. Banks and businesses in the West were only too eager to sign deals with the USSR after the Great Depression of autumn. Up-to-date machinery was imported, especially from the USA and Germany. Contracts were signed, too, for large foreign firms to supply expertise to assist with the construction of new Soviet enterprises. The American Ford car company, the greatest symbol of world capitalism, signed a deal to help to build a gigantic automotive works in Nizhni Novgorod.[11]

Stalin hardly needed to be nudged towards allaying Western fears about Soviet international intentions. Under the NEP he had made a name for himself with the slogan of 'Socialism in One Country'. Repeatedly he had suggested that the USSR should avoid involvement in capitalist countries' affairs while building a socialist society and economy at home. Foreign policy during the Five-Year Plan was made subordinate to domestic policy more firmly than ever.

Bukharin came to agree with Trotski that Stalin had abandoned the objective of European socialist revolution. The unequivocality of this judgement was incorrect. In 1928, most communists grew to believe in the imminent collapse of capitalism. Stalin went along with them so long as nothing was done to endanger the USSR's security. The German Communist Party contained many leaders who wanted to break with the policy of a 'united front' with other socialist parties in Germany, and in the first year of the Five-Year Plan it was hard to dissuade these leaders from thinking revolutionary thoughts. Under a certain amount of pressure from the German communist leadership, the Comintern at the Sixth Comintern Congress in 1928 laid down that an instruction was given that the parties such as the German Social-Democrats and the British Labour Party should be treated as communism's main political adversaries. Thus the Comintern took 'a turn to the left'.[12] The European political far right, including Hitler's Nazis, was largely to be disregarded. The task for the German Communist Party was to build up its strength separately so that it might seize power at some future date.

Among Stalin's several motives in supporting the international turn to the left was a wish to cause maximum discomfort to Bukharin, who was closely identified as the NEP's advocate at home and abroad. Throughout 1928–9 Bukharin was humiliated by being forced to condemn 'rightist' policies among the various member parties of Comintern. This was of considerable help to Stalin in the imposition of the Five-Year Plan at home. Bukharin was no longer the ascendant star of official world communism.

Constantly the Politburo quickened the projected pace of industrialization. Cheap labour was made available by peasants fleeing the villages. They came for work and for ration-cards, and their arrival permitted a lowering of the wages of labourers; for the commitment to raising wages was soon found unrealistic. In spring 1929 Stalin, seeking still cheaper labour, appointed a Central Committee commission under N. Yanson to explore opportunities for convicts to work on projects in the USSR's less hospitable regions.

The prisons were already crammed with peasants who had resisted being pushed into collective farms: Yanson recommended their transfer to the forced-labour camps subject to the OGPU.[13] Among the first results was the formation of the 'Dalstroi' trust in the Far East which ran the notorious gold mines of Kolyma.

The Politburo also resolved the question as to how to handle those peasants who remained in the countryside. After two successive winters of grain seizures, the peasants would not voluntarily maintain their sown area. Bolsheviks already believed that collective farms, with large production units and electrically-powered machinery, were the solution to agrarian backwardness. Thus the Politburo majority, against Bukharin's counsel, came to the opinion that compulsory collectivization should be initiated (although the fiction was maintained in public that coercion would not be used). To Molotov was entrusted the job of explaining this to the Central Committee in November 1929. Bukharin was sacked from the Politburo at the same meeting and, in the following month, Stalin's fiftieth birthday was celebrated with extravagant eulogies in the mass media. By January 1930 the Politburo was insisting that a quarter of the sown area should be held by collective farms within two years. An agricultural revolution was heralded.

And yet both agriculture and industry were altogether too chaotic to be described without reservation as being integrated within 'a planned economy'. For example, the Five-Year Plan of 1928–33 was drawn up six months after it was said to have been inaugurated (and the Plan was said to be completed a year before it was meant to end). Rough commands were of a more practical importance than carefully-elaborated planning; and the commands were based on guesses, prejudices and whims. At best the officials of Gosplan could rectify the worst mistakes before too much damage was done. But huge human suffering occurred before any particular experiment was halted on the grounds of being dyseconomic.

'Class struggle' was intensified through a governmental assault upon the so-called kulaks. It was laid down that the collective farms should be formed exclusively from poor and middling peasant households. Kulaks stood to lose most from collectivization in material terms; they tended also to be more assertive than average. At least, this is how Stalin saw things. He set up a Politburo commission to investigate how to decapitate kulak resistance. Its proposals were accepted by him and incorporated in a Sovnarkom decree of February 1930. Kulaks were to be disbarred from joining collective farms and divided into three categories. Those in category one were to be dispatched to forced-labour settlements or shot. Category two comprised households deemed more hostile to the government; these were to go to distant provinces. Category three consisted of the least 'dangerous' households, which were allowed to stay in their native district but on a smaller patch of land. Between five and seven million persons were treated as belonging to kulak families.[14]

The decree could not be fulfilled without magnifying violence. The Red Army and the OGPU were insufficient in themselves and anyway the Politburo could not depend on the implicit obedience of their officers of rural origins.[15] And so tough young lads from the factories, militia and the party went out to the villages to enforce the establishment of collective farms. About 25,000 of them rallied to the Politburo's summons. Before they set out from the towns, these '25,000-ers' were told that the kulaks were responsible for organizing a 'grain strike' against the towns. They were not issued with detailed instructions as to how to distinguish the rich, middling and poor peasants from each other. Nor were they given limits on their use of violence. The Politburo set targets for grain collection, for collectivization and for de-kulakization, and did not mind how these targets were hit.

But when they arrived in the villages, the '25,000-ers' saw for themselves that many hostile peasants were far from being rich. The central party apparatus imaginatively introduced a special category of 'sub-kulaks' who were poor but yet opposed the government.[16] Sub-kulaks were to be treated as if they were kulaks. Consequently Stalin's collectivizing mayhem, involving executions and deportations, was never confined to the better-off households. The slightest resistance to the authorities was met with punitive violence. With monumental insincerity he wrote an article for *Pravda* in March 1930, 'Dizzy with Success', in which he called local functionaries to task for abusing their authority. But this was a temporizing posture. For Stalin, the priority remained mass collectivization. By the time of the harvest of 1931, collective farms held practically all the land traditionally given over to cereal crops. Stalin and the Politburo had won the agrarian war.

The price was awful. Probably four to five million people perished in 1932–3 from 'de-kulakization' and from grain seizures.[17] The dead and the dying were piled on to carts by the urban detachments and pitched into common graves without further ceremony. Pits were dug on the outskirts of villages for the purpose. Child survivors, their stomachs swollen through hunger, gnawed grass and tree-bark and begged for crusts. Human beings were not the only casualties. While the government's policies were killing peasants, peasants were killing their livestock: they had decided that they would rather eat their cattle and horses than let them be expropriated by the collective farms. Even some of Stalin's colleagues blanched when they saw the effects with their own eyes. For instance, Ordzhonikidze was aghast at the behaviour of officials in eastern Ukraine;[18] but he felt no need to criticize mass compulsory collectivization as general policy.

Collectivization was a rural nightmare. It is true that the average harvest in 1928–30 was good.[19] But this was chiefly the product of excellent weather conditions. It certainly did not result from improved agricultural management; for often the collective farm chairmen were rural ne'er-do-wells or inexpert party loyalists from the towns. Nor did the state fulfil its promise to supply the countryside with 100,000 tractors by the end of the Five-Year Plan. Only half of these were built,[20] and most of them were used inefficiently through lack of experienced drivers and mechanics.

With the exception of 1930, mass collectivization meant that not until the mid-1950s did agriculture regain the level of output achieved in the last years before the Great War. Conditions in the countryside were so dire that the state had to pump additional resources into the country in order to maintain the new agrarian order. Increased investment in tractors was not the only cost incurred. Revenues had to be diverted not only to agronomists, surveyors and farm chairmen but also to soldiers, policemen and informers. Moreover, 'machine-tractor stations' had to be built from 1929 to provide equipment and personnel for the introduction of technology (as well as to provide yet another agency to control the peasantry). Otherwise the rickety structure of authority would have collapsed. No major state has inflicted such grievous economic damage on itself in peacetime.

Yet Stalin could draw up a balance sheet that, from his standpoint, was favourable. From collectivization he acquired a reservoir of terrified peasants who would supply him with cheap industrial labour. To some extent, too, he secured his ability to export Soviet raw materials in order to pay for imports of industrial machinery (although problems arose with foreign trade in 1931–2). Above all, he put an end to the recurrent crises faced by the state in relation to urban food supplies as the state's grain collections rose from 10.8 million tons in 1928–9 to 22.8 million tons in 1931–2.[21] After collectivization it was the countryside, not the towns, which went hungry if the harvest was bad.

Stalin was still more delighted with the record of industry. The large factories and mines had been governmentally-owned since 1917–19, but the number of such enterprises rose steeply after 1928. Thirty-eight per cent of industrial capital stock by the end of 1934 was located in factories built in the previous half-dozen years.[22] Simultaneously the smaller manufacturing firms – most of which had been in private hands during the NEP – were closed down. The First Five-Year Plan was meant to end in September 1933; in fact its completion was announced in December 1932. Mines and factories were claimed to have doubled their production since 1928. This was exaggeration. Yet even sceptical estimates put the annual expansion in industrial output at ten per cent between 1928 and 1941; and the production of capital goods probably grew at twice the rate of consumer goods during the Five-Year Plan.[23] The USSR had at last been pointed decisively towards the goal of a fully industrialized society.

Stalin the Man of Steel boasted that he had introduced 'socialism' to the villages. The nature of a collective farm was ill-defined; no Bolshevik before 1917 – not even Lenin – had explained exactly what such farms should be like. There was much practical experimentation with them after 1917: at one end of the range there were farms that required their employees to take decisions collectively and share land, housing, equipment and income equally, regardless of personal input of labour; at the other end it was possible to find arrangements allowing peasant households to form a co-operative and yet keep their land, housing and equipment separately from each other and to make their own separate profits.

The idea of peasants taking most of their own decisions was anathema to Stalin. The government, he insisted, should own the land, appoint the farm chairmen and set the grain-delivery quotas. His ideal organization was the *sovkhoz*. This was a collective farm run on the same principles as a state-owned factory. Local authorities marked out the land for each sovkhoz and hired peasants for fixed wages. Such a type of farming was thought eminently suitable for the grain-growing expanses in Ukraine and southern Russia. Yet Stalin recognized that most peasants were ill-disposed to becoming wage labourers, and he yielded to the extent of permitting most farms to be of the kolkhoz type. In a kolkhoz the members were rewarded by results. If the quotas were not met, the farm was not paid. Furthermore, each peasant was paid a fraction of the farm wage-fund strictly in accordance with the number of 'labour days' he or she had contributed to the farming year.

And so the kolkhoz was defined as occupying a lower level of socialist attainment than the sovkhoz. In the long run the official expectation was that all kolkhozes would be turned into sovkhozes in Soviet agriculture; but still the kolkhoz, despite its traces of private self-interest, was treated as a socialist organizational form.

In reality, most *kolkhozniki*, as the kolkhoz members were known, could no more make a profit in the early 1930s than fly to Mars. Rural society did not submit without a struggle and 700,000 peasants were involved in disturbances at the beginning of 1930.[24] But the resistance was confined to a particular village or group of villages. Fewer large revolts broke out in Russia than in areas where non-Russians were in the majority: Kazakhstan, the North Caucasus, Ukraine and parts of Siberia. Yet the official authorities had advantages in their struggle against the peasants which had been lacking in 1920–22.[25] In the collectivization campaign from the late 1920s it was the authorities who went on the offensive, and they had greatly superior organization and fire-power. Peasants were taken by surprise and counted themselves lucky if they were still alive by the mid-1930s. Battered into submission, they could only try to make the best of things under the new order imposed by the Soviet state.

An entire way of life, too, was being pummelled out of existence. The peasant household was no longer the basic social unit recognized by the authorities. Grain quotas were imposed on the collective farm as a whole, and peasants were given their instructions as individuals rather than as members of households.

Industrial workers were fortunate by comparison. Except during the famine of 1932–3, their consumption of calories was as great as it had been under the NEP. But although conditions were better in the towns than in the countryside, they were still very hard. The quality of the diet worsened and food rationing had to be introduced in all towns and cities: average calory levels were maintained only because more bread and potatoes were eaten while consumption of meat fell by two thirds. Meanwhile wages for blue-collar jobs fell in real terms by a half in the course of the Five-Year Plan.[26] Of course, this is not the whole story. The men and women who had served their factory apprenticeship in the 1920s were encouraged to take evening classes and secure professional posts. Consequently many existing workers obtained material betterment through promotion. About one and a half million managers and administrators in 1930–33 had recently been elevated from manual occupations.[27]

This was also one of the reasons why the working class endured the Five-Year Plan's rigours without the violent resistance offered by peasant communities. Another was that most of the newcomers to industry, being mainly rural young men who filled the unskilled occupations, had neither the time nor the inclination to strike for higher wages; and the OGPU was efficient at detecting and suppressing such dissent as it arose. Go-slows, walk-outs and even occasional demonstrations took place, but these were easily contained.

Of course, Stalin and OGPU chief Yagoda left nothing to chance. The OGPU scoured its files for potential political opponents still at large. Former Mensheviks and Socialist-Revolutionaries were hunted out even though their parties had barely existed since the 1922 show-trial of the Socialist-Revolutionaries. But whereas Lenin had trumped up charges against genuinely existing parties, Stalin invented parties out of the air. A show-trial of the imaginary 'Industrial Party' was staged in November 1930. The defendants were prepared for their judicial roles by an OGPU torturer; they were mainly persons who had worked for the Soviet regime but had previously been industrialists, high-ranking civil servants or prominent Mensheviks and Socialist-Revolutionaries. In 1931 a trial of the fictitious 'Union Bureau' of the Menshevik party was organized. Trials were held in the major cities of Russia and the other Soviet republics. Newspapers were stuffed with stories of professional malefactors caught, arraigned and sentenced.

Stalin glorified the changes in the political environment by declaring that the party had 're-formed its own ranks in battle order'. Administrators with 'suspect' class origins or political opinions were sacked from their jobs. Workers were hallooed into denouncing any superiors who obstructed the implementation of the Five-Year Plan. A witch-hunt atmosphere was concocted. For Stalin used the party as a weapon to terrify all opposition to his economic policies. He needed to operate through an institution that could be trusted to maintain political fidelity, organizational solidity and ideological rectitude while the Soviet state in general was being transformed and reinforced. In the late 1920s only the party could fulfil this function.

But the party, too, needed to be made dependable. Expulsions started in May 1929, resulting in a loss of eleven per cent of the membership. A recruitment campaign began at the same time, and the party expanded its number of members from 1.3 million in 1928 to 2.2 million in 1931.[28] Party secretaries at the various local levels were the Politburo's local chief executives. Republican party leaders were handpicked by the Politburo for this role; and in the RSFSR Stalin constructed a regional tier in the party's organizational hierarchy which brought together groups of provinces under the reinforced control of a single regional committee.[29] Thus the Mid-Volga Regional Committee oversaw collectivization across an agricultural region the size of the entire United Kingdom. Party secretaries had been virtually the unchallengeable economic bosses in the localities since the middle of the Civil War. But there was also a large difference. In the 1920s private agriculture, commerce and industry had been widespread; under the Five-Year Plan only a few corners of non-state economic activity survived.

Yet still the central leadership could not regard the party with equanimity. The picture of over-fulfilled economic plans painted by the newspapers involved much distortion. And where there was indeed over-fulfilment, as in steel production, its quality was often too poor for use in manufacturing. Wastage occurred on a huge scale and the problem of uncoordinated production was ubiquitous. The statistics themselves were fiddled not only by a central party machine wishing to fool the world but also by local functionaries wanting to trick the central party machine. Deceit was deeply embedded in the mode of industrial and agricultural management.

It has been asserted that shoddy, unusable goods were so high a proportion of output that official claims for increases in output were typically double the reality. If the increase in output has been exaggerated, then perhaps Stalin's forced-rate industrialization and forcible mass collectivization were not indispensable to the transformation of Russia into a military power capable of defeating Hitler in the Second World War. An extrapolation of the NEP's economic growth rate into the 1930s even suggests that a Bukharinist leadership would have attained an equal industrial capacity. This is not the end of the debate; for as the First Five-Year Plan continued, Stalin diverted investment increasingly towards the defence sub-sector. Nearly six per cent of such capital was dedicated to the Red Army's requirements: this was higher than the combined total for agricultural machines, tractors, cars, buses and lorries.[30] It was easier for Stalin to bring this about than it would have been for Bukharin who wanted peasant aspirations to be taken into account.

Yet Bukharin would have ruled a less traumatized society, and been more able to count on popular goodwill. Bukharin's perceptiveness in foreign policy might also have helped him. Stalin's guesses about Europe were very faulty. In the German elections of 1932 the communists were instructed to campaign mostly against the social-democrats: Hitler's Nazis were to be ignored. There were comrades from Berlin such as Franz Neumann who questioned Stalin's judgement. But Stalin calmly replied: 'Don't you think, Neumann, that if the nationalists come to power in Germany, they'll be so completely preoccupied with the West that we'll be able to build up socialism in peace?'[31] Stalin's judgement did not lack perceptiveness: he correctly anticipated that Hitler would stir up a deal of trouble for the Allies who had imposed the Treaty of Versailles – and since the end of the Great War it had been Britain and France, not Germany, which had caused greatest trouble to Soviet political leaders.

Yet when due allowance is made, his comment underestimated the profound danger of Nazism to the USSR and to Europe as a whole. It also displayed the influence of Leninist thinking. Lenin, too, had asserted that the German extreme right might serve the purpose of smashing up the post-Versailles order;[32] he had also stressed that Soviet diplomacy should be based on the principle of evading entanglement in inter-capitalist wars. The playing of one capitalist power against another was an enduring feature of Soviet foreign policy.[33] This does not mean that Lenin would have been as casual as Stalin about Adolf Hitler. Yet as socialism was misbuilt in the USSR, silence was enforced by the Politburo about the risks being taken with the country's security.

Stalin had tried to root out every possible challenge to both domestic and foreign policies. His suspicions were not without foundation. Many party and state functionaries had supported his rupture with the NEP without anticipating the exact policies and their consequences. Most of them had not bargained for famine, terror and Stalin's growing personal dictatorship. Small groupings therefore came together to discuss alternative policies. Beso Lominadze and Sergei Syrtsov, one-time supporters of Stalin, expressed their disgruntlement to each other in autumn 1929. An informer denounced them and they were expelled from the Central

Committee.[34] In 1932 another group was formed by Mikhail Ryutin, who sought Stalin's removal from power; and yet another group coalesced under A. P. Smirnov, Nikolai Eismont and V. N. Tolmachev. Both groups were detected by the OGPU and arrested; but their existence at a time when the punishments for 'factionalism' were increasing in severity showed how restive the party had become.

Then there were the oppositionist leaders waiting for a chance to return to the Politburo: Kamenev and Zinoviev had publicly recanted and been allowed to return to the party in 1928; Bukharin had avoided expulsion from the party by publicly accepting official party policy in November 1929. Their professions of loyalty convinced no one, and Trotski wasted no time in publishing his *Bulletin of the Opposition* from abroad and in initiating a secret correspondence with several disaffected communist officials.[35] All these disgraced former leaders knew that they could count on many existing party functionaries, activists and rank-and-file members to support them if ever an opportunity arose.

They might also be able to appeal to the persons who had walked out on the party or had been expelled: there were about 1,500,000 such individuals by 1937.[36] In addition, the Socialist-Revolutionaries had possessed a million members in 1917, the Mensheviks a quarter of a million. Dozens of other parties in Russia and the borderlands had also existed. Huge sections of the population had always hated the entire Bolshevik party. Whole social strata were embittered: priests, shopkeepers, gentry, mullahs, industrialists, traders and 'bourgeois specialists'. Among these 'former people' (*byvshie lyudi*), as the Bolsheviks brusquely described persons of influence before the October Revolution, hatred of Bolshevism was strong. Many peasants and workers had felt the same. And Stalin had made countless new enemies for the party. Collectivization, de-kulakization, urban show-trials and the forced-labour penal system had wrought suffering as great as had occurred in the Civil War.

Stalin had engineered a second revolution; he had completed the groundwork of an economic transformation. But his victory was not yet totally secure. For Stalin, the realization of the First Five-Year

Plan could only be the first victory in the long campaign for his personal dictatorship and his construction of a mighty industrial state.

10

Fortresses under Storm: Culture, Religion, Nation

Stalin's ambition was not confined to economics and politics. Like other Bolsheviks, he had always seen that the creation of a communist society necessitated further changes. Communist leaders also aspired to raise the level of education and technical skills in the population. They wished to expand the social base of their support; they had to dissolve Soviet citizens' attachment to their national identity and religion. Bolshevism stood for literacy, numeracy, internationalism and atheism, and this commitment was among the reasons for the replacement of the NEP with the First Five-Year Plan.

Of all the regime's achievements, it was its triumph over illiteracy that earned the widest esteem – and even anti-Bolsheviks were among the admirers. Education was treated as a battlefront. Only forty per cent of males between nine and forty-nine years of age had been able to read and write in 1897; this proportion had risen to ninety-four per cent by 1939.[1] The number of schools rose to 199,000 by the beginning of the 1940–41 academic year.[2] They were built not only in major areas of habitation like Russia and Ukraine but also in the most far-flung parts of the country such as Uzbekistan. Pedagogical institutes were created to train a generation of young teachers to take up their duties not only in schools for children and adolescents but also in polytechnics, night-schools and factory clubs for adults. Compulsory universal schooling was implemented with revolutionary gusto. The USSR was fast becoming a literate society.

As workers and ex-peasants thronged into the new educational institutions, they could buy reading materials at minimal cost. *Pravda* and *Izvestiya* in the 1930s were sold daily for ten kopeks, and the print-run of newspapers rose from 9.4 million copies in 1927 to 38 million in 1940.[3] Other literature, too, was avidly purchased. The poet Boris Slutski recalled: 'It may have been stupid economically, but books were sold for next to nothing, more cheaply than tobacco and bread.'[4]

Revenues were also channelled into the provision of inexpensive facilities for relaxation. By the end of the 1930s the USSR had 28,000 cinemas.[5] Football, ice-hockey, athletics and gymnastics were turned into major sports for both participants and spectators. All-Union, republican, regional and local competitions proliferated across the country. For those who wanted quieter forms of recreation, 'houses of culture' were available with their own reading-rooms, notice-boards, stages and seating. Each medium-sized town had its theatre. Drama and ballet became popular with a public which looked forward to visits by companies on tour from Moscow. The authorities also laid aside space for parks. Families took Sunday strolls over public lawns – and the largest of all was the Park of Culture, which was named after the novelist Maksim Gorki, in the capital.

As in other industrial countries, the radio was becoming a medium of mass communication. Performers and commentators based in Moscow became celebrities throughout the USSR. News reports vied for attention with symphony concerts and variety entertainments. The telephone network was widened. Communications between district and district, town and town, republic and republic were impressively strengthened.

The foundation of new cities such as Magnitogorsk was celebrated (although *Pravda* was not allowed to report that a segment of the labour-force used for the construction consisted of Gulag prisoners).[6] Housing was not built as fast as factories. But Russian towns whose houses had been chiefly of wooden construction were becoming characterized by edifices of brick and stone; and most new dwellings were apartments in immense blocks whose heating was supplied by communal boilers. The steam escaping through air-vents was a feature of the broad thoroughfares. The internal combustion engine took the place of horse-drawn vehicles for people going about their working lives. Goods were transported in lorries. In Moscow, the first section of the underground railway came into operation in 1935. A fresh style of life was introduced in remarkably short time so that Stalin's slogan that 'there are no fortresses the Bolsheviks cannot storm!' seemed justified.

Thus a triumph for 'modernity' was claimed as the USSR advanced decisively towards becoming an urban, literate society with access to twentieth-century industrial technology; and Stalin's adherents declared their modernity superior to all others by virtue of its being collectivist. The typical apartment block contained flats called *kommunalki*. Each such flat was occupied by several families sharing the same kitchen and toilet. Cafeterias were provided at workplaces so that meals need not be taken at home. The passenger vehicles produced by automotive factories were mainly buses and trams rather than cars – and such cars as were manufactured were bought mainly by institutions and not by individuals. State enterprises, which had a monopoly of industrial output from the end of the NEP, were steered away from catering for the individual choices of consumers. Whereas capitalism manufactured each product in a competitive variety, communism's rationale was that this competition involved a waste of resources. Why waste money by developing and advertising similar products?

And so a pair of boots, a table, a light-bulb or a tin of sardines bought in Vladivostok or Archangel or Stavropol would have the same size and packaging. Clothing, too, became drab; local styles of attire disappeared as kolkhozniki were issued with working clothes from the factories and as village artisans ceased production. Standardization of design, too, was a basic governmental objective. Uniformity had been installed as a key positive value. Stalin was proud of his policies. Brazenly he announced to a mass meeting: 'Life has become better, life has become gayer!'[7]

The changes in life were not better or gayer for everyone. Wage differentials had been sharply widened; material egalitarianism, which had anyway not been practised even in the October Revolution, was denounced. The administrative élites were amply rewarded in a society which had undergone huge structural change since the NEP. Spivs, grain-traders, shopkeepers and workshop owners had gone the way of the aristocracy, the gentry and the 'big bourgeoisie'. The administrators had the cash to pay for goods in the sole retail outlets where high-quality consumer goods were on legal sale. These were state shops belonging to the *Torgsin* organization. In a Torgsin shop a previously well-off citizen could deposit some family heirloom which the shop would sell at a commission on the citizen's behalf.[8] Stalin's economy was not all tractors, tanks and canals; it was also luxury goods, albeit luxury goods that were not being made in Soviet factories but were being sold on by individuals who had fallen on hard times since 1917.

By means of these blandishments the Politburo aimed to ensure that the stratum of newly promoted administrators would remain keen supporters of the NEP's abandonment; and such persons were a large proportion of the fourfold increase in the number of state employees in institutions of education, health, housing, and public administration between 1926 and the end of the 1930s. But life was tough even for the middle-ranking administrators. The new schools, apartment blocks, hotels and kindergartens took years to build. Most working-class people, moreover, had yet to benefit at all from the general improvements promised by the Politburo. A generation was being asked to sacrifice its comfort for the benefit of its children and grandchildren. Hunger, violence and chaos were widespread, and the rupture of social linkages drastically increased the sense of loneliness in both the towns and the countryside. This was not a society capable of being at ease with itself.

Stalin, too, felt uneasy lest political opposition might arise inside or outside the party to exploit the situation. His attitude to Martemyan Ryutin, who was arrested in 1932 for leading a secret little group of communists who denounced his despotic rule and called for his removal from power, supplied a terrifying signal of his intentions. The fact that Ryutin had once belonged to the Central Committee apparently did not stop Stalin from calling for his execution. The Politburo instead ordered him to be sentenced to ten years' detention in the Gulag. This treatment of an oppositionist was horrific by most standards, but was much too light for Stalin's taste.

Yet he felt compelled to yield somewhat to the warnings being given, inside and outside the party, that failure to reduce the tempos of economic development would result in disaster. Even many of his central and local supporters stressed that conditions in industry were altogether too chaotic for the Second Five-Year Plan, introduced at the beginning of 1933, to be fulfilled in most of its objectives. A hurried re-drafting took place and a lower rate of growth was accepted. The new expectation was for a doubling of the output of industrial producers' goods in the half-decade before the end of 1937. This was still a very rapid growth, but not at the breakneck speed of the First Five-Year Plan. The Politburo began to lay its emphasis upon completing the construction of the half-built factories and mines and getting them into full production. Consolidation of existing projects became the priority in the industrial sector.[9]

As policy was being modified in 1932, Bukharin was appointed chief editor of *Izvestiya*. Meanwhile Sergo Ordzhonikidze, as Chairman of the Supreme Council of the National Economy in 1930–32 and as People's Commissar for Heavy Industry from 1932, protected managers and engineers from persecution.[10]

These modulations in official stance were extended to agriculture, which was in a frightful condition. In 1932 the fantastic scheme to increase state grain procurements by nearly thirty per cent over the previous year was quietly abandoned. The total of cereal crops actually obtained by the state did not rise at all, but dropped by nearly a fifth.[11] A decree was passed in the same year permitting the establishment of 'kolkhoz markets', where peasants could trade their surplus produce so long as they worked on those few kolkhozes which had fulfilled their quota of deliveries to the state. Another decree in 1933 allowed each household in a kolkhoz to cultivate a garden allotment for personal consumption or sale. Private profit was reintroduced even though it was banned from official terminology. In any case, these concessions were restricted to the margins of economic activity. Most industry, agriculture and commerce remained under strict state control; and the mass deportation of kulaks was intensified in the Kuban region and the North Caucasus. Yet the lesson had been learned that not even the economy of Stalin's USSR could function without some residual components of the market.

And so the hope was inspired in some observers that Stalin's demeanour during the First Five-Year Plan had been an aberration and that he would revert to less severe methods. Perhaps the party was about to return to the NEP. When he told the Central Committee plenum in January 1933 that he would not 'go on whipping the country', he was heard with relief by most of his listeners.[12]

Yet at the same plenum he bared his tigrine fangs as he advanced the following proposition: 'The abolition of classes is not obtained through the elimination of class struggle but through its reinforcement.'[13] For Stalin, his victory in the First Five-Year Plan was an occasion for the intensification rather than the relaxation of state violence. He pounced on his friend Ordzhonikidze for objecting to trials being held of officials from the People's Commissariats for Heavy Industry and Agriculture. According to Stalin, Ordzhonikidze was guilty of hooliganism while Kaganovich, who was not unsympathetic to Ordzhonikidze, was accused of joining 'the camp of the party's reactionary elements'.[14] The Boss, as his associates referred to him, was prowling with menace. The gravest snub he suffered face to face came not from an associate but from his wife Nadezhda, who seems to have agreed with Bukharin that the countryside had been ravaged by mass collectivization. Nor was she willing to tolerate his alleged flirtations with other women. After an altercation with him in November 1932, she had gone outside and shot herself.[15]

He had always been a solitary fellow, but the suicide of Nadezhda, whom he had loved despite their stormy relationship, shoved him further into himself. Stalin's early life had been hard. Born to a Georgian couple in the little town of Gori near Tiflis, his real name was Iosif Dzhugashvili. His birthday was given out officially as 21 December 1879; but the parish records indicate that he entered this world a year earlier.[16] Why he wished to alter the date remains a mystery; but, whatever his reasons, such a desire was in keeping with a man who liked to manipulate the image that others held of him.

Iosif's father was a child-beating drunkard who died leaving the family penniless; but Katerina Dzhugashvili, the mother of Iosif, managed to have him enrolled in the Tiflis Ecclesiastical Seminary. He quickly picked up the Russian language and the rhythms of the catechism; but he was also rebellious: like thousands of adolescents of his generation, he preferred revolutionary literature to the Bible. After being expelled from the seminary, he wandered over the Transcaucasus picking up odd jobs and getting involved with clandestine political circles. When news of the split of the Russian Social-Democratic Labour Party reached him, he sided with the Bolsheviks whereas most Georgian Marxists became Mensheviks. Young Dzhugashvili, whose pseudonym was first Koba and then Stalin (or 'Man of Steel'), reacted positively to themes of dictatorship, terror, modernity, progress and leadership in Lenin's writings.

Stalin became an organizer for the Bolsheviks and so underwent arrest several times. His articles on the 'national question' commended him to Lenin as 'the wonderful Georgian', and he was co-opted to the Bolshevik Central Committee in 1912. He was sent to St Petersburg to edit the legal Bolshevik newspaper *Pravda*, but was quickly captured and exiled to Siberia. There he stayed until 1917. A street accident he had suffered as a lad left him with a slightly shortened arm, and because of this he escaped conscription into the Imperial Army.

Returning to the Russian capital after the February Revolution, he was not fêted to the extent of Lenin and the *émigré* veterans. He seemed unimpressive alongside them. Unlike them, he had made only brief trips abroad. He could not speak German or French or English. He was a poor orator, a plodding theorist and a prickly character. Yet his organizational expeditiousness was highly valued, and he joined the inner core of the Central Committee before the October Revolution. Thereafter he became People's Commissar for Nationalities in the first Sovnarkom and served uninterruptedly in the Party Politburo from 1919. In the Civil War he was appointed as leading political commissar on several fronts and was regarded by Lenin as one of his most dependable troubleshooters, acquiring a reputation for a fierce decisiveness. In 1920 he added the chairmanship of the Workers' and Peasants' Inspectorate to his list of posts, and in 1922 became General Secretary of the Party Central Committee.

Stalin's rivals in his own party would soon pay dearly for their condescension. He was crude and brutal even by Bolshevik standards, and was proud of the fact. On the Southern front in 1918 he had put villages to the torch to terrorize the peasantry of an entire region, and but for Lenin's intervention would have drowned scores of innocent former Imperial Army officers on a prison barge moored on the river Volga.

But Stalin's rivals had no excuse for underestimating Stalin's intelligence. His lack of intellectual sophistication did not mean that he was unmotivated by ideas; and he was conscious enough of the gaps in his education to take on Jan Sten as a private tutor in philosophy in the 1920s.[17] He was also a voracious reader, supposedly getting through a daily quota of 500 pages.[18] Although his objects of study changed, his orientation was constant. He despised middle-class experts, believing that the regime could train up its own 'specialists' in short order. The 'filth' from the old days ought to be cleansed (or 'purged'); social, economic and political problems should not be allowed to await solution. Those persons deemed responsible for the survival of such problems had to be physically exterminated. Let saboteurs and renegades perish! Let there be steel, iron and coal! Long live comrade Stalin!

That this maladjusted character, whose mistrustfulness was close to paranoia, should have won the struggle to succeed Lenin boded ill for his opponents past and present and for his potential opponents as well. It has been speculated that his vengefulness was influenced by the beatings he supposedly had received from his father or by the traditions of honour and feud in the Caucasian region. Yet his fascination with punitive violence went far beyond any conditioning by family or national customs. Stalin supposedly remarked: 'To choose one's victims, to prepare one's plans minutely, to slake an implacable vengeance, and then to go to bed . . . there is nothing sweeter in the world.'[19]

He also had a craving for adulation. As his doings were celebrated in the public media, only his ageing mother, to whom he dutifully sent packets of roubles, was oblivious of his status. Official history textbooks by Nikolai Popov and Emelyan Yaroslavski exaggerated his importance. Articles were published on the Civil War which treated the battles around Tsaritsyn in 1918, when Stalin was serving on the Southern front, as the turning point in the Red Army's fortunes. Already in 1925, Tsaritsyn had been renamed Stalingrad. The phrase was put into circulation: 'Stalin is the Lenin of today.' Ostensibly he shrugged off claims to greatness, complaining to a film scriptwriter: 'Reference to Stalin should be excised. The Central Committee of the party ought to be put in place of Stalin.'[20] He also repudiated the proposal in 1938 that Moscow should be renamed as Stalinodar (which means 'Stalin's gift')![21] His modesty on this and other occasions was insincere, but Stalin knew that it would enhance his popularity among rank-and-file communists: in reality he was extremely vainglorious.

Egomania was not the sole factor. The cult of Stalin was also a response to the underlying requirements of the regime. Russians and many other nations of the USSR were accustomed to their statehood being expressed through the persona of a supreme leader. Any revolutionary state has to promote continuity as well as disruption. The First Five-Year Plan had brought about huge disruption, and the tsar-like image of Stalin was useful in affirming that the state possessed a strong, determined leader.

Full regal pomp was nevertheless eschewed by him; Stalin, while inviting comparison with the tsars of old, also wished to appear as a mundane contemporary communist. Audiences at public conferences or at the Bolshoi Ballet or on top of the Kremlin Wall saw him in his dull-coloured, soldierly tunic – as he mingled with delegates from the provinces to official political gatherings – and he always made sure to have his photograph taken with groups of delegates. The display of ordinariness was a basic aspect of his mystique. The incantations of public congresses and conferences included not only

Stalin but also 'the Leninist Central Committee, the Communist Party, the Working Class, the Masses'. It was crucial for him to demonstrate the preserved heritage of Marxism-Leninism. The heroism, justice and inevitability of the October Revolution had to be proclaimed repeatedly, and the achievements of the First Five-Year Plan had to be glorified.

There is no doubt that many young members of the party and the Komsomol responded positively to the propaganda. The construction of towns, mines and dams was an enormously attractive project for them. Several such enthusiasts altruistically devoted their lives to the communist cause. They idolized Stalin, and all of them – whether they were building the city of Magnitogorsk or tunnelling under Moscow to lay the lines for the metro or were simply teaching kolkhozniki how to read and write – thought themselves to be agents of progress for Soviet society and for humanity as a whole. Stalin had his active supporters in their hundreds of thousands, perhaps even their millions. This had been true of Lenin; it would also be true of Khrushchëv. Not until the late 1960s did Kremlin leaders find it difficult to convince a large number of their fellow citizens that, despite all the difficulties, official policies would sooner or later bring about the huge improvements claimed by official spokesmen.[22]

Stalin's rule in the early 1930s depended crucially upon the presence of enthusiastic supporters in society. Even many people who disliked him admired his success in mobilizing the country for industrialization and in restoring Russia's position as a great power. There was a widespread feeling that, for all his faults, Stalin was a determined leader in the Russian tradition; and the naïvety of workers, peasants and others about high politics allowed him to play to the gallery of public opinion more easily than would be possible for Soviet leaders in later generations.

But enthusiasts remained a minority. Most people, despite the increase in cultural and educational provision, paid little mind to communist doctrines. They were too busy to give politics more than a glancing interest. It was a hard existence. The average urban inhabitant spent only an hour every week reading a book or listening to the radio and twenty minutes watching films or plays.[23] Adulatory newsreels were of limited help to Stalin while there remained a paucity of spectators. Furthermore, in 1937 there were still only 3.5 million radios in the country.[24] The authorities placed loudspeakers on main streets so that public statements might be broadcast to people as they travelled to work or went shopping. But this was rarely possible in the countryside since only one in twenty-five collective farms had access to electrical power.[25] Several weeks passed in some villages between visits from officials from the nearby town, and *Pravda* arrived only fitfully. The infrastructure of intensive mass indoctrination had not been completed before the Second World War.

The underlying cause for the ineffectiveness of official propaganda, however, was the hardship caused by official measures. The non-Russian nationalities were especially embittered. The assertiveness of national and ethnic groups in the 1920s had been among the reasons for the NEP's abolition. Several imaginary anti-Soviet organizations were 'discovered', starting with the Union for the Liberation of Ukraine in July 1929.[26] Artists, scholars and novelists were arraigned in Kiev and sentenced to lengthy years of imprisonment. Analogous judicial proceedings took place in Belorussia, Georgia, Armenia and Azerbaijan. Communist officials thought to have shown excessive indulgence to the sentiments of nations in their republics suffered demotion. The prime victim was Mykola Skrypnik in Ukraine. In 1933 he was dropped as Ukraine's People's Commissar of Enlightenment, and committed suicide. Simultaneously those writers and artists who had developed their national cultures under the NEP were subject to ever stricter surveillance.

Nor was the menace of Russian nationalism ignored. In 1930 the historians S. F. Platonov and E. V. Tarle, famous Russian patriots, were put on trial and imprisoned for leading the non-existent All-People's Union of Struggle for Russia's Regeneration.[27] Three thousand Red Army commanders who had been officers in the Imperial Army were also arrested.[28] Russian-language literary figures, too, were persecuted. Novels dealing sensitively with the peasants, rural customs, spirituality and individual emotions had appeared in the 1920s and had offered consolation to readers who disliked Marxism-

Leninism. With the occasional exception such as Mikhail Sholokhov's stories of Cossack life in *Quiet Flows the Don*, this artistic trend was eradicated. The field was dominated during the First Five-Year Plan by writer-activists belonging to the Russian Association of Proletarian Writers. Works depicting working-class selflessness and internationalism flooded from Soviet publishing houses.

Each nationality felt itself to be suffering worse than all the others: such is the norm for national and ethnic groups in times of stress and privation. In 1934 some daredevils in the Russian city of Saratov produced an illicit poster of a broad river with two bands of men lining up on opposite banks to give battle to each other. On one bank stood Trotski, Kamenev and Zinoviev, all of them being Jewish; the other was held by the Georgians: Stalin, Yenukidze and Ordzhonikidze. Underneath was the caption: 'And the Slavs fell into dispute over who was to rule in Old Russia.'[29] The message was that Russians, Ukrainians and Belorussians were being humiliated in their own lands. Even under Stalin, in the early 1930s, the composition of the central party leadership failed to mirror the country's demography even though it was not so much out of focus as previously. To a popular tradition of anti-Semitism was added a resentment against the nations of the Transcaucasus.

In reality the Georgians were tormented along with the other peoples. The local OGPU chief in Tbilisi, the Georgian Lavrenti Beria, was winning plaudits from Stalin for his ruthlessness towards Georgian nationalist dissent and peasant resistance. And those Jewish institutions of the USSR which had flourished in the 1920s were either emasculated or crushed. Winter followed the springtime of the nations.

This did not mean that nations suffered equally. Most deaths caused by the Soviet state during the First Five-Year Plan were brought about by the collectivization of agriculture. Consequently the less urbanized nationalities were victimized disproportionately. For example, it is reckoned that between 1.3 million and 1.8 million Kazakh nomads died for this reason;[30] and the imposition of agricultural quotas upon such a people led to the destruction of an entire way of life. Kazakhs, who knew nothing of cereal cropping, were ordered to cultivate wheat on pain of execution. The Soviet economy's patchwork quilt was being replaced by a blanket cut from a single bloodied cloth. Several victim-nations concluded that Stalin was bent on genocide. Not only Kazakhs but also Ukrainians suspected that he aimed at their extermination under cover of his economic policies. Collectivization, according to surviving nationalists, was Stalin's equivalent of Hitler's 'Final Solution'. Purportedly, the difference was that Stalin had it in for the Ukrainians whereas Hitler wished to annihilate all Jews.

Certainly Ukraine was subject to perniciously peculiar dispensations. Passenger traffic between the Russian and Ukrainian republics was suspended in 1932 and the borders were sealed by Red Army units.[31] From village to village the armed urban squads moved without mercy. 'Kulaks' were suppressed and the starving majority of the Ukrainian peasantry had to fulfil the state's requirements or else face deportation. Famine was the predictable outcome. It is true that the central authorities cut the grain-collection quotas three times in response to reports of starvation. Yet the cuts were a long, long way short of the extent sufficient to put a quick stop to famine. Horrendous suffering prevailed over Ukraine in 1932–3.

Were not these official measures therefore genocidal? If genocide means the killing of an entire national or ethnic group, the answer has to be no. The centrally-imposed quotas for grain deliveries from Ukraine were in fact somewhat reduced from the second half of 1932. The evidence of millions of starving people gave even the Politburo some pause for thought. It must be stressed that the reductions were nothing like enough to end the famine; but the occurrence of any reductions at all casts doubt on the notion that Stalin had from the start intended to exterminate the Ukrainian nation. Furthermore, Ukrainians were only seventy-four per cent of the Ukrainian Soviet Republic's population before the First Five-Year Plan, and to this extent the infliction of famine was not nationally specific.[32] In any case Stalin needed Ukrainians as well as Russians to take up jobs in the factories, mines and railheads being opened in Ukraine and elsewhere.

Indeed Stalin did not go as far as banning their language from the local schools. To be sure, Russian-language schooling assumed much greater prominence than in the 1920s; and the ability of Ukrainian educationists and writers to praise specifically Ukrainian cultural achievements was severely limited. Nevertheless Stalin – albeit with great reservations – accepted Ukrainian linguistic and cultural distinctness as a fact of life (and in 1939 he sanctioned sumptuous celebrations of the 125th anniversary of the birth of the great Ukrainian national poet and anti-tsarist writer Taras Shevchenko). But Stalin also wanted to teach Ukraine a political lesson; for Ukraine had always appeared to Bolsheviks as the black heart of kulakdom and national separatism. The bludgeoning of its inhabitants, going as far as the killing of a large number of them, would serve the purpose of durable intimidation.

A logical corollary was the resumed persecution of the Ukrainian Autocephalous Church. Indeed the authorities were zealous in smashing the foundations of organized religion of all kinds and in all places. The God of the Christians, Muslims and Jews was derided as that 'nice little god'. The limited tolerance afforded to religion since the middle of the NEP was thrown aside.

Unlike de-kulakization, de-clericalization was not explicitly announced as a policy, and there were no quotas for elimination. Yet a licence was given for physical attacks on religious leaders. Stalin thought godlessness the beginning of righteousness and had no compunction about the mass slaughter of clerics. The number of killings during the First Five-Year Plan outdid even the record of the Civil War. In the Russian Orthodox Church alone the number of active priests tumbled from around 60,000 in the 1920s to only 5,665 by 1941. No doubt many of them fled in disguise to the towns in order to escape the attentions of the armed squads that were searching for them. But many priests were caught unawares and either imprisoned or executed.[33] Thousands of other Christian leaders, mullahs, both Shi'ite and Sunni, and rabbis were also butchered. The one-ideology state was imposed with a vengeance.

Political pragmatism as well as a philosophy of militant atheism spurred on the campaign. Stalin and his associates remembered that in 1905 a demonstration headed by Father Gapon had touched off an avalanche that nearly buried the monarchy. Churches, mosques and synagogues were the last large meeting-places not entirely controlled by the state authorities after the October Revolution of 1917.

The feasts of the religious calendar also stood as marking points for the farming year. Particularly in Russia the tasks of ploughing, sowing, reaping and threshing were deemed incomplete unless a priest was present to pray for success. Agriculture and religious faith were intimately entwined. From its own fanatical standpoint, the League of the Militant Godless had logic on its side in pressing for the demolition of the houses of 'god'. Priest and mullah and rabbi were vilified as parasites. In reality most parish clergy were as poor as church mice and, after the separation of Church from state in 1918, depended entirely on the voluntary offertories from their congregations. The same was usually true of other faiths. Clerics of all religions were integral parts of social order in their small communities. They welcomed children into the world, blessed marriages and buried the dead. They alternately rejoiced and commiserated with ordinary peasants. A village without a church, mosque or synagogue had lost its principal visible connection with the old peasant world. A countryside deprived of its priests, shrines, prayers and festivities was more amenable to being collectivized.

The destruction continued through the 1930s. Only one in forty churches was functioning as such by the decade's end; the others had been reduced to rubble or recommissioned for secular purposes.[34] Equally significantly, no place of worship was built in the new cities and towns arising in the Soviet Union. Stalin and Kaganovich, as the capital's party first secretary from 1930 to 1935, implemented schemes for the re-creation of the vista of central Moscow. They knocked down the little streets around the Kremlin so that great parades might be held along broad new avenues. The Cathedral of Christ the Saviour was blown up; the plan was to use the site for the construction of the world's tallest building, which would house a Palace of Soviets with a massive statue of Lenin on its roof.[35] Kaganovich, a Jewish atheist, had no compunction in assailing a Russian Orthodox Church notorious for its anti-Semitism before

1917. But even he was wary, and instructed that the demolition of the Cathedral should take place secretly at dead of night.

The leaders of the various faiths had been traumatized. The Acting Russian Orthodox Church Patriarch Sergei lived in perpetual fear of arrest. The violence threw the communist party's campaign for cultural and national reconstruction into grotesque relief. Indisputable gains were made in literacy, numeracy, industrial skills and urban infrastructure. The account-sheet, however, was in debit: both culturally and nationally there had been more destruction than construction. A society had gone into semi-dissolution. Nations, religions and popular traditions had been ground into the dust.

Among the reasons for this was Stalin's desire to produce 'Soviet' men and women and create a 'Soviet' people. As a follower of Marx and Engels, he held that the ultimate antidote to conflicts among national groups was the 'fusion' of all nations. The post-national compound would supposedly include ingredients from each nationality. Among Stalin's acolytes during the First Five-Year Plan there had been several who assumed the moment of fusion to be imminent in the USSR. But Stalin recognized that this might damage the last elements of cohesion in society. Some binding factor had to be introduced. By 1934 he had come to the opinion that the Soviet state, for reasons of security, needed to foster Russian national pride. Russians were fifty-two per cent of the USSR's population in the late 1930s.[36] A large number of them lived in each republic, especially after the migration of people during the First Five-Year Plan; and they were disproportionately well-represented in administrative posts. Russians were anyhow used to inhabiting a state larger than mere Russia as defined by Soviet communists and had no wish to see this state dismembered.

Already in 1930 the communist versifier Demyan Bedny had been reprimanded for insulting the Russian people in one of his doggerel verses. Marxism-Leninism was not to be used as a cover for humiliating a nation whose workers had been the vanguard of the October Revolution; limits existed on the deprecation of Russianness.

It was in 1934 that the privileging of Russian nationhood began in earnest. Concerns about the USSR's security had been growing in the early 1930s; and Stalin and the leadership felt edgy about Ukraine, about Polish infiltration into the western borderlands and about the threat posed by Adolf Hitler and the Third Reich. Russian national feelings were nurtured more warmly, and nowhere was this more obvious than in the writing of history. The doyen of the academic profession until his death in 1932 had been M. N. Pokrovski, who had waged a vendetta in his books and in university administration against writers who failed to put class struggle at the centre of their interpretations. He had insisted, too, that Russian imperial expansion over the centuries had brought harm to the non-Russian peoples. This approach now fell into official disrepute; and Professor E. V. Tarle, the non-Marxist historian and Russian patriot, was released from prison to reoccupy his university chair in Moscow.

It remained obligatory to analyse the Soviet period predominantly in terms of class struggle, but the distant Russian past could now be handled more flexibly. Stalin himself was an admiring reader of the best works that appeared. As Russian emperors and commanders came in for gentler treatment, scholars still had to criticize their faults but were also required to accentuate the benefits brought to Russians by the tsarist unification of Muscovy and to the non-Russians by the growth of the Russian Empire. The Russian language was given heightened status. In the academic year 1938–9 it became one of the compulsory subjects of instruction in all schools; and from the late 1930s a campaign was begun to alter the various non-Russian languages to a Cyrillic-style alphabet on the Russian model. Thus in 1940 the Uzbek tongue was no longer allowed to be written in Arabic characters.[37]

Yet there were restrictions on the expression of Russian patriotism. Ivan the Terrible and Peter the Great could be praised, but not Nicholas II; and the aristocracy, gentry, merchantry and other so-called 'former people' had to be denounced. The expression of contemporary Russian nationhood, moreover, excluded the Orthodox Church. It rejected most village traditions. In literature it incorporated Alexander Pushkin and Maksim Gorki, but rejected the

Christian nationalist Fëdor Dostoevski.[38] For the central political leaders in the 1930s remained wary lest Russian national pride might get out of hand. They were willing to modify Marxism-Leninism and even to distort it by adding Russian national ingredients to it; but they insisted that Marxism-Leninism should remain at the core of the state ideology.

Russians anyway did not always do better than other peoples in the USSR. The famine that devastated society in Ukraine in 1932–3 was also grievous in southern Russia. The Russian nation, despite the accolades it received, could reasonably perceive itself as a victim people. Territorially the Russian Soviet Federal Socialist Republic (RSFSR) abruptly lost much of its status. In 1936 the internal borders of the USSR were redrawn. The Transcaucasian Federation was dissolved and Georgia, Armenia and Azerbaijan became republics on a par with the RSFSR. At the same time a huge chunk of the RSFSR was hacked away when the territory previously known as the Turkestan Region became the Kazakh Socialist Soviet Republic, thereby supplanting Ukraine as the USSR's second largest republic. Most significantly, the new republic of Kazakhstan acquired its own communist party whereas the RSFSR remained without one.

For Stalin feared a New Russia as much as the Old. He wielded the knout to discourage certain aspects of Russianness while waving a flag to foster others. But he could not do this without increasing the self-awareness of Russians as Russians. The process was driven also by other forces. Chief among these were urbanization and mass literacy; for as Russian-speaking peasants poured into the towns and as Russian-speaking workers moved from one town to another in search of jobs, so millions of Russians discovered how much they had in common.

A certain administrative measure gave unintended impetus to the process. From December 1932 urban inhabitants had to acquire identity booklets (or 'internal passports') specifying personal particulars. Item No. 5 referred to nationality. Labour books and other documents had long contained such information; but, unlike them, the new passports were mandatory for all town-dwellers. Many individuals might previously have described themselves as peasants or workers, as natives of Samara or Nakhichevan, as Christians or Muslims. They now had to make a definitive choice of their nationality. Should they be of mixed parentage, they had to opt for either the paternal or the maternal line of descent. Aleksei Kulichenko, whose father was Ukrainian and mother was half-Russian and half-Tatar, decided to put 'Ukrainian' in his passport; and Avraam Epshtein, a Jew from the Belorussian capital Minsk who had lost his faith and was at ease linguistically in Russian, registered himself as a Russian.

The passports had been introduced to control the surge of villagers into the towns in search of industrial work. The kolkhozniks were denied the automatic right to obtain them. More generally, passports were a signal of the party leaders' concern that society remained outside their full control. The First Five-Year Plan had intensified state authority beyond precedent. The Politburo under Stalin decided every great aspect of policy in foreign affairs, security, politics, administration, economy, science and the arts. No organized hostile group, except for a few bands of Basmachi in central Asia, endured. Yet somehow the peoples of the USSR had resisted being pummelled into the shape prescribed by the Kremlin.

Thus the first half-decade of the 1930s was a time of sharp contrasts. Cultural work was strengthened, but in an atmosphere that induced fear among school-teachers, writers and even party propagandists; and the peoples of the USSR had succeeded in preserving their traditions and beliefs against the pressure of official Soviet doctrines. Economic relaxations were announced, but generally the methods of obtaining food supplies by intimidation and violence was kept in place. National and religious leaderships and organizations were attacked; and yet there was also an increasing indulgence to Russian nationhood. Internationalism and Russian semi-nationalism were engaged in uneasy cohabitation. The First and Second Five-Year Plans were meant to secure the voluntary allegiance of workers, peasants, administrators and intellectuals to the regime. But although some enthusiasm for Stalin's policies undoubtedly existed, hostility was much more widely disseminated. The integration of the aspirations of party, state and society was a very distant goal. The USSR was a country in travail and the compound of the Soviet order had yet to be stabilized sufficiently for the central party leadership's comfort of mind.

11

Terror upon Terror (1934–1938)

It was in this volatile situation that the engine of a Great Terror was cranked up and set in motion. The exact calculations of Stalin and his associates have not been recorded for posterity, but undoubtedly several leaders had been made edgy by the situation confronting them after the First Five-Year Plan. They knew that resentment of their rule in the rest of society was deep and wide, and they feared lest former Bolshevik oppositionists might exploit this circumstance. Stalin's allies felt deeply insecure, and shared a rising sense of frustration. They were annoyed by the chaos that prevailed in the network of public institutions – and they had doubts about the loyalty of party, governmental, military and managerial officials, even including those who had implemented the First Five-Year Plan. They had few scruples about applying their repressive power. The thought, practices and institutions of the Civil War had set precedents for the horrors of the late 1930s.

Indeed state violence was already being applied widely under the First and Second Five-Year Plans. 'Kulaks', railwaymen-'wreckers', 'nationalists' and managerial 'saboteurs' were being arrested in large numbers. Nearly a million Soviet citizens languished in the forced-labour camps and colonies of the OGPU by 1933, and further millions were in prisons, deportation camps and compulsory resettlement areas.[1] Consequently the Great Terror of 1937–8 was not a thunderclap in a cloudless sky but the worsening of a storm that was already raging.

None the less the Great Terror would not have taken place but for Stalin's personality and ideas. He it was who directed the state's punitive machinery against all those whom he identified as 'anti-Soviet elements' and 'enemies of the people'. Among his purposes was a desire to use his victims as scapegoats for the country's pain; and in order to sustain his mode of industrialization he also needed to keep his mines, timber forests and construction sites constantly supplied with slave labour.[2] It was probably also his intention to take pre-emptive measures against any 'fifth column' operating against him in the event of war.[3] These considerations, furthermore, fitted into a larger scheme to build an efficient Soviet state subservient to his personal dictatorship – and to secure the state's total control over society. Such was the guiding rationale of the Great Terrorist.

Back in 1933, not even Stalin had been urging repression on that scale: he was still selecting specific 'anti-Soviet elements' as targets for the OGPU. Yet official violence was never absent from the Politburo's agenda for long, and Stalin reprimanded his Politburo colleagues whenever they failed to support him. The tensions in public life were maintained. Stalin and his most trusted associates saw a tightening of discipline as the main means to attain economic success and political stability. Repeatedly they affirmed the need to root out class enemies, saboteurs and spies.

This did not happen without dissension in the Politburo. Three great power-bases had been consolidated during the First Five-Year Plan: the All-Union Communist Party, the People's Commissariats and the OGPU. Relations between the party and the commissariats caused heated controversy. To Stalin's fury, Ordzhonikidze as People's Commissar of Heavy Industry prevented local party bodies from interfering in the activity of factory directors.[4] But at the same time Stalin was angered by the power of the party at its lower levels, power that was frequently used to thwart the central party apparatus's instructions. So that Stalin was unhappy with both the party and the government. Debate about this in the Politburo ensued in the winter of 1933–4 and the balance of opinion was in favour of letting the commissariats get on with fulfilling the Second Five-Year Plan without interference by local party bodies.[5]

But how could this be achieved without losing control of the commissariats? Kaganovich suggested that the party should be given a crucial supervisory role at the local level. Thus the party committees would establish an internal department for each major branch of the economy. The task of the departments would be to check on the implementation of central economic objectives at the local level without taking over the functions of detailed management.

Kaganovich's proposal had the virtue, from Stalin's standpoint, of strengthening compliance with the Second Five-Year Plan. Each local party secretary would be reduced in authority when his committee was turned into 'a small apparatus subordinate to the People's Commissar',[6] and the party as a whole was subjected to greater control from the centre. In 1933 yet another purge of the membership was undertaken, resulting in the withdrawal of party cards from 854,300 persons identified as careerists, drunkards, idlers and unrepentant oppositionists.[7] While all this was sweet music to Stalin's ears, there remained much to annoy him. Firstly, the trimming of the party's sprawling powers served to increase hostility to Stalin's policies and mode of leadership among many party secretaries in the provinces. Stalin was less and less their hero. Secondly, the enhanced autonomy of the governmental organs made them still less amenable to Stalin's control. Stalin was not the sort of leader who found this a tolerable situation.

Basic questions about how to consolidate the regime were therefore yet to be resolved. The Politburo reserved the right to take any definitive decision. No one was allowed to refer directly to these questions at the Seventeenth Congress of the All-Union Communist Party, which opened in Moscow on 26 February 1934. The press had indicated that it would be a Congress of Victors. The internal communist oppositions had been defeated; industrialization and agricultural collectivization had been imposed; military security had been reinforced. The party's unity under its great leader was to be celebrated.

Stalin in his speech to the Congress, however, indicated that he was not going to be gracious in victory: 'Consequently it is necessary not to sing lullabies to the party but to develop its vigilance, not to send it to sleep but to keep it in a condition of militant readiness, not to disarm but to arm it.'[8] He warned against complacency about the party's economic achievements and against indulgence towards the former oppositionists. His associates were equally intransigent. Molotov asserted that 'vestiges of capitalism' continued to affect thinking in the party; Kaganovich added that anti-Leninist deviations still threatened the party.[9] Lesser figures added to the belligerent chorus. M. F. Shkiryatov suggested that the central leadership needed to intervene more vigorously to make improvements in local party life; and R. I. Eikhe declared that Bukharin had not done enough to prevent the emergence of 'Ryutin and other counter-revolutionary swine'.[10]

They did not have everything their own way. Politburo members Kuibyshev and Mikoyan refrained from calling for a sharpening of political struggle.[11] Similar reluctance was shown by influential regional party first secretaries including Pëtr Postyshev of Ukraine, I. M. Vareikis of the Central Black-Earth Region and B. P. Sheboldaev of the Azov-Black Sea Region.[12] Molotov bridled at any such signs of diminishing militancy, and in his report on the economy he proposed – presumably with Stalin's approval – to raise the projected annual industrial growth rate by another five per cent.[13] Ordzhonikidze's intervention led to a limitation of the increase to three per cent.[14] The intensity of the dissension between Molotov and Ordzhonikidze ought not to be exaggerated. Nevertheless the Congress's other decisions were generally in favour of slackening the political tensions, and it would seem that Leningrad party boss Sergei Kirov, too, was popular among Congress delegates for favouring such a relaxation. Pointedly Kirov had stated in his main speech: 'The fundamental difficulties are already behind us.'[15]

There is also fragmentary evidence that Stalin did so poorly in the elections to the new Central Committee that the number of votes cast for each candidate was withheld from publication. Another story is that several Congress delegations asked Kirov to stand against Stalin for the General Secretaryship – and that Kirov declined the request.[16] The full truth remains beclouded. What is clear is that Stalin lost his title of General Secretary and was redesignated simply as Secretary, and that Kirov was given the same rank.[17] On the other hand, it remains far from clear that Kirov's policies were really very different from those of Stalin and Molotov. Certainly he eulogized Stalin in his same speech to the Congress;[18] and probably, too, he actually tried to resist his own promotion to Central Committee Secretary.[19] Nevertheless Stalin had not had the enjoyable time during and after the Congress which he had thought his due: this much appears clear. His usual reaction in such a situation was to search for ways to settle accounts finally with those whom he regarded as his enemies.

From spring to autumn 1934 some impression was given that Stalin was making compromises just as Lenin had done in introducing the NEP. Kirov went on speaking in support of increased rations for workers, greater respect for legal procedures and an end to the violent extortion of grain from peasants.[20] Restrictions were placed on the arbitrary arrest of economic experts.[21] The OGPU lost its separate institutional status, and its activities and personnel were transferred under the control of the People's Commissariat of Internal Affairs (NKVD). Thus the state's mechanisms of arbitrary repression appeared to have been weakened. Yet the changes for the better were nugatory. Massive instrumentalities of violence remained intact, and the NKVD's engorgement of the OGPU had the result of constructing an even mightier centralized organ for policing and security. Political passions therefore remained high: the Congress had ultimately resolved little.

On 1 December 1934 an astonishing event triggered an upward ratcheting of the level of repression. A young ex-Zinovievite, Leonid Nikolaev, walked into Kirov's office in Leningrad, pulled out a revolver and shot him. Stalin exploited the assassination as a pretext to rush through a set of decrees granting full authority to the NKVD to arrest, try and execute at will. This gave rise to the belief that Stalin connived in the killing. Nikolaev had previously been caught in possession of a firearm in suspicious circumstances. He was executed before any exhaustive interrogation could take place and an improbably large proportion of those who handled Nikolaev after Kirov's death, including the van-drivers, quickly perished in mysterious circumstances. Yet Stalin's complicity in the Kirov murder remains unproven. What is beyond dispute is that the assassination enabled him and his associates to begin to move against the somewhat less militant among the Stalinists and their tacit supporters.

Stalin first took revenge upon Zinoviev and Kamenev, who were accused of conniving in Kirov's death. They agreed to accept moral and political responsibility for their former minor adherent in return for an assurance that they would receive a light sentence. Their trial was held in camera in January 1935. On Stalin's orders Zinoviev and Kamenev were consigned to ten and five years of imprisonment respectively. Stalin's prisons were not rest-homes. Furthermore, 663 past supporters of Zinoviev in Leningrad were seized and sent into exile in Yakutia and other bleak Siberian locations. Over 30,000 deportations of members of social groups regarded as hostile to the communism in Leningrad and other cities as the security agencies intensified its years-old campaign against undesirables.[22]

Stalin was cranking up the motor of prophylactic repression. Neither the exiled communist ex-oppositionists nor the deported former middle-class city dwellers had been conspiring against Stalin. But Stalin did not want to give them the chance to do so. His desire for complete control was even extended to ordinary communists who had never belonged to an oppositional faction. Yet another clear-out of undesirable rank-and-file members was ordered in 1934 and a block was placed on recruitment for the second half of the year. Coming after the purge of 1933, this measure was a sign of the Secretariat's undispelled concern about the revolutionary 'vanguard'. In January 1935, as Kamenev and Zinoviev received their prison sentences, a general exchange of party cards was announced. This would be a purge under a different name: the aim was to identify and remove those many members who did nothing for the party while deriving advantage from having a card. In consequence, by May 1935, 281,872 persons had ceased being Bolsheviks.[23]

This fitted the schemes of Andrei Zhdanov, who had become a Central Committee Secretary in 1934 and Leningrad party chief after Kirov's murder. Zhdanov wanted to restore the authority of the party at the expense of the people's commissariats; he saw the internal party purge as a prerequisite of this task. Once it had been 'cleansed', the party would be in a condition to resume its role as the supreme institution of the Soviet state. At a practical level, Zhdanov aimed to reverse the Seventeenth Party Congress's decision to reorganize the departments of party committees on parallel lines to the economic branches of government. The local party committees, according to Zhdanov, should reclaim their role in propagating Marxism-Leninism, mobilizing society and in selecting personnel for public office. His implicit argument was that the Soviet order could not safely be entrusted to the people's commissariats.

Zhdanov's success was an episode in the struggle among institutions. The Soviet economy was run on the basis of central command, and it was important that the people's commissariats maximized their power to impose their will. Yet there was a danger that this power might be used against the wishes of the central political leadership. And so the party had to be retained to control the commissariats. But the party might lack the necessary expertise. As central politicians tried to resolve this dilemma, they alternated in their preferences between the people's commissariats and the party. Indeed this had become the perennial institutional dilemma of the one-party, one-ideology state and the state-owned economy of the USSR.

Yet Stalin had his own motives in supporting Zhdanov. Apparently Zhdanov wished to box off the party purge from the concurrent arrests of ex-oppositionists. But Stalin rejected any such demarcation, and on 13 May 1935 the Secretariat sent out a secret letter to local party committees asserting that party cards had got into the hands of many adventurers, political enemies and spies.[24] Thus persons expelled from the party could now find themselves accused of espionage, for which the punishment was either execution or years of forced labour. On 20 May, the Politburo issued a directive for every former Trotskyist to be sent to a labour camp for a minimum of three years. On 20 November, Trotski, Kamenev and Zinoviev were accused of spying for foreign powers.[25] Stalin, designedly or not, was moving towards a violent general resolution of the political tensions. Apparently not even Kaganovich or Zhdanov or even Molotov, his closest associates, were demanding the extension of terror. But by then none of them dared deny Stalin something upon which his mind was fixed.[26]

Not only political administration but also economic management became more hazardous. For it was also in 1935 that an extraordinary campaign was introduced to raise industrial productivity. In the Don Basin, in eastern Ukraine, the miner Aleksei Stakhanov hewed 102 tons of coal in a six-hour stint in August. This feat was fourteen times the norm set by his enterprise. When the news reached Moscow, Stalin and Molotov perceived that a summons to all industrial labourers to emulate Stakhanov would help to break the spine of the objections by managers, technical experts and workers to the Politburo's policies.

Stakhanov was hailed as a worker-hero; a Stakhanovite movement was founded. Suddenly it was found that practically every industrial machine could be made to function much, much faster. Even the boilers of steam-trains started to perform wonders. Managers and administrative personnel were intimidated into altering patterns of work to accommodate attempts on records; and the workers were put under pressure to change their working procedures.[27] Critics of Stakhanovism in any enterprise were not merely reprimanded but arrested as 'wreckers'. Ordzhonikidze as a Politburo member had immunity from such a sanction, and he pointed out that Stakhanov and his emulators could perform miracles only by means of the deployment of other workers to service their needs. Yet he was ignored. The Stakhanovite movement suited Stalin, who wanted to foster utopian industrial schemes by terrorizing doubters and encouraging enthusiasts.

His hostility to factory directors, local party chiefs and former oppositionists was coalescing into a single repressive campaign. It would take little to impel Stalin into action. Politics had been dangerously volatile for years as institutional interests clashed and rivalries among the leaders intensified. In 1935–6 there was again a dispute in the Politburo about tempos of economic growth.[28] As usual, Stalin was strongly in favour of increasing the tempos. At the same time there was administrative chaos and popular resentment in the country. And then suddenly, in summer 1936, Stalin was driven frantic by evidence obtained by the NKVD that Trotski had been keeping contact from abroad with clandestine groups of supporters and that these groups had been negotiating with supporters of Bukharin, Kamenev and Zinoviev.[29] For an extremely suspicious and vengeful person such as Stalin, this threat called for massive retaliation. In the rest of the year he sought to settle accounts bloodily with all those whom he identified as his enemies.

First he moved against Kamenev and Zinoviev. On 29 June 1936, a secret letter was sent by the Central Committee Secretariat to the local party bodies alleging the discovery of 'the terrorist activities of the Trotskyist-Zinovievite counter-revolutionary bloc'.[30] In August 1936, Kamenev and Zinoviev were dragged from their cells and re-tried. This time the proceedings were held in public. The defendants were privately threatened with the death sentence unless they 'confessed' to having set up an Anti-Soviet Trotskyist-Zinovievite Centre that organized assassinations. Supposedly Stalin was next on their list after Kirov. They duly confessed, and Stalin duly broke his promise. The court condemned them to death and sentence was carried out early next morning.

This was the first execution of anyone who had belonged to the Party Central Committee. Stalin's campaign was relentless. He sacked Yagoda in September on the grounds that he was four years behind in catching enemies of the people. His replacement was Nikolai Yezhov a rising figure in the central party apparatus. The atmosphere in the Soviet leadership was not relaxed by the economic news. The 1936 grain harvest turned out to be twenty-six per cent smaller than the harvest of the previous year;[31] and in November a massive explosion occurred at the Kemerovo coal-mine. Many such troubles in agriculture and industry were the product of the technical disruptions brought about by Stalin's management of the economy. But he blamed the troubles on wreckers and anti-Soviet elements and strengthened his resolve to stick to his methods.

Ordzhonikidze and Kuibyshev, who themselves had supported the brutal industrialization during 1928–32, were disconcerted by Stalin's continued brutality.[32] But Kuibyshev, a heavy drinker, died of a heart attack (or was he poisoned on Stalin's orders?) in January

1935. Ordzhonikidze was becoming isolated in the Politburo. Others who had their doubts – Mikoyan, Voroshilov and Kalinin – were threatened back into submission. And so Stalin had the preponderant influence in the central party organs. The Politburo, which had convened weekly during the First Five-Year Plan, met only nine times in 1936.[33] Despite losing his title of General Secretary in 1934, Stalin still dominated the Secretariat. He also had his own office, headed by A. N. Poskrëbyshev, which kept hold of its own long-established links with the NKVD.

Even Stalin, however, needed a sanction stronger than his signature as Party Secretary in order to start a systematic extermination of communist oppositionists. He was not yet a dictator. The party was the regime's most influential institution, and Stalin still had to get his strategy, ill-defined as it was, approved by the rest of the Politburo. Ordzhonikidze was a source of difficulty. Stalin attacked him in a particularly nasty fashion by putting Pyatakov, former oppositionist and presently Ordzhonikidze's deputy in the People's Commissariat of Heavy Industry, on show-trial alongside fellow ex-oppositionist Karl Radek. Under intense psychological pressure Pyatakov and Radek confessed to leading an imaginary Parallel Anti-Soviet Trotskyist Centre aiming to restore capitalism in Russia. Pyatakov was shot and Radek sent to a labour camp. In February, unhinged by Pyatakov's execution, Ordzhonikidze shot himself – or possibly he was murdered on Stalin's orders.

Ordzhonikidze's death freed Stalin to present his ideas to the lengthy Party Central Committee plenum that stretched from the end of February into mid-March 1937. He wasted no words of sympathy on Ordzhonikidze. Stalin also declared that the local party leadership was a tap-root of the Soviet state's problems. He castigated the cliental system of appointments: 'What does it mean if you drag a whole group of pals along yourself? It means you've acquired a certain independence from local organizations and, if you like, a certain independence from the Central Committee.'[34]

This was no longer a prim administrative point because Stalin at the same time asserted that wreckers, spies and assassins had insinuated themselves into influential party posts, forming Trotskyist groups and aiming at a capitalist restoration. Allegedly, enemies of the people existed in every locality and party organization. The First Party Secretary in Ukraine, Pëtr Postyshev, had for weeks been rejecting this extraordinary claim. Postyshev had previously been a close supporter of Stalin; and Stalin, being determined to have implicit obedience from his supporters, made a public example of Postyshev by declaring that he had allowed enemies of the people to infiltrate the Kiev party apparatus.[35] This was a hair's breadth from denouncing Postyshev as an enemy of the people, and the plenum was cowed. Having achieved the desired effect, Stalin appeared to show magnanimity by only calling for Postyshev to be removed from the Politburo.[36]

The shooting of Pyatakov and the humiliation of Postyshev terrified every Central Committee member, and it was almost with relief that the plenum listened to Zhdanov's parallel proposal to inaugurate a campaign for 'democratization' in local party organizations. The fact that the projected 're-elections' might end the political careers of most of the audience was overlooked.[37] For the number of arrested oppositionists and economic officials increased sharply in spring 1937, and Stalin deftly obviated any last obstacle to his wishes in the Politburo by getting sanction for the creation of a commission which could take decisions on the Politburo's behalf. The commission consisted exclusively of leaders who by then accepted the case for intensified terror: Molotov, Voroshilov, Kaganovich, Yezhov (who was not even a Politburo member at the time) and Stalin himself.[38]

Thus empowered, Stalin expanded the scope of terror: no institution in the Soviet state failed to incur his suspicion. The next group picked by him for repression were the Red Army leaders. Stalin's aim was to ensure that the armed forces were incapable of promoting policies in any way different from his own, and Marshal Tukhachevski laid himself open to trouble by arguing for a more adventurous military strategy for the USSR.[39] He and several high-ranking commanders were arrested in May and beaten into confessing to plotting a *coup d'état*. Stalin called them all spies at a meeting of the Military Soviet of the People's Commissariat of Defence, and they were shot in mid-June. On the same occasion he announced that Bukharin, Tomski and Rykov were guilty of espionage.[40] Stalin repeated these charges against these former leaders of the Right Deviation at a Central Committee plenum starting on 23 June, where he stated that the NKVD had collected information sufficient to merit judicial proceedings.

At this Osip Pyatnitski, who had first been elected a Central Committee member in 1912 before Stalin himself became one, protested. An intermission was called so that Molotov and Kaganovich, Stalin's intermediaries at the plenum, might bring Pyatnitski to his senses.[41] Pyatnitski opted for death before dishonour. Thereupon Yezhov took not only Bukharin and Pyatnitski but also his own NKVD predecessor Yagoda into his care.

Yezhov enjoyed the technical chores of administering repression, devising instructions that anticipated most practical snags. Since 1927 he had risen to ever more senior posts in the Central Committee Secretariat. At the age of forty-three years he was a living caricature of gleeful fanaticism. He was 'short of stature, almost a dwarf, with a piercing voice and bandy legs'.[42] His associates played on the verbal associations of his name in the Russian language by dubbing him the Iron Hedgehog. On 2 July, at Stalin's instigation, the Politburo passed a resolution 'On Anti-Soviet Elements', and Yezhov scuttled back to the Politburo on 31 July with the scheme for the NKVD to arrest 259,450 persons over the following four months.[43] In mid-August 1937 torture was sanctioned as a normal procedure of interrogation in Soviet prisons. The Great Terror was raging. It did not cease until the end of 1938.

Central direction was constantly involved. On 27 August, when the Krasnoyarsk Regional Committee wrote to him about a grain-store fire, Stalin telegrammed back within hours: 'Try the guilty [*sic*] persons in accelerated order. Sentence them to death.'[44] His method was systematically arbitrary; for the Politburo decision of 31 July 1937 assigned arrest-quotas to each major territorial unit of the USSR. No serious effort was made to catch and punish people for offences they had really committed; and it was laid down that 72,950 of victims – twenty-eight per cent – should be shot and the rest given 'eight to ten' years in prison or labour camp.[45] A Central Committee plenum in January 1938 momentarily seemed to terminate the madness by passing a resolution calling for greater scrupulousness to be shown in decisions to expel individuals from the party, decisions which by then were normally a preamble to arrest by the NKVD.[46] But the relief was illusory, and on 15 March 1938 an additional target of 57,200 'anti-Soviet elements' was introduced. Fully 48,000 of them were marked for execution this time.[47]

The victims were tried by trios (*troiki*), typically consisting of the local NKVD chief, party secretary and procurator. Trials were derisorily brief and sentences were carried out without right of appeal. In searching out 'anti-Soviet elements', troiki were enjoined to capture escaped kulaks, ex-Mensheviks, ex-Socialist-Revolutionaries, priests, pre-revolutionary policemen and former members of non-Russian parties.[48] As the Great Terror was intensified, the resolution 'On Anti-Soviet Elements' was applied to virtually anyone who had been active in or sympathetic to a communist oppositionist faction; and soon pretty well everybody who held a political, administrative or managerial post lived in fear. Not a single institution was unscathed by the NKVD's interrogators. The quota system was applied not merely to geographical areas but also to specific public bodies. The objective was to effect a 'cleansing' throughout the state. The NKVD was not to restrain itself by notions about an individual's possible innocence: the point was to eliminate all the categories of people believed by Stalin and Yezhov to contain the regime's enemies.

According to official central records, 681,692 persons were executed in 1937–8.[49] This may well be an underestimate, but the total number of deaths caused by repression in general was anyway much higher as people also perished from the inhuman conditions of their captivity. Between one million and one and a half million persons, it is tentatively reckoned, were killed by firing squad, physical maltreatment or massive over-work in the care of the NKVD in those two years alone.[50] The Jews and Gypsies exterminated by Hitler knew that they were dying because they were Jews and Gypsies. Stalin's terror was more chaotic and confusing: thousands went to their deaths shouting out their fervent loyalty to Stalin.

Even Hitler's Gestapo had to trick Jews to travel peacefully to the gas-chambers, and Stalin had to be still more deceitful: the risible fiction had to be disseminated throughout the country that a conspiracy of millions of hirelings of foreign states existed. Victims usually had to sign a confession mentioning participation in a terrorist conspiracy headed by Trotski and Bukharin and directed by the British, American, Japanese or German intelligence agencies. An immense punitive industry was developed with guaranteed employment for torturers, jailors, stenographers, van-drivers, executioners, grave-diggers and camp-guards. Meticulous records were kept, even though the blood of the signatories occasionally smudged the documents.[51]

Bukharin, who was put on show-trial in March 1938, was one of the luckier ones inasmuch as he was not physically abused. But he was nevertheless put under acute psychological duress to 'confess'. Bukharin surrendered as part of a deal to save the lives of his wife and son. The protracted rigmarole of denunciations, confessions, trials and sentencings in any event made the immense stratum of surviving officials complicit in the Terror. Even Nikita Khrushchëv, a rising party official in the 1930s who lived to denounce Stalin posthumously in 1956, was heavily involved; and Georgi Zhukov was exceptional among Red Army generals in refusing to make allegations of criminal activity against fellow generals.[52] At the central level Stalin's civilian associates competed with each other in the stylistic flourish with which they confirmed death sentences. Among Molotov's favourite addenda was: 'Give the dog a dog's death!'

Vans and lorries marked 'Meat' or 'Vegetables' could carry the victims out to a quiet wood, such as the one near Butovo twenty-five kilometres north of Moscow, where shooting-grounds and long, deep pits had been secretly prepared. Plenty of work could be found for prisoners spared capital punishment. Cattle-trucks were commandeered for journeys to the labour camps of the Gulag in Siberia, Kazakhstan and arctic Russia. The trains rumbled through towns at night-time to avoid public curiosity. Food and drink on the journey were grievously inadequate. The convicts were treated as badly as the Negro slaves who had been shipped to the West Indies. On arrival at their camp they sawed timber, dug for gold, mined coal and built towns. Their meals left them constantly famished: Yezhov's dieticians had estimated a provision of calories barely enough to sustain men and women who were not doing strenuous physical labour with wholly inadequate clothing and medical care in some of the USSR's most inhospitable regions.[53]

The exact death-rate of inmates is not known, but was indubitably high. Contingent after contingent of fresh (or rather newly-battered) prisoners were needed to replenish a labour-force that afforded a crucial portion of the state's industrial output. Not even Stalin, an enterprising proponent of the virtues of penal servitude, turned over his camps to agriculture. The kolkhozes and sovkhozes were already so close to being labour camps that the transfer of wheat cultivation to the Gulag would have brought no advantage. In times of famine, indeed, peasants in Vologda province were reduced to begging for crusts of bread from the convoys of prisoners in the locality.

And so it would seem that by 1939 the total number of prisoners in the forced-labour system – including prisons, labour camps, labour colonies and 'special settlements' – was 2.9 million.[54] In each camp there were gangs of convicted thieves who were allowed by the authorities to bully the 'politicals'. The trading of sexual favours was rife. Many inmates would kill or maim a weaker fellow victim just to rob him of his shoes. Alexander Solzhenitsyn, who was arrested after the Second World War, later wrote that experience of the camps could ennoble the character of prisoners. But Solzhenitsyn served most of his sentence in a camp in the Moscow suburbs where the inmates were given unusually light conditions in order to carry out scientific research. More typical for the Gulag inmates were the camps outside central Russia where it was every person for himself and moral self-control was rarely practised.

This convulsion of Soviet state and society had the severest consequences. Only one in thirty delegates to the Seventeenth Party Congress in 1934 returned to the Eighteenth Congress in 1939. The loss from the Central Committee was also drastic: just sixteen out of seventy-one members survived.[55] Another devastated institution was the Red Army. Tens of thousands of officers fell into the grip of Yezhov's 'hedgehog gloves', including fifteen out of the sixteen army commanders.

These figures are most easily compiled for high and medium-ranking functionaries. But other folk could also get caught by the mass repression. In his pursuit of political security Stalin resumed and expanded the policy of national deportations. Especially vulnerable were national and ethnic groups which had a large number of people living beyond the USSR's frontiers: Stalin was concerned lest they might prove disloyal in the event of war. Thus the Poles were removed from Soviet Ukraine by a secret decree of April 1936, roughly deposited in Kazakhstan and left to build their settlements. In the following year the Kurds were driven out from the North Caucasus, and the Koreans from eastern Siberia. Uninhabited tracts of Kazakhstan became a dumping ground for all peoples which incurred Stalin's suspicion.[56] As Yezhov carried out his master's command, countless deportees died before reaching their destination.

The impact of the Great Terror was deep and wide and was not limited to specific political, administrative, military, cultural, religious and national groups. Even a harmless old Russian peasant woman muttering dissatisfaction with conditions in the kolkhoz or her young worker-son blurting out complaints about housing standards would be dispatched to the horrors of the Gulag. No trace of 'anti-Soviet agitation' was meant to survive. Casual jokes against Stalin, the communist party or the Soviet state were treated as the most heinous form of treason. In this fashion practically all Soviet citizens were extirpated who had displayed an independent mind about public affairs.

Yet Stalin's very success brought about a crisis of its own. The original purpose of his clique in the central leadership had been to reconstruct the state so as to secure their authority and impose their policies. In carrying through this design, the clique came close to demolishing the state itself. The blood-purge of the armed forces disrupted the USSR's defences in a period of intense international tension. The arrest of the economic administrators in the people's commissariats impeded industrial output. The destruction of cadres in party, trade unions and local government undermined administrative co-ordination. This extreme destabilization endangered Stalin himself. For if the Soviet state fell apart, Stalin's career would be at an end. He had started the carnage of 1937–8 because of real hostility to his policies, real threats to his authority, a real underlying menace to the compound of the Soviet order. Yet his reaction was hysterically out of proportion to the menace he faced.

Stalin had a scarily odd personality. He was in his element amidst chaos and violence, and had learned how to create an environment of uncertainty wherein only he could remain a fixed, dominant point of influence. His belief in the rapid trainability of functionaries and experts, furthermore, gave him his equanimity when butchering an entire administrative stratum. The Stalin of the Civil War and the First Five-Year Plan lived again in the Great Terror. His hyper-suspicious, imperious temperament came to the fore. No one coming into frequent contact with him in the late 1930s had a chance to become disloyal: he had them killed before such thoughts could enter their heads. He was unflustered about murder. When his old comrade Vlas Chubar telephoned him out of concern lest he be arrested, Stalin warmly reassured him; but Chubar was arrested the same day and, after disgusting physical torment, executed.

By then Stalin was privately identifying himself with the great despots of history. He was fascinated by Genghis Khan, and underlined the following adage attributed to him: 'The deaths of the vanquished are necessary for the tranquillity of the victors.' He also took a shine to Augustus, the first Roman emperor, who had disguised the autocratic character of his rule by refusing the title of king just as Stalin was permitting himself at most the unofficial title of Leader.[57]

Other rulers who tugged at his imagination were the Russian tsars Ivan the Terrible and Peter the Great. He admired them with the critical eye of a twentieth-century dictator: 'One of Ivan the Terrible's mistakes was to overlook the five great feudal families. If he had annihilated those five families, there would definitely have been no Time of Troubles. But Ivan the Terrible would execute someone and then spend a long time repenting and praying. God got in his way in this matter. He ought to have been still more decisive!'[58] And, when proposing a toast at a celebratory banquet in honour of the Bulgarian communist Georgi Dimitrov in 1937, Stalin declared that any party member trying to weaken the military might and territorial integrity of the USSR would perish: 'We shall physically annihilate him together with his clan!' He summarized his standpoint with the war-cry: 'For the destruction of traitors and their foul line!'[59]

This was a leader who took what he wanted from historical models and discarded the rest – and what he wanted apparently included techniques for the maintenance of personal despotism. No candidate for the Lenin succession in the mid-1920s would have done what Stalin did with his victory a decade later in the Great Terror. Nadezhda Krupskaya, Lenin's widow, quipped that if he had not died in 1924, he would be serving time in one of Stalin's prisons.

Lenin would surely have been appalled at the NKVD's bacchanalia of repression. But it must not be overlooked how much Stalin had learned and inherited from Lenin. Stalin continued to admire Lenin even though Lenin on his death-bed wished to sack him from the General Secretaryship. Lenin's ideas on violence, dictatorship, terror, centralism, hierarchy and leadership were integral to Stalin's thinking. Furthermore, Lenin had bequeathed the terroristic instrumentalities to his successor. The Cheka, the forced-labour camps, the one-party state, the mono-ideological mass media, the legalized administrative arbitrariness, the prohibition of free and popular elections, the ban on internal party dissent: not one of these had to be invented by Stalin. Lenin had practised mass terror in the Civil War and continued to demand its application, albeit on a much more restricted basis, under the NEP. Not for nothing did Stalin call himself Lenin's disciple.

It is hard to imagine Lenin, however, carrying out a terror upon his own party. Nor was he likely to have insisted on the physical and psychological degradation of those arrested by the political police. In short, Lenin would have been horrified by the scale and methods of the Great Terror.

He would also have been astounded by its autocratic insouciance.

Stalin over the years reviewed 383 lists of the most important arrested persons in bound booklets he endearingly called albums, and his self-assigned chore was to append a number to each name. A number '1' was a recommendation for execution, a '2' indicated ten years in the camps, a '3' left it to Yezhov's discretion. A single album might contain 200 names, and the technique of reviewing cases 'in the album fashion' was copied at lower rungs of the ladder of state repression.[60] Also attributable to Stalin personally was the insistence that leading victims should not be shot until they had been thoroughly humiliated. In one of his last pleas to Stalin, Bukharin wrote asking what purpose would be served by his death. This question must have given profound satisfaction to Stalin, who kept the letter in his desk until his own death in 1953. Countless unfortunates across the USSR were similarly robbed of every shred of dignity by interrogators who extracted a grovelling confession before releasing them to the firing squad.

Stalin had an extraordinary memory, but not even he could know the biographies of every real or potential antagonist. His method of rule had always been to manufacture a situation which induced local officials to compete with each other in pursuit of his principal aim. It gladdened him that troiki in the provinces sometimes appealed against centrally-assigned arrest quotas, conventionally known as 'the limits', that they regarded as too low.[61] Nor did he punish local officials who went beyond their quotas. Between August and September 1938, for instance, the security police in Turkmenia carried out double the originally-assigned number of executions.[62]

Thus the Great Terror followed the pattern of state economic planning since 1928: central direction was accompanied by opportunities for much local initiative. While aiming to reach their 'limits', NKVD officials were left to decide for themselves who were the 'anti-Soviet elements' in their locality. Neither Stalin nor even Yezhov could ensure that these 'elements' fell precisely into the categories defined in their various instructions. Nor were even the local NKVD officials entirely free to choose their own victims. As well as personal jealousies there were political rivalries in play. Conflicts at the local level among leaders, among enterprises and among institutions could suddenly be settled by a nicely-timed letter of 'exposure'. There was little incentive to delay in denouncing an enemy; for who could be sure that one's enemy was not already penning a similar letter? Old scores were murderously paid off. And it greatly simplified the task of repression, once a fellow had been arrested, to compile a list of his friends and associates and arrest them too.

But if vile behaviour was widespread, it was at its worst among the employees of the NKVD. Neither Stalin nor Yezhov in person directly inflicted pain on those under arrest. But the duties of the NKVD attracted some enthusiastic physical tormentors. One such was Lavrenti Beria who became Yezhov's deputy in July 1938. He had a collection of canes in his office, and Red Army commanders ruefully talked of such interrogations as occasions when they went 'to have a coffee with Beria'.[63] This newcomer to Moscow was notorious in Georgia, where he beat prisoners, sentenced them to death and gratuitously had them beaten again before they were shot.[64] And Beria was by no means the worst of the gruesome sadists attracted to the NKVD's employment.

Furthermore, the morbid suspiciousness of the Kremlin dictator was internationalized as Stalin turned his attention to the world's communist parties. The irony was that he did this during a period of improvement of the USSR's relations with several major foreign states. Formal diplomatic ties had been agreed with the United Kingdom, France and the USA in 1933. Entrance had been effected to the League of Nations in 1934 and treaties signed with France and Czechoslovakia. In the same year the Politburo also overturned its injunction to foreign communist parties to concentrate their hostility upon rival socialists; instead they were to form 'popular fronts' with such socialists in a political campaign against fascism. The containment of the European far right had become a goal in Soviet foreign policy. The reorientation was affirmed at the Seventh Congress of the Comintern in August 1935.

While making this adjustment in foreign policy, Stalin demanded vigilance from Europe's communists, and the Comintern was ordered to rid its ranks of Trotskyist and Bukharinist 'traitors'. Until 1937 this was a strictly political process because only the All-Union

Communist Party in Moscow was a governing communist party with a secret police which could arrest those party members who had been expelled. This meant that while communists were being tortured in the USSR for long-past associations with members of left-of-centre political parties, communists abroad were expelled from their own parties as Trotskyists if they refused to collaborate with other parties on the left.

There was certainly reason for Stalin to worry about the world situation. Germany and Japan signed an Anti-Comintern Pact in November 1936, increasing the menace of a war against the USSR on two fronts. In the same year Hitler had wrecked the Treaty of Versailles in Europe by occupying the Rhineland and offering military support to the fascist forces of General Franco in the Spanish Civil War. The USSR's call for intervention by the parliamentary democracies of Europe in concert with the Soviet state was ignored. Stalin sent equipment and advisers to Spain all the same. Official Soviet propagandists praised the principled stand being taken by the Kremlin. The USSR was the only state willing to translate its anti-fascist rhetoric into action and Stalin enhanced his prestige among those sections of Western political opinion which bridled at the passivity of the British and French governments.

As Soviet assistance reached Spain in 1937, however, so too did Soviet political practices. The Spanish and foreign volunteers fighting for the Madrid republican government did not consist exclusively of members of parties belonging to the Comintern: there were also liberals, social-democrats, socialists, Trotskyists and anarchists. Stalin, while wanting to preserve the policy of 'popular fronts' against fascism, rejected co-operation with rival far-left groupings; and he instructed his emissaries to conduct the same bloody terror against the Trotskyists, anarchists and others that he was applying to them in the USSR. Thousands of anti-fascist fighters were arrested and executed at the behest of the Soviet functionaries.

Stalin wanted to increase the influence of the world-wide communist movement, but only insofar as it in no way damaged the USSR's interests as he perceived them. In 1938 he took the otherwise incomprehensible decision to wipe out the leading cadre of the Polish

Communist Party. The victims were by then resident in Moscow, and the few surviving figures were those lucky enough to be in prison in Warsaw (and one of these, Władisław Gomułka, was destined to become the Polish communist leader in 1945). Stalin, knowing that many comrades from Poland had sympathized with leftist communist factions in Moscow in the 1920s, aimed to crush insubordination before it recurred. Moreover, the NKVD infiltrated their agents into groups of political *émigrés* from the Soviet Union. Assassinations were frequent. Trotski, immured in his own armed compound in Coyoacán in Mexico, survived for a while; but even his defences were penetrated on 20 August 1940, when his killer, Ramon Mercader, plunged an ice-pick into the back of his head.

All this time the situation around the USSR's border became more threatening. While fighting a war against China, the Japanese military command was not averse to provoking trouble with the USSR. Violent clashes occurred in July 1937. Another series of incidents took place between July and August 1938, culminating in the battle of Lake Khasan on the Manchurian border. A truce was arranged, but there was no guarantee that Japan would desist from further aggression. In the same year, Hitler made Germany the most powerful state in Europe by occupying all of Austria and the Sudetenland in Czechoslovakia.

Yet it was also in 1937–8 that Stalin chose to liquidate practically the entire high command of his armed forces. Nothing more vividly demonstrates that his was the statesmanship of the madhouse. By late 1938 even Stalin was coming to the conclusion that the scale of state terror had to be reduced. The most obvious sign of this was given on 19 November 1938, when Yezhov unexpectedly resigned from the NKVD after a brief interview with Stalin. He retained a job as People's Commissar for Water Transport, but began to while away the meetings of Sovnarkom by folding paper aeroplanes and flying them around the room. Acquaintances were puzzled as to whether he had finally gone off his head or was an accomplished actor; but Stalin was not one to leave such things to guesswork: Yezhov was arrested in April 1939 and executed in the following February.[65]

The Iron Hedgehog's disappearance signalled the closing of the floodgates of the Great Terror. It was not the end of extensive terror; on the contrary, Stalin used it liberally for the rest of his career. But at the end of 1938 he had decided that the arrests should be fewer. He did not explain his changed position; and yet surely even he must have been shaken by the many practical effects of the blood-purge. There is still much uncertainty about the physical volume of industrial output in 1937–8; but certainly the rate of growth was severely curtailed. There may even have been an absolute decrease in production.[66] The disorganization was extraordinary. Even the purgers of the purgers of the purgers had been arrested in some places. There are hints that Stalin recognized his own proneness to being too suspicious for his own good; he was to mutter in Khrushchëv's presence several years later: 'I trust nobody, not even myself.'[67]

Yet such comments were rare. On the whole Stalin gave the impression that abuses of power were not large in number and that anyway they were Yezhov's fault. Consequently no action was taken against people who referred to the Great Terror as the Yezhovshchina.[68] For this term distracted unpleasant attention from Stalin. And Stalin, having used Yezhov to do his dirty business, emerged as Soviet dictator in all but name.

He had broken the party as an independent, supreme political agency. Five years passed after the Seventeenth Party Congress in 1934 before he would permit another Congress to convene, and he restricted the Central Committee to one plenum in 1939. The Politburo was ceasing to meet on a regular, formal basis: Stalin preferred to hold discussions with whatever group of Politburo members suited his purposes at the time.[69] The NKVD's star had risen while the party's had fallen; and Beria, when replacing Yezhov, entered the small circle of Stalin's close advisers. The 'organs', as the security police were known, were at Stalin's elbow whenever he needed them. Fearsome as it was, moreover, the NKVD itself operated in dread of Stalin. In consequence of the Great Terror of 1937–8, therefore, Stalin had succeeded in elevating himself above party, people's commissariats, army, trade unions and police.

He fostered tension among these powerful institutions so as to maintain his towering position. Communists had typically given little mind to the demarcation of functions among state bodies since the October Revolution; they despised such pernicketiness as an obstacle to communist progress. Stalin exploited this attitude to his personal advantage. The NKVD conflicted with the Red Army, the Red Army with various People's Commissariats, the Commissariats with the Central Council of Trade Unions and the Central Council with the Party Central Committee.

After 1938 these clashes were mainly bureaucratic squabbles; they often involved differing orientations of policy, but they were less frequently accompanied by mass arrests. All public institutions, while abjectly professing loyalty to Stalin, were confirmed in their power over the rest of society. The Soviet state was authoritative as never before. Satisfied that he had brought the party to heel, Stalin restored its prestige and authority somewhat. The salaries of its functionaries were raised. In December 1938 the NKVD was ordered to seek permission from the party apparatus before taking any official of the party into custody; and, at the Eighteenth Party Congress in March 1939, Beria stressed that not all the economic problems of the USSR were attributable to sabotage. It was even admitted that a great many expulsions from the party – which in 1937–8 had typically led to arrests – had been unjustified. Stalin confirmed the fresh attitude by asserting the necessity to 'value cadres like the gold reserves of the party and state, esteem them, have respect for them'.[70]

The applause which greeted this statement of monumental hypocrisy stemmed from a feeling of relief that the party might again enjoy durable favour. Other institutions were similarly reassured; but the party remained rather special. It incarnated continuity with the October Revolution, with Lenin, with Marxism-Leninism, with the Communist International. It provided the ideological cement to help to maintain the Soviet state. Its cohesive capacity was equally important organizationally: holders of governmental, administrative and military office were virtually obliged to be party members and to operate under the party's discipline; and the party apparatus, at the centre and elsewhere, helped to co-ordinate state institutions.

Furthermore, citizens of the USSR were acutely aware of their state's immense and pervasive powers. The Great Terror, following quickly after the violent campaigns of collectivization and industrialization, left no one in doubt about the consequences of overt disobedience. The kind of conversation held by the visiting American engineer John Scott with Soviet managers in the early 1930s about the inefficiency of a particular coal-mine no longer took place. Similarly, the complaining talk among workers recorded at the beginning of the decade by the ex-Menshevik Viktor Kravchenko became more discreet by its end. Oppositional leaflets of discontented party activists, which still appeared as late as 1933, had become antiquarian artefacts. Officials in every institution and at every level were wary of saying the slightest thing that might conceivably be interpreted as disloyal. The traumatization had been profound, and the carnage of 1937–8 left a mark on popular consciousness that endures.

12

Coping with Big Brothers

By the late 1930s the term totalitarianism was being widely used to describe the kind of state and society engineered by Iosif Stalin. Benito Mussolini had used it in reference to his own fascist Italy nearly two decades before. Commentators on Soviet politics, while recognizing contrasts of ideology, saw the similarities among fascism, nazism and communism in their methods of rule. In Moscow as in Berlin there was a dominant leader and a one-party state. Both countries had witnessed a merciless crushing of internal opposition. The state not only monopolized the instrumentalities of coercion but also dominated the means of mass communication. It allowed no challenge to the single official ideology. There was persecution of any independent individual, organization or institution standing between the central state bodies and ordinary citizens. Total, unmediated pervasion of society by his power was each leader's aspiration.

That something close to this had been Stalin's underlying objective in carrying through the Great Terror there can be little doubt. Yet his power was not absolute. Those who had carried out the bloody purges knew that, in order to survive, they had to use the practices of patronage and mutual protection which Stalin had hoped to eradicate. And Stalin himself had had to scale down his totalist aims in the course of the Terror. Concessions to Russian national pride had been strengthened. Moreover, not all public entertainments were heavily political: frivolity existed even in Stalin's USSR. Stalin felt the need to identify himself with the aspirations of the people he governed. This fearsome dictator had fears of his own.

Yet he could take comfort from the knowledge that he had

promoted a vast number of newly-trained young activists. The central nomenklatura of personnel involved in state economic management had risen to 32,899 posts. Of these, 14,585 at the beginning of 1939 had been appointed in the past two years – forty-seven per cent of the total. In the Red Army the proportion was also remarkable: Stalin had purged the officer corps at its highest levels with particular thoroughness. The apparatus of the party, too, had been overhauled. Four out of five provincial committee first secretaries had joined the party after Lenin's death; ninety-one per cent of them had yet to reach the age of forty (and sixty-two per cent were less than thirty-five years old).[1] A cohort of young men gained advancement who were later to govern the country through to the early 1980s: Mikhail Suslov, Dmitri Ustinov, Leonid Brezhnev, Aleksei Kosygin and Nikolai Podgorny. It was a new élite and it was Stalin's élite.

Most of its members were workers or peasants who had taken the opportunities offered by the Soviet authorities to get themselves educated. Over half of the voting delegates to the Eighteenth Party Congress in 1939 had completed their secondary schooling.[2] Their adult life and their politics marked them off from the generation of Old Bolsheviks: they had not operated in the clandestine Bolshevik groups before 1917; they had not made the October Revolution or fought in the Civil War; and their Marxism was not their intellectual passion but a crude creed purveyed to them by the party's agitation-and-propaganda departments.

They were taught to obey and be vigilant; their obligation was not only to 'unmask' traitors but also to engage in 'self-criticism' whenever they could not fulfil orders. Simultaneously they were cajoled to clamber up the ladder of promotion. The administrative hierarchy in the USSR was much simpler than in advanced capitalist societies: the duties, perks and authority accompanying each post were evident to every ambitious man and woman. The Soviet Union was distinguished by a uniformity of work-style and by great symbolism and ceremony. Not only military but also civilian medals were worn in normal public life: even Molotov sported a Hero of the Soviet Union badge on his suit's lapel. Outstanding actors, opera singers and clowns were awarded the title of 'People's Artist of the

USSR'; and when national gatherings were held in the capital, ritual obeisance to Stalin was compulsory: the major decisions had been taken in advance by the party leadership.

The promotees could hardly believe their luck. Most of them were persons who had not dreamed of staying in a hotel or even having a healthy diet earlier in their lives. As the Great Terror came to an end, they became able to enjoy their privileged conditions. The gap between the rulers and the ruled widened. In 1940, Stalin approved the introduction of fees to be paid by parents for students in the last three years of secondary school and at university. High-ranking administrators were in a better position to find the necessary finance than any other group in society. A new social class was in the process of formation.[3]

Its members acclaimed Stalin as the world's outstanding philanthropist, leader and theorist. In the 1930s he attempted no lengthy contribution to the canon of Bolshevism: he was too busy killing Bolsheviks. Many among the party's writers who might have written textbooks for him fell victim to his butchery. A new explication of the principles of Marxism-Leninism was essential for the regime. As regional party secretary M. M. Khataevich had put it in 1935, there was a need for 'a book of our own, in place of the Bible, that could give a rigorous answer – correct and comprehensible – to the many important questions of the structure of the world'.[4] Khataevich perished in the Great Terror; and the project for a grand treatise on Marxism was not realized until after Stalin's death. In the meantime the gap was filled by a book with a narrower title, *The History of the All-Union Communist Party: A Short Course*.

The main authors were veteran party loyalists V. G. Knorin, E. M. Yaroslavski and P. N. Pospelov. But Stalin closely supervised the contents and personally wrote the sub-chapter on 'dialectical and historical materialism'. To most intents and purposes he was the textbook's general editor and hid behind the pseudonym of 'a commission of the Central Committee'.

The *Short Course* traced the rise of the Bolsheviks from the political struggles against the Romanov monarchy through to Stalin's ascendancy. The last section of the final chapter dealt with 'the

Liquidation of the Remnants of the Bukharinite-Trotskyist Gang of Spies, Wreckers and Traitors to the Country'. Hysterical self-righteousness imbued the book. Stalin wanted to stress that Marxism provided the sole key to understanding both the social life of humanity and even the material universe, and that only Stalin's variant of Marxism was acceptable. Just as prophet followed prophet in the Old Testament, the *Short Course* traced a lineage of authentic scientific communism from Marx and Engels through Lenin down to Stalin. According to Stalin, Bolshevism had triumphed predominantly through struggle, often bloody, merciless struggle, and unceasing vigilance.[5]

Purportedly its victories had also resulted from the virtues of its leadership. Lenin and Stalin, and subsequently Stalin by himself, had led the Central Committee. The Central Committee had led the communist party and the party had led the masses. In each period of the party's history there had been maleficent communists such as Trotski and Bukharin who had linked up with kulaks, priests, landlords and tsarist officers at home and capitalist espionage agencies abroad. But in vain! For Comrade Stalin had rooted out the traitors and pointed the party in the direction of the attainment of a perfect society!

The book divided everything between black and white (or, as Stalin preferred, White and Red). There was no palette of colours in this Stalinist catechism. Violence, intolerance, pitilessness, command, discipline, correctness and science were the central themes. In the USSR of the 1930s this was a conservative set of recommendations. Current holders of office could act without qualms. Stalin's infallibility meant that they need not question their consciences, even when taking up the posts of innocent dead men and buying up their possessions in the special shops runs by the NKVD. By obeying the Leader, they were acting in complete accord with the requirements of patriotism, class struggle and History. Their power and their privileged life-style were in the natural order of things, and the existence of an impregnable, terrifying Soviet state was the guarantee of the October Revolution's preservation. The *Short Course* was a manifesto for Stalin's style of communist conservatism.

According to Lenin, however, the communist dictatorship would wither away and be succeeded by a society without any state bodies whatsoever. Stalin brazenly declared that much progress had already been made towards that ultimate goal. The bourgeoisie no longer existed, and a new social and economic order had been built.

Now it was stated that only three social classes existed: the working class, the peasantry and the 'working intelligentsia' (which included everyone with an administrative, managerial or educational post). Therefore the Soviet Union was still a society of classes. But supposedly it was different from all such previous societies inasmuch as the three classes had no reason to conflict with each other. Thus the working class, the peasantry and the intelligentsia had 'non-antagonistic' interests and drew common benefit from the state's provision of employment, education, health care, nutrition and shelter.[6] In November 1936, when introducing a new Constitution for the USSR, Stalin proclaimed: 'Socialism, which is the first phase of communism, has basically been realized in our country.'[7] He therefore proposed that the electoral franchise should be made universal. The 'deprived ones' (*lishentsy*) – including former kulaks, White Army officers and priests – should be allowed to vote.[8]

Universal civil rights were introduced on paper, and the freedoms of thought, the press, religion, organization and assembly were guaranteed. Furthermore, Stalin insisted that economic rights were as important as political ones. In particular, he drew attention to the guarantees of employment given in the Soviet Union. This led him to claim that the new Constitution proved that the USSR was the most democratic country in the world.

Stalin was being monumentally insincere. The lishentsy were picked out for repression when the Great Terror began in full earnest in mid-1937. Moreover, the new Constitution itself was laden with stipulations that restricted the exercise of civil freedoms. In the first place, the USSR was defined as 'a socialist state of the workers and peasants'. Thus the rights of citizens were made entirely subsidiary to the determination to preserve the existing structure and orientation of the Soviet state. No clause in the Constitution expressly sanctioned the All-Union Communist Party's political monopoly; but only the existing public institutions, including the communist party, were allowed to put up candidates in elections. Formal approval was given in this indirect fashion to the one-party state. Stalin carefully supervised the wording of the final draft and, when introducing the Constitution, specified that the communist dictatorship was not going to be weakened.[9]

Not surprisingly the Constitution was not taken seriously by citizens of the USSR.[10] Its main admirers were gullible foreigners. The most notorious of them were Sidney and Beatrice Webb, whose *Soviet Communism: A New Civilization?* sought to defend Stalin against the charge that dictatorship of any kind existed in the USSR![11] In the meantime Molotov bluntly affirmed that years would pass before full implementation of all the civil freedoms granted by the Constitution;[12] and already in 1933 Stalin himself had contended that, as the party advanced to victory after victory, so the state required strengthening against the bitter onslaughts of its foes at home and abroad. In 1939 he expatiated on this point at the Eighteenth Party Congress: 'Will our state be retained also in the period of communism? Yes, it will be retained unless capitalist encirclement is liquidated and unless the danger of a military attack from abroad is liquidated.'[13]

This contradicted Marxist doctrine inasmuch as communism was supposed to involve the 'withering away of the state'. But Stalin ignored such a nicety; his overriding aim was to reinforce the regimentative aspects of Bolshevism. The Congress delegates were anyway not the sort to worry about interpretations of Marxism. They were also well accustomed to the fact that the USSR was a terror-state. At the same Eighteenth Congress Stalin alluded to this in his po-faced comment that, whereas the elections to the USSR Supreme Soviet yielded a 98.6 per cent vote in favour of the regime after the sentencing of Tukhachevski in 1937, the proportion rose to 99.4 per cent after Bukharin's trial in 1938.[14]

Stalin, needless to say, knew that the more favourable vote derived not from the cogency of the evidence against the alleged traitors but from the intimidating example of their execution. Not even he, however, ruled exclusively through the violence of his security and judicial machinery. He had his equivalent of an old boys' network, consisting of cronies who had supported him in his past battles and who served him through to his death. The first in political seniority was Molotov. Then came Kaganovich and Mikoyan, who had joined him in the early 1920s. Others included pre-revolutionary party veterans such as Andrei Zhdanov, Andrei Andreev, Nikolai Bulganin and Kliment Voroshilov. Nor did Stalin neglect the young: Lavrenti Beria, Nikita Khrushchëv and Georgi Malenkov were hauled up by him from the lower political echelons and promoted to supreme party and government posts.

The central leadership was like a gang, and Stalin as its leader relied upon his fellow members to organize the state's institutions. Competence and obedience remained prerequisites of gang membership. The penalty for disagreement with Stalin was constant: 'seven grams of lead' in the head.

Stalin continued to make occasional arrests of cronies. Like Al Capone, he knew how to 'keep the boys in line'.[15] For instance, he asked Khrushchëv whether it was true that he was really a Pole.[16] This was quite enough to terrify Khrushchëv, who knew that in 1938 Stalin had executed the Polish communist *émigrés* in Moscow. The nearer someone was to the apex of power, the more directly he was intimidated by Stalin. People's commissars trembled at meetings of Sovnarkom. Stalin's ploy was to get up from the long green-baize table and pad up and down in his soft leather boots behind the seats of his colleagues. It was an unnerving experience. In reply to Stalin's enquiry about the number of recent plane crashes, air force commander Rychagov, being the worse for drink, blurted out: 'There will continue to be a high level of accidents because we're compelled by you to go up in flying coffins.' The room fell silent as a graveyard, and after a long pause Stalin murmured: 'You shouldn't have spoken like that.' Rychagov was shot a few days later.[17]

Yet the uppermost élite lived in greater safety than in 1937–8. Stalin could not afford to reduce his associates to the condition of robots: he needed them to accompany their self-abasement before him with a dynamic ruthlessness in the discharge of their tasks – and to give orders on their own initiative. Laws, decrees, regulations and commands were produced in profusion in this period of frightful legal abusiveness.[18] But, as under Lenin, office-holders were given to understand that they would not be assessed on the basis of their adherence to procedural norms. What would ultimately count for or against them was their record of practical results.

At the supreme and middling levels they had to combine the talents of cardinals, *condottieri* and landed magnates: they had to be propagators of Marxism-Leninism; they had to fight for the policies of the party; and each of them had to assemble a band of followers who would carry out orders throughout the area of their patron's responsibility. The unavoidable result was that Stalin had to settle for a less amenable administration than he had aimed to establish by means of the Great Terror. Just as he needed his cronies, so they needed cronies of their own. The cliental groupings therefore stayed in place. For example, Postyshev's team in the Ukrainian party leadership gave way to Khrushchëv's team when Stalin sent Khrushchëv to Kiev in 1938; and Beria likewise cleared out Yezhov's team from the NKVD and installed his own: it was the only available way to ensure the substitution of reliable anti-Yezhovites.

Not only vertically but also horizontally the old administrative practices stayed in place. In June 1937 Stalin had complained: 'It's thought that the centre must know everything and see everything. No, the centre doesn't see everything: it's not like that at all. The centre sees only a part and the remainder is seen in the localities. It sends people without knowing these people one hundred per cent. You must check them out.'[19] But new local 'nests' or 'family circles' were formed almost as soon as Stalin destroyed the existing ones. Wheeling and dealing occurred among the heads of party, soviet, police, army and enterprise management; local officials protected each other against the demands made by central authorities. More than ever, lying to Moscow was a skill crucial for physical survival. Institutions had to fiddle the accounts so as to exaggerate achievements enough to win acclaim, but not to the point that the following year's quotas would be raised intolerably high.

Such evasiveness was not confined to officialdom. A black market existed in those many types of product which were in severe deficit in the USSR. Moisei Kaganovich, brother of Stalin's close associate, loudly objected to the general evidence of disobedience: 'The earth ought to tremble when the director walks around the plant!' In theory the managerial stratum was obliged to give its work-forces a harder time than since the October Revolution. But the potential for harshness was limited outside the forced-labour camps by the chronic shortage of skilled free labour. Strict time-keeping and conscientious work could not be enforced if hired labourers could simply wander off and find employment elsewhere. A kind of social concordat was established whereby managers overlooked labour indiscipline so long as they could hang on to their workers. Records were written to over-state a worker's technical qualifications or his hours of attendance or his output. Managers had to break the law in order to fulfil their own quotas.[20]

In every branch of the economy it was the same story. Even in the kolkhozes and the sovkhozes the local authorities found it convenient to make compromises with the work-forces. A blind eye was turned to the expansion of the size of peasants' private plots.[21] Regular contribution of 'labour days' was not always insisted upon. Illicit borrowing of the farm's equipment was overlooked by the chairman who needed to keep the peasants on his side in order to fulfil the governmental quotas.

The central political leadership had been encouraging the workers and kolkhozniki to denounce factory directors and farm chairmen for their involvement in sabotage; but the end of the Great Terror led to a renewed emphasis on labour discipline. Increasingly draconian punishments were introduced. Managers in town and countryside were threatened with imprisonment if they failed to report absenteeism, lack of punctuality, sloppy workmanship as well as theft and fraud. According to a decree of December 1938, labourers who were late for work three times in a month should be sacked. Another decree in June 1940 stated that such behaviour should incur a penalty of six months' corrective labour at their place of work.[22] Stalin also tightened his grip on the collective farms. A decree of May 1939 ordered local authorities to seize back land under illegal private cultivation by kolkhozniki.[23] But the fact that such measures were thought necessary showed that, at the lower levels of administration, non-compliance with the demands of the central authorities was widespread. Sullen, passive resistance had become a way of life.

The Soviet order therefore continued to need a constant dosage of excitation in order to keep functioning. Otherwise the institutions of party and government would tend to relapse into quietude as officials pursued personal privilege and bureaucratic compromise. Ideological apathy would also increase. The provision of dachas, nannies, special shops and special hospitals was already well developed in the 1920s; and, with the termination of the Great Terror, these benefits were confirmed as the patrimony of Stalin's ruling subordinates. How to ensure a lively discomfort among the central and local nomenklaturas?

Or indeed among all sections of the USSR's society? Denunciation by ordinary workers became a routine method of controlling politicians and administrators. Stalin knew that anonymous letter-writing was open to abuse; and yet he fostered the practice in order to keep all leaders in a state of trepidation. Likewise he reinforced *Pravda*'s custom of carrying out muck-raking investigations in a specific locality. The idea was that an exposé of malpractice would stimulate the eradication of similar phenomena elsewhere. Stalin and his colleagues were attracted to a campaigning style of work. Time after time the central political authorities imposed a fresh organizational technique or a new industrial product, and used the press to demand enthusiastic local obedience. Reluctantly they had accepted that Stakhanovism caused more disruption than increase in output; but the pressurizing of managers and workers to over-fulfil plans was an unchanging feature.[24]

These traditions had existed since 1917; but Stalin relied upon them to a greater extent than Lenin. Organizational pressure and ideological invocation, in the absence of the predominant stimulus of the market, were the principal instruments available to him apart from resort to the security police. A structural imperative was at work. Stalin's preferences gave strength to the practices, but the practices were also necessary for the maintenance of the regime.

The central authorities aimed at the total penetration of society.

The Great Terror had smashed down nearly all associations that competed with the regime for popularity. The only surviving potential challenge of an organized nature came from the religious bodies, and all of these were in a deeply traumatized condition. It was the aim of the authorities that no unit of social life – not only the tribe and the clan but also even the family – might be left free from their control. Within the walls of each family home there could be talk about the old days before the October Revolution and about values and traditions other than the Marxist-Leninist heritage. Discussions between parents and their children therefore became a matter for governmental concern. In 1932 a fourteen-year-old village boy called Pavlik Morozov had denounced his father for fraud. The peasants on the same kolkhoz were enraged by such filial perfidy, and lynched the lad. Young Pavlik became a symbol of the official duty of each citizen to support the state's interest even to the point of informing upon his parents.

Other groups, too, attracted Stalin's persecution. No recreational or cultural club was permitted to exist unless it was run by the state; and harmless groups of philatelists, Esperantists and ornithologists were broken up by the arrest of their members. Labourers had to watch their tongues when gathering together over a glass of vodka in taverns; intellectuals were wary of sharing their thoughts with each other in the kommunalki in case their neighbours might overhear them. NKVD informers were everywhere and everyone learned to exercise extreme caution.

Lower than this level, however, the Soviet state found it difficult to achieve its goals. The plan was to maximize the influence over people as individuals. Citizens were permitted to act collectively only when mobilized by party and government. But the groups based on family, wider kinship, friendship, leisure and a common culture were molecules resistant to disintegration into separate atoms.[25] The difficulties for the authorities were compounded by the abrupt, massive process of urbanization: a third of the population of the USSR lived in towns and cities by 1940: this was double the proportion three decades earlier. The newcomers from the villages brought with them their folk beliefs, their religion and even their forms of organizations; for some of them, when leaving their villages, stayed together in *zemlyachestva*, which were the traditional groups based upon geographical origin. In the short term the influx had a 'ruralizing' effect as former villagers introduced their habits and expectations to the towns.[26]

If customary patterns of behaviour caused problems for the political leadership, so too did newer ones. Under the First Five-Year Plan there had been a drastic loosening of moral restraints and social ties. Juvenile delinquency reportedly increased by 100 per cent between 1931 and 1934. Hooliganism was rife not only in the new shanty-cities under construction but also in the old metropolitan centres. In 1935 there were three times as many abortions as births. The incidence of divorce rose sharply. Promiscuity was rampant. Vital social linkages were at the point of dissolution.[27]

Even before the Great Terror the authorities had seen the risks of this situation. Measures were taken to restore a degree of stability. Respect for parents and teachers was officially stressed from 1935. There were curtailments of the rights to get a divorce and to have an abortion in 1936. Awards were to be made to 'mother-heroines' who had ten or more children. School uniforms were reintroduced for the first time since 1917. Discipline at school, at work and at home was officially demanded and most of the new inhabitants of the towns went along with this. But their behaviour displeased the authorities in other respects. Peasants were thought unhygienic, ignorant and stupid. They needed, in the contemporary phrase, to become *kul'turnye* ('cultured'). Campaigns were organized to rectify the situation. People were instructed to wash their hands and faces, brush their teeth and dress smartly in the dourly Soviet manner. Men were told that beards were unmodern. Even Kaganovich, at Stalin's behest, had to shave off his beard.[28]

It was therefore for pragmatic reasons that political leaders began in the mid-1930s to give encouragement to the family and to rather traditional proprieties. But this shift in policy occurred within carefully-maintained parameters. Stalin was determined that it should not culminate in the disintegration of the October Revolution.

He similarly aimed to hold expressions of Russian nationhood under control. His particular stratagem was to attempt to amalgamate 'Russian' and 'Soviet' identities. Thus Russians were to be induced to take much pride in Russia but even greater pride in the USSR. There were indeed many achievements about which the Soviet state could boast in the 1930s. Daring expeditions were made to the frozen Russian north, where gold, oil and other precious deposits were discovered. Records were broken by Valeri Chkalov and other aviators who flew over the North Pole. Gymnastic displays were frequent and football became a major sport across the USSR. The Moscow Metro was renowned for its sumptuous frescos, candelabra and immaculate punctuality. Almost every edition of *Pravda* carried a large photograph of some young hero who had accomplished some great feat – and in 1937–8 there were more pictures of such persons than of Stalin himself on the first page of the newspaper.[29] The popularity of such successes was among the reasons why he got away with his bloody mass purges.

Science, mathematics and technology were also celebrated. Bolsheviks had always dreamed of engineering an entirely new physical environment, and Lenin had minted the slogan: 'Communism equals electrification plus soviet power.' Under the NEP, few advances were made either in academic research or in the diffusion of up-to-date technology. But things changed under Stalin, who put the resources of the Soviet state firmly behind such efforts.

The authorities demanded that scientists should produce work that would benefit the economy. The goals included not only electrification but also 'radiofication' and 'tractorization'. Close control was imposed upon research, often with baleful results: many researchers languished in Siberian labour camps. At the same time the fraudulent geneticist Timofei Lysenko, exploiting his access to Stalin, built up a sparkling career; and one particular foreign adventurer is alleged to have been given funds for the rearing of herds of giant rabbits.[30] (This was surely the most hare-brained of all Stalinist schemes!) Nevertheless science in general made immense progress in the USSR and acquired world renown. Pëtr Kapitsa did brilliant work on low-temperature physics and became director of the Institute of Physical Problems in Moscow. Aleksei Bakh was a founding father of biochemistry. The veteran physiologist Ivan Pavlov remained at work through to his death in 1935, and other giants of the period were the physicists Lev Landau and Yevgeni Lifshits. Promising youths such as Andrei Sakharov were being trained by them to serve the country's interests.

Literature, too, was accorded prestige; but, as with science, Stalin supported activity only insofar as it assisted his ulterior purposes and this naturally affected its quality. Notoriously, he dragooned Maksim Gorki and others to write a eulogistic account entitled 'Stalin's White Sea–Baltic Canal'.[31] Other participating writers included Mikhail Zoshchenko, Valentin Kataev, Aleksei Tolstoy and Viktor Shklovski. All artistic figures went in fear of their lives. Many of the country's most glorious poets, novelists, painters, film directors and composers came to an untimely end. Isaak Babel was shot; Osip Mandelshtam perished in the Gulag; Marina Tsvetaeva, whose husband and son were slaughtered by the NKVD, committed suicide. The despairing Mikhail Bulgakov died of nephritis outside prison. Anna Akhmatova and Boris Pasternak lived a living death, not knowing why they had been spared the fate of others.

Just a few works of merit, such as Andrei Platonov's stories, were published in the late 1930s. Bulgakov's *The Master and Margarita*, with its phantasmagoric portrayal of the clowns and bureaucrats of contemporary Moscow, lay in his desk drawer. None of the wonderful elegies by Mandelshtam, Pasternak and Tsvetaeva on the fate of their country appeared in print. Pasternak wanted to survive and, if this involved keeping his decent poems to himself, he understandably thought it a price worth paying. In 1934 the founding Congress of the Union of Writers was held and the principle of 'socialist realism' became officially mandatory. This meant that 'the truthfulness and historical concreteness of artistic portrayal must be in harmony with the objective of the ideological transformation and education of the workers in the spirit of socialism'. Above all, the arts had to be optimistic. The typical novel would involve a working-class hero who undertakes a task such as the construction of a dam or a housing block and fulfils it against near-miraculous odds.

Reconditeness in theme or style was forbidden not only in literature but also in music. Stalin wanted melodies that were whistlable, and wonderful composers and Marxist-Leninist sympathizers such as Dmitri Shostakovich fell into disgrace for their atonalities and discords. Stalin's taste leant in the direction of the less demanding pre-revolutionary Russian classics: he adored Glinka and Chaikovski. Indeed the ballet and the symphony concert were becoming the favourite evening entertainment for the central party élite. Patriotic (nay, chauvinistic!) films such as Sergei Eisenstein's *Ivan the Terrible* and novels about the tsars by Aleksei Tolstoy were also admired. Lighter mental fare, too, was provided. Spy novels, patriotic doggerel and folk-songs were popular, and many theatres specialized in 'light entertainment'. Love ditties were particular favourites with the audiences. Jazz and Western ballroom dancing were also increasingly common.[32]

The opportunities for cultural self-edification and recreation were widely welcomed; but what most people wanted above all else was an improvement in their material situation. Food shortages had troubled most Soviet citizens since the beginning of the First Five-Year Plan. And things were gradually getting a little better. Bread, meat, sugar were among several staple products no longer rationed from 1934–5. All rationing was abolished in 1936, and material provision improved for most non-arrested people in the late 1930s. Cheap food in work-place cafeterias also made a difference to the average diet. Admittedly consumption per head of the population was still three per cent lower in 1940 than in 1928.[33] But the general trend was towards betterment in the late 1930s. The network of free educational and medical establishments was also expanded and people in employment received their work-clothes free of charge. Such changes proved a surer means of ensuring acquiescence than compulsory study of the *Short Course*.

Many workers and kolkhozniki were anyway pleased by the repression of peremptory, privileged administrators. Sometimes there was a xenophobic aspect to popular attitudes – and *Pravda* played cunningly upon worries about spies and about the military threats from abroad. Furthermore, the Bolsheviks who had made the October Revolution included a disproportionate number of non-Russians, especially Jews.[34] Indeed many relished the discomfiture of such people. At last the biters were being bitten. Nor were the mass media always disbelieved when they claimed that 'wreckers' and 'spies' existed in a countless quantity.[35] Practically everyone had experienced a breakdown in factory machinery, in public transport or in the supply of food. The years of industrialization and collectivization had been exceptionally turbulent, and it was not hard to persuade people that sabotage was widespread. Moreover, Russian peasants had a tradition of dealing severely with the wrongdoers in their midst. There was a certain amount of popular approval for the harsh punishment of those whom Stalin purged.

The survival of old social attitudes was important in enabling Stalin to carry out the Great Terror and to deflect blame from himself. Among Russians there was a centuries-old assumption that, if the policies of the tsar were unfair, the fault lay with his malevolent advisers. Stalin persistently induced people to think that he had their interests at heart. It was necessary, he had declared, 'to listen carefully to the voice of the masses, to the voice of rank-and-file party members, to the voice of the so-called "little people", to the voice of simple folk.'[36]

Nevertheless it is unclear whether his pose won him friends even among the most simple-minded of citizens. Of course, Stalin's message appealed to the newly-promoted members of the various élites. Of course, too, it was attractive to youngsters who had been schooled to revere him and whose parents were too terrified to say anything even privately against him. But rural hatred of Stalin was visceral.[37] He had identified himself so closely with agricultural collectivization that he could not easily disassociate himself from its horrors. And in the towns there were millions of inhabitants who had no reason whatsoever to regard the period of his rule with affection. Religious belief remained a solace for most people. In the USSR census of 1937, fifty-seven per cent of the population disclosed that they were believers – and the real percentage was probably a lot greater in view of the state's aggressive promotion of atheism.[38] All in all, little political acquiescence would have been obtained if people had not been afraid of the NKVD: silent disgruntlement was the norm.

Most adults in the Soviet Union knew all too well how far official rhetoric was at variance with their direct experience. Real wages per person in 1937 were about three fifths of what they had been in 1928.[39] The material improvement for the average family since the mid-1930s was mainly the result of more members of each family taking up paid employment.[40] People knew they were working much harder for their living. They also retained a keen memory of the military-style collectivization, the famine, the persecution of religion and the bludgeoning of all dissent, near-dissent and imaginary dissent. It is difficult to quantify the degree of hostility to Stalin's regime. Who but a fool or a saint talked openly about these matters? But the NKVD did not delude itself that the voluntary communion of Stalin, the party and the masses was a reality. Police informers in Voronezh province, for example, indicated that the contents of the 1936 Constitution were widely regarded as not being worth the paper they were printed upon.[41]

The conclusion must be that the Soviet state was far from its goal of reshaping popular opinion to its liking. But a caveat must be entered here. Interviews with Soviet citizens who fled the USSR in the Second World War showed that support for welfare-state policies, for strong government and for patriotic pride was robust – and this was a sample of persons who had shown their detestation of Stalin by leaving the country.[42] Some elements in the regime's ideology struck a congenial chord while others produced only disharmony. This was not a settled society, far less a 'civilization'. People knew they lacked the power to get rid of the Societ order. While hoping for change, they made the best of a bad job. Probably most of them ceased to dream of a specific alternative to Stalinism. They tried to be practical in an efford to survive. All the more reason for Stalin to reward the men and women who staffed the institutions that administered society on his behalf. Insofar as it was a durable system, this was to a large extent because a hierarchically graduated system of power and emoluments held their loyalty. Even many doubters thought that the regime's nastiness was not unreformable. Hope, too, endured in the USSR.

A wilder misjudgement of Stalin is hard to imagine. Stalin was unembarrassed about the need to use force in order to maintain his rule. In August 1938, as the penal terms of a generation of convicts drew to a close, he playfully asked the USSR Supreme Soviet whether such convicts should be released on time. He declared that 'from the viewpoint of the state economy it would be a bad idea' to set them free since the camps would lose their best workers. In addition, convicts on release might re-associate with criminals in their home towns and villages. Better for them to complete their rehabilitation inside the Gulag: 'In a camp the atmosphere is different; it is difficult to go to the bad there. As you know, we have a system of voluntary-compulsory financial loans. Let's also introduce a system of voluntary-compulsory retention.'[43] And so just as free wage-earners had to agree to 'lend' part of their wages to the Soviet government, so camp inmates would have to agree to the lengthening of their sentences.

And so control over people came nearest to perfection in relation to two groups: those at the very bottom and those at the very top. Camp inmates had no rights: their daily routine ensured compliance with the instruction of their guards on pain of death. Politburo members, too, lacked rights, and their physical proximity to Stalin necessitated an unswerving obedience to the whim of the Leader. Molotov, Kaganovich, Malenkov, Beria and their colleagues could never safely object to a line of policy which Stalin had already approved.

But in between there were gradations of non-compliance which were possible and common. Policies could be obfuscated, modified and even emasculated. Choices could be made between one official priority and another; for there was practically no message from the Kremlin that was not said to be a priority of the Politburo. Furthermore, the entire structure of public information, surveillance and enforcement was patchy. Such a state and such a society were clearly not totalitarian if the epithet involves totality in practice as well as in intent. Compliance with the supreme communist leadership was greater in politics than in administration, greater in administration than in the economy, greater in the economy than in social relations. The totalitarian order was therefore full of contradictions.

Perfect central control eluded Stalin. The Soviet compound was a unity of extremely orderly features and extremely chaotic ones.

It is plain that Stalin in the 1930s was driven by the will to destroy the old relationships and to build new ones within a framework entirely dominated by the central state authorities. He did not entirely succeed. Nor did his mirror-image adversary Adolf Hitler in Germany. But the goal was so ambitious that even its half-completion was a dreadful achievement.

13

The Second World War (1939–1945)

Stalin had always expected war to break out again in Europe. In every major speech on the Central Committee's behalf he stressed the dangers in contemporary international relations. Lenin had taught his fellow communists that economic rivalry would pitch imperialist capitalist powers against each other until such time as capitalism was overthrown. World wars were inevitable in the meantime and Soviet foreign policy had to start from this first premiss of Leninist theory on international relations.

The second premiss was the need to avoid unnecessary entanglement in an inter-imperialist war.[1] Stalin had always aimed to avoid risks with the USSR's security, and this preference became even stronger at the outbreak of the Spanish Civil War in mid-1936.[2] The dream of Maksim Litvinov, People's Commissar for External Affairs, of the creation of a system of 'collective security' in Europe was dissipated when Britain and France refused to prevent Germany and Italy from aiding the spread of fascism to Spain. But what could Stalin do? Complete diplomatic freedom was unfeasible. But if he dealt mainly with the victor powers of the Great War, what trust could he place in their promises of political and military co-operation? If he attempted an approach to Hitler, would he not be rebuffed? And, whatever he chose to do, how could he maintain that degree of independence from either side in Europe's disputes he thought necessary for the good of himself, his clique and the USSR?

Stalin's reluctance to take sides, moreover, increased the instabilities in Europe and lessened the chances of preventing continental war.[3] In the winter of 1938–9 he concentrated efforts to ready the USSR for such an outbreak. Broadened regulations on conscription raised the size of the Soviet armed forces from two million men under arms in 1939 to five million by 1941. In the same period there was a leap in factory production of armaments to the level of 700 military aircraft, 4,000 guns and mortars and 100,000 rifles.[4]

The probability of war with either Germany or Japan or both at once was an integral factor in Soviet security planning. It was in the Far East, against the Japanese, that the first clashes occurred. The battle near Lake Khasan in mid-1938 had involved 15,000 Red Army personnel. An extremely tense stand-off ensued; and in May 1939 there was further trouble when the Japanese forces occupied Mongolian land on the USSR–Mongolian border near Khalkhin-Gol. Clashes occurred that lasted several months. In August 1939 the Red Army went on to the offensive and a furious conflict took place. The Soviet commander Zhukov used tanks for the first occasion in the USSR's history of warfare. The battle was protracted and the outcome messy; but, by and large, the Red Army and its 112,500 troops had the better of the Japanese before a truce was agreed on 15 September 1939.[5]

Hitler was active in the same months. Having overrun the Sudetenland in September 1938, he occupied the rest of Czechoslovakia in March 1939, thereby coming closer still to the USSR's western frontier. Great Britain gave guarantees of military assistance to Poland in the event of a German invasion. All Europe already expected Warsaw to be Hitler's next target, and the USSR engaged in negotiations with France and Britain. The Kremlin aimed at the construction of a military alliance which might discourage Hitler from attempting further conquests. But the British in particular dithered over Stalin's overtures. The nadir was plumbed in summer when London sent not its Foreign Secretary but a military attaché to conduct negotiations in Moscow. The attaché had not been empowered to bargain in his own right, and the lack of urgency was emphasized by the fact that he travelled by sea rather than by air.[6]

Whether Stalin had been serious about these talks remains unclear: it cannot be ruled out that he already wished for a treaty of some kind with Germany. Yet the British government had erred; for even if Stalin had genuinely wanted a coalition with the Western democracies, he now knew that they were not to be depended upon. At the same time Stalin was being courted by Berlin. Molotov, who had taken Litvinov's place as People's Commissar of External Affairs in May, explored the significance of the German overtures.[7] An exchange of messages between Hitler and Stalin took place on 21 August, resulting in an agreement for German Foreign Minister Ribbentrop to come to Moscow. Two lengthy conversations occurred between Stalin, Molotov and Ribbentrop on 23 August. Other Politburo members were left unconsulted. By the end of the working day a Nazi-Soviet Non-Aggression Treaty had been prepared for signature.

This document had two main sections, one made public and the other kept secret. Openly the two powers asserted their determination to prevent war with each other and to increase bilateral trade. The USSR would buy German machinery, Germany would make purchases of Soviet coal and oil. In this fashion Hitler was being given *carte blanche* to continue his depredatory policies elsewhere in Europe while being guaranteed commercial access to the USSR's natural resources. Worse still were the contents of the secret protocols of the Non-Aggression Treaty. The USSR and Germany divided the territory lying between them into two spheres of influence: to the USSR was awarded Finland, Estonia and Latvia, while Lithuania and most of Poland went to Germany. Hitler was being enabled to invade Poland at the moment of his choosing, and he did this on 1 September. When he refused to withdraw, Britain and France declared war upon Germany. The Second World War had begun.

Hitler was taken aback by the firmness displayed by the Western parliamentary democracies even though they could have no hope of rapidly rescuing Poland from his grasp. It also disconcerted Hitler that Stalin did not instantly interpret the protocol on the 'spheres of influence' as permitting the USSR to grab territory. Stalin had other things on his mind. He was waiting to see whether the Wehrmacht would halt within the area agreed through the treaty. Even more important was his need to secure the frontier in the Far East.

Only on 15 September did Moscow and Tokyo at last agree to end military hostilities on the Soviet-Manchurian frontier. Two days later, Red Army forces invaded eastern Poland.

This was to Germany's satisfaction because it deprived the Polish army of any chance of prolonging its challenge to the Third Reich and the USSR had been made complicit in the carving up of north-eastern Europe. While Germany, Britain and France moved into war, the swastika was raised above the German embassy in Moscow. Talks were resumed between Germany and the USSR to settle territorial questions consequent upon Poland's dismemberment. Wishing to win Hitler's confidence, Stalin gave an assurance to Ribbentrop 'on his word of honour that the Soviet Union would not betray its partner'.[8] On 27 September 1939, a second document was signed, the Boundary and Friendship Treaty, which transferred Lithuania into the Soviet Union's sphere of interest. In exchange Stalin agreed to give up territory in eastern Poland. The frontier between the Soviet Union and German-occupied Europe was stabilized on the river Bug.

Stalin boasted to Politburo members: 'Hitler is thinking of tricking us, but I think we've got the better of him.'[9] At the time it seemed unlikely that the Germans would soon be capable of turning upon the USSR. Hitler would surely have his hands full on the Western front. Stalin aimed to exert tight control in the meantime over the sphere of interest delineated in the Boundary and Friendship Treaty. The governments of Estonia, Latvia and Lithuania were scared by Stalin and Molotov into signing mutual assistance treaties which permitted the Red Army to build bases on their soil.

On 30 November 1939, after the Finns had held out against such threats, Stalin ordered an invasion with the intention of establishing a Finnish Soviet government and relocating the Soviet-Finnish border northwards at Finland's expense. Yet the Finns organized unexpectedly effective resistance. The Red Army was poorly co-ordinated; and this 'Winter War' cost the lives of 200,000 Soviet soldiers before March 1940, when both sides agreed to a settlement that shifted the USSR's border further north from Leningrad but left the Finns with their independence. Thereafter Stalin sought to strengthen his grip on the other Baltic states. Flaunting his military hegemony in the region, he issued an ultimatum for the formation of pro-Soviet governments in Estonia, Latvia and Lithuania in June. Next month these governments were commanded, on pain of invasion, to request the incorporation of their states as new Soviet republics of the USSR. Also in July 1940, Stalin annexed Bessarabia and northern Bukovina from Romania.

The Sovietization of these lands was conducted with practised brutality. Leading figures in their political, economic and cultural life were arrested by the NKVD. Condemned as 'anti-Soviet elements', they were either killed or consigned to the Gulag. The persecution also affected less exalted social categories: small traders, school-teachers and independent farmers were deported to 'special settlements' in the RSFSR and Kazakhstan;[10] 4,400 captured Polish officers were shot and buried in Katyn forest. Thus the newly-conquered territory, from Estonia down to Moldavia, lost those figures who might have organized opposition to their countries' annexation. A Soviet order was imposed. A communist one-party dictatorship was established, and factories, banks, mines and land were nationalized.

Stalin and his associates felt safe in concentrating on this activity because they expected the war in western Europe to be lengthy. Their assumption had been that France would defend herself doughtily against the Wehrmacht and that Hitler would be in no position to organize a rapid attack upon the Soviet Union. But Holland, Belgium, Denmark and Norway had already been occupied and, in June 1940, French military resistance collapsed and the British expeditionary forces were evacuated at Dunkirk. Even so, the USSR's leadership remained confident. Molotov opined to Admiral Kuznetsov: 'Only a fool would attack us.'[11] Stalin and Molotov were determined to ward off any such possibility by increasing Soviet influence in eastern and south-eastern Europe. They insisted, in their dealings with Berlin, that the USSR had legitimate interests in Persia, Turkey and Bulgaria which Hitler should respect; and on Stalin's orders, direct diplomatic overtures were also made to Yugoslavia.

But when these same moves gave rise to tensions between Moscow and Berlin, Stalin rushed to reassure Hitler by showing an ostentatious willingness to send Germany the natural materials, especially oil, promised under the two treaties of 1941. The movement of German troops from the Western front to the Soviet frontier was tactfully overlooked, and only perfunctory complaint was made about overflights made by German reconnaissance aircraft over Soviet cities. But Richard Sorge, a Soviet spy in the German embassy in Tokyo, told the NKVD that Hitler had ordered an invasion. Winston Churchill informed the Kremlin about what was afoot. Khrushchëv, many years later, recalled: 'The sparrows were chirping about it at every crossroad.'[12] Stalin was not acting with total senselessness. Hitler, if he planned to invade had to seize the moment before his opportunity disappeared. Both Soviet and German military planners considered that the Wehrmacht would be in grave difficulties unless it could complete its conquest of the USSR before the Russian snows could take their toll.

Convinced that the danger had now passed, Stalin was confident in the USSR's rising strength. Presumably he also calculated that Hitler, who had yet to finish off the British, would not want to fight a war on two fronts by taking on the Red Army. In any case, the cardinal tenet of Soviet military doctrine since the late 1930s had been that if German forces attacked, the Red Army would immediately repel them and 'crush the enemy on his territory'.[13] An easy victory was expected in any such war; Soviet public commentators were forbidden to hint at the real scale of Germany's armed might and prowess.[14] So confident was Stalin that he declined to hasten the reconstruction of defences in the newly annexed borderlands or to move industrial plant into the country's interior.

Throughout the first half of 1941, however Stalin and his generals could not overlook the possibility that Germany might nevertheless attempt an invasion. Movements of troops and equipment in German-occupied Poland kept them in a condition of constant nervousness. But Stalin remained optimistic about the result of such a war; indeed he and his political subordinates toyed with the project for the Red Army to wage an offensive war.[15] At a reception for recently-trained officers in May 1941, Stalin spoke about the need for strategical planning to be transferred 'from defence to attack'.[16] But he did not wish to go to war as yet, and hoped against hope that an invasion by the Wehrmacht was not imminent. Soviet leaders noted that whereas the blitzkrieg against Poland had been preceded by a succession of ultimatums, no such communication had been received in Moscow. On 21 June Beria purred to Stalin that he continued to 'remember your wise prophecy: Hitler will not attack us in 1941'.[17] The brave German soldiers who swam the river Bug to warn the Red Army about the invasion projected for the next day were shot as enemy agents.

At 3.15 a.m. on 22 June, the Wehrmacht crossed the Bug at the start of Operation Barbarossa, attacking Soviet armed forces which were under strict orders not to reply to 'provocation'. This compounded the several grave mistakes made by Stalin in the previous months. Among them was the decision to shift the Soviet frontier westward after mid-1940 without simultaneously relocating the fortresses and earthworks. Stalin had also failed to transfer armaments plants from Ukraine deeper into the USSR. Stalin's years-old assumption prevailed that if and when war came to the Soviet Union, the attack would be quickly repulsed and that an irresistible counter-attack would be organized. Defence in depth was not contemplated. Consequently no precautionary orders were given to land forces: fighter planes were left higgledy-piggledy on Soviet runways; 900 of them were destroyed in that position in the first hours of the German-Soviet war.[18]

Zhukov alerted Stalin about Operation Barbarossa at 3.25 a.m. The shock to Stalin was tremendous. Still trying to convince himself that the Germans were engaged only in 'provocational actions', Stalin rejected the request of D. G. Pavlov, the commander of the main forces in the path of the German advance, for permission to fight back. Only at 6.30 a.m. did he sanction retaliation.[19] Throughout the rest of the day Stalin conferred frenetically with fellow Soviet political and military leaders as the scale of the disaster began to be understood in the Kremlin.

Stalin knew he had blundered, and supposedly he cursed in despair that his leadership had messed up the great state left behind by

Lenin.[20] The story grew that he suffered a nervous breakdown. Certainly he left it to Molotov on 22 June to deliver the speech summoning the people of the USSR to arms; and for a couple of days at the end of the month he shut himself off from his associates. It is said that when Molotov and Mikoyan visited his dacha, Stalin was terrified lest they intended to arrest him.[21] The truth of the episode is not known; but his work-schedule was so intensely busy that it is hard to believe that he can have undergone more than a fleeting diminution of his will of steel to fight on and win the German-Soviet war. From the start of hostilities he was laying down that the Red Army should not merely defend territory but should counter-attack and conquer land to the west of the USSR. This was utterly unrealistic at a time when the Wehrmacht was crashing its way deep into Belorussia and Ukraine. But Stalin's confirmation of his pre-war strategy was a sign of his uncompromising determination to lead his country in a victorious campaign.

The task was awesome: the Wehrmacht had assembled 2,800 tanks, 5,000 aircraft, 47,000 artillery pieces and 5.5 million troops to crush the Red Army. German confidence, organization and technology were employed to maximum effect. The advance along the entire front was so quick that Belorussia, Lithuania, Latvia and Estonia were under German occupation within weeks. The Russian city of Smolensk was overrun with a rapidity that left the party authorities no time to incinerate their files. By the beginning of September, the Wehrmacht had cut off Leningrad by land: transport to and from the Soviet Union's second city had to be undertaken over Lake Ladoga. To the south, huge tracts of Ukraine were overrun: Kiev was captured in mid-August. After such success Hitler amassed his forces in the centre. In September, Operation Typhoon was aimed at the seizure of Moscow.

In the first six months of the 'Great Fatherland War', as Soviet leaders began to refer to the conflict, three million prisoners-of-war fell into German hands.[22] There had been a massive loss to the USSR in its human, industrial and agricultural resources. Roughly two fifths of the state's population and up to half its material assets were held under German dominion.

A political and military reorganization was rushed into place. For such a war, new forms of co-ordination had to be found. On 30 June it was decided to form a State Committee of Defence, bringing together leading Politburo members Stalin, Molotov, Beria, Malenkov and Voroshilov. The State Committee was to resolve all major political, economic and strategical questions and Stalin was appointed as its chairman. On 10 July he was also appointed Supreme Commander (although no immediate announcement was made since Stalin wanted to avoid being held popularly culpable for the continuing military débâcle). In addition, he became chairman of the High Command (*Stavka*) on 8 August.[23] Stalin was attempting to be the Lenin and Trotski of the German-Soviet conflict. In the Civil War Lenin had operated the civilian political machinery, Trotski the military. Stalin wished to oversee everything, and dispatched several of his central civilian colleagues to secure his authority over the frontal commands.

It was a gruelling summer for the Red Army. The speed of the German invasion induced Stalin to contemplate moving the capital to the Volga city of Kuibyshev (once and now called Samara), 800 kilometres to the south-east of Moscow. Foreign embassies and several Soviet institutions began to be transferred. But suddenly in late October, the Wehrmacht met with difficulties. German forces on the outskirts of Moscow confronted insurmountable defence, and Stalin asked Zhukov whether the Red Army's success would prove durable. On receiving the desired assurances from Zhukov, Stalin cancelled his emergency scheme to transfer the seat of government and intensified his demand for counter-offensives against the Wehrmacht.[24]

Hitler had already fallen crucially short of his pre-invasion expectations. His strategy had been based on the premiss that Moscow, Leningrad and the line of the river Volga had to be seized before the winter's hard weather allowed the Red Army to be reorganized and re-equipped. The mud had turned to frost by November, and snow was not far behind. The supply lines of the Wehrmacht were overstretched and German soldiers started to feel the rigours of the Russian climate. Soviet resolve had already been demonstrated in abundance. On 3 July, Stalin made a radio-broadcast speech, addressing the people with the words: 'Comrades! Citizens! Brothers and Sisters!' He threatened the 'Hitlerite forces' with the fate that had overwhelmed Napoleon in Russia in 1812. 'History shows,' he contended, 'that invincible armies do not exist and never have existed.'[25] In the winter of 1941–2 his words were beginning to acquire a degree of plausibility.

Yet Stalin knew that defeat by Germany remained a strong possibility. Nor could he rid himself of worry about his own dreadful miscalculations in connection with Operation Barbarossa. On 3 October 1941 he blurted out to General Konev: 'Comrade Stalin is not a traitor. Comrade Stalin is an honest person. Comrade Stalin will do everything to correct the situation that has been created.'[26] He worked at the highest pitch of intensity, usually spending fifteen hours a day at his tasks. His attentiveness to detail was legendary. At any hint of problems in a tank factory or on a military front, he would talk directly with those who were in charge. Functionaries were summoned to Moscow, not knowing whether or not they would be arrested after their interview with Stalin. Sometimes he simply phoned them; and since he preferred to work at night and take a nap in the daytime, they grew accustomed to being dragged from their beds to confer with him.

As a war leader, unlike Churchill or Roosevelt, he left it to his subordinates to communicate with Soviet citizens. He delivered only nine substantial speeches in the entire course of the German-Soviet war,[27] and his public appearances were few. The great exception was his greeting from the Kremlin Wall on 7 November 1941 to a parade of Red Army divisions which were on the way to the front-line on the capital's outskirts. He spent the war in the Kremlin or at his dacha. His sole trip outside Moscow, apart from trips to confer with Allied leaders in Tehran in 1943 and Yalta in 1945, occurred in August 1943, when he made a very brief visit to a Red Army command post which was very distant from the range of gunfire.

The point of the trip was to give his propagandists a pretext to claim that he had risked his life along with his soldiers. Khrushchëv was later to scoff at such vaingloriousness; he also asserted – when

Stalin was safely dead and lying in state in the Mausoleum on Red Square – that the office-based mode of leadership meant that Stalin never acquired a comprehension of military operations. The claim was even made by Khrushchëv that Stalin typically plotted his campaigns not on small-scale maps of each theatre of conflict but on a globe of the world. At best this was an exaggeration based upon a single incident. If anything, Stalin's commanders found him excessively keen to study the minutiae of their strategic and tactical planning – and most of them were to stress in their memoirs that he gained an impressive technical understanding of military questions in the course of the war.

Not that his performance was unblemished. Far from it: not only the catastrophe of 22 June 1941 but several ensuing heavy defeats were caused by his errors in the first few months. First Kiev was encircled and hundreds of thousands of troops were captured. Then Red Army forces were entrapped near Vyazma. Then the Wehrmacht burst along the Baltic littoral and laid siege to Leningrad. All three of these terrible set-backs occurred to a large extent because of Stalin's meddling. The same was true in the following year. In the early summer of 1942, his demand for a counter-offensive on German-occupied Ukraine resulted in the Wehrmacht conquering still more territory and seizing Kharkov and Rostov; and at almost the same time a similar débâcle occurred to the south of Leningrad as a consequence of Stalin's rejection of Lieutenant-General A. N. Vlasov's plea for permission to effect a timely withdrawal of his forces before their encirclement by the enemy.

Moreover, there were limits to Stalin's military adaptiveness. At his insistence the State Committee of Defence issued Order No. 270 on 16 August 1941 which forbade any Red Army soldier to allow himself to be taken captive. Even if their ammunition was expended, they had to go down fighting or else be branded state traitors. There could be no surrender. Punitive sanctions would be applied to Soviet prisoners-of-war if ever they should be liberated by the Red Army from German prison-camps; and in the meantime their families would have their ration cards taken from them. Order No. 227 on 28 July 1942 indicated to the commanders in the field that retreats, even of a temporary nature, were prohibited: 'Not one step backwards!' By then Stalin had decided that Hitler had reached the bounds of his territorial depredation. In order to instil unequivocal determination in his forces the Soviet dictator foreclosed operational suggestions involving the yielding of the smallest patch of land.

Nor had he lost a taste for blood sacrifice. General Pavlov, despite having tried to persuade Stalin to let him retaliate against the German invasion on 22 June, was executed.[28] This killing was designed to intimidate others. In fact no Red Army officer of Pavlov's eminence was shot by Stalin in the rest of the German-Soviet war. Nor were any leading politicians executed. Yet the USSR's leaders still lived in constant fear that Stalin might order a fresh list of executions. His humiliation of them was relentless. On a visit to Russia, the Yugoslav communist Milovan Djilas witnessed Stalin's practice of getting Politburo members hopelessly drunk. At one supper party, the dumpy and inebriated Khrushchëv was compelled to perform the energetic Ukrainian dance called the gopak. Everyone knew that Stalin was a dangerous man to annoy.

But Stalin also perceived that he needed to balance his fearsomeness with a degree of encouragement if he was to get the best out of his subordinates. The outspoken Zhukov was even allowed to engage in disputes with him in Stavka. Alexander Vasilevski, Ivan Konev, Vasili Chuikov and Konstantin Rokossovski (who had been imprisoned by Stalin) were more circumspect in their comments; but they also emerged as commanders whose competence he learned to respect. Steadily, too, Stalin's entourage was cleared of the less effective civilian leaders. Kliment Voroshilov, People's Commissar for Defence, had been shown to have woefully outdated military ideas and was replaced. Lev Mekhlis and several other prominent purgers in the Great Terror were also demoted. Mekhlis was so keen on attack as the sole mode of defence in Crimea that he forbade the digging of trenches. Eventually even Stalin concluded: 'But Mekhlis is a complete fanatic; he must not be allowed to get near the Army!'[29]

The premature Soviet counter-offensive of summer 1942 had opened the Volga region to the Wehrmacht, and it appeared likely that the siege of Stalingrad would result in a further disaster for the

Red forces. Leningrad in the north and Stalingrad in the south of Russia became battle arenas of prestige out of proportion to their strategical significance. Leningrad was the symbol of the October Revolution and Soviet communism; Stalingrad carried the name of Lenin's successor. Stalin was ready to turn either city into a Martian landscape rather than allow Hitler to have the pleasure of a victory parade in them.

Increasingly, however, the strength of the Soviet Union behind the war fronts made itself felt. Factories were packed up and transferred by rail east of the Urals together with their work-forces. In addition, 3,500 large manufacturing enterprises were constructed during the hostilities. Tanks, aircraft, guns and bullets were desperately needed. So, too, were conscripts and their clothing, food and transport. The results were impressive. Soviet industry, which had been on a war footing for the three years before mid-1941, still managed to quadruple its output of munitions between 1940 and 1944. By the end of the war, 3,400 military planes were being produced monthly. Industry in the four years of fighting supplied the Red forces with 100,000 tanks, 130,000 aircraft and 800,000 field guns. At the peak of mobilization there were twelve million men under arms. The USSR produced double the amount of soldiers and fighting equipment that Germany produced.

In November 1942 the Wehrmacht armies fighting in the outer suburbs of Stalingrad were themselves encircled. After bitter fighting in wintry conditions, the city was reclaimed by the Red Army in January 1943. Hitler had been as unbending in his military dispositions as Stalin would have been in the same circumstances. Field-Marshal von Paulus, the German commander, had been prohibited from pulling back from Stalingrad when it was logistically possible. As a consequence, 91,000 German soldiers were taken into captivity. Pictures of prisoners-of-war marching with their hands clasped over their heads were shown on the newsreels and in the press. At last Stalin had a triumph that the Soviet press and radio could trumpet to the rest of the USSR. The Red Army then quickly also took Kharkov and seemed on the point of expelling the Wehrmacht from eastern Ukraine.

Yet the military balance had not tipped irretrievably against Hitler; for German forces re-entered Kharkov on 18 March 1943. Undeterred, Stalin set about cajoling Stavka into attacking the Germans again. There were the usual technical reasons for delay: the Wehrmacht had strong defensive positions and the training and supply of the Soviet mobile units left much to be desired. But Stalin would not be denied, and 6,000 tanks were readied to take on the enemy north of Kursk on 4 July 1943. It was the largest tank battle in history until the Arab-Israeli War of 1967. Zhukov, who had used tanks against the Japanese at Khalkhin-Gol, was in his element. His professional expertise was accompanied by merciless techniques. Penal battalions were marched towards the German lines in order to clear the ground of land-mines. Then column after column of T-34 tanks moved forward. Red Army and Wehrmacht fought it out day after day.

The result of the battle was not clear in itself. Zhukov had been gaining an edge, but had not defeated the Wehrmacht before Hitler pulled his forces away rather than gamble on complete victory. Yet Kursk was a turning point since it proved that the victory at Stalingrad was repeatable elsewhere. The Red Army seized back Kharkov on 23 August, Kiev on 6 November. Then came the campaigns of the following year which were known as the 'Ten Stalinist Blows'. Soviet forces attacked and pushed back the Wehrmacht on a front extending from the Baltic down to the Black Sea. Leningrad's 900-day siege was relieved in January and Red forces crossed from Ukraine into Romania in March. On 22 June 1944, on the third anniversary of the German invasion, Operation Bagration was initiated to reoccupy Belorussia and Lithuania. Minsk became a Soviet city again on 4 July, Vilnius on 13 July.

As the Red Army began to occupy Polish territory, questions about the post-war settlement of international relations imprinted themselves upon Soviet actions. On 1 August the outskirts of Warsaw were reached; but further advance was not attempted for several weeks, and by that time the German SS had wiped out an uprising and exacted revenge upon the city. About 300,000 Poles perished. Stalin claimed that his forces had to be rested before freeing Warsaw from the Nazis. His real motive was that it suited him if the Germans destroyed those armed units of Poles which might cause political and military trouble for him.

The USSR was determined to shackle Poland to its wishes. In secret, Stalin and Beria had ordered the murder of nearly 15,000 Polish officers who had been taken captive after the Red Army's invasion of eastern Poland in 1939. Subsequently Soviet negotiators had been suspiciously evasive on the question of Poland's future when, in July 1941, an Anglo-Soviet agreement was signed; and the British government, which faced a dire threat from Hitler, had been in no position to make uncompromising demands in its talks with Stalin. Nor was Stalin any more easily controllable when the USA entered the Second World War in December 1941 after Japan's air force attacked the American fleet in Pearl Harbor and Hitler aligned himself with his Japanese partners against the USA. The USSR's military contribution remained of crucial importance when the Anglo-Soviet-German war in Europe and the Japanese war of conquest were conjoined in a single global war.

There was an exception to Stalin's chutzpah. At the end of 1941 he had ordered Beria to ask the Bulgarian ambassador Ivan Stamenov to act as an intermediary in overtures for a separate peace between the USSR and Germany.[30] Stalin was willing to forgo his claims to the territory under German occupation in exchange for peace. Stamenov refused the invitation. Stalin would anyway not have regarded such a peace as permanent. Like Hitler, he must have calculated that the Wehrmacht's cause was ultimately lost if Leningrad, Moscow and the Volga remained under Soviet control. A 'breathing space' on the model of the Treaty of Brest-Litovsk would have been more advantageous to Stalin in 1941–2 than to Lenin in 1918.

Naturally Stalin kept this gambit secret from the Western Allies; and through 1942 and 1943, he expressed anger about the slowness of preparations for a second front in the West. Churchill flew to Moscow in August 1942 to explain that the next Allied campaign in the West would be organized not in France or southern Italy but in north Africa. Stalin was not amused. Thereafter a meeting involving Churchill, Roosevelt and Stalin was held in Tehran in November 1943 – the greatest distance Stalin had travelled from Moscow in three decades. Churchill flew again to Moscow in October 1944, and in February 1945 Stalin played host to Roosevelt and Churchill at Yalta in Crimea. At each of these meetings, he drew attention to the sacrifices being borne by the peoples of the USSR. Not even the D-Day landings in Normandy in June 1944 put an end to his habit of berating the other Allies; for he knew that his complaints about them served the purpose of distracting attention from his designs upon eastern Europe.

All this notwithstanding, Stalin had been receiving considerable military and foodstuffs assistance from the USA and the United Kingdom to plug the gaps in Soviet production. The German occupation of Ukraine deprived the USSR of its sugar-beet. Furthermore, Stalin's pre-war agricultural mismanagement had already robbed the country of adequate supplies of meat; and his industrial priorities had not included the development of native equivalents to American jeeps and small trucks. In purely military output, too, misprojections had been made: the shortage of various kinds of explosive was especially damaging.

From 1942, the Americans shipped sugar and the compressed meat product, Spam, to Russia – and the British naval convoys braved German submarines in the Arctic Ocean to supplement supplies. Jeeps, as well as munitions and machinery, also arrived. The American Lend-Lease Programme supplied goods to the value of about one fifth of the USSR's gross domestic product during the fighting – truly a substantial contribution.[31] Yet Allied governments were not motivated by altruism in dispatching help to Russia: they still counted upon the Red Army to break the backbone of German armed forces on the Eastern front. While the USSR needed its Western allies economically, the military dependence of the USA and the United Kingdom upon Soviet successes at Stalingrad and Kursk was still greater. But foreign aid undoubtedly rectified several defects in Soviet military production and even raised somewhat the level of food consumption.

There was a predictable reticence about this in the Soviet press.

But Stalin and his associates recognized the reality of the situation; and, as a pledge to the Western Allies of his co-operativeness, Stalin dissolved the Comintern in May 1943. Lenin had founded it in 1919 as an instrument of world revolution under tight Russian control. Its liquidation indicated to Roosevelt and Churchill that the USSR would cease to subvert the states of her Allies and their associated countries while the struggle against Hitler continued.

While announcing this to Churchill and Roosevelt, Stalin played upon their divergent interests. Since Lenin's time it had been a nostrum of Soviet political analysis that it was contrary to the USA's interest to prop up the British Empire. Roosevelt helped Stalin by poking a little fun at Churchill and by turning his charm upon Stalin in the belief that the USSR and USA would better be able to reach a permanent mutual accommodation if the two leaders could become friendlier. But Stalin remained touchy about the fact that he was widely known in the West as Uncle Joe. He was also given to nasty outbursts. Churchill walked out of a session at the Tehran meeting when the Soviet leader proposed the execution of 50,000 German army officers at the end of hostilities. Stalin had to feign that he had not meant the suggestion seriously so that the proceedings might be resumed.

At any rate, he usually tried to cut a genial figure, and business of lasting significance was conducted at Tehran. Churchill suggested that the Polish post-war frontiers should be shifted sideways. The proposal was that the USSR would retain its territorial gains of 1939–40 and that Poland would be compensated to her west at Germany's expense. There remained a lack of clarity inasmuch as the Allies refused to give *de jure* sanction to the forcible incorporation of Estonia, Latvia and Lithuania into the USSR. But a nod and a wink had been given that the Soviet Union had special interests in parts of eastern Europe that neither Britain nor the USA cared to challenge.

This conciliatory approach was maintained in negotiations between Churchill and Stalin in Moscow in October 1944. Japan had not yet been defeated in the East, and the A-bomb stayed at an early experimental stage. Germany was still capable of serious counter-offensives against the Allied armies which were converging on the Third Reich. It made sense to divide German-occupied Europe into zones of influence for the immediate future. But Churchill and Stalin could not decide how to do this; each was reluctant to let the other have a completely free hand in the zone accorded to him. On his Moscow trip, therefore, Churchill put forward an arithmetical solution which appealed to Stalin. It was agreed that the USSR would gain a ninety per cent interest in Romania. She was also awarded seventy-five per cent in respect of Bulgaria; but both Hungary and Yugoslavia were to be divided fifty-fifty between the two sides and Greece was to be ninety per cent within the Western zone.

Very gratifying to Stalin was the absence of Poland from their agreement, an absence that indicated Churchill's unwillingness to interfere directly in her fate. Similarly Italy, France and the Low Countries were by implication untouchable by Stalin. Yet the understanding between the two Allied leaders was patchy; in particular, nothing was agreed about Germany. To say the least, the common understanding was very rough and ready.

But it gave Stalin the reassurance he sought, and he scrawled a large blue tick on Churchill's scheme. The interests of the USSR would be protected in most countries to Germany's east while to the west the other Allies would have the greater influence. Churchill and Stalin did not specify how they might apply their mathematical politics to a real situation. Nor did they consider how long their agreement should last. In any case, an Anglo-Soviet agreement was insufficient to carry all before it. The Americans were horrified by what had taken place between Churchill and Stalin. Zones of influence infringed the principle of national self-determination, and at Yalta in February 1945 Roosevelt made plain that he would not accede to any permanent partition of Europe among the Allies.

But on most other matters the three leaders could agree. The USSR contracted to enter the war against Japan in the East three months after the defeat of Germany. Furthermore, the Allies delineated Poland's future borders more closely and decided that Germany, once conquered, should be administered jointly by the USSR, USA, Britain and France.

Stalin saw that his influence in post-war Europe would depend upon the Red Army being the first force to overrun Germany. Soviet forces occupied both Warsaw and Budapest in January 1945 and Prague in May. Apart from Yugoslavia and Albania, every country in eastern Europe was liberated from German occupation wholly or mainly by them. Pleased as he was by these successes, his preoccupation remained with Germany. The race was on for Berlin. To Stalin's delight, it was not contested by the Western Allies, whose Supreme Commander General Eisenhower preferred to avoid unnecessary deaths among his troops and held to a cautious strategy of advance. The contenders for the prize of seizing the German capital were the Red commanders Zhukov and Konev. Stalin called them to Moscow on 3 April after learning that the British contingent under General Montgomery might ignore Eisenhower and reach Berlin before the Red Army. The Red Army was instructed to beat Montgomery to it.

Stalin drew a line along an east-west axis between the forces of Zhukov and Konev. This plan stopped fifty kilometres short of Berlin. The tacit instruction from Stalin was that beyond this point whichever group of forces was in the lead could choose its own route.[32] The race was joined on 16 April, and Zhukov finished it just ahead of Konev. Hitler died by his own hand on 30 April, thwarting Zhukov's ambition to parade him in a cage on Red Square. The Wehrmacht surrendered to the Anglo-American command on 7 May and to the Red Army a day later. The war in Europe was over.

According to the agreements made at Yalta, the Red Army was scheduled to enter the war against Japan three months later. American and British forces had fought long and hard in 1942–4 to reclaim the countries of the western coastline of the Pacific Ocean from Japanese rule; but a fierce last-ditch defence of Japan itself was anticipated. Harry Truman, who became American president on Roosevelt's death on 11 April, continued to count on assistance from the Red Army. But in midsummer he abruptly changed his stance. The USA's nuclear research scientists had at last tested an A-bomb and were capable of providing others for use against Japan. With such a devastating weapon, Truman no longer needed Stalin in the Far East, and Allied discussions became distinctly frosty when Truman, Stalin and Churchill met at Potsdam in July. On 6 August the first bomb was dropped on Hiroshima, on 9 August a second fell on Nagasaki.

Yet Stalin refused to be excluded from the war in the Far East. Alarmed by the prospect of a Japan exclusively under American control, he insisted on declaring war on Japan even after the Nagasaki bomb. The Red Army invaded Manchuria. After the Japanese government communicated its intention to offer unconditional surrender, the USA abided by its Potsdam commitment by awarding southern Sakhalin and the Kurile Islands to the Soviet Union. Thus the conflict in the East, too, came to an end. The USSR had become one of the Big Three in the world alongside the United States of America and the United Kingdom. Her military, industrial and political might had been reinforced. Her Red Army bestrode half of Europe and had expanded its power in the Far East. Her government and her All-Union Communist Party were unshaken. And Stalin still ruled in the Kremlin.

'Spring Sowing in Ukraine.'

A cartoon (1942) showing Hitler and a German soldier planting a whip-carrying German government official in a Ukrainian village.

CODA

14

Suffering and Struggle (1941–1945)

The USSR would not have achieved its military victory if the country had not become one of the world's great industrial powers by 1941. It outranked Germany in material output and natural resources, and had a population nearly three times greater. Soviet educational attainments and applied technological expertise were impressive. The USSR had institutions, policies and experience that could exploit such advantages in war. Consequently Hitler had taken a risk in attacking the USSR, and he had done this not only as a result of his ideological obsessions but also because he wanted to strike before the Red Army could recover from the Great Terror and the Soviet-Finnish war. It was for this reason that the Russians and the other *Untermenschen* of the USSR were paid the compliment of having three quarters of Hitler's divisions concentrated against them.

Yet the human cost of Stalin's industrial strategy had been huge throughout the 1930s. Deaths occurred in their millions. The diet and health of the surviving population was poor, and popular hostility to the government had been intensified. Nor can it be wholly discounted that the USSR would have been able to achieve about the same volume of output from its factories and mines if the New Economic Policy had been maintained.[1] State violence had not been a prerequisite of the country's industrialization: such violence was really the product of the wishes and interests of Stalin and his close supporters in the communist party leadership. It is true that Stalin in the 1930s managed to give a priority to the defence sector of industry that had been lacking in the previous decade. But account must also be taken of the fact that Stalin's blunders in June 1941 threw away a great portion of the USSR's hard-won military and industrial achievements when Ukraine, Belorussia and western Russia fell under foreign occupation.

Nor was there comprehensive success for the Soviet economy in the remainder of the German-Soviet war. The USSR demonstrated its excellence at producing tanks and aircraft while proving itself woefully inadequate in the feeding of its population. Moscow workers in the hardest manual occupations in 1943 were receiving only 2,914 calories per day; they needed at least 3,500 for mere subsistence.[2] If the widespread drought of 1946 had occurred three or four years earlier, the result of the war itself might have been different.[3] Stalin's collective farms were the worst imaginable form of wartime food production. The USSR was in some ways at its peak of efficiency in the Second World War; but it was at its lower depths in others.

The regime's self-inflicted damage was not confined to the economy. In 1941 Stalin ordered the deportation of the Volga Germans from their autonomous republic in the RSFSR. Two years later, as the Wehrmacht was beginning to retreat into the eastern parts of Ukraine and Belorussia, the process was repeated. Karachai, Kalmyks, Ingushi, Chechens, Balkars, Crimean Tatars, Meshketian Turks and Greeks of Crimea were arrested and deported from their native lands in the North Caucasus and other southern parts of the RSFSR. Men, women and children were crammed into freezing cattle-trucks and transported to inhospitable areas of Kazakhstan, where they were abandoned without the rudimentary means of sustenance. Stalin secretly branded whole nationalities as traitors, and the NKVD was instructed to round them up in a lightning military operation; and Beria was able to report to Stalin on the fulfilment of these instructions by NKVD General I. A. Serov.[4]

Armed groups of Chechens and others had indeed rendered active assistance to the Wehrmacht. But this was not the whole story; for thirty-six Chechens had been decorated as Heroes of the Soviet Union for their conspicuous valour as Red Army soldiers.[5] Moreover, even the Third Reich did not trust the Volga Germans. They had settled in Russia in the eighteenth century and Nazi officials classified them according to four categories of Germanhood – and the fourth category embraced those who were impervious to Nazi ideas and were to be handed over to the Gestapo.[6] And vastly more Ukrainians than Volga Germans or Chechens had started by warmly greeting the German invasion. Nevertheless the Ukrainian nation was not subsequently deported. Presumably even Stalin blanched at the scale of resources that he would have to divert from the war against Hitler. Probably, too, he was using the maltreatment of small nationalities as a signal to the larger ones to accord the maximum co-operation to the Soviet authorities.

Stalin also caused wholly needless resentment even among Russians. Lieutenant-General A. N. Vlasov, whom the German forces had captured in 1942, was infuriated by Stalin's refusal to allow him to retreat in time from an unavoidable encirclement. Vlasov the unquestioning Stalinist turned into an anti-Stalin Russian patriot who agreed to organize a Russian Liberation Army out of Soviet POWs. Vlasov was a dupe. His intention was for these armed units to fight on the Eastern front, overthrow Stalin and then turn on the Nazis, driving them out of Russia and installing a government committed to moderate socialist policies; but Hitler foresaw such a trick and restricted Vlasov's men mainly to guard duties in the Channel Islands. Yet the Russian Liberation Army's very existence testified to the hatred stirred up by Stalin, and Vlasov's comrades undertook the most concerted endeavour ever made by Russians to bring him down.[7]

Thus the ultra-authoritarian features of the Soviet regime caused harm to its war effort. Britain and the USA were states which lacked a capacity to enforce their political, social and economic commands before entering the war. This had not impeded them from carrying out the necessary wartime reorganization. Indeed a democratic state probably benefits from needing to secure voluntary acceptance of centralization and discipline. An elected political leadership, buoyed up by popular consent, has small reason to use violence on its own citizens.

Such considerations were odious to Stalin and his cronies. Already having been a highly 'militarized' society before 1941, the USSR became co-ordinated as if it were simply a great armed camp wherein the Red Army itself was but the most forward and exposed contingent. 'Everything for the Front!' was the state's rallying slogan. The NKVD unconcernedly reduced the dietary provision in the Gulag system by a further thirty per cent. The new norms for prisoners were far below the level of subsistence, and 622,000 of them are reckoned to have died in the penal-labour camps between 1941 and 1945.[8] Food distribution had also become a powerful instrument for the control of the free population: urban inhabitants were eligible for official ration-cards, which could be withdrawn for acts of delinquence. For a brief and unique time in Soviet history, factories and mines had dependable work-forces.

The increased compliance did not mean that the previous informal patterns of organization were eliminated. The opposite was the case: both the cliental 'tails' and the 'family circles' were indispensable to the operation of administrative machinery in wartime, when abrupt movements of the military front could cut off a city, province or whole region from commands from Moscow. The vertical and horizontal linkages which Stalin had tried to uproot in the Great Terror had been replanted in 1939–41; they were crucial to the state's ability to organize its military effort.

And so committees of defence were formed in all cities, typically involving the leading figures in the party, soviet, police and army command. The precise relationships among institutions behind the front line underwent modification and the further enhancement of the party's authority was particularly noteworthy. Nikolai Patolichev, who served successively in Yaroslavl and Chelyabinsk as first secretary of the party province committee, later recorded how he had intervened in factories when industrial targets were not being met. He countermanded instructions from military commanders and the local NKVD for the good of the cause. Patolichev knew that, if his judgement was called into question, he could get on the phone to Moscow and seek central political support.[9] Party committees were not as dominant as they had been in the course of the First Five-Year Plan: they had to share power with other institutions at the local level. Yet the reinforcement of the communist party's authority was none the less substantial.

Stalin used cunning to restrict the potential for insubordination to himself. He made appointments from rival cliental groups to the most important institutions, localities and fronts. This brought him several advantages. It ensured a lively competition to fulfil his orders. It gave ample opportunity, too, for denunciations of one group by another: the slightest sign of disloyalty to Stalin would be reported to him. He also kept watch over the Red Army through political commissars whose main task was to check on the obedience of military officers.

Yet at the same time he reduced some of the annoyance given to such officers. In November 1942 he decreed that the commissars should become mere deputies to their commanders and no longer be their equals. Moreover, the best-nourished citizens were those on active service. Each soldier, in addition to his daily ration, was given a 100-cc tot of vodka to steady the nerves and keep out the cold.[10] The officers were looked after still more carefully, and the central state organs ensured that their families were given additional privileges.[11] Epaulettes were restored to uniforms. The practice of saluting superiors was reintroduced. A swagger returned to the gait of generals. Stalin had little alternative but to treat them better than before 1941. The losses in the officer corps were grievous in the Second World War. According to Red Army records, 1,023,093 commissioned officers were killed and 1,030,721 were invalided out of service.[12]

The plight of the armed forces in summer 1941 was such that thousands of officers convicted as 'spies' were recalled from Siberian labour camps, given a couple of square meals and recommissioned to fight against their alleged spymasters. These were the lucky ones. Other inmates who had not been officers before their arrest were also released, but only on condition that they served in the dreaded penal regiments which marched out in front of their own side's tanks and armoured vehicles, clearing the enemy's minefields at the high risk of their lives. They were motivated by patriotism as well as by a desire to erase the undeserved shame of a prison sentence: the regulations of the penal regiments allowed them to earn their freedom in reward for acts of conspicuous bravery.[13] They also saw the frightful dangers as being more tolerable than the living death of Gulag labour on starvation rations.

Not that the Gulag system was dismantled: the great majority of camp prisoners were given no chance to fight Hitler. The exact number of them at the moment of the German invasion and through the war is still uncertain; but probably there was a decline by two fifths in the three years after January 1941. Thereafter the camps were replenished with fresh intakes. By January 1945 the estimated total came to nearly nine tenths of the pre-war one.[14]

Slave labour had become a permanent category of Stalin's thought and a permanent mode of his governance. None of his associates dared to challenge this. The timber still needed felling and the gold mining; the new factory sites still had to be completed in the Urals and Siberia. Confidential official discussions started from the premiss that the economy would be seriously dislocated if the Gulag camps were to be closed and emptied of their prisoners. A certain industrial administrator, when his department had difficulty in hitting its production target, was heard to remark: 'The fact is that we haven't yet fulfilled our plans for imprisonments.'[15] It is therefore hardly surprising that many prisoners felt they had nothing to lose by rebelling. In January 1942 an uprising was led by Mark Retyunin in the Vorkuta.[16] The insurgents were put down with exemplary savagery and the terror-regime was reinforced.

Repression continued through the war. Soviet citizens were warned to continue to treat foreigners warily, including citizens of the Allied countries. After December 1941, when the USA entered the war, a new offence was created by the NKVD: the praising of American technology (*voskhalenie amerikanskoi tekhniki*). An unguarded, admiring comment about an American jeep could lead to someone being consigned to the labour camps.[17] By 1943, as the Red Army reconquered the western USSR, the security police arrested not only those Soviet citizens who had collaborated with the Germans but even those who had just been taken prisoner-of-war by them. Victories in battle also encouraged Stalin to resume campaigns for Marxist-Leninist indoctrination in the armed forces themselves. Soldiers had previously been ordered only to fight well. Now they had to think acceptable thoughts too.[18] Evidently Stalin had already decided that the pre-war regime was to be reinstated in all its brutality as soon as was possible.

Nevertheless this was not yet obvious to most people. What many of them preferred to note was that Stalin had introduced several concessions since the beginning of the German-Soviet war. And hopes grew that the regime would become more humane once Germany had been defeated.

This mood was encouraged by the concessions made in culture. Artists were permitted to create what they wanted so long as their works avoided direct criticism of Marxism-Leninism and had a patriotic resonance. The magnificent Leningrad Symphony was written in the city of that name by composer and part-time fire-warden Shostakovich, who had been in trouble with the official authorities before 1941. Writers, too, benefited. One was among the century's greatest poets, Anna Akhmatova, whose innocent son had died in the NKVD's custody. She continued to compose without fear, and the following stanza drew forth an ovation from within the Hall of Columns in Moscow:[19]

It's not awful to fall dead under the bullets.
It's not bitter to be left without shelter –
We will preserve you, Russian speech,
Great Russian word.
We will bear you free and pure
And hand you to our grandchildren, and save you forever from captivity.

Many ordinary working citizens were attracted to high art as never before, and the link that bound the arts and politics became a source of strength for the state authorities.

Stalin also somewhat moderated his rough approach to the religious faith of most Soviet citizens. At a time when he needed the maximum co-operation in the war effort it made no sense to give unnecessary offence to such believers, and the word was put about that the authorities would no longer persecute the Russian Orthodox

Church. In its turn the Church collected money for military needs and its priests blessed tank divisions on their way from the factories to the Eastern front.

The shift in policy towards organized religion was formalized in September 1943, when Metropolitan Sergei was summoned to the Kremlin. To his bemusement, he was given the good news that permission was being given by the Soviet authorities for the Russian Orthodox Church to hold an Assembly and elect the first Patriarch since the death of Tikhon in 1925. Stalin playfully affected surprise that the Metropolitan had so few priests escorting him – and the Metropolitan forbore to mention that tens of thousands of priests would have been available had they not been killed by the NKVD. In fact Metropolitan Sergei died soon after being confirmed as Patriarch and he was succeeded in 1944 by Metropolitan Aleksi of Leningrad. But both Sergei and Aleksi followed a policy of grateful accommodation to Stalin's wishes.

The Russian Orthodox Church was helpful to Stalin as an instrument whereby he could increase popular acquiescence in his rule. It was also pressed by him into the service of suppressing other Russian Christian sects as well as those Christian denominations associated with other nationalities. As the Red Army moved into Ukraine and Belorussia, nearly all ecclesiastical buildings were put under the authority of Patriarch Aleksi. The Russian Orthodox Church became one of the main beneficiaries of Stalinism. Real authority, it need hardly be added, remained with Stalin, whom Aleksi grotesquely described as a 'God-given leader'.[20]

While making manipulative compromises with religion, Stalin extended those he had been offering to Russian national sensitivities. In June 1943 the *Internationale* was dropped as the state anthem. Stalin ordered the composition of a less internationalist set of verses which began:

> An indestructible union of free republics
> Has forever been welded by Russia the Great.
> Long live the land created by the will of the peoples:
> The united, powerful Soviet Union!

Cheap copies of it were reproduced on postcards for soldiers to send back from the front. Stalin also tried to appeal more generally to Slavic peoples, including not only Ukrainians but also Czechs, Serbs and Poles. The bonds between the Slavs were stressed by official Soviet historians. Stalin wanted to increase the Red Army's popular welcome in eastern Europe as it moved on Berlin. Russia's role as past protector of the Slav nations was emphasized (and, it must be added, exaggerated).[21]

Special praise was showered upon the Russians for their endurance and commitment to the defeat of Hitler. An unnamed partisan gave an account to *Pravda* about German atrocities in a provincial city; his conclusion was defiant: 'Pskov is in chains. Russian history knows that the people have more than once broken the chains welded on to a free town by the enemy.'[22]

The Russian nation was encouraged to believe that it was fighting for its Motherland (and Fatherland: propagandists used the terms indiscriminately), and that this included not only Russia but the entire USSR. Political commissars urged troops to charge into action shouting in unison: 'For the Motherland, for Stalin!' It is doubtful that most of them really mentioned Stalin in their battle-cries; but certainly the idea of the Motherland was widely and enthusiastically accepted by Russians on active service. They would have taken this attitude even if the regime had not given its encouragement. The German occupation of Ukraine, Belorussia and the Baltic republics in the first two years of the war meant that the great majority of Red Army soldiers perforce originated from the RSFSR and were Russians; and such soldiers needed little convincing that the Russian contribution was uniquely crucial to the struggle against Hitler.[23]

Yet the eulogies of the Russians also had to avoid giving offence to other nations whose young men had been conscripted into the Red Army. Multinational harmony was emphasized in the following appeal to the Uzbek people: 'The home of the Russian is also your home; the home of the Ukrainian and the Belorussian is also your home!'[24] Such invocations were not without their positive impact upon several peoples belonging to the USSR. The war induced an unprecedented sense of co-operation among nations.[25]

But this was very far from meaning that a 'Soviet people' was created. Most national and ethnic groups experienced an increase in their sense of distinctness in the heat of the war. The brutal policies before 1941 had induced permanent hatred of Stalin among most non-Russians. Antagonism was especially noticeable both among the deported nationalities but also among peoples living in states which had recently been independent from Moscow. Western Belorussians, for example, were reported as being keen to fight against Hitler but not to swear a military oath of loyalty to the USSR. 'Why,' some of them asked, 'is our nation being trampled upon?' Romanians from Moldavia took a similar attitude; they especially objected to being prohibited from singing their own patriotic songs on campaign and being forced to learn the officially-approved Russian ones.[26] For such conscripts, talk of the Soviet Motherland was a disguised way of advocating Russian imperialism.

Yet still they fought in the ranks of the Red Army; for they judged Hitler's defeat to be the supreme goal. The Soviet regime exploited this situation and anti-German sentiments were given raucous expression in the mass media. A poem by Konstantin Simonov ended with the words:

Then kill a German, kill him soon –
And any time you see one, kill him.

Propagandists who had portrayed Germans as honorary Russians during the two years of the Nazi-Soviet Non-Aggression Treaty came to treat the entire German people as the enemy; and most citizens of the USSR readily condoned this in the light of the barbarities of the Nazis.

They also approved of certain alterations in economic policy. For example, the authorities earned a degree of popularity by quietly dropping the May 1939 restriction on the size of private plots on kolkhozes: there was recognition that the goodwill of the peasantry was vital to halt the steep decline in agricultural output. In practice, too, peasants were allowed to trade their produce not only in the legal private markets but also illicitly on street corners. The Soviet state continued to bear responsibility for the supply of all kinds of food to the armed forces; but only an extremely small range of products, mainly bread, was guaranteed to urban civilians, who had to supplement their diet in whatever fashion they could. Sanction was given for the marking out of vegetable allotments outside factory buildings and on the outskirts of towns. The potatoes grown on these little patches of ground prevented many families from starving to death.[27]

Only in Stalin's USSR could such meagre concessions to cultural, religious, national and economic aspirations be regarded as startling indulgences on the part of the authorities. If conditions had not been so hard for most people, the concessions would also have been discerned as a sign of the inability of the state authorities to exert total, detailed control over society. This inability, which had already been observable before 1941, attained even greater salience during the German-Soviet war: Stalin had learned the need for a dose of pragmatism in his choice of policies.

Urban conditions were appalling. Hunger was incessant for most townspeople in the regions held by the Red Army. There was a very high rate of mortality; and human corpses in some places were used by the living to survive a little longer. Cattle, pigs and poultry had gone first; then dogs, cats and rats, followed by any berries and herbs and then nettles, grass and tree bark. So that dead people were sometimes quite literally a last resort. Geographical factors had a deep and direct influence on things. Leningrad was the city worst supplied with food: the courageous convoys sent over the ice of Lake Ladoga could not always get through the German siege. But malnutrition and disease affected all urban areas; and houses demolished by artillery and bombing from the air were not replaced; sanitation was ruined. Precious few families escaped the loss of loved ones: even Stalin's son Yakov was killed by the Germans.

In the countryside it was mainly old women and men judged unfit for military conscription who worked on the farms. Most of the twelve million military volunteers and conscripts came from the villages;[28] and appeals were made also for able-bodied men and women to enter industrial employment so that the factory labour-force increased by a third between 1942 and 1945.[29] The consequence was a further depopulation of the countryside. Not only that: the tractor drivers who were needed for the maintenance of large-scale arable cultivation were among the earliest lads to be pressed into the Red Army. The technical core of collective farms imploded; whole rural areas collapsed to a level of production insufficient to meet the subsistence requirements of the villages. On farms in the vicinity of the military fronts there was usually total devastation. Homes, byres and barns were bombed into oblivion, and it was common for peasants to live out the war sheltering in holes in the ground.[30]

So whence came this capacity to endure and resist? The answer cannot lie only with the industrial might and organizational efficiency of the regime, even when allowance is made for the informal institutional patterns and the modified policies that enhanced performance. What was crucial was the reaction of countless millions of Soviet citizens to the news of what was going on in the vast area of the USSR currently under German occupation. Above all, they learned that the policies of Hitler were even more ghastly than those of Stalin. They learned that defeat by the German forces would bring about consequences of almost unimaginable horror.

Thus the Gestapo and Wehrmacht had the task of killing every Jew and Gypsy. Captured communist party members were to be summarily executed. There was piteous slaughter at Babi Yar in Ukraine where 33,771 Jews were machine-gunned to death over the edge of a ravine; and around the town of Cherkessk alone there were 'twenty-four vast pits filled with the corpses of men, women and children tortured and shot by the German monsters'.[31] Further millions of people – Jews, Ukrainians, Belorussians and Russians – were deported to labour camps such as Auschwitz where all but very few met their deaths through brutal labour, starvation and beatings. The author of *Mein Kampf* did not merely despise the Russians and other Slavs: he classified them as sub-human. About eleven million Soviet citizens died under German occupation, and of these roughly five million perished in captivity.[32]

Not all governments in the eastern half of Europe were simply victims of German oppression. Hungary and Romania, albeit under pressure from Berlin, provided contingents for the invasion of the Soviet Union. Hitler also gave favoured status to Croats in what had been pre-war Yugoslavia; and the Germans encouraged Estonian, Latvian and Lithuanian volunteers to form SS units that sought revenge for their sufferings at Stalin's hands. The Wehrmacht was warmly received, too, further south. Ukrainian peasants offered bread and salt as a traditional sign of welcome to their invaders in the hope that Hitler would break up the collective farms and abolish the state quotas for grain deliveries.

In fact the Ostministerium, which Hitler established to govern the territory seized from the USSR, refused to de-nationalize the collective farms and large industrial enterprises but instead transferred them into the property of the Third Reich.[33] But other concessions were forthcoming. Elections were held to local administrative posts. German officials held such functionaries under ruthless control, but at least a semblance of self-administration existed for some months. In addition, former entrepreneurs could apply for licences to run their workshops and cafés again: small-scale private business was restored to the economy.[34] The Ostministerium also authorized the reopening of churches. In contrast to the Soviet authorities, the Germans prevented the re-emergence of the Russian Orthodox Church and gave preference to Ukrainian and Belorussian denominations (although these, too, were highly restricted in their public activities).[35] Thus the Ostministerium endeavoured to alleviate the tasks of the Wehrmacht on the Eastern front.

Initially collaborators were not hard to find. Many deportees and ex-prisoners were persuadable to work for the Nazis. For example, a policeman called Noga from Prokovskoe district in southern Ukraine enthusiastically informed on 'the people who interested the Germans'. Noga, having served out six years of Siberian exile, eagerly took his chance to beat a captured partisan to death.[36] Plenty of such persons volunteered their services to the German occupiers; and inhabitants of the western provinces of Ukraine and Belorussia (which had recently been annexed to the USSR) deserted the Red Army in large numbers.[37] In December 1941 Hitler sanctioned the recruitment of volunteer military units from among the non-Slav nationalities. The Turkestani, Armenian, Azerbaijani, Georgian, Tatar and North Caucasian legions were quickly formed. Even a Cossack unit came into existence since Hitler's racial theorists rejected the incontrovertible fact that the Cossacks were descended from runaway Russian peasants and from Russian soldiers who had completed their military service.

Most of the conquered peoples soon learned by direct experience that one of three destinies had been planned for them: execution; deportation for forced labour; or starvation. In the kolkhozes the German delivery quotas were raised even above the levels imposed by Stalin before 1941. Field-Marshal Reichenau implacably explained to the Wehrmacht: 'To supply local inhabitants and prisoners-of-war with food is an act of unnecessary humanity.'[38]

There was astonishment at the savagery ordered by Hitler. Ferocious conflicts had taken place between the Russian and Ottoman Empires in the previous two centuries; but the butchery had by and large been confined to the fields of battle. The last time when Russians confronted an external enemy disposed to take hostages as a normal method of war was in the campaigns against the Chechens in the 1820s and 1830s – and the Chechens were the objects of Russian aggression, not themselves the invaders. In the 1930s it had been the unconscious assumption of Soviet politicians and ordinary citizens alike that if ever war broke out with Germany, the fighting would be no dirtier than in the First World War. They failed to anticipate that an advanced industrial society, even one that had been infected with belligerent racism, could resort to mass inhumanities on Hitler's scale.

Resistance intensified as Hitler's intentions became public knowledge, and the German-occupied zone was never free from military conflict. Even in many areas where non-Russians were the majority of the population and where the Wehrmacht had initially been welcomed, there was a spirit of defiance. Groups of armed men formed themselves in the woods and made sporadic attacks on German armed units. By mid-1942 there were 100,000 partisans active against the Wehrmacht.[39] German soldiers and airmen could never forget that they were detested by local inhabitants determined to see the back of them and to push a bayonet between their shoulder-blades for good measure. The student Zoya Kosmodeyanskaya was hailed as a national heroine. Captured by the Germans after setting fire to their billets in the village of Petrishchenko, she was tortured and hanged. On the scaffold she called out defiantly: 'German soldiers, give yourselves up before it's too late!'[40]

Yet even where the partisans had minor successes, terrible retaliation was effected upon nearby towns and villages. The Wehrmacht and the SS applied a rule that a hundred local inhabitants, usually randomly selected, would be shot in reaction to every killing of a German soldier. The result was that the Soviet partisan groups did not cause decisive damage to German power even when, from 1943, munitions and guidance started to reach them from Moscow.

In practical terms, then, it was the attitude to the war taken by civilians and soldiers in Soviet-held territory that was the crucial component of the USSR's victory. They had quickly understood what was in store for them if Hitler were to win. They got their information from conversations with refugees, soldiers and partisans as well as from the mass media. Reporters such as Vasili Grossman, who was at double risk as a Jew and a communist party member, travelled to the front areas, and the facts as discovered by them were so terrible that the newspapers were allowed to reveal them without the usual official distortions. The regime, moreover, had the sense not to over-fill the press with eulogies to Stalin, Marxism-Leninism and the October Revolution. Only after the battle of Kursk, when it was already clear that the Red Army was likely to win the war, was the 'cult' of the great Stalin resumed in its pre-war devoutness.[41]

There was always an abundance of volunteers to join the Red Army. The war gave many people who were deeply dissatisfied with the Soviet regime a reason at last for co-operating with the authorities.[42] This was especially noticeable among refugees whose minds burned with the ambition to fight their way back to their home towns and villages to rescue their families before it was too late.[43] Thus the hostility caused by Stalin's policies since the late 1920s could, at least to some extent, be put into suspension. The will to beat the Germans had a unifying effect.

Militant patriotism was in the air. Russians in particular acquired a more intense sense of nationhood as millions of them came together as soldiers and factory workers. Many other peoples of the USSR, furthermore, displayed the same toughness and resilience. All drew upon reserves of endurance associated with a life-style that, by the standards of industrial societies in western Europe, was already extraordinarily harsh. The Civil War, the First Five-Year Plan and the Great Terror had habituated Soviet citizens to making the best of an extremely bad lot: hunger, disease, low wages, poor shelter and state violence had been recurrent features in the lives of most of them. Their material expectations were low even in the good times. The difference in 1941 was that the torment originated from without rather than within the country. This time it was a foreign Führer, not a Soviet General Secretary, who was the source of their woes.

The genocidal intent of Nazism impelled both Russians and the other peoples living in the regions unoccupied by the Wehrmacht to put up the sternest defence. If it had not been for Hitler's fanatical racism, the USSR would not have won the struggle on the Eastern front. Stalin's repressiveness towards his own citizens would have cost him the war against Nazi Germany, and the post-war history of the Soviet Union and the world would have been fundamentally different.

PART THREE

‘Whether you believe it or not, I’m telling you that there really was an occasion when I managed to get a quick interview with the boss here.’

A comment in the magazine Krokodil *in 1952 about the relentless growth of queues in administrative offices after the war. It is a mild satire; but not every official statement in the Soviet Union claimed that all was well in the running of society.*

15

The Hammers of Peace (1945–1953)

The compound of the Soviet order had been put under an excruciating test from abroad and had survived. Not only was Stalin still in power but also the one-party, one-ideology state was intact. There also remained a state-owned economy orientated towards the production of industrial capital goods and armaments. The mechanisms of the police state were in place; and, as before, it was not even a police state where due process of law was respected.

Yet there were features of the Soviet compound that had proved their ineffectiveness during the war even from a pragmatic viewpoint. Political, economic, national, social and cultural difficulties were acute. In the subsequent twenty-five years the political leaders tried various answers. Stalin simply reimposed the pre-war version of the compound and crushed any hopes of incipient change. His successors under Khrushchëv tried to remove certain elements in a campaign of reforms. But Khrushchëv introduced deep instabilities and fellow leaders came to regard his policies and techniques as a threat to the regime's long-term durability. After sacking him, they attempted to conserve the compound by policies which trimmed the commitment to reform. All these changes, furthermore, were made while Soviet leaders wrestled with problems of geo-politics, technological modernization, popular indoctrination and their own power and its legitimization as a group and as individuals. Their constant quest was to conserve the compound in a manner that suited their interests.

For the world in 1945 had changed beyond retrieval since 1939. Adolf Hitler had shot himself in his Berlin bunker. Benito Mussolini had been hanged by Italian partisans and Hideki Tojo was awaiting trial before American judges. German, Italian and Japanese racist militarism had been shattered. The USA, the USSR and the United Kingdom had emerged as the Big Three in global power.

It was they who established the United Nations in October 1945. Without the Big Three, no major international project could be brought to completion. Britain had incurred huge financial debts to the Americans in the Second World War and already was a junior partner in her relationship with them. The crucial rivalry was therefore between the Big Two, the USA and the USSR, a rivalry which at times threatened to turn into all-out military conflict. Fortunately the Third World War did not break out; and the American-Soviet rivalry, while constituting a constant danger to global peace, became known as the Cold War. Global capitalism confronted global communism. President Harry S Truman, Roosevelt's successor, was determined to assert the superiority of free markets and electoral politics over the Soviet system; but the likelihood of capitalism's eventual victory in this struggle was far from being self-evident.

Multitudes of people in the USSR and Eastern Europe detested communist government, and there was no paucity of commentary in the West about Stalin. The horrors of his rule were vividly described by journalists and diplomats. Quickly the admiration of the USSR for its decisive contribution to the defeat of Hitler gave way to revulsion from the policies and practices of the Soviet regime after 1945.

Yet the Soviet Union of 'Uncle Joe' Stalin continued to attract a degree of approval. It still seemed to many observers that the USSR served as a model for enabling the emergence of industrial, literate societies out of centuries of backwardness. Central state planning had acquired global respect during the war. But whereas most countries with capitalist economies tended to restrict such planning after 1945, the USSR persisted with it on the grounds that it obviated the social evils characteristic of the West. Unemployment did not exist in the USSR. Among the large capitalist economies after the defeat of Germany and Japan, only a few such as Britain and Sweden sponsored a comprehensive system of state welfare-assistance. Furthermore, the new communist authorities in Eastern Europe commenced a campaign of universal education and took steps so that the local nationalisms which had helped to cause the First and Second World Wars might be prevented from exploding again into violence.

The world communist movement followed the USSR's example: even the Chinese communist party, which took power in Beijing in September 1949, acknowledged the USSR's hegemony. The large communist parties in Italy and France had fought their own partisan struggles against Fascism and Nazism; but they, too, obeyed Moscow's line of the day; their relationship with the All-Union Communist Party was more filial than fraternal. The Soviet Union was a military power of the first rank. In the post-war years, through to the break-up of the USSR, pride in the Soviet armed forces' victory over Hitler and in their ability to compete with the USA's nuclear power pervaded the regime . The resonance of her ideology reached parts of the globe where it had been unknown. Soviet political institutions had never been stronger, and the confidence of the country's leaders never greater.

If Stalin and his confederates were to maintain their image around the world, however, they had to curtail the world's knowledge about their country. The consequences of war were dreadful. Stalin sent NKVD investigators into all the areas that had ever been under German occupation to draw up an account of Soviet losses, and their reports made for depressing reading. Roughly twenty-six million citizens of the USSR lay dead as the direct result of the Second World War.[1] The western regions of the USSR suffered disproportionate damage: perhaps as much as a quarter of the population of Ukraine and Belorussia failed to survive the war. The losses in Russia itself were also enormous. The number of Russians killed in wartime is not yet known; but indisputably it was huge. The Germans had occupied large regions of central, northern and southern Russia for lengthy periods and 1.8 million civilians were killed by them on the territory of the RSFSR.[2] This was half the number of such deaths in Ukraine; but it should not be forgotten that Russians constituted one tenth of Ukraine's population in 1939.[3] In any case the RSFSR, where four fifths of citizens were Russians, had supplied most of the conscripts to a Red Army which suffered grievous losses throughout the Soviet-German war.

The dead were not the only victims. Russia and the rest of the USSR teemed with widows, orphans and invalids. Innumerable families had been destroyed or disrupted beyond repair. The state could not cope with the physical rehabilitation of those veterans left disabled at the end of military hostilities. Nor could it secure adequate food and shelter for the waifs and strays on Soviet streets. And since many more men than women had been killed, there would inevitably be a demographic imbalance between the sexes. The USSR's people appeared more like the losers than the victors of the Second World War.

The urban landscape throughout the western Soviet Union was a ruin. Minsk, Kiev and Vilnius had become acres of rubble. In the RSFSR, Stalingrad was a blackened desert. The Red Army had implemented a scorched-earth policy in its rapid retreat in 1941. But the damage done by the Wehrmacht on its own long retreat in 1944–5 was vastly more systematic. Hardly a factory, collective farm, mine or residential area was left intact; 1710 towns were obliterated along with about 70,000 villages. Whole rural districts were wrecked so thoroughly that agriculture practically ceased in them.[4] In Cherkessk in Stavropol region, for instance, the Soviet investigative commission reported the demolition of thirty main buildings, including the party and soviet headquarters, the furniture factory, the radio station, the saw-mill and the electricity-generating plant. Hospitals and clinics had been put out of action. The town's thirty-five libraries had been blown up along with their 235,000 books. The commission added in a matter-of-fact fashion: 'All the good new schools were turned into stables, garages, etc.'[5]

It had been Nazi policy to reduce the Russians and other Soviet nations to starvation, poverty and cultural dissolution. And so, as the Wehrmacht and Gestapo moved out of north-western Russia, they paused at Petrodvorets in order to annihilate the palace built for the Empress Elizabeth to the design of the Italian architect Rastrelli. No one who has visited that now-reconstructed great palace is likely to forget the records of vandalism: pictures defaced, wall-coverings burnt, statues bludgeoned to smithereens.

Displaced civilians and disattached soldiers swarmed on to the highways and rail-routes leading to Moscow. The Smolensk Road, from Warsaw to Moscow, was crammed with Soviet troops making their way back home and often carrying war booty. Lorries, cars, horses and even railway carriages were commandeered by them. The chaos of administration increased at the end of military hostilities, and total detailed dominance by the Kremlin was unobtainable. The police state was at its most efficient in Moscow; but the Soviet security police was overstretched by its recently-acquired responsibility for conducting surveillance over the countries of Eastern Europe. An attempt had been made in 1943 to rationalize the NKVD's functions between two agencies: the NKVD itself and a new NKGB (People's Commissariat of State Security). But the workload was enormous, and the result was that in many towns and most villages of the USSR there was a temporary relief from the state's interference on a day-to-day basis.

A depiction of the scene comes to us from the Italian writer Primo Levi. Having escaped from the Auschwitz concentration camp, Levi had to make his own arrangements to get back to his native Turin. He wandered into Warsaw, where thieving and black-marketeering were rife. He walked on from Warsaw into Belorussia, and yet again he found that illegal private bartering was the only way to stay alive. After much haggling, he exchanged a few trinkets with peasants for one of their chickens. Of the party-state's presence there was little sign.[6]

For Stalin, therefore, military victory in 1945 presented many risks.[7] The material and social damage would take years to mend, and disorder might occur in Russia or any other Soviet republic or indeed any country of Eastern Europe. Stalin's discomfort was sharpened by the reports that broad segments of society yearned for him to abandon the policies and methods of the past. The Red Army soldiers who had marched into Europe had seen things that made them question the domestic policies of their own government. Greeting fellow soldiers of the Western Allies on the river Elbe or in

Berlin, they had been able to learn a little about foreign ways. Those other citizens, too, who had never crossed the boundaries of the USSR had had experiences which increased their antagonism to the Soviet regime. Partisans and others had resisted Hitler without needing to be compelled by the Kremlin; and Stalin's near-catastrophic blunders in 1941–2 had not been forgotten.

Then there were those who had objections of an even more immediate nature: the kulaks, priests and national leaders repressed during the 1930s; the Gulag inmates; the deported nationalities of the Second World War; the peoples of the annexed Baltic states, western Ukraine and Moldavia; the Red Army soldiers captured as prisoners-of-war by the Germans. Countless millions of Soviet citizens would have been delighted by the collapse of Stalin's party and government.

The sentiment was popular, too, that the wartime rigours applied by the Soviet political leadership for the defeat of Hitler should be removed. Otherwise the war would not have been worth fighting. This sense was strong among men and women who had become adults in 1941–5; for they, unlike their parents, had no direct experience of the purges of 1937–8. They felt fear, but it was not always the petrifying fear common to their parents.[8] There was also less tension than in earlier times between the working-class and the intelligentsia. In particular, the soldiers on campaign had shared appalling conditions regardless of social origin, and they wanted policies to be changed not just for a section of society but for everyone. Courageous individual spirits had been produced by the war. It is no accident that some of the most durable critics of the ascendant party leadership in the 1960s and 1970s, including Alexander Solzhenitsyn and Roy Medvedev, had been young veterans in the war.[9]

At the USSR Supreme Soviet elections in 1946, people privately complained that there was no point in voting since there was only a single candidate for each seat and the electoral results would not affect decisions of policy. In the countryside rumours spread like wildfire that the kolkhozes were about to be disbanded,[10] and peasant households went on appropriating land from the farms and growing produce for personal consumption and black-market trade.[11] There was disgruntlement with the abject remuneration for farm-work. The same mutterings were heard in the towns, especially after the raising of food-ration prices in 1946.[12]

Stalin ordered his intimates 'to deliver a strong blow' at any talk about 'democracy', talk which he thought to be the unfortunate result of the USSR's wartime alliance.[13] He was striking before opposition got out of hand. No unifying political vision existed among the peasants; factory workers, low-ranking administrators, teachers and other professional people were equally vague about what needed to be done. It is true that bands of guerrillas challenged Soviet rule in the newly-annexed regions of the USSR – in western Ukraine they held out until the mid-1950s. But such resistance was rare in the older parts of the USSR. In Russia it was virtually non-existent, and only a very few clandestine dissentient groups were formed. These consisted mainly of students, who were quickly arrested. In any case, such students were committed to a purer version of Leninism than Stalin espoused: the communist dictatorship had lasted so long that young rebels framed their ideas in Marxist-Leninist categories. Lenin, the planner of dictatorship and terror, was misunderstood by such students as a libertarian. The groups anyway failed to move beyond a preliminary discussion of their ideas before being caught and arrested by the security police.

Most other citizens who detested Stalin were grumblers rather than insurrectionaries. Police phone-tappers recorded the following conversation between General Rybalchenko and General Gordov:

> Rybalchenko: So this is the life that has begun: you just lie down and die! Pray God that there won't be another poor harvest.
>
> Gordov: But where will the harvest come from? You need to sow something for that!
>
> Rybalchenko: The winter wheat has been a failure, of course. And yet Stalin has travelled by train. Surely he must have looked out of the window? Absolutely everyone says openly how everyone is discontented with life. On the trains, in fact everywhere, it's what everyone's saying.[14]

This loose talk led to their arrest. But no matter how many persons were caught in this way, the resentment against the regime persisted. A local party secretary, P. M. Yemelyanov, gave this confidential warning: 'There are going to be revolts and uprisings, and the workers will say: "What were we fighting for?"'[15] Even Stalin seemed to feel the need to choose his words with circumspection. In a speech on 24 May 1945 he acknowledged that society had had every right in mid-1941 'to say to the Government: you have not justified our expectations; get out of here altogether and we shall install another government which will conclude a peace with Germany'.[16]

Yet this was a long way from being a fulsome confession. On the contrary, he was inculpating the Soviet government as if he himself had not led that government. Nor did he relent in his practical campaigns of mass repression. Estonia, Latvia, Lithuania, Moldavia, western Ukraine were subjected to a resumed quota of deportations. Those persons who had collaborated with the German occupying forces were imprisoned, and the Soviet security forces hunted down 'bandits' and 'kulaks'.[17] The arrests were not confined to overt opponents. Prominent among the victims were also persons guilty of no other crime than the fact that they belonged to the political, economic and cultural élites of the local nationality. According to the police files, 142,000 citizens of the three formerly independent Baltic states were deported in 1945–9. Most of the deportees were dispatched to 'special settlements' in the Russian far north, Siberia and Kazakhstan.[18]

This meant that Russians, too, came to learn of Stalin's continued application of terror even though the violence was at its most intense outside the RSFSR in the USSR's 'borderlands'. Many gained such knowledge still more directly if they happened to have had relatives taken prisoner by the Wehrmacht. Vlasov, the Russian Liberation Army leader, fell into Soviet captivity and was hanged. His soldiers were either shot or sent to labour camps, usually for terms of between fifteen and twenty-five years.[19] But Stalin did not restrict himself to military renegades. The infamous Order No. 270 that defined as a traitor anyone taken captive by the Germans had not been repealed. Emaciated by their suffering in Hitler's concentration camps, 2,775,700 former Red Army soldiers were taken into Soviet custody upon their repatriation. After being interrogated by the Department of Verification-Filtration Camps, about half of them were transferred into the Gulag system.[20]

The usual pressure to guarantee a supply of inmates to the forced-labour camps had been intensified by Stalin's predictable decision to catch up with the Americans and British in nuclear-bomb capacity.[21] He had put Beria in charge of the bomb research project, commanding him to build testing-sites, to assemble scientists (including captured Germans), to collect American secrets by means of the Soviet spy network, to discover and mine the necessary natural resources. Hundreds of thousands of Gulag prisoners were deployed in the secret quest for uranium.[22]

The technology of war had changed, and Stalin's simple response was to want the USSR to stay abreast of the transformation. Yet even Stalin perceived that several major political and economic questions did not offer easy answers. Debate was allowed in his inner circle of leaders about the difficulties; academics and journalists were also allowed, within prescribed limits, to offer their opinions to the leadership in books, journals and newspapers. Such deliberations, especially in 1945–7, were lively enough to strengthen the hope among some of the participants that Stalin might be contemplating a permanent softening of his political style. These were, as the last tsar had said in 1895 about projects for reform, 'senseless dreams'. The one-party, one-ideology state; the retention of the peoples of the USSR and Eastern Europe under Soviet imperial control; the Stalinist personal dictatorship: these basic features of the compound of the Soviet order as modified in the course of Stalin's rule were held firmly beyond the scope of permissible discussion.

Yet some questions of immense importance had to be kept under collective review: even Stalin did not trust himself to anticipate everything. In foreign policy, he felt nervous about the USA's ambitions. Potential flashpoints in Soviet-American relations existed not only in Japan, China and Iran but also in Europe. The Soviet leadership had to decide whether to support revolutionary movements in France, Italy and Greece. Jenö Varga, Director of the Institute of the World Economy and World Politics, urged caution and argued that a parliamentary road to communism was in any case a realistic possibility in Western Europe. By contrast, Politburo member Zhdanov argued that revolutionary movements should be encouraged wherever they might arise – and he warmed to the Yugoslav communist leaders who criticized the slowness of the political and economic changes being imposed by communist parties elsewhere in Eastern Europe.[23]

Issues at home were equally vexatious. The problems of state organization that had arisen in the 1930s remained unresolved. The party's role was yet again controversial and this time the protagonists were Zhdanov and Malenkov. Zhdanov wished to restore the party's role in selecting governmental cadres and in mobilizing society whereas Malenkov opposed an increase in the party's authority and wished to keep the party organized along the lines of branches of the economy.[24] Their dispute was only in part a competition to become Stalin's prime adjutant. It was also the result of the inherent structural tensions within the one-party state.

This was not the only dissension in the Soviet political leadership. On industry, there was severe disagreement about regional policy. At first it was the Politburo's policy to accelerate the development of Siberia and central Asia; but Molotov and Voznesenski apparently preferred to concentrate resources in the traditional European manufacturing regions where the costs of production were smaller and where the population was greater. And while the priority for capital-goods production was fixed, the precise proportion of expenditure to be left for the requirements of civilian consumers was contentious. Mikoyan advocated the boosting of light-industrial production. On agriculture, Khrushchëv felt the collective farms were too small and called for amalgamations that would lead to the establishment of 'agrotowns'. Andreev argued the opposite, proposing the division of each farm's work-force into several groups (or 'links') that would take responsibility for particular tasks.[25]

The agenda for deliberations at the highest level was therefore large. Its major items included the following: the military and diplomatic competition with the USA; the security of Soviet frontiers; Eastern Europe; the communist movement in Western Europe;

industrial planning and investment; agricultural organization; the scope of national and cultural self-expression. Decision-making was complicated because the various items intersected with each other. And this was not a static situation: the post-war world was in rapid flux.

Soviet politicians operated in an environment that was exceedingly unsettling. Molotov, Zhdanov, Malenkov, Khrushchëv, Voznesenski and Beria had to compete for Stalin's approval. After the war it was Zhdanov who was his favourite. Zhdanov returned to the Central Committee Secretariat in Moscow in 1946. He brought with him the prestige of a leader who had spent time in Leningrad while it was under siege by the Germans. Malenkov's career went into eclipse. But Zhdanov, sodden with drink, died in August 1948. An alliance was formed between Malenkov and Beria. Together they plotted the demise of Zhdanov's protégés. Practically the entire Leningrad and Gorki party leadership was executed in 1949. Even Politburo member and native Leningrader Voznesenski, who had argued against some of Zhdanov's proposals, was incarcerated. Voznesenski was shot in 1950. Civilian political struggle was resuming its bloody pre-war characteristics.

Zhdanov's scheme for a resurgent communist party was abandoned and the authority of the economic agencies of the government was confirmed. The USSR was still a one-party state; but the party as such did not rule it. The Politburo rarely met. No Party Congress was held after the war until 1952. The party was pushed back into the role proposed for it by Kaganovich in the mid-1930s: it was meant to supervise the implementation of policy, not to initiate it and certainly not to interfere in the detailed operation of governmental bodies. The infrequency of meetings of the party's supreme bodies – the Congress, the Central Committee and the Politburo – meant that Stalin no longer accorded great significance to its tasks of supervision.

In any case, Zhdanov had not challenged the priority of the capital-goods sector, which in 1945–50 amounted to eighty-eight per cent of all industrial investment.[26] The Fourth Five-Year Plan's first draft, which had taken consumers' aspirations into more favourable consideration than at any time since the NEP, was ripped up.[27] Capital goods output, including armaments, rose by eighty-three per cent in the half-decade after the Second World War.[28] This towering priority was enhanced in subsequent years. The budget of 1952 provided for a forty-five per cent increase of output for the armed forces in comparison with two years before.[29] Meanwhile the Soviet team of nuclear scientists led by Sergei Kurchatov and controlled by Beria had exploded an A-bomb at the Semipalatinsk testing-site in Kazakhstan in August 1949. Beria was so relieved at the sight of the billowing mushroom cloud that he momentarily abandoned his haughtiness and gave Kurchatov a hug.[30]

The priority for the armed forces meant that factory production for the ordinary consumer was starved of investment. Although output in this sector was doubled in the course of the Fourth Five-Year Plan, this was an increase from the pitifully low level of wartime.[31] Machine-tools, guns and bombs took precedence over shoes, coats, chairs and toys. The supply of food was also terribly inadequate. The grain harvest reaching the barns and warehouses in 1952 was still only seventy-seven per cent of the 1940 harvest.[32]

Schemes were introduced to raise additional revenues. Stalin sucked back citizens' personal savings into the state's coffers on 16 December 1947 by announcing a nine tenths devaluation of the rouble. Extra taxes, too, were invented. Among them was a charge on the peasant household for each fruit tree in its kitchen garden. Owners of cattle, pigs, sheep and hens were also subjected to punitive taxation. In 1954, fully a year after Stalin's death, the monthly pay for a typical kolkhoznik remained lower than a sixth of the earnings of the average factory worker: a miserable sixteen roubles.[33] To be sure, many kolkhozniki found other means of income; and some urban inhabitants were able to eke out their miserable wages by means of land allotments on which they grew potatoes and even kept the odd chicken. But conditions were generally abysmal. There was famine in Ukraine and Moldavia, a famine so grievous that cases of cannibalism occurred.

Many rural families elsewhere were left with so little grain after delivering their quotas to the government that they themselves had to buy flour in the towns. Innumerable farms in any case failed to comply with the state's procurement plan. Agriculture recovery had hardly begun. This meant that it was not unusual for kolkhozniki to receive no payment whatsoever from one year's end to the next. Such individuals would have no money to buy things from shops.

In the towns, too, there was great hardship. Stalin's ministers planned a programme of apartment construction (for which his successors took exclusive credit) but little was achieved in the early post-war years. The Soviet welfare state was not universal: social misfits and mentally-unstable individuals were neglected; and pensions were set at a derisory level. Furthermore, they were claimable by only a million people as late as 1950. Certain occupations in the towns offered just twenty roubles monthly, considerably below the poverty level as defined by the United Nations. Admittedly these were the worst-paid jobs. But official statistics also indicated that the average urban wage in 1952 was still no higher than it had been in 1928. Pressure therefore existed not only to get a job but also to seek promotion to higher posts.[34]

And a similar economic system was simultaneously being imposed on many other countries by the Soviet armed forces and security police and Eastern Europe's fraternal communist parties. The decisions of Allied political leaders at Moscow and Yalta in 1945 divided the European continent into broad zones of military responsibility; there had also been an assumption that the respective basic interests of the USSR, the USA, the UK and France would be safeguarded after the last shot of the Second World War had been fired.

The Yugoslav communist fighter Milovan Djilas has given a record of Stalin's musings: 'This war is not as in the past; whoever occupies a territory also imposes his own social system on it. Everyone imposes his own system as far as his army can reach. It cannot be otherwise.'[35] Initially Stalin had to act stealthily since until August 1949 the USSR, unlike the USA, had no A-bomb at its disposal. Initially he therefore geared his diplomacy to protecting his gains in Eastern Europe, where his forces had occupied Poland, Czechoslovakia, Romania, Bulgaria, Albania, Hungary and eastern Germany in 1944–5. Among his goals was the arrangement of communist parties' entrance to government in these countries. Having conquered an outer empire, he intended to reinforce his sway over it; and many Soviet citizens, however much they distrusted him, were proud that the USSR had defeated mighty Germany and had to all intents and purposes acquired an empire stretching across half the continent. Russians in particular had a pride in this military achievement and imperial consolidation lasted through to and beyond the last years of the USSR's existence.

Still needing to avoid trouble with the Western Allies, he imposed restraints upon the Italian, French and Greek communist parties in the West. These parties had played the major role in the resistance to Nazism in their countries, and several communist leaders assumed that military victory would be followed by political revolution. Palmiro Togliatti consulted with Stalin before returning to Italy after the war,[36] and Maurice Thorez anyway accepted anything laid down in the Kremlin for France. In Greece, the communists ignored Stalin's cautionary instructions and tried to seize power. They paid dearly for their insubordination. Stalin ostentatiously stood aside while the USA and the UK aided the Greek monarchist forces in their defeat of communist guerrillas.

But what to do about the countries directly under Soviet occupation? At the Potsdam Conference of Allied leaders in July 1945 Stalin, on his last ever trip outside the USSR, secured the territorial settlement he demanded. The boundaries of Lithuania and Ukraine were extended westward at the expense of pre-war Poland while Poland was compensated by the gift of land previously belonging to the north-eastern region of Germany.[37] Yet the Western Allies refused to recognize the USSR's annexation of Lithuania, Latvia and Estonia. Wishing to affirm that the post-war boundaries would be permanent, Stalin therefore decided that Königsberg and the rest of East Prussia would belong not to Lithuania or Poland but to the RSFSR. Consequently a 'Russian' territory was to act as a partial wedge between Poland and Lithuania. The RSFSR would have a military base and an all-season port at Königsberg – now renamed as Kaliningrad – in order to deter any attempt to redraw the map of Europe.

The Soviet occupying authorities also inserted communists into the coalition government formed in Poland at the war's end. The same process occurred in Hungary even though the communist party received only seventeen per cent of the votes in the November 1945 election. Elections in Czechoslovakia were delayed until May 1946, when the communists won nearly two fifths of the vote and were the most successful party. A coalition government led by communist Clement Gottwald was established in Prague.

In all countries where the Red Army had fought there were similar arrangements: communists shared power with socialist and agrarian parties and the appearance of democratic procedures was maintained. In reality there was unremitting persecution of the leading non-communist politicians. Everywhere in Eastern Europe the Soviet security police manipulated the situation in favour of the communists. Defamatory propaganda, jerrymandering and arrests were the norm. Teams of police operatives were sent to catch the large number of people who had actively collaborated with the Nazis. In Germany a Soviet organization was installed to transfer industrial machinery to the USSR. Local communist leaders were carefully supervised from the Kremlin. They were selected for their loyalty to Stalin; and they in turn knew that, with the exception of Yugoslavia and Czechoslovakia, their positions of influence in their own countries would be fragile in the absence of support from the Soviet armed forces.

Yet these same leaders were aware of the awful effects of Stalin's policies on his own USSR. Polish communists wanted to avoid mass agricultural collectivization; and even the Yugoslav comrades, who generally rebuked the East European communist parties for a lack of revolutionary resolve, refused to de-kulakize their villages. Several parties, including the Poles, Hungarians and Czechoslovaks, aimed to form left-of-centre governmental coalitions; there were few proponents of the need for the immediate formation of one-party states. The Soviet road to socialism was not regarded by them as wholly desirable.[38]

Stalin went along with these divergences from Marxism-Leninism-Stalinism in 1945–6 while the general world situation remained in flux. But he was unlikely to tolerate heterodoxy for long, and it was only a matter of time before he moved to strap an organizational strait-jacket around European communist parties. Furthermore, in 1946 there was a hardening of the USA's foreign policy. President Truman resolved to contain any further expansion of Soviet political influence; he also decided in 1947, on the suggestion of his Secretary of State George Marshall, to offer loans for the economic reconstruction of Europe, East and West, on terms that would provide the USA with access to their markets. Stalin was aghast at the prospect. As he saw things, the problem in Eastern Europe was that there was too little communism: a resurgent market economy was the last thing he wanted to see there. The Marshall Plan was regarded by him as an economic device to destroy Soviet military and political hegemony over Eastern Europe.

Relations between the USSR and the former Allies had worsened. The USA, Britain and France were resisting demands for continued reparations to be made to the USSR by regions of Germany unoccupied by Soviet forces, and Germany's partition into two entirely separate administrative zones was becoming a reality. Stalin feared that the western zone was about to be turned into a separate state that would re-arm itself with the USA's encouragement and would belong to an anti-Soviet alliance. In the Far East, too, the USA seemed interested mainly in rehabilitating Japan as an economic partner. As in the 1930s, Stalin felt threatened from both the Pacific Ocean and central Europe.

Stalin could do little about the Far East except build up his military position on Sakhalin and the Kurile Islands acquired at the end of the Second World War; and in March 1947 he decided to withdraw from northern Iran rather than risk confrontation with Britain and the USA. But in Europe he was more bullish. On 22 September 1947 he convoked a conference of communist parties from the USSR, Poland, Yugoslavia, Czechoslovakia, Bulgaria, Romania, Hungary, France and Italy. The venue was Szklarska Poręba in eastern Poland. Soviet politicians dominated the proceedings. Stalin was not present, but was kept closely informed by his Politburo associates Zhdanov and Malenkov about what was said. The organizational aim was to re-establish an international communist body, which would be called the Information Bureau. Several delegates were uneasy about the proposal and stressed the need to co-operate with non-communists in their country and to avoid agricultural collectivization.

But in the end they agreed to the creation of an Information Bureau, which quickly became known as Cominform. Ostensibly it was a very different body from the defunct Comintern: Cominform was to be based not in Moscow but in Belgrade; it was to involve only the parties present at the Conference and to have no formal control over these parties.[39] Yet Stalin clearly intended to use Cominform so as to impose his will on the communist leaderships with delegates at the Conference.

In 1948, as he continued to harden his purposes towards the communist parties in Eastern Europe, he sanctioned the replacement of the various coalition governments with communist dictatorships. One-party communist states were formed by a mixture of force, intimidation and electoral fraud; and the Soviet security police operated as overseers. If Ukraine and other Soviet republics were the inner empire ruled from Moscow, the new states were the outer imperial domains. They were officially designated 'people's democracies'. This term was invented to emphasize that the East European states had been established without the civil wars which had occurred in Russia.[40] Thus the Soviet Army inhibited any counter-revolution and the social and economic reconstruction could proceed without obstruction. The term also served to stress the subordination of the East European states to the USSR; it was a none too discreet way of affirming imperial pride, power and cohesion.

The main impediment to cohesion in the politics of Eastern Europe was constituted not by anti-communists but by the Yugoslav communist regime. Its leader Josip Broz Tito was a contradictory figure. On the one hand, Tito still refused to de-kulakize his peasantry; on the other, he castigated the slow pace of the introduction of communism to other countries in Eastern Europe. Both aspects of Tito's stance implied a criticism of Stalin's policies for Eastern Europe after the Second World War. Stalin was accustomed to receiving homage from the world's communists whereas Tito tried to treat himself as Stalin's equal.

There was also a danger for Stalin that Tito's independent attitude might spread to other countries in Eastern Europe. In 1946–7 Tito had been canvassing for the creation of a federation of Yugoslavia and other communist states in south-eastern Europe. Stalin eventually judged that such a federation would be hard for him to control. Tito also urged the need for active support to be given to the Greek communist attempt at revolution. This threatened to wreck the understandings reached between the USSR and the Western Allies about the territorial limits of direct Soviet influence. And so Stalin, in June 1948, ordered Yugoslavia's expulsion from the Cominform. Tito was subjected to tirades of vilification unprecedented since the death of Trotski. This communist leader of his country's resistance against Hitler was now described in *Pravda* as the fascist hireling of the USA.

In the same month there were diplomatic clashes among the Allies when Stalin announced a blockade of Berlin. The German capital, which lay in the Soviet-occupied zone of Germany, had been divided into four areas administered separately by the USSR, the USA, Britain and France. Stalin was responding to an American attempt to introduce the Deutschmark as the unit of currency in Berlin, an attempt he regarded as designed to encroach on the USSR's economic prerogatives in the Soviet zone. His blockade, he expected, would swiftly produce the requested concessions from the Western powers. But no such thing happened. After several weeks he had to back down because the Americans and her allies airlifted food supplies to their areas in the German capital. Neither side in the dispute wished to go to war over Berlin, and tensions subsided. But lasting damage had been done to relations between the USSR and USA.

The expulsion of the Yugoslavs from the fraternity of world communism and the recurrent clashes with the USA terrified the communist governments of Poland, Czechoslovakia, Bulgaria, Albania, Romania and Hungary into servility. None was allowed to accept Marshall Aid. Instead, from January 1949 they had to assent to the formation of the Council for Mutual Economic Assistance (Comecon). In October 1949 Stalin also decided that, if the USA was going to dominate western Germany, he would proceed to form a German Democratic Republic in the zone occupied by Soviet armed forces. Private economic enterprise, cultural pluralism and open political debate were eliminated throughout Eastern Europe. Exceptions persisted. For example, agricultural collectivization was only partially implemented in Poland. But in most ways the Soviet historical model was applied with ruthlessless to all these countries.

Furthermore, Władisław Gomułka, who had shown an independent turn of mind at the Cominform Conference in 1947, was pushed out of power in Warsaw and arrested. Another delegate to the Conference, Hungary's Internal Affairs Minister László Rajk, was arrested in June 1949. Bulgarian former deputy premier Trajcho Kostov was imprisoned in December 1949 and Rudolf Slánsky, Czechoslovakia's Party General Secretary, was imprisoned in December 1952. Of these leaders only Gomułka escaped execution. Bloody purges were applied against thousands of lower party and government officials in each of these countries from the late 1940s through to 1953.

Soviet and American governments used the most intemperate language against each other. At the First Cominform Conference in September 1947 a resolution was agreed that the USA was assembling an alliance of imperialist, anti-democratic forces against the USSR and the democratic forces. On the other side, the Western powers depicted the USSR as the vanguard of global communist expansion. Soviet self-assertion increased in subsequent years after the successful testing of a Soviet A-bomb in August 1949 had deprived the Americans and British of their qualitative military superiority. Stalin's confidence rose, too, because of the conquest of power in Beijing by the Chinese Communist Party led by Mao Zedong in November. The People's Republic of China quickly signed a Treaty of Friendship, Alliance and Mutual Assistance. A great axis of communism stretched from Stettin on the Baltic to Shanghai in the Far East. A quarter of the globe was covered by states professing adherence to Marxism-Leninism.

Since 1947, furthermore, Stalin had begun to license the French and Italian communist parties to take a more militant line against their governments. He remained convinced that 'history' was on the side of world communism and was willing to consider schemes that might expand the area occupied by communist states.

One such possibility was presented in Korea in 1950. Korea had been left divided between a communist North and a capitalist South since the end of the Second World War. The Korean communist leader Kim Il-Sung proposed to Stalin that communist forces should take over the entire country. Stalin did not demur, and gave support to Kim in a civil war that could eventually have involved the forces of the USSR and the USA facing each other across battlefields in the Far East. Mao Zedong, too, was in favour. Given the political sanction and military equipment he had requested, Kim Il-Sung attacked southern Korea in June 1950. Foolishly the Soviet Union temporarily withdrew its representative from the debate on the Korean civil war at the Security Council of the United Nations. Thus Stalin robbed himself of the veto on the United Nations' decision to intervene on the southern side with American military power. China supplied forces to assist Kim Il-Sung. A terrible conflict ensued.[41]

Kim Il-Sung seemed invincible as he hastened southwards, but then the arrival of the Americans turned the tide. By mid-1951 there was a bloody stalemate across Korea. Soviet forces were not seriously involved; but President Truman justifiably inferred that the USSR had rendered material assistance to Kim. Millions of soldiers on both sides were killed in 1952–3.

But how had the USSR and the USA allowed themselves to come so close to direct armed collision so soon after a world war in which they had been each other's indispensable allies? The apologists for either side put the respective cases robustly. Indeed it took no great skill to present the actions of either of them as having been responsible for the onset of the Cold War. The Americans had acted precipitately. They formed a separate state in western Germany; they flaunted the possession of their nuclear weaponry; they built up Japan as an ally and established the North Atlantic Treaty Organization. The Soviet Union had also behaved provocatively. It had terrorized Eastern Europe, delayed its withdrawal from Iran and supported Kim Il-Sung. Each successive crisis left the two sides ever more intransigent in their postures towards each other. Clashes between American and

Soviet diplomats became normal over every matter of global politics.

Yet it would have taken little short of a miracle to avoid a Cold War. The USSR and the USA were states with diametrically-opposite interests. Both states, indeed, aimed to expand their global power and were not too scrupulous about the methods used. They also had opposing ideologies. Each thought the principles of human betterment were on its side. Each was armed to the teeth. Each operated in an environment of considerable ignorance about the politicians and society of the other side. So was the balance of responsibility equal? No, because the USSR depended much more directly than its rival upon militarism, terror and injustice to get its way. There was as much financial blandishment and political persuasion as manipulativeness and force at work in the American domination of Western Europe. But manipulativeness and force, involving systematic savagery, was the predominant method of the USSR in Eastern Europe.

The USSR and Eastern Europe were an armed camp confronting the Western Allies. The USSR itself was an armed camp charged with maintaining the subjugation of Eastern Europe. In the USSR, the Soviet political order applied the most brutal repression to its society. Stalin's domestic order was inescapably militaristic; and only by maintaining such a posture in its foreign relations could it contrive to justify and conserve its power at home. Stalin expected to find trouble in the world and was not averse to seeking it out.

16

The Despot and his Masks

Stalin could not dominate by terror alone. Needing the support of the elites in the government, the party, the army and the security police, he systematically sought favour among them. The privileges and power of functionaries were confirmed and the dignity of institutions was enhanced. By keeping the gulf between the rulers and the ruled, Stalin hoped to prevent the outbreak of popular opposition. What is more, he tried to increase his specific appeal to ethnic Russians by reinforcing a form of Russian nationalism alongside Marxism-Leninism; and Stalin cultivated his image as a leader whose position at the helm of the Soviet state was vital for the country's military security and economic development.

Such measures could delay a crisis for the regime; they were not a permanent solution. In any case Stalin did not adhere to the measures consistently. He was far too suspicious of his associates and the country's élites to provide them with the entirely stable circumstances that would have alleviated the strains in politics, the economy and society. His health deteriorated after the Second World War. His holidays in Abkhazia became longer, and he sustained his efforts much more concentratedly in international relations than in domestic policy. But he could intervene whenever he wanted in any public deliberations. If an open debate took place on any big topic, it was because he had given permission. If a problem developed without reaction by central government and party authorities, it was either because Stalin did not think it very important or did not think it amenable to solution. He remained the dictator.

He so much avoided flamboyance that he refrained from giving a single major speech in the period between mid-April 1948 and October 1952. At first he declined the title of Generalissimus pressed upon him by Politburo colleagues. In a characteristic reference to himself in the third person, he wondered aloud: 'Do you want comrade Stalin to assume the rank of Generalissimus? Why does comrade Stalin need this? Comrade Stalin doesn't need this.'[1]

But assume it he did, and he would have been angry if the torrents of praise had dried up. His name appeared as an authority in books on everything from politics and culture to the natural sciences. The Soviet state hymn, which he had commissioned in the war, contained the line: 'Stalin brought us up.' In the film *The Fall of Berlin* he was played by an actor with luridly ginger hair and a plastic mask who received the gratitude of a multinational crowd which joyfully chanted: 'Thank you, Stalin!' By 1954, 706 million copies of Stalin's works had been published.[2] In 1949 a parade was held in Red Square to celebrate his seventieth birthday and his facial image was projected into the evening sky over the Kremlin. His official biography came out in a second edition, which he had had amended so as to enhance the account of his derring-do under Nicholas II. His height was exaggerated in newsreels by clever camera work. The pockmarks on his face were airbrushed away. This perfect 'Stalin' was everywhere while the real Stalin hid himself from view.

Among the peoples of the USSR he strained to identify himself with the ethnic Russians. In private he talked in his native tongue with those of his intimates who were Georgian; and even his deceased wife Nadezhda Allilueva had Georgian ancestors.[3] He ran his supper parties like a Georgian host (although most such hosts would not have thrown tomatoes at his guests as Stalin did).[4] But publicly his origins embarrassed him after a war which had intensified the self-awareness and pride of Russians; and his biography referred just once to his own father's nationality.[5] Stalin placed the Russian nation on a pedestal: 'Among all peoples of our country it is the leading people.'[6] Official favour for things Russian went beyond precedent. The lexicographers were told to remove foreign loan-words from the dictionaries. For instance, the Latin-American tango was renamed 'the slow dance'.[7] The history of nineteenth-century science was ransacked and – glory be! – it was found that practically every major invention from the bicycle to the television had been the brainchild of an ethnic Russian.

Simultaneously the Soviet authorities re-barricaded the USSR from alien influences. Polina Zhemchuzhina, Molotov's wife, was imprisoned for greeting the Israeli emissary Golda Meir too warmly. The poet Boris Pasternak was terrified when the Russian-born British philosopher, Isaiah Berlin, then serving as a diplomat in Moscow, paid him a visit at home. Stalin expressed the following opinion to Nikita Khrushchëv: 'We should never allow a foreigner to fly across the Soviet Union.'[8] After the war, Kliment Voroshilov placed a ban on the reporting of Canadian ice-hockey results.[9] Great Russia always had to be the world's champion nation. A propaganda campaign was initiated to stress that there should be no 'bowing down' before the achievements and potentiality of the West.

All national groups suffered, but some suffered more than others. The cultures of Estonians, Latvians and Lithuanians – who had only recently been re-conquered – were ravaged. The same occurred to the Romanian-speaking Moldavians; in their case even their language was emasculated: first it was equipped with a Cyrillic alphabet and then its vocabulary compulsorily acquired loan-words from Russian so as to distinguish it strongly from Romanian.[10] The Ukrainian language was decreasingly taught to Ukrainian-speaking children in the RSFSR.[11] More sinister still was the experience of a philologist who was imprisoned simply for stating that some Finno-Ugric languages had more declensions than Russian. Historiography became ever more imperialist. Shamil, the leader of the nineteenth-century rebellion in the North Caucasus against tsarism, was depicted unequivocally as a reactionary figure. Anyone dead or alive who since time immemorial had opposed the Russian state was prone to be denounced.[12]

The nationality which underwent the greatest trauma were the Jews. The Anti-Fascist Jewish Committee was closed down without explanation, and its leader and outstanding Yiddish singer Solomon Mikhoels was murdered in a car crash on Stalin's orders. Several prominent Soviet politicians who happened to be Jewish, such as Semën Lozovski, disappeared into prison.

Stalin, starting with his article on the national question in 1913, refused to describe the Jews as a nation since, unlike the Ukrainians or Armenians, they did not inhabit a particular historic territory. In 1934 he sought to give them a territory of their own by establishing a 'Jewish Autonomous Region' in Birobidzhan and asking for volunteers to populate it. But Birobidzhan lay in one of the coldest regions of eastern Siberia. Little enthusiasm was invoked by the project, and after the war there was tentative talk about turning Crimea instead into a Jewish homeland. But in the 1940s Stalin's unease about the Jews had increased to the point that he cursed his daughter Svetlana for going out with a Jewish boyfriend. Particularly annoying to him was the admiration of many Soviet Jews for the Zionist movement which had founded the state of Israel in 1948. Stalin responded by denouncing 'cosmopolitanism' and 'rootlessness'. He ignored the fact that Marxists had traditionally opposed nationalism in favour of cosmopolitan attitudes. Restrictions were introduced on the access of Jews to university education and professional occupations. Soviet textbooks ceased to mention that Karl Marx had been Jewish.

Russian chauvinism was rampant. The first party secretary, the police chief and the governmental chairmen in other Soviet republics such as Ukraine and Kazakhstan were invariably of Russian nationality. There was similar discrimination in appointments to other important public offices. Russians were trusted because they, more than any other nation, were thought to have a stake in the retention of the USSR in its existing boundaries.

This imperialism, however, was not taken to its fullest imaginable extent. Ordinary Russians lived as meanly as Ukrainians and Kazakhs; indeed many were worse off than Georgians and other peoples with higher *per capita* levels of output of meat, vegetables and fruit than Russia. Furthermore, Stalin continued to limit the expression of Russian nationhood. Despite having distorted Marxism-Leninism, he also clung to several of its main tenets. He continued to hold the Russian Orthodox Church in subservience, and practising

Christians were debarred from jobs of responsibility throughout the USSR. Stalin also exercised selectivity towards Russian literary classics and allowed no nostalgia about pre-revolutionary village traditions. His version of Russian national identity was so peculiar a mixture of traditions as to be virtually his own invention. The quintessence of Russia, for Stalin, was simply a catalogue of his own predilections: militarism, xenophobia, industrialism, urbanism and gigantomania.

It also embraced a commitment to science. But as usual, Stalin gave things a political twist. His spokesman Zhdanov, despite negligible training, breezily denounced relativity theory, cybernetics and quantum mechanics as 'bourgeois' and 'reactionary'. Crude, ideologically-motivated interventions were made in the research institutes for the natural sciences. The relativist concepts of Einstein were an irritant to the monolithism of Marxism-Leninism-Stalinism. Zhdanov proclaimed the axiomatic status of absolute notions of space, time and matter; he insisted that an unshifting objective truth existed for all organic and inorganic reality.[13]

Persecution of scholarship was accompanied by the continued promotion of cranks. By the 1940s the pseudo-scientist Lysenko was claiming to have developed strains of wheat that could grow within the Arctic circle. His gruff manner was attractive to Stalin. The result was disaster for professional biology: any refusal to condone Lysenkoite hypotheses was punished by arrest. Where biology led, chemistry, psychology and linguistics quickly followed. Physics escaped this mauling only because the scientists employed on the Soviet nuclear weapon project convinced Beria that the USSR would not acquire an A-bomb unless they were allowed to use Einstein's concepts. Stalin muttered to Beria: 'Leave them in peace. We can always shoot them later.'[14] This grudging indulgence proved the rule. Researchers of all kinds, in the arts as well as in the sciences, were treated as technicians investigating problems strictly within the guidelines prescribed by the state authorities.

Stalin made this crystal clear when he intruded himself into erudite debates among linguisticians. In his quirky booklet of 1950, *Marxism and Questions of Linguistics*, he took it upon himself to insist that the Russian language originated in the provinces of Kursk and Orël.[15] The entire intelligentsia was constrained to applaud the booklet as an intellectual breakthrough and to apply its wisdom to other fields of scholarship. Writers scrambled to outdo each other in praise of Stalin's injunctions.

The arts suffered alongside the sciences and the wartime cultural semi-truce was brought to an end. Zhdanov again led the assault, describing the poet Anna Akhmatova as 'half-nun, half-whore'. The short-story writer Mikhail Zoshchenko, who had avoided trouble by writing predominantly for children, was also castigated. Shostakovich could no longer have his symphonies performed. Zhdanov noted that several artists had withheld explicit support for the official ideology, and he announced that this 'idea-lessness' (*bezideinost*) would no longer be tolerated. Essentially he was demanding overt adherence to a single set of ideas, 'Marxism-Leninism-Stalinism'. The various official organizations of creative artists were trundled into action. Tikhon Khrennikov, chairman of the Union of Musicians, was rivalled only by Alexander Fadeev, leader of the Union of Writers, in fawning before Zhdanov's judgements on particular composers, painters, poets and film directors. Such cheerleaders cried that the arts should be the conveyor-belt for the regime's commands.

Only rarely did Stalin intervene in Zhdanov's campaign for Marxist-Leninist compliance. But when he did, his effect was terrifying. For instance, in 1947 Stalin, Zhdanov and Molotov paid a visit to the director Sergei Eisenstein, who was filming the second instalment of his two-part depiction of *Ivan the Terrible*. To Stalin's mind, Eisenstein had failed to stress that Tsar Ivan's terror against the aristocracy had been justified; he urged Eisenstein to 'show that it was necessary to be ruthless'. The intimidated director – who already had a chronic cardiac complaint – asked for further detailed advice; but Stalin would only reply, in false self-deprecation: 'I'm not giving you instructions but expressing the comments of a spectator.' Eisenstein was deeply scared by the conversation. He died a few months later.[16]

Meanwhile only a few works that were critical of social and

economic conditions were permitted. Among the most interesting were the sketches of collective-farm life published by Valentin Ovechkin under the title *Rural Daily Rounds*. And so Stalin, probably at Khrushchёv's instigation, permitted a portrait of the troubles of contemporary farming to appear in *Pravda*. This seepage through the Stalinist cultural dam occurred solely because Politburo members themselves were in dispute about agrarian policy. For the most part, in any case, official propagandists remained utterly self-satisfied, asserting that all Soviet citizens were living in comfort. A massive cookbook was produced in 1952, *The Book of Delicious and Healthy Food*, which took as its epigraph a quotation from Stalin: 'The peculiar characteristic of our revolution consists in its having given the people not only freedom but also material goods as well as the opportunity of a prosperous and cultured life.'[17]

The beneficiaries of the Soviet order were not the 'people', not the workers, kolkhozniki and office-clerks. Even doctors, engineers and teachers were poorly paid. But one group in society was certainly indebted to Stalin. This was constituted by the high and middling ranks of the bureaucracy in the ministries, the party, the armed forces and the security organs. The material assets of functionaries were small by the standards of the rich in the West. But they knew how hard life was for the rest of society; they also understood that, if they were unlucky in some way in their career, they might suddenly enter prison despite being innocent of any crime. Immediate pleasure was the priority for them.[18]

The tone of their lifestyle was set by Politburo members as the ballet and the opera were given the imprimatur of official approval. Stalin patronized the Bolshoi Theatre, favouring its singers with coveted awards. The families of the Politburo went to the spa-town Pyatigorsk in the North Caucasus to take the waters. Occasionally they went to Karlovy Vary in Czechoslovakia. Flats were done up with wallpaper, lamps and chairs that were unobtainable in general stores such as GUM on Red Square. Special shops, special hospitals and special holiday-homes were available to persons of political importance. The compulsory fees that had been introduced in 1940 for pupils wishing to complete their secondary schooling meant that the proportion of working-class entrants to universities fell from forty-five per cent in 1935 to just above twenty-five by 1950.[19] The central and local nomenklaturas were steadily turning into a hereditary social group.

But the nomenklatura did not yet flaunt their perks which had to be enjoyed discreetly in deference to the official ultimate aim of social egalitarianism. The Politburo took care to wear modest tunics or dull suits and hats. Ordinary people were given no hint about the tables creaking under the weight of caviar, sturgeon and roast lamb served at Kremlin banquets. Stalin himself lived fairly simply by the standards of several Politburo members; but even he had a governess for his daughter, a cook and several maids, a large dacha at Kuntsevo, an endless supply of Georgian wine and so few worries about money that most of his pay-packets lay unopened at the time of his death. Armed guards secured the privacy of the apartment blocks of the central political élite. Only the domestic servants, nannies and chauffeurs knew the truth about the lifestyle of the nomenklatura.

No wonder the emergent ruling class was determined to keep the foundations of the Soviet order in good repair. The mood of most functionaries was triumphalist; they felt that the USSR's victory in the Second World War had demonstrated the superiority of communism over capitalism. They themselves were by now better qualified than before the war; they were more literate and numerate and most of them had completed their secondary education. But this in no way diminished their ideological crudity. Far from it: they did not distinguish between the interests of the regime and their own, and they would brook no challenge to their exploitative, repressive measures.

Stalin and his subordinates still talked about the eventual realization of communism, reaffirming that 'the state will not last forever'.[20] But how to create a communist society was not a question under consideration. Far from it. The specific aspirations of the Soviet working class no longer figured prominently in Soviet propaganda. Workers in the rest of the world were called upon to engage in revolutionary struggle, but not in the USSR. At home the main requirement was for patriotism. Stalin implicitly laid down this line even in his *Marxism and Questions of Linguistics*. For example, he stressed the need to reject the notion that language was the product of class-based factors. This notion had conventionally been propagated by communist zealots who declared that words and grammar were the product of the social imperatives of the ruling class of a given society. Stalin instead wanted Soviet schoolchildren to admire the poetry of the nineteenth-century writer Alexander Pushkin without regard to his aristocratic background. Patriotism was to count for more than class.[21]

Here Stalin was clarifying the doctrines of communist conservatism prominent in his thought immediately before the Second World War. As ruler and theorist he wished to emphasize that no transformation in the Soviet order was going to happen in the foreseeable future. The attitudes, policies and practices of the post-war period were meant to endure for many more years.

Nowhere was this more obvious than in the discussions in 1950–51 among 240 leading scholars about a projected official textbook on political economy. Dauntlessly many of the 240 participants took issue with the premisses of current state policy.[22] Stalin entered the debate in 1952 by producing yet another booklet, *The Economic Problems of Socialism in the USSR*. He laid down that the objective 'laws' of economics could not be ignored by governmental planners and that there were limits on what was achievable by human will. This was a rebuff to S. G. Strumilin, who had been among his scholarly supporters at the end of the 1920s. On the other hand, Stalin offered no hope for the relaxation of economic policy. Taking issue with L. D. Yaroshenko, he argued that the primacy of capital goods in industrial planning was unalterable; and he reprimanded V. G. Venzher and A. V. Sanina for proposing the selling-off of the state-owned agricultural machinery to kolkhozes.[23]

Stalin made no mention of topics such as the party, the government, elections, relations between classes, participation, international communism, authority or terror. On a single great subject he was expansive: global capitalism. He began by declaring that the economies of war-beaten Germany and Japan would soon recover. This accurate prediction was accompanied by a prognosis which has proved awry:

namely that after communism's victory in China, the market for global capitalism would be too limited for capitalist countries to be able to expand their economies. According to Stalin, the result would be yet another world war among the major non-communist powers, and he reaffirmed Lenin's thesis on the inevitable recurrence of such wars so long as capitalist imperialism endured. Stalin repeated that the most acute danger of a Third World War occurring lay in rivalry between one capitalist coalition and another and not between communism and capitalism.[24]

His plan was to go on and compose a broader work; but it is unlikely that he would have tugged such a work out of the rut worn by his previous writings. Stalin had accommodated his thought to the kind of Soviet state that already existed. He ruled over this state, but needed also to rule through it.

And so relations among the various public bodies by the late 1940s were entering a stable period by the measure of the past two decades. In order to indicate that revolutionary disturbance would not recur in the institutional framework, Stalin in 1946 renamed the People's Commissariats as Ministries. He also ordered that the Red Army should henceforward be called the Soviet Army. This emphasis on continuity with the pre-revolutionary state was reinforced artistically. In 1948 the octocentenary of Moscow's foundation was celebrated, and a statue of the medieval patriot Prince Dolgoruki was commissioned for erection on Gorki Street. Dolgoruki's stern visage and muscular limbs gave monumental expression to Stalin's vision of Soviet statehood.[25] Architects abetted the process. The power and dignity of the USSR acquired visible form in the vast granite buildings, topped by fairy-castle decorations. Six of them were constructed in central Moscow. A seventh was added in Warsaw, as if to emphasize Poland's inclusion in the Soviet imperial domain.

And yet Stalin could not afford to allow institutional stabilization to be carried too far. As he well understood, his despotism required him periodically to re-agitate the elements in the Soviet order. In the post-war years there remained much to worry him. Those vertical clienteles and horizontal local groups were an object of continuing concern. So, too, was the fact that each of the great organizations of state was developing its own corporate identity. Soviet Army officers, like their predecessors in the tsarist forces, had begun to see themselves almost as a separate caste. The same phenomenon – albeit to a lesser degree – was visible in the economic ministries, the security police and the party.

Furthermore, the indoctrination of administrative, professional and intellectual functionaries was far from satisfactorily achieved. Some of them had ideas which sat uncomfortably alongside Marxism-Leninism-Stalinism and which came from a variety of sources. People were influenced by folk customs and by stories and memories recounted within families. Military veterans had had a glimpse of a different way of life abroad – and their conclusions were often to the USSR's discredit. Many others continued to be motivated by national and religious traditions. Even officially-approved publications could give rise to un-Stalinist thoughts. Scientific textbooks propounded rules of investigation and validation at variance with Stalin's claim that Marxism was based on premisses of eternal verity. Despite the heavy censorship exercised by Glavlit, moreover, citizens could glean unorthodox ideas from the approved Russian literary classics: Pushkin's poems and Tolstoy's novels teemed with discussions about religion, philosophy, nationhood and – last but not least – politics.

How well Stalin was acquainted with this information is unknown; but certainly he acted to rearrange the pattern of Soviet politics. His despotic will was undiminished. When his personal physician V. N. Vinogradov advised him to run down his official duties on grounds of failing health, Stalin had him arrested. Stalin did not want others to know that he was no longer up to the job. He also turned against the chief of his bodyguards N. S. Vlasik and his personal assistant A. N. Poskrëbyshev. His isolation increased. He rarely saw his beloved daughter Svetlana and had not remarried since his second wife's death in 1932. Stalin trusted nobody.

As his suspicions grew, so too did his anti-Semitic tendencies. Several other Kremlin physicians were arrested in 1952 after being denounced by a certain Lidya Timashuk. Most of the thirteen detainees in this Doctors' Plot had Jewish names and the tirades in the press against the 'assassins in white coats' produced an anti-Semitic hysteria. Individual Jews were subjected to verbal abuse by their neighbours throughout the country. It made no difference that many of them no longer practised their religion: the fact that their passports recorded them as Jewish made it easy for their persecutors to identify them. Meanwhile Stalin was giving confidential consideration to a scheme to round up all Jews and force them to live in the Jewish Autonomous Region established in eastern Siberia. Polina Zhemchuzhina, Molotov's Jewish wife, was brought back from a camp and re-interrogated. The prospects for Soviet Jewry grew very bleak.

Nevertheless Jews were not Stalin's sole intended victims. The treatment of Zhemchuzhina raised the question how long it might be before Politburo member Molotov, too, would share her fate. Stalin also appeared to be planning to move against past and present leaders of the Soviet security organs. Beria was a notable potential target. In 1951, arrests had begun of party and governmental officials of Mingrelian origin. Mingrelians are an ethnic division of the Georgian nation, and the fact that Beria was their most famous son was not coincidental. A bloody purge of some kind was in the offing even though its exact nature and scale remained unclear. Almost certainly something broader than the Leningrad purge of 1949 was in Stalin's mind. The shadow cast over Molotov and Beria might well eventually reach many other persons at the apex of the Soviet state. It cannot be excluded that his ultimate purpose was to conduct yet another great bloody purge of personnel in government, party, army and police.

Probably his exact purposes will never be discovered. Certainly he did not confide them to the Nineteenth Party Congress in October 1952. The biggest event was the change of name from the All-Union Communist Party (Bolsheviks) to the Communist Party of the Soviet Union. Stalin left it to Malenkov to give the Central Committee report; and the contributions not only by Malenkov but also by everyone else emphasized that Stalin's wise leadership had their unanimous approval and gratitude. Apparently not the slightest disagreement on policy existed in the Kremlin.

Yet while offering obeisance to the officially-tabled resolutions,

Stalin's associates used indirect language to indicate their respective differences of opinion. Malenkov wanted greater attention to be paid to light-industrial investment and to the development of intensive methods of agriculture. Beria highlighted the desirability of treating the non-Russians more carefully. After propounding his agricultural schemes, Khrushchëv declared that every party member should display 'vigilance': a conventional code-word for support of political repression. A careful reader of the *Pravda* reports could therefore discern that tensions existed at the apex of the Soviet communist party. Stalin made no attempt to arbitrate among them. Most of the delegates anyway did not care: they had come to the Congress mainly to catch a glimpse of Stalin and to pass the resolutions with unanimity. At the very mention of Stalin's name they applauded, and several times in the course of the Congress they gave him standing ovations.

Only at the Central Committee elected by the Congress did Stalin at last reveal his impatience. Firstly he asked to resign as Central Committee Secretary. Malenkov was chairing the session and turned white with dread lest the Central Committee members failed spontaneously to rise to their feet to deny Stalin his request. Luckily for him, they did.[26]

Then Stalin gave an impromptu address. Still speaking of his weariness, he gave the impression that he knew this might be the last speech he made. In particular, he rambled through his memories of the Treaty of Brest-Litovsk in 1918: 'And what about Lenin? Just you read again what he said and what he wrote at that time. He let out a roar at that time, in so incredibly grievous a situation; he thundered, he was scared of no one. Thundered, he did.' In almost the same breath Stalin considered his own career. While almost begging the Central Committee to compare him favourably with Lenin, he also wanted to appear as the party's modest and dutiful leader. 'Once this task has been entrusted to me,' he declared, 'I carry it through. But not in such a way that it's accredited only to me. I've not been brought up that way.'[27]

This was a man anticipating his obituary. Stalin, too, wanted to be remembered as a leader of courage and foresight, a leader who thundered. These were not the characteristics which immediately sprang to mind among those who knew him at close quarters: he had not been notably brave, foresightful or devoid in vanity.

Weary or not, Stalin continued to pose a deadly threat to his colleagues. Halfway through his Central Committee address he suddenly accused Molotov and Mikoyan of political cowardice.[28] They rejected his criticisms as tactfully as they could in the circumstances, and the topic was dropped. Nevertheless Central Committee members had been shocked by the episode. Many of them concluded that Stalin wanted at the very least to prevent these two veteran leaders from succeeding him. This impression was strengthened by other moves he made at the Central Committee plenum. For example, he redesignated the Politburo as a Presidium and increased the number of its members to twenty-five. The sinister aspect of the change was that Stalin simultaneously secured the appointment of a seven-person Bureau of the Presidium which, by involving mainly the younger leaders, would allow him to drop the veterans at a convenient moment in the future.

Several central politicians already had reason to expect to be arrested before he collapsed in his dacha at Kuntsevo on 1 March 1953. The sudden, secret nature of his indisposition gave rise to rumours that someone, perhaps Beria, had ordered some skulduggery. Certainly Beria and fellow Politburo members took an unconscionably long time to make a serious attempt to resuscitate Stalin over the next few days.[29] The kindest interpretation is that they were too afraid to intervene in decisions on his medical care. Finding him on the floor of his bedroom, they dithered as to what to do with his body; and after doctors pronounced him definitely dead on 5 March, there was much weeping over his passing. Their Boss had entranced as well as horrified them.

Their grief was shared in homes and on the streets after the radio announcement was made on 6 March. Stalin's funeral took place on Red Square three days later. Foreign statesmen attended as Molotov, Malenkov and Beria pronounced eulogies to the deceased dictator. Molotov, despite having a wife held in prison on Stalin's orders, was visibly distraught. Malenkov was better composed. But Beria in private dropped all pretence of respect for Stalin and cursed his memory. After the speeches, Stalin's corpse, embalmed by experts from the same institute as had developed the technique for Lenin, was displayed in what was renamed as the Lenin-Stalin Mausoleum. A silence was meant to descend over Moscow. But such was the crowd in the nearby streets that a commotion broke out. The pressure of bodies led to dozens of fatalities. From under the glass the chemically-treated corpse could still terminate innocent lives.

And so Stalin's accomplices came into a disturbing inheritance. It is true that the Soviet Union was still a superpower. It dominated Eastern Europe. It had the world's second largest industrial capacity; its population was literate and acquiescent. The armed forces, the security organs, the party and the ministries of government were calmly able to confront their duties. If Soviet leaders were going to face trouble in 1953, it would arise only because they had grossly mishandled opinion among the élites or fallen out irretrievably among themselves – and the leaders could at least take consolation from the fact that Stalin's death had pre-empted the immediate possibility of a massive purge that would lead to the deaths of leaders, their cliental groups and perhaps millions of other people.

Yet enormous problems had been bequeathed by him, and not the least of them was agricultural. Malenkov had asserted at the Nineteenth Party Congress that wheat production had recovered to the level of 1940 and that the country's grain problem had been solved 'definitively and forever'. This was nonsense. The statistics were a wild exaggeration of reality since they were based upon what was known as the 'biological yield'. This was a calculation derived from observations of the crop before it was harvested. Subsequent loss of grain in fact often occurred through bad weather; and it always took place because the harvest was stored so badly. Furthermore, whole regions of Russia had fallen out of cultivation. The kolkhozniki were under-paid and over-taxed, and the demographic structure of countless villages was distorted by the exodus of most able-bodied men and the young of both sexes. The neglect of rural problems could not be allowed to persist.

Even the forced-labour system presented difficulty. Discontent was on the rise in the prisons, camps, colonies and 'special settlements' where 5.5 million prisoners were still held.[30] A rebellion in Kolyma in 1949 was followed by another near Krasnoyarsk in 1951 and yet others in Labytnangi and Ozerlag in 1952.[31] Permanent quiescence in the Gulag could no longer be taken for granted.

At the same time it was questionable whether the 'free' industrial sector could continue as previously. Workers were too afraid to go on strike, but resented their conditions of labour, their low wages and poor diet and housing. There was little that administrators could do to make them more conscientious; and the administrators themselves were constrained by patterns of organization inimical to honesty and independent thought. Wasteful methods of production persisted in factories, mines and other enterprises. Stalin, furthermore, had rejected advice to invest substantially in chemical industries or in natural gas. His projections had become extremely inflexible. Capital goods in general and armaments in particular were given reinforced priority: expenditure on the armed forces, their weaponry and equipment, was forty-five per cent more in 1952 than two years earlier. This was a great strain upon the Soviet budget and was not indefinitely sustainable.

National problems, too, had accumulated. Acute, lasting embitterment had been caused by Stalin's deportations of nationalities during and after the Second World War; and the elevation of the prestige of the Russians above the other peoples of the USSR also caused lasting offence. Science and culture, too, were subjected to excessive supervision. Not only writers and scientists but also teachers, engineers, lawyers and managers worked in fear. Initiative from below was thwarted. The disgruntlement among administrative, professional and intellectual groups was intensifying. They especially wanted to work without fear of imprisonment. Only terror at the punitive repercussions held them back from complaining publicly.

All in all, Stalin's system of rule was not at its most effective when dealing with an increasingly complex society. The government, the party, the army and the security police – at metropolitan as well as local levels – were run on principles of the most rigid hierarchy. The scope for constructive consultation and collaboration had been severely reduced. The Soviet state as a whole was vastly over-centralized. Policies were decided by a tiny group of leaders, and the danger that they might blunder was acute. The leadership itself was subject to permanent intimidation; none of its members could fail to be mindful of the power of the security organs. For years the various Politburo members had taken objection to official policies but never dared to express themselves openly. Stalin had scared them rigid. In short, there was too much fear and too little trust for such a system to endure indefinitely.

The world outside was also dangerous. East European nations resented their subjugation to the Soviet Union. The USA and its allies in NATO had no intention of rescuing them from this position; but resistance to further communist expansion was a firm objective. The Korean War was a suppurating sore in relations between the USSR and the USA.

These were among the problems left behind by Stalin. They existed in every area of public life: politics, economy, ethnic relations, culture, security and continental and global power. And they complicated and aggravated each other. It is true that the Soviet order was not on the verge of collapse. But if several of these problems were not tackled within the next few years, a fundamental crisis would occur. Stalin's legatees were justified in feeling nervous, and knew that the next few months would be a period of great trial for them. The uncontainable surge of crowds on to the streets of Red Square as he was laid to rest alongside Lenin in the joint Lenin-Stalin Mausoleum had been a warning to his successors about the passions lurking under society's calm surface. This was the first act of self-assertion by the people since the inception of Stalin's dictatorship. It was by no means clear how the Kremlin leaders would respond to the challenge.

17
'De-Stalinization' (1953–1961)

The people, however, had only a brief walk-on role in the drama. The major parts were jealously grabbed by Stalin's veteran associates, who wanted to consolidate their positions of power as individuals and to preserve the compound of the Soviet order. Their common goals were to maintain the one-party, one-ideology state, to expand its economy, to control all public institutions and their personnel, to mobilize the rest of society, to secure the Soviet Union's domination of Eastern Europe and to expand communist influence around the world. And several of these veterans were convinced that such goals were unattainable unless a reform programme were quickly to be implemented.

There was dispute about this, but at first it did not matter because all the veteran leaders had a transcendent interest in securing their power at the expense of the younger rivals whom Stalin had promoted to high office. The veterans agreed tactics before convoking a combined meeting of the Council of Ministers, the USSR Supreme Soviet and the Party Central Committee on 6 March 1953. They had already decided among themselves on the size and composition of the various leading political bodies. In particular, they arranged a decrease in the number of members of the Presidium of the Central Committee from twenty-five to ten. The purpose of this was to remove the younger leaders from the Presidium and reduce their authority. Among the older figures who asserted themselves were the three leaders – Molotov, Mikoyan and Beria – who had appeared likely to be arrested before Stalin's death.

Malenkov benefited most from the new division of posts. He was appointed as both Chairman of the Council of Ministers and Party Central Committee Secretary. His Deputy Chairmen in the Council of Ministers were to be Beria and Molotov. Beria was to lead the Ministry of Internal Affairs (MVD), and this institution was merged with the Ministry of State Security (MGB) into an enlarged MVD. Molotov was promoted to Minister of Foreign Affairs and Khrushchëv kept his post as Party Central Committee Secretary. They were ruthless, ambitious men, but at the time there seemed little to stop Malenkov from becoming the dominant leader in succession to Stalin.

While outward loyalty was shown to Stalin's memory, his policies were already undergoing reconsideration. Malenkov wanted quieter relations with the West; he also favoured the boosting of industrial consumer-goods production and the intensification of agricultural techniques. Beria agreed with this and went further by demanding that concessions be made to the non-Russians in terms of political appointments in the USSR and that a lighter grip should be maintained in Eastern Europe (and secretly he resumed contact with Tito in Yugoslavia). Malenkov, Beria and Khrushchëv backed a curtailment of the security police's arbitrariness. Khrushchëv's particular priority was agriculture, and he urged the ploughing up of virgin lands in Kazakhstan as a cheap way to raise output rapidly. Only a couple of Presidium members, Molotov and Kaganovich, opposed reform. The dynamism in the central political leadership belonged to Malenkov, Beria and Khrushchëv.[1]

Beria organized an exhibition for Central Committee members where tapes of Stalin's conversations with the security police were played. Stalin's guilt in arresting innocent officials was established.[2] The general public had no access to the exhibition; but when the MVD announced that the accused professors in the Doctors' Plot had been freed, it was evident that the Soviet supreme leadership wished to attenuate its reliance on terror. Articles appeared in *Pravda* proclaiming that the masses rather than single leaders made history. Marxism-Leninism was stated to be hostile to any 'cult of the individual' and to favour 'collective leadership'. The barely disguised object of such commentary was Stalin.

Simultaneously the main reformers were locked in struggle about the rest of their reforms. On 14 March, Malenkov was compelled to choose between his respective posts in party and government. He stepped down as Central Committee Secretary, calculating that his job as Chairman of the Council of Ministers held the greater political authority. This handed the Central Committee Secretariat into the keeping of Khrushchëv, who thereby acquired an incentive to strengthen the party's authority. At the time, however, the thoughts of most leaders were preoccupied not with Khrushchëv but with Beria, who embodied a double threat to all of them. First, his radical plans for reform endangered the interests of influential institutions and could even have destabilized the entire Soviet order; second, his position in the MVD gave him the capacity to deal violently with any political rivals. Beria was a complex politician. But most of his colleagues did not ponder his complexities: they simply feared him.

The reforming projects of Beria came thick and fast. He also obtained republican-level appointments in both the MVD and the communist party for his nominees; and when he introduced MVD troops to Moscow to deal with a mass outbreak of larceny (caused by his release of thousands of petty criminals from the Gulag camps!), Khrushchëv and others guessed that Beria was about to use the troops to carry out a *coup d'état*. They were not willing to wait to see whether their speculation was correct: Beria's past career marked him out as a danger to everyone.

Khrushchëv has left us his account of what happened next. Not unexpectedly, he appears as the hero of the drama. Apparently Khrushchëv first cajoled Malenkov into joining a plot against Beria, and Voroshilov wept with relief when told of their plans. Mikoyan had his doubts but went along with the rest of the Party Presidium. On 26 June the Presidium met in the Kremlin. Khrushchëv had arranged for Marshals Zhukov and Moskalenko to hide outside the door until an agreed signal for them to burst in and grab Beria. If Beria had a fault as a potential single leader, it was over-confidence. He was taken by surprise, bundled into the back of a car and held in military custody. Army commanders enthusiastically took possession of their past tormentor-in-chief. Party officials, too, were delighted at the news. Both central and local politicians felt relief that an incubus had been removed from Soviet politics.

A Central Committee plenum was held on 2 July, where Beria's actions as head of the security police were denounced. Khrushchëv's proposal for the MVD to be placed directly under the party's control was given warm sanction. Party officials could no longer be arrested except with permission of the party committee to which they belonged. Beria himself was accused of having been an anti-Bolshevik agent in the Civil War (which may have been true) and a British agent after the Second World War (which was nonsense). From prison he mewled to Malenkov that Khrushchëv had tricked the Presidium.[3] But he also acknowledged his many abuses of political power and admitted to having raped young girls. Once arrested, Beria was never very likely to emerge alive. In December 1953 he was convicted in camera and shot.

The process was rich in ironies. For the movement away from Stalin's legacy had been engineered by typically Stalinist tactics: Beria's judicial sentence was imposed in advance by politicians and the allegation that he was a British spy was a Stalin-style fatuity. Nevertheless the times were a-changing. The first drastic adjustment of institutional relationships since the 1930s took place as the communist party fully subordinated the state's policing agencies to itself. A few months later, in March 1954, the gigantic Ministry of Internal Affairs was broken up into two institutions. One was still to be called the MVD and was to deal with problems of ordinary criminality and civil disorder; the other would be the Committee of State Security (KGB): as its name suggested, it was charged with the protection of the USSR's internal and external security. No doubt the Presidium calculated that any resultant rivalry between the MVD and the KGB would render the police agencies easier to control.

Such changes were the product of decisions taken at the apex of the Soviet political system: the party leaders wanted no interference in their claim to govern. Most citizens followed developments warily. There were no illicit posters, no strikes, no demonstrations. Fear of retribution remained pervasive. Only in the camps, where the inmates had nothing left to lose, was a challenge thrown down to the authorities. In Norilsk and Vorkuta there were uprisings which were suppressed only by the introduction of armed troops who mowed down the defenceless rebels with tanks and machine guns.[4] Yet the uprisings had some effect inasmuch as discipline in the camps was relaxed somewhat. Mention of these events was forbidden in the mass media; but politicians had been given a lesson that repression alone was not enough to keep regular control even over prisoners. All the more reason for changing policy before popular discontent got out of hand.

The reformers kept their advantage in the Presidium. After Stalin's death a leavening of the cultural and social atmosphere was allowed to occur. Permission was given for the appearance of an article by Vladimir Pomerantsev calling for greater sincerity in literature. The deceits and self-deceits in literature and the mass media were widely denounced, and a sensation was caused by Ilya Erenburg's short novel *The Thaw*, which described the problems of administrators and intellectuals in the Stalin period.

But the conflict intensified between Malenkov and Khrushchëv over the nature of the reforms to be adopted. Already in April 1953, Malenkov had lowered retail prices for both food and industrial consumer products; and in August he presented a budget to the Supreme Soviet cutting taxes on agriculture and raising the prices paid to the collective farms for their output. By October he was arguing that the consumer-oriented sector of industry should expand faster than armaments and capital goods. But Khrushchëv countered with his own projects. At the September Central Committee plenum he successfully proposed the cultivation of the virgin lands. Nor did he do himself any harm by giving the impression that no one else was quite as keen as he to end rule by police terror. The plenum rewarded him for his initiative in the Beria affair by designating him as First Secretary of the Central Committee.

His elevation came from his daring; but this would have counted for little unless his policies had been attractive to influential political constituencies. Unlike Malenkov, he did not advocate peaceful coexistence with world capitalism. Nor did he propose to alter the existing investment priorities; and, in contrast with Malenkov, he proudly described the central and local party apparatus as 'our underpinning'.[5] Deftly he gained more friends than Malenkov in the heavy-industrial ministries, the armed forces and the communist party. Furthermore, he had shown a large capacity for shouldering responsibility. He obviously had a talent for setting himself clear practical objectives in a situation of extraordinary flux.

The dangers were not restricted to internal Kremlin disputes. The tensions between the USSR and the USA remained acute, and the Korean War had not ended. In 1952 American scientists had attained a further stage of destructive military capacity by producing a hydrogen bomb. Their Soviet counterparts fortified their competing research programme. In the meantime Stalin had made moves to effect a settlement in Korea lest the conflict might erupt into a Third World War. His successors maintained this approach. The Korean War was brought to a close and Korea was divided between a communist North and a capitalist South. But the Cold War between the Soviet and American governments continued. In March 1954 the USA successfully tested a hydrogen bomb that could be delivered by long-range aircraft. But the USSR was catching up. Already in August 1953 Soviet scientists had tested its own hydrogen bomb and they were conducting research on long-range aircraft capable of delivering it.[6]

The Soviet regime had sharp difficulties not only with the USA but also with several countries in Eastern Europe. The industrial workers in Berlin, sensing that Stalin's death gave them an opportunity to express their discontent with the political and economic policies of the German Democratic Republic, went on strike in midsummer 1953. There were riots, too, in Plzeň in Czechoslovakia; and rumblings of discontent were reported in Poland and Hungary. The Soviet Party Presidium members made material concessions while ruthlessly suppressing overt opposition; but all of them recognized the dangers of the international situation: they were confronted by instabilities and threats which needed handling with decisiveness.

Khrushchëv had this quality aplenty; but his eventual victory in the dogfight in the Kremlin was not yet guaranteed: he had to continue making his own luck. Among his manoeuvres was the establishment of a commission under P. N. Pospelov to investigate the crimes of the 1930s and 1940s. The Leningrad purge of 1948–9 came under particular scrutiny. This was not the greatest case of blood-letting in Stalin's time, but for Khrushchëv it had the advantage that Malenkov had been involved as a perpetrator of repression. Malenkov was a politician on the slide. The harvest of summer 1954 was a good one, and the success was attributed to Khrushchëv even though the virgin lands contributed next to nothing to the improvement. By December, Malenkov's authority in the Presidium had been so weakened that he was compelled to resign as Chaïrman of the Council of Ministers.

Although the Presidium steadily came under Khrushchëv's personal influence, he still had to show restraint. Malenkov's post in the Council of Ministers was given in February 1955 to Nikolai Bulganin, who had allied himself with Khrushchëv but was not his protégé. Furthermore, the Ministry of Defence – which until then had been led by Bulganin – was handed over to Marshal Zhukov, who had never been known to kowtow to civilian politicians. But Khrushchëv was in irrepressible mood. Together with Bulganin he visited Yugoslavia despite having executed Beria for having written letters to Tito. Khrushchëv's pre-eminence was on display in Belgrade: his boisterous vulgarity left no room for ambiguity for observers. Nor did he fail to stress that, as Stalin's successor, he would frame his policies to compete with the USA. In May 1955 the Soviet government convoked a meeting of East European communist leaders and formed the Warsaw Pact in reaction to the permission given by NATO for West Germany to undertake its rearmament.

Khrushchëv had to watch his back. Gradually Malenkov shifted back into an alliance with Molotov and Kaganovich: having lost the struggle to be the supreme reformer, he settled for becoming an associate of communist reactionaries. There was much uneasiness about Khrushchëv. His enemies understood, above all else, that the Soviet edifice as reconstructed by Stalin was held together by tightly-interlocked structures and that any improvised architectural alterations might bring the roof down on everyone's head.

But how to stop Khrushchëv's mischief? In foreign policy Molotov as yet had little objection to Khrushchëv, who had helped him to repudiate Malenkov's contention that any nuclear war would bring about 'the destruction of world civilization'. Khrushchëv's weakness in 1955 lay instead in domestic economic policy. In pursuit of his virgin lands scheme Khrushchëv had replaced the Kazakhstan communist party leadership in Alma-Ata, and sent his follower Leonid Brezhnev there to secure policy on his behalf. He recruited 300,000 'volunteers', especially from among students, for summer work in Kazakhstan and western Siberia. As a consequence Khrushchëv's survival in power depended on the germination of wheat seed in the ploughed-up steppe of central Asia. Fortunately for him, the 1955 grain harvest across the USSR was twenty-one per cent higher than in the previous year.[7]

What is more, Khrushchëv had kept his ability to surprise. On 13 February 1956, a day before the Twentieth Congress of the Communist Party of the Soviet Union, he proposed to the Presidium that a speech should be delivered on 'the Cult of the Individual and its Consequences'. This constituted a call for discussion of the horrors of the Stalin period. Khrushchëv argued not from moral but from pragmatic premisses: 'If we don't tell the truth at the Congress, we'll be forced to tell the truth some time in the future. And then we shan't be the speech-makers; no, then we'll be the people under investigation.'[8] Molotov's counter-proposal was for the speech to be made on the theme 'Stalin the Continuer of Lenin's Work'. But Khrushchëv had a majority, and arrangements were made for his speech to be given at a closed session of the Congress.[9]

This decision was not mentioned by Khrushchëv in his general report at the start of the Congress on 14 February. It was not Khrushchëv but Mikoyan who stirred things up by making some derogatory remarks about Stalin. But behind the scenes Khrushchëv was preparing himself. The Pospelov commission had made a deposition to the Presidium in late January detailing many of Stalin's abuses. Khrushchëv wanted to increase trenchancy of the commission's criticisms and to offer an account of Stalin throughout his rule. With this in mind he recruited D. T. Shepilov, fellow Central Committee Secretary and a former *Pravda* editor, to head a drafting group.[10] Presidium members eyed the process with trepidation. As Stalin's adjutants, they knew about the mass repressions: all of them – including Khrushchëv – had blood on their hands. They could only hope that Khrushchëv was right that it was better to raise the Stalin question sooner rather than later.

On 25 February he spoke, as planned, to a closed session of the Congress: only delegates from the Communist Party of the Soviet Union were allowed to attend. Journalists were banned. Even distinguished foreign communists such as Togliatti were prohibited from being present. The Presidium exercised the greatest possible control of the occasion.

The speech, which lasted four hours, was a turning-point in the USSR's politics. Its unifying topic was Stalin. Khrushchëv informed the Congress about Lenin's call in 1923 for Stalin's removal from the General Secretaryship. The rest of the speech was given over to the abuses perpetrated by Stalin in the following three decades. The repressions of 1937–8 were itemized. Khrushchëv stressed that Stalin was a blunderer as well as a killer. The failure to anticipate Hitler's invasion in mid-1941 was given as a particularly gross example. Wanting to demonstrate the persistence of Stalin's terrorism, Khrushchëv described the ethnic deportations of the Second World War and the post-war carnage in the Leningrad Affair, the Doctors' Plot and the Mingrelian Affair. Stalin had brought about a drastic decline in internal party democracy. Thirteen years elapsed between the Eighteenth and Nineteenth Party Congresses. After 1945 the Central Committee rarely met, and the Politburo fell into desuetude.

Khrushchëv had agreed to exculpate the current Presidium. Allegedly Stalin had decided everything. Only fitfully did Khrushchëv yield to the temptation to score points off fellow Presidium members. For instance, he mentioned the difficulties in Ukraine in the Second World War when an appeal was made to Stalin for increased supplies of equipment. Malenkov had given the following answer on Stalin's behalf: 'You have to arm yourselves.' The revelation of so curt a response, even if Malenkov had merely been relaying a message, reflected badly upon him. Khrushchëv was casting a shadow over the reputation of his most powerful rival.

Otherwise he heaped the blame on Stalin and the conveniently dead leaders of the security police. On the Great Terror he declared to the Congress: 'The majority of Politburo members did not, at the time, know all the circumstances in these matters and therefore could not intervene.' He suggested that only a handful of associates helped Stalin in his dastardly activity: the security-police leaders Yezhov, Beria, Abakumov (and subordinates of theirs such as the 'bird-brained' Rodos).[11] Supposedly the repressions could not have been stopped by well-meaning communist party leaders because they lacked the necessary information about the purges undertaken by Stalin and his police cronies. Khrushchëv, who had helped to organize the terror in Moscow and Ukraine in 1937–8,[12] was lying shamelessly; but this is what he knew he needed to do if he was to retain his reputation and ruin Stalin's.

For the supreme intention was to knock Stalin from the pedestal of public esteem. Stalin was portrayed as a capricious autocrat. As an example of Stalin's megalomania he recalled the comment: 'I'll wag my little finger, and Tito will be no more!' Stalin, moreover, had been extremely distrustful. 'Why,' he would enquire of his associates, 'are your eyes so shifty today?'

Khrushchëv's analysis was focused more upon personality than upon policy. He stipulated that the bloodshed had started only after the assassination of Kirov in 1934. Indeed Khrushchëv proposed that, before the mid-1930s, Stalin had performed 'great services to the party, to the working class and the international labour movement'. Thus the horrors committed in the Civil War, the NEP and the First Five-Year Plan were ignored. Agricultural collectivization, despite all the deaths and deportations, was condoned. In addition, the burden of Khrushchëv's message was that mostly it was prominent officials who had been Stalin's victims. There had been, he suggested, 'several thousand' functionaries of party, government and army; he gave no hint that millions of people, many of whom did not hold any rank at all in public life, had died.

His undeclared purpose was to show the Congress that the attack on Stalin would not involve a dismantlement of his entire system. Arbitrary arrests and executions would cease; but the communist one-party state would be preserved, alternative ideologies would be suppressed and state economic ownership would remain intact. In Khrushchëv's presentation, this would involve a reversion to the days of Lenin, when supposedly all the working people of the USSR had luxuriated in the beneficent farsightedness of Marxism-Leninism. The future for the USSR lay in a return to the past.

By reassuring, flattering and inspiring the Congress, Khrushchëv won support from its delegates even though many of them were so shocked by the contents of the closed-session speech that they fainted. Molotov could frighten them, Malenkov confuse and sedate them. Only Khrushchëv had had the animal boldness to exhilarate them; and, having pulled off this achievement, he turned his attention to the rest of the country. Confidential briefings of party members were given to activists in local party organizations. Khrushchëv gave transcripts to foreign communist party leaders as they departed home. As if suspecting that several of the recipients might censor its contents, he also arranged for the KGB to ensure that the CIA should obtain a copy, and the London *Observer* scooped the world by printing a full version.

In the West his policies were dubbed de-Stalinization. This was understandable since Khrushchëv had devoted an entire report to denouncing Stalin. But Khrushchëv himself talked instead of a campaign to eliminate 'the cult of the individual'.[13] This was not an inappropriate term even though it was so euphemistic. For Khrushchëv kept Stalin's kolkhozes in agriculture and his capital-goods priority in industry; he also refrained from rehabilitating Trotski, Bukharin and the various other communists alleged to have been foreign spies. Much remained in place that would have been congenial to Stalin.

Despite the limited nature of the closed-session speech, however, Khrushchëv was already experiencing difficulty in Moscow, where the Presidium baulked at his efforts to publicize the report. Only a brief summary was published in the press. Even this caused a furore. Many citizens were astounded by what was revealed about the 1930s and 1940s. It was not news to them that abuses of power had occurred: practically every household in the land had at least one relative who had fallen victim to the Gulag. But not everyone, especially amidst the generations born and educated under Stalin, had known that Stalin was the instigator of the horrors recounted by Khrushchëv. In Georgia he was venerated as a national hero although he had executed many Georgians. A riot took place in Tbilisi. Yet by and large, the revelations evoked an enormous sense of relief, and the decrease in overt political intimidation was enjoyed even by Stalin's admirers.

Nevertheless Khrushchëv and his historians, crafty as they had been in formulating the case against Stalin, had not been quite crafty enough. They had done an efficient job solely in relation to the pre-war USSR. Since Lenin had founded the Soviet state, a 'return to Lenin' was an attractive path to recommend to comrades at home. But this could not be the case for the other countries of Eastern Europe or indeed for Estonia, Latvia and Lithuania. They had been conquered not in the Civil War but in Stalin's military campaigns of 1944–5 – and now Khrushchëv, the Soviet communist leader, was claiming that Stalin was a mass murderer. The closed-session speech gusted away the rags of legitimacy claimed by communism in the countries of the Warsaw Pact.

First to express discontent were Polish industrial workers. As the rumours spread in Poland about Khrushchëv's closed-session speech, they went on strike. Poles had always known that Stalin had been a wrong 'un, but Khrushchëv's confirmation of this gave them irrefutable grounds for revolt. Compromises were swiftly agreed. Władisław Gomułka, the veteran communist imprisoned by Stalin in 1948 for showing too much care for Polish national interests, was released and, with much grumpiness, Khrushchëv assented to his becoming First Secretary of the Polish United Workers' Party.[14] This manoeuvre was combined with police action in Warsaw. The strikes faded and order was restored. But the episode was yet another indication of the unpopularity of the Soviet Army, the Communist Party of the Soviet Union and the KGB throughout Eastern Europe. No Presidium member took seriously the official Soviet trumpetings about the fraternal feelings felt by the peoples of the Warsaw Pact towards the USSR.

Gomułka's transfer to supreme power was the most spectacular example of the trend towards compromise. The Kremlin already in Beria's time had slackened the pace of 'Sovietization' in Eastern Europe. Changes of personnel had been undertaken so as to hasten the acceptance of reforms. In particular, campaigns for agricultural collectivization had been halted. Recalcitrant Stalinists had been reprimanded in mid-1953, and told to adopt the Kremlin's new course of policies.

But things went badly for the USSR. Rákosi was replaced as governmental premier by Imre Nagy but remained leader of the Hungarian party. Only after Khrushchëv's speech to the Twentieth Congress in Moscow was Rákosi at last constrained to step down entirely. By then Budapest's workers and intellectuals were pressing for the regime's fundamental reform.[15] Nagy's Hungarian patriotism proved stronger than his Marxism-Leninism and he went along with the crowds, trusting that Moscow would not resort to forcible intervention. He also assumed that the West would lean on the Soviet Union to respect Hungary's sovereignty. On 23 October a popular disturbance took place in Budapest. In the following week a revolt against Soviet domination occurred; and the courageous but naïve Nagy, a communist who had fallen foul of Rákosi in the late 1940s, continued to believe that a political compromise could be reached with Moscow. Visits by Mikoyan, Malenkov and Yuri Andropov, the Soviet ambassador to Budapest, failed to induce a more realistic judgement.

On 4 November 1956 the tanks of the Soviet Army moved against the rebels. Resistance was fierce but futile. The Hungarian revolt was castigated by Khrushchëv as a counter-revolution inspired by the West, and Nagy fled to the safety of the Yugoslav embassy; but he was tricked into leaving it and taken into custody – he was executed in 1958 for refusing to repent of his actions. The NATO countries refused to intervene on Hungary's side. The joint attack by British, French and Israeli forces on the Suez Canal preoccupied the West at the time; but in any case the major powers flinched from risking the outbreak of a Third World War. A tame Hungarian regime was set up in Budapest under János Kádár, and the countries of the Warsaw Pact were put on notice that, under Khrushchëv as under Stalin, no challenge to the Kremlin's dominance would be tolerated.

The prestige of Khrushchëv, who had been hailed around the world as the hero of the Twentieth Party Congress, tumbled; but this did not bother him as much as the criticism he suffered in the Presidium. Already in June he had been compelled to agree to an official resolution playing down the abuses of power by Stalin. The Polish strikes and the Hungarian revolt gave further stimulus to his critics. Printed copies of the closed-session report were destroyed before they could be distributed. Legal publication in the USSR did not occur until the rule of Gorbachëv, and for this reason the report became known as 'the secret speech'. Khrushchëv began to avoid overt commitment to reform; such was his discomfiture that at the end of the year he denounced anti-Stalinist novels such as Vladimir Dudintsev's *Not by Bread Alone* as being anti-Soviet. Khrushchëv had not attained supreme office to preside over the collapse of the post-war order in the USSR and its subject states.

But it was only a matter of time before Molotov, Malenkov and Kaganovich mounted an assault on him. On 18 June 1957 they struck. At a Presidium meeting lasting three days, Khrushchëv was outnumbered and defeated. Rather than simply sack him, Molotov and his friends had hit on the device of abolishing the post of Party First Secretary.[16] In this way they hoped to win over those leaders alarmed by the renewal of dissension in the Kremlin. For any other contender for the leadership this might have been the end of the matter, but Khrushchëv staunchly insisted that the right to dismiss him lay with the Central Committee. With the assistance of Marshal Zhukov as Minister of Defence, Central Committee members were flown to Moscow to attend an emergency plenum. Some of them banged on the doors of the Presidium as it discussed Khrushchëv's fate. The Central Committee plenum commenced on 21 June and resulted in a resounding victory for Khrushchëv.

Molotov, Malenkov and Kaganovich – along with their last-minute ally D. T. Shepilov – were dismissed from the Presidium by the Central Committee. Into the Presidium came Zhukov, Frol

Kozlov and other figures who had stood by Khrushchëv in the crisis. Khrushchëv had won because his amalgam of policies continued to appeal to Central Committee members. Also important was the suspicion that his opponents, were they to achieve victory, might revert to terror. After the plenum, Kaganovich had rung up Khrushchëv pleading for mercy. Khrushchëv issued a contemptuous retort: 'Your words yet again confirm what methods you intended to use for your vile ends . . . You measure other people by your own standard. But you are making a mistake.'[17] Such self-righteousness would have been more plausible if Khrushchëv had not had Beria shot in 1953. In his favour, however, it deserves stress that his mercy towards the 'Anti-Party Group' was an important break with Stalin's practices. Khrushchëv guaranteed that internal élite disputes should be conducted without manacles and rifles.

Khrushchëv had fun at the losers' expense chiefly by subjecting them to humiliating demotions. Molotov became ambassador to Mongolia, Malenkov director of a hydro-electric power station in Kazakhstan and Kaganovich director of a Sverdlovsk cement works. Khrushchëv's ascendancy led to a disgorging of victims of Stalin's purges from the Gulag penal camps. Until 1956 only some 7000 reprocessed cases had resulted in judicial rehabilitation of prisoners. (Molotov's wife had been among the first of them.) Within a few months, between eight and nine million people had been rehabilitated.[18] It is true that this good fortune came to most of Stalin's victims posthumously. Even so, the releases from the camps became a mass phenomenon after the Twentieth Congress, and they deepened popular knowledge about the past.

The policy of 'socialist legality' had been proclaimed since 1953. This did not signify that the USSR was meant to become a law-based state: Khrushchëv provided a system under which the constitution and the law would be enforced solely insofar as communist party rule was preserved. The Presidium's dominance over high state policy remained in place. If Hungary needed invading or a summit with the American president arranging or a new crop imposing on the kolkhozes, this was normally done by the Presidium. Thus the Central Committee was able to intervene in discussions on policy only at the Presidium's request – and this happened most decisively when the Presidium was itself divided. Yet the Central Committee had had a taste of power; and Mikhail Suslov, when pleading with the Central Committee to vote for Khrushchëv at the June 1957 plenum, took the liberty of noting the need for Khrushchëv to end his sharp-tongued, overbearing behaviour towards colleagues.[19]

For a while Khrushchëv seemed to take Suslov's words to heart. He consulted often with Presidium and Central Committee members and published the proceedings of Central Committee plenums. Power at the centre was exercised more formally than before 1953. Party bodies met regularly and asserted control over the other public institutions. The party inherited by Khrushchëv grew in size as a recruitment campaign gathered strength. When Stalin died, there were nearly 6.1 million members; by 1961 there were 9.7 million.[20] Khrushchëv also started to show considerable contempt for the desk-bound bureaucracy of the communist party apparatus. He wanted action in society, and he set an example by visiting factories, mines and kolkhozes. The party had to be mobilized so that the party might mobilize society.

The change in the party's condition, however, had its limits. The party set policies, but these policies continued to be conditioned by the existing interests of groups, organizations and institutions. Thus the Soviet Army impeded a reconsideration of military priorities. Khrushchëv preferred nuclear weapons to the more traditional armed forces on grounds of cheapness as well as deterrence. Marshal Zhukov argued strongly against Khrushchëv. From Khrushchëv's standpoint, Zhukov had outlived his usefulness as soon as the Anti-Party Group had been defeated. Khrushchëv moved with dispatch. In October 1957 a startled Zhukov was pitched into retirement. Nevertheless the Soviet Army command remained a serious constraint on the Presidium's freedom to govern. So, too, were the economic ministries that could in practice choose which of the various priorities set for them by the Presidium they would pursue.

While the Presidium could push its policies upon the ministers as party members, the ministers in their turn had access to the party's decision-making; and, much as he altered the party's apparatus,

Khrushchëv retained the system of economic departments in the Secretariat.[21] As ever, the officials in such departments did little to inhibit the inclinations of 'their' ministries. The entanglement of party and government was strengthened in March 1958 when Khrushchëv, having waited his chance to get rid of Bulganin who had supported the Anti-Party Group, took over the post of Chairman of the Council of Ministers. The head of the party now also became head of the government.

Having worsted the Anti-Party Group, Khrushchëv at last felt well placed to rectify the inadequacies in consumer-goods production in Soviet factories.[22] Malenkov's priority became his own. This adjustment of policy, however, unsettled the institutional support that had facilitated his rise to power since Stalin's death; the traditional lobbies in the army and the heavy-industrial civilian administrations were appalled by what they saw as his treachery. Conflict was avoided mainly because Khrushchëv did not push his wishes too hard. In any case he adhered to his original contention that agricultural improvements remained more urgent than changes in industrial investment policy. He expressed his opinion as follows: 'It is important to have good clothing and good footwear, but it is still more important to have a tasty dinner, breakfast and lunch.'[23] Khrushchëv also vetoed suggestions that Soviet automotive plants should produce cars for purchase by the private citizen.[24]

Thus his basic economic preferences were much more conventional than appeared from his declarations about the need to satisfy all the aspirations of Soviet consumers. The incidence of such declarations increased in the late 1950s, and his confidence in his own judgement on the entire range of official policies was extreme. Khrushchëv, the Party First Secretary and the Chairman of the Council of Ministers, led from the front.

His colleagues noticed the paradox that the politician who denounced the 'cult of the individual' was zealous in accumulating prestige. A day would not pass without his picture appearing in the press. The practice was resumed of prefacing books with mandatory eulogies to the party's leader. Khrushchëv secured additional publicity for himself by appointing his son-in-law Aleksei Adzhubei as editor of *Izvestiya*. He had a keen eye for self-advertisement (although the photograph of him wrapped in a bearskin rug probably confirmed the Western image of the threat posed by each Soviet leader!). Significantly, he stopped short of commissioning a full-scale biography: presumably his criticism of Stalin's vanity-publishing ventures dissuaded him from such an attempt. But this was a rare instance of restraint. Khrushchëv demanded and obtained adulation from the press, radio, cinema and television.

It was this ebullience that had powered his rise from unpropitious social origins. As a lad in the village of Kalinovka in Kursk province, Khrushchëv had worked as a shepherd. In adolescence he had drifted – like many other young Russians – to the Don Basin and signed on as a miner. In the First World War he was active in the labour movement. In the Civil War he fought on the Red side, becoming a Bolshevik in 1918. His exuberant intelligence was coupled to ambition. After rising through the local party network in Ukraine, in 1929 he undertook training at the Industrial Academy in Moscow. Despite his inadequate formal education, he made further headway after taking up the cudgels against Bukharin in the struggle over the First Five-Year Plan. Kaganovich, who already knew him in Ukraine, helped to bring him to the attention of Stalin himself.

By 1935 Khrushchëv was leading the Moscow City Party Committee and three years later he became First Secretary of the Communist Party of Ukraine. In the Great Terror he was an unflinching purger, but he was also a dynamic administrator. In 1941 he became the main political commissar on the Southern front. His career was not without its setbacks. Stalin's moods were hard to anticipate and Khrushchëv had sometimes carried metal-working instruments in his jacket in case he were suddenly to be cast down from office and were to need to seek factory employment.[25] Yet Khrushchëv survived, and was honoured with the joint appointment as leader of the party and the government of Ukraine in February 1944. In December 1949, when he was recalled to Moscow as Central Committee Secretary, it had obviously been Stalin's intention to use him as a political counterweight to Malenkov.

He relished the grandeur of supreme authority from the mid-1950s, and was delighted when his grandson enquired: 'Grandad, who are you? The tsar?'[26] He also liked his vodka and was given to earthy anecdotes and crude outbursts. A more careful First Secretary would not have said to Western politicians: 'We will bury you!' Nor would any alternative Soviet leader in 1960 have banged a shoe on his desk at the United Nations to interrupt a speech by the delegate from the Philippines. In power, he had a wonderful time. He adored gadgets, and welcomed scientists to his dacha. Never having been an avid reader, he got distinguished authors to read their works aloud to him. He fancied himself as a thinker with a practical bent. Going to the USA in September, he admired the fertile plains of maize and on his return he instructed all kolkhozes and sovkhozes to grow it. Khrushchëv was ever the enthusiast.

But his impulsiveness irked his colleagues. The maize campaign was a case in point. Leading Soviet agronomists told him that it was a crop unsuited to many regions of the USSR. But he rejected their advice. Khrushchëv, like Stalin before him, always assumed he knew best, and he disrupted the work of any institution which opposed his policies. Even the Party Central Committee's activities were impaired. Since Khrushchëv was not always able to secure its approval, he introduced outsiders to its proceedings so that they might help to put pressure on its members. In the process he undermined the very patterns of consultation and procedural regularity that he had once helped to establish.

Thus, having used the party apparatus as a means of taking supreme power, he attempted to reduce its capacity to constrain him; and he convinced himself that the party's problems stemmed from the kind of officials he had inherited from Stalin. In 1961 he brought in a rule confining them to three periods of tenure of office:[27] job insecurity for his erstwhile supporters increased. At the same time he was a sucker for flattery. A. M. Larionov, the first party secretary in Ryazan province, inserted himself into Khrushchëv's affections by claiming an unprecedented expansion in local meat production. Larionov had achieved this only by killing off an inordinate number of livestock and by buying the remainder from outside his area. Found out, Larionov committed suicide in 1960. But

Khrushchëv blundered on regardless. A vast turnover of personnel occurred in the late 1950s.

In economics, too, Khrushchëv made his imprint. In 1953 his personal objective had been the exploitation of the virgin lands, and he had implied that no large diversion of finances would be needed to turn agriculture out of its Stalinist rut. It was quite a campaign. Within three years of Stalin's death an additional 36 million hectares were put under the plough. This was as large as the cultivated area of Canada and represented a staggering extension of Soviet cereal agriculture. Khrushchëv also returned to one of his pet schemes by carrying out the amalgamation of kolkhozes into bigger units. The number of such farms consequently dropped from 125,000 to 36,000.[28] Khrushchëv wanted the biggest possible units of agricultural production. He also strove to turn kolkhozes into sovkhozes, thereby increasing the number of peasants employed directly as state employees; and he severely reduced the area under cultivation in private plots.

For Khrushchëv, in his own way, was a communist believer who wished to demonstrate the superiority of communism. While he tried to increase central state intervention in some ways, he also tried to liberate rural initiative. The machine-tractor stations were abolished in 1958. Kolkhozes were to be allowed to run their affairs without excessive local interference. The annual harvest figures, which were the key test of Khrushchëv's agricultural policy, were generally encouraging. Wheat output rose by over fifty per cent between 1950 and 1960. Milk and meat production had increased by sixty-nine and eighty-seven per cent respectively in the seven years after Stalin's death.[29]

Food was consumed in the greatest quantity in the country's history; but such an improvement was not the end of the matter for Khrushchëv. He wanted adjustments in the economy that would afford an even fuller satisfaction of the needs of ordinary consumers. He felt that the ministries in Moscow prevented any solution. They were detached from everyday questions of production and remained careless of local needs. In 1957 he secured the Presidium's sanction to break up the central ministries and to allocate their functions to

105 regional economic councils (*sovnarkhozy*). Khrushchëv's idea was that this new administrative tier would introduce more dynamic planning and management. In 1958, too, he secured a reconsideration of priorities for industrial investment. Capital goods were still projected to expand production at a faster rate than consumer goods: Khrushchëv did not touch this sacred cow. But he adjusted priorities so as to boost those sectors – especially oil, gas and chemicals – that had been neglected by Stalin.

Soviet economic achievements under Khrushchëv were undeniable. An ambitious Seven-Year Plan came into effect in 1959. Gross national income had grown by fifty-eight per cent by 1965 and industrial output by eighty-four per cent. Even consumer goods went up by sixty per cent. There were spectacular successes for the USSR, especially in 1957 when the first sputnik was sent up to circle the earth; in 1960 Yuri Gagarin followed this with the first manned orbit of the globe. Gagarin had a film star's good looks, but Khrushchëv was his equal as a showman, habitually holding public receptions for cosmonauts when they returned from subsequent missions.

In agriculture, his over-confidence remained incorrigible. He interfered persistently with crop-rotation patterns. Even more damaging were his further restrictions on the size of the private plots which could be allocated to kolkhozniki. Since two fifths of Soviet vegetables were grown on them it took little expertise to foresee that shop shelves would soon become empty unless his policy was reversed. The same picture was discernible in industry. For instance, he disrupted co-ordination in Moscow and other cities by arbitrarily raising targets for the construction of apartment blocks; and, when he simultaneously downgraded the priority for bricks, he brought chaos to his already outlandish schemes.[30] Khrushchëv was brought up in the Stalinist tradition of command and did not alter his habits after denouncing Stalin. Never the most self-questioning of men, he assumed he knew best; his bossiness had been hardened into an essential feature of his mode of rule.

There were disappointments for Khrushchëv even by the standards of his own Seven-Year Plan as introduced in 1959. The virgin lands were so over-ploughed that parts of Kazakhstan were turned into a dust-bowl, and Khrushchëv's authority was diminished by poor harvests across the USSR: agricultural output in 1963 was only ninety-two per cent of the total achieved in 1958. Consumer products were not coming out of the factories in the quantity and with the quality he desired. The investment in capital goods continued to be skewed heavily towards military needs, still more heavily than the Plan required. Khrushchëv's attempt to associate himself with youth, science and progress was belied by the survival of economic priorities and practices from the 1930s.

So long as the official aim was to achieve military parity with the USA, it was difficult to alter economic policy to any great extent. Yet Khrushchëv, after his early refusal to support Malenkov's plea for more relaxed relations with the American government, began to reconsider the situation. By the late 1950s Khrushchëv, too, was advocating 'peaceful coexistence'. Professional historians dutifully ransacked the archives for evidence that Lenin had strongly believed that global socialism and global capitalism could peacefully coexist. In fact Lenin had mentioned such an idea only glancingly.[31] In any case Khrushchëv did not unequivocally repudiate the traditional Leninist thesis on the inevitability of world wars until global capitalism had been brought to an end.[32] But certainly he preferred to put his practical stress on the need for peace. Repeatedly he argued that competition between the communist East and the capitalist West should be restricted to politics and ideology.

The Soviet-American relationship was at the crux of deliberations in the Presidium. The USSR and the USA were left as the only superpowers. As the old empires crumbled, the Presidium sought to befriend the emergent African and Asian states. The opportunity overlooked by Stalin was grasped by Khrushchëv. Together with Bulganin, he had toured India, Burma and Afghanistan in 1955. Nine years later he went to Egypt and offered President Nasser a subsidy sufficient to build the Aswan Dam. In 1959 the guerrilla movement led by Fidel Castro seized power in Cuba and associated itself with the USSR.

At last the original Bolshevik objective to promote the interests of the colonial peoples was being vigorously pursued. Yet the nations of Eastern Europe felt that the Soviet Union was itself an 'imperialist' power. There was also an edginess elsewhere, especially in the West, about Soviet pretensions in central Europe. Admittedly the USSR co-signed the peace treaty in 1955 which involved the Soviet Army's withdrawal from Austria; and West German Chancellor Konrad Adenauer went to Moscow in the same year and secured the release of the thousands of German POWs not yet repatriated to West Germany. But the Soviet forces' suppression of the Hungarian popular revolt revived old fears. Also intimidating was the USSR's refinement of its H-Bomb after its first successful test in August 1953. The USSR had the personnel, ideology and technology to threaten the heart of the continent, and the USA made clear that it would retaliate with nuclear weaponry if any NATO state were to be attacked.

Khrushchëv tried to relieve the tensions between the USSR and the USA. A conference was held in Geneva in 1955 attended by himself and President Eisenhower. In 1959 Khrushchëv permitted an exhibition of the American way of life in Moscow which included a model kitchen. There, the ebullient First Secretary of the Communist Party of the Soviet Union participated in a televised impromptu discussion with American Vice-President Richard Nixon on the respective virtues of communism and capitalism, and Khrushchëv enhanced his popularity at home and abroad by his readiness to debate directly with foreign leaders. Khrushchëv, accompanied by his wife and a host of advisers, reciprocated with a visit to the USA in September 1959.

Soviet politicians were gradually ceasing to seem utopian fanatics or mindless automatons. But mutual suspicions were not entirely dispelled. Far from it: a summit meeting of Khrushchëv and Eisenhower that had been planned for mid-1960 was ruined by the shooting down of an American U-2 spy-plane over Soviet airspace. The fact that the American pilot Gary Powers had been captured gave Khrushchëv and his spokesmen an irresistible opportunity to upbraid the Americans for their diplomatic untrustworthiness. Yet he still wanted peaceful coexistence with the West. In the 1960 American elections Nixon was defeated by John Kennedy; and Khrushchëv arranged a summit with him in Vienna in June 1961. This proved to be not the easiest of meetings since Khrushchëv did not hide his condescension towards the younger man. But eventually the two leaders agreed to move towards introducing greater predictability and harmony to relations between their countries.

Khrushchëv no longer faced serious domestic challenge to his foreign policy. His control was such, he boasted, that he could instruct Foreign Minister Andrei Gromyko to take down his trousers and sit on a block of ice and Gromyko would meekly comply. He also knew that Soviet nuclear capacity was as yet nowhere near to parity with the Americans' despite the claims made by Kennedy in his electoral campaign; he could therefore count on considerable support in the Presidium for a cautious handling of affairs with the USA.[33]

Yet the Soviet rapprochement with the USA caused upset in the 'world communist movement', especially in the People's Republic of China. Tensions had existed for years. Mao had never forgotten his demeaning treatment at Stalin's hands. A Soviet-Chinese agreement was signed in 1959 which promised Soviet technical and financial aid in an attempt to buy off Chinese criticism. But it did not work. In 1960 Mao fulminated against those who based their policies on the priority to avoid nuclear war. Such a war, according to Mao, would in fact be both survivable and winnable. Once the mushroom clouds of the H-bombs had lifted, 'a beautiful system' would be created in place of capitalist imperialism. As this tacit critique of Khrushchëv continued, other communist parties were appalled by the growing breach in the international communist movement; and, although the militarist recklessness of Mao was widely rejected, there remained several foreign leaders who had waited for years to oppose Khrushchëv for his insults to Stalin's memory. The conference of eighty-one parties held in Moscow in 1961 did little to rally Marxist-Leninist global unity.

And so Khrushchëv, despite his dominance, was beset by problems by the early 1960s. His political and economic changes were not as effective as he had anticipated, and his foreign policy was running into obstacles. By removing aspects of Stalin's heritage and undertaking a semi-return to Leninism, he was solving a few problems but avoiding most. His failure was in some measure his fault. He had an erratic, autocratic personality and a deeply authoritarian outlook. Yet his quarter-reforms of the Soviet order were probably the maximum that his close colleagues and the rest of the central and local élites would have tolerated at the time. The upholders of this order were too powerful, accomplished and confident for any more radical transformation.

18

Hopes Unsettled (1961–1964)

Khrushchëv still believed that history was on the side of communism. His confidence was infectious and attracted a lot of lower-echelon party functionaries and ambitious youngsters to his side. Like Stalin in the 1930s, he persuaded such people that the problems for communism in the USSR could be solved by a more rigorous application of the basic principles of Marxism-Leninism. This, he suggested, would necessarily involve a rejection of Stalin and a reversion to the ideals of Lenin. There were many people who responded to his summons to join the party and to help to change public life. The enthusiasts among them were known as 'Children of the Twentieth Congress'.

They believed that a reformed Soviet order would quickly demonstrate its political and economic superiority over its Western rivals; they agreed with Khrushchëv that capitalism was like 'a dead herring in the moonlight, shining brilliantly as it rotted'.[1] Khrushchëv himself assumed that popular gratitude for his liberating influence would engender co-operation between the central political élite and society. He was proud of the achievements made for the average Soviet citizen. High-rise apartment blocks were put up in all cities. Diet went on improving. Meat consumption rose by fifty-five per cent between 1958 and 1965 alone.[2] Fridges, televisions and even washing-machines entered popular ownership. The hospital and education services were free and universally available; rents, home heating and cooking fuel were very inexpensive. Labour discipline was relaxed.[3] Unemployment was practically unknown. Wages rose after 1953 and kept on rising; in the RSFSR between 1959 and 1962, for instance, they increased by seven per cent.[4]

General financial provision had also been introduced for those who had retired from work. In fact the minimum annual pension was set at thirty roubles and was barely sufficient for subsistence;[5] but Khrushchëv had made a start in tackling the problem and jobs were anyway available for many elderly citizens as concierges, doorkeepers and hotel cleaners. The retention of cheap urban cafeterias meant that neither pensioners nor the working poor starved.

Recreational clubs flourished. Lev Yashin, the soccer goalkeeper, was one among the many sportsmen adored by the population. Escapist entertainment was heard on Soviet radio. A very popular ditty began with the words:

> Let there always be sunshine,
> Let there always be sky,
> Let there always be mama,
> Let there always be me!

Such songs had been allowed even under Stalin; the difference was that they were heard much more frequently. Another novelty was Khrushchëv's permission for a change in the design of apartment blocks so that a family might have its privacy. The shared kitchens and corridors of Stalin's kommunalki had prevented this; but now parents could speak to their children without fear of being overheard. Nor was it any longer dangerous to take an interest in foreign countries. Hobbies such as philately and Esperanto became activities that did not lead to arrest by the KGB. One of the most popular film series, *Fantomas*, was a French sci-fi thriller with Russian subtitles; and the authorities began to allow specially-trusted citizens, usually party members, to travel to the West in tourist groups.

Yet much stayed unchanged. Although Khrushchëv rehabilitated millions he punished only a handful of Stalin's intimates for the abuses of power he regularly condemned. Apart from Beria and the security-police leaders, apparently, there were no serious transgressors in the entire Soviet state. It would, of course, have been difficult to arraign all those whose activities had led to arrests and deaths under Stalin: the result would have been an anti-Gulag as big as the Gulag – and Khrushchëv would have been a convict. Nevertheless his evasiveness had the effect of maintaining public distrust of politicians.

The media of public communication continued to blare out messages of support for the communist party. News programmes stuck closely to the party line of the day. Alternatives to Soviet Marxism-Leninism were banned: Khrushchëv, while getting rid of some of Stalin's rigidities, introduced rigidities of his own. Doctrinal orthodoxy remained an unquestionable objective, and the authorities did not give up the habit of lecturing society about everything from nuclear-bomb test negotiations to methods of child-care. Day-to-day dispensation of justice was improved and a proliferation of legal reforms took place.[6] But arbitrariness remained a basic feature of the management of society. The dense network of informers was maintained in every corner of society: the USSR was still a police state. Those Soviet citizens who travelled abroad exemplify the point. They had to write reports on foreigners they met on their holidays; they were also constrained to leave behind a close member of their family as a surety that they would return to the USSR. The state continued to hold its society in suspicion.

Consequently people did not feel grateful to Khrushchëv for long. Material and social conditions had got better, but life in general remained hard – and the political, economic and cultural order was still extremely authoritarian. Khrushchëv in his frequent, lengthy speeches showed that he underestimated the depth of popular grievances.

In the countryside he failed to grasp that the amalgamation of the kolkhozes into super-kolkhozes produced enormous social distress.[7] His campaign to build quasi-urban settlements for compulsory inhabitation by all farmworkers nearly finished off a peasantry bludgeoned to its knees by Stalin. No kulaks survived to be dekulakized, and the KGB did not pile trouble-makers into cattle-trucks bound for Siberia and Kazakhstan. But deportations of a kind occurred as villages were bulldozed and large settlements were established to form the centres of the enlarged farms. The avowed intention was that schools, shops and recreational facilities should simultaneously be attached to each super-kolkhoz; and probably Khrushchëv genuinely believed that the amalgamations would bring benefit to the rural population. But, as usual, the regime was better at destruction than creation. The new rural facilities always fell short of Khrushchëv's promises in number and quality.

If peasants had no love for him, he received little greater affection from urban inhabitants. All towns across the USSR were dreary, ill-appointed places to live. Even Khrushchëv's record in building apartments was ridiculed. The new flats were referred to as *khrushch-ëby*, a pun on his surname and the Russian word for slums. Furthermore, the increase in industrial output was achieved at huge cost to the environment. In Kazakhstan his neglect of the effects of nuclear testing led to the deaths of thousands of people. A repertoire of private satirical commentary circulated. Millions of Gulag inmates returned from the camps with bitter jokes about the Soviet order, but most people did not need to have had this penal experience to mock the authorities. The Presidium and the KGB took preventive action against trouble. On days of official celebration, such as May Day or the October Revolution anniversary, the security police regularly cleared the streets of likely trouble-makers. Individuals waving critical placards or clutching petitions of complaint were swiftly arrested.

The authorities could maintain their one-party, one-ideology state; but they were unable to secure acquiescence in their more mundane demands on a daily basis – and the extent of non-collaboration was worrisomely broad in a society wherein no social, economic or cultural activity was officially considered innocent of political implications.

Non-compliance rather than direct resistance was the norm and many social malaises survived from the 1920s. Turnover of workers at the country's factories peaked at one fifth of the labour-force per annum, and official invocations to stay at an enterprise for one's working life were despised.[8] Financial deals struck to dissuade persons from leaving were the convention. This was illegal, but the economy would have come to a halt if such deals had been eradicated. Enterprises, district councils and local party organizations gave the appearance solely of subservience to the central political authorities. Misinformation remained a pervasive feature of the Soviet order: the trend remained to supply inaccurate data to higher bodies in order to obtain low production targets in the following year. Cliental groups and local nests of officials conspired to impede the Kremlin's decrees. The frequent sackings of party, governmental and police officials served only to bind their successors together in a campaign to save their new jobs.

These phenomena were well known to Khrushchëv, who fitfully tried to eliminate them. But at best, a sullen acceptance of his policies was replacing the initial enthusiasm he had evoked. The difficulty was that the Soviet order did not and could not welcome autonomous initiative in political, social and economic life: spontaneity of thought and behaviour would threaten the entire structure of the state. How, then, could he inspire people again?

In facing up to this problem, he saw that he had to propound his own positive vision of communism. The closed-session speech of 1956 was a denunciation of Stalin, not a delineation of new and inspiring ideas. Before the Twenty-Second Party Congress in Moscow in October 1961 he began to address the task by rewriting the Party Programme, which had been the communist political credo under Stalin (and indeed under Lenin, since it had been accepted in 1919). A team of theorists, editors and journalists had been assembled under B. N. Ponomarëv to produce a draft. Khrushchëv edited its contents.[9] He insisted that it should avoid incomprehensible abstraction: ordinary people had to be able to understand its wording and its goals. More dubiously, he overrode his advisers' objection to the inclusion in the Programme of precise quantitative predictions and ideological schedules that were ludicrously over-ambitious.[10]

The proceedings of the Twenty-Second Congress were ructious. A verbal barrage was aimed at Stalin's record, and this time there was no sparing of those among the deceased dictator's associates who had belonged to the so-called Anti-Party Group: Molotov, Malenkov and Kaganovich were reviled for their complicity in mass murder. An Old Bolshevik, D. A. Lazurkina, took the platform to recount a dream she had had the previous night in which Lenin had appeared to her saying how unpleasant it was for him to lie next to Stalin's corpse.[11] This stage-managed sentimentality led to a decision to remove Stalin from the Lenin-Stalin Mausoleum and to bury him under a simple plinth and bust outside the Kremlin Wall.

The Party Programme accepted by the Congress described the USSR as an 'all-people's state' which no longer needed to use dictatorial methods.[12] Data were adduced on Soviet achievements in production, consumption and welfare. Massive future attainments were heralded: by the end of the 1960s, according to the Programme's prediction, the per capita output of the USA would be overtaken; by 1980 the 'material-technical basis' of a communist society would have been laid down. Full communism would be in prospect. Khrushchëv asserted that the USSR had already reached a point where the 'all-out construction' of such a society could begin.[13] Thus there would be complete freedom for individuals to develop their talents to the full along with the complete satisfaction of every person's needs. The Soviet Union would enter an age of unparalleled human happiness.

Khrushchëv's ideas were jumbled. Under communism as projected by Lenin's *The State and Revolution*, the state would wither away and society would become entirely self-administering; and Lenin implied political organizations would cease to exist once the dictatorship of the proletariat came to an end. Khrushchëv by contrast expected that the party would increase in influence as the communist epoch came nearer; he never revealed how and why the party would ever give up being the vanguard of communism. Furthermore, it was difficult to see the logic in his argument that dictatorship had ended if freedom of belief, publication, assembly and organization had yet to be realized.

He was less exercised by theory and logic than by the desire to issue an effective summons to action. He called upon all Soviet citizens to participate in public life. The lower organizational units of the party, the Komsomol and the trade unions were to meet more regularly, and new voluntary associations were to be formed. (Interestingly, there was no reference to the KGB.) The most notable innovation were the so-called *druzhinniki,* which were groups of citizens acting as a vigilante force for law and order on urban streets. Needless to add, Khrushchëv's summons was delivered on the strict condition that the authority of himself, the Presidium and the entire Soviet order was respected. Mass participation, he assumed, had to be heavily circumscribed. It was consequently hardly surprising that most citizens felt that the main result of his policy was to encourage the busybodies in each town and city to become still more intrusive than ever.

But Khrushchëv's optimism was unabated, and the Programme eulogized the achievements of the 'Soviet people'. The opening section proclaimed the October Revolution as the first breach in the wall of imperialism and stressed that the vast majority of workers, peasants and soldiers had supported the Bolsheviks through the years of the Civil War and the NEP. The Five-Year Plans were depicted as the crucible of unrivalled industrial, cultural and even agricultural progress; and the resilience of the Soviet order was said to have been proven by the USSR's destruction of Nazism in the Second World War.

This was a forceful blend of patriotic and communist rhetoric. Yet the Programme also stated that mimicry of the USSR's experience was no longer treated as compulsory. It was even conceded that, while the non-communist countries would have to come to socialism through a revolution of some kind, there was no inevitability about civil war. But there was a limit to Khrushchëv's ideological tolerance. Yugoslavia's 'revisionism' was condemned. 'Dogmatism', too, was castigated: he did not name names here, but his obvious target was the People's Republic of China. Even more odious, however, was the USA. The Americans were the bastion of imperialist oppression around the globe. Peaceful coexistence would prevent a Third World War taking place; but non-violent competition between the two systems would continue. Capitalism was entering its terminal crisis.

The reasoning behind this prognosis was not explained; and indeed there were incompletenesses and confusions throughout the Programme. This was especially obvious in the treatment of the 'national question'. While one paragraph referred to 'the Soviet people' as a single unit, another noted that a large number of peoples lived in the USSR. By fudging the terminology, Khrushchëv presumably had it in mind to avoid giving offence to national and ethnic groups. The Programme explicitly conceded that class distinctions took a shorter time to erase than national differences. Thus the convergence (*sblizhenie*) of the country's nations would not happen in the near future; and Khrushchëv, unlike Stalin, refrained from picking out the Russians for special praise. Unlike Lenin, however, he omitted to hail the 'fusion' (*sliyanie*) of all nations as an ultimate communist objective. Consequently the Programme left it unclear how it would be possible to build a communist society within just a few years.

But Khrushchëv was undeterred by logical considerations of this kind. His aim was to carry his listeners and readers on the wave of his enthusiasm. He aimed to revive the political mood of the 1920s, when Bolsheviks had thought no task to be impossible. The Programme, at his insistence, boldly declared: 'The party solemnly declares: today's generation of Soviet people will live under communism!'[14]

Khrushchëv had published a charter for Soviet patriotism, party authoritarianism, economic conservatism and mass participation. But he was mortified to find that most people were uninspired by it. Radical anti-Stalinists were worried by its silence about the KGB. Peasants were demoralized by its plan to turn kolkhozes into sovkhozes; and the emphasis on increased industrial productivity alarmed workers. Russians pondered why the Programme no longer gave them a higher status than the other nations of the USSR while the other nations – or at least sections of each of them – bridled at being classified as part of 'the Soviet people'. Traditional communists were equally agitated: the Programme constituted a serious threat to their prerogatives if implemented in full. For nearly all sections of society, furthermore, Khrushchëv's ideas would involve an increase in the burden of work. Few people were happy about the prospect.

Khrushchëv's boastful projections were especially inappropriate in the light of the economic difficulties of 1961–2. Prices paid by the state since 1958 to the collective farms were below the cost of production. This was financial idiocy. Shortages of meat, butter and milk had resulted and the Presidium decided to raise the prices. In order to balance the budget it was also resolved, on 31 May 1962, to increase the prices charged to the urban consumers. It was officially pointed out that these prices had been held at the same level since the First Five-Year Plan;[15] but the economic explanation did not interest most people. Life was hard and was about to get harder. Popular opinion was outraged.

There had been urban disturbances before, notably in Karaganda in 1958 where building workers protested against their dreadful living conditions. In 1962, popular disturbances broke out in Riga, Kiev and Chelyabinsk. The hostile mood existed in most major cities, and on 1 June 1962 an uprising took place in Novocherkassk. Several party and police officials were lynched before order was restored by Soviet Army units. The thousands of demonstrators were fired upon, and twenty-three were killed. Presidium members Mikoyan and Kozlov were dispatched to tell the city's inhabitants that the Kremlin understood their feelings; but only the military action to put Novocherkassk in quarantine and suppress the 'terroristic' activity stopped the trouble spreading to the rest of the Soviet Union. KGB chairman Semichastny confidentially informed the Presidium that the majority of rebels were young male workers. Without such people on his side Khrushchëv could never realize his dream of a consensus between government and the governed.[16]

For a time he had success with the intelligentsia. Under Khrushchëv the creative arts flourished as at no time since the 1920s. Novelists, painters, poets and film-makers regarded themselves as Children of the Twentieth Congress. After his closed-session speech of 1956 Khrushchëv was given the benefit of the doubt; for it was appreciated that he had a less oppressive attitude to high culture than his rivals in the Soviet political leadership at the time.

Certain works of art were published that, but for him, would never have seen the light of day. New words were written for the state anthem: at the Melbourne Olympic games in 1956 the previous version had had to be played without being sung, because of its eulogy to Stalin. The young Siberian poet Yevgeni Yevtushenko wrote *Babi Yar*, which denounced not only the Nazi mass murder of Jews in Ukraine but also the Stalinist terror-regime. Anti-Semitism re-emerged as a topic of debate. Andrei Voznesenski, another young writer, composed his *Antiworlds* cycle of poems which spoke to the emotions of educated teenagers and said nothing about Marxism-Leninism. Jazz was heard again in restaurants. Painters started to experiment with styles that clashed with the severely representational technique approved by the authorities. Poet-guitarists such as Bulat Okudzhava satirized bureaucratic practices. Yevtushenko and Voznesenski became famous, filling large theatres with audiences for their poetry recitations; they were treated by their fans as were pop stars in the West.

Easily the most explosive event in the arts was touched off by a middle-aged former Gulag inmate. In 1962 Alexander Solzhenitsyn brought out his story *One Day in the Life of Ivan Denisovich*. This was a vivid account of twenty-four hours in the life of a construction worker in one of Stalin's camps. Solzhenitsyn's emphasis that his story was about a comparatively benign day in Ivan Denisovich Shukhov's life enhanced the literary effect: readers were left wondering what the other days were like. Solzhenitsyn, a reclusive fellow, instantly acquired international renown.

Yet *Ivan Denisovich* was the peak of the concessions made to cultural freedom. Khrushchëv continued to approve the ban placed upon writers such as Anna Akhmatova and Boris Pasternak. When Pasternak was awarded a Nobel Prize in 1958 for his *Doctor Zhivago*, Presidium member Suslov persuaded Khrushchëv to compel the writer to refuse the honour. Thereafter political difficulties with his colleagues made the First Secretary regress towards even sterner censorship. In 1963 he visited a modern art exhibition on the Manège below the Kremlin. Wading among the artists' stands, Khrushchëv described their paintings as 'shit'. On another occasion he lost his temper with Andrei Voznesenski and other writers. Khrushchëv ranted: 'Mr Voznesenski! Off you go! Comrade Shelepin [as KGB chairman] will issue you with a passport!'[17]

Subjects such as political science and sociology, moreover, were forbidden. The same was true of national studies; only the 'ethnographic' analysis of small, non-industrialized peoples could be undertaken. The machinery of censorship stayed in place. Typescripts had to be submitted to Glavlit before being published; film rushes and even musical scores had to be similarly vetted. Writers of a politically critical bent had to content themselves with writing only 'for their desk drawer'.

Yet the contrast with the Stalin period must not be overlooked. Until 1953 it had been dangerous even to write for desk drawers; there really had been a loosening of official ideological constraints under Khrushchëv. The works of poet-troubadour Sergei Yesenin were published again. Novels by the nineteenth-century writer Fëdor Dostoevski were reprinted and historians writing about tsarist Russia were also permitted a somewhat slacker framework of interpretation. Moreover, not all the intellectual critics of Khrushchëv had entirely given up hope in him. Writers such as the historian Roy Medvedev, the physicist Andrei Sakharov and the journal editor Alexander Tvardovski hoped that Khrushchëv might be persuaded to resume a more relaxed posture on the arts and scholarship. Even the novelist Alexander Solzhenitsyn, who quickly took a dim view of Khrushchëv, continued to submit manuscripts for publication.

Hopefulness was more evident in Russia than in the other Soviet republics, where nationalism complicated the situation. In the Baltic region the memory of pre-war independence and of post-war armed resistance was alive. Estonians, Latvians and Lithuanians thought little of the industrial advance they made as parts of the Soviet economy. Instead they noticed the influx of Russians and other Slavs to the factories being built in their countries. Latvia was a prime example. By 1959 twenty-seven per cent of the republic's population was Russian.[18] The Baltic region was virtually being colonized by retired Russian generals and young working-class Russian men and women who refused to learn the local language.

The Kremlin leaders proclaimed that this national intermingling was simply a sign of socialist internationalism at work; but they were being disingenuous. In reality they were pumping Russians into the other republics as a means of holding together the vast multi-national state. Russian people, more than any other nation, were capable of identifying their own aspirations with the interests of the USSR. Khrushchëv, unlike Stalin, did not put Russian officials in charge practically everywhere. But Russians were none the less in key positions of authority and control. Khrushchëv customarily appointed them to posts such as second party secretaryships; and nearly always the KGB chiefs in the non-Russian republics were Russians. He also set up a Bureau for the RSFSR within the Party Central Committee; it had little autonomous authority, but its existence was a quiet signal that Russian interests were never overlooked in the Kremlin. Above all, he punished any cases of anti-Russian discrimination. Thus he conducted a large peaceful purge of the Communist Party of Latvia in 1959–61 on the grounds that functionaries had been promoted there purely because they happened to be Latvians. This was a warning to other republics that crypto-nationalist tendencies would not be tolerated.

Khrushchëv consolidated his approach educationally. Going further than Stalin, he stipulated that parents had the right to exempt their children from native-language classes in the non-Russian Soviet republics. This reform, carried through in 1958–9, fortified the attempt to promote the study of Russian in schools. Among non-Russian nationalists, consequently, the name of Khrushchëv was mud. In Kiev, where he had spent many years, he was detested for restricting the expression of Ukrainian national pride.

Even so, the traffic of policy was not unidirectional. In 1954 he transferred Crimea from the RSFSR to Ukraine on the grounds that the local links of transport and economic co-operation were closer with Kiev than with Moscow;[19] but he also aimed to give honour to Ukraine and to increase its interest in the maintenance of the Soviet order. Crimea, which had been seized by the Russians from the Turks in the eighteenth century, was prominent in the annals of Russian military valour. Furthermore, Khrushchëv expressed regret for the abuses suffered by the deported nationalities in 1943–4, and sanctioned the repatriation of the Balkars, Chechens, Ingushi, Kalmyks and Karachai. It must be added that Khrushchëv's magnanimity was not comprehensive. Not only the Volga Germans but also the Crimean Tatars and the Meshketian Turks were refused permission to return home from Kazakhstan. Probably he was unwilling to show friendliness to Germans so soon after the war; the Meshketians, moreover, lived near the Turkish border and were presumably regarded as a menace to Soviet security.

The reasons for Khrushchëv's overtures to Ukrainian popular opinion are not hard to guess. It was already obvious that, if current trends prevailed, the Russians would cease to constitute a majority of the USSR's society. The Presidium assumed that common linguistic origins, culture and history united the Russians, Ukrainians and Belorussians. These three peoples were seventy-six per cent of the population in 1959 and were tacitly regarded as the backbone of the Soviet state.[20]

Yet the authorities curtailed and controlled the public expression of nationhood; for Ukraine was a hindrance as well as a help to the Soviet supreme leadership. Too much concession to national feeling might encourage separatist aspirations, and Ukraine's very size – it contained the largest non-independent nation in Europe – would endanger the USSR's integrity if a national movement got out of hand. Consequently only a limited celebration of the nineteenth-century poet Taras Shevchenko was permitted. The policy was the same elsewhere. The anti-tsarist Muslim rebel Shamil, who had been defamed in Stalin's last years, became a respectable historical figure again in the north Caucasus – but only up to a certain point: emphasis was still given to the benefits brought to the Muslim peoples after their conquest by the Russian Imperial Army. The Presidium knew that the USSR had many deep, ethnically-based enmities; but these had been put into the freezer by the communist party dictatorship: they were not seen boiling in the pot. And, as the regime's advocates untiringly pointed out, the incidence of national intermarriages had reached ten per cent and was therefore not insignificant.[21]

Most wedding ceremonies, furthermore, were civil affairs conducted by local government functionaries. Encouragement was given to newly-weds to follow their ceremony with visits to monuments to the dead of the Second World War. Soviet patriotism and secular ceremony were meant to supplant religious practice. For the persistence of belief in God was displeasing to the atheistic state and was also regarded as a potential instrument for covert political opposition.

Khrushchëv mounted a crude assault upon religion. On his instructions Christian churches of all denominations were demolished across the country. Only 7,560 were left standing by the mid-1960s.[22] The Russian Orthodox Church, which Stalin had exempted from his earlier excesses after the Second World War, suffered from Khrushchëv's attacks. Yet not even Khrushchëv could do without the Russian Orthodox Church as a tool of foreign and domestic policy. The State Committee of Religious Affairs interfered in its appointments and organization; and the KGB kept dozens of bishops as informers. The Patriarch Aleksi was compelled to travel the world on behalf of the Soviet campaign for 'peaceful coexistence'. Furthermore, the hierarchy of the Russian Orthodox Church remained corrupted by its continued occupation of cathedrals previously owned by other denominations. This ecclesiastical imperialism was flagrant in Ukraine where both the Greek Catholic (Uniate) Church and the Ukrainian Autocephalous Church were kept locked out of their own buildings.

Not only in the Baltic region but also in Moldavia, Georgia and Armenia the official authorities reinforced persecution and suborned, demoralized and exploited the priesthood as in Russia. But not all the religious groups succumbed. Certain of them gathered adherents precisely because they were unwilling to collaborate with the regime. The Catholic Church in Latvia and Lithuania was indomitable, and in Russia the Baptists gained in popularity.

Khrushchëv was also ruthless towards non-Christian believers. He allowed only 12,000 mosques and 60 synagogues to survive, and the Buddhists in Siberia were harassed. The anti-religious campaign of the regime involved a further undermining of social morale and cohesion, especially in rural areas. Khrushchëv was not the sole threat to religion: urbanization in the USSR strengthened secularist tendencies in Soviet society just as it did in other advanced industrial countries. What saved these faiths from extinction was the reluctance of local party and government officials to be quite as brutal to people of their own ethnic group as central party policy demanded. In

Tajikistan and in the villages of Azerbaijan there was general revulsion at the intrusion of militant Marxism-Leninism. Many functionaries themselves continued to practise Islam in the privacy of their homes.

This situation makes it impossible to know how many religious believers existed. A later survey carried out in Moscow province in 1970 suggested that 16 per cent of men and 45 per cent of women held a faith in God.[23] The younger generation believed less than the older. Furthermore, people lower down the social hierarchy believed more than those higher up, and villagers believed more than urban inhabitants. If this was the pattern of religious belief in a highly-urbanized province such as Moscow, it must be assumed that religion was much more densely practised elsewhere.

Khrushchëv was furious. While lowering the number of political prisoners in the Gulag, he showed no mercy to religious activists: 1,500 of them, at the very lowest estimate, were locked up by the early 1960s. A troublesome pair of Orthodox archbishops, Andrei of Chernigov and Iov of Kazan, were put to forced labour.[24] That so many harmless Soviet citizens were subjected to such maltreatment is a sign that the state was very far from succeeding in indoctrinating society. There is a paradox here. Enthusiastic Marxist-Leninists tended to be newcomers – including Mikhail Gorbachëv – to the positions of power. But most of the sons and daughters of the current generation of high-ranking central officials did not give a fig for the Party Programme; and when such youngsters of privileged backgrounds had an opportunity to visit foreign parts, many of them returned with a hankering for Western jeans and pop music. The language of Marxism-Leninism was used by them in furtherance of careers; but in their homes they avoided such verbiage. The worm had entered the apple: the offspring of the nomenklatura despised the state ideology.

Meanwhile all was not well within officialdom itself. The pre-war and wartime cohort of functionaries in party, police, army and government were disoriented by the recent innovations; they were uncomfortable, too, with the recurrent attacks on Stalin, who was venerated by many of them. As the years passed, they tended to forget that Stalin had killed a large number of persons like themselves. Khrushchëv increasingly annoyed them. While they desired certainty and reassurance, he brought them only disturbance.

This was true not only in Moscow but also in the provinces. Few party secretaries had more than a brief party-school education. Local politicians flattered Khrushchëv at Congresses and fawned upon him whenever he paid a visit to their locality. No ruler in Russian history, not even the energetic Peter the Great, had gone to so many parts of his country. But once out of the range of his surveillance, they gave priority to their personal comforts. They drank and ate; they used the special shops which were barred to the general public. They were chauffeured everywhere. They took well-appointed holidays by the Black Sea and participated in official Soviet delegations to the countries of Eastern Europe. They grabbed access to higher education and to professional jobs for members of their families regardless of their qualifications. They lived in cantonments separate from the common run of humanity.

Khrushchëv himself delighted in occupying his palatial dacha at Pitsunda; he gladly received gifts from foreign statesmen, especially if they were rifles or scientific instruments.[25] (How he would have loved hand-held computer games!) Nor did he refrain from dispensing jobs, titles and privileges to close relatives. This proponent of communism would never have liked communist egalitarianism in reality, and he was so accustomed to the luxuries of office that he was incapable of recognizing his hypocrisy.

What irked Khrushchëv was not so much the morality of officials in the provinces as their uncontrollability. But his own measures in fact contributed to the problem. The combination of economic decentralization and political consultation served to strengthen localist tendencies. Aping Lenin and Stalin, Khrushchëv set up special supervisory bodies. One such was the Committee of Party-State Control; but this was no more able to bring institutions and their officials to heel than any of its predecessors. The custom of fudging figures on industrial and agricultural output according to self-interest was ineliminable. Khrushchëv, like his predecessors, reacted with campaigns of mass mobilization. Ordinary party members and the general public were encouraged to blow the whistle on illegalities and disobedience. The difficulty was that the entire Soviet order exerted a pressure on everyone to be deceitful in everyday life. Eradication of all the fiddles would really have necessitated a revolution.

At the lowest levels of society the joke went the rounds: 'They pretend to pay us and we pretend to work!' Soviet workers saw no point in being more punctual, co-operative and conscientious than they absolutely had to be. Theft from farms and factories was not regarded with popular disapproval. Individuals looked after themselves, their families and their close friends. Khrushchëv, who had expected that people would toil tirelessly for the communist common weal, was deeply frustrated; but the Novocherkassk uprising had shown that, unless he slackened his demands on society, the entire political status quo might be challenged.

An ever-growing menace to his position and his plans came from higher levels. Ostensibly he was unchallengeable. The ministries, the KGB, the trade unions and the party shared his commitment to maintaining the Soviet order; and these same institutions were subject to the Party Presidium. They could select representatives to put their case to the Presidium. Khrushchëv could even brow-beat the Soviet Army. He not only sacked Zhukov in 1957 but also reduced the number of troops from 5.8 million to 3.7 million in the second half of the decade.[26] His justification was that the USSR's nuclear weaponry provided a more adequate base for the country's defence than conventional land and air forces. Khrushchëv had depended upon the Soviet Army's assistance in his struggle against the Anti-Party Group; and Zhukov, at the moment of his sacking, had warned Khrushchëv that even Marshal Moskalenko, one of Khrushchëv's favourites, had been talking about the desirability of a *coup d'état*.[27] But Khrushchëv refused to be bullied by such talk. He was totally confident that power at last lay firmly in the hands of the civilian politicians.

His willingness to think the unthinkable was proved in September 1962 when he permitted a debate in *Pravda* on economic reform. The main participant, Yevsei Liberman, urged the desirability of according greater autonomy to factory managers in decisions about production, sales and labour inputs. This project would have impinged upon the prerogatives of Gosplan and the entire police-party-military-industrial complex. Not since the 1920s had managers enjoyed the authority proposed by Liberman.

Whether Khrushchëv's heart lay in so basic a reform is questionable. As Stalin's legatee, he never seriously tried to lower the proportion of the country's gross investment in the capital-goods sector. Resources were poured into defence production in particular. Rather than offer autonomy to managers, he suggested yet another institutional reorganization in September 1962. The agency he picked to mobilize economic advance was the party. In a note written to the Presidium, Khrushchëv suggested that each local party committee should be split into two separate committees to deal respectively with industry and agriculture. This bipartition, he argued, would concentrate attention upon both sectors of economic production in each province. His colleagues regarded it as a bureaucratic nonsense which would make demarcation of responsibilities even more complicated than at present; but they yielded to him when he insisted on implementing the scheme.

He had raised most members of the central political élite to their posts: Frol Kozlov, Leonid Brezhnev and Nikolai Podgorny were his protégés; and other figures who had built careers independently of him, notably Mikhail Suslov and Aleksei Kosygin, had gained additional promotion through his efforts. He grossly underestimated their dislike of his interminable reorganizations, a dislike that was shared at lower levels of the party's hierarchy. The scheme for the party's bipartition caused particular irritation in the localities. Each provincial party secretary who had previously run the party throughout a province was being asked to choose between industry and agriculture in his province. No official welcomed this abrupt reduction in power.

Khrushchëv had become too isolated to discern this. Certainly he was careful to consult colleagues on foreign policy. In August 1961, for example, he obtained the preliminary sanction of the Presidium for the building of a wall between the Soviet and Western sectors of

Berlin. For years there had been an exodus of the German Democratic Republic's citizens to West Germany, and one of the results had been the loss of doctors, engineers and other professional people. Khrushchëv rather shamefacedly argued that the German Democratic Republic 'had yet to reach a level of moral and material development where competition with the West was possible';[28] but the building of the Berlin Wall was disastrous for Soviet prestige around the world. In trying to put pressure on the NATO governments, moreover, he resumed the testing of Soviet nuclear bombs. He wanted to show that the USSR was capable of defending its interests under his guidance.

He also had the Presidium's consent in trying to extend the country's influence elsewhere in the world. Soviet leaders had always been angry about the USA's placement of nuclear missile facilities in Turkey on the USSR's borders. The communist revolution under Fidel Castro gave rise to a plan for the Soviet Union to construct similar facilities on the Caribbean island of Cuba, not far from the Florida coast. Khrushchëv and his advisers, with Castro's enthusiastic participation, made the necessary preparations in 1962.

American spy-planes picked out the unusual construction-work being carried out in Cuba. In October 1962 President Kennedy, before the Soviet missiles could complete their voyage to the Caribbean, declared that Cuba would be placed in military quarantine. Soviet ships would be stopped and searched for missiles. Castro recklessly urged Khrushchëv to bomb American cities, but was brushed aside as a madman.[29] For a few days the diplomats of the USSR and the USA faced the possibility of a Third World War. Khrushchëv had badly underestimated Kennedy's will. The old dog, far from intimidating the young pup, had to give way. The ships were turned back, and the Soviet regime was humbled in the eyes of the world. In fact Kennedy had made a substantial concession to Khrushchëv by promising both to dismantle the Turkish facilities and never to invade Cuba. The snag was that this compromise was to be a secret between the American and Soviet administrations.

Presidium members had been consulted by Khrushchëv throughout the crisis; but it was he who had brought the Cuban proposal to their attention, and therefore it was he alone who was blamed by them for the USSR's humiliation. Khrushchëv had run out of luck. All the main economic data indicated that his policies were running into trouble. The harvest of 1963 was nine per cent lower than in the previous year. The fodder crop was so inadequate that imports had to take place for the first time – a deeply-annoying development at a time when the Presidium needed to use its hard-currency funds for the purchase of Western industrial technology.[30]

There was scarcely a group, organization or institution that did not hate Khrushchëv. He had offended the party, the economic ministries, the generals, the diplomatic service, the intelligentsia, the managers and the security police. His achievements were undeniable, especially in the ending of terror and the raising of the general standard of living. But further improvement was not forthcoming; and Khrushchëv's futurological boasts, his idiosyncratic bossiness and his obsessive reorganizations had taken their toll on the patience of practically everyone. He was a complex leader. At once he was a Stalinist and anti-Stalinist, a communist believer and cynic, a self-publicizing poltroon and a crusty philanthropist, a trouble-maker and a peacemaker, a stimulating colleague and domineering bore, a statesman and a politicker who was out of his intellectual depth. His contradictions were the product of an extraordinary personality and a lifetime of extraordinary experiences.

Yet it must be appreciated that his eccentricities in high office also resulted from the immense, conflicting pressures upon him. Unlike his successors, he was willing to try to respond to them by seeking long-term solutions. But the attempted solutions were insufficient to effect the renovation of the kind of state and society he espoused. Reforms were long overdue. His political, economic and cultural accomplishments were a great improvement over Stalin. But they fell greatly short of the country's needs.

19

Stabilization (1964–1970)

The Soviet political system since 1917 had developed few fixed regulations. When Lenin died there was no assumption that a single successor should be selected. The same was true at Stalin's death. No effort had yet been made to establish rules about the succession even though it was by then taken for granted that whoever was appointed to lead the Secretariat would rule the country. In mid-1964, as Khrushchëv's colleagues wondered what to do about him, this uncertainty persisted and they also had the problem that the Party First Secretary was not dead but alive and capable of retaliating.

Khrushchëv returned from trips to Scandinavia and Czechoslovakia in summer. Sensing nothing afoot, he took a break at Pitsunda by the Black Sea in October. He was still fit for a man of seventy. His Presidium colleagues had recently congratulated him at his birthday celebrations and wished him well in political office, and the First Secretary took them at their word. Mikoyan popped over to chat with him and hinted to him not to be complacent. But Khrushchëv ignored the allusion; instead he waited with bated breath for news that the latest team of Soviet cosmonauts had returned safely to earth. As was his wont, he arranged to greet them in person. Everything seemed well to him despite an alarm raised by a chauffeur who had overheard details of a plot to oust the First Secretary.[1] He who had outplayed Beria refused to believe that he might one day meet his match.

The Presidium had in fact put together a peaceful plot involving older colleagues like Brezhnev and Suslov as well as the younger ones such as Shelepin and Semichastny. KGB chief Semichastny's betrayal was crucial since it was properly his duty to inform Khrushchëv of any such conspiracy. The plotters had also used former Central Committee Secretary Nikolai Ignatov, who had been sacked by Khrushchëv, to take discreet soundings among Central Committee members. Nothing was left to chance.

The only thing left to decide was about the timing. After several false starts, Suslov made a phone call to Khrushchëv on 12 October 1964 and requested that he fly to Moscow for an unscheduled Presidium discussion of agriculture. At last Khrushchëv guessed what was in store; for he said to Mikoyan: 'If it's me who is the question, I won't make a fight of it.' Next day, when his plane landed at Vnukovo 2 Airport, Semichastny's men isolated him and rushed him to a Presidium meeting in the Kremlin. Initially Mikoyan worked for a compromise whereby Khrushchëv would lose the First Secretaryship but remain Chairman of the Council of Ministers. But the rest of the Presidium wanted Khrushchëv completely retired. Eventually the old man buckled under the strain and tearfully requested: 'Comrades, forgive me if I'm guilty of anything. We worked together. True, we didn't accomplish everything.' Unconditional surrender followed: 'Obviously it will now be as you wish. What can I say? I've got what I deserved.'[2]

On 14 October, an emergency Central Committee plenum was held. It was attended by 153 out of 169 members. Brezhnev was in the chair since the Presidium had already agreed that he should become Party First Secretary. After briefly referring to Khrushchëv's 'cult of the individual' and 'voluntaristic actions', he vacated the podium so that Suslov might make a report. The Central Committee needed to hear from someone who had no close association with Khrushchëv.[3]

Suslov asserted that what Lenin had said about Stalin's crudity and capriciousness was also applicable to Khrushchëv. The principles of collective leadership had been infringed, and Khrushchëv had intrigued to set colleague against colleague. Policy had been changed without consultation. Khrushchëv had arbitrarily introduced outsiders to Central Committee meetings. He had promoted members of his family and taken them on expensive foreign trips. His interventions in industry were bad, in agriculture even worse. His reorganizations had damaged the party, and he had behaved high-handedly towards the countries of the Warsaw Pact. He had replaced the Stalin cult with a Khrushchëv cult. 'So there you have it,' declaimed Suslov. 'Not leadership but a complete merry-go-round!' Suslov's tone was softened only towards the end when he read out a letter from Khrushchëv recognizing the validity of the criticisms.[4]

Emotions in the audience were highly charged and several Central Committee members shouted out that Khrushchëv should undergo punishment of some sort. But Brezhnev was already assured of victory, and ignored such demands. Khrushchëv, depressed and contrite, was shunted into comfortable retirement. He was hardly mentioned in the press again in his lifetime. In the contemporary Western term, he became a 'non-person' overnight.

Khrushchëv none the less came to regard the manner of his going with some satisfaction. No guns, no executions. Not even many sackings apart from his own. Brezhnev would head the Central Committee Secretariat and Kosygin the Council of Ministers; Podgorny, as chairman of the Presidium of the Supreme Soviet was to become head of state. They and their associates approved of the general line taken by the party since 1953; but they wished to introduce greater stability to policies and institutions. New themes appeared in *Pravda*: collective leadership, scientific planning, consultation with expert opinion, organizational regularity and no light-headed schemes. At Khrushchëv's going there was no popular commotion. On the contrary, there was a widespread feeling of relief; even the dour image cultivated by Brezhnev, Kosygin and Podgorny seemed admirable after Khrushchëv's unsettling ebullience. Most Soviet citizens, including the intellectuals, anticipated a period of steady development for Soviet economy and society.

Certain early decisions on policy were predictable. The Central Committee plenum in October 1964 forbade any single person from holding the two supreme posts in the party and government simultaneously. In November the bipartition of local party committees was rescinded. In the winter of 1964–5 overtures were made to Mao Zedong to close the breach between the USSR and the People's

Republic of China. In October 1965 the sovnarkhozes were abolished and the old central ministries were restored.

Yet there was no consensus about what substantial innovations should be made. Shelepin, who was made Presidium member after helping to organize Khrushchëv's dismissal, made a bid for the supreme leadership in February 1965 by calling for a restoration of obedience and order. He disliked the concept of the 'all-people's state'; he wanted to resume an ideological offensive against Yugoslavia; and he showed a fondness for the good old days in his confidential support for the rehabilitation of Stalin's reputation.[5] 'Iron Shurik', as he was nicknamed, got nowhere in the Presidium. He did not help himself by parading his contempt for his older colleagues and by proposing to cut back the perks enjoyed by party office-holders. Brezhnev was not yet strong enough to remove him from the Presidium; but in 1967 he directed him out of harm's way by moving him from the Committee of Party-State Control to the USSR Central Council of Trade Unions.

The Presidium member who struggled the hardest for any positive sort of reform was Kosygin. Brezhnev had kept up an interest in agriculture since guiding the virgin lands campaign in Kazakhstan; but mainly he busied himself with internal party affairs. It was Kosygin who initiated a reconsideration of economic policy. Yevsei Liberman's proposal of 1962 for an increase in the rights of factory managers was dusted down and presented by Kosygin to the Central Committee in September 1965.[6]

Kosygin did not open the door to complete managerial freedom: even Liberman had avoided that, and Kosygin as a practising politician was yet more cautious. Yet the implications of his reforms were large. If the heads of enterprises were to operate with reduced interference by Gosplan, then the authority of economic ministries and the party would decline. Kosygin's long-standing advocacy of the consumer-goods sector of industrial investment increased his colleagues' suspicion of him. Party officials were especially annoyed at his proposal to reduce the authority of economic-branch departments in the Central Committee Secretariat. The post-war organizational dispute between Malenkov and Zhdanov was re-emerging as Kosygin challenged the interests of the central party apparatus. If Kosygin had had his way, the premisses of economic policy would stealthily be shifted towards profit-making, managerial initiative and ministerial freedom from the party's interference.

Brezhnev decided that his best stratagem was not to confront Kosygin but to position himself between Kosygin and Shelepin until he could bring his own appointees into the Presidium. With Brezhnev's approval, the Central Committee gave formal permission to Kosygin to go ahead with the reforms; but all the while Brezhnev, both at the plenum and afterwards, impeded him with unhelpful modifications.

He quietly went about enhancing his own authority, ringing up provincial party secretaries for their opinion at each stage. He often spent a couple of hours each day on such conversations. His modesty seemed impressive. On the Kremlin Wall he was indistinguishable from the other late middle-aged men in staid suits and staider hats. At the March 1965 Central Committee plenum he displayed his preferences in policy by getting a larger share of the budget for agriculture (which was another sign that Kosygin's industrial proposals were not going to be allowed to work). Brezhnev regarded chemical fertilizers and advanced mechanical equipment as the main solution to the grain shortage. He had concluded that budgetary redistribution rather than Khrushchëvian rhetoric and reorganization was the most effective instrument of progress. His primary objective was to make the existing system work better and work harder.

Brezhnev's stabilization of politics and administration after the upsets of Khrushchëv also led him to clamp down on cultural freedom. As Khrushchëv had become more illiberal, many intellectuals had taken to meeting in little groups and circulating typescripts of poems, novels and manifestos that were certain to be refused publication. This method of communication was known as *samizdat* (or self-publishing); and it was to acquire a broader technical range when tape-recorder cassettes became available. The latter method was known as *magnitizdat*.

The participants in such groupings grew in number as access to official publication narrowed. Roy Medvedev's book on the Great Terror, which itemized previously-unknown details of Stalin's activity, was banned from the press. The same fate befell Viktor Danilov's opus on agricultural collectivization at the end of the 1920s. Alexander Solzhenitsyn wrote two lengthy novels, *The First Circle* and *Cancer Ward*, describing the lower levels of the political and social hierarchy under Stalin. He, too, had his works rejected or even 'arrested' by the KGB. Andrei Sakharov wrote letters to the Presidium requesting freedom of opinion and self-expression, but to no avail. A lesson was given to them that the avenues of consultation with the country's supreme political leadership that had been kept semi-open under Khrushchëv were being closed. The cultural spring turned to autumn without an intermediate summer.

And a chilly winter was imminent. In September 1965 the KGB arrested two writers, Andrei Sinyavski and Yuli Daniel, who had circulated some satirical tales in samizdat about the Soviet state. They were put on trial in the following February and charged under Article No. 70 of the Criminal Code with spreading 'anti-Soviet propaganda'. Sinyavski and Daniel were unyielding, and sympathizers demonstrated on their behalf outside the Moscow court building. Yet they were found guilty and sentenced to forced labour in the Gulag.[7]

The principal embarrassment to the Presidium was that the trial had lasted so long. New articles were therefore added to the Code so as to expedite matters in the future. The result was that dissenters could quickly be branded as common criminals, parasites or even traitors. The dissenters referred to themselves as 'other-thinkers' (*inakomyshlyashchie*). This was a neat term which encapsulated the origin of their predicament: namely that they disagreed with the postulates of the ruling ideology. Certainly it was more accurate than the word favoured in the West, 'dissidents'. The etymological root of dissidence implies a sitting apart; but Soviet 'other-thinkers' were by no means distant from the rest of society: indeed they shared the living conditions of ordinary citizens; even a leading scientist such as Sakharov had most of his comforts withdrawn as soon as he became a dissenter. What was different about the dissenters was their willingness to make an overt challenge to the regime.

Starting in 1968, the samizdat journal *The Chronicle of Current Events* appeared. It was produced on typewriters with sheaves of carbon paper tucked into them. In 1970 a Human Rights Committee was formed by Andrei Sakharov, Valeri Chalidze and Andrei Tverdokhlebov. In 1971 an Estonian National Front was created in Tallinn. In Moscow, the priests Gleb Yakunin and Dmitri Dudko gathered Christian followers who demanded freedom of faith. Jewish organizations were established for the purpose of gaining visas to emigrate to Israel.

By the mid-1970s there were reckoned to be about 10,000 political and religious prisoners across the Soviet Union. They were held in grievous conditions, most of them being given less than the intake of calories and proteins sufficient to prevent malnutrition. Punishments for disobedience in the camps were severe and the guards were both venal and brutal. But labour camps were not the sole methods used by the KGB. Punitive psychiatry, which had been used under Khrushchëv, was extended after 1964. Medicine became an arm of coercive state control as doctors were instructed to expect an influx of cases of 'paranoiac schizophrenia' shortly before public festivals; and many persistent dissenters were confined for years in mental asylums. Meanwhile the KGB maintained a vast network of informers and *agents provocateurs*. No group operated for long without being infiltrated by them, and the security police also tried to demoralize camp inmates into repenting their past.

Yet Brezhnev and his colleagues refrained from all-out violent suppression. They had not forgotten how the Great Terror had affected party leaders such as they had now become. Furthermore, they did not want to incur greater hostility from the intelligentsia than was absolutely necessary; they continually stressed that they would treat the opinions of professional experts seriously. Consequently dissent was not eliminated, but was held at a low level of intensity.

Brezhnev himself had a kindly reputation among political colleagues and in his family; and he can hardly have been consistently anti-Semitic since his wife Viktoria was Jewish.[8] But first and foremost he was an *apparatchik*, a functionary of the party apparatus, and an ambitious, energetic one at that. When appointed as First Secretary, he was fifty-eight years old. He had been born to a Russian working-class family in Ukraine in 1906 and had no involvement in the October Revolution or Civil War. He became a communist party member towards the end of the First Five-Year Plan and qualified as an engineer in 1935. He had just the background to enter politics in Dneprodzherzhinsk as the Great Terror raged. By 1939 he was working in the party apparatus in Dnepropetrovsk in Ukraine. In the Second World War he served as a commissar on both the Southern and Ukrainian fronts. Attaining the rank of Major-General, he made impression enough on Khrushchëv to be taken under his patronage and marked out for rapid promotion.

No one who had held this succession of posts could have been over-endowed with moral sensitivity. Collusion in repression was a job specification. So, too, was an ability to trim to the changing winds of official policy; and most functionaries of the pre-war generation were more like Brezhnev than Khrushchëv: they had learned to avoid being seen to have independent opinions. Brezhnev's guiding aim was to avoid getting himself into trouble with higher authority.

He therefore stamped ruthlessly upon the 'bourgeois nationalism' of Romanian speakers when appointed as the Moldavian Communist Party First Secretary in 1950. He was put on the Presidium by Stalin in 1952 as a member of the younger generation of Soviet leaders. Losing this status on Stalin's death, he rejoined the Presidium after the Twentieth Party Congress. By then he had played a major part in the virgin lands campaign, and photographs of him by Khrushchëv's side became frequent in *Pravda*. Meanwhile he built up his own power-base by recruiting personnel from among his associates from his time as Dnepropetrovsk Province Party Secretary. He had a handsome look with his generous grin and his shock of black hair – and he was proud of his appearance. Only his pragmatic need to subsume his personality under the demands of 'collective leadership' stopped him from shining in the glare of the world's media.

And yet it would have been a brightness of style, not of substance; and the style, too, would have been dulled by Brezhnev's defects as a public speaker. He had no oral panache. He was also very limited intellectually, and acknowledged this in private: 'I can't grasp all this. On the whole, to be frank, this isn't my field. My strong point is organization and psychology.'[9] This comment hit the mark. For indeed Brezhnev was masterly at planning an agenda so as to maximize consensus. Always he strove to circumvent direct conflict with colleagues. Even when he decided to get rid of someone, he carried out the task with charm.

Such qualities were embarrassingly narrow for the leader of one of the world's superpowers. And Brezhnev's vanity was extraordinary. For instance, he shunted the Moscow City Party Secretary N. G. Yegorychev into an obscure ambassadorship for refusing to sing his praises.[10] Moreover, he was indifferent to problems of corruption. 'Nobody,' he casually opined, 'lives just on his wages.'[11] He permitted his family to set a grotesque example. His daughter Galina was a promiscuous alcoholic who took up with a circus director running a gold-bullion fraud gang. Brezhnev himself outdid Khrushchëv in the nepotism for which he had criticized him. Nor did he forget to be generous to himself. His passion was to add to his fleet of foreign limousines donated to him by the leaders of states abroad. He drove them on the roads between his dacha and the Kremlin with flagrant disregard for public safety.

Yet it was initially a distinct point of attraction for his central party colleagues that Brezhnev was so undistinguished. Each Presidium member expected to be able to guide the First Secretary in policy-making. They had underestimated him. Shelepin and Kosygin were steadily being worn down. Podgorny, who wanted Brezhnev kept in check, had no personal following in the Presidium; and Suslov apparently had no ambition to become the supreme leader, preferring to exercise influence behind the scenes.[12] Brezhnev's fellow leaders perceived that he was becoming more than *primus inter pares* among them only when it was too late to reverse the process.

Brezhnev had helped to make his own luck. But he was also assisted by the trends of current economic data. Khrushchëv had lost his political offices partly as a result of the poor grain harvest of 1963. He was sacked just before the encouraging news of the harvest of 1964 had become fully available. The improvement continued in the immediately following years. Between 1960 and 1970 Soviet agricultural output increased at an annual average of three per cent.[13] Industry, too, enhanced its performance. At the end of the Eighth Five-Year Plan period of 1966–70 the output of factories and mines was 138 per cent greater than in 1960.[14] At the same time the regime was effective in maintaining strict political control. There were several disparate strikes, but nothing remotely akin to the Novocherkassk uprising of 1962. The authorities had a tight grip on society, and Brezhnev's prestige grew among members of the Soviet political élite.

The Twenty-Third Party Congress, which began on 29 March 1966, changed the name of the Presidium back to the Politburo and allocated eleven members to it. The post held by Brezhnev was redesignated as the General Secretaryship (as it had been known in the 1920s). This hint at continuity with the Stalin era was meant to emphasize that the disruptions of Khrushchëv's rule were at an end. Since Brezhnev wanted to avoid the Politburo turning on him as he and his colleagues had turned upon Khrushchëv, very few sackings occurred in the central party leadership. For a while only the most dangerous opponents were removed. In particular, Shelepin's ally Semichastny was replaced by Yuri Andropov as KGB chairman in May 1967; and Shelepin himself was moved out of the Committee of Party-State Control in June and out of the Party Secretariat in September.

The Politburo was still feeling its way towards settled policies. This was especially obvious in its handling of those countries in Eastern Europe where economic reforms were being implemented. Hungarian party leader János Kádár had introduced measures similar to those advocated by Kosygin in the USSR. He got away with this because he had moved stealthily while Khrushchëv was in power and because he had Kosygin's protection after Khrushchëv's retirement. By 1968 a New Economic Mechanism which included limited permission for the creation of retail markets had been introduced.

In Poland a different approach was taken. Władisław Gomułka had failed to fulfil his promises of industrial and agricultural growth and was removed in favour of Eduard Gierek in 1970. The new Polish government raised huge Western loans to facilitate the rapid expansion of heavy industry. Financial support and technological transfer, Gierek argued, would unblock the country's economic bottlenecks.

The Soviet communist leaders gave approval to both the Hungarian and the Polish experiments not least because the USSR could ill afford to maintain its massive subsidy of the East European countries in the form of cheap oil and gas exports. In any case the basic structures of the centrally-planned economy remained in place in both countries.

Less contentment was shown by the Soviet Politburo with the policies adopted by the communist leadership in Czechoslavakia. At first there had been little cause for concern. Czechoslovak party leader Antonin Novotný had become as unpopular as Gomułka in Poland, and Brezhnev on his visit to Prague in December 1967 refused to intervene in the factional dispute. Novotný resigned in January 1968 and was succeeded by Alexander Dubček. The consequence was the 'Prague Spring'. Dubček and his colleagues allowed the emergence of independent pressure groups; they allowed the mass media to criticize the Czechoslovak official authorities, not excluding himself. The trade unions resumed the role of defence of workers' interests, and market reforms of the Hungarian type were treated as a minimum short-term aim. Dubček, hoping to create a 'socialism with a human face', still thought of himself as a Leninist. But by introducing so many checks on the communist party dictatorship, he was unknowingly rejecting the main tenets of Lenin's thought and practice.

His cardinal error lay in assuming that he could pull the Soviet Politburo along with him. In Moscow, the Czech reforms were seen as threatening the existence of one-party rule, the centrally-planned economy and the survival of Eastern Europe as an exclusively communist zone. Brezhnev sent his emissaries to Prague over the summer to pull him back into line. But Dubček ignored all the hints that his intransigence would incur a military penalty.

On the night of 20–21 August 1968 the tanks of the Warsaw Pact rolled into Czechoslovakia. The decision had been taken in the Soviet Politburo. Kosygin had wavered earlier in the summer, remembering the complications around the world that had followed the suppression of the Hungarian revolt.[15] Brezhnev, too, had not always been enthusiastic. But the vote in the Politburo was unanimously in favour of invasion. Brezhnev was later to affirm that 'if I hadn't voted in the Politburo for military intervention, I probably wouldn't be sitting here now'. In the meantime Hungarian leader Kádár had tried to dispel Dubček's naïvety: 'Don't you understand what kind of people you are dealing with?' Dubček rebuffed the warning; and when the tanks arrived in Prague, he was taken prisoner and flown to Russia, where he was injected with drugs and threatened with execution unless he complied with the USSR's orders. Dubček succumbed, but with obvious heavy reluctance, and in spring 1969 the Soviet Politburo put the compliant Gustav Husak in power.

After a brief period as Czechoslovak ambassador to Turkey, Dubček was demoted to the job of local forest administrator. A bloodless purge of the participants in the Prague Spring was put in hand. No country of the Warsaw Pact was permitted to follow policies involving the slightest derogation from the premisses of the one-party state, Marxism-Leninism and Warsaw Pact membership. The Brezhnev Doctrine was imposed, whereby upon any threat to 'socialism' in any country of the Pact, the other member countries of the Pact had the right and duty to intervene militarily.

The invasion of Czechoslovakia had baleful consequences for the political and economic debates in the USSR. Ideological retrenchment was inevitable. This was appreciated by dissenters outside the party such as Pavel Litvinov, who led a small group of protesters on Red Square on 23 August. The participants were seized by police, put on trial in October and sentenced to three years in prison camps.[16] Litvinov's treatment could easily have been worse; but within the Politburo there was reluctance to resort to greater repression than was deemed completely necessary. The measures were anyway severe enough for the intelligentsia to lose any remaining illusions about

Brezhnev. Khrushchëv, who spent his days at his dacha telling tales to visitors who came out to picnic in the woods, was becoming a figure of nostalgia among artists and scholars. A siege mentality gripped the regime: if a Gorbachëv had existed in the Kremlin in 1968, he would have been arrested.

The USA assured the USSR that the invasion of Czechoslovakia would not cause a world war and that Western political revulsion would not get in the way of negotiations between the superpowers. The Nuclear Non-Proliferation Treaty was signed in 1969 and Strategic Arms Limitation Talks (SALT) were begun in the same year. By 1970 the USSR had caught up with its rival in the number of its intercontinental ballistic missiles. But both Moscow and Washington were keen that competition in military preparedness should occur in a predictable, non-violent fashion.

Yet the Czechoslovak invasion damaged the USSR irreparably inside the global communist movement. Hopes for a reconciliation with China had been slim since 1966, when Mao Zedong had castigated Moscow as a 'centre of modern revisionism' that had betrayed the principles of Marx, Engels and Lenin. After 1968 the number of critics grew. Albania, Romania and Yugoslavia condemned the Brezhnev Doctrine; and when seventy-five communist parties met in Moscow in June 1969, the polemics were incessant. Only sixty-one parties agreed to sign the main document at the conference. World communism had definitively become polycentric. Indeed border skirmishes broke out along the Siberian border with the People's Republic of China. All-out war was a possibility until Moscow and Beijing each concluded that a diplomatic settlement was in its interest. The Politburo was finding relations with China as intractable as at any time under Khrushchëv.

Not that everything in foreign affairs was problematical. Kosygin, Brezhnev and Podgorny followed Khrushchëv's precedent by visiting several foreign countries. In 1966 the USSR had brought India and Pakistan together under Kosygin's chairmanship in Tashkent to settle their recurrent conflicts. The Soviet-Indian relationship was especially warm.[17] Furthermore, Cuba remained defiantly pro-Soviet despite an American diplomatic and economic embargo, and in 1970 the Marxist coalition leader Salvador Allende came to power in Chile. In Asia, North Vietnam, fighting with Soviet military equipment, was wearing down the American-supported regime in South Vietnam. In Europe, the USSR had its successes even after the Soviet-led invasion of Czechoslovakia. As soon as Willy Brandt was elected German Chancellor in Bonn in 1969, he made overtures to the Kremlin. A treaty was signed between the USSR and the Federal Republic of Germany in the following year giving formal recognition to the separate German Democratic Republic.

Elsewhere in the non-communist world the attempts to increase Soviet power and prestige were not quite so productive. In Ghana, Kwame Nkrumah was chased from power in 1966. His departure left the USSR without friends in Africa except for Egypt. Then Egypt, too, fell away. In 1967 Soviet influence in the Middle East was undermined when Israeli forces defeated an Arab military coalition in the Six-Day War. President Nasser of Egypt died in 1970 and was succeeded by Anwar Sadat, who saw no advantage in keeping close ties with the USSR. The Soviet-Egyptian alliance rapidly collapsed. Countries of the Third World were finding that the USSR might be able to supply them adequately with military equipment but could not sustain them economically. It was increasingly understood around the globe that occasional acts of munificence such as the financing of the Aswan Dam did not generate long-term industrial and agricultural development.

Yet the campaign to increase Moscow's influence abroad was sustained. At home, furthermore, central political prerogatives were asserted. The Politburo abandoned the decentralizing experiments of Khrushchëv. In 1966 its members scrapped the sovnarkhozes. Inside the party, the Bureau of the RSFSR in the Central Committee – established by Khrushchëv – was abolished. Thus the largest republic by far in the USSR lost its co-ordinating party body. The other republics still had their own parties, central committees and first secretaries. The humbling of the RSFSR signified that no national political unit, not even the Russian, was immune to the Politburo's supra-national demands.

Accordingly, the other republics were placed under tight discipline.

Eighteen well-known Ukrainian nationalist and intellectual dissenters were brought to court in Kiev in August 1965 – a full month before the arrest of Daniel and Sinyavski in Moscow. They refused to disown their beliefs and received harsh prison sentences. Also in 1965 there was a large demonstration in Erevan, protesting about past and present injustices against the Armenian people. It was suppressed by armed force. The subsequent invasion of Czechoslovakia horrified nationalist opinion, especially in the Baltic Soviet republics and Ukraine. A student was arrested in the Estonian city of Tartu for daubing a cinema wall with the declaration: 'Czechs, we are your brothers.' But disturbances also occurred independently of the Prague events. Riots broke out in the Uzbek capital of Tashkent, in 1969. Several officials of Russian nationality were murdered before sufficient troops arrived to restore control.

In the Politburo there were lively discussions. It would seem that Alexander Shelepin and Dmitri Polyanski took the strongest line in advocating the eradication of national dissent among non-Russians. It was rumoured that Polyanski's ideas were virtually those of a Russian nationalist. On the other side there was Petro Shelest, First Secretary of the Ukrainian Central Committee, who believed that any further scouring of Ukrainian culture would open wounds that would turn the Ukrainian speakers of his republic into irretrievable opponents of a 'Soviet Ukraine'. Shelest himself had a deep sympathy for the traditions of the Cossacks.

Brezhnev steered a middle course between them. In November 1967 he called for the 'convergence' of the Soviet Union's peoples, but stressed that this would involve highly-sensitive decisions and that hastiness had to be avoided. Even so, neither Brezhnev nor even Shelest was diffident about quelling overt opposition whether it came in mass demonstrations or in poems, songs and booklets. This meant that the basic problems of a multinational state were suppressed rather than resolved. Russian nationalists resented the fact that their culture was not allowed to develop outside the distortive framework imposed by the Politburo. Among the non-Russians, nationalists resented what they perceived as the Politburo's Russian chauvinism;

their grievances were ably summarized in Ivan Dziuba's lengthy memorandum to the Ukrainian party and government, *Internationalism or Russification?*[18]

Ostensibly most republic-level communist party leaders endorsed the suppression of nationalism in the various Soviet republics. Eduard Shevardnadze, who was installed as Party First Secretary in Georgia in 1972, rhapsodized that 'the true sun rose not in the East but in the North, in Russia – the sun of Leninist ideas'. Sharaf Rashidov, the First Secretary of the Uzbekistan Communist Party, eulogized the Russian people as 'the elder brother and true friend' of the Uzbeks.[19]

When at home in Uzbekistan, Rashidov was not so self-abasing; on the contrary, he was promoting his fellow clan members into high office and ensuring that they could benefit from the perks of office without Moscow's interference. The same had been happening in Georgia under Shevardnadze's predecessor V. P. Mzhavanadze – and Shevardnadze's subsequent struggle against corruption had only limited success. Even Dinmukhammed Kunaev, First Secretary of the Kazakhstan Communist Party and boon companion of Brezhnev, covertly gave protection to emergent national aspirations. Rashidov, Mzhavanadze and Kunaev zealously locked up overt nationalist dissenters in their respective republics; but they increasingly themselves selected and organized the local élites on a national principle. Such phenomena were also on the rise in the RSFSR, whose internal autonomous republics were allowed much freedom to promote the interests of the local national majority.

The Politburo's own commitment to 'stability of cadres' contributed to the difficulties of holding together the USSR as a multinational state. Brezhnev assured officials in the party and major governmental institutions that their jobs were secure so long as they did not infringe current official policies. He wanted to avoid the enmity incurred by Khrushchëv's endless sackings of personnel; he also contended that officials needed stable working conditions if the Politburo's objectives were to be realized in the localities. Consequently Mzhavanadze's replacement by Shevardnadze was a rare direct attempt to indicate to the official leaderships of the non-Russian republics that there were limits to the Kremlin's indulgence.

A general lightness of touch was applied in the Russian provinces of the RSFSR. Leningrad Party Secretary V. S. Tolstikov was sacked in 1970. Tolstikov had drawn attention to himself as a communist arch-conservative, but the reason for his dismissal was not politics but his sexual escapades on a yacht in the Gulf of Finland.[20] Brezhnev anyway punished him gently by sending him as Soviet ambassador to Beijing. Elsewhere in the RSFSR there was bureaucratic tranquillity. Typical province-level party secretaries were either left in post or else promoted to higher party and governmental offices. Cliental systems of personnel were fortified, and local officials built their 'nests' of interests so tightly that Central Committee emissaries could seldom unravel the local scams. Brezhnev sometimes talked about the need to 'renew' the cadres of party and government; but self-interest discouraged him from putting an end to the immobilism he detected. He did not want to risk alienating lower-level officialdom.

By the end of the 1960s Politburo members were united in their broad approach. They did not abandon Khrushchëv's basic policies; but they erased his eccentricities and pencilled in what they thought to be sound alternatives. Stalin had been too brutal, Khrushchëv too erratic. They did not want to revert to the bloody fixities of the post-war years; they were glad that the unsettling reorganizations after 1953 had been terminated.

It was their assumption that such an approach would effect a successful stabilization of the Soviet order. They acted out of optimism, and still believed in the superiority of communism over its competitors. They could point to the military security and economic advance achieved since 1964. They were confident about having checked the rise of dissent and having brought the intelligentsia and the working class under control. They were not entirely hostile to experimentation in their measures at home and in Eastern Europe. But the scope for novelty was brusquely narrowed after the Warsaw Pact's invasion of Czechoslovakia. And already the Soviet leaders were becoming entangled in complications which they had not anticipated. They confronted deepening problems in politics, economics, society, culture, nationalism and international relations. Little did they know that the price of their attempt at stabilizing the Soviet order was about to be paid.

PART FOUR

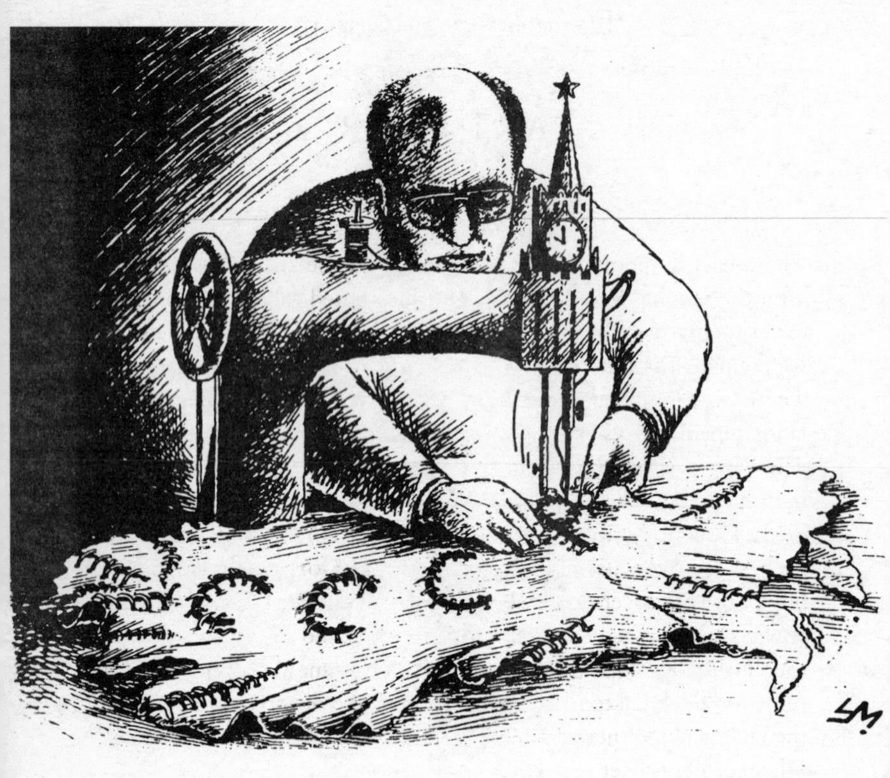

A. Umyarov in Krokodil *sees Gorbachëv as a tailor trying to stitch together the torn cloth of the USSR.*

20

'Developed Socialism' (1970–1982)

The Soviet compound, as it emerged from the successive changes after the Second World War, had only a limited capacity for radical experimentation. Brezhnev and his fellow leaders understood and welcomed this. But the problems about the compound persisted. There was political frustration and resentment throughout the USSR, including its party, government and other public institutions. There were economic set-backs. There was social alienation and national, religious and cultural embitterment. Only when Brezhnev died was there a serious reconsideration of the compound's problems. At first this was attempted cautiously. But Gorbachëv, coming to power in 1985, overlooked the internal necessities of the compound. Always he assumed that experimentation could be open ended. In the end he developed an audacious programme of comprehensive reforms which led to the dissolution of the Soviet compound and to the emergence of new forms of state and society in Russia and the other former Soviet republics.

But back in 1970, despite its growing problems, the Soviet Union was still a stable entity and was treated by the rest of the world as a permanent feature of the international landscape. Statesmen, scholars and commentators took it for granted that Soviet armed strength and political militance were too great to be ignored. The USSR had nearly reached military parity with the United States, and the Soviet economy had the world's second greatest industrial capacity and already produced more steel, oil, pig-iron, cement and even tractors than any other country.[1] British Prime Minister Harold Macmillan had trembled at the possibility that Russia's centrally-planned industry might succeed in outmatching advanced capitalist countries in other sectors of industry. The skills and equipment developed for the Soviet Army, he thought, might one day be diffused to the rest of the country's factories. Not only he but still more sceptical observers of the Soviet economy warned against underestimating the USSR's capacities.

Not everyone subscribed to this conventional wisdom. The NATO countries continued to refuse to recognize Stalin's annexation of Estonia, Latvia and Lithuania in 1940, and *émigré* groups of various nationalities continued to argue that the USSR was an illegitimate state. They exposed the repressive record from Lenin to Brezhnev. Some thought that the Soviet order would fall apart if only the Western powers would cease to make diplomatic and commercial compromises.

At any rate few people in the West had any affection for the USSR. Too much was known about the brutality and immobilism of Soviet communism for it to shine out as a beacon of political freedom and social justice. Even the Italian and Spanish communist parties abandoned their ideological fealty to Moscow and formulated doctrines hostile to dictatorship. Especially after the USSR-led invasion of Czechoslovakia in 1968, the number of admirers of Lenin was getting smaller in states not subject to communist leaderships. Moreover, changes in the Third World were steadily diminishing the international appeal of the USSR because most of the world's colonies had by then been given their independence. Meanwhile the grinding poverty widespread in several European countries, such as Spain, was being overcome: capitalism was found to be more adaptable to welfare economics than had previously been supposed possible.

Nevertheless some optimists contended that the Soviet political system could be softened and that a convergence between communism and capitalism might occur as capitalist states resorted increasingly to central economic planning and governmentally-provided welfare. This was rejected by others who asserted that basic reform was incompatible with the maintenance of the communist order. Supposedly no Politburo leader would attempt such a reform.

Certainly Brezhnev was not of a mind to undermine the party he served as General Secretary, and the development of the relationship between the USSR and the USA for several years appeared to justify his stance. As he took control of Soviet foreign policy he exchanged visits with American presidents. Richard Nixon went to Moscow in 1972 and 1974, Gerald Ford to Vladivostok in 1976. Brezhnev himself was received in New York in 1973. The Strategic Arms Limitation Talks after protracted negotiations produced an Anti-Ballistic Missiles Treaty in 1972. The trust between the two superpowers steadily increased. In order to stress that a warmer relationship than Khrushchëv's 'peaceful coexistence' had been attained, a new phrase was coined, 'détente' (in Russian, *razryadka*), which referred to the slackening of the tensions of the Cold War. Brezhnev confidently proposed to American Secretary of State Henry Kissinger that the two superpowers could maintain a global condominium if they had the sense to reinforce détente.

Moreover, not all events elsewhere in the world were unfavourable to Soviet interests. The Kremlin's resolve was strengthened in 1970 when the coalition led by the communist Salvador Allende acceded to power in Chile. When Ethiopia, too, had a revolution in 1974, military equipment was supplied from Moscow; and the Portuguese Empire's disintegration in Africa gave the USSR and its Cuban ally a further opportunity to intervene in civil wars in Angola and Mozambique. At successive Party Congresses Brezhnev asserted the USSR's willingness to support struggles for national liberation in Asia, Africa and South America.

The USA meanwhile suffered from the demoralizing effects of its unsuccessful war in Vietnam, even after the withdrawal of its troops in 1973. In the same year the American economy was buffeted by the decision of the Organization of Petroleum-Exporting Countries (OPEC) to introduce a massive rise in the price of oil. All advanced capitalist economies suffered from this; but the USSR, despite not having influenced OPEC's decision, gained enormous revenues from her energy exports outside Eastern Europe. Undoubtedly the USA's *rapprochement* with the People's Republic of China in the early 1970s caused a tremor among Soviet policy-makers. Yet even this event had its positive aspect. Politburo members were able to see the Americans' need for Chinese support as proof of the relative decline of the USA as a superpower. Soviet General Secretary and American President bargained as equals at their summits.

Nevertheless the USA extracted concessions from the USSR. Military and economic deals with Moscow were made dependent on the Politburo allowing Soviet Jews to emigrate if they so desired. Such would-be emigrants became known in the West as the refuseniks on account of their having been refused permission to emigrate on the grounds that they had had previous access to secret information vital to the state's interests; a quarter of a million of them left the USSR under Brezhnev's rule. The Western powers also sought to place limits on the regime's oppression of Soviet citizens in general. In 1975 the Helsinki Final Act was signed as the culmination of several years of negotiations to settle Europe's post-war territorial boundaries and to make provision for economic and scientific co-operation between West and East. The Final Act's commitment to the free passage of information was to prove a valuable instrument for dissenters in the Soviet Union to embarrass the Politburo.

For the USA and the USSR, much as they wanted to eliminate the danger of nuclear war, remained rivals. Intensive development of weaponry continued in both countries. In 1977 the Soviet Union stationed its newly-tested SS-20 missiles in Eastern Europe, missiles which had a capacity to attack Western Europe. The USA reacted by setting up facilities for the basing of Cruise missiles in the United Kingdom and West Germany and for the introduction of Pershing missiles to West Germany. The danger and costliness of all this were evident to politicians in Moscow and Washington, who simultaneously aimed at achieving agreement in the second stage of the Strategic Arms Limitation Talks, known by the acronym SALT 2. By 1979 it looked as though the negotiators had elaborated a draft that would be acceptable to both sides.

The expansion of the USSR's global influence served to enhance Brezhnev's personal authority in the Politburo. In agricultural policy he reinforced the conventional methods for organizing the collective farms. The central imposition of quotas of output was maintained, and instructions on what to sow and when came to the villages from Moscow. The policy of amalgamating farms was prolonged by Brezhnev, who shared with Khrushchëv a belief that bigger kolkhozes would increase productivity. At the same time Brezhnev insisted that agriculture should have a massive increase in the government's financial support. Collective farms in the 1970s received twenty-seven per cent of all state investment – and even this figure did not include the revenues being channelled into the production of tractors, chemical fertilizers and other farm equipment. In 1981 the budgetary allocation constituted the 'highest food-and-agriculture subsidy known in human history', amounting to 33,000 million dollars at the contemporary official exchange rate.[2]

Gross agricultural output by 1980 was twenty-one per cent higher than the average for 1966–70. Cereal crops in particular rose by eighteen per cent in the same period.[3] This allowed Brezhnev to bask in the praise heaped upon him. On closer inspection, the improved results were not encouraging. The usual criterion for assessing the effectiveness of Soviet agriculture had been and still was the grain harvest. In fact the imports of cereals, which had been started by Khrushchëv, had become a regular phenomenon. When it became difficult to seal commercial deals with the USA in 1974, the USSR's foreign-trade officials began to make hole-in-the-corner purchases in Argentina and elsewhere. This was necessary because Soviet domestic production was severely deficient in fodder crops. There were also problems in other important sectors; for instance, the sugar-beet harvest, far from rising, declined by two per cent in the decade prior to 1980.

Brezhnev's attempted solution was to increase state investment. Reform-minded central party functionaries were cowed by the fate of Politburo member G. I. Voronov. For years Voronov had advocated the division of each farm work-force into 'links' or teams which would be entrusted with specific functions. A link might, for instance, run a farm's dairy unit. Voronov's argument was that work-forces were so vast that individual kolkhozniki felt little sense of responsibility for the work on the farm. Accordingly, the link system, accompanied by suitable material incentives, would introduce conscientiousness and lead to an expansion of output. This proposal had been put to Stalin unsuccessfully by A. A. Andreev in the 1940s and had been opposed by Khrushchëv both before and after Stalin's death. Voronov was equally ineffective in trying to convince Brezhnev about the need for such a reform. Indeed Brezhnev removed Voronov from the Politburo in April 1973.

Experimentation with agricultural links was not totally disallowed on a local basis (and among the party officials who tried them out was the young Stavropol Region Party Secretary, Mikhail Gorbachëv). Yet central policy was otherwise unimaginative and incompetent. In 1976 the Politburo issued a resolution 'On the Further Development of Specialization and Concentration of Agricultural Production on the Basis of Inter-Farm Co-operation and Agro-Industrial Integration'. The resolution called for several kolkhozes in a given district to combine their efforts in production; it was therefore not a cure but a prescription for aggravated difficulties by virtue of adding yet another administrative layer to agricultural management. Meanwhile the state's food-and-agriculture subsidy did not prevent many kolkhozes from operating at a loss; for although the prices paid for farming produce were raised, the costs charged for fuel and machinery also rose. Oil, for example, cost eighty-four per cent more in 1977 than in the late 1960s – and the price of certain types of seed-drills more than doubled.[4]

Agricultural policy was therefore very confused, and in such a situation Khrushchëv would probably have made yet another assault on the private plots of kolkhozniki. Brezhnev was not so misguided, but instead in 1977 and 1981 issued two decrees to expand the maximum size of each plot to half a hectare. These measures removed a large obstacle to the expansion of agricultural output. Under Brezhnev the private plots yielded thirty per cent of total production while constituting only four per cent of the USSR's cultivated area.

Both ideological tradition and political interests impeded Politburo members from recognizing this as proof that de-collectivization was essential to an expansion of agricultural production. They were so nervous about private plots that the 1977 decree was withheld from publication for a whole year.[5] The underlying problems therefore lay unresolved: the shortage of skilled labour; the wrecked rural culture; the payment of farmworkers by quantity of work without regard to its quality; the roadless countryside; the central imposition of quotas for planting, harvesting and procurement; the technology and machinery too large for their functions on Soviet farms; the memory of the horrors of collectivization from the late 1920s. Apart from throwing money at the problems, Brezhnev could only propose grandiose schemes of land reclamation, irrigation and of river diversion. He listened to flattering advisers who deflected attention from any endeavour to address those underlying problems.

At the same time he eased his leading opponents out of high office. Not only Voronov but also Shelest were discarded in 1973. Shelepin at last went the same way in 1975. Each had had disagreements about policy with Brezhnev and eventually paid a personal price. The forced retirement of rivals continued. Membership of the Politburo was withdrawn from D. S. Polyanski in 1976, Nikolai Podgorny in 1977 and K. T. Mazurov in 1978. The long-serving Chairman of the Council of Ministers, Aleksei Kosygin, resigned because of ill-health in 1980. Meanwhile Brezhnev had been recruiting associates to fill the empty seats. Dinamukhammed Kunaev and Volodymyr Shcherbytskiy became full members of the Politburo in 1971, Konstantin Chernenko in 1978 and Nikolai Tikhonov in 1979 (and Tikhonov took over the Council of Ministers at Kosygin's departure). Their claim to preference was the accident of having worked amicably with Brezhnev in Dnepropetrovsk, Moldavia and Kazakhstan between the 1930s and 1950s. The Politburo was being remade in the General Secretary's image.

Brezhnev was extolled as a dynamic leader and intellectual colossus. The removal of Podgorny enabled him to occupy the additional post of Chairman of the Presidium of the USSR Supreme Soviet and thereby become head of state. When Kosygin died in December 1980, *Pravda* postponed the reporting of the news until after the celebration of Brezhnev's birthday. In May 1976 he had been made Marshal of the Soviet Union. In 1979 he published three volumes of ghost-written memoirs which treated minor battles near Novorossisk as the decisive military theatre of the Second World War; and his account of the virgin lands campaign of the 1950s barely mentioned Khrushchëv.

The growing cult of Brezhnev was outrageously at variance with actuality. His physical condition was deteriorating. He was addicted to sleeping pills; he drank far too much of the Belorussian 'Zubrovka' spirit and smoked heavily; to his embarrassment, he was also greatly overweight.[6] From 1973 his central nervous system underwent chronic deterioration, and he had several serious strokes.[7] At the successive ceremonies to present him with Orders of Lenin, Brezhnev walked shakily and fumbled his words. Yevgeni Chazov, Minister of Health, had to keep doctors in the vicinity of the General Secretary at all times: Brezhnev was brought back from clinical death on several occasions. The man in the East whose finger was supposed to be on the nuclear-war button inside the Soviet black box was becoming a helpless geriatric case. He was frequently incapable of rudimentary consecutive thought even in those periods when he was not convalescing.

His cronies had cynically decided that it suited them to keep Brezhnev alive and in post. The careers of Chernenko, Tikhonov and others might suffer if Brezhnev were to pass away. Even several Politburo members who were not friends of his – Central Committee Secretary Suslov, Defence Minister Ustinov and Foreign Minister Gromyko – feared the uncertainties of any struggle to succeed him. Such figures also recognized that their unhappiness with the General Secretary's policies impinged only on secondary matters. Brezhnev's Lazarus-like returns from physical oblivion allowed them to hold in place the policies agreed in the second half of the previous decade.

The central political leadership had turned into a gerontocracy. By 1980 the average age of the Politburo was sixty-nine years.[8] Each member, surrounded with toadying assistants, wanted an old age upholstered by material comfort and unimpeded power. The idea of preparing a younger generation of politicians to take over the state leadership was distasteful to them. Fifty-year-old Konstantin Katushev was demoted from the Central Committee Secretariat in 1977 and his promising career was nipped in the bud. Grigori Romanov had become a full member of the Politburo at the age of fifty-three in 1976; Mikhail Gorbachëv did the same when he was forty-nine in 1980. But these were exceptions to the norm. Brezhnev's Politburo was composed mainly of Stalin's ageing promotees. Their fundamental attitudes to politics and economics had been formed before 1953. They were proud of the Soviet order and present achievements. Change was anathema to them.

Already in 1969 there had been an attempt by Brezhnev and a majority of Politburo members to rehabilitate Stalin's reputation. They were not proposing a reversion to the terror of the 1930s and 1940s; but as they grew old in office, their unpleasant memory grew dimmer and they became nostalgic about their own contribution to the glorious past. It would seem that whereas Shelepin had hoped to use Stalin as a symbol for the robust restoration of order, Brezhnev and his friends wanted to use him more as the personification of the USSR's achievements in industrialization in the early 1930s and in victory in the Second World War. Only strenuous representations to the Politburo by foreign communist parties brought about a last-minute reversal of the decision on Stalin's rehabilitation.[9]

Nevertheless the Politburo still had to supply citizens with its analysis of the country's current condition. The favoured terms were 'really existing socialism', 'real socialism', 'mature socialism' and 'developed socialism'.[10] Really existing socialism was too wordy. Real socialism invited an undesirable comparison with surrealist socialism; mature socialism sounded altogether too decrepit a note. And so from 1966 the propagandists increasingly claimed that the country had entered the stage of 'developed socialism'. This term, while avoiding the over-optimism of Khrushchëv's Party Programme, highlighted achievements already made and objectives yet to be attained. The authorities looked back with pride on the October Revolution, the Five-Year Plans and the Second World War; they anticipated a future involving an incremental improvement of living standards, of technology and of social and political integration throughout the USSR.

Developed socialism was a term used in Brezhnev's opening report to the Twenty-Fourth Party Congress in March 1971. In a purple passage he declared: 'Accounting for its work in this very important direction of activity, the Central Committee of the Party has every justification to say that the Soviet people, having worthily completed the Eighth Five-Year Plan, has taken a new great step forward in the creation of the material-technical base of communism, in the reinforcement of the country's might and in the raising of the standard of living of the people.'[11]

His report offered an agenda for step-by-step improvement; and as the concept was elaborated in later years, the Politburo acknowledged that developed socialism would constitute a 'historically protracted period'. A tacit indication was being given that roughly the same kind of state order would prevail for the duration of the lives of Soviet citizens. In the course of the construction of a communist society as projected by Khrushchëv there was no scheme for the party to become obsolete; the party was even more crucial to Brezhnevite developed socialism. Article 6 of the Soviet Constitution, which was introduced in 1977, announced: 'The leading and guiding force of Soviet society and the nucleus of its political system, its state organizations and public organizations is the Communist Party of the Soviet Union.' Stalin's 1936 Constitution had mentioned the party's authority only in relation to electoral arrangements. The USSR had always been a one-party state; but the new Article 6 gave the most formal validation to this reality to date.[12]

Not even Brezhnev entirely stopped calling for higher levels of participation by ordinary members of society in public life or talking about a future communist society. But his statements on such topics were ritualistic verbiage. He was much more serious when he stressed the need for hierarchy and planning. The party, under the Politburo's leadership, would formulate the policies and give the guidance. Society's main duty was to supply the orderly obedience.

A 'scientific-technical revolution' would be accomplished, and central state planning would prove its superior rationality. Official theorists stressed that already the USSR outmatched capitalism in bettering the human condition. The Soviet state guaranteed employment, health care, shelter, clothing and pensions; and citizens were brought up to respect the general interests of society and to avoid selfish individualism. Not that the USSR's leaders wanted to be seen as complacent. There was a recognition that the Soviet economy had fallen behind the advanced capitalist countries in civilian technology. It was also admitted that much needed to be done to meet the material aspirations of ordinary consumers and that the political organs of the Soviet state, including the party, had to become more responsive to the people's wishes. Indeed there had to be a perfecting of all mechanisms of governance and welfare. 'Developed socialism' had to be brought to its triumphant maturity.

No basic novelty in industrial and agricultural measures was contemplated. The options were limited by the Politburo's diversion of massive resources to the state food-subsidy and to the nuclear arms race. But the very word reform caused most Soviet leaders to shudder. After the defeat of Kosygin's endeavour to widen managerial freedom in 1965, no one tried to pick up his banner.

Although the 1970s were a lost decade for potential reformers, however, not everything was static. Not quite. The Ninth Five-Year Plan was the first to project a slightly higher rate of increase in the output of industrial consumer products than of industrial capital goods. Watches, furniture and radios were at last meant to be manufactured in abundance. Yet the Plan still left the predominant bulk of investment at the disposal of capital-goods production. And in practice the economic ministries and the rest of the party-police-military-industrial complex managed to prevent the Plan's consumer-oriented investment projects from being fully realized.[13] By 1975, for example, consumer goods had expanded at a rate nine per cent slower than capital goods.[14] This thwarting of the Politburo's policy continued throughout the decade despite Brezhnev's reaffirmation of his commitment to the rapid shift of investment towards satisfying the needs of Soviet consumers at both the Twenty-Fifth Party Congress in February 1976 and the Twenty-Sixth Congress in February 1981.

And so only the most minuscule steps were taken in the modification of policy. In 1973 a decree was issued to draw factories with complementary activities into 'associations' (*ob"edineniya*). The idea was that enterprises would be enabled to serve each other's needs without resort to permission from Gosplan and the ministries in Moscow. Associations were also expected to operate on a self-financing basis and recurrent deficits in their accounts were no longer to be tolerated. By 1980 there were 4,083 associations in the USSR, producing slightly over a half of total industrial output. Yet self-financing was never fully realized. An experiment along these lines had been started at the Shchëkino Chemical Association as early as 1967; yet the reluctance of the central authorities to abandon control over decisions on investment, prices, wages and hiring and firing had condemned it to a fitful performance.

In 1979 another general decree on industry was issued which emphasized the need for scientific planning and for the avoidance of deficits in annual factory accounts. But this yielded miserable results. Soviet economic trends became ever more depressing. The contemporary official statistics gave a different impression: industrial output was still said to have risen by 4.4 per cent per annum in 1976–80. Yet even these statistics indicated a steady decrease in the rate of expansion. The supposed annual rise in 1966–70 had been 8.5 per cent.

In fact the official statistics took no account of the inflation disguised by the trick of slightly altering products and then selling them at higher prices. The statistics also hid the plight of manufacturing industry in comparison with extractive industry. Unwittingly the oil-producing Arab states had rescued the Soviet budget in 1973 by increasing the world-market prices for oil. The USSR was a major exporter of oil, petrol and gas. The reality was that the country, so far from catching up with the advanced capitalist West, was as reliant upon the sales abroad of its natural resources as it had been before 1917; and, in contrast with the tsarist period, it could no longer find a grain surplus for shipment to the rest of Europe. There can as yet be no exact statement of the percentage of industrial growth achieved. The sceptics suggest that no growth at all occurred. Be that as it may, nobody denies that by the end of the 1970s chronic absolute decline was in prospect.

The Politburo's modifications were still more pathetic in other sectors of the economy. No fresh thinking was applied to banking, insurance, transport, personal services, construction or foreign trade. Policy was so motionless that it was rarely a topic for glancing comment in *Pravda* or even in the scholarly economic journals. The claims that, by avoiding Khrushchëv's utopianism, the USSR could make steady economic advance were being tested and found wanting.

Only very dimly were Brezhnev and his colleagues aware that doing nothing was a recipe for political disaster. If they needed proof of the regime's vulnerability, they had only to look to the country adjacent to the Soviet western border. Poland was seething with working-class opposition. Strikes and demonstrations occurred in the Gdansk shipyards in 1970 under the leadership of Lech Wałesa. Repression worked only briefly: by 1976 the authority of the Polish government was again being challenged. Other countries in Eastern Europe were also restless. Yugoslavia and Romania recurrently criticized the Soviet communist leadership. Albania did the same and reaffirmed her support for the People's Republic of China. But what could Brezhnev and his colleagues do about anti-Soviet developments in Eastern Europe? The Politburo had no principled objection to the project of a Warsaw Pact invasion, but the experience of Czechoslovakia since 1968 showed that military occupation was not a solution in itself.

Problems also persisted about the potential for working-class unrest in the USSR. Since the Novocherkassk rebellion of 1962 the Politburo had feared lest the 'party of the workers' should be challenged by the Russian working class. Central party leaders concluded that timely concessions, if necessary, should always be made; and Brezhnev, while not espousing egalitarianism in wages policy, sanctioned a narrowing of formal differentials. He also ensured that blue-collar workers were paid better than several professional groups. For example, a bus driver in the 1970s earned 230 roubles, a secondary schoolteacher 150 roubles.[15]

Brezhnev wanted workers to be materially comfortable; and although the investment in the industrial consumer-goods sector fell behind projections, the expansion in output was enough to improve the conditions of ordinary people. Refrigerators were owned by thirty-two per cent of households in 1970 and by eighty-six per cent in 1980. Ownership of televisions rose from fifty-one to seventy-four per cent in the same decade.[16] Trade unions opened further holiday centres for their members on the Baltic and Black Sea coasts. Trusted workers could travel on officially-organized trips to Eastern Europe and, if they were extremely lucky, to the West. Prices in the shops for staple products such as bread, potatoes, meat and clothing, as well as apartment rents and gas were held low, indeed barely higher than they had been during the First Five-Year Plan. Workers had never known it so good. Nor had the kolkhozniki; for the state pension system had been extended to them in 1964 and they were given internal passports from 1975.[17]

The Politburo also had to appeal to the middling groups in society. A persistent source of their dissatisfaction were those remaining aspects of official educational policy which provided sons and daughters of workers with preferential access to university education. The Politburo abolished all such discrimination. In the same spirit, measures were introduced to move away from Khrushchëv's highly vocational orientation in the schools. The economic ministries and even many factory directors came to feel that the pendulum was swinging too far in the opposite direction; but, after a spirited debate, only a halfway return towards vocational training in schools was sanctioned in 1977.[18]

Yet the Politburo was failing to maintain active support in society even at previous levels. It therefore sought to intensify the recruitment of communist party members. In 1966 there had been 12.4 million rank-and-filers; by 1981 this had risen to 17.4 million.[19] Thus nearly one in ten Soviet adults were party members. Their assigned duty was to inspire and mobilize the rest of society. The idea was that the more members, the better the chance to secure universal acquiescence in the status quo. As ever, the result was not a compact political vanguard but a party which reflected the diverse problems of broad social groups. Politburo leaders contrived to overlook the problem. For them, the dangers of further change outweighed the risks of keeping things as they were. Indeed the contemplation of change would have required a concentration of intellectual faculties that hardly any of them any longer possessed. And those few, such as Andropov, who had even mildly unorthodox ideas kept quiet about them.

Despite being inclined towards caution in domestic affairs, they were still tempted to undertake risky operations abroad. In 1978–9 they had been disconcerted by the course of a civil war in Afghanistan across the USSR's southern frontier. Afghan communists repeatedly asked the Soviet leadership to intervene militarily; but Brezhnev and his associates, sobered by the knowledge of the mauling meted out to the USA in Vietnam, rejected their pleas;[20] and Jimmy Carter, who had assumed office as American President in 1977, saw this as evidence that détente was a force for good throughout the world.

In December 1979, however, the Politburo's inner core decided that failure to support Afghan communist forces would leave the way open for the USA to strengthen the military position of their Islamist adversaries. Soviet Army contingents were sent from Tajikistan to support the communist-led Afghan regime. President Carter felt deceived by the USSR, and ordered a substantial rise in the USA's military expenditure. The policy of détente collapsed. In 1980, Moscow's troubles increased when the Polish independent trade union Solidarity led strikes against the government in Warsaw. Poland was becoming virtually ungovernable, and in December 1981 General Wojciech Jaruzelski, who was already the Party First Secretary and Prime Minister, obtained the USSR's sanction to mount a *coup d'état* to restore order. The eventual alternative, as Jaruzelski understood, would be that Warsaw Pact forces would invade Poland. But Solidarity, though damaged, did not crumble. Deep fissures were beginning to open in the communist order of Eastern Europe.

The Soviet Union's international position was shaken further when Ronald Reagan, the Republican Party's right-wing candidate, defeated Carter in the American presidential elections in 1980. The Politburo was put on notice to expect a more challenging attitude on the part of the USA. Domestic and foreign policies which had seemed adequate in the 1970s were about to be put to their stiffest test.

21

Privilege and Alienation

The Soviet political leaders did not feel insecure in power. There were occasional acts of subversion, such as the detonation of a bomb in the Moscow Metro by Armenian nationalists in 1977. But such terrorism was not only rare; it was also usually carried out by nationalists on the territory of their own republics. Russians, however hostile they were to the Politburo, had an abiding horror of political upheaval. Civil war, inter-ethnic struggles and terror were the stuff not of medieval folklore but of stories told by grandparents and even fathers and mothers.

The KGB's repressive skills remained at the ready. In 1970 the biologist and dissenter Zhores Medvedev was locked up in a lunatic asylum. Only the timely intervention of his twin brother Roy and others, including Andrei Sakharov and Alexander Solzhenitsyn, secured his release.[1] Human-rights activist Viktor Krasin and the Georgian nationalist Zviad Gamsakhurdia were arrested, and they cracked under the KGB's pressure on them to renounce their dissenting opinions. Another method was employed against the young poet Iosif Brodski. Since his works were banned from publication and he had no paid occupation, the KGB took him into custody and in 1964 he was tried on a charge of 'parasitism'. In 1972, after being vilified in the press, he was deported. Solzhenitsyn, too, was subjected to involuntary emigration in 1974. Vladimir Bukovski suffered the same fate a year later in exchange for imprisoned Chilean communist leader Luis Corvalan. In 1980 Sakharov was subjected to an order confining him to residence in Gorki, a city which it was illegal for foreigners to visit.

Yet the members of the various clandestine groups appreciated the uses of publicity. Within a year of the signature of the Helsinki Final Act in 1975, informal 'Helsinki groups' in the USSR were drawing the world's attention to the Soviet government's infringements of its undertakings. Western politicians and diplomats picked up the cause of the dissenters at summit meetings; Western journalists interviewed leading critics of the Politburo – and, to the KGB's annoyance, several writers let their works appear abroad. The Soviet government did not dare to stop either Solzhenitsyn in 1970 or Sakharov in 1975 from accepting their Nobel Prizes.

Three figures stood out among the dissenters in Russia: Sakharov, Solzhenitsyn and Roy Medvedev. Each had achieved prominence after Stalin's death and had tried to persuade Khrushchëv that basic reforms were essential. Initially they were not recalcitrant rebels; on the contrary, they were persons promoted by the political establishment: they did not seek confrontation. But all eventually concluded that compromise with the Politburo would not work. They were unique and outstanding individuals who could not be broken by the weight of material and psychological pressures that were brought to bear upon them. But they were also typical dissenters of the 1970s. In particular, they shared the characteristic of deriving a spiritual forcefulness from their acceptance of their precarious living and working conditions; they had the advantage of truly believing what they said or wrote, and were willing to endure the punishments inflicted by the state.

They gained also from the country's traditions of respect for relatives, friends and colleagues. Before 1917, peasants, workers and intellectuals kept a wall of confidentiality between a group's members and the 'powers', as they referred to anyone in official authority over them. Russians were not unique in this. All the peoples of the Russian Empire had coped with oppressive administrators in this way. The informal ties of the group were reinforced in the Soviet period as a defence against the state's intrusiveness, and the dissenters latched on to the traditions.

What Sakharov, Medvedev and Solzhenitsyn had in common was that they detested Stalin's legacy and knew that Brezhnev's Politburo had not entirely abandoned it. But on other matters their ideas diverged. Sakharov had contended in the late 1960s that the world's communist and capitalist systems were converging into a hybrid of both. But steadily he moved towards a sterner assessment of the USSR and, being committed to the rights of the individual, he saw democracy as the first means to this end.[2] This attitude was uncongenial to Medvedev, a radical communist reformer who argued that there was nothing inherently wrong with the Leninism enunciated by Lenin himself.[3] By contrast, Solzhenitsyn put his faith in specifically Christian values and Russian national customs. Solzhenitsyn's nuanced anti-Leninism gave way to strident attacks not only on communism but also on virtually every variety of socialism and liberalism. He even rehabilitated the record of the last tsars.[4] Thus he infuriated Sakharov and Medvedev in equal measure.

By 1973 these disputes were ruining their fellowship, and the situation was not improved by the differential treatment of dissenters by the authorities. Sakharov had once received privileges as a nuclear scientist. The fact that he and his wife had an austere life-style did not save them from Solzhenitsyn's carping comments, at least until Sakharov and his wife were dispatched into exile to the city of Gorki. Of the three leading dissenters, it was Medvedev who received the lightest persecution. His detractors claimed that although the security police pilfered his manuscripts, he had defenders in the central party leadership who felt that the time might come when his brand of reformist communism would serve the state's interests.

Yet the efforts of the dissenters at co-ordination were insubstantial. The Moscow-based groups had some contact with the Jewish refuseniks in the capital; but they had little connection with the clandestine national organizations in Ukraine, the Transcaucasus or the Baltic region. And when in 1977 Vladimir Klebanov founded a Free Trade Union Association, he and his fellow unionists conducted their activities almost entirely in isolation from the intellectual dissenters. Few ordinary citizens had copies of their samizdat works. Occasionally it looked as if the KGB, by focusing efforts upon them, unnecessarily increased their significance. This was true to some extent. But the USSR was an authoritarian ideocracy; any failure to extirpate heterodoxy would be taken as a sign of weakness. The snag was that Brezhnev was not Stalin, and understood that persuasion to support the regime would not be effective if persecution were to be increased.

Key ideas of the dissenters continue to leech into the minds of many thousands of citizens. Some heard the ideas on Radio Liberty, the BBC World Service or the Voice of America in the periods when foreign radio stations ceased to be jammed. Others in Estonia could pick up and understand Finnish television. Still others knew people who knew people who had read the original works in samizdat. Having refrained from killing the leaders of dissent, the Politburo had to live with the consequence that their ideas could not be kept wholly in quarantine.

The dissenters probably had less impact on opinion in society than critics of the regime who stayed on the right side of the KGB. In the literary journals a host of writers appeared. In Russia, Vladimir Soloukhin and Valentin Rasputin wrote about the ruination of agriculture and village life. Vasil Bykaw did the same in Belorussia. Despite recurrent disagreements with the party, all of them successfully demanded respect for the pre-revolutionary customs and beliefs. Such writers were known as the 'ruralists' (*derevenshchiki*).[5] Some of them involved themselves in public debates on ecology. They were joined by the Kyrgyz novelist Chingiz Aitmatov, who described the ravaging of nature and traditional culture in central Asia. Nor was it only living writers whose arguments against the designs of communism had an influence. Classics of Russian literature, such as Fëdor Dostoevski's novels, continued to provide material for a strong critique of Marxism-Leninism.[6]

In every branch of the arts it was the same. The film directors Andrei Tarkovski and Tengiz Abuladze; the science-fiction writers Arkadi and Boris Strugatski; the musical composer Alfred Schnittke; the sculptor Ernst Neizvestny; the theatre director and performer Vladimir Vysotski: none of them belonged to the groups of overt dissent, but their works offered an alternative way of assessing Soviet reality. And they had a depth of analysis and emotion greater than most of the artists whom Khrushchëv had promoted to eminence.

There was resentment among natural scientists, too, about their working conditions. Distinguished physicists queued up in the Academy of Sciences Library in Leningrad to read copies of the London scientific weekly *Nature* with the advertisements cut out (which meant that crucial bits of articles on the other side of the excised pages were removed).[7] Even more strictly supervised were historians, economists and political scientists. Politburo member Suslov kept a sharp eye on them and punished delinquents with demotion: his favourite sanction was to transfer them to a pedagogical institute and stop their books from being published. He also interviewed the novelist Vasili Grossman about the manuscript of his *Life and Fate*, which exposed both the dictatorial essence of Leninism as well as the anti-Semitism of Stalin's policies. Suslov predicted that the novel would not be printed for 300 years. (As things turned out, his prophecy was wildly wrong because *Life and Fate* was published in 1989.)

Although professional people were fed up with the humiliating customs of subordination, they usually complied with the summons to cast their votes in favour of single candidates from a single party in Soviet elections: any failure to do this would attract unpleasant attention from the KGB. For similar reasons it was difficult to refuse to join the Communist Party of the Soviet Union if invited. By the late 1970s approximately forty-four per cent of 'the party' was constituted by white-collar employees.[8]

Thus the state was regarded with suspicion by practically everybody and lying and cheating remained a popularly approved mode of behaviour. The fish rotted from the head. Brezhnev was a cynic and his family was corrupt. But even if he had been a communist idealist, he would have had no remedy. The old problems remained. In order to fulfil the quotas assigned by the Five-Year Plan, factories still needed to bend regulations. Skilled workers still had to be paid more than was centrally intended. Unskilled sections of the labour-force still had to be indulged in relation to punctuality, conscientiousness and sobriety. The flitting of workers from one job to another was an ineradicable feature in industry; the absence of unemployment meant that the state had no serious counter-measure. Factories, mines and offices were staffed by salaried and waged personnel who put greater effort into the protection of their indolence than into the discharge of their duties. A work-shy attitude was characteristic of both administrators and workers.

The Politburo was given no credit for the material improvements secured in the 1970s, and the cheap provision of food, shelter, clothing, sanitation, health care and transport was taken for granted. Brezhnev's successes were noted more for their limitations than their progress beyond the performance before 1964. He earned neither affection nor respect.

Soviet citizens concentrated on getting what enjoyment they could out of their private lives. Families operated as collective foragers in an urban wilderness. Turning up at a restaurant was seldom enough unless a booking had been made or a bribe been offered. And so Granny was dispatched to queue for hours in the ill-stocked food shop; young Yevgeni missed a morning at the pedagogical institute to dig the potatoes at the family dacha; and Dad (or 'Papa') took a set of spanners he had acquired from the factory and swapped them for an acquaintance's armchair. The people who carried the greatest burden were the women. Years of propaganda had not bettered their lot even though many had entered occupations once reserved for men. Wives were simply expected to do their new job while also fulfilling the traditional domestic duties. It was not a sexual liberation but a heavier form of patriarchy.

Consequently Soviet citizens, while remaining resolutely slack at work, had to be indefatigable in obtaining alleviation of their living conditions. They had no other option even if they aimed only to semi-prosper. They had to become very enterprising. Each looked after himself or herself and relatives and close friends. On the inside, this collectivistic society fostered extreme individualism.

When all was said and done, however, ordinary Russians could only make the best of a bad situation. They were powerless to effect a general change. Rates of alcoholism, mental illness, divorce and suicide went on rising inexorably. The deterioration of the physical environment continued; diseases were on the increase and hospital services worsened. The living space accorded to the normal urban family remained cramped: just 13.4 square metres per person in 1980.[9] Thousands of Moscow inhabitants had no resident permits, and many of them inhabited shacks, doorways and parked trams. The diet of most citizens, furthermore, ceased to improve in the late 1970s. Rationing of staple food products returned to Sverdlovsk (which was then under the rule of local party secretary Boris Yeltsin) and several other large cities.[10]

Not surprisingly the society of the USSR turned a flinty eye upon the propagandists sent out by party organizations. Attitudes had changed a lot since Stalin had claimed that 'life is getting gayer'. An anecdote illustrates the point neatly. A young woman was seized by the burly militiamen next to Lenin's Mausoleum for distributing a pamphlet of protest. The pamphlet was discovered to be full of blank pages. Asked to explain herself, the woman replied: 'Why bother writing? Everybody knows!'

Marxism-Leninism had never become the world-view of most citizens. The authorities knew this from the reportage on popular opinion delivered by the KGB. In the 1960s they were sufficiently worried that they allowed random-sample social surveys to be undertaken and published despite the ban on sociology as a subject in institutions of higher education. The results were troubling to the Ideological Department of the Party Central Committee Secretariat. In Moscow, according to the results of a questionnaire, only one in eleven propagandists believed that their audiences had absorbed the Marxist-Leninist content of lectures as their personal convictions. Nor did it help that many propagandists carried out their duties with obvious reluctance. For example, forty per cent of those polled in Belorussia gave talks or lectures only as a party obligation.[11] This was a problem stretching back to the 1920s. Fifty years on, it had not been solved.

Politburo member Suslov had played a prominent part in the mummification of the notions of Marx, Engels and Lenin; but even Suslov did not stand in the way of Marxism-Leninism's retreat from earlier standpoints. The natural sciences were freed to a somewhat greater extent from ideological interference. Researchers continued to suffer impediments and indignities since contacts with foreign colleagues remained difficult. Yet at least they were no longer compelled to accept a single official party-approved version of biology, chemistry and physics.

In the social sciences, which in Russia includes philosophy and literature as well as history, party control was tighter. Lenin's interpretations of the literary classics were compulsory ingredients of scholarship; and, although historical accounts of the Assyrian Empire could be published with merely cursory mention of Marxism, the same was not true about the history of Russia – and especially the decades of Soviet rule. No subject was more jealously guarded from heterodoxy than the theory and practice of the communist party. From one end of the telescope it appeared that extraordinary concessions were being made to non-Marxist opinion. But from the other end things looked different: sceptics were less impressed by the licence gained by Assyriologists than by the unchallengeability of the official party historians who affirmed that, from 1917 to the present day, the party leadership had largely avoided error. Anything new written about Assurbanipal mattered a thousand times less than the fixed catechism about Lenin.

This was indeed a contradictory situation. On the one hand, Marxism-Leninism's self-restrictions signalled a diminishing official confidence. On the other, Suslov and his subordinate ideologists were eradicating any surviving liveliness in interpretations of Lenin, the October Revolution, Soviet history and current official policies. The authorities had given up ground to its critics, but made a bitter defence of the remaining ideological terrain.

Even Lenin's books were handled with caution. The fifty-five volumes of the fifth edition of his collected works had been brought to completion in 1965. But in the late 1970s an unpublicized official ban was placed on the sale of the edition in second-hand bookshops.[12] Many of Lenin's statements were at variance with many of the party's contemporary doctrines. Consequently the authorities preferred to use excerpts from his writings, carefully chosen to fit in with Brezhnev's policies. It was a funny old Leninist world where Lenin had become a suspect author. Yet only a few Russians bothered about this paradox since Lenin's writings were abundantly available at least in some fashion or another. This was not true of thousands of authors who still attracted unconditional disapproval; and the regime had not abandoned its key dogmas on politics, economy and society.

The systematic curtailment of information affected even the pettiest aspects of daily life. KGB operatives were attached to harmless groups of tourists visiting the West, and the card-indexed files of the security organs bulged with reports by its unpaid informers as well as by its own officials. Not even telephone directories were on sale, but were held behind the counter of 'information kiosks' – and the employees in these kiosks were not permitted to tell the ordinary enquirer the phone number of foreign embassies. What is more, the Politburo dedicated large financial resources to the development of the technology of control. The KGB's bugging devices were especially sophisticated. At the same time Soviet citizens were prevented from acquiring equipment that might enable them to pass information among themselves without official permission. Walky-talky radios, photocopiers and word-processing computers were not purchasable in the shops.

These barriers to communication, however, were only partially effective. Citizens had their own direct experience of Soviet history and politics, and were in an excellent position to pass private judgement on the words of party propagandists. Hardly a family existed without relatives who had been killed in Stalin's time. And everyone could remember the boasts made by successive rulers. After decades in power it was hard for the Politburo to claim that the country's problems were not the party's fault to a decisive extent.

And so this most politicizing of states had induced a pervasive political apathy. The messages and the methods of official ideology were deeply unappealing. On Soviet TV, the female continuity announcer's rigid, bouffant hairdo and humourless mien set the tone; and there was a steam-rolling pomposity about series such as 'For You, Parents' and 'For You, Veterans'. Most TV programmes were heavily didactic. But the public reacted unenthusiastically to them. Sport, crime thrillers, variety shows, science-fiction films and melodramas were much more popular: even Politburo members were scunnered by any media output that was intellectually demanding. Brezhnev liked 'low-brow' entertainment as much as did ordinary citizens. Ice-hockey games between the Soviet Union and Canada were much more to his liking than the theory of 'developed socialism'.

Much leisure in any case was spent outside the home. The Soviet Union, like other communist states, linked its international prestige closely to the performance of its sports teams. The network of facilities was the envy of foreign countries. Soviet youngsters had access to well-funded premises, training and equipment; they knew that, if they had talent, they would be rewarded by privileges which would not fade when they retired: the typical ex-athlete would move into the profession of trainer. The football goalkeeper Lev Yashin and the weightlifter Aleksei Vlasov remained major personalities in Soviet public life.

The state also provided several institutions for daily recreation and annual holidays. Trade unions provided beach vacations in Crimea and Georgia to members who showed a high level of activism and obedience (and children could be sent separately by their parents to summer camps). Workers achieving the monthly production quotas had their names placed on their factory's Roll of Honour. The state continued to award badges for all manner of public services, and bemedalled war veterans were allowed to go to the head of queues in shops. Members of the USSR Academy of Sciences – who had their own special badge – were each provided with a chauffeur-driven car. The hierarchy of honour and privilege paralleled the hierarchy of job occupations. A large enough minority of citizens benefited sufficiently from these perks to give considerable solidity to the Soviet order.

Yet the long-term dissolvent tendencies in society were unmistakable. The villages went on losing their skilled males to the towns since the improvement in the conditions of kolkhozniki failed to stem the exodus from the countryside. Tractor drivers could nearly always better themselves in the urban work-force. The kolkhozniki, who were typically female and either late middle aged or elderly, had neither the morale nor the energy to organize harvests adequate to feed an industrial country. In the towns and cities a different set of problems prevailed. Workers entering employment in the 1930s and 1940s could reasonably expect promotion to white-collar jobs if they worked and studied hard and obeyed the political authorities. In the 1950s the number of posts in management was ceasing to expand; in the 1970s the holders of these posts hung on to them: mere incompetence was scarcely ever deemed due cause for an individual to be sacked. Social rigidification was setting in: once a worker, always a worker.[13]

Simultaneously the structure of families in many regions of the USSR was causing trepidation. Across Russia, as well as the other Slavic republics and the Baltic region, married couples increasingly limited themselves to having one child. The inadequate living-space and the financial pressure upon wives to stay in the labour-force were the causes. The main birth-control technique was itself a problem: abortion. It was far from unusual for a woman to endure a dozen aborted pregnancies before reaching the menopause. This was terrible enough; but the long-term prospect was equally dispiriting since the proportion of the population supporting their pensioner relatives in Russia and other such regions was going into decline.

In January 1981 Kosygin's successor as Chairman of the Council of Ministers, Nikolai Tikhonov, acknowledged that 'demographic policy' was one of the weakest areas of his government's activity. In reality he was referring to the 'national question'; for Tikhonov's unstated worry was that not enough Russians were being born. Many people, including non-communists, sympathized with him. If current trends continued, the Russian nation would soon constitute a minority in the Soviet Union. The evidence was provided by a census, which revealed that ethnic Russians had dropped from fifty-five per cent of the USSR's population in 1959 to fifty-two per cent in 1979.[14] For the attitude to family size in the Transcaucasus and central Asia had not followed the pattern of Russia. Tajiks and Uzbeks, who had gained better medical services from the hands of the Soviet state, produced more children than ever who survived to adulthood. The idea circulated among Russians that they would soon be outnumbered and politically downgraded by 'orientals'.

Such language was racist; it was also rather laughable since several of the supposedly oriental cities, such as the Georgian capital Tbilisi, are located on a line of longitude to the west of cities in central Russia! Nevertheless the feeling behind the words was deep. Russians had for decades been treated as the primary nation of the USSR. Not only did they feel superior to the other peoples but also they considered that their contribution to the development and preservation of the USSR had been the greatest.

The Russian nation's resentments could no longer be totally ignored, and the Politburo became increasingly frantic to assuage them. Anti-Semitism, which had been approved by Stalin not long before he died, was given semi-official respectability again. Already in 1963 the central party leadership had permitted the Ukrainian writer T. Kichko to publish *Judaism without Veneer*, an anti-Jewish tract which provoked still more citizens of Jewish origin to apply for exit visas. Brezhnev had let hundreds of thousands leave the country, but solely in order to placate the American administration: on the whole he preferred to reassure Russians that he was on their side. Among the central party leaders in Moscow only Alexander Yakovlev, who served in the Central Committee apparatus, strenuously opposed the condoning of Russian nationalism and demanded a more resolutely internationalist official policy. His position was made so uncomfortable for him that an agreement was made that he should become Soviet ambassador to Canada.[15]

None the less there was a still higher standard of living in Georgia and Estonia than across the RSFSR. This naturally caused many Russians to believe that current policies were injurious to the Russian national interest. The policy of elevating personnel of the major local nationality to high office was maintained. Ukrainians administered Ukraine, Uzbeks Uzbekistan and Latvians Latvia. Certainly very severe controls remained: the Politburo continued to position ethnic Russians – or sometimes especially trusted Ukrainians or Belorussians – as deputy leaders in virtually every republican party, government and the KGB. Yet local 'national' functionaries were also prominent; and the policy of 'stability of cadres', which had been started in 1964, was prolonged through the 1970s.

The result, as time went on, was that the majority nationalities in each republic were able to augment their dominance over other local national and ethnic groups. Stern campaigns against administrative and financial malpractice were maintained by Eduard Shevardnadze in Georgia and Geidar Aliev in Azerbaijan; but neither Shevardnadze nor Aliev did much to protect the position of minorities: in Georgia the Abkhazians and the Adzharians suffered considerable discrimination; in Azerbaijan, the Armenian-inhabited enclave of Nagorny Karabakh was starved of funds. Nor were such tensions absent from the RSFSR. A glaring example was the attempt by Bashkirian communist leaders to 'Bashkirize' the education and culture of the Tatar population in their vicinity.[16]

Ostensibly these disintegrative trends in other republics were prevented from manifesting themselves in the same fashion in the RSFSR's Russian provinces. The RSFSR shared a capital with the USSR and was altogether too vast to be permitted to follow a line of action disapproved by the central political authorities. The RSFSR had a formally separate government, but real power was denied it; and the ban on the establishment of a separate communist party remained in force. But there had long been ambivalences in the policies of the Politburo. In particular, Russian intellectuals were accorded greater latitude for cultural self-assertion than were their non-Russian counterparts. Russia's pride of place among the nations of the USSR continued to be officially affirmed. And whereas Russians had important posts in the local political administrations of the other Soviet republics, ethnic Russians had a monopoly in the administrative apparatus of the RSFSR's provinces.

The policy of stability of cadres, moreover, encouraged officials in the localities to ignore uncongenial central demands. The province-level party committee (*obkom*) secretary retained crucial local power and the fact that functionaries from the non-central party apparatus occupied a third of the places at the Twenty-Fifth Party Congress in 1976 was an index of their influence.[17]

Thus the local 'nests' were also reinforced. For a manager running a factory of national significance could always threaten to appeal to his minister; and a KGB chief in a border area or a commander of a military district might easily cause trouble if the obkom secretary interfered excessively in security affairs. But few local 'nests' of officials were very disputatious; for a common local interest existed in keeping the 'centre' from prying into the locality. Ordinary Soviet citizens who wrote to the Politburo and the Secretariat exposing an abuse of power in their town or village were sometimes rewarded with a *Pravda* campaign on their behalf; but such campaigns were ineffectual in transforming general practice – and sometimes such citizens found themselves victimized by the local officials whom they had exposed. At any rate the central authorities remained loyal to the policy of only sacking functionaries in cases of extreme disobedience to the Kremlin's demands.

The old paradox endured. On the one hand, there was a frantic profusion of official demands for observance of legality, and under Brezhnev – according to one estimate – the number of 'normative acts' of legislation in force across the USSR had risen to 600,000;[18] on the other hand, infringements of legality were pervasive. The key common goal of political leaders in the Kremlin was to minimize shifts of policy and avoid damaging internal controversy. Transfers of personnel, if they were on a large scale, would destabilize the relations among central and local public groups in the various institutions. The Soviet compound was entering a stage of degradation.

Nevertheless this is not how it seemed to most wielders of power at either the central or local levels. Even among those of them who were minded to introduce reforms there was little acceptance that basic reform was overdue; instead they tended to believe that it would be enough to modify existing policies, to sack the most incompetent of Brezhnev's cronies and introduce younger blood. Above all, they felt that Brezhnev himself had served in office too long. The condition of his health was in fact even worse than most of the rumours about it. The handful of officials who came into regular, direct contact with him could see for themselves that he was a dreadfully ill old man. The scribblings in his personal diary showed a lingering interest in television programmes and sport; and his punctuation and spelling would have disgraced a schoolchild.[19]

Brezhnev had stayed in office after bowing to pressure from some of his Politburo associates; and this had postponed the jostling among them over the question of the political succession. Essentially Gromyko, Ustinov, Suslov and Andropov were governing the country through a consensus among themselves. Brezhnev's closest aide and confidant, Politburo member Chernenko, had also acquired an influence. Crucial Politburo decisions were being taken by them in his absence.

But Brezhnev's health worsened drastically in the winter of 1981–2 and the Politburo pondered who eventually was to take his place as General Secretary. The choice would have been influenced by Suslov, who was a senior Central Committee Secretary. But Suslov died aged seventy-nine in January 1982. KGB chairman Andropov was given Suslov's place in the Central Committee Secretariat in May, and quickly it became obvious that he would make a strong bid to succeed Brezhnev. Stories about corrupt practices in Brezhnev's family and entourage started to circulate.[20] The stories came from Andropov's associates in the KGB. Evidently Andropov was trying to create a mood in the Politburo that would ruin the chances of one of Brezhnev's boon companions emerging as a serious rival to his own candidature.

By his actions Andropov showed that he no longer feared incurring Brezhnev's hostility. Through spring, summer, autumn 1982 the General Secretary rarely appeared in public. The official pretence was maintained that he was not seriously ill; but his doctors, together with his nurse (who for years had been his mistress), despaired that he would ever recover. Brezhnev was sinking fast. On 10 November 1982, he suffered a final relapse and died.

The Politburo instructed that he should be buried outside the Kremlin Wall on Red Square. Statesmen from all over the world attended. His wife and family were accompanied to the funeral by the central party leadership – and daughter Galina outraged spectators by refraining from wearing sombre garb. Brezhnev had been dressed in his Marshal's uniform with all his medals. But the careless way the coffin was dropped into his grave was taken as a sign that not all Politburo leaders wished to be seen to regret that at last he had left the political stage. In truth it was hard to feel very sorry for Brezhnev. When he had succeeded Khrushchëv, he was still a vigorous politician who expected to make the party and government work more effectively. He had not been inactive; he had not been entirely inflexible. But his General Secretaryship had turned into a ceremonial reign that had brought communism into its deepest contempt since 1917.

22

Towards Reform (1982–1985)

Yuri Andropov had played an astute hand in the last months of Brezhnev's life, and it was he who was chosen by the Politburo as the new General Secretary on 12 November 1982. He had waited many years to occupy the supreme party office and had no intention of governing in the fashion of Brezhnev. Andropov believed changes in policy to be vital.

As General Secretary, however, he had to take feelings in the Politburo into account. The Politburo contained a rump of Brezhnev's promotees who could cause him trouble: Tikhonov, Shcherbytskiy, Grishin and Chernenko had an iron-plated complacency about current policies and disliked virtually any proposal for change. Yet several other influential members of the Politburo, Dmitri Ustinov and Andrei Gromyko, did not stand in Andropov's way when he demanded a modification of official policies. Ustinov had been Defence Minister since 1976, Gromyko had led the Foreign Affairs Ministry since 1957. With their acquiescence, Andropov intensified his campaign against corruption. Political and social discipline, he argued, were the prerequisites for economic expansion – and economic expansion was needed if the Soviet standard of living was to be raised and military parity with the USA to be retained.

Andropov was the brightest party leader of his generation. Born in 1914, he was of Cossack descent.[1] He had a conventional background except inasmuch as his father had been a railway administrator and not a worker. He quickly rose up the hierarchy of the Komsomol and the party; by the end of the Second World War he was second party secretary for the Karelo-Finnish Soviet Republic. The post-war purges of communist functionaries in Leningrad had repercussions in that republic and many of Andropov's colleagues were shot.[2] He counted himself lucky to survive; and in 1954 he was appointed as Soviet ambassador to Hungary. He was in Budapest during the Hungarian uprising of 1956 and stayed there until 1957, when Khrushchëv recalled him to work in the central party apparatus in Moscow. A decade later he was picked by Brezhnev to take over the KGB.

An associate described him as having 'an enormous forehead, which looked as if it had been specially shaven clean on both sides of his temples, a large, impressive nose, thick lips and a cleft chin'.[3] He took little pleasure in food and sport and was a teetotaller. His taste for well-tailored suits was his only sign of self-indulgence, and occasionally he let himself go by penning stanzas of doggerel to his advisers – and his humour could be lavatorial.[4] But generally he refrained from such ribaldry. Not even fellow Politburo members saw much of his lighter side. He would not even accept an invitation to a supper party unnecessarily.[5] His ideological severity was emphatic. Andropov believed in Marxism-Leninism and was offended by the laxities permitted by Brezhnev: he could not abide the incompetent gerontocrats in the Kremlin. The problem was that he, too, was old and was troubled by ill-health. A chronic kidney complaint was becoming acute. If he was going to have an impact, action had to be swift.

And so Andropov announced the reimposition of discipline and order as his immediate priority. He instituted judicial proceedings against leading ne'er-do-wells in the Ministry of Internal Affairs. He also punished the more mundane misdemeanours of ordinary citizens: the police cleared the streets of drunks; lack of punctuality at work was also penalized and random inspections were made so that people might not leave their place of work in working hours. Conscientious fulfilment of professional duties was demanded of everybody in society, right from the central party leaders down to ordinary citizens. Such measures were stern in general, but they inflicted special hardship on Soviet wives and mothers. Most women in the USSR went out to work and yet had to undertake all the domestic chores; it was difficult for them to cope with the queuing in the shops unless they could take time off in working hours.

Not that Andropov was a complete killjoy. He did not mind if people had a tipple; on the contrary, he permitted the introduction of a cheap new vodka, which was known as 'Andropovka'.[6] He also genuinely aimed to improve living conditions. He gave the following summary of his purposes to his physician: 'First we'll make enough sausages and then we won't have any dissidents.'[7]

Such a remark was not made by someone who was bent upon a fundamental revision of Marxism-Leninism. Accordingly, then, the slogan of 'developed socialism' was retained. But differences in style quickly appeared. For example, Andropov admitted that the party leadership needed 'to acquire an understanding of the society in which we live'.[8] This was a cognitive humility uncharacteristic of previous leaders of the Communist Party of the Soviet Union. Andropov stressed that he had not come to office with ready-made, easy solutions and that he intended to learn from as many people as he could. Thus in February 1983 he visited a Moscow lathe-making factory and held brief conversations with workers.[9] It was a mundane event in itself. (It was also highly contrived: the workers knew that they had to say things that would not irritate the General Secretary.) But the contrast with Brezhnev's later years was unmistakable.

Replacements were being made in the Kremlin's personnel. Andropov surrounded himself with personal advisers who, by contemporary official standards, were free thinkers. Typically they were academics or journalists. They were loyal communist party members; all for a long time had argued that official policies needed to be altered. Andropov also showed his impatience in his changes of political personnel at the centre. Mikhail Gorbachëv and Yegor Ligachëv were lively party officials from a younger generation for whom he secured further advancement; he also plucked Nikolai Ryzhkov from the State Planning Commission and transferred him to party duties. Gorbachëv, Ligachëv and Ryzhkov were appointed as Central Committee Secretaries so that Andropov could ensure compliance with his wishes throughout the central party apparatus. Gorbachëv retained oversight over agriculture and gained it over the entire economy. Ryzhkov, who headed a new Economic Department, was made responsible specifically for industry. Ligachëv led the Organizational Department.[10]

Andropov was aiming – in his secretive way – to explore possible ways to modify the Politburo's measures; he knew that the economy cried out for regeneration. But he was far from sure about which measures to adopt. He therefore asked Gorbachëv and Ryzhkov to conduct confidential, detailed research on his behalf and to make suitable recommendations.[11]

Probably Andropov did not wish to venture far along the route of reforms. A decree was passed in July 1983 to provide industrial associations with somewhat greater autonomy from the central planning authorities.[12] Yet the clauses were still not as radical as the proposals of Kosygin in 1965; and the enduring closeness of his friendship with Minister of Defence Ustinov indicated that Andropov hardly wanted to transform the entire system of power.[13] He kept his more independently-minded advisers well under control. Indeed several scholars outside his entourage felt that he was entirely failing to appreciate the critical nature of the country's problems. In particular, a group of Novosibirsk sociologists and economists under Tatyana Zaslavskaya produced its own treatise on the need for reform. The authors argued that administrative arbitrariness lay at the centre of the difficulties in Soviet society and its economy. Zaslavskaya's mild ideas were so audacious in the USSR of the early 1980s that she was in jeopardy of being arrested when the treatise fell into the KGB's hands.[14]

At any rate, Andropov was a naturally cautious man. Certainly he gave no licence to Gorbachëv and Ryzhkov, his adjutants in the quest for economic regeneration, to take up the analysis provided by the Novosibirsk group. In short, he wanted change, but insisted that it should be undertaken at no risk to the existing state order. Domestic policy was to be revised with gradualness and with due appreciation of all possible difficulties.

Andropov showed greater enterprise in foreign policy. On becoming General Secretary, he issued proposals thick and fast. He especially strove to reanimate the international understandings of détente which had been ruined by the Soviet military intervention in the Afghan Civil War in 1979. Andropov called for a summit with American President Reagan, for an arms reduction agreement between the USSR and the USA and for a ban on nuclear tests. At a Warsaw Pact meeting in Prague in January 1983 Andropov made a still more startling suggestion. This was that the USSR and the USA should sign an accord that each should formally undertake not to attack any country belonging to the other's alliance or even any country within its own alliance.[15] No doubt Andropov deliberately chose to make his suggestion in Prague, capital of the Warsaw Pact country invaded by the USSR in 1968.

But Reagan was as yet of no mind to see anything positive in Soviet overtures. He regarded the USSR as an 'evil empire' and former KGB chief Andropov as an emperor as demonic as any of his predecessors in the Kremlin. Far from improving, relations between the superpowers deteriorated after Brezhnev's death. On 23 March 1983, President Reagan announced he was going to finance research on a Strategic Defence Initiative (or 'Star Wars' Initiative, as it quickly became known). According to Reagan, this would serve no offensive purpose whatever but would be an exclusively defensive system for the detection and destruction of nuclear missiles aimed at the USA. Reagan promised that the technological developments would be shared with the USSR. Unsurprisingly Andropov felt unable to accept him at his word: there was no guarantee that the system would indeed be confided to the Soviet Union. The Politburo resolved to subsidize a parallel research programme, and competition in military technology was set to grow fiercer.

Tension between the USSR and the USA increased on 1 September when a South Korean airliner, KAL-007, strayed into Soviet airspace and was shot down by the forces of Air-Defense Command. Furious recriminations occurred between Moscow and Washington; the diplomatic strains were intensifying to the point of rupture. Andropov was advised by Sovet intelligence organs abroad that Reagan might be about to order a nuclear strike on the USSR. The suspicion was that the imminent NATO exercise of 2 November might be used as a cover to attack Moscow. Andropov felt he had no alternative but to order his nuclear forces to assume a condition of heightened alert.[16] This emergency, unlike the Cuban missiles crisis, was kept secret from the Soviet and American publics. But the politicians in the two capitals knew how near the world had come to the brink of a Third World War; and it was clear that robust, clear-sighted leadership was required if such incidents were not to recur.

Robustness could no longer be provided by Andropov. The decay of his kidneys could not be slowed and the frequency of his attendance at official meetings was already decreasing in spring and summer 1983: colleagues had to communicate with him by letter as he convalesced at his dacha. Greater authority therefore passed into the hands of the second secretary of the Central Committee, Chernenko, who chaired the Politburo in Andropov's absence. This job was also sometimes carried out by Gorbachëv. In the discreet struggle for the succession, Andropov's preference was for Gorbachëv over Chernenko. He appended a note to this effect on one of his last memoranda to the Central Committee. But Chernenko's supporters excised the note from the version presented to the Central Committee, and Andropov died on 9 February 1984 before he could consolidate Gorbachëv's chances.[17]

For his protégés, Andropov's passing was a tragic loss for the USSR. Even the dissenter Roy Medvedev felt that great changes had been in prospect under Andropov.[18] This was excessive optimism. It is true that Andropov had succeeded in sacking one fifth of province-level party first secretaries – a vital process of replacement if ever the Brezhnevite complacency was to be dispelled.[19] Furthermore, industrial output was five per cent higher in 1983 than in the previous year; and the value of agricultural production rose by seven per cent.[20] Yet although the duration of Andropov's tenure had not been enough for him to take a grip on economic policies, he was far too traditionalist to be able to do much more than he had already accomplished.

After kidney-patient Andropov it was Chernenko, already debilitated by emphysema, who became General Secretary. Gorbachëv had to be content with being his informal deputy. Chernenko was not the most highly qualified of General Secretaries. Flimsilyeducated and uninspiring, he had served in lowly party ranks until he met Brezhnev in Moldavia in the early 1950s. After years of service as Brezhnev's personal aide, he was rewarded by being made a Central Committee Secretary in 1976 and a full Politburo member two years later. His talents had never stretched beyond those of a competent office manager and his General Secretaryship was notable for woeful conservatism. The sole change to the composition of the Politburo occurred with the death of Ustinov in December 1984 – and such was the disarray of the central party leadership that Ustinov was not replaced. Chernenko's single innovation in policy was his approval of an ecologically pernicious scheme to turn several north-flowing Siberian rivers down south towards the Soviet republics of central Asia.

His Politburo colleagues had chosen Chernenko as their General Secretary because his frailty would enable them to keep their own posts and to end Andropov's anti-corruption campaign. The Central Committee, being packed with persons promoted by Brezhnev, did not object to this objective. But the choice of Chernenko caused concern. Chernenko was left in no doubt about the contempt felt for him by members of the Central Committee when they refrained from giving him the conventional ovation after his promotion to General Secretary.[21] But Chernenko was old, infirm and losing the will to live, much less to avenge himself for such humiliation.

It was Gorbachëv who led the Politburo and the Secretariat during Chernenko's incapacitation. Behind the scenes, moreover, Gorbachëv and Ryzhkov continued to elaborate those measures for economic regeneration demanded of them by Andropov.[22] Other Politburo members were disconcerted by Gorbachëv's status and influence. Tikhonov persistently tried to organize opposition to him; and Viktor Grishin decided to enhance his own chances of succeeding Chernenko by arranging for a TV film to be made of Chernenko and himself. Chernenko was so ill that he lacked the presence of mind to shoo Grishin away. Another of Gorbachëv's rivals was Politburo member and former Leningrad party first secretary Grigori Romanov; and, unlike the septuagenarian Grishin, Romanov was a fit politician in his late fifties. Both Grishin and Romanov were hostile to proposals of reform and wished to prevent Gorbachëv from becoming General Secretary.

Chernenko died on 10 March 1985. If Brezhnev's funeral had been distinguished by farce when the coffin slipped out of the bearers' grasp at the last moment, Chernenko's was not memorable even for this. Opinion in the party, in the country and around the world sighed for a Soviet leader who was not physically incapacitated.

Yet it was not the world nor even the Communist Party of the Soviet Union as a whole but the Politburo that would be deciding the matter at 2 p.m. on 11 March.[23] Behind the scenes Ligachëv was organizing provincial party secretaries to speak in Gorbachëv's favour at the Central Committee. In the event Gorbachëv was unopposed. Even Tikhonov and Grishin spoke in his favour. Foreign Minister Andrei Gromyko was chairing the session and was unstinting in his praise of Gorbachëv. There were the usual rumours of conspiracy. It was noted, for example, that Volodymyr Shcherbytskiy, who was not among Gorbachëv's admirers, had found it impossible to find an Aeroflot jet to fly him back from the USA for the Politburo meeting. But the reality was that no one in the Politburo was willing to stand against Gorbachëv. The Politburo's unanimous choice was to be announced to the Central Committee plenum in the early evening.

At the plenum, Gromyko paid tribute to Gorbachëv's talent and dependability: little did he know that Gorbachëv would soon want rid of him.[24] Whatever else he was, Gorbachëv was a brilliant dissimulator: he had attended the court of Leonid Brezhnev and managed to avoid seeming to be an unsettling reformer. Only under Andropov and Chernenko had he allowed his mask to slip a little. In a speech in December 1984 he used several words soon to be associated with radicalism: 'acceleration', 'the human factor', 'stagnation' and even '*glasnost*' and 'democratization'.[25] But nobody in the Politburo, not even Gorbachëv himself, had a presentiment of the momentous consequences of the decision to select him as General Secretary.

Mikhail Sergeevich Gorbachëv had been born in 1931 and brought up in Privolnoe, a small village of Stavropol region in southern

Russia. His family had been peasants for generations. Relatives of Gorbachëv had been persecuted in the course of mass agricultural collectivization. One of his grandfathers, who was a rural official, was arrested; the other was exiled for a time. He had a straitened childhood on the new kolkhoz, especially under the Nazi occupation in 1942–3; his memory of his early life was far from sentimental: 'Mud huts, earthen floor, no beds.'[26] But he survived. During and after the war Gorbachëv worked in the fields like the other village youths, and in 1949 his industriousness was rewarded with the Order of the Red Banner of Labour. He was highly intelligent, receiving a silver medal for his academic achievements at the local school and gained a place in the Faculty of Jurisprudence at Moscow State University.

He graduated in 1955 with first-class marks, but recently-introduced rules prevented him from working for the USSR Procuracy in Moscow.[27] He therefore dropped his plans for a career in the law and opted to enter politics. Returning to Stavropol, he joined the apparatus of the Komsomol and then the party. Two decades of solid organizational work followed for Gorbachëv and his wife Raisa. He enjoyed rapid promotion. By 1966 he was heading the City Party Committee and four years later was entrusted with the leadership of the entire Stavropol Region. He was not yet forty years old and had joined an élite whose main characteristic was its advanced age. Both he and his wife were ambitious. A story is told that they had the same dream one night. Both had a vision of him clambering up out of a deep, dark well and striding out along a broad highway under a bright sky. Gorbachëv was perplexed as to its significance. Raisa unhesitatingly affirmed that it meant that her husband was destined to be 'a great man'.[28]

Khrushchëv's closed-session speech to the Twentieth Party Congress had given him hope that reform was possible in the USSR.[29] But he kept quiet about these thoughts except amidst his family and with his most trusted friends. In any case, he was vague in his own mind about the country's needs. Like many of his contemporaries, he wanted reform but had yet to identify its desirable ingredients for himself.[30]

In the meantime he set out to impress the central leaders who visited the holiday resorts adjacent to Stavropol; and he was making a name for himself by his attempts to introduce just a little novelty to the organization of the region's kolkhozes. By virtue of his post in the regional party committee in 1971 he was awarded Central Committee membership. In 1978 he was summoned to the capital to lead the Agricultural Department in the Secretariat. Next year he became a Politburo candidate member and in 1980 a full member. Two years later he was confident enough to propose the establishment of a State Agro-Industrial Committee. This was a cumbersome scheme to facilitate the expansion of farm output mainly by means of institutional reorganization. It was hardly a radical reform. But it was criticized by Tikhonov, Kosygin's successor as Chairman of the Council of Ministers, as an attempt to form 'a second government', and the Politburo rejected it. Gorbachëv was learning the hard way about the strength of vested interests at the summit of Soviet politics.[31]

His career anyway did not suffer: the preferment he enjoyed under Brezhnev was strengthened by Andropov. Word had got around that Gorbachëv was a man of outstanding talent. He was not a theorist, but his openness to argument was attractive to the intellectual consultants who had advised Andropov. So, too, was Gorbachëv's reputation as a decisive boss. He had not in fact achieved much for agriculture either in Stavropol or in Moscow; but he was given the benefit of the doubt: he could not do what Brezhnev would not have allowed.

Gorbachëv's practical ideas in 1985 were as yet very limited in scope. He resumed the economic and disciplinary orientation set by Andropov; he also gave priority to changes of personnel.[32] But already he had certain assumptions that went beyond Andropovism. In the 1970s he had visited Italy, Belgium and West Germany in official delegations and taken a three-week car-touring holiday in France with Raisa. The impression on him was profound. He learned that capitalism was not a moribund economic system and that, despite many defects, it offered many sections of its societies a breadth of material goods unrivalled in the USSR.[33] He had also been rethinking his attitude to the Soviet order since 1983, when he had studied Lenin's last works on bureaucracy and had come to understand that the bureaucratic problems of the 1920s had not disappeared.[34] His private assumptions and understandings would at last have room to develop into policies when Gorbachëv became General Secretary.

By temperament he was a gambler, and the very fact that he had not elaborated his strategy left him open to suggestions to take ever larger risks. The night before going to the Politburo meeting which selected him as General Secretary, he stated: 'Life can't be lived like this any longer.'[35] But he said this solely to his wife Raisa, in the garden of their dacha where he could be confident of not being bugged.[36] He could not afford to be too frank about his intention to repudiate Brezhnev's heritage: on 11 March 1985 he soothed the Central Committee with his statement that policies did not need changing.[37] Yet on the quiet he was looking for substantial changes. He had no detailed objectives, but he was impatient to achieve something fast.

His first task was to assemble a group of influential supporters. At the next Central Committee plenum, on 23 April 1985, he gave favour to fellow protégés of Andropov: Central Committee Secretaries Ryzhkov and Ligachëv were promoted to full membership of the Politburo, and KGB chairman Viktor Chebrikov rose from being candidate to full member of the Politburo. When the Central Committee met again in July, two local party leaders, Lev Zaikov of Leningrad and Boris Yeltsin of Sverdlovsk, were appointed to the Secretariat. Romanov, Gorbachëv's chief rival of pre-pensionable age, was sacked from the Politburo; and Eduard Shevardnadze, Georgian communist party leader and a friend of Gorbachëv, was raised from candidate to full Politburo membership. These were persons who shared his sense of urgency. A year before, in conversation with Gorbachëv on Pitsunda beach in Crimea, Shevardnadze had put their common approach into a few blunt words: 'Everything's rotten. There must be change.'[38]

Shevardnadze was then appointed Soviet Foreign Minister in place of Gromyko. For Gromyko at the age of seventy-six there was the consolation of being made Chairman of the Supreme Soviet

Presidium and thereby becoming head of state; but Gorbachëv was not so generous towards the eighty-year-old Nikolai Tikhonov, who was compelled to retire and whose job was taken by Nikolai Ryzhkov. In October the leadership of the State Planning Commission (Gosplan) passed from Nikolai Baibakov, who had held the post for two decades, to Nikolai Talyzin.

Already Gorbachëv had removed the most powerful of Brezhnev's cronies, got rid of Romanov and installed a group of experienced administrators at the centre who were dedicated to the regeneration of the Soviet economy. Within months he had accomplished a turnover of personnel that Stalin, Khrushchëv and Brezhnev had taken years to carry out. The average age of the Politburo fell from sixty-nine years at the end of 1980 to sixty-four by the end of 1985.[39] Another aspect of change was the background of the supreme party leadership. All the newcomers, unlike many leaders in Brezhnev's generation, had completed at least their secondary education. Most of them also had until recently lived in 'the localities'. Yeltsin had worked for most of his career in the Urals, Ligachëv in mid-Siberia, Shevardnadze in Georgia. They brought to the capital an awareness of day-to-day provincial actuality. They were confident that collectively they could solve the country's problems.

Gorbachëv was the most worldly-wise of all of them. His ability to adjust his style to unfamiliar surroundings astonished foreign politicians. In 1984 the British Prime Minister Mrs Thatcher declared: 'I like Mr Gorbachëv. We can do business together.'[40] Gorbachëv and his wife were a vivacious couple, and Raisa's wardrobe excited interest in Western newspapers. The new General Secretary transparently wanted to govern a USSR which no longer invited hatred and ridicule beyond its frontiers.

But how were he and his colleagues in the Kremlin going to achieve this? Initially they followed Andropov's general line and concentrated efforts upon the economy. Discipline and order also returned to the agenda. The Politburo, persuaded by Ligachëv, even took the risk of discouraging alcohol consumption. Threefold increases in the price of vodka were decreed and vineyards were hacked down in Georgia, Moldavia and Ukraine. This was not the last time that

Gorbachëv fell out of touch with social opinion: on this occasion he was nicknamed the Mineral Secretary for asserting the superiority of mineral water over booze. Yet he was mocked more than resented. Nearly all Soviet citizens were delighted by his unceremonial dumping of the Brezhnevite time-servers. He was also admired for his visits to cities outside Moscow and his willingness to engage bystanders in conversation. *Pravda* editorials became as compulsive reading as the sport, chess and quizzes at the back of the newspaper.

Gorbachëv, whose main economic slogan was 'acceleration', looked like a man in a hurry. But actual measures were slower to emerge. His first move was made in November 1985, when a super-ministry for the cultivation and processing of foodstuffs was formed along the lines unsuccessfully proposed by Gorbachëv in Brezhnev's time. Named as the State Committee for the Agro-Industrial Complex (*Gosagroprom*), it was to be led by one of Gorbachëv's political clients, Vsevolod Murakhovski. This had been one of Gorbachëv's pet projects in Brezhnev's lifetime, but until he became General Secretary he encountered resistance from the Council of Ministers.[41] Now he could realize his wishes.

But this meant he was aiming to renovate Soviet agriculture chiefly by reorganizing its central governmental institutions. As he should have known from Zaslavskaya's Novosibirsk Report in 1983, the regeneration of the economy required much more than administrative measures. Kolkhozniki and sovkhozniki remained subject to a system of peremptory orders and of weak material incentives; and they had no positive influence over the running of the collective farm: they were bossed by farm chairmen and the chairmen themselves were bossed by Moscow. Gosagroprom was not going to dislodge a single brick in this bureaucratic wall. Quite the opposite: by giving additional authority to a central body such as Gosagroprom, Gorbachëv would increase the wall's solidity. The General Secretary acted as if a group of new officials, a structural experiment and a campaign of public exhortation would do the trick; his orientation was centralist, hierarchical, administrative and command-based.

If agriculture was the economy's Achilles' heel, industry was its severely bruised knee. In Gorbachëv's first months there was no equivalent reorganization of the manufacturing sector. Nevertheless a re-jigging of budgetary aims took place. The Twelfth Five-Year Plan was scheduled to begin in 1986, and the Politburo declared that an increase in the quantity and quality of industrial output required the maximizing of investment in the machine-building sector. Ryzhkov and Gorbachëv were the principal advocates of this strategy. They were putting into effect the ideas elaborated by the two of them under Andropov's encouragement.

Increasingly, however, Gorbachëv recognized that such calculations were inadequate to the solution of the country's problems. On his various tours to the provinces he spoke off the cuff and tagged new priorities to the formally-agreed economic agenda. By late 1985 there was scarcely an industrial sector not mentioned by the General Secretary as deserving of large, additional investment.[42] Ryzhkov, a former deputy chairman of Gosplan, perceived that such promises were a budgetary impossibility: Gorbachëv had simply not done his sums. Yet Ryzhkov, too, lacked a workable strategy and continued to advocate an unrealizably rapid expansion in the output of industrial consumer goods; for his diversion of vast revenues into machine-construction could not yield results until after several years, perhaps even decades. The draft Twelfth Five-Year Plan presented by Ryzhkov to the Twenty-Seventh Party Congress in February 1986 was based upon false economic premisses.

The central communist leadership would be frustrated until the ideas on economic reform underwent more basic revision. Gorbachëv sometimes hinted that he was considering this option. In Leningrad in May 1985 he announced to fellow communists: 'Obviously, we all of us must undergo reconstruction, all of us . . . Everyone must adopt new approaches and understand that no other path is available to us.'[43] Within a year the notion of reconstruction (or *perestroika*, as it became known in all languages) was the condiment in every dish of policy served up by the General Secretary.

Gorbachëv was fighting harder than any of his colleagues to radicalize the regime's policies. As his ideas changed, he left several of Andropov's appointees bemused; and inside the Politburo he could initially count only upon Shevardnadze as an unconditional ally. Gorbachëv remained unclear as to what he wanted. But although he took time to discover a positive set of aims, at least he knew what he was against. He hated the obstacles being put in his way by upholders of the ideas and practices of the Brezhnev period. Debate was lively among the central party leaders and Gorbachëv was in his element. In November 1985 he briskly persuaded the Politburo to sack Grishin, giving his place to Yeltsin in both the Politburo and in the Moscow City Party Committee. Yeltsin declared war on corruption and indolence throughout the capital's administration, and sacked Grishin's placemen as opponents of perestroika. Gorbachëv had promoted someone he hoped would be a permanent supporter in the Politburo.

Yet the struggle for reform had only just begun. At the Twenty-Seventh Party Congress in February 1986 Gorbachëv had to tread carefully in recommending fresh policy initiatives. The new Party Programme accepted at the Congress would hardly have discomfited Gorbachëv's predecessors in office: the 'perfecting' of 'developed socialism' was set to remain the main political slogan.[44] Yet immediately after the Congress he showed that he would not permanently be denied. Local officialdom was to be brought into line with his thinking: by the middle of 1986 two thirds of province-level party secretaries had not had the same jobs a half-decade earlier.[45] He was convinced that the vigorous support of such appointees would guarantee his success.

He was equally optimistic in his conduct of international relations in 1985–6. He had set his mind on sorting out Soviet domestic affairs, and had used the occasion of Chernenko's funeral to call a meeting of leaders of the Warsaw Pact countries and to announce his commitment to non-interference in their political life. According to Gorbachëv, these countries were thenceforward to have independent control of their internal development.[46] This was already a striking contrast with Soviet foreign policy since 1945. Even Andropov had offered to relax the USSR's grip on Eastern Europe solely on condition that the USA made analogous concessions in its regional spheres of influence.[47] Gorbachëv's statement was not tied to a public bargaining position with the USA: it was delivered exclusively to an audience of the USSR's allies in Eastern Europe. He wanted them to know that they were responsible for their own fate.

This was not a sign that Gorbachëv thought that communism was doomed in the USSR and Eastern Europe. The exact opposite was true. Gorbachëv was still at that time a Marxist-Leninist believer: he contended that the Soviet communist order was in many ways already superior to capitalism; he was unshaken in his opinion that the Soviet type of state provided its citizens with better health care, education and transport. The task in the USSR and Eastern Europe was consequently to renovate communism so as to match capitalism in other areas of public life. Gorbachëv assumed that he would be able to persuade fellow communist leaders in Eastern Europe to follow his example. There was to be no repetition of the invasions of Hungary in 1956 and Czechoslovakia in 1968. Renovation had to occur voluntarily. Despite Gorbachëv's eloquence, however, the Warsaw Pact leaders did not take him seriously and treated his speech as ceremonial rhetoric.[48]

The Politburo was learning to take his words more literally. In October 1985 he was already suggesting to its members that a way had to be found for the Soviet Army to be withdrawn from the war in Afghanistan.[49] Presumably he wished to have freedom to alter conditions in the USSR without international distractions. The material and human costs of the Afghan war were running out of control. Gorbachëv felt he could build the kind of socialism in his country that would cause the rest of the world to marvel.

He therefore refused to be downcast by the attitude taken by US President Reagan, who had secured a second term of office in 1984 and persisted with the development of his Strategic Defence Initiative. Gorbachëv continued to believe that Soviet science and industry would cope with the challenge and match the USA's technology. To the despair of his own more sceptical advisers, he even convinced himself that he could undertake major economic reform while supplying the Ministry of Defence with the immense additional resources needed to develop and deploy the USSR's equivalent to Reagan's project.[50] Since the end of the Second World War, Soviet scientists had always succeeded in emulating American military technology.

Gorbachëv felt that there was no reason to doubt that they could do the same in the mid-1980s. Gorbachëv began his reforms as a buoyant optimist.

Yet the Strategic Defence Initiative, while not instigating Gorbachëv's domestic perestroika, was indisputably going to make a tough task tougher, and Gorbachëv was not so stupid as to think that a vast new programme of military research would not divert expenditure from the civilian industrial sector. It would obviously therefore be far better for the USSR if the USA could be persuaded to abandon its Initiative altogether in return for firm and binding agreements on nuclear disarmament.

Although Gorbachëv had no experience as a diplomat, he intuitively sensed that personal contact with the American President might produce a transformation in relations between the superpowers. He was certainly lucky in his choice of moment to make the attempt. For Reagan himself, influenced by both Margaret Thatcher and his wife Nancy, was starting to look for signs that Soviet foreign policy might be more amenable to American political overtures. Gorbachëv and Reagan were therefore pleased to be able to arrange to meet each other in Geneva in November 1985. Their fireside conversations were courteous, even congenial. The two men liked each other and a rising degree of trust was noticeable between them. Nevertheless Reagan remained on his guard. While talking reassuringly to Gorbachëv, he licensed subordinates such as Caspar Weinberger and Richard Perle to make whatever menacing remarks they wanted about the USSR. The patience of Soviet negotiators was tested severely.

Yet Gorbachëv continued his line of reconciliation. At the Twenty-Seventh Party Congress in February 1986 he stressed that his country was 'ready to do everything it could to change the international situation radically'.[51] While asserting that Soviet defences would be strengthened to meet any foreign threat, Gorbachëv went out of his way to plead the case for global peace and for a process of disarmament.

Like most politicians in East and West, he assumed that the danger of nuclear technology was confined to bombs. His concentration on the military risks was understandable, but misplaced. There had been several explosions in Soviet civilian nuclear power stations since they had first been built under Khrushchëv. The lessons had not been learned: supervision and training of staff remained lamentable and no mention of past explosions was allowed in the USSR's press. The astute dissenting scientist, Zhores Medvedev, had deduced that there had been a nuclear disaster in the Urals from the indirect data on fauna and flora available in recondite Soviet academic journals; but he was living in emigration in London.[52] Discussion of his warnings was prohibited and his book was banned from publication. Consequently Gorbachëv was barely any better informed about the situation than his ordinary fellow citizens.

On 26 April 1986 a horrific jolt was delivered to official Soviet complacency when an accident occurred at the nuclear power station near the Ukrainian town of Chernobyl. The core of the reactor had overheated and the station's staff, instead of instantly shutting down the reactor, tried out various cooling measures. Their incompetence caused an explosion.

The result was catastrophic radiation. The local politicians panicked, and some of them secretly moved their families out of Ukraine. But the winds carried the radioactive particles northwards and westwards. Belorussia and eastern Poland were affected and Scandinavian newspapers revealed that a nuclear disaster had taken place somewhere in the USSR. As the clamour of public opinion grew around the world, the assumption was that the Politburo was deliberately pretending that nothing untoward had happened. This had been conventional Soviet practice to date whenever a nuclear accident or even an airplane crash had occurred. But in this instance, the Politburo itself had difficulty in getting rapid, accurate information. As the enormity of the event started to become evident, Gorbachëv announced the dispatch to the area of an investigative team from Moscow. Ryzhkov, the Chairman of the Council of Ministers, courageously visited Chernobyl in person.

For Gorbachëv, their reports were almost as appalling as the human and natural devastation wrought by the accident. A long chain of negligence, incompetence and disorganization was to blame.

Workers were careless; technicians were ill-trained; local politicians were ignorant; and central ministers and scientific consultants had omitted to put a reasonable set of safeguards into operation.

In 1921 Lenin had declared that the Kronstadt mutiny was the flash that led to the New Economic Policy. Gorbachëv made no similar statement. But the Chernobyl nuclear explosion undoubtedly had a deep impact on him. He could no longer fail to understand that the defects of the regime could not be corrected by administrative tinkering.[53] Misinformation, indiscipline and organizational manipulation were intrinsic to its workings. The lethal atmosphere over Chernobyl was a metaphor for the conditions in Soviet public life. A ventilation of the country's problems was no longer merely desirable; it was crucial for the medium-term survival of the USSR as a superpower. People were not protesting out on the streets. The declining economy was not already battered to the ground and the governing élites had not yet been demoralized into acceptance of fundamental reform. Yet Gorbachëv had had enough. Reform was going to be basic and fast, and the General Secretary was readying himself for a historic contest.

He and his group of supportive colleagues and advisers were embarrassed about the ineffectual, drifting methods of recent leadership. There was also confidence that the situation could be reversed. As General Secretary, Gorbachëv had no intention of presiding over the dissolution of the USSR or over the dismantlement of the communist political system. The economic, social and cultural problems were dire. But he was confident they could be solved.

The Politburo in 1985–6 agreed that new methods had to be formulated. Its members recognized their fundamental difficulties in achieving economic development, social acquiescence, ideological commitment, administrative efficiency, inter-ethnic harmony, control over Eastern Europe and peace between the superpowers. Each difficulty aggravated the others. But why did the Politburo go beyond the limits of Andropovite policy? External pressures played a part, especially the aggressive diplomacy of President Reagan and his Strategic Defence Initiative. Unpredictable events, particularly the Chernobyl explosion, were also important. Even so, the movement towards basic reforms was not inevitable. Gorbachëv would not have lost power if he had opted to conserve the heritage of Andropov. The collective outlook of his Politburo and Secretariat colleagues was not as open minded as his own, and the impact of this single individual over the course of Soviet politics was decisive.

He had no grand plan and no predetermined policies; but if Gorbachëv had not been Party General Secretary, the decisions of summer 1986 would have been different. The USSR's long-lasting order would have endured for many more years, and almost certainly the eventual collapse of the order would have been much bloodier than it was to be in 1991. The irony was that Gorbachëv, in trying to prevent the descent of the system into general crisis, proved instrumental in bringing forward that crisis and destroying the USSR.

23

Glasnost and Perestroika (1986–1988)

By mid-1986 Gorbachëv had concluded that his early economic and disciplinary measures offered no basic solution; he was also coming to recognize that it would not be enough merely to replace Brezhnev's personnel with younger, more energetic officials. The attitudes and practices of the Communist Party of the Soviet Union needed changing. The problem was that most party officials refused to recognize the acuteness of the problems faced by the USSR. This was a reflection of their self-interest; but it also derived from their ignorance. And this ignorance was not confined to officialdom. Soviet society had for decades been prevented from acquiring comprehensive knowledge of the country's past and current problems.

It was for this reason that Gorbachëv initiated a series of public debates. The policy was encapsulated in the slogan of glasnost. This is a difficult word to translate, broadly connoting 'openness', 'a voicing' and 'a making public'. Gorbachëv's choice of vocabulary was not accidental. Glasnost, for all its vagueness, does not mean freedom of information. He had no intention of relinquishing the Politburo's capacity to decide the limits of public discussion. Moreover, his assumption was that if Soviet society were to examine its problems within a framework of guidance, a renaissance of Leninist ideals would occur. Gorbachëv was not a political liberal. At the time, however, it was not so much his reservation of communist party power as his liberating initiative that was impressive. Gorbachëv was freeing debate in the USSR to an extent that no Soviet leader had attempted, not even Khrushchëv and certainly not Lenin.

Glavlit, which censored all printed materials prior to publication, was instructed from June 1986 to relax its rules. The USSR Union of Writers held a Congress in the same month and welcomed the relaxation of rules on the press. But new novels took time to be written. Consequently the leading edge of *glasnost* was sharpened mainly by weekly newspapers and magazines. Chief among these were *Moscow News*, *Ogonëk* ('Little Spark') and *Arguments and Facts*. None of them had been characterized by radicalism until, in 1986, they acquired new editors – Yegor Yakovlev, Vitali Korotich and Vladislav Starkov respectively – on recommendation from Gorbachëv's Party Secretariat. The incumbents were told to shake the press out of its torpor.[1]

Gorbachëv had to discover a large number of like-minded radicals able to help him refashion public opinion. Yeltsin was already doing this as Moscow Party City Committee First Secretary: from time to time he travelled, in company with a photographer, to his office by bus rather than chauffeur-driven limousine; he also sacked hundreds of corrupt or idle functionaries in the party and in local government, and his harassment of metropolitan bureaucracy was acclaimed by the ordinary residents of the capital. Another radical was Alexander Yakovlev, who served as a department chief in the Secretariat from 1985 and became a Central Committee Secretary in 1986. The problem for Gorbachëv was that such figures were rarities in the party apparatus. Most communist officials wanted only minimal reforms and were horrified at the thought of changing their methods of rule. Gorbachëv therefore turned for help to the intelligentsia. He was placing a wager on their loyalty and skills in communication in his struggle to win support from fellow party leaders and Soviet society as a whole.

His preference was for those who, like him, believed that Marxism-Leninism had been distorted since Lenin's time. He did not have to look very far. Since the 1960s there had been several scholars, writers and administrators whose careers had been blighted by their commitment to reforming the Soviet order. While sympathizing with Roy Medvedev, few of them had joined the overt dissenters. Instead they had lived a life of dispiriting frustration under Brezhnev, trusting that basic reform could not be delayed forever.

Yegor Yakovlev and others had worked as jobbing journalists.

Others had found sanctuary in research academies such as the Institute of the World Economic System under Oleg Bogomolov and the Novosibirsk Institute of Economics under Abel Aganbegyan. A few had bitten their tongues hard and continued to work as advisers to Politburo members: among these were Georgi Shakhnazarov and Alexander Bovin. By the mid-1980s this was a late middle-aged generation; most of them were persons in their fifties and sixties. They had been young adults when Khrushchëv had made his assault upon Stalin and referred to themselves as 'Children of the Twentieth Congress'. But although they were admirers of Khrushchëv, they were by no means uncritical of him: they felt that he had failed because his reforms had been too timid. Without the zeal of such supporters, Gorbachëv's cause would already have been lost.

They were better acquainted with developments in the rest of the world than any Soviet generation in the previous half-century. Most had travelled in tourist groups to non-communist countries, and Western scholarly literature had been available to several of them in their working capacities. They were also avid listeners to foreign radio stations and so were not entirely dependent on the Soviet mass media for their news of the day.

This was a generation awaiting its saviour; and they found him when Gorbachëv, like Superman pulling off his Clark Kent suit, revealed himself as a Child of the Twentieth Congress. Quickly he indicated that his urgent priority was to subject Soviet history to public reconsideration. Permission was given for the release of the phantasmagoric film *Repentance*, whose Georgian director Tengiz Abuladze satirized the Stalin years. The playwright Mikhail Shatrov's drama *Onward! Onward! Onward!* portrayed the parlousness of Lenin in the face of Stalin's machinations. Gorbachëv felt that until there was comprehension of the past, little could be done by him in the present. He saw a brilliant way to highlight his attitude: on 16 December 1986 he lifted the phone and spoke to the dissenting physicist Andrei Sakharov and invited him to return from exile in Gorki.[2] One of the regime's most uncompromising opponents was to return to liberty.

Economic measures were not forgotten by Gorbachëv and Ryzhkov. A Law on the State Enterprise was being drafted to restrict the authority of the central planning authorities. There were simultaneous deliberations on the old proposal to introduce the 'link' system to agriculture. A commission was also set up to draft a Law on Co-operatives. But Gorbachëv himself, while pushing Ryzhkov to hurry forward with proposals, put his greatest effort into ideological and political measures. He did this in the knowledge that substantial progress on the economic front would be impeded until he had broken the spine of opposition to his policies in the party, including the Politburo. It took months of persuasion in 1986 before Gorbachëv could cajole the Politburo into agreeing to hold a Central Committee plenum in order to strengthen the process of reform.

When the plenum began on 27 January 1987, Gorbachëv went on to the offensive and called for changes in the party's official ideas. 'Developed socialism' was no longer a topic for boasting; it was not even mentioned: instead Gorbachëv described the country's condition as 'socialism in the process of self-development'.[3] Implicitly he was suggesting that socialism had not yet been built in the USSR. Democratization was now proclaimed as a crucial objective. This meant that the Soviet Union was no longer touted as the world's greatest democracy – and it was the General Secretary who was saying so. Gorbachëv called for the 'blank spots' in the central party textbooks to be filled. He denounced Stalin and the lasting effects of his policies. Despite not naming Brezhnev, Gorbachëv dismissed his rule as a period of 'stagnation' and declared that the leaving of cadres in post had been taken to the extremes of absurdity.[4]

Gorbachëv gained assent to several political proposals: the election rather than appointment of party committee secretaries; the holding of multi-candidate elections to the soviets; the assignation of non-party members to high public office. He succeeded, too, with an economic proposal when he insisted that the draft Law on the State Enterprise should enshrine the right of each factory labour-force to elect its own director. Gorbachëv aimed at industrial as well as political democratization.[5] This was not a leader who thought he merely had to learn from capitalist countries. Gorbachëv still assumed he could reconstruct the Soviet compound so that his country would patent a new model of political democracy, economic efficiency and social justice.

In June 1987 he presented the detailed economic measures at the next Central Committee plenum, which adopted the draft Law on the State Enterprise. Apart from introducing the elective principle to the choice of managers, the Law gave the right to factories and mines to decide what to produce after satisfying the basic requirements of the state planning authorities. Enterprises were to be permitted to set their own wholesale prices. Central controls over wage levels were to be relaxed. The reform envisaged the establishment of five state-owned banks, which would operate without day-to-day intervention by the Central State Bank.[6] As under Lenin's NEP, moreover, there was to be allowance for a private sector in services and small-scale industry. The reintroduction of a mixed economy was projected. Although there would still be a predominance of state ownership and regulation in the economy, this was the greatest projected reform since 1921.

Gorbachëv's argument was that the country was in a 'pre-crisis' condition.[7] If the USSR wished to remain a great military and industrial power, he asserted, then the over-centralized methods of planning and management had to be abandoned. He persuaded the plenum that the proposed Law on the State Enterprise was the prerequisite for 'the creation of an efficient, flexible system of managing the economy'. The plenum laid down that it should come into effect in January 1988.[8]

But Central Committee resolutions were one thing, their implementation quite another. Whereas communist intellectuals were attracted to the General Secretary, communist party functionaries were not. Gorbachëv's own second secretary and ally Ligachëv was covertly trying to undermine Gorbachëv's authority. Gorbachëv also had problems from the other side. Yeltsin in the Moscow Party City Committee was urging a faster pace of reform and a broader dimension for glasnost. Gorbachëv found it useful to play off Yeltsin and Ligachëv against each other. Of the two of them, Ligachëv was the more problematical on a regular basis; for he was in charge of ideological matters in the Secretariat and acted as a brake upon historical and political debate. But the more immediate problem was Yeltsin. His sackings of Moscow personnel left scarcely anyone in a responsible job who had held it for more than a year.

Ligachëv talked to Politburo colleagues about Yeltsin's domineering propensities; but Gorbachëv tried to protect Yeltsin. For a while Gorbachëv succeeded. But Yeltsin made things hard for himself by stressing his desire to remove the privileges of Mikhail and Raisa Gorbachëv. In his justified criticisms of the status quo, he lacked tactical finesse. Indeed he lacked all tact. He was a troubled, angry, impulsive individual. He also had no coherent programme. As an intuitive politician, he was only beginning to discover his purpose in politics, and his explorations were exhausting the patience of the General Secretary.

In October 1987 Gorbachëv accepted Yeltsin's resignation as a candidate member of the Politburo. Yeltsin had threatened to leave on several occasions, and this time Ligachëv made sure that he was not allowed to withdraw his resignation. And so the supreme party leadership lost Yeltsin. A few days later a conference of the Moscow City Party Organization was called. Although Yeltsin was in hospital recovering from illness,[9] he was pumped full of drugs and dragged along to attend: on a personal level it was one of the most disgraceful of Gorbachëv's actions. Yeltsin acknowledged his faults, but the decision had already been taken: a succession of speakers denounced his arrogance and he was sacked as party secretary of the capital. Only at this point did Gorbachëv take him sympathetically by the arm. He also showed mercy by appointing Yeltsin as Deputy Chairman of the State Construction Committee. But both of them assumed that Yeltsin's career at the centre of Soviet politics had ended.

Gorbachëv was more than ever the solitary fore-rider of reform. During his summer holiday in Crimea, he had edited the typescript for his book *Perestroika*; he began, too, to prepare a speech to celebrate the October Revolution's seventieth anniversary. In the weeks after the Central Committee plenum a large number of journalists, novelists, film-makers, poets – and yes, at last, historians – filled the media of public communication with accounts of the terror of the Stalin era and the injurious consequences of Brezhnev's rule. Gorbachëv sought to encourage and direct the process.

In November he published his book and delivered his speech. In both of them he denounced the regime's 'command-administrative system', which he described as having emerged under Stalin and having lasted through to the mid-1980s. He hymned the people more than the party. He treated not only the October Revolution but also the February Revolution as truly popular political movements. He also expressed admiration for the mixed economy and cultural effervescence of the New Economic Policy. He praised Lenin as a humanitarian, representing him as having been a much less violent politician than had been true. Despite lauding the NEP, moreover, Gorbachëv continued to profess the benefits of agricultural collectivization at the end of the 1920s. For Gorbachëv still equivocated about Stalin. In particular, the industrial achievements of the First Five-Year Plan and the military triumph of the Second World War were counted unto him for virtue.[10]

Certainly he had set out a stall of general objectives; but he had not clarified the details of strategy, tactics and policies. And he still regarded the objectives themselves as attainable without the disbandment of the one-party, one-ideology state. As previously, he refused to consider that the party and the people might not voluntarily rally to the cause of renovating Marxism-Leninism and the entire Soviet order. Nor did he take cognizance of the role of the Soviet Union as an imperial power both within its own boundaries and across Eastern Europe. The most he would concede was that 'mistakes' had been made in Hungary in 1956 and Czechoslovakia in 1968 – and he coyly blamed them on the 'contemporary ruling parties'.[11] No accusation was levelled at Kremlin leaders of the time. And Gorbachëv declined to reject the traditional class-based analysis of international affairs of the world as a whole.

These contradictions stemmed both from the pressures of his Politburo colleagues and from ambivalence in the mind of the General Secretary. Yet the general direction of his thought was evident. He required a yet deeper process of democratization. He declared that a new political culture and an insistence on the rule of law were required in the Soviet Union. He called for a fresh agenda for Eastern Europe. He also asserted that his country's foreign policy throughout the world should be based on 'common human values'.[12]

This was extraordinary language for a Soviet leader. Gorbachëv was diminishing the significance accorded to class-based analysis, and his emphasis on 'common human values' clashed with the Leninist tradition. Lenin had contended that every political culture, legal framework, foreign policy and philosophy had roots in class struggle. Leninists had traditionally been unembarrassed about advocating dictatorship, lawlessness and war. Gorbachëv hugely misconceived his idol. He was not alone: the reform communists, including well-read intellectuals, had persuaded themselves of the same interpretation to a greater or lesser extent and were transmitting their ideas to the General Secretary. Politics were being transformed on the basis of a faulty historiography. But what a transformation was involved! If it were to be accomplished, the USSR would adhere to legal, democratic procedures at home and pacific intentions abroad. Such changes were nothing short of revolutionary.

Much as he rethought his policies, however, Gorbachëv was also a disorganized thinker. His knowledge of his country's history was patchy. His sociological understandings may have been more impressive since his wife, who was his political as well as marital partner, had written a dissertation on contemporary rural relationships;[13] even so, his public statements continued to treat Soviet society as an inchoate whole and to make little allowance for the different interests of the multifarious groups in an increasingly complex society. His comprehension of economic principles was rudimentary in the extreme.

Nowhere was his complacency more baleful than in relation to the 'national question'. Superficially he seemed to understand the sensitivities of the non-Russians: for example, he excluded favourable mention of the Russians from the 1986 Party Programme and affirmed the 'full unity of nations' in the USSR to be a task of 'the remote historical future'.[14] This gave reassurance to the non-Russian peoples that there would be no Russification campaign under his leadership.

But no other practical changes of a positive kind followed. Gorbachëv himself was not a pure Russian; like his wife Raisa, he was born to a couple consisting of a Russian and a Ukrainian.[15] But this mixed ancestry, far from keeping him alert to national tensions in the USSR, had dulled his understanding of them. He was comfortable with his dual identity as a Russian and as a Soviet citizen; and this produced casualness that gave much offence. For example, when he visited Ukraine for the first time as General Secretary in 1986, he spoke about Russia and the USSR as if they were coextensive. Ukrainian national sensitivities were outraged.

The problem was exacerbated by the fact that non-Russians had been prevented from expressing their grievances. Inter-ethnic difficulties were the hatred that dared not speak its name. Gorbachëv and other central party leaders were slow to perceive the inherent risks involved in campaigning against corruption in the republics while also granting freedom of the press and of assembly. Much resentment arose over the appointment of Russian functionaries in place of cadres drawn from the local nationalities. In addition, more scandals were exposed in Kazakhstan and Uzbekistan than in Russia. The Kazakhstan party first secretary Dinmukhammed Kunaev, one of Brezhnev's group, had been compelled to retire in December 1986; even Geidar Aliev, brought from Azerbaijan to Moscow by Andropov, was dropped from the Politburo in October 1987. Eduard Shevardnadze was the sole remaining non-Slav in its membership. The Politburo was virtually a Slavic men's club.

An early sign of future trouble was given in Kazakhstan, where violent protests in Alma-Ata were organized against the imposition of a Russian, Gennadi Kolbin, as Kunaev's successor. The Kazakh functionaries in the republican nomenklatura connived in the trouble on the streets; and the intelligentsia of Kazakhstan were unrestrained in condemning the horrors perpetrated upon the Kazakh people in the name of communism. The nationalist resurgence had been quieter but still more defiant in Lithuania, Latvia and Estonia. The titular nationalities in these countries had a living memory of independence. Bilateral treaties had been signed in 1920 with the RSFSR and Stalin's forcible incorporation of the Baltic states in the USSR in

1940 had never obtained official recognition in the West. Demonstrations had started in Latvia in June 1986. Cultural, ecological and political demands were to the fore. A victory was won by the environmental protest against the hydro-electric station proposed for Daugavpils.

Then the dissenters in Lithuania and Estonia joined in the protest movement. Not all their leaders were calling for outright independence, but the degree of autonomy demanded by them was rising. In August 1987, demonstrations were held to mark the anniversary of the 1939 Nazi-Soviet Non-Aggression Treaty. The example of Latvia, Lithuania and Estonia stimulated national movements elsewhere. Discontent intensified in Ukraine after Chernobyl and Gorbachëv was so concerned about the political destabilization that might be produced by Ukrainian cultural, religious and environmental activists that he retained Shcherbytskiy, friend of Brezhnev, as the republican party first secretary. Ukraine was held firmly under Shcherbytskiy's control.

The USSR, furthermore, contained many inter-ethnic rivalries which did not predominantly involve Russians. Over the winter of 1987–8, disturbances occurred between Armenians and Azeris in the Armenian-inhabited area of Nagorny Karabakh in Azerbaijan. In February 1988 the two nationalities clashed in Sumgait, and dozens of Armenians were killed. Threats to the Politburo's control existed even in places that experienced no such violence. In June 1988 the Lithuanian nationalists took a further step by forming *Sajudis*; other 'popular fronts' of this kind were formed also in Latvia and Estonia. The Belorussian Communist Party Central Committee tried to suppress the popular front in Minsk, but the founding members simply decamped to neighbouring Lithuania and held their founding congress in Vilnius.

The tranquillity in Russia and Ukraine gave grounds for official optimism since these two republics contained nearly seven tenths of the USSR's population. Most Soviet citizens were not marching, shouting and demanding in 1988. Not only that: a considerable number of people in the Baltic, Transcaucasian and Central Asian regions did not belong to the titular nationality of each Soviet republic. Around twenty-five million Russians lived outside the RSFSR. They constituted thirty-seven per cent of the population in Kazakhstan, thirty-four per cent in Latvia and thirty per cent in Estonia.[16] In all three Baltic Soviet republics so-called 'Interfronts' were being formed that consisted mainly of Russian inhabitants who felt menaced by the local nationalisms and who were committed to the maintenance of the Soviet Union.

Shcherbytskiy prevented *Rukh*, the Ukrainian popular front, from holding its founding congress until September 1989. In Russia there was no analogous front; for there was no country from which, according to Russian nationalists, Russia needed to be separated in order to protect her interests. There was, however, much nationalist talk. An organization called *Pamyat*, which had been created with the professed aim of preserving Russian traditional culture, exhibited anti-Semitic tendencies; unlike the popular fronts in the non-Russian republics, it had no commitment to democracy. But Gorbachëv reasonably judged that the situation was containable. What he underestimated was the possibility that Ligachëv and his associates, too, might play the linked cards of Soviet state pride and of Russian nationalism. Ligachëv was affronted by the relentless public criticism of the Stalin years, and he was looking for an opportunity to reassert official pride in the Russian nation's role during the First Five-Year Plan and the Second World War. Many other party leaders felt sympathy with him.

Ligachëv bided his time until March 1988, when Gorbachëv was about to leave for a trip to Yugoslavia. A letter had reached the newspaper *Sovetskaya Rossiya* from an obscure Leningrad communist named Nina Andreeva, who demanded the rehabilitation of Stalin's reputation and implied that the country's woes after the October Revolution had been chiefly the fault of the Jewish element in the party leadership's composition. Despite this anti-Semitism, Ligachëv facilitated the letter's publication and organized a meeting of newspaper editors to impress on them that the season of free-fire shooting at communism past and present was at an end.

Gorbachëv conducted an enquiry on his return; but Ligachëv lied about his actions, and Gorbachëv accepted him at his word and resumed his own policy of glasnost.[17] Yet he also took precautions against any repetition of the event. Most importantly, he enhanced the position of Alexander Yakovlev, who had been a Politburo member since mid-1987 and became the radical-reformer counterweight to Ligachëv in the central party apparatus after Yeltsin's departure. Yakovlev supervised the publication of material about abuses under Brezhnev as well as under Stalin. A number of articles also appeared about Bukharin, who was depicted as the politician who had deserved to succeed Lenin.[18] The image of Bukharin as harmless dreamer was at variance with historical reality; but Gorbachëv believed in it – and, for both pragmatic and psychological purposes, he needed positive stories about Soviet communism to balance the exposés of the terroristic practices of the 1930s.

The problem for him was that the new journalism excited the reading public without managing to enlist its active political participation. The reformist magazines were inadvertently bringing all existing Soviet politicians, with the notable exception of Gorbachëv, into disrepute. If only the first decade of the USSR's history was officially deemed to have been beneficial, how could the Politburo justify its continuing rule?

Gorbachëv had hoped to avoid such a reaction by pensioning off those older politicians who had been prominent under Brezhnev. In his first year in power he had imposed new first secretaries on twenty-four out of seventy-two of the RSFSR's provincial party committees. Between April 1986 and March 1988 a further nineteen such appointments were made. Hardly any of these appointees came from Stavropol.[19] Gorbachëv wanted to break with the Soviet custom whereby a political patron favoured his career-long clients. Most of the appointees had recently been working under his gaze in Moscow and appeared to have the necessary talent. The snag was that the new incumbents of office made little effort to alter local practices and attitudes. On arrival in their localities, Gorbachëv's newcomers typically went native. The fact that they were younger and better educated than their predecessors made no difference to their behaviour.

In another way Gorbachëv himself was acting traditionally. Since

January 1987 it was official policy that local party organizations should elect their own secretaries; and yet Gorbachëv persisted in making his own appointments through the central party apparatus.

So why was he infringing his own policy for internal party reform? The answer highlights the scale of the obstacles in his path. He knew that party committees throughout the USSR were blocking the introduction of multi-candidate elections. Only one in every eleven secretaryships at all the various local levels was filled by such competition in 1987–8. Worse still, merely one per cent of province-level secretaries obtained posts in this fashion. And the fresh air ventilating public discussions in Moscow seldom reached the 'localities': the provincial press clamped down on the opportunities of glasnost. It is therefore unsurprising that Gorbachëv did not relinquish his powers of appointment in favour of elections. If he had left the local party committees to themselves, he would never have achieved the political and economic goals he had set for the communist party.

Nor could Gorbachëv lightly overlook the danger posed by Ligachëv and other leaders who opposed further radicalization of reforms. The January 1987 Central Committee plenum had taken the decision to convoke a Party Conference. Gorbachëv hoped that such a Conference, scheduled to meet in mid-1988, would change the composition of the Central Committee. For the Central Committee elected in 1986 still consisted mainly of functionaries appointed in the Brezhnev years. The 'nests' had selected anti-perestroika delegates to the Conference; and indeed, while Gorbachëv was meeting President Reagan in Vladivostok, the communist party rank-and-file in the same city rebelled against their corrupt provincial party secretary. Gorbachëv spoke up for the rebels. He also signed letters of reference for prominent Moscow-based supporters of his policies such as the historian Yuri Afanasev.

He also made a further advance with economic reform. The Law on the State Enterprise had come into effect in January 1988; and in May the Law on Co-operatives had been passed whereby co-op members could set their own prices and make their own deals both in the USSR and abroad. Certainly the fiscal disincentives were strong, and the local soviets were entitled to deny official registration to the co-ops. Yet the Law's significance was undeniable. For the first time in six decades it was permitted to set up urban manufacturing and service-sector enterprises that were not owned by the state.

Gorbachëv confidently opened the Nineteenth Party Conference on 28 June 1988 even though he had only half-succeeded in getting his supporters elected as delegates. His theses called for a strict functional separation between the party and the soviets. At the Conference he defined this more closely. He wanted to disband the economic departments in the Central Committee Secretariat and to reduce the size of the party apparatus in Moscow. At the same time the Supreme Soviet, which had had only an honorific role, was to become a kind of parliament with over 400 members who would be in session most of the year and be chosen from a Congress of People's Deputies consisting of 2,250 persons. As a sop to the Party Conference, Gorbachëv proposed that while two thirds of the deputies should be elected through universal suffrage, one third should be provided by 'public organizations' including the communist party.[20]

His assault on the party's prerogatives was relentless. Among his most startling suggestions was that local party first secretaries should automatically submit themselves for election to the parallel soviet chairmanship. He gave the impression that he expected such secretaries to retain their personal power. Yet privately he hoped that the electorate would use their votes to get rid of his opponents in the party.

Gorbachëv's audience consisted of delegations led by precisely the sort of communist party officials he wished to eliminate. The implications of his proposal were understood and resented by them; and whereas Ligachëv received a rapturous reception from the Conference, Gorbachëv was applauded only at the few points where he made comments of a conservative content. And then something unexpected occurred which enraged his critics still further: back from political oblivion came Boris Yeltsin. Uncertain that he would be allowed to address the Conference, he came down to the foot of the platform waving his party card. Gorbachëv made a gesture to him to take a seat in the front row of the hall until there was an opportunity for him to speak; and on this occasion Yeltsin chose his words with care, endorsing practically all Gorbachëv's proposals and humbly asking to be rehabilitated as a leader.

Critics were angry that Yeltsin should be picking up the pieces of his political career. After a pause in the Conference proceedings, Ligachëv led the counter-attack.[21] Yeltsin's record was torn to shreds. Even his career as a provincial party secretary in Sverdlovsk was mocked. Summing up the case for the prosecution, Ligachëv asserted: 'You, Boris, are not right!' The Conference took Ligachëv's side and Yeltsin was refused his request to be re-admitted to the supreme party leadership.

Gorbachëv had already dropped his plan to change the Central Committee's composition at the Conference; but he would make no further concessions to Ligachëv and insisted that the Conference should ratify his draft theses. And he had a final trick up his sleeve. Or rather he had it in his pocket. At the end of the Conference he pulled out a scrap of paper on which was scribbled his schedule for implementing the constitutional amendments. Without this, the central and local party apparatuses would have engaged in endless procrastination. Gorbachëv wanted the amendments to be in place by autumn 1988 and a general election to be held in spring 1989, followed by republican and local elections in the autumn. The internal reorganization of the party was set to occur by the end of 1988. Gorbachëv resumed his masterful tone: 'That's how the draft resolution comes out. It seems to me simply vitally necessary to accept this resolution, comrades.'[22] The delegates gave their approval before being given a chance to think about the consequences. Change was coming, and coming fast.

The Conference decisions embodied an important reorientation of Gorbachëv's strategy. The party was being dropped as the vanguard of perestroika. Instead Gorbachëv wished to rule through a Congress of People's Deputies elected by the people. The size and functions of the central party apparatus were sharply diminished at a Central Committee plenum held in September 1988. The same plenum left Vadim Medvedev instead of Ligachëv in charge of ideology and gave Yakovlev a supervisory role on the party's behalf in international affairs. Gromyko was pushed into retirement in

October and replaced as Chairman of the USSR Supreme Soviet by Gorbachëv himself (who refrained from redesignating the office as President until March 1990). The Soviet Union remained a one-party state; but the party as such had abruptly lost much of its power.

The Politburo was preoccupied by this domestic transformation. Not even Ligachëv – nor even, come to mention it, Yeltsin – badgered Gorbachëv about developments in Eastern Europe. The common feeling of Soviet political leaders was that the USSR's affairs should have priority of attention. Gorbachëv had set down the general line. On coming to power, he had advised the various leaderships of Warsaw Pact countries that the USSR would no longer interfere in their affairs.[23] But beyond this his comments on Eastern Europe were of a general nature. In 1985 he was still not averse to praising the anti-reform economic policies of the German Democratic Republic. Thereafter he spoke more fervently in favour of reforms in Eastern Europe. But his working assumption was that the communist leaderships of each country in the region had to find their own most suitable mode of political and economic transformation. He studiously avoided instructing the Warsaw Pact countries to follow the specific model of the USSR.

Gorbachëv held to his belief that the Soviet-style compound, once reconstituted, would flourish in Eastern Europe. He showed his priorities by his choice of places to visit and politicians to meet. In November 1985 he travelled to meet President Reagan in Geneva and in October 1986 they met again in Reykjavik. Not until April 1987 did Gorbachëv visit East Berlin and Prague. And in March 1988 he took a trip to Belgrade. In each of these East European capitals he was fêted by crowds. It was obvious to him and his entourage that people were using his public appearances as an opportunity to manifest their resentment of their own communist regimes.

Nevertheless Gorbachëv, Shevardnadze and Yakovlev continued to shape policy towards Eastern Europe without offering direct criticism of their counterparts in these countries. They even avoided leaning very hard on the parties and governments to replace their leaders. When the Bulgarian communist reformer Petar Mladenov approached Gorbachëv for advice as to how to replace the ageing hierarch Todor Zhivkov, Gorbachëv cut short the conversation.[24] Gorbachëv would have preferred Mladenov to Zhivkov as Bulgaria's leader; but the Soviet General Secretary wanted to avoid being seen to intervene. Thus he confirmed that what he had said confidentially to Warsaw Pact leaders in March 1985 had been intended seriously: non-interference was a reality. Even as late as his Prague trip, in April 1987, Gorbachëv fastidiously stated: 'We are far from intending to call on anyone to imitate us.'[25] So glasnost and perestroika were not commodities for obligatory export. But what, then, was meant to happen in Eastern Europe?

Zhivkov and his fellow veterans in the region asked the same question. They hated Gorbachëv's perestroika. Erich Honecker in the German Democratic Republic and Gustáv Husák in Czechoslovakia, who was nationally hated for doing the USSR's dirty business for years, felt betrayed. Even János Kádár in Hungary was troubled by the prospect of the introduction of political and cultural freedoms on the current Soviet paradigm. Yet Gorbachëv still desisted from openly attacking them. He contented himself with destabilizing the political compounds and standing back to observe the consequences. This was like a trainee chemist running amok in a laboratory. He was dealing with ingredients which, once tampered with, became volatile and unpredictable. If there remained doubts that Gorbachëv would go further than Khrushchëv in reforming foreign policy, a glance at the disintegrating communist order in Eastern Europe dispelled them.

It is mysterious how Gorbachëv persuaded himself that his version of 'communism' would emerge in a strengthened condition. The main explanation seems to be that he and Foreign Minister Shevardnadze simply overestimated the inherent attractiveness of their ideas. Probably, too, they were distracted by the cardinal significance they attached to relations with the USA. Negotiations with President Reagan took precedence over all other aspects of foreign policy. As the hidden dimensions of the USSR's domestic problems became apparent to Gorbachëv, so did his need for a drastic reduction in Soviet military expenditure. In practical terms this could be achieved only if both superpowers agreed to an end to the 'arms race' between them.

In October 1986 a summit meeting was held in Reykjavik, where Gorbachëv won over Reagan to a proposal for all nuclear weapons to be destroyed within ten years. But at the last moment Reagan's aides, who wished to bargain from a position of military superiority, dissuaded him from signing the preliminary agreement. The two men parted, unable to look one another in the face. Yet Reagan continued to wish Gorbachëv well. The denunciations of Stalin and Brezhnev; Sakharov's release from exile; the lightening grip on Eastern Europe: all these things counted in Gorbachëv's favour among Western governments. So that the amicable relations between the USA and the USSR survived the débâcle in Reykjavik. By December 1987 Gorbachëv and Reagan were able to co-sign the Intermediate Nuclear Forces Treaty in Washington whereby all ground-based intermediate nuclear weapons would be destroyed. The Cold War was gradually being ended; it was not yet a full peace, but it was no mere truce either.

In April 1988 the USSR announced its intention to make a swift, complete withdrawal of its forces from Afghanistan. Constantly Gorbachëv emphasized his commitment to 'new thinking' in international relations. Despite the primacy of the USSR-USA relationship, moreover, he wanted also to remove tensions from the Soviet Union's relations with other regions. Feelers were put out to the People's Republic of China. In an overture to Western Europe he spoke of 'the common European home'. On a visit to Vladivostok he spoke of the Pacific as 'our common home' and asked for friendlier links with Japan. If he had gone to the North Pole, he would no doubt have charmed the polar bears with his commitment to 'the common Arctic home'.

On 7 December 1988 Gorbachëv laid out the parameters of his foreign policy in a speech to the United Nations Assembly in New York. Marxist-Leninist concepts were tacitly rejected.[26] The need for global peace, Gorbachëv asserted, transcended support for class struggle. The world had become an 'interdependent' place. 'Common human values' had to triumph. Unlike his book *Perestroika*, the speech scarcely mentioned Lenin. In order to authenticate his commitment to peace and reconciliation, Gorbachëv announced a unilateral cut in the size of the Soviet Army by a tenth; he also promised the recall of six divisions from Eastern Europe. Mikhail Gorbachëv mounted to a peak of popularity abroad. Every agreement between Washington and Moscow had made global international relations safer and more controllable. If he had died in New York, he would already have secured a reputation as one of the great figures of the twentieth century.

In the USSR, too, he had effected what had once been a virtually inconceivable metamorphosis of politics and culture. Citizen talked unto citizen. Dangerous opinions could be shared outside the narrow boundaries of the family or group of friends. Soviet public life had been uplifted. Hidden issues had been dragged into the open air. Institutional complacency had been disturbed. Personnel had been re-appointed, policies redesigned. The entire structure of state had been shaken, and Gorbachëv let it be known that more walls had to be brought down before he could properly rebuild as he wished.

While battering the system in 1986–8, he hoped to change the Soviet order and secure popular approval and political legitimacy throughout society. He still aimed, in his confused fashion of thought, to preserve the Soviet Union and the one-party state. Lenin and the October Revolution were meant to remain publicly hallowed. But he failed to understand that his actions were strengthening the very phenomena which he was trying to eliminate. Glasnost and perestroika were undermining the political and economic foundations of the Soviet order. Localism, nationalism, corruption, illegal private profiteering and distrust of official authority: all these phenomena, which had grown unchecked under the rule of Brezhnev, had been reinforced by the dismantlement of central controls undertaken by Gorbachëv. He was Russia's 'holy fool', and like the 'holy fool' he did not know it.

24
Imploding Imperium
(1989)

By late 1988 the optimism of even Gorbachëv had been dented. As a full member of the Politburo since 1980 he had been privy to many statistics denied to the general public. But not even the Politburo had been given reliable information. Reports were automatically pruned of anything very discouraging, and anyway every local branch of administration misled the centre about the real situation.[1]

There had been a constant official prescription that crises were the exclusive characteristic of capitalism and that they could not occur under 'developed socialism'. In reality practically every index of economic performance was depressing. The technological gap between the USSR and industrially-advanced capitalist countries was widening in every sector except the development of armaments: the Soviet Union had been left far behind in both information technology and biotechnology. The state budget in the last years of Brezhnev would have been massively insolvent if the government had not been able to derive revenues from domestic sales of vodka. The Ministry of Finance depended heavily on popular consumption of alcohol. It relied to an even greater extent on the export of petrochemical fuels at high prices. Oil and gas constituted eighteen per cent of exports in 1972 and fifty-four per cent by 1984.[2]

The USSR resembled a Third World ex-colony in these and other respects. Agriculture remained so inefficient that two fifths of hard-currency expenditure on imports were for food.[3] By the early 1980s, revenues earned by exports to the West could no longer be used mainly to buy advanced industrial technology and equipment: two fifths of the USSR's hard-currency purchases abroad were of animal feed; and the purchase of energy by the countries of Eastern Europe at lower than the world-market prices deprived the USSR of the full value of its trade. Its very industrial achievements had occurred at grievous ecological expense. Large areas became unfit for human habitation. The Caspian Sea, Lake Baikal and the river Volga had been poisoned and the air in major cities such as Chelyabinsk was dangerous to breathe.

Yet while fighting the cause of economic reforms, Gorbachëv had made many mistakes. First the anti-alcohol campaign and then the excessive investment in the machine-tool industry in 1985–6 had depleted state revenues without producing long-term gains in output. Nor was this the end of his mismanagement. The openness of the debate conducted by the authorities in 1987–8 on the need to raise retail prices had the undesired effect of inducing consumers into buying up and hoarding all manner of goods. Shortages in the shops were increasing. And the Law on the State Enterprise, by empowering workers to elect their own managers, led to a steep rise in wages. Payments to urban work-forces increased by nine per cent in 1988 and thirteen per cent in 1989.[4] The Soviet budget was massively in deficit. Foreign indebtment and domestic inflation increased sharply; a decline in industrial output set in. The USSR was entering a state of economic emergency.

Gorbachëv's choice of collaborators, too, was far from ideal. Ryzhkov, his Chairman of the Council of Ministers, was a reformer, but a reformer who wanted 'to go to the market' at a snail's pace. And whereas Ryzhkov at least believed in a further movement to reform, Ligachëv did not. Gorbachëv erred, when demoting Ligachëv in the party leadership in September 1988, in putting him in charge of agriculture. This was like trusting the fox to guard the hen-house. Under Ligachëv's guidance not even the size of the private plots was increased.

Even if Gorbachëv had avoided such errors, however, he would also have needed a much better run of luck than he received. On 8 December 1988, a day after he had made his triumphant address to the United Nations Assembly, the cities of Leninakan and Spitak in Armenia were devastated by an earthquake. More than 25,000 people died. Ryzhkov phoned to New York to relay the news to Gorbachëv. Projected diplomatic negotiations were abandoned. Gorbachëv left the USA for Moscow next day and straightway hurried to Armenia. He and his wife talked to ordinary Armenians near the rubble of their former homes. The Gorbachëvs shed tears over the plight of the population. But they were totally unprepared for one thing: the fact that Armenians to a man and woman were agitated more about the politics of Karabakh than about the effects of the earthquake.[5]

Radical economic reform was therefore being attempted in a very unpropitious situation. The war in Afghanistan continued to involve massive expenditure until the last Soviet soldier returned home in February 1989. The Chernobyl nuclear explosion was a financial as well as a human and ecological disaster. Now the USSR's resources, already stretched to breaking point, had to cope with the task of recovery from the Armenian earthquake. Gorbachëv could have been forgiven for cursing his misfortune.

It must be mentioned that there had been a rise in the USSR's net material product by eleven per cent in the half-decade after 1983; but this had been obtained primarily through the tightening of labour discipline and the sacking of incompetent, corrupt officials. Such a strategy had been initiated by Andropov and resumed by Gorbachëv. It had a distinctly limited potential for the permanent enhancement of economic performance; and certainly it was unsustainable once the decentralizing decrees of 1987–8 started to have an impact. Between 1988 and 1990 net material product tumbled by nine per cent. The per capita consumption of factory-produced goods rose annually by less than 2.5 per cent in the five years after 1985. For food, the increase was 1.4 per cent; and – admittedly, mainly because of the anti-alcohol campaign – there was a decrease by 1.2 per cent for beverages and tobacco. Urban housing space per person rose merely by twelve per cent to a pitiful 13.1 square metres in the 1980s.[6]

The reorientation of the industrial sector towards the needs of civilian consumers was an unattained goal. Gorbachëv had promised much material improvement, but delivered deterioration. Instead of an advance to universal material well-being there was a reversion to food-rationing. Soviet queues, already legendary for their length, became longer and angrier in the course of 1989.

A rationing system had existed for food products in certain provincial cities even before 1985: it was one of Ligachëv's taunts at Yeltsin that, during his tenure of the local party secretaryship, he had issued the inhabitants of Sverdlovsk with ration-cards to do their shopping. Steadily the system was geographically extended. Already at the end of 1988, meat was rationed in twenty-six out of fifty-five regions of the RSFSR. Sugar was even scarcer: only two regions managed to get by without rationing.[7] At the same time the hospitals were reporting shortages of medicines and there was no end in sight to inadequate provision of housing and everyday services. It is true that the annual growth in the output of agriculture rose from one per cent in the first half of the decade to just under two per cent in the second.[8] But production remained inadequate for the needs of consumers. Throughout the 1980s, agricultural imports constituted a fifth of the population's calorific intake.

To the stupefaction of the Politburo (and nearly all commentators in the USSR and the West), a full-scale economic crisis had occurred. Its abruptness was as impressive as its depth. Suddenly Gorbachëv was faced with two life-or-death alternatives: either to abandon the reforms or to make them yet more radical. He never gave serious consideration to the former; his experience in his Stavropol days and subsequently had proved to him that Brezhnev's policies would lead only to a widening of the gap in technology and organization between the USSR and the capitalist West.

Boldness therefore seemed to him the only realistic choice. When the Law on the State Enterprise and other measures failed to produce the desired results, Gorbachëv talked about the need to go further and create a 'socialist market economy' – and while he refrained from defining the term, several of his advisers suggested that it should involve more market than socialism. Perhaps Gorbachëv was at his most relaxed when speaking about agriculture. Already in 1986, for instance, he had authoritatively proposed that each sovkhoz and kolkhoz should be run on the basis of 'family contracts'.[9] By this he meant that a family or household would take over a particular function on the farm and be rewarded for any increase in productivity. As his critics noted, this would involve a reversion to peasant forms of farming; but Gorbachëv faced them down by openly advocating the need to turn the peasant into 'master of the land'.[10]

But this change in ideas was not yet realized in policy, far less in practice. Basic positive changes in agriculture did not occur, and the situation in industry and commerce was no more inspiring. On the contrary, officials in every republic, region and province implemented only such aspects of legislation as did not damage their immediate interests. Initially their inclination was to show outward enthusiasm for Gorbachëv while disobeying his instructions. But in some localities the attitude was sterner and officials engaged in blatant sabotage. For example, the Leningrad city administration gave orders to withdraw sausages from the fridges in its warehouses and bury them in a specially-dug trench on the city's outskirts. These were the politics of criminal provocation. Life without beef and chicken was bad enough for ordinary citizens; without sausages it became intolerable, and Gorbachëv got the blame.

Even so, the central party and governmental bodies remained powerful enough to secure the establishment of a rising number of small private-sector co-operatives in most major cities. The trouble was that these new enterprises were distrusted by the rest of society, especially by people on low fixed incomes: the pensioners, the war invalids, the poorly-paid unskilled workers. The co-ops had a reputation as scams for speculation, and certainly they did little to expand manufacturing output. This was not exclusively their fault since the local political authorities usually withheld licences for private industrial enterprises. Co-ops operated mainly in the economy's service and retail sectors and flourished in the form of private restaurants and clothes-kiosks which bought up goods in supply and put a large mark-up on them.

The consequence was that these same goods were not being sold in state-owned enterprises. The co-ops aggravated the shortages in the shops and raised the cost of living. They also added to the problems of law-breaking since their owners had to bribe local government officials in order to be allowed to trade; and often it was impossible for them to obtain raw materials and equipment except by colluding with venal factory directors. The Kremlin reformers called ineffectually for honesty. But the reality was that they would have found it even more difficult to install co-ops if the members of local administrative élites had not benefited materially from them. Illegality had to be accepted as companion to the re-emergence of private economic activity.

By the approach of winter 1989–90, all this brought notoriety to the Politburo's reforms. Milk, tea, coffee, soap and meat had vanished from state retail outlets even in Moscow. The dairy-product shops were hit particularly badly. They often had to function for days at a time without anything to sell: cartons of milk had ceased to reach them, and the staff had nothing to do but explain to an ill-tempered public that they had nothing to sell.

Not all citizens were willing to tolerate their plight. A great strike was organized by coal-miners in Kemerovo in the Kuz Basin and their example was followed by the work-force of the mines in the Don Basin – and the miners in Karaganda in Kazakhstan also struck in the first half of 1989. A further strike occurred in November in the mines around Norilsk in the Siberian far north.[11] All these strikes were settled in favour of the strikers, who demanded higher wages and improved living conditions; and in contrast with Soviet political practice since the Civil War no repressive sanctions were applied against the strike leaders.[12] Independently-elected strike committees were in operation. The Council of Ministers under Ryzhkov did little else in these months but try to effect a reconciliation with those segments of the working class which threatened to do it damage. The government feared that a Soviet equivalent of Poland's Solidarity was in the making.[13]

But the Soviet authorities weathered the storm. The strikers lived in far-flung areas, and Ryzhkov and his fellow ministers managed to isolate them from the rest of society by quickly offering them higher wages. Yet the government was faced by a society embittered against it. Elections to the Congress of People's Deputies had duly occurred in March 1989, and the result administered the greatest electoral shock to the communists since the Constituent Assembly polls in 1917–18. Across the country thirty-eight province-level party secretaries were defeated.[14] So, too, were city secretaries in the republican capitals in Kiev, Minsk and Alma-Ata. Even Yuri Soloviev, Politburo candidate member and Leningrad communist party boss, was rejected by voters. Unlike Lenin, Gorbachëv did not overturn the elections. To those of his party comrades who had incurred the people's disapproval he signalled that they should step down from their posts in the party and other institutions.

None the less the Congress was not without its problems for Gorbachëv. Eighty-eight per cent of the delegates were full or candidate members of the Communist Party of the Soviet Union, and most of these disliked proposals for further reforms.[15] Yuri Afanasev, who was committed to just such reforms, denounced the Congress as a 'Stalinist-Brezhnevite' body with 'an aggressively obedient majority'.[16] Gorbachëv thought him ungrateful and irresponsible; for Afanasev had needed his protection to consolidate himself in public life.

Gorbachëv also felt betrayed by criticisms he suffered in the non-Russian republics. In November 1988 the Estonian Supreme Soviet declared its right to veto laws passed in Moscow; in January 1989 Lithuanian nationalists held a demonstration against the continued location of Soviet Army garrisons in Lithuania. The official authorities in these countries decided to drop Russian as the state language. Latvia was not far behind: in the course of the elections there was a protest rally in Riga against the Latvian Communist Party Central Committee's repudiation of 'anti-Soviet and separatist' trends of thought in Latvia. The mood of the majority nationalities in the Baltic republics was shared in the Transcaucasus, but with fatal consequences. A demonstration in favour of national independence was held in the Georgian capital Tbilisi in April 1989. Gorbachëv returned from abroad in the course of the crisis, but his efforts to prevent bloodshed were frustrated by Georgian communist leaders and Soviet Army commanders. Nineteen unarmed civilians were killed.[17]

There was further trouble in the republics before the Congress of People's Deputies convened. The Soviet Army was dispatched to

Uzbekistan, Estonia and Latvia in reaction to the possibility of protests on the Georgian model. The Soviet 'empire' was going to be maintained by force. Such actions were not guided primarily by Russian nationalism: the Politburo would have done the same in Leningrad or Saratov or Kursk. But this is not the way it appeared to the republican protesters. In June, Estonia proclaimed its economic autonomy and Lithuania declared its right to overrule the USSR's legislation. Even quiet Moldavia had a popular front that rejected the area's annexation by the Soviet Union in 1940.

So that the Congress, whose first session lasted from 25 May to 9 June, reflected the political divisiveness in the country. What once had been said privately in living-rooms was given full-throated public utterance. The proceedings were transmitted live on television and work stopped in factories and offices when sensitive issues were debated. Every citizen wanted to enjoy the spectacle. Most deputies were neither radicals nor out-and-out conservatives (in the sense of Soviet politicians wishing to avoid radical reforms). It was the middle-ranking politicians, administrators, managers and scholars who occupied a majority of the Congress seats. Such people were willing, on the whole, to support the General Secretary; but they would no longer offer automatic obedience. Shrugging off the tight discipline of previous years, they spoke passionately about the policies that bothered them. Gorbachëv had to deploy much charm, guile and patience to hold them on his side in the elaboration of reforms.

He got his way. The specific form of this vast Congress had been of Gorbachëv's own making: it appealed to his sense of Russian traditions, notably the mass political gatherings of Lenin's time. He was looking back to the October Revolution with rose-tinted glasses; in particular, he did not perceive that the soviets in 1917–18 had been a forum for endless, chaotic disputes as workers, peasants, soldiers and intellectuals discussed the issues of the day.

The turbulence of the Congress of People's Deputies surprised him. But once created, the Congress had to be made to function. Having arranged that he should be elected Chairman of the Supreme Soviet, Gorbachëv chaired most sessions of the Congress; for he rightly judged that only he had the personal authority and mental agility to prevent debates from running out of control. The fact that a Congress of People's Deputies had been elected at all was a massive achievement even though the elections were marred by gerrymandering by central and local political élites. But this was not an end in itself. Gorbachëv needed to use the Congress as an institution for the ratification of his strategy for political and economic reform; he had to pre-empt its becoming simply a verbal battleground between conservatives and radicals.

Yeltsin again caused trouble. Standing as a candidate in Moscow, he had run a brilliant campaign against the sleazy lifestyle of the nomenklatura and had won nine tenths of the city's vote. But this victory did not endear him to the Congress; and when it came to the Congress's internal elections to the 542 seats of the new USSR Supreme Soviet, a majority rejected him. He obtained a seat only when an elected member of the Supreme Soviet voluntarily yielded his own seat to him. Gorbachëv went along with this improvised compromise; he wanted to show that his own slogan of democratization was sincere: Yeltsin had to be seen to be treated decently.

Yeltsin and the Congress radicals showed Gorbachëv no gratitude; they were determined to use the Congress as a means of constituting a formal opposition to the communist regime despite the fact that most of them were still communist party members. Around 300 of them gathered together in an Inter-Regional Group led by Yeltsin, Sakharov, Afanasev and the economist Gavril Popov. It included liberals, social-democrats, greens and even some communists; its unifying purpose was to push Gorbachëv into making further moves against his conservative central and local party comrades. But the Inter-Regional Group itself could not throw off all caution. Its members were outnumbered by the conservative-communist rump at the Congress; and if they had seriously tried to undermine Gorbachëv's dominance, the only result would have been to destabilize his control over the communist party and to wreck the cause of reform.

The Inter-Regional Group also faced problems outside the Congress. Active popular opposition to communist conservatism was strongest in the non-Russian Soviet republics. It is true that political associations had been formed in Moscow and other Russian cities since 1987. These associations were known as the 'informals' (*neformaly*) since the USSR Constitution gave formal public recognition solely to the Communist Party of the Soviet Union. Some 'informals' had local and ecological interests; others were motivated primarily by particular credos: patriotism, anti-Stalinism, democracy, civil rights and socialism. In 1988 there were attempts to co-ordinate such activities and a 'Klub Perestroika' was created. Another such oppositionist organization was the Democratic Union. But neither the Club nor the Union had many branches in other cities of the RSFSR.[18] Rivalries of ideology, region, class and personality inhibited the birth of a unified Russian radical movement.

This was a disadvantage not only for the Inter-Regional Group but also for Gorbachëv. The various reformers in Russia were unable to stimulate much popular participation in their projects, and the *neformaly* had only a few thousand members. In such a situation it would not be impossible for Ligachëv, were he ever to oust Gorbachëv from the communist party leadership, to close down the Congress of People's Deputies and re-establish the traditional structures of the communist regime.

Not that Russians were untouched by the excitement of the times. A religious and cultural renaissance had begun. The millenium of the Russian Orthodox Church was celebrated in 1988 and Gorbachëv met Patriarch Pimen and transferred several churches and monasteries out of state control. The Church hierarchy had not covered itself in glory in earlier years and had regularly been castigated by the writer Alexander Solzhenitsyn as well as by parish priests such as Dmitri Dudko and Gleb Yakunin for its failure to stand up to the Politburo. But this sorry history started to be forgotten, and cathedrals and churches were packed out with the believing few and the inquisitive many. Old ladies could safely stand by the kerb with ecclesiastical collecting boxes; clerics began to be invited on to TV and radio discussion programmes. Christian philosophical literature was produced in abundance. The Bible was put on open sale.

Not all developments were so high minded. Salacious booklets such as *The Lovers of Catherine II* were sold from stalls at Moscow metro stations; and publishing houses increasingly preferred to invest in Agatha Christie and John Le Carré than in the Russian literary classics. Russia was also acquiring a paperback trade in works on astrology, pet-rearing, horticulture, crossword puzzles and tarot cards. Pop music was broadcast on TV stations, and Paul McCartney recorded a special album for the Soviet market. Meanwhile Russian rock stars showed greater willingness to comment on issues of the day than their Western models. Youth did not revolt against authority; it despised and ignored it. Indeed citizens, both young and old, treated politics as a spectator sport but not a process deserving their participation. The quest for private pleasure outdid the zeal for public service.

This dispiriting situation was readily explicable. People were exhausted by queues, food shortages and administrative chaos. Life was getting more arduous day by day. Despite this, Gorbachëv was still the country's most popular politician (and it was not until mid-1990 that Yeltsin overtook him in this respect).[19] Yet politicians generally were not respected. Gorbachëv inadvertently added to the effect by his tactics: he held no trials of oppressive rulers of the 1950s, 1960s and 1970s; even the torturers, false delators and political killers of the 1930s and 1940s escaped with only verbal criticism. The pensions and honours of the victimizers remained untouched, and Vyacheslav Molotov and Lazar Kaganovich lived out their old age without interference: Molotov even had his party membership restored to him. The result was that while the mass media blared out their critique of past abuses in general terms, little was changed in the lives of the surviving victims. Historical unfairness remained in place. The practical and mental catharsis of Soviet society had been only half accomplished.

No wonder that most people remained quietly cynical. They had their own quiet, private aspirations. After years of being bored by stuffy Marxism-Leninism, their ideal of Freedom was not the freedom to join a political party and attend open meetings on city squares. They wanted to stay at home and enjoy the freedom to be frivolous, apolitical, unmobilized.

Such a desire was especially prevalent in Russia; but things stood somewhat differently in the other Soviet republics. Middle-aged citizens in the Baltic region could remember a time when Estonia, Latvia and Lithuania had been independent states. This was the case only for the very elderly in the Transcaucasus. Nevertheless there was trouble in store for the Kremlin in all republics. Each of them had been territorially demarcated according to ethnic demography; each of them had enhanced its sense of individuality by emphasizing the importance of the local national language and culture. The Leninist mode of organizing a state of many nations was at last displaying its basic practical weakness. Everywhere nationalist dissent was on the rise. Its leaders were succeeding in convincing their local electorates that the problems of their respective nation were insoluble unless accompanied by economic and administrative reforms.

Few Russians felt similarly uncomfortable to be living in the USSR; and, to a greater extent than non-Russians, they tended to worry lest a further reform of the economy might deprive them of such state-provided welfare as was currently available. Moreover, ethnic Russians were numerically predominant throughout the traditional institutions of the Soviet state. In party, government and armed forces they held most of the key positions. In the newer institutions, by contrasts, they were beginning to lose out. Only forty-six per cent of the USSR Congress of People's Deputies, and indeed only a third of the members of the Politburo itself when it underwent reform in 1990, were ethnic Russians.[20]

A further peculiarity of Russians, in comparison with the other nations of the Soviet Union, was the highly contradictory mélange of ideas that came from their cultural figures. Gorbachëv's supporters no longer went unchallenged in their propagation of reformist communism. Several artistic and political works also appeared which attacked communism of whatever type. For example, Vasili Grossmann's novel on the Soviet past, *Forever Flowing*, was serialized in a literary journal. So, too, was Alexander Solzhenitsyn's history of the labour-camp system, *The Gulag Archipelago*. Both works assailed Lenin and Stalin with equal intensity. A film was made of the labour camp on the White Sea island of Solovki, which was filled with political prisoners from the 1920s. A sensation was caused, too, by Vladimir Soloukhin's *Reading Lenin*. By analysing volume thirty-eight of the fifth edition of Lenin's collected works, Soloukhin showed Lenin to have been a state terrorist from the first year of Soviet government.

An attempt was made by officially-approved professional historians to repulse the assault on Leninism. But most of such historians before 1985 had put political subservience before service to historical truth. Even those among them who had experienced official disfavour under Brezhnev obtained little popularity with the reading public. Communism in general was falling into ever greater disrepute, and the official fanfares for Lenin, Bukharin and the New Economic Policy were treated as fantasias on a tired theme.

Gorbachëv's measures of political democratization inevitably added to his difficulties. The Congress of People's Deputies and the Supreme Soviet had the right to supervise and veto the activities of government – and he encouraged them to use the right. High politics came under open critical scrutiny. The Tbilisi massacre was the first subject of several exhaustive investigations. Hardly a day passed without ministers and other high-ranking state officials, including even Ryzhkov, being harangued when they spoke to the Congress; and, to their chagrin, Gorbachëv did little to protect them. The result was less happy than he assumed. Unified central executive authority was steadily weakened and traditional structures were dismantled without the creation of robust substitutes. Policies were sanctioned with no bodies ready and able to impose them.[21]

Furthermore, the reorganizations were unaccompanied by a clear demarcation of powers. By 1989 Gorbachëv was talking a lot about the need for a 'law-based state', and universal civil rights were added to his set of objectives. But as yet there was no law on press freedom. Far from it: when in May 1989 *Arguments and Facts* published an inaccurate opinion poll indicating that his popularity had plummeted, Gorbachëv summoned editor Vladislav Starkov and threatened to have him sacked. The fact that Gorbachëv left Starkov in post was a credit to his self-restraint, not a sign of the practical limits of his power.[22]

Others displayed no such caution. Public organizations had never had greater latitude to press for their interests. Local party secretaries, republican chiefs, factory managers, generals, scholars and KGB chiefs had belonged to the USSR's representative state organs since the Civil War. But previously they had had little autonomy from the central political leadership. The Congress of People's Deputies and the Supreme Soviet gave these various figures a chance to speak their mind. In particular, Colonel Viktor Alksnis complained about the deterioration in the prestige and material conditions of Soviet armed forces after the final, humiliating withdrawal from the war in Afghanistan. Alksnis addressed the Congress as an individual, but he rightly claimed that other officers in the Soviet Army shared his feelings. Such tirades at least had the merit of frankness. Above all, they increased political awareness amidst a population that had been starved of information judged injurious to the regime.

The old élites were rallying to defend themselves. The humiliation of the communist party in the Congress elections was only partial: local communist apparatuses remained largely in place and aimed to retain their authority. Other public institutions, too, had scarcely been touched by the campaign of propaganda to make them more responsive to society's demands. The personnel and structures of communism had survived the storms of perestroika largely intact.

Of course, important additions had been made to the wings of the USSR's political edifice. The KGB, while not dismantling its great network of informers, was no longer arresting citizens for lawful acts of political dissent. An independent press of sorts had been constructed. Whereas *Arguments and Facts* and *Ogonëk* had been established by the Soviet state, the journal *Glasnost* arose from the initiative of Sergei Grigoryants. Moreover, the cultural intelligentsia was writing, painting and composing in a liberated mood; and its organizations reflected the diversity of its objectives. Thus the Union of Writers of the RSFSR acted more or less as a megaphone for Russian nationalism. Similarly, the party and governmental machines in the non-Russian republics were consolidating themselves as instruments of the aspirations of the local majority nationality. All this constituted a menace to Gorbachëv's ultimate purposes. Interest groups, organizations and territorial administrations functioned with scant interference; and most of them either disliked reform or wanted a type of reform different from Gorbachëv's vision.

The trend had an arithmetical precision. The greater the distance from Moscow, the bolder were nations in repudiating the Kremlin's overlordship. The communist regimes of Eastern Europe had been put on notice that they would have to fend politically for themselves without reliance on the Soviet Army. This knowledge had been kept secret from the populations of the same states. If the news had got out, there would have been instantaneous revolts against the existing communist regimes. No wonder the Soviet General Secretary was seen by his foreign Marxist-Leninist counterparts as a dangerous subversive.

This was also the viewpoint on him taken by fellow central leaders in the USSR. Rebelliousness and inter-ethnic conflict were on the rise in non-Russian republics. In June 1989 there were riots between Uzbeks and Meshketian Turks in Uzbekistan. In the following months there was violence among other national groups in Georgia, Kazakhstan and Tajikistan. Gorbachëv appeared on television to declare that the stability of the state was under threat. In the Georgian Soviet republic there was violence between Georgians and Abkhazians as well as marches in Tbilisi in favour of Georgian national independence. In August a dramatic protest occurred in the three Baltic republics when a human chain was formed by one million people joining hands across Estonia, Latvia and Lithuania in commemorative protest against the Nazi-Soviet Pact of 1939. Yet Gorbachëv refused to contemplate the possibility of the Baltic republics seceding from the USSR. Ultimately, he assumed, their citizens would perceive their economic interests as being best served by their republics remaining within the Union.[23]

In September 1989 the Ukrainian giant stirred at last with the inauguration of Rukh. At this Gorbachëv panicked, flew to Kiev and replaced Shcherbytskiy with the more flexible Vladimir Ivashko. Evidently Gorbachëv recognized that the clamp-down on Ukrainian national self-expression had begun to cause more problems than it solved. At this moment of choice he preferred concession to confrontation; but thereby he also took another step towards the disintegration of the USSR. Neither of the alternatives offered Gorbachëv a congenial prospect.

Movement occurred in the same direction for the rest of the year. In October the Latvian Popular Front demanded state independence; in November the Lithuanian government itself decided to hold a referendum on the question. Next month the Communist Party of Lithuania, concerned lest it might lose every vestige of popularity, declared its exodus from the Communist Party of the Soviet Union. Tensions increased between resident Russians and the majority nationalities in the Baltic republics: the Estonian proposals for a linguistic qualification for citizenship of Estonia were especially contentious. In Estonia and Latvia, furthermore, the nationalist groupings won elections by a handsome margin. The situation was even graver for Gorbachëv in the Transcaucasus. In December 1989 the Armenian Supreme Soviet voted to incorporate Nagorny Karabakh into the Armenian republic. In January 1990 fighting broke out in the Azerbaijani capital Baku. The Soviet Army was sent to restore order, and attacked the premises of the Azerbaijani Popular Front.

But the deployment of the armed forces did not deter trouble elsewhere: inter-ethnic carnage was already being reported from Uzbekistan and Tajikistan in February. The possibility that the USSR might implode under these pressures began to be discussed in the press. The more rhetorical of politicians warned against any actions that might lead eventually to civil war across the USSR.

This worry distracted the minds of Soviet citizens from foreign affairs. If it had not been for the preoccupations of the domestic economic, political and national environment, attention would have been paid to events of epochal importance in Eastern Europe. Since the defeat of Hitler in 1945 the Soviet Army had maintained a vast zone of political and economic dominion and military security in the countries to the east of the river Elbe. Every VE-Day after 1945 had been celebrated on the assumption that this zone was an inviolable feature of the European map. Over the years of his power

Gorbachëv had indicated, in language that became ever more explicit, that the peoples of the Warsaw Pact countries should be empowered to choose their political system for themselves. But even he was astonished by the rapidity with which communist governments collapsed in country after country in the second half of 1989.

The process began in Poland. After an agreement to submit themselves to contested elections, the communists had been soundly defeated in June, and in August meekly joined a coalition under the anti-communist Tadeusz Mazowiecki. In September the Hungarian communist government allowed tens of thousands of East Germans to cross its frontiers and seek asylum in Austria; in October the ageing Erich Honecker was sacked as party boss in the German Democratic Republic. Within weeks the reformed communist leadership was permitting its citizens unimpeded transit to the Federal Republic of Germany. Meanwhile Todor Zhivkov retired in Bulgaria. The Czechoslovak government, too, was replaced. In the last month of this remarkable year, President Gustáv Husák resigned and the dissenting dramatist Vacláv Havel was elected by parliament to take his place (while the communist leader of the 'Prague Spring' of 1968 Alexander Dubček returned to head the Federal Assembly).

The dominoes were tumbling fast. The fall of any communist regime made the surviving ones more susceptible to collapse. And yet *Pravda* noted the succession of events with studied calmness. Such reportage was the sharpest sign to date that Gorbachëv was predominantly engaged with Soviet internal affairs and would pull no chestnuts out of the fire for the USSR's post-war allies. Gorbachëv had not intended to preside over the end of communism in Eastern Europe; but he did not act to prevent the last scenes in the drama from being enacted.

Events in Romania took a dramatic turn in December 1989, when Nicolae Ceauşescu appeared on his palace balcony to address a loyal Bucharest crowd. Ceauşescu was challenged in a scene akin to a spaghetti Western movie: he was catcalled. When he failed to intimidate the assembled crowd, he leapt into a helicopter before trying to flee the country in a fast-driven limousine; but he was captured and summarily tried and executed. Gorbachëv had often confidentially expressed his horror of the Romanian terror-regime; indeed he had tried, just a few days earlier in a Moscow meeting with Ceauşescu, to persuade him that his regime would eventually incur the people's wrath. But Ceauşescu had spurned him, making little attempt to hide his disapproval of the USSR's perestroika. The grotesque finale to communism in Romania was thought by Gorbachëv to settle their argument in his own favour.

It was a remarkable denouement. At the beginning of 1989 most countries in Europe east of the river Elbe were ruled by communists. At the year's end the sole remaining European communist state to the west of the USSR was Albania – and Albania had been hostile to the USSR since Khrushchëv's period of office.

Gorbachëv could have sent the Soviet Army to suppress the anti-communist movements earlier in the year. He would, needless to emphasize, have paid a great price. In particular, he would have forfeited the diplomatic support he had from Western countries; certainly he would have reinstigated tensions with the USA, which would have led to yet another race to construct new forms of nuclear weaponry. And yet any one of Gorbachëv's predecessors would not have blanched at a resumption of the Cold War. That he chose to avoid such a course was among his momentous choices. It took exceptional determination to stand by policies involving the minimum of violence when this resulted in the demise not only of old-style communism but even of those communist leaders in Eastern Europe who were his political allies. He had not set out to achieve this end; rather it was the unwilled result of his activity as it developed. But great was the work of his hands.

25

Hail and Farewell
(1990–1991)

Gorbachëv wanted to prevent the disappearance of self-styled communist leaderships in Eastern Europe being repeated in the USSR. His domestic achievements were already enormous. Official party policies in the USSR would have been compelled to get nastier if left intact. Economic decline, political conflict, national embitterment, social alienation and environmental degradation: all these would have increased. The communist party apparatus might well have reverted to a clumsy version of Stalinism or might even have stumbled into a clash with the USA at the risk of a Third World War.

Instead Gorbachëv had been working at the renewal of the Soviet compound by means of reform. But reform implies a series of modifications which leave the basic political, economic and social order intact. In fact Gorbachëv's rule already involved change of a much greater dimension. Several of the principal features of communism in the USSR were being undermined by his activity: the one-party state, the mono-ideological controls, the militant atheism, the centralized administration, the state economic monopoly and the suspendability of law. Perestroika was no longer a project for partial alterations but for total transformation. It was scarcely surprising that many Soviet leaders, including several who owed him their promotion to the Politburo, were aghast. Gorbachëv was no longer what he had claimed to be. By his actions, if not by his deliberate purpose, he was abetting the disintegration of the existing compound.

His intuitive brilliance did him little good; he remained hampered by his background from foreseeing where his path of transformation was leading. While wanting a market economy, he did not think this would involve much capitalism. While approving of national self-expression, he had set his face against any republic seceding from the USSR. While wishing to replace traditional communist functionaries with energetic newcomers, he often chose newcomers who had no commitment to serious reform. While aiming at an institutional division of powers, he induced chaos in governance. His personal confusion had practical consequences. Although he radicalized his proposals, he did this always more slowly than the pace of the deepening crisis over the economy, the republics, the administration and the personnel of the Soviet order. And this made his eventual fall all the more likely.

About Gorbachëv's dedication there was no doubt: 'I'm doomed to go forward, and only forward. And if I retreat, I myself will perish and the cause will perish too!'[1] He expected the same self-sacrifice from his associates. His group of intimates included several of his promotees to the Politburo: Alexander Yakovlev, Eduard Shevardnadze, Vadim Medvedev and Vadim Bakatin. Also important to him were aides such as Georgi Shakhnazarov and Anatoli Chernyaev; and he derived indispensable intellectual and emotional support from his wife Raisa despite her unpopularity with politicians and public alike.

But whereas he had once led from the front, by the end of the decade he was operating from the centre. Gorbachëv's technique was to calm the communist radicals, convince his loyalists and reassure the conservatives. In practical terms he aimed to dissuade as many critics as possible from leaving the party and campaigning against him. For this purpose he opted to remain in the party as its General Secretary; he argued that the alternative was to abandon the party and let his critics use it as an instrument to struggle for the rejection of his reformist measures. It was an uncongenial task. Most central and local functionaries incurred his contempt: 'They're careerists; all they want is their hands on power and their snouts in the feeding trough!'[2] But he said no such thing in public, and hoped that his patience would be rewarded by success in making the process of reform irreversible.

Within his entourage, Yakovlev argued against his refusal to leave the party. Yeltsin agreed with Yakovlev. So, too, did the dissenter Andrei Sakharov from outside the ranks of communism. Better, they all urged, to make a clean break and form a new party. But Gorbachëv spurned the advice. He increasingly thought of Yakovlev as unsound of judgement and Yeltsin as irresponsible. He had a higher estimate of Sakharov, who was widely acclaimed as Russia's liberal conscience. Gorbachëv was not averse to cutting off Sakharov's microphone when he did not like what he heard.[3] But by and large he ensured that this frail, croaky-voiced scientist should be given a hearing at the Congress of Soviets; and when Sakharov died in mid-December 1989, Gorbachëv paid his respects at his coffin.

Nevertheless Gorbachëv did not alter his mind about the communist party and continued to work for its fundamental reform from within. In February 1990 he produced a 'platform' for the Central Committee which was entitled 'Towards a Humane, Democratic Socialism' and which used his most extraordinary language to date: 'The main objective of the transitional period is the spiritual and political liberation of society.'[4] Gorbachëv's implication was that the USSR had always been a despotism. His vision of a socialist future, moreover, barely mentioned Lenin and Marxism-Leninism. None too gently Gorbachëv was repudiating most of the Soviet historical experience. Communism was no longer the avowed aim. Since Lenin, socialism had been depicted as merely a first post-capitalist stage towards the ultimate objective: communism. Now socialism itself had become the ultimate objective; and Gorbachëv's socialism would be a socialism antagonistic to dictatorship, to casual illegality, to a hypertrophied state economy and to cultural and religious intolerance. Indeed the draft platform was strongly reminiscent of Western social-democracy.

This similarity was not lost on Gorbachëv's critics. Provincial party secretary Vladimir Melnikov had already accused him of sculpting policies so as 'to appeal to the bourgeoisie and the Pope in Rome'.[5] Most critics, however, were more restrained. At the February 1990 Central Committee plenum they desisted from undertaking a frontal attack on the draft platform; they even acquiesced in Gorbachëv's demand for the repeal of Article 6 of the 1977

USSR Constitution, which guaranteed the political monopoly to the Communist Party of the Soviet Union. No rival party had been permitted to operate in the country since the early 1920s: Gorbachëv was breaking with the dictatorial heritage of his hero Lenin.

Gorbachëv was still but weakly aware of the implications of his activities; he continued to talk of going off to 'confer with Lenin' for inspiration.[6] But the rupture with Leninism was real. On 27 February 1990 Gorbachëv addressed the USSR Supreme Soviet and obtained its sanction for multi-party politics. The third convocation of the Congress of People's Deputies ratified the change on 14 April. The one-party state defended by communist apologists since the Civil War was relegating itself to oblivion. Gorbachëv reversed Lenin's policy as deftly as Lenin had introduced it. And while being innocent in his understanding of essential Leninism, Gorbachëv also needed to display much deviousness in order to get the institutional changes he desired. Otherwise he would never have succeeded in manipulating the central party apparatus, the ministries, the local administrations, the military high command and the security organs into accepting the step-by-step transformation of the Soviet state.

Yet the communist radicals were disgruntled with him. Yeltsin, who was still a Party Central Committee member as well as a leader of the Inter-Regional Group, was the most vociferous in demanding faster and deeper reform; and he grasped an opportunity to press his case when, in March 1990, he stood for election to the RSFSR Supreme Soviet and became its Chairman. Politically he was playing the 'Russian card'. Unable to challenge Gorbachëv directly at the level of the USSR, he asserted himself in the organs of the RSFSR.

The communist-conservative enemies of perestroika reacted furiously. Wanting to put pressure on Gorbachëv as well as to strike down Yeltsin, they adopted the device of forming a Communist Party of the Russian Federation. Their leader was Ivan Polozkov, Krasnodar Regional Party First Secretary. Why, asked Polozkov, should the RSFSR be denied a party tier long ago given to Ukraine and Uzbekistan? Gorbachëv accepted the validity of the question and assented to the foundation of the Russian party. Its first congress was held in June, and Polozkov became its First Secretary. Polozkov tried to take up the role of leading the party traditionalists, a role lost by Ligachëv after his successive demotions in 1989. Yet Polozkov was a much less prepossessing figure than Ligachëv. Gorbachëv kept him firmly in his place by refusing to intervene on his behalf to secure a suitable apartment for him in Moscow. Polozkov, a grumpy fellow, did little to enhance the popularity of his ideas in his few public appearances.

The dispute between Yeltsin and Polozkov took some of the heat off Gorbachëv. One of Gorbachëv's devices was to occupy a position above all the country's politicians and exploit their disagreements to his own advantage. He also had an interest in refraining from protecting any rivals from nasty accusations. Newspapers claimed that Ligachëv had made pecuniary gain from the corruption in Uzbekistan. Similarly it was alleged at the Congress of People's Deputies that Ryzhkov had been involved in shady industrial deals. Gorbachëv did nothing to help either of them.

Yeltsin, too, complained that dirty tricks were being played against him. In September 1989, when he was touring the USA, *Pravda* had reported him as having been drunk at Johns Hopkins University. Yeltsin claimed the problem to have been the tablets he was taking for his heart condition;[7] but he was less convincing about another incident, which happened upon his return to the USSR next month. As he walked late at night towards a dacha in Uspenskoe village near Moscow, he inexplicably tumbled into a river. His supporters claimed that this was an assassination attempt on him. Yet Yeltsin omitted to complain to the authorities. The conclusion of dispassionate observers might have been that there is no smoke without fire, but in Russia Yeltsin's predilection for vodka was not frowned upon. The Chairman of the Russian Supreme Soviet continued to be hailed as the people's champion. If anything, his escapade was regarded as near-martyrdom, and his prestige rose higher.

Speaking on behalf of the RSFSR, he assured Estonia, Latvia and Lithuania that he did not seek their forcible retention within the Soviet Union (whereas Gorbachëv's hostility to secession was the despair of his radical counsellors). In June 1990 Uzbekistan declared its sovereignty. On Yeltsin's initiative, so did the RSFSR. The disintegrative process affected even the internal affairs of the RSFSR when the autonomous republics of Tatarstan and Karelia demanded recognition as wholly independent states. The USSR's entire constitutional basis was being undermined. The threat no longer came mainly from defeated *émigré* nationalists but from active Soviet politicians.

By September, when even obedient Turkmenistan declared its sovereignty, it had become the general trend. Everywhere the republican leaderships were calling for democracy and national self-determination. In some cases, such as Estonia, there was a genuine commitment to liberal political principles. In most, however, the high-falutin terms disguised the fact that local communist party élites were struggling to avoid the loss of their power. The national card had been played by them quietly in the Brezhnev period. Republican assets had been regarded by the respective élites as their own patrimony; and, after they had seen off the anti-corruption campaigns of Andropov in 1982–4 and Gorbachëv in the mid-1980s, they settled down to enjoy their privileges. While detesting Gorbachëv's perestroika, they used his democratization of public affairs as a means of reinforcing their position and increasing their affluence. By announcing their independence, they aimed to seal off each republic from Moscow's day-to-day interference.

Gorbachëv held tight to his strategy. The Twenty-Eighth Party Congress met from 2 June 1990 and discussed the de-Leninized party platform approved by the Central Committee in February. This time Gorbachëv's critics shouted angrily at him, and delegates for the Russian Communist Party led a successful campaign to vote Alexander Yakovlev off the Central Committee. But Gorbachëv was retained as General Secretary by a huge majority and his platform was ratified by the Congress. When the election was held for the new post of his deputy in the party, Ligachëv was defeated by Ukrainian party first secretary Ivashko, whom Gorbachëv favoured, by 3,109 to 776 votes.

The Congress had granted that the Politburo should no longer intervene in day-to-day politics and that the USSR Presidency ought to become the fulcrum of decision-making. But Gorbachëv's victory did not satisfy Yeltsin and other communist radicals. They were annoyed by the down-grading of Yakovlev and urged Gorbachëv yet again to leave the communist party. When he refused, they walked out. Thus the Soviet President's support was narrowed at the very moment of his triumph. He repeated that if he left the communist party, its central and local officials would carry out a coup against him and his reforms. Was this plausible? The attempted coup in August 1991 was to show that his fears were not imaginary. But this in itself does not vindicate Gorbachëv's judgement. For the coup leaders would have had much greater difficulty if they had confronted a Soviet social-democratic party under Gorbachëv that had split from the communist party.

But Gorbachëv had made his political choice to stay with the Communist Party of the Soviet Union. Among other things, this had the consequence that drastic economic measures would be postponed and that popular living standards would go on falling. The industrial, commercial and financial sectors were on the edge of collapse. Even according to official figures, output from manufacturing and mining enterprises in 1990 fell by one per cent over the previous year.[8] Retail trade was reduced to pitiful proportions. Massive state loans were contracted with Western banks. Imports of grain and industrial consumer goods increased. Gorbachëv refused to allow any factory or kolkhoz to go to the wall, and there were no bankruptcies. But the general economic condition was dire. Most Soviet citizens could hardly believe that so rapid a deterioration had taken place. Industry was on the verge of collapse. Inflation was rising; banking and commerce were in disorder.

They blamed Gorbachëv. What counted for them was not that the economy had basically been in long-term decline long before 1985 but that they themselves were worse off than for decades. Even if they were unaware of the huge technical flaws in the Law on the State Enterprise, they knew from direct experience that the attempt at reform had not worked and that Gorbachëv's promises of economic regeneration had not been fulfilled. By 1990, people were wondering whether they would soon be starving. There had not been such fear about the popular living conditions since the end of the Second World War.

At this point of crisis there was danger to Gorbachëv if he was cautious and danger if he was daring. He would have had a somewhat easier time if he had known his mind on the economy. Although he wanted some basic reform, he was unclear about exact measures and schedules. Nor did he recognize the need to dispense with the services of Ryzhkov as Chairman of the Council of Ministers. Ryzhkov had voiced his unhappiness about extensive denationalization and monetary reform in December 1989.[9] By June 1990 Ryzhkov yielded somewhat, but still called in opaque terms for a 'regulated market'; he also announced that he would soon be introducing an increase in food prices so as to correct the gross imbalance in the state budget. Ryzhkov's position combined the worst of both worlds: a half-hearted, drawn-out privatization programme and a further rise in the cost of living. The most radical among Gorbachëv's advisers argued that the economy's collapse was imminent. According to them, measures had to be deep, had to be rapid, had to be consistently imposed.

Even Gorbachëv's agile mind had failed to assimilate basic economic concepts, and he simply refused to accept that consensus was unobtainable. In August 1990 he got permission from the USSR Supreme Soviet to create a commission to elaborate a plan for industrial, agricultural and commercial recovery – and Yeltsin agreed to co-operate with the commission. The result was the '500 Days Plan', composed chiefly by Stanislav Shatalin. Gorbachëv supported it, but then vacillated under pressure from Ryzhkov. In September he ordered a reworking of the '500 Days Plan' by Abel Aganbegyan to effect a compromise between the positions of Shatalin and Ryzhkov. This was like mating a rabbit with a donkey. Aganbegyan produced a predictably unworkable mixture of radical language and conservative ideas. But he had helped Gorbachëv out of his political complications, and in October the Supreme Soviet gave its assent to the set of 'Basic Guidelines' he presented to it.

At the time his angriest adversaries were the conservatives in the Congress of People's Deputies who formed their own *Soyuz* ('Union') organization in October 1990.[10] Most Soyuz members were Russians, but otherwise they were a diverse group. They included not only communist party members but also Christian believers, nationalist writers and ecological activists, and some of them were simply Russian functionaries who lived outside the RSFSR and were terrified about their personal prospects if ever the Soviet Union fell apart. Soyuz's unifying belief was that the Soviet Union was the legitimate successor state to the Russian Empire. Its members were proud of the USSR's industrial and cultural achievements of their country; they gloried in the USSR's defeat of Nazi Germany. For them, Gorbachëv was the arch-destroyer of a great state, economy and society.

Gorbachëv was more disturbed by Soyuz than by those of his own supporters who wanted him to be still more radical. He knew that Soyuz had many undeclared sympathizers and that these were even to be found among central political and economic post-holders. Having backed down over Shatalin's '500 Days Plan' for the economy, he was sufficiently worried to give ground also in politics. One by one, he dispensed with prominent reformers in his entourage.

Alexander Yakovlev ceased to be one of Gorbachëv's regular consultants after his bruising treatment at the Twenty-Eighth Party Congress. Yakovlev and Gorbachëv ceased to appear publicly together. In November, Vadim Bakatin was asked by Gorbachëv to step down as Minister of Internal Affairs. Gorbachëv also lost his close party colleague Vadim Medvedev. Bakatin and Medvedev had been constant proponents of the need to take the reforms further and faster. Then, Eduard Shevardnadze followed. In his case he went without being pushed; but unlike the others he did not go quietly. In an emotional speech to the Congress of People's Deputies on 20 December he declared that, unless Gorbachëv changed his present course, the country was heading for dictatorship. Thereafter Nikolai Petrakov, Gorbachëv's economics adviser, also departed. Even Ryzhkov left the political stage, laid low by a heart condition.

Ryzhkov's job as Chairman of the Cabinet of Ministers was taken by Valentin Pavlov, the Minister of Finances. Pavlov was even more suspicious of reform than Ryzhkov; and the new Minister of Internal

Affairs was Boris Pugo, who was known as an advocate of repressive measures. Gorbachëv's choice of Gennadi Yanaev, who agreed with Pavlov and Pugo, as Vice-President of the USSR was another indication that Shevardnadze's fears were not entirely misplaced. Furthermore, on 13 January 1991, Soviet special forces in Lithuania stormed the Vilnius television tower. Fifteen people were killed in this flagrant attempt to deter separatist movements throughout the USSR. Gorbachëv disclaimed any knowledge of the decision to use force, and the blame was placed upon officials at the local level.

Yet Gorbachëv retained his determination to protect the territorial integrity of the USSR. On 17 March he organized a referendum on the question: 'Do you consider necessary the preservation of the Union of Soviet Socialist Republics as a renewed federation of equal sovereign republics in which the rights and freedom of the individual of any nationality will be guaranteed?' Gorbachëv's phrasing made it difficult for reform-minded citizens to vote against sanctioning the Union. But in other aspects of public life Gorbachëv was beset by trouble. Another Russian miners' strike had broken out days earlier. In March, furthermore, supporters of Polozkov called an emergency session of the Russian Congress of People's Deputies in a bid to oust Yeltsin; and Gorbachëv, still leaning in the direction of Pavlov and Pugo, allowed 50,000 Ministry of Internal Affairs troops to be introduced to the capital to prevent a demonstration in Yeltsin's favour. For a brief time Moscow seemed near to upheaval. But Gorbachëv baulked at the potential violence needed to restore direct control. He was also impressed by the 200,000 Muscovites who took the risk of turning out for a rally in support of Yeltsin. At last – alas, far too late! – Gorbachëv definitively reverted to the agenda of reform.

A *rapprochement* with Yeltsin ensued. Gorbachëv and Yeltsin announced that they would work together with common purpose. On 23 April a meeting of nine republican leaders was arranged at Gorbachëv's dacha at Novo-Ogarëvo to draft a new Union Treaty that would augment political and economic powers of the governments of the Soviet republics. The final version was to be signed on 20 August. This tried the patience of Polozkov and his supporters beyond their limits, and they vehemently criticized him at the Central Committee of the USSR Communist Party on 24–5 April. Their comments enraged Gorbachëv in turn. At one point he handed in his resignation as General Secretary; only a petition in his favour organized by Bakatin and sixty-nine other Central Committee members persuaded him to stay in office. Polozkov lacked the nerve to push him out.[11] The result was victory for Gorbachëv: the terms of the proposed Union Treaty were accepted in principle by the Central Committee. The date of signature was set for 20 August.

A delighted Yeltsin travelled around the RSFSR urging the autonomous republics to 'take whatever helping of power that you can gobble up by yourselves'.[12] When submitting himself to a presidential election in Russia on 12 June, he won a massive majority. His running-mate Alexander Rutskoi, an army colonel, became Russian vice-president. Other prominent associates were Ivan Silaev and Ruslan Khasbulatov: Silaev was appointed the RSFSR Prime Minister and Khasbulatov the Speaker of the Russian Supreme Soviet. On 20 July Yeltsin pressed home his advantage by issuing a decree banning communist party organizations from keeping offices in administrative institutions and economic enterprises in Russia. This so-called 'de-partization' was not approved by Gorbachëv; but even he was exasperated by his party's resistance to self-reform, and he arranged for another Party Congress to be held to determine a permanent strategy.

But Gorbachëv had scarcely any credit left with Soviet society. The economy was collapsing in every sector. Industrial output fell by eighteen per cent in 1991, agriculture by seventeen per cent. Even energy production, whose exports had supplied the backbone of state revenues in previous years, went down by ten per cent. The USSR budget deficit was between twelve and fourteen per cent of gross domestic product whereas it had been only four per cent in 1990. The result was a decline in the government's ability to sustain the level of imports of consumer goods. The USSR's towns and villages also experienced a shortage in fuel supplies. Consumers were further troubled by Pavlov's decision at last to start raising the prices for food products in state shops. The result was highly unpleasant for a population unaccustomed to overt inflation. Across the year, it is reckoned, prices in such shops almost doubled.[13]

The hero of the late 1980s was regularly pilloried by his fellow Soviet citizens. He was much more popular abroad than at home. But even in international affairs he was buffeted: when in July 1991 he appealed to the 'Group of Seven' leading economic powers in London for assistance, he received much sympathy but no promise of a quick loan large enough to give relief to the traumatized Soviet economy. Gorbachëv's demeanour appeared to many Soviet citizens as that of a cap-in-hand beggar. Yeltsin, who urged that Russia should get up off her knees, gained in popularity.

Several leading colleagues of Gorbachëv had long ago concluded that the USSR's domestic chaos and international parlousness resulted from an excess of reform. Oleg Shenin, who had taken over the Central Committee Secretariat in the absence of both Gorbachëv and the physically-ailing Ivashko, called in January 1991 for an 'end to the careless, anarchic approach' to party affairs. USSR Vice-President Gennadi Yanaev talked often about the need for at least 'elementary order' in the country. Oleg Baklanov, Deputy Chairman of the Defence Council, regretted the arms agreements made with the USA. Prime Minister Valentin Pavlov at the April 1991 Central Committee plenum demanded the declaration of a state of emergency on the railways, in the oil and metallurgical industries and in several whole regions of the USSR. At the Supreme Soviet, in June, he undermined the Novo-Ogarëvo negotiations by stating that the sovereignty demanded by the various Soviet republics could not be unconditional.

Gorbachëv was a tired man, too tired to take full cognizance of the dangers. He had often heard Shevardnadze and Yakovlev warning of an imminent *coup d'état*; yet nothing had ever happened. In late June 1991, when American Secretary of State James Baker sent him a message naming Pavlov, Kryuchkov and Yazov as possible conspirators, Gorbachëv refused to become alarmed, and went off in early August for an extended vacation in the dacha he had had built for himself in the Black Sea village of Foros.[14]

He underrated the extraordinary political discontent he left behind. On 23 July 1991 the newspaper *Sovetskaya Rossiya*, which had carried Nina Andreeva's letter in March 1988, published 'A Word to the People' signed by twelve public figures.[15] Army generals Boris Gromov and Valentin Varennikov were among them: Gromov was First Deputy Minister of Internal Affairs, Varennikov was Commander of Soviet Ground Forces. Another signatory was Soyuz leader Yuri Blokhin. Russian nationalists such as the film director Yuri Bondarëv and writers Alexander Prokhanov and Valentin Rasputin were also present. Others included Gennadi Zyuganov (member of the Politburo of the Russian Communist Party), Vasili Starodubtsev (chairman of the USSR Peasants' Union) and Alexander Tizyakov (President of the Association of State Enterprises and Associations). None was at the peak of public eminence, but all were major Soviet personages.

Their 'Word to the People' railed against current conditions in the Soviet Union: 'An enormous, unprecedented misfortune has occurred. The Motherland, our country, the great state entrusted to us by history, by nature and by our glorious forebears is perishing, is being broken up, is being plunged into darkness and oblivion.'[16] All citizens were entreated to help to preserve the USSR. A wide variety of social groups was addressed: workers, managers, engineers, soldiers, officers, women, pensioners and young people.

No reference was made to Lenin and the October Revolution. The signatories appealed instead to patriotism and statehood: the Army, whose feat in vanquishing Nazi Germany was recorded, was the only institution selected for praise. Nor was any disrespect shown towards religion. The appeal was explicitly directed equally at Christians, Muslims and Buddhists.[17] Ostensibly, too, the contents indicated no preference for any particular nation. But out of all countries and regions of the USSR, only Russia was mentioned as 'beloved'. And indeed the appeal opened with the following phrase: 'Dear Russians! Citizens of the USSR! Fellow countrymen!' Here was a fusion of Russian and Soviet identities reminiscent of Stalin in the Second World War. Without saying so, the signatories firmly trusted that Russians would prove the national group that would act to save the USSR from the disaster of the projected Union Treaty.

They had practically written the manifesto for a *coup d'état*. It is inconceivable that they were publishing their feelings in the press without the knowledge of other governmental personages. Gorbachëv's refusal to recognize how things stood was surprising: the only precaution he took in summer 1991 was to ask Yeltsin informally to stay in Moscow while the Gorbachëv family took a holiday in Crimea. Yeltsin was meant to mind the shop, as it were, in the owner's absence. Such casualness later gave rise to rumours that Gorbachëv had secretly been planning to have a pretext to tear up the deal with Yeltsin. Perhaps he even wanted a coup to be attempted so that he might return as the mediator between all the contending forces. All this is far fetched. The likeliest explanation lies in Gorbachëv's over-confidence. He trusted his fellow ministers because they were his own appointees. He had out-manoeuvred them year after year: he simply could not believe that they eventually might dance rings around him.

And so Mikhail and Raisa Gorbachëv went off to enjoy themselves in Foros with their daughter, son-in-law and two grandchildren. Every day they walked six kilometres. (Much as he Americanized his image, Gorbachëv laudably refrained from the practice of TV-accompanied jogging.) Even on holiday, of course, he was a working President. In particular, he prepared a speech and an article on the Union Treaty to be signed on 20 August 1991.

On 18 August his quietude was interrupted, when he was visited unexpectedly by Shenin, Baklanov, Varennikov and his own personal assistant Valeri Boldin. On their arrival he noted that the telephones at his dacha were not functioning. This was the first sign that a conspiracy was afoot. His visitors told him that an emergency situation would shortly be declared, and that it would be appreciated if he would transfer his powers temporarily to Vice-President Yanaev. Baklanov assured him that they would restore order in the country and that he could subsequently return as President without having had to carry out the 'dirty business' himself. But Gorbachëv was intransigent. If he had misjudged his collaborators, they had got him wrong to an equal extent; and he swore at them lustily before sending them packing.[18] Varennikov flew on to Kiev to inform Ukrainian political leaders that a state of emergency was being declared and that Gorbachëv was too ill to stay in charge. Baklanov, Shenin and Boldin returned to Moscow to confer with the other principal plotters.

Meanwhile KGB Chairman Kryuchkov and Interior Minister Pugo had been busy persuading functionaries to join them in the State Committee for the Emergency Situation. Vice-President Yanaev, Prime Minister Pavlov and Defence Minister Yazov were courted strongly. All eventually agreed even though Pavlov and Yanaev needed preliminary infusions of vodka. Along with them were Baklanov, Starodubtsev and Tizyakov. Kryuchkov had tried in vain to get Anatoli Lukyanov, the Supreme Soviet speaker and Gorbachëv's friend since their university days, to join them. But at least Lukyanov handed the plotters an article criticizing the Union Treaty which could be broadcast by television early next morning;[19] he also signalled to the plotters that he would prevent opposition arising in the Supreme Soviet.

From the night of 18–19 August nothing went right for the conspiracy. The plan for the creation of a State Committee for the Emergency Situation was to be announced in the morning. Explanations were to be sent out to the army, the KGB and the Soviet communist party. Then the members of the State Committee were set to appear at a televised press conference. In fact the press conference was a shambles. Yanaev, while declaring himself Acting President, could not stop his fingers from twitching. Pavlov was too drunk to attend. Outlandish incompetence was shown after the conference. Meetings of public protest were not broken up in the capital. The Moscow telephone network was allowed to function. Fax messages could be sent unimpeded. Satellite TV continued to be beamed into the USSR; foreign television crews moved around the city unhindered. The tanks sent into the streets contained naïve young soldiers who were disconcerted by the many bystanders who asked them why they were agreeing to use force upon fellow citizens.

The State Committee's project for a *coup d'état* had not been unrealistic. Disillusionment with Gorbachëv in Russia was pervasive by summer 1991; order and tranquillity were universally demanded. Kryuchkov, Yanaev and their associates also had the cunning to gain popularity by releasing basic consumer products to be sold in the shops at rock-bottom prices. Moreover, every Soviet citizen knew that traditional institutions of coercion were at the disposal of the State Committee: resistance to the attempted coup would require considerable bravery.

Yet radical politicians showed exactly that quality. The State Committee had blundered in failing to arrest Yeltsin, Rutskoi, Silaev and Khasbulatov. Yeltsin, on hearing of the coup, phoned his colleagues and prepared a proclamation denouncing the State Committee as an illegal body and calling for Gorbachëv's liberation. He also contacted Pavel Grachëv, Commander of Soviet Airborne-Ground Forces to request physical protection.[20] The State Committee had erred yet again; for they had put Grachëv in charge of military operations in Moscow without testing his political loyalty. Grachëv's refusal to abandon Gorbachëv and Yeltsin was to prove crucial. Yeltsin got into a car and raced along country roads to the RSFSR Supreme Soviet building – which was becoming known as the White House – in central Moscow. There he rallied his associates, and a crowd of tens of thousands began to gather outside. Barricades of rubble, old trucks and wire were constructed around the building.

Yeltsin's instincts told him what to do next. Tall and bulky, he strode out from the White House at one o'clock in the afternoon and clambered on to one of the tanks of the Taman Division stationed at the side of the road. From this exposed position the Russian President announced his defiance of the State Committee. The State Committee leaders had expected that the merest show of force, with perhaps only seventy arrests in the capital, would give them victory. Most of them, including Kryuchkov and Pugo, did not want to be responsible for a great number of deaths.

Their *coup d'état* had therefore depended on immediate total implementation. This scheme had not succeeded. The State Committee's sole alternative was to intensify military operations. Above all, the White House had to be stormed. The suppression of resistance in Moscow would have the effect of intimidating all the Soviet republics into compliance. Unfortunately for the State Committee, 'Acting President' Yanaev was already losing his nerve and trying to avoid trouble. Baklanov, Kryuchkov and Pugo therefore decided to ignore him and direct their troops against the White House. Yeltsin, who had for years been well acquainted with the State Committee leaders, phoned them on a direct line to warn of the unpleasant international consequences. He also predicted that they would not be forgiven at home either. But the core of the State Committee's membership held firm. Late on 19 August army commanders were asked to draw up a plan for the storming of the Russian White House.

At the same time the Taman Tank Division besieging the building was talking to Yeltsin's Vice-President Alexander Rutskoi.[21] Yanaev's will cracked. At a State Committee meeting at 8 p.m. he ordered that no action should be started against the White House.[22] But the State Committee again ignored him, recognizing that any failure to arrest Yeltsin would bring ruin on themselves. Commands were given for further troop movements. In the night of 20–21 August tanks moved around the Garden Ring Road of Moscow. Crowds of citizens tried to block their path; and in an incident near the White House, three young civilian men – Dmitri Komar, Ilya Krichevski and Vladimir Usov – were killed.

A violent outcome seemed inevitable as Yeltsin and his associates got ready to resist an attack on the White House. Weapons were smuggled inside. The cellist Mtsislav Rostropovich joined Yeltsin in the building, playing his instrument to stiffen morale. Eduard Shevardnadze and Alexander Yakovlev arrived to show solidarity. They all did this in the knowledge that they might not come out alive. Crowds of Muscovites, mainly youngsters, formed a human chain around the perimeter of the White House. They had no means of apprehending that in the early hours of 21 August the State Committee's confidence was on the point of collapse. One after another, the military commanders withheld assistance from the State Committee: even the Alpha Division, which had been ordered to storm the White House, had become uncooperative. Yazov as Minister of Defence called off the military action; and Kryuchkov – to

Baklanov's disdain – refused to seize back control from Yazov.[23]

By midday on 21 August the sole effective aspect of the State Committee's activity was its maintenance of a news black-out on its decisions. In fact its leaders had decided to terminate the coup, and at 2.15 p.m. Kryuchkov and three other State Committee members along with Anatoli Lukyanov boarded a plane for the south. Their purpose was to plead their case directly with Gorbachëv in Foros. Gorbachëv refused to see most of them, but agreed to a brief meeting with Lukyanov. Having asked why Lukyanov had not convened the USSR Supreme Soviet in protest against the State Committee, Gorbachëv called him a traitor and showed him the door.[24] Yeltsin's Vice-President Rutskoi, too, had meanwhile arrived at Foros to take custody of the various plotters. Gorbachëv and his family – including Raisa, who had had a severe collapse of some kind – immediately returned to Moscow. Kryuchkov and others were put on the same plane by Rutskoi to ensure that military sympathizers of the State Committee did not take it into their heads to fire upon them.[25]

At four minutes after midnight on 22 August, Gorbachëv stepped down from the plane at Moscow's Vnukovo Airport. He came back to a changed USSR. Yet Gorbachëv refused to lay blame on the Communist Party of the Soviet Union despite the evidence that many of its officials had collaborated with the 'putsch'. He filled some of the posts of the putschists with figures who were as odious to the White House's defenders as the putschists had been. At the funeral of Komar, Krichevski and Usov, it was Yeltsin rather than Gorbachëv who captured the public mood by asking forgiveness of their bereaved mothers for not having been able to protect their sons.

On 5 September the Congress of People's Deputies set up yet another temporary central authority, the State Council, which comprised Gorbachëv and the leaders of those Soviet republics willing to remain part of the Union.[26] Gorbachëv's resilience was truly remarkable: both his sense of duty and his will to retain power were unabated. But the putsch had altered the constellation of politics. Estonia, Latvia, Lithuania and Moldova had conducted a campaign of passive resistance to the State Committee of the Emergency

Situation. Kazakhstan and Ukraine had been less forthright in opposing the Committee, but nevertheless had not co-operated with it. Only a minority of the USSR's Soviet republics, notably Turkmenistan, had welcomed the putsch. In the RSFSR, Tatarstan under its leader Mintimer Shaimiev took a similar position; but most of the other internal autonomous republics refused to collaborate. When the putsch failed, even Turkmenistan's President Niyazov started again to demand independence for his country.

No State Council would be able to impose central authority to the previous degree. Estonia, Latvia and Lithuania appealed to the rest of the world to give them diplomatic recognition; and Yeltsin, unlike Gorbachëv, had long since supported their right to complete independence. At last the West gave the three states what they wanted. Meanwhile the humbling of Gorbachëv continued in Moscow. Having suffered at Gorbachëv's hands in October 1987, Yeltsin had no reason to be gentle. At any rate he had never been a gracious victor. When the two of them had appeared together at the Supreme Soviet of the RSFSR on 23 August, Yeltsin ordered the Soviet President about as if he were the junior office-holder. With a peremptory gesture of his hand he rasped out that the recently-compiled list of the State Committee's collaborators should be made public: 'Read them out!' A doleful Gorbachëv had no choice but to release the list to the media.

No politician in twentieth-century Russia had effected so stupendous a comeback as Yeltsin. No one was as daring as he. Nor was anyone luckier. Gorbachëv could easily have finished him off politically in 1987. Certainly Ligachëv would have done just that. But Gorbachëv, once he had defeated Yeltsin, showed a degree of magnanimity which no previous Soviet leader had exhibited towards vanquished opponents.

Good fortune had blessed Yeltsin several times in his life. Born in a tiny village in Sverdlovsk province in 1931, he nearly died at his baptism when a tipsy priest dropped him in the font. His grandmother plucked him out to stop him drowning.[27] Young Boris was a rascal. Once he and his pals played with a hand-grenade they found in the woods. There was an explosion, and Boris lost two fingers of his left hand.[28] Yet his personality was irrepressible. His father had been sentenced to three years of forced labour for criticizing conditions of construction-site workers in Kazan;[29] but the young lad managed to keep this quiet when he entered the Urals Polytechnical Institute to train as a civil engineer. A natural athlete, he was quickly picked for the city's volleyball team. In the vacations he travelled widely in Russia despite his poverty by climbing on to train carriage-tops and taking a free ride. He never lived life by the rules.

On graduating, he worked in the construction industry. In 1968 he switched careers, joining the Sverdlovsk Province Party Committee apparatus. Eight years later he was its first secretary, and in 1981 became a Central Committee member. Sverdlovsk (nowadays known by its pre-revolutionary name, Yekaterinburg) is Russia's fifth largest city. Yeltsin was its boisterous leader in the communist party tradition: he ranted and threatened. He broke legal and administrative procedures to achieve results for his province. He also used charm and guile. In search of finance for an underground rail-system in Sverdlovsk, he asked for an audience with Brezhnev and whispered his case into the ailing General Secretary's ear. Sverdlovsk obtained the funds for its metro.[30]

It was already evident that his style had a populistic streak. In Sverdlovsk he had turned public ceremonies into carnivals. Whole families walked in parade on the October Revolution anniversary and Yeltsin addressed them on the city's main square. One year on the eve of the anniversary, when his car swerved into a ditch sixty kilometres from Sverdlovsk, he bounded over the fields to the nearest village and commandeered a tractor and a drunken tractor-driver to get them to the morning parade on time.[31] On his transfer to the capital in 1985 he was already an audacious crowd-pleaser. His anti-corruption campaign in Moscow made him an object of hatred among the existing party personnel. But he did not mind about their criticisms; he understood that his popularity rose every time he was victimized by the Politburo from 1987. The more dangers he ran, the better he was liked in ordinary homes.

He had a mercurial personality. As Moscow party chief in 1985–7, he had been a bully and had sacked officials in their thousands without investigation of individual cases. But subsequently the Inter-Regional Group in the Congress of People's Deputies since 1990 had given him an education in consultative procedures, and he learned how to listen and to act as a member of a team: this was not typical behaviour for a communist party official.

His apparent goal, after the arrest of the putschists, was the inception of a combination of democratic politics and capitalist economy in a Russia unrestrained by the USSR. On 23 August he suspended the legal status of the Communist Party of the Soviet Union in Russia. Gorbachëv complied by laying down the office of Party General Secretary. Yeltsin's pressure was unremitting. On 28 October he made a lengthy, televised speech to the Russian Congress of People's Deputies declaring his intention to implement an economic programme based upon the principles of the market. A few days later, on 6 November, he issued a decree banning the Soviet communist party altogether. He stipulated, too, that the ministers of the RSFSR had precedence over those of the USSR; and he applied a veto on any USSR appointments he disliked. Between 6 and 8 November he announced the composition of his full cabinet. He himself would be RSFSR prime minister while Yegor Gaidar, a proponent of *laissez-faire* economics, would be his Finance Minister and a Deputy Prime Minister. It would be a cabinet for drastic economic reform.

None the less Yeltsin had yet to reveal his purposes about the USSR. Publicly he denied any wish to break up the Union, and he accepted the invitation to return to the Novo-Ogarëvo negotiations. Yet Yeltsin's aides had been working on contingency plans for Russia's complete secession even before the August coup; and subsequently Yeltsin lost no chance to weaken the draft powers of the Union he was discussing with Gorbachëv. So what did Yeltsin really want?

Gorbachëv's proposal was that the USSR should give way to a 'Union of Sovereign States'. There would still be a single economic space and a unified military command; there would also be regular consultations among the republican presidents. Gorbachëv concurred that the Union President would not be allowed to dominate the others. His despair was such that he offered to step down in Yeltsin's favour as Union President if only Yeltsin would agree to maintain the Union. 'Let's talk man to man about this,' he implored Yeltsin.[32] But Yeltsin was inscrutable. There were reasons for him to keep his options open. Of special importance was the refusal of Leonid Kravchuk, the Ukrainian President, to join the discussions. On 18 October, when a Treaty on the Economic Commonwealth had been signed, Ukraine declined to send a representative.[33] In such a situation, on 24 November, Yeltsin rejected Gorbachëv's request to him and to the other republican leaders to initial the Union Treaty.[34]

The people of Ukraine, including most of its Russian inhabitants, were terminally exasperated with Gorbachëv, and on 1 December they voted for independence in a referendum. The voters cast their ballots for a variety of reasons. Supporters of radical economic reform wanted freedom to carry it out fast; opponents of such reform advocated independence because they, too, wished to be liberated from Gorbachëv. And Ukrainian nationalists simply wanted independence. The result of the referendum was a disaster for the proposed Union of Sovereign States. Without Ukraine, such a Union was unrealizable.

Yeltsin arranged an emergency meeting with Ukrainian President Kravchuk and Shushkevich, Chairman of the Supreme Soviet of Belarus (as Belorussia now insisted on being called), in the Belovezhskaya Pushcha near the Belarusian capital Minsk. On 8 December, Yeltsin and Kravchuk persuaded Shushkevich to agree to the formation of a Commonwealth of Independent States (CIS), an even weaker combination than the very weakened version of the Union lately proposed at Novo-Ogarëvo.[35] The Commonwealth would maintain a unified economic area and unified strategic military forces. But it would have its central offices not in Moscow but in Minsk, and there would be no president. The declaration of the three Slavic republics presented the other republics with a *fait accompli*. They could either join the Commonwealth or go it alone. On 21 December eight further Soviet republics assented to membership: Armenia, Azerbaijan, Kazakhstan, Kyrgyzstan, Moldova, Tajikistan, Turkmenistan and

Uzbekistan. The dissenting republics were the three Baltic states and Georgia.

Perhaps the Ukrainian referendum was the pretext that Yeltsin had been waiting for to break up the USSR in line with a basic hidden strategy. More likely is the possibility that he simply had a keen wish to get rid of Gorbachëv and to assume unconditional authority in Moscow. It may also be that, being a very impulsive leader, he was merely reacting to situations as the mood took him.

What was indisputably clear was that the game was up for Gorbachëv. If there was not even to be a Union of Sovereign States, he had no function to discharge except the declaration of his retirement. He bowed to the inevitable and accepted that the Soviet republics were about to go their own ways. He did this with a heavy heart, predicting that the break-up of the Union would lead to military and political strife as well as economic ruin. But he had fought for the Union, and lost. On 25 December he gave a short speech on television. He spoke with simple dignity: 'I leave my post with trepidation. But also with hope, with faith in you, in your wisdom and force of spirit. We are the inheritors of a great civilization, and now the burden falls on each and every one that it may be resurrected to a new, modern and worthy life.'[36] The USSR would be abolished at midnight on 31 December 1991.

Into oblivion would pass a state which had caused political tremors abroad by its very existence in the 1920s. A state whose borders were roughly the same as those of the Russian Empire and whose population embraced an unparalleled number of nations, religions and philosophies. A state which had built a mighty industrial base in the 1930s and had defeated Germany in the Second World War. A state which became a superpower, matching the USA in military capacity by the late 1970s. A state whose political and economic order had introduced a crucial category of the lexicon of twentieth-century thought. From the beginning of 1992, that state was no more.

Zhirinovski's newspaper Liberal *ridicules Yeltsin as a saint leading a truck full of Western products such as Pepsi Cola. The truck is painted with the sign 'Market'.*

26

Power and the Market (1992–1993)

The Soviet Union had ended not with a bang but with a whimper. Its communist party, its ideology, its flag and state anthem and its October Revolution disappeared. All this had occurred with extraordinary abruptness. Nobody, not even those at the apex of public power, had had a chance to ponder the general significance of the events in all their momentousness.

Politics remained volatile; a premium was still placed upon the swift implementation of fundamental reforms. But in the person of Yeltsin, Russia had a leader who had always been decisive. After the Soviet Union's dismantlement, moreover, he had an incentive to display this characteristic. Having played a prominent part in the demise of the old order, he had to show that he could create a better economy and society. His room for choice in policies was at its greatest in his first few months of unrivalled power when his popularity was at its peak. The first half of 1992 was crucial for his prospects. Two main options were discussed by him and his advisers. The first was for him to call fresh elections so as to obtain an unequivocal political mandate for economic reform; the second was to proceed with economic reform in expectation of an eventual approval at elections to be held later.

Yeltsin selected the second alternative; and on 2 January 1992 he permitted Gaidar, his First Deputy Prime Minister, to introduce free-market prices for most goods in the shops of the Russian Federation. Thus the government gave up its right to fix prices for consumers. It was a big change of stance. Gaidar indicated that 'price liberalization' would be just the first of a series of reforms which would include measures to balance the budget, eliminate state subsidies and privatize virtually the whole economy. A transformation of industry, agriculture, commerce and finance was heralded.

It is easy to see why Yeltsin selected the second option. Imperious and impulsive, he had an aversion to Gorbachëv's procrastinations; he must also have sensed that the political, economic and national élites at the centre and in the localities might retain a capacity to distort the results of any election he might at that stage have ordained. To Yeltsin, economic reform by presidential decree appeared the surer way to bring about the basic reform he required in the Russian economy. The choice between the two options was not a straightforward one; but Yeltsin's decision to avoid the ballot-box probably caused more problems for him than it solved. It inclined him to use peremptory methods of governance which previously he had castigated. It also compelled him to operate alongside a Russian Supreme Soviet which had been elected in 1990 and whose majority was constituted by persons who had little sympathy with his project to create a full market economy.

Yeltsin and Gaidar made things worse for themselves by refusing to explain in any detail how they would fulfil their purposes. They reasoned among themselves that citizens were fed up with the publication of economic programmes. Yet Gaidar's reticence induced widespread suspicion of the government. As prices rose by 245 per cent in January 1992,[1] suspicion gave way to fear. Russians worried that Gaidar's 'shock therapy' would lead to mass impoverishment. Moreover, they had been brought up to be proud of the USSR's material and social achievements and its status as a superpower. They were disorientated and humbled by the USSR's disintegration. Russians had suddenly ceased to be Soviet citizens, becoming citizens of whatever new state they lived in; and their bafflement was such that when they spoke about their country it was seldom clear whether they were referring to Russia or the entire former Soviet Union.

Gaidar appeared on television to offer reassurance to everyone; but his lecturely style and abstract jargon did not go down well. Nor did viewers forget that earlier in his career he had been an assistant editor of the Marxist-Leninist journal *Kommunist*. Gaidar had never experienced material want; on the contrary, he had belonged to the Soviet central nomenklatura. Even his age – he was only thirty-five years old – was counted against him: it was thought that he knew too little about life.

Yeltsin knew of Gaidar's unappealing image, and endeavoured to show that the government truly understood the popular unease. Aided by his speech-writer Lyudmila Pikhoya, he used words with discrimination. He ceased to refer to the Russian Soviet Federal Socialist Republic as such; instead he usually called it the Russian Federation or simply Russia. At the same time he strove to encourage inter-ethnic harmony. He addressed his fellow citizens not as *russkie* (ethnic Russians) but as *rossiyane*, which referred to the entire population of the Russian Federation regardless of nationality.[2] While denouncing the destructiveness of seven decades of 'communist experiment', he did not criticize Lenin, Marxism-Leninism or the USSR by name in the year after the abortive August coup. Evidently Yeltsin wanted to avoid offending the many citizens of the Russian Federation who were not convinced that everything that had happened since 1991, or even since 1985, had been for the better.

The Russian President eschewed the word 'capitalism' and spoke in favour of a 'market economy'.[3] It would also have been impolitic for Yeltsin to recognize that the USA and her allies had won a victory over Russia: he refrained from mentioning 'the West' as such; his emphasis fell not on the East-West relationship but on Russia's new opportunities to join 'the civilized world'.[4]

Yeltsin towered above his team of ministers in experience. This was inevitable. The most illustrious ex-dissenters were unavailable. Sakharov was dead. Solzhenitsyn insisted on finishing his sequence of novels on the Russian revolutionary period before he would return home. Roy Medvedev's reputation had been ruined by his role as adviser to Lukyanov, a collaborator of the putschists. In any case, the veteran dissenters – including the less prominent ones – adapted poorly to open politics: their personalities were more suited to criticizing institutions than to creating them. Yeltsin retained some of Gorbachëv's more radical supporters. After the August coup, with Yeltsin's encouragement, Gorbachëv had brought back Shevardnadze as Soviet Foreign Minister and Bakatin as chairman of the KGB, and these two stayed on with Yeltsin for a while. But Shevardnadze went off to Georgia in 1992 to become its President, and Bakatin resigned after the dissolution of the USSR.[5]

Necessarily the team around Yeltsin and Gaidar consisted of obscure adherents: Gennadi Burbulis, Anatoli Chubais, Andrei Kozyrev, Oleg Lobov, Alexander Shokhin, Sergei Shakhrai and Yuri Skokov. Most of them were in their thirties and forties, and few expected to hold power for long. Only Vice-President Rutskoi and the Speaker in the Russian Supreme Soviet Khasbulatov had previously held influential posts. Rutskoi was contemptuous of the youthful ministers, calling them 'young boys in pink shorts and yellow boots'.[6]

But the young boys shared Yeltsin's enthusiasm to effect change. The fact that they assumed that their tenure of office was temporary made them determined to make a brisk, ineradicable impact. What they lacked in experience they made up for in zeal. Yeltsin was raring to give them their opportunity. Where Gorbachëv had feared to tread, Yeltsin would boldly go. Having seized the reins of Great Russia's coach and horses, he resolved to drive headlong along a bumpy path. Yeltsin saw himself as the twentieth-century Peter the Great, tsar and reformer.[7] Those who knew their eighteenth-century history trembled at the comparison. Peter the Great had pummelled his country into the ground in consequence of his dream to turn Russia into a European power and society. Would Yeltsin do the same in pursuit of an economic transformation approved by the International Monetary Fund?

Yeltsin and his cabinet knew that the old communist order had not entirely disappeared with the USSR's abolition. The Communist Party of the Soviet Union had vanished; Marxism-Leninism and the October Revolution were discredited. But much else survived from the Soviet period. The Russian Supreme Soviet contained a large rump which hated Yeltsin. The local political and economic élites, too, operated autonomously of Moscow; they worked with criminal gangs to promote their common interests as the market economy began to be installed. In the internal non-Russian republics of the RSFSR the leaderships talked up nationalist themes and gained local support.

The methods of communism were used by Yeltsin to eradicate traces of the communist epoch. He rarely bothered with the sanction of the Supreme Soviet, and he visited it even more rarely. He confined deliberations on policy to a small circle of associates. These included not only Gaidar and his bright fellow ministers but also his bodyguard chief Alexander Korzhakov (who was his favourite drinking mate after a day's work). He sacked personnel whenever and wherever his policies were not being obeyed. In provinces where his enemies still ruled he introduced his own appointees to bring localities over to his side. He called them variously his 'plenipotentiaries', 'representatives', 'prefects' and – eventually – 'governors'. These appointees were empowered to enforce his will in their respective provinces. In the guise of a President, Yeltsin was ruling like a General Secretary – and indeed with less deference to 'collective leadership'![8]

To his relief, price liberalization did not lead to riots on the streets. The cost of living rose; but initially most people had sufficient savings to cope: years of not being able to buy things in Soviet shops meant that personal savings kept in banks were still large. Although Yeltsin's popularity had peaked in October 1991,[9] there was no serious rival to him for leadership of the country. He intended to make full use of his large latitude for the strategic reorientation of the economy. Nor did the industrial and agricultural directors object strongly to his proposals. For they quickly perceived that the liberalization of prices would give them a wonderful chance to increase enterprise profits and, more importantly, their personal incomes. Politicians from the Soviet nomenklatura, furthermore, had long been positioning themselves to take advantage of the business opportunities that were becoming available.[10]

Confidently Yeltsin and Gaidar proceeded to further stages of economic reform. The two most urgent, in their estimation, were the privatization of enterprises and the stabilization of the currency. The first of these was to be privatization. Its overseer was to be Anatoli Chubais, who was Chairman of the State Committee for the Management of State Property. His essential task was to put himself out of a job by transferring state enterprises to the private sector.

Chubais published projects on the need to turn factories, mines and kolkhozes into independent companies, and seemed to be about to facilitate the development of 'popular capitalism'. But the crucial question remained: who was to own the companies? In June 1992, Chubais introduced a system of 'vouchers', which would be available to the value of 10,000 roubles per citizen and which could be invested in the new companies at the time of their creation. He also enabled those employed by any particular company, whether they were workers or managers, to buy up to twenty-five per cent of the shares put on the market; and further privileges would be granted to them if they should wish to take a majority stake in the company. But Chubais's success was limited. At a time of rapid inflation, 10,000 roubles was a minuscule grant to individual citizens; and the facilitation of internal enterprise buy-outs virtually guaranteed that managers could assume complete authority over their companies; for very few workers were in a mood to struggle with their managers: strikes were small scale and few.[11]

Chubais and Gaidar had ceded ground because the economic and social forces ranged against the government were too strong. The administrative élite of the Soviet period remained in charge of factories, kolkhozes, shops and offices. In particular, twenty-two per cent of the Russian Congress of People's Deputies had come from the highest echelons of party and governmental agencies of the USSR; thirty-six per cent were officials of a middling level; and twenty-one per cent were drawn from local political and economic management.[12] Although about a quarter of deputies in early 1992 were committed to basic reforms, there was a drift into the embrace of the thirteen anti-reformist caucuses in the Russian Supreme Soviet in the course of the year.

Outside the Congress, furthermore, several dozens of parties had recently been formed. Lobbying organizations emerged to increase the pressure on the government. Trade unions of workers had little influence. Only the miners caused trepidation to ministers – and even miners did not bring them to heel. But directors of energy, manufacturing and agricultural companies were more effective in pressurizing Yeltsin. Their lobbyists were men who had walked the corridors of power before the end of the USSR. Most famous of them was Arkadi Volsky, who headed the Russian Union of Industrialists and Entrepreneurs. Another was Viktor Chernomyrdin, chairman of the vast state-owned gas company known as Gazprom. Even more remarkable was the decision of the Agrarian Union to choose Vasili Starodubtsev as their leader despite his having been imprisoned for belonging to the State Committee of the Emergency Situation in August 1991. Throughout the first six months of 1992 such lobbyists raised the spectre of economic collapse if existing enterprises were allowed to go to the wall.

They proved willing to bargain with Chubais. Their basic demand was that if the government was going to insist on the denationalization of companies, this should be done without ending state subsidies and without threatening the immediate interests of the directors or workers. It was only when Chubais gave way on this that the Supreme Soviet ratified his programme of privatization on 11 June. This was the last success of the radical economic reformers for a year.[13] They knew that they had made compromises. But their rationale was that they had introduced enough capitalism to ensure that the members of the old Soviet nomenklatura would not permanently be able to shield themselves from the pressures of economic competition.[14] Market relationships, they trusted, would eventually entail that the previous cosy relationships within whole sectors of industry, agriculture, finance, transport and trade would break down. Thus a revived Russian capitalism would consign the communist order to oblivion.

Rutskoi and Khasbulatov thought otherwise and aimed to continue stymieing Chubais's programme. From midsummer 1992, both cast themselves in the semi-open role of opponents of Yeltsin. Usually they took care to criticize him by castigating Gaidar. But it was primarily Yeltsin whom they sought to harm.

Yeltsin gave ground to the preferences of Rutskoi and Khasbulatov. In May he had promoted Chernomyrdin, Gazprom's chairman, to the post of Energy Minister. In July Yeltsin appointed Viktor Gerashchenko as head of the Central Bank of Russia. Whereas Gaidar wanted to decelerate inflation by restricting the printing of paper roubles, Gerashchenko expanded the credit facilities of the great companies. Inflation accelerated. Yet the public heaped the blame not on Gerashchenko but on Gaidar. In June Yeltsin had made him Acting Prime Minister in order to stress that economic reforms would somehow continue. But vehement hostility to Gaidar remained in the Russian Supreme Soviet, which rejected Yeltsin's subsequent recommendation that Gaidar should be promoted to the post of Prime Minister. In December, Yeltsin yielded to the Supreme Soviet and instead nominated Chernomyrdin to the premiership. On 5 January 1993 Chernomyrdin introduced a limit on the rates of profit on several goods – and some of these goods also had governmental price controls applied to them. Rutskoi and Khasbulatov were delighted.

They had plentiful reason to think that Yeltsin had been given a shock that would permanently deter him. Disenchantment with him was spreading throughout society in 1992. Food production was only nine per cent down on the previous year;[15] but the funds of the government were so depleted that most kolkhozes were unpaid for their deliveries to the state purchasing agencies.[16] Industrial production continued to fall. Output in the same year was down by eighteen per cent on 1991.[17] Inflation was 245 per cent in January.[18] Whereas kolkhozniki could survive by means of their private plots and sales of their surplus products at the urban markets, workers and office employees were hard pressed unless they had nearby dachas where they could grow potatoes and vegetables. Some folk simply cut out a patch of land on the outskirts of towns to cultivate produce or keep rabbits, pigs or even cows.

Others moonlighted from their jobs, selling cigarettes at Metro stations. Factories, mines and offices no longer asserted work-discipline: like the kolkhozes, they frequently lacked funds to pay their workers; and, being unable to maintain regular production, they no longer needed everyone to be on site in working hours. Pensioners eked out a living similarly. Many of them queued for hours in shops to buy basic products and to sell them on the pavement at double the price to busy passers-by.

The economy was reverting to ancient techniques of barter. Foreigners were astounded by the adaptiveness of ordinary Russians; but this was because they had taken too much account of official Soviet propaganda. Petty thefts from enterprises had been an established way of life in the USSR: grocery-shop counter staff kept back the best sausages; bookshop salespeople secreted the most sensational books; factory workers went home with spanners and screwdrivers. Such prized acquisitions could be traded among friends. Capitalism had not existed in the Soviet Union since the 1920s; but personal commerce had never been eliminated. Under Yeltsin, the attempt was no longer made to harass those who tried, legally or even illegally, to gain a few little luxuries in an economy where such luxuries were in constant deficit. The militia might occasionally clear the streets of pedlars, but this was usually in order to receive the bribes that were their method of surviving on inadequate wages.

Such trading was one thing; it was much harder to kick-start a market economy into motion on a larger scale. For most people, the replacement of communism with capitalism was most obviously manifested in the tin kiosks erected in all towns and cities. The goods they sold were a curious assortment: soft-drinks, alcohol, bracelets, watches, Bibles, pens and pornographic magazines. The kiosks also got hold of goods of domestic provenance which were in chronic under-supply such as razors, flowers and apples. At first there was a flood of imports, but Russian enterprises became active in production, often presenting their goods in fictitious foreign packaging (including allegedly non-Russian vodka). Prices were high, profits large.

And so popular disgruntlement grew even though the kiosks' operations were helping to end the perennial shortage of products. Poverty of the most dreadful kind was widespread. Tent-settlements of the homeless sprang up even in Moscow. Beggars held out their hands in the rain and snow. Most of them were frail pensioners, orphans and military invalids. Without charitable donations from passers-by they faced starvation. The incidence of homelessness increased. Meanwhile everyone – not only the poor – suffered from the continuing degradation of the environment. In areas of heavy industry such as Chelyabinsk, the rise in respiratory and dermatological illnesses was alarming. Spent nuclear fuel was casually emitted into the White Sea. Not since the Second World War had so many citizens of Russia felt so lacking in care by the authorities. The old, the poor and the sick were the victims of the governmental economic programme.

Virtually everyone who had a job, however, kept it. The exceptions were the soldiers of the Soviet Army who were being brought back from the garrisons of Eastern Europe since 1990, and many were compelled to retire from service. Conditions were often dire for those who remained in the armed forces. The state construction of housing blocks had more or less ceased, and in the worst cases, public lavatories were requisitioned as military residences. Through 1992, too, contingents of the Soviet Army were divided among the newly-independent states of the CIS and a Russian Army was formed.

Russian Army contingents, however, were located not only in Russia but across the entire former Soviet Union, and uncertainty persisted as to what should be done with them. In Moscow, crowds gathered daily outside the Lenin Museum off Red Square protesting at the USSR's dismemberment. Stalinists, Russian nationalists and monarchists mingled. There was even a man with a huge billboard offering all and sundry a cheap cure for AIDs. This congregation was menacing, but also a little ridiculous: its dottiness outdid its activism. But its members were nostalgic for the Soviet Union, for orderliness and for Russian pride and power that was echoed amidst the population of the Russian Federation. Naturally this feeling was strongest among ethnic Russians. They constituted eighty-two per cent of the Russian Federation,[19] and many of them worried about the potential fate of relatives and friends now living in what were formally foreign countries.

They worried, too, about the situation in Russia. Not since the Second World War had life been so precarious. By the mid-1990s the life expectancy of Russian males had fallen to fifty-nine years and was still falling. Alcohol abuse was widespread. But most problems faced by most citizens were beyond their control: declining health care; the pollution and lack of industrial safety standards; and the fall in average family income. Even those people who had jobs were not always paid. Salary and wages arrears became a national scandal.

In other ways, too, life was precarious. As the criminal and governmental organizations got closer, the use of direct violence became commonplace. Several politicians and investigative journalists were assassinated. Entrepreneurs organized the 'contract killings' of their entrepreneurial rivals; and elderly tenants of apartments in central city locations were beaten up if they refused to move out when property companies wished to buy up their blocks. Criminality was pervasive in the development of the Russian market economy. Governmental officials at the centre and in the localities were routinely bribed. The police were utterly venal. Russian generals sold their equipment to the highest bidder, sometimes even to anti-Russian Chechen terrorists. Illicit exports of nuclear fuels and precious metals were made; the sea-ports of Estonia were especially useful for this purpose. Half the capital invested abroad by Russians had been transferred in contravention of Russian law. The new large-scale capitalists were not demonstrably keen to invest their profits in their own country.

And so Russia did not build up its economic strength as quickly as neighbouring Poland and Czechoslovakia; and its legal order was a shambles. Sergei Kovalëv, the Russian government's human rights commissioner, was increasingly isolated from ministers. The Constitutional Court retained a degree of independence from the President, but generally the goal of a law-based state proved elusive. Everywhere there was uncertainty. Arbitrary rule was ubiquitous, both centrally and locally. Justice was unenforceable. The rouble depreciated on a daily basis. It appeared to Russian citizens that their entire way of existence was in flux. On the streets they were bargaining with American dollars. At their kiosks they were buying German cooking-oil, French chocolate and British alcohol. In their homes they were watching Mexican soap-operas and American religious evangelists. A world of experience was being turned upside-down.

Nor were the problems of Russians confined to the Russian Federation. Twenty-five million people of Russian ethnic background lived in other states of the former Soviet Union. In Tajikestan (as its government now spelled its name), the outbreak of armed inter-clan struggle amongst the Tajik majority induced practically all Russian families to flee for their lives back to Russia. In Uzbekistan the local thugs stole their cars and pushed them out of prominent jobs. In Estonia there was discussion of a citizenship law which would have deprived resident Russians of political rights. Large pockets of Russians lived in areas where such intimidation was not quite so dramatic: north-western Kazakhstan and eastern Ukraine were prime examples. But Russians indeed had a difficult time in several successor states in the former Soviet Union.

Yeltsin hinted that he might wish to expand Russia at the expense of the other former Soviet republics, but foreign criticism led him to withdraw the remark. Other politicians were not so restrained. Vladimir Zhirinovski, who had contested the 1991 Russian presidential elections against Yeltsin, regarded the land mass south to the Indian Ocean as the Russian sphere of influence. Widely suspected of being sheltered by the KGB, Zhirinovski's Liberal-Democratic Party had been the first officially-registered non-communist political party under Gorbachëv; and Zhirinovski had supported the State Committee of the Emergency Situation in August 1991. His regret at the USSR's collapse was shared by communist conservatives who obtained a decision from the Constitutional Court in November 1992 allowing them to re-found themselves under the name of the Communist Party of the Russian Federation. Its new leader Gennadi Zyuganov and his colleagues cut back its ideology of internationalism and atheism while maintaining a commitment to the memory of Lenin and even Stalin.

The threat to Yeltsin came from such self-styled patriots. Unequivocal advocacy of liberal political principles became rarer. Several prominent critics of authoritarianism fell into disrepute: the most notable example was Gavriil Popov, mayor of Moscow, who resigned in 1992 after accusations were made of financial fraud. Sergei Stankevich, who had seemed the embodiment of liberalism, became gloomier about the applicability of Western democratic traditions to Russia – and he too was charged with being engaged in fraudulent deals. The few leading surviving liberals such as Galina Starovoitova and Sakharov's widow Yelena Bonner were voices crying in the wilderness.

Russian politics were gradually becoming more authoritarian; and Yeltsin's shifting policy towards Russia's internal republics reflected this general development despite the amicable signature of a Federal Treaty in March 1992. Chechnya had been a sore point since its president, Dzhokar Dudaev, had declared its independence in November 1991. Tatarstan, too, toyed with such a project. Several other republics – Bashkortostan, Buryatiya, Karelia, Komi, Sakha (which had previously been known as Yakutia) and Tuva – insisted that their local legislation should take precedence over laws and decrees introduced by Yeltsin. North Osetiya discussed the possibility of unification with South Osetiya despite the fact that South Osetiya belonged to already independent Georgia. Yeltsin also had to contend with regionalist assertiveness in the areas inhabited predominantly by Russians. In summer 1993 his own native region, Sverdlovsk, briefly declared itself the centre of a so-called Urals Republic.[20]

Yeltsin, the man who had urged the republics to assert their prerogatives against Gorbachëv, asserted the prerogatives of 'the centre'. Taxes would be exacted. No separatist tendencies would be tolerated: the frontiers of 'Russia' were non-infringible. National, ethnic and regional aspirations were to be met exclusively within the framework of subordination to the Kremlin's demands. A firm central authority needed to be reimposed if the disintegration of the Russian state was to be avoided during the implementation of economic reforms.

Furthermore, Yeltsin did not intend to go on giving way to the demands of Rutskoi, Khasbulatov and the Russian Supreme Soviet. He tried to shunt Vice-President Rutskoi out of harm's way by assigning him agriculture as his legislative responsibility just as Gorbachëv had got rid of Ligachëv in 1989. There was less that could be done about Khasbulatov, the Supreme Soviet Speaker, who gave plenty of parliamentary time to deputies who opposed Gaidar's monetarist economic objectives.[21] But at least Yeltsin prevented Chernomyrdin, the Prime Minister since December 1992, from adopting policies still closer to those advocated by Khasbulatov. Yeltsin insisted that Chernomyrdin should accept Gaidar's associate Boris Fëdorov as Minister of Finances; and the cabinet was compelled, at Yeltsin's command, to adhere to Chubais's programme of privatization. Yeltsin was biding his time until he could reinforce the campaign for a full market economy.

To outward appearances he was in trouble. His personal style of politics came in for persistent criticism from the newspapers and from the large number of political parties which had sprung up. For example, it was claimed that Russia was governed by a 'Sverdlovsk Mafia'. Certainly Yeltsin was operating like a communist party boss appointing his clientele to high office; and he steadily awarded himself the very perks and privileges he had castigated before 1991. He was chauffeured around in a limousine and his wife no longer queued in the shops. He founded his own select tennis club: he seemed ever more secluded from other politicians in the country.[22]

Yet Yeltsin made a virtue of this by stressing that he would always ignore the brouhaha of party politics. Like Nicholas II and Lenin, he habitually denounced politicking. Yeltsin had backed Gaidar in 1991-2, but not to the point of forming a party with him. He was a politician apart and intended to remain so. Moreover, the great blocks of economic and social interests in Russia had not yet coalesced into a small number of political parties. The problem was no longer the existence of a single party but of too many parties. The distinctions between one party and another were not very clear; their programmes were wordy and obscure and the parties tended to be dominated by single leaders. The far-right Liberal-Democratic Party was described in its official handouts as 'the Party of Zhirinovski'.[23] Russia had not yet acquired a stable multi-party system, and this circumstance increased Yeltsin's freedom of manoeuvre.

In March 1993 the Russian Supreme Soviet provided him with the kind of emergency in which he thrived by starting proceedings for his impeachment. Yeltsin struck back immediately, and held a referendum on his policies on 25 April 1993. Fifty-nine per cent of the popular turn-out expressed confidence in Yeltsin as president. Slightly less but still a majority – fifty-three per cent – approved of his economic policies.[24] Yeltsin drew comfort from the result, but not without reservations; for fifty per cent of those who voted were in favour of early presidential elections: not an unambiguous pat on the back for the existing president. Yet in general terms he had gained a victory: his policies were supported despite the unpleasantness they were causing to so many people. Undoubtedly Yeltsin had outflanked the Supreme Soviet; he could now, with reinforced confidence, claim to be governing with the consent of voters.

The trouble was that he would still need to rule by decree in pursuit of a fuller programme of economic reform leading to a market economy. Furthermore, Rutskoi and Khasbulatov were undaunted by the referendum. They still had strong support in a Supreme Soviet which could thwart the introduction of any such programme; they could also use the Supreme Soviet to prevent Yeltsin from calling early political elections. The result was a stalemate. Both sides agreed that Russia needed a period of firm rule; but there was irreconcilable disagreement about policies, and each side accused the other of bad faith in their negotiations.

Characteristically it was Yeltsin who took the initiative in breaking the stalemate. He plotted simply to disperse the Supreme Soviet, hold fresh parliamentary elections and propose a new Russian Constitution to the electorate. The plan was his own, and he approached his military and security ministers about it at the last moment in summer 1993. Chernomyrdin was on a trip to the USA when the discussions were held, and was told of them only upon his return.[25] Yeltsin planned to lock the Supreme Soviet deputies out of the White House. But he had made no allowance for his plan being leaked to Rutskoi and Khasbulatov. At least this is the kinder interpretation of his activity; the other possibility is that he was out to provoke a violent showdown with his adversaries and therefore wanted them to know of his intentions.[26] What is beyond dispute is that he flaunted his intention to resume the government's campaign for a market economy; for on 18 September he pointedly brought back Yegor Gaidar as First Deputy Prime Minister.[27]

In any case, when on 21 September the President duly issued his Decree No. 1400, Rutskoi and Khasbulatov were ready for him. Together with hundreds of Supreme Soviet deputies, they barricaded themselves inside the White House: they had arms, food and a determination to topple Yeltsin. Immediately Yeltsin, hero of the peaceful defence of the White House in August 1991, ordered his Defence Minister Grachëv to lay siege to the same building. In fact there continued to be much entering and leaving of the White House, and the White House's defenders attracted a group of prominent *enragés* to their side, including Albert Makashov, Vladislav Achalov and Viktor Anpilov. Makashov and Achalov were army generals who had long wanted Yeltsin deposed by fair means or foul; Anpilov had founded a Russian Communist Workers' Party which rejected Zyuganov's Communist Party of the Russian Federation as being altogether too respectable. A violent outcome was not inevitable, but neither side was greatly predisposed towards reconciliation.

Rutskoi and Khasbulatov had become hostile to any compromise with Yeltsin and by now thought of themselves as protectors of parliament and legality; and indeed Yeltsin's act of dispersal was a breach of the limits of his constitutional authority.[28] Yeltsin for his part affirmed that the parliament had been elected in 1990 whereas he had put his policies to a referendum in April 1993. The country's government, he added, should not be held permanently in abeyance because of the perpetual stalemate between president and parliament.

Doubtless most citizens of the Russian Federation would have preferred a compromise. But it was not to be. Rutskoi, cheered by the crowd of supporters outside the White House, thought that a popular majority was on his side; he declared himself Acting President and announced that Achalov was his Defence Minister: it did not occur to him that this was bound to throw a wavering Grachëv into the arms of Yeltsin. On Sunday, 3 October, Makashov's armed units tried to storm the Ostankino TV station in Moscow, and Rutskoi recklessly urged the crowd outside the White House to march on the Kremlin. Yeltsin resorted to direct armed action. In the early hours of 4 October, he and Chernomyrdin pushed Grachëv into retaking the White House.[29] A gaping hole was blasted in the building before Rutskoi, Khasbulatov and their supporters would concede defeat. They were arrested and detained in the same Sailors' Rest Prison where several of the August 1991 plotters were still being held.

These 'October Events' were quickly exploited by Yeltsin, who sanctioned further steps towards the construction of a market economy. According to an optimistic calculation, average personal incomes had recovered by the end of 1994 to a level only ten per cent lower than they had held in 1987.[30] Privatization of companies, under Chubais's direction, proceeded apace. By the end of 1994 two fifths of the working population in the Russian Federation were employed by private enterprises.[31] Shops, stalls and street-vendors began to offer a variety of consumer products not seen on open sale for over six decades. Even more remarkable was what happened in the bakeries. The need to secure cheap basic foodstuffs for the towns had troubled governments in the Russian capital throughout the century. The question of grain supplies had been the touchstone of every ruler's claim to efficient governance. Yeltsin put his confidence on parade: in the last quarter of 1993 the remaining price controls on consumer products were lifted; in particular, bakeries were at last permitted to charge what they wanted for bread.

Not everything went his way. Gross domestic product in 1993 fell by twelve per cent over 1992.[32] And although there was a rise in general comfort in Moscow, things were much more unpleasant in most other cities, towns and villages. To some extent, the fault did not lie with Yeltsin's government. He had taken office with the expectation that the Western powers would provide finance to enable him to set up a 'stabilization fund'. Such a fund would have been of important assistance during the period of transition to a market economy: it would have helped both to sustain social-security benefits and to make the rouble freely convertible into the world's other currencies. The Western powers, however, were impressed more by the limitations than the achievements of the Russian economic reforms.

Such limitations were considerable. Massive state subsidy was retained for the gas and oil industries; the fact that Prime Minister

Chernomyrdin remained on friendly terms with his former colleagues in Gazprom made it unlikely that the subsidy would quickly be withdrawn. The kolkhozes, despite having been turned into private economic organizations of one kind or another, were another sector which continued to receive easy credit from the government. Ministers also refrained from introducing the long-awaited legislation on land privatization. Furthermore, there were persistent constraints upon entrepreneurial activity. The government did precious little to impose the rule of law. Businessmen did not have the predictable framework for their operations which they craved. The powers given to local administrations to grant or withhold trading licences impeded the emergence of an untrammelled market economy.

Yet much had been achieved under the premiership of Chernomyrdin, and Yeltsin acted to maximize his political advantage after the 'October Events' by arranging national and local elections and a constitutional referendum. The arrest of his Vice-President and Speaker removed his two most awkward antagonists from contention, and seemed to leave him free to devise a strategy unimpeded by considerations of compromise with the Supreme Soviet. He aimed to endorse the newly-formed political party of Yegor Gaidar, Russia's Choice (*Vybor Rossii*); his favoured option was to go for a more drastic economic reform than Chernomyrdin approved. But Yeltsin had reckoned without the widespread revulsion caused by his action on the White House. The 'October Events' were an unsolicited gift to those of his opponents who claimed that he was violent and unpredictable.

Yet despite its roughness and imperfections, this was the first Russian parliamentary election where nearly all political parties could operate freely. The problem was that Russia still had a superfluity of parties, and it made sense for electoral pacts to be formed among them. Russia's Choice led a block committed to rapid economic liberalization. The *Yabloko* ('Apple') block favoured a somewhat slackened pace of change and a retention of subsidies for state-owned industry. There were also three blocks which brought together communist sympathizers; these were led respectively by the Communist Party of the Russian Federation itself and by the Agrarian

Party and Women of Russia. Others stayed outside all blocks. Chief among these was the Liberal-Democratic Party, whose leader Vladimir Zhirinovski insisted that only his organization was not somehow linked to 'the authorities'.

A bias in Gaidar's favour was recognizable in both the amount and the content of central TV reportage. This was important; for rallies were few, posters were flimsy and unplentiful, newspapers were delivered intermittently and the local networks of the parties were patchy. Citizens got most of their information from their television sets. Yeltsin left nothing to chance: he even issued an instruction that no political broadcast could be made on television that referred critically to the draft Constitution.

Seemingly he obtained most of what he wanted. His Constitution draft secured the necessary approval of the electorate, albeit by a narrow majority. This meant that Yeltsin had virtually unrestricted authority to appoint his prime minister, to prorogue parliament and rule by decree. The static warfare between parliament and president appeared unlikely to recur. The new parliament was to be renamed the Federal Assembly. This Assembly would be bi-cameral: the first chamber was the State Duma, the second was the Council of the Federation. And the Council of the Federation, being constituted by leading figures in the legislatures and administrations of the republics and provinces, would be heavily influenced by the President's wishes and would act as a check upon the State Duma. Of the 450 seats in the State Duma, furthermore, half were elected by local constituencies and half by national party lists. This system was designed to limit the ability of local political élites, especially those of a communist orientation, to resist the brave capitalist boys of Tsar Boris.

But not everything went well for Yeltsin. There had been signs of problems during the electoral campaign. In particular, Gaidar, a stilted public speaker at the best of times, was out of his depth. His pudgy, shiny face had never endeared itself to most voters and his language was as incomprehensible as ever; and even Yeltsin, appealing at the last moment for a vote in favour of his proposed Constitution and his preferred parties, looked uncomfortable in his addresses to the public on television.

By contrast Zhirinovski, having conjured up funds to buy time on the broadcast media, showed panache. He was the only politician who could speak the language of the man and woman in the street. His vulgar aggressiveness appealed to those Russian citizens who had suffered from the effects of Yeltsin's policies, especially the provincial industrial workers, the middle aged and the serving officers. Zhirinovski was not the only threat to Yeltsin's plans. There was also Zyuganov and the Communist Party of the Russian Federation. Zyuganov was an unprepossessing speaker and a writer of some of the stodgiest prose in the Russian language. And yet like Zhirinovski, he exposed the political and economic dislocation that had occurred in 1991. His charisma was negligible; but his party stood well with those sections of the electorate which were discomfited by Russia's separation from the former USSR, her decline in global power and her inability to guarantee general material well-being.

The surge of support for Yeltsin's adversaries was hidden by the ban on the divulgence of public-opinion surveys in the last weeks of the electoral campaign. But the talk in Moscow on 15 December, when voters went to the polls in the mildly snowy weather, indicated that Yeltsin was in trouble. Although he won sanction for the Constitution, he was troubled by the other results. To his consternation, the State Duma contained sixty-four deputies from the Liberal-Democratic Party and 103 from the block led by the Communist Party of the Russian Federation under Gennadi Zyuganov. Russia's Choice supplied only seventy deputies. There had been much unfair manipulation before voting day and probably there was downright fraud in the counting of the votes; but still the results were compiled with a sufficient degree of fairness for a snub to be delivered to Boris Yeltsin.

27

The Lowering of Expectations (1994–1999)

Yeltsin had adopted democratic ideas late in life and in a superficial fashion. The electorate's unhappiness with the results of his reforms quickly induced him to go back to more authoritarian habits. Surveys of popular opinion in the early 1990s made depressing reading for him and his government. Citizens of the Russian Federation had started by welcoming political democracy and being willing for market economics to be given a try.[1] As real average incomes went into steep decline, people resented the top stratum of an elite which had become rich and powerful beyond the wildest dreams of officialdom under communism. As Yeltsin's popularity waned, so nostalgia grew for the safe and stable conditions remembered from the years before 1985. Brezhnev's rule began to be recalled with enthusiasm.[2] The disintegration of the USSR was regretted. People were bewildered by the denigration of military, economic and cultural achievements of the Soviet period. The floor was giving way beneath the Kremlin reformers, and Yeltsin found it difficult to introduce his policies without extensive consultation with the representative bodies – the State Duma and the Council of the Federation – which had been established by his own new Constitution.

He stuffed his successive governments with politicians who lacked qualms about this approach. The dogged Viktor Chernomyrdin was retained as Prime Minister, and Yeltsin never attempted to bring Gaidar back to power. Nevertheless Yeltsin treated Chernomyrdin pretty shabbily, frequently indicating dissatisfaction with the government's performance; but it was not until March 1998 that he risked replacing him with an economic radical in Gaidar's mould. This was Sergei Kirienko, still in his mid-thirties, from Nizhni Novgorod. The financial collapse of August 1998 did for Kirienko and the State Duma's intransigence induced Yeltsin to appoint Yevgeni Primakov to the premiership. Primakov's willingness to have dealings with the Communist Party of the Russian Federation irked Yeltsin. Equally annoying was the Prime Minister's high standing in popular opinion. In May 1999 Primakov was dropped and his post was given to former Minister of the Interior Sergei Stepashin. But when Stepashin refused to keep the state anti-corruption investigators away from the Yeltsin family's affairs, he too was removed from office. In August 1999 the obscure Vladimir Putin, ex-head of the Federal Security Service (FSB), became Prime Minister. It was a giddying carousel on the fairground of Russian governance.

Yeltsin's hands at the controls grew ever shakier, apart from when it came to decisions about sacking his associates. He was resorting extravagantly to the comforts of the vodka bottle, and in Berlin in 1994 he drunkenly snatched a conductor's baton and led an orchestra through a rendition of the folksong 'Kalinka'. His drinking aggravated a chronic heart ailment. Suffering a collapse on a flight across the Atlantic in the same year, he was too ill to meet the Irish Taoiseach at Dublin airport.[3] For the duration of the 1996 presidential electoral campaign he had to be pumped full of palliative medicines. Afterwards a quintuple cardiac bypass operation proved necessary.

Neither Yeltsin nor his governments retained much support in the country. Prime Minister Chernomyrdin formed a party, the archly named Our Home's Russia, to contest the Duma elections of December 1995. He had a huge advantage over the opposition since the new party had unrivalled financial resources and powers of patronage and secured unobstructed access to TV news programmes. Yet Chernomyrdin took only 65 seats out of 450. The lacklustre Gennadi Zyuganov and his Communist Party of the Russian Federation obtained 157, and the allies of the communists – the Agrarian Party and Women of Russia – added a further 23. This made Zyuganov the leader of the largest block in the Duma. Yeltsin, however, refused to compromise with him and insisted on keeping Chernomyrdin as Prime Minister. Zyuganov, filled with new confidence, denounced both Yeltsin and Chernomyrdin. The Duma elections, he declared, supplied a popular mandate for a reversal of the whole reform agenda. The USSR should never have been abolished. Economic privatization had reduced millions of households to poverty. The country's assets and interests had tumbled into the grasp of Russian plutocrats and the IMF, and Yeltsin and Chernomyrdin were the agents of this dénouement. Zyuganov made the case for a government of communists to restore well-being in state and society.

The Communist Party of the Russian Federation had been widely thought to be at death's door since it drew its support mainly from pensioners and from workers in the decaying sectors of industry. Yet there was a tenacity about Zyuganov, and his increasingly Russian nationalist statements continued to attract popular approval. His party comrades in the Duma, moreover, were well-organized and one of them, Gennadi Seleznëv, became its Speaker. Despite having equipped himself with abundant powers under the 1993 Constitution, President Yeltsin had to let his governments come to terms with Zyuganov whenever the communists stirred up controversy in the Duma about his behaviour, health or policies. Yeltsin and Chernomyrdin continued to trim back the project of reforms. The headlong rush into capitalism was slowed. The inclination to perceive Russia's national interests in international relations as identical to those of the leading Western powers faded. The chaotic relationship between the centre and the republics and provinces in the Russian Federation began to be regularized. Yeltsin more and more rarely devoted his speeches to the theme of the communist totalitarian nightmare between 1917 and 1991.[4]

Although these adjustments came easily to the opportunistic President, he did not want to concede more than was absolutely necessary. He and his coterie were determined to hold on to power. In spring 1996, when Zyuganov was beating him in the national opinion surveys, he contemplated a plan to suspend the presidential election. His aide and chief bodyguard Alexander Korzhakov encouraged him, arguing that a communist restoration had to be prevented at all costs. A 'red scare' atmosphere was fostered in newspapers and on television. A decree of suspension was drafted. Not until the last moment was Yeltsin persuaded that he would do more damage than good by trampling on democratic procedures.[5] Not that he stopped being devious. He agreed a secret deal with Boris Berezovski and a handful of other exceptionally wealthy businessmen who were commonly known as 'the oligarchs' whereby they would receive a lucrative stake in state-owned mining enterprises in return for bailing out the state budget and financing Yeltsin's electoral campaign.[6] He also came to an agreement with rival presidential candidate Alexander Lebed. With his booming voice and confident comportment, Lebed had a substantial following in the country. As reward for urging his supporters to vote in the second round for Yeltsin, Lebed was to become Secretary of the Security Council and principal negotiator for the Russian side in the conflict with Chechnya.

Zyuganov had started the electoral campaign with advantages. Even though he fought it with obsolete techniques, he was confronting an incumbent whose health problems were acute. Nevertheless the second round of the voting in July 1996, after the other candidates had been knocked out, gave a thumping victory to Yeltsin. Money, patronage and a brilliant media campaign had done the trick for him.

Despite his good performance in the presidential polls, though, Yeltsin lacked a stable, loyal majority for his policies in the State Duma.[7] He did not attend its proceedings or negotiate with its leaders, leaving it to his prime ministers to manage some kind of accommodation. Chernomyrdin worked behind the scenes offering attractive deals to groups of deputies. Party politics lost much importance as various leading figures were bought off. Vladimir Zhirinovski and the Liberal-Democratic Party noisily criticized the government but did not always vote against it. Duma debates commanded little public respect or attention. Press and TV were concentrated upon the President and ministers except when something scandalous was happening in the chamber. Zhirinovski increased his notoriety in 1996 by physically assaulting a female Duma deputy; but his party's fortunes did not benefit in subsequent elections. The situation was staider in the Council of the Federation but hardly more helpful in easing the passage of Chernomyrdin's legislation unless he gave in to their demands for special concessions to region after region. This was pork-barrel politics *par excellence*.[8]

Of all the republics in the Russian Federation it was Chechnya which caused the greatest trouble for Moscow. Having declared unilateral independence in 1991, its leader Dzhokar Dudaev had continually cocked a snook at Yeltsin. He had presided over the thorough criminalization of economic activity in Chechnya and given haven to Chechen protection racketeers operating in Russia's cities. He permitted the application of Sharia law. He declined to pre-empt Islamist terrorist raids from inside Chechnya upon nearby Russian areas. While Dudaev was right that Chechnya had remained with Russia solely because of the superior military power of tsars and commissars, he was not the simon-pure democrat and liberator depicted in his propaganda.[9]

In December 1994 Yeltsin's Minister of Defence Pavel Grachëv had persuaded him that the Russian Army would quickly crush the Chechen rebellion. The motives for the invasion were murky. Grachëv wished to divert attention from his corrupt management of the armed forces' finance and equipment. Powerful members of Moscow's business elite also aimed to secure tighter control over their oil assets in the Chechen capital Grozny. Yet Grachëv had misled everybody about the readiness of his troops to take on the Chechens. After Grozny fell to artillery assault by land and air, Dudaev and his commanders organized resistance in the mountains. Terrorist actions were intensified in Russian cities. Moscow TV stations and newspapers had reporters in Chechnya who told of the Russian army's incompetence and of the atrocities carried out by its troops. Such was the confidence of the Chechen fighters that even after Dudaev was killed, having been traced through his satellite-connected mobile phone, the armed struggle continued. But the cost in human lives mounted, and a truce was arranged for the duration of the presidential campaign; and Lebed soon succeeded in producing a peace agreement which left both sides with their honour intact. Military hostilities would cease; the Chechens would in practice govern Chechnya without interference and the independence question would simply be deferred.

No one really thought that the threshold had been crossed to a solution. Already the implications were dire for Russia's self-liberation from the authoritarian past. Leading liberals Grigori Yavlinski and Yegor Gaidar were among the few politicians to censure the invasion. Yeltsin recognized his blunder over Chechnya too late and was a shadow of his former self. Practically the entire political establishment had casually accepted the use of massive and at times indiscriminate violence in pursuit of the state's ends. There was scant appreciation of the damage done to the prospects for a healthy civil society to emerge.

The usually critical leaders of the Western powers did little more than go through the motions of upbraiding the Russian government. The perception was that Yeltsin, warts and all, was the best President available and that his economic and diplomatic achievements earned him the right to prolonged support. It was noted too that Chernomyrdin, while abandoning the *laisser-faire* zeal of Gaidar, continued to strengthen the roots of capitalism in Russia. Even Gaidar had avoided genuine 'shock therapy' for the ailing economy for fear that a drop in people's living conditions might provoke civil disturbances. Chernomyrdin maintained the policy of enormous state subsidies for fuel, lighting, telephones and transport, and he ensured that tenants should receive the deeds to their apartments without charge. He also devoted resources to keep the prices of farm produce low. Moreover, fiscal regulations gave incentives to firms to eschew sacking employees; the incidence of unemployment stayed low.[10] At the same time Chernomyrdin and his successors pressed ahead with economic measures which brought little benefit to anyone outside the tiny circles of the wealthy. By 1995 sixty-five per cent of industrial enterprises had been privatized. The market economy had been installed.

Markets in Russia, however, were of a very distorted kind. Competition was cramped by the dominance of a few 'oligarchs' over the banks and the media as well as the energy and rare metals sectors. Criminal gangs and corrupt administrative clientèles compounded the difficulty. The rule of law was seldom enforced. The economic environment was so unpredictable and indeed downright dangerous that the most successful entrepreneurs stashed away their profits in Swiss bank accounts. Fraud was rampant. About half the funds loaned to Russia by the IMF were illegally expropriated by powerful individuals and diverted abroad.

Not all the economic data were gloomy. Although gross domestic output continued to diminish after 1993, the rate of diminution was slowing. In comparison with most states of the CIS, indeed, Russia had an economy that seemed very vibrant. Tajikestan and Georgia were in desperate straits and even Ukraine could not afford to pay its debts to Russia for gas and petrol. The Ministry of Economics in Moscow in 1995 predicted that the Russian economy would at last start to expand again in the following year. The prognosis was proved wrong. Among the problems was the justified reluctance of foreign enterprises to set up branches in Russia while contracts were hardly worth the paper they were printed on. The government's financial management also left much to be desired. In 1997 it issued state bonds to balance the budget. The terms were hopelessly disadvantageous to the government if ever the rouble fell under severe pressure. Global financial markets were febrile at the time and the dreaded run on the rouble duly occurred in August 1998. Russia unilaterally defaulted on its international loan repayments and Sergei Kirienko, despite not having been Prime Minister when the state bonds had been issued, stepped down.[11]

Yeltsin's reputation was in tatters, but the Russian financial collapse quickly turned out to be a blessing in disguise. The devaluation of the rouble increased the costs of imported goods and inadvertently provided a stimulus to domestic manufacturing and agriculture. Shops and kiosks bought up and sold Russia's own products. By 1999 the beginnings of economic recovery were unmistakable and gross domestic output was rising; and these small steps forward were rightly treated as success.

Nevertheless the economic crisis was not simply an accidental result of the vagaries of financial markets at home and abroad; for the government's incompetent policies had made a bad situation a lot worse. Such strength as the Russian Federation retained in the world economy anyway rested on the export of its natural resources.

Oil and gas were in the lead. Not far behind came gold, diamonds and nickel. Wood pulp too was sold abroad – the result was a shortage in the supply of paper for Russian newspapers! The only finished industrial goods to be sold in any amount across Russian borders were armaments, and even in this sector there was the difficulty that the government was constrained by the Western powers to stop selling weaponry to traditional customers such as Iraq and Iran. Such an economic strategy had been followed by governments from Gaidar's onwards. Indeed the structure of Soviet foreign trade had similarly been built on the export of natural resources. What was new after the collapse of the USSR, as Zyuganov pointed out, was the process of de-industrialization. Russian factories no longer produced as much output as in 1990 (which was a poor year for the Soviet economy). The Communist Party of the Russian Federation urged the need for tariff walls for the restoration of industrial production.

Communists were brisker in supplying criticism than practical policies. Indeed they appeared reconciled to permanent opposition, and their willingness to abandon tenets of Marxism-Leninism was remarkable. Zyuganov declared himself a Christian believer; his prolific pamphleteering was inspired more by anti-communists like Nikolai Berdyaev, Arnold Toynbee and Oswald Spengler than by Lenin.[12] One prominent communist even owned a casino.

Such a party had become ever more incapable of reversing the changes made since 1991. Its most telling criticisms in the State Duma were aimed at the government's foreign policy. Yeltsin had planned with Foreign Minister Andrei Kozyrev to sustain Russia as a power in alliance with the most influential Western countries: both believed in the need for a warm partnership with the USA and Yeltsin spoke confidently about his 'friend Bill' when reporting on his summit meetings with President Clinton. Yet the partnership was never remotely near to being an equal one. Russian economic distress disabled the government from competing with American technological advance, military power and global diplomacy. The only residue of old glory lay in Russia's possession of ageing nuclear weapons: this was the sole reason why Clinton bothered to hold summit meetings. The Russian financial system's dependence on the USA's sanction for the IMF to go on lending to Russia meant that Yeltsin could never easily refuse an American diplomatic demand. Kozyrev's 'Atlanticist' orientation was put under assault in the Duma and the press.

Yeltsin responded in characteristic fashion by publicly rebuking Kozyrev as if he himself had not had a hand in setting the orientation. He spoke about the need to protect the singular interests of the Russian state, and both he and Kozyrev warned that the government could not stay indifferent when other states of the former USSR discriminated against their ethnic Russians. The stringent linguistic and cultural qualifications for Estonian citizenship became a bone of contention. Within the CIS, moreover, Russia increasingly used its supply of oil and gas to neighbouring countries as an instrument to keep them within the Russian zone of political influence.

Hardening the line of foreign policy, Yeltsin sacked Kozyrev in December 1995. Yet he could do little about the series of encroachments by Western powers. Finland had joined the European Union earlier in the year and schemes were made for the eventual accession of many countries in Eastern Europe in the twentieth-first century. This was embarrassing enough. Worse for the Russian government was the NATO's refusal to disband itself after the Cold War's end and the Warsaw Pact's dissolution. Quite the contrary: NATO set about territorial expansion. Poland, the Czech Republic and Hungary became members in 1999. NATO forces were sent into action in Bosnia in 1993–1995 and Kosovo in 1999 as inter-ethnic violence intensified. In both cases the Russian government protested that insufficient effort had been invested in diplomacy. Yeltsin sent Chernomyrdin as his personal envoy to Belgrade to plead with Serbia's President Slobodan Milosević to come to terms with the Americans and avoid the bombing of his capital. But to no avail. Having lost its position as a global power, Russia was ceasing to carry much weight even in Eastern Europe.

The Russian Foreign Ministry and various Moscow think-tanks recognized that policy should be formulated on the basis of a realistic appreciation of Russia's reduced capabilities. They recommended that Russia should seek other partners in world diplomacy without alienating the USA. The benefits of 'multipolarity' in global politics and economics were touted. The European Union, China and India were courted by Russian diplomats with a revitalized enthusiasm.

Nothing about this steady endeavour was going to capture the imagination of a public unaccustomed to seeing its government treated casually by the USA. It was Yeltsin's good fortune that few public bodies took him to task. The Russian Orthodox Church supported his invasion of Chechnya and his diplomatic stand on the Kosovo question. Its hierarchy had little interest in the routine of politics. At times of national emergency, especially in late 1993, Patriarch Alexi II offered himself as an intermediary between Yeltsin and his enemies; but generally the Church, needing the government's assistance in defending itself against the resurgence of other Christian denominations, was quiescent. So too was the Russian Army. Yeltsin never had to face the overt criticism by serving officers that Gorbachëv endured. Military critics no longer held seats in representative public institutions. The platform of criticism had been sawn from under them. The armed forces performed poorly in Chechnya. Although their finances had been savagely reduced, there was no excuse for their incompetence and brutality in the taking of Grozny. Even the media were easy on Yeltsin's regime. They exposed corruption in his family; the NTV puppet show *Kukly* ('Dolls') satirized him as a bumbling idiot. But his policies rarely suffered assaults of a fundamental nature.

The reason was that Church, high command and media had more to lose than gain by the regime's removal. A communist restoration would have disturbed their comforts at the very least. Yeltsin had prevented any such disturbance. He had also not needed to resort to violence again in Moscow. The order of Russian state and society was beginning to settle into a durable mould.

At the central level of politics it had proved not unduly difficult for former members of the Soviet nomenklatura to establish themselves in the new Russian elite. Typically, they were persons who had been in the early stage of a career when the USSR fell. In business circles too there were many entrepreneurs with a solid background in the communist party or the Komsomol before 1991. Newcomers were not excluded. Most of the 'oligarchs', for example, had worked in posts outside any nomenklatura.[13] This mixture of old and new in the post-communist establishment was also observable in the localities. Mintimer Shaimiev had moved smoothly from being communist party first secretary of the Tatar Provincial Party Committee to installing himself as President of Tatarstan.[14] So blatant a transition was in fact unusual in the Russian Federation. (It was much more common in ex-Soviet Central Asia.) But whoever emerged to lead a republic or a province was likely to bring along an entourage with administrative experience from the Soviet period. Patronage remained an important feature of local public life, and traditions of 'tails' and 'nests' were little affected by recurrent elections. The ruling group in nearly every locality used whatever trickery – or even illegality – was needed to hold on to power.[15]

The prime beneficiaries of the 'new Russia' were politicians, businessmen and gangsters. In some cases the individual might be all three things at once. Wealth was celebrated in public life. Successful sportsmen such as Yevgeni Kafelnikov or entertainers like Alla Pugachëva led an extremely luxurious life. Sumptuous dachas were built. Apartment blocks were bought up and renovated to the highest standards of opulence. Children were sent to English private schools. Domestic servants, chauffeurs and personal hairdressers were employed. Foreign limousines, clothing and holidays were treated as nothing out of the ordinary by families who had suddenly got rich as capitalism flooded all over Russia. The ultra-rich were seldom eager to keep their wealth a secret and were determined to keep their gains exclusively for themselves. They bought yachts and villas on the Mediterranean – the Black Sea had become too vulgar for them. Forsaking the Russian countryside, they purchased mansions in Hampstead and estates in the English home counties. They dressed in Versace or Prada outfits. Their limousines were Mercedes. Not since 1914 had the excesses of Russian material abundance been shown off so excessively.

Magazines sprang up to cater for such tastes. Most people who bought them were not wealthy; but they had to have an above-average income to afford a copy and ogle at how the 'new Russians' expected to live. As fortunes were made the competition grew to show them off. Birthday parties were celebrated by paying American or British rock stars to give private performances. Sons and daughters of the oligarchs were treated as celebrities.

At the same time there remained a possibility that wealth won so quickly and often so illicitly might one day soon be confiscated or stolen. Big businessmen protected themselves with personal bodyguards and financial sweeteners to influential politicians and police. They surrounded their dachas with hi-tech surveillance equipment. The poodle was for indoor companionship; in the grounds, the Rottweilers were the patrol dogs of choice. The danger usually came from fellow businessmen. Courts were only for the 'little people'. Defence of funds and property effectively depended on firepower if bribery of officials failed, and company owners remained vulnerable unless they could assemble adequate means of defence. At restaurants and night-clubs no one was surprised to see guards with Kalashnikovs in the foyers. The atmosphere at the stratospheric level of Russian business was frantic. This in turn induced its practitioners to enjoy their earnings to the full in case they suffered a financial or personal disaster. Most oligarchs felt notoriously little inclination to share their wealth with charities. With a few exceptions their civic commitment was negligible.

A disproportionate number of them were non-Russians, especially Jews, which provided parties on the political far right with the pretext to make anti-Semitic propaganda. Russians ignored the fascists even while detesting the oligarchs. More congenial to Russian popular opinion were measures directed against people from the north and south Caucasus. Yeltsin, in a breach of multinational tolerance, backed Moscow mayor Yuri Luzhkov's attempts to eject Azeris, Armenians and others from the capital. Demagogic tactics of this kind reflected an awareness of the widening resentment of the new street vendors and entrepreneurs – and people from the south of the former Soviet Union were prominent among the capital's stallholders.

A long ladder separated the families at its top from the vast impoverished majority of citizens at its base. Russia – like other societies – had its wealthy, middling and poor strata. But the poor were a disturbingly large section of society. By the end of the twentieth century about two-fifths of the population lived below the poverty level as defined by the UN.[16] The data were geographically diverse. Moscow and, to a lesser extent, St Petersburg had an economic buoyancy denied to the rest of the country. Inhabitants of big cities, moreover, did better materially than the rest of society. The Russian north and most parts of Siberia suffered especially badly as the state subsidies for salaries and accommodation in places of harsh climatic conditions were phased out. The standard of living also plummeted even in central cities whose economy depended on an industrial specialization which was beaten down by superior foreign imports. Machine tool production slumped in the Urals and the mid-Volga region with appalling consequences for the employees and their families. Large industrial firms in the USSR had provided cafeterias, kindergartens and sports facilities, and trade unions had organized holidays for their members. A whole way of making existence bearable was put in jeopardy.

Most people took shelter in the systems of mutual support that had helped them survive in the Soviet decades. Families and friends stuck together as they had always done. Cliental groups remained intact. The alternative was for individuals to take their chances on their own; but there was much risk so long as economic opportunities were outrageously unequal in society and political and judicial bias was flagrantly in favour of the rich and mighty. Limitations on freedom remained in Russian reality.

No greater limitation existed on life in general than conditions of employment. Wages fell far below the rocketing rate of inflation. Few Russian citizens could buy the imports of Western industrial products or even the bananas or oranges that had suddenly appeared in the kiosks. Workers in the factories and mines were lucky if they were paid at the end of the month. Teachers, doctors and often even civil servants suffered the same. Pensioners were treated abysmally. Privatization of state enterprises was accomplished by the issuance of vouchers for shares to all adults; but the vouchers lost value in the inflationary times. Directors tended to do much better than the other employees because of their inside knowledge. Some of the sting was removed from popular resentment by laws granting apartments to residents as private property; but building blocks fell into disrepair for want of continued finance by local authorities. Life remained hard for most people for bigger part of the decade and they coped by the well-worn methods of eking out a diet of bread and sausages, bartering their possessions and hoping that conditions would eventually improve. De-communization exhausted society.

Bit by bit, though, the situation eased somewhat. Staple foods in the shops increased in attractiveness and variety. Beer and vodka remained cheap; and breweries, distilleries and bakeries were among the most dynamic sectors of the consumer-oriented economic sectors. Basic clothes became more attuned to the aspirations of fashion.

Resistance to the general trends was therefore very weak. The labour movement, which had begun to arrest itself under Gorbachëv, fizzled out after 1991. The Federation of Independent Trade Unions called for a general strike in October 1998 with uninspiring results.[17] Across the economy the advantage remained on the side of the employers. Not every segment of Russian business went along with the policy of privatization. Notable opponents were the collective farm directors, who obstructed the government's desire to break up the kolkhozes into small, privately owned farms. By the mid-1990s the number of such farms had stabilized at only a quarter of million.[18] Most kolkhozes simply redesigned themselves as agricultural co-operatives with the same director in charge and the same workforce under him. The point was that very few rural inhabitants welcomed the chance to go it alone: credit facilities were poor and the supply of the necessary equipment and fuel was unreliable. Yet if the countryside with its demoralized and ageing population was predictably conservative in outlook, the towns too disappointed those radical reformers who had believed that the abolition of the Soviet political structures would induce mass support for rapid change.

Russians made the best of a bad situation, as they always had done. Their energies were given mainly to their domestic conditions.

They practised their DIY skills. They gardened (and produced food for their own tables). They took up hobbies, bought pets and watched TV. Western popular culture – rock music, sport and pornography – flooded into the country.

This caused affront to the established cultural elite, but younger writers relished the change and wrote incisive commentaries on the blending of the old and the new in Russian society. The satirical novels of Victor Pelevin caused a stir; and the poignant ballads of Boris Grebenshchikov and his rock group Akvarium searched for meaning in Russian history from its origins to the present day.[19] Two of Grebenshchikov's stanzas ran as follows:[20]

Eight thousand two hundred versts of emptiness,
And still there's nowhere for me to stay the night with you.
I would be happy if it wasn't for you,
If it wasn't for you, my motherland.

I would be happy, but it makes no odds any more.
When it's sky-blue everywhere else, here it's red.
It's like silver in the wind, like a sickle to the heart –
And my soul flies about you like a Sirin.

The words reprise Soviet motifs of redness and the sickle. The old tsarist measure of length – the verst – is introduced. A still more ancient figure like the mythic Sirin (who was half-woman, half-bird) appears. The style brings together Soviet balladeering and the songs of Bob Dylan. The concern with Russian national themes was also favoured by novelists; and the film director Alexander Sokurov's *Russian Ark* depicted current reality through the metaphor of a vessel trying to preserve the best of national culture and history from a life-threatening flood.[21]

Russians for two centuries had been accustomed to accepting moral guidance from their artists. Few young artists or poets felt comfortable about such a public role. The removal of the Soviet political and ideological lid decompressed the cultural order in Russia. Ideas of extreme diversity and experimentalism became the norm. Post-modernism flourished.

The intelligentsia in any case was losing its leverage on public opinion. Even Alexander Solzhenitsyn ceased to be taken seriously. Returning from America in 1994, he was given a weekly show on TV; but his humourless sermons on the need to restore Orthodox Christian values were unpopular and he was taken off air. Writers in general found it hard to touch the hearts of their public. Meanwhile the national press was beset by problems with paper supply and with distribution facilities. Billionaires who bought newspapers seldom wanted columnists who subjected the new capitalism to a thorough critique. Intellectuals themselves were baffled by the nature of the changes since 1991. Many sought to make what they could out of the marketplace; they were ceasing to act as the conscience of the nation. The Russian Orthodox Church enjoyed expanded congregations in comparison with earlier years when persecution had been intense. But secularism proved to be a tenacious phenomenon and the clergy's refusal to renew liturgy or doctrines restricted the possibility of appealing to people who had no prior knowledge of Christianity. Scientists and other scholars too lost prominence in public life as the struggle to earn their daily bread acquired precedence over involvement in politics. The Russian Academy of Sciences in Moscow retained its old prestige but without the former impact.

The government sought to fill the media with its vision of Russia. The attack on communism continued but patriotism was more increasingly emphasized. Electoral disappointments indicated that a gap had widened between official policies and popular expectations. Chernomyrdin was no man of ideas and had no inkling about how to regain the trust of Russians. His remedy in July 1996 was to announce a competition, with a $1,000 prize (which was more than two years' wages for an office worker at the time), to answer the question: 'What is Russia?' The search was on for a fresh definition of 'the Russian idea'. Hundreds of diverse entries appeared in the governmental newspaper. If Chernomyrdin was baffled before posing the question, he was just as confused when he read the attempted answers. The winner, philologist Guri Sudakov, offered bland words about Motherland and spirituality.[22] Meanwhile Russians elsewhere went on disputing the whole topic with their usual gusto and there was never any prospect of a broad consensus.

The pluralism in culture high and low testified to the vivacity of Russian society below the carapace fixed upon it by the political and economic authorities. This vivacity had existed before Gorbachëv's *perestroika* but it was only after 1985 that it came fully into the open. The pity was that the ruling group under Yeltsin made little attempt to enlist such energy and enthusiasm in the cause of fundamental reform. Probably the chances of success were very small. The invitation to participate in the country's reformation had been extended by Gorbachëv and had evoked an inadequate response. But at least Gorbachëv had gone on trying. What obstructed him were the effects of decades, indeed centuries of political oppression which had made most people reluctant to engage at all in affairs of state. Increasingly Yeltsin, ill and distracted, had not bothered to try – and it may reasonably be asked whether his commitment to fundamental reform had ever been deeply felt. Certainly there were several influential members of his entourage who had always disliked aspects of the reform project.

The movement towards a more authoritarian political style accelerated in August 1999 when Yeltsin replaced Sergei Stepashin with Vladimir Putin as Prime Minister. At first the change in personnel did not seem to matter. Both Stepashin and Putin had backgrounds in the security agencies. Furthermore, Putin was obliged to behave as obsequiously to the President in public as every Prime Minister since Chernomyrdin. Continuity in policy and practice appeared the likely outcome.

Putin came to office with an agenda for the north Caucasus. Already Stepashin had secretly been planning a second invasion of Chechnya. In September there were bomb explosions in Moscow apartment blocks which were blamed on Chechen terrorists. The circumstantial evidence pointed away from Chechens and towards a provocation by the Federal Security Service, and the explanations offered by Bureau director Nikolai Patrushev were derisorily implausible. Nevertheless they were believed at the time by most Russians. The authorities had the pretext it needed, and Putin, in consultation with Yeltsin, ordered the Russian Army into Chechnya. Lessons had been learned from the 1994–1996 campaign. This time the government closely controlled news reporting. Firepower was maximized and, as Russian armed forces approached Grozny, warnings were given for civilians to evacuate the city. Piloting his own plane, Putin went down to visit troops near the front line. His popularity soared as total military victory appeared in sight. Yeltsin was already treating him as his heir. And then, on 31 December 1999, the entire county was taken by surprise when the President in a dignified address announced his retirement.[23] Putin was to become Acting President with immediate effect. The Yeltsin cavalcade was over.

28

And Russia? (From 2000)

Vladimir Putin achieved an impressive victory in the presidential election of March 2000. He had left nothing to chance against challengers who matched his zeal to promote Russian state interests and national pride. Yuri Luzhkov, the mayor of Moscow, let it be known he was ready to stand on behalf of the Fatherland party. Immediately the government-controlled TV stations released charges about his political and personal integrity. Then Yevgeni Primakov offered a further threat after bringing together the Fatherland and All Russia parties and announcing his candidacy for the presidency. Yet again Russian television stations conducted an operation against the challenger, and Primakov too decided to withdraw his candidacy. This left Zyuganov and Zhirinovski to put forward their standard hopeless case. Opinion polls universally predicted an electoral landslide and Putin made a virtue of refusing to campaign. His nonchalance was counterfeit currency at a time when his subordinates were working hard at conveying his image of cherubic militancy in the news bulletins and suppressing any untoward reports from the Chechnya front. A flattering biography was prepared and rushed into print. Youthfulness, sobriety, competence, persistence, patriotism: these were the qualities which commended themselves to voters. No second round of voting was required. Putin had already won the election in the first round, receiving fifty-three per cent of all votes cast.

Yeltsin and Patriarch Aleksi II gave their blessing at the Kremlin inauguration ceremony. Down the aisle of the St Andrew's Hall walked Putin like a hunter eyeing the trees on either side of him for quarry. His address to the audience, televised live, indicated a determination to set a new tone in public life. He spoke about democracy and the rule of law. But much more insistent was his emphasis on state power and institutional order. Compliance with higher authority was going to be demanded. Russia's place in the world would be asserted. Putin was combative in appearance and mode of delivery. He had not needed to go cap in hand to wealthy businessmen to get himself elected. Diminutive in stature, he towered over the proceedings and restored dignity to his office.

Putin was proud of being the product of a Soviet upbringing. He described the dismantling of the USSR as 'the greatest geopolitical catastrophe of the twentieth century'; he hated the blizzard-like deprecation of the USSR's achievements. Born in Leningrad in 1952, he had a father who had fought in the Second World War and a grandfather who had cooked for Lenin. As an adolescent he became a judo champion in his native city. He also applied for recruitment to the KGB, but was told that the KGB expected to approach individuals, not to be approached by them. But his enthusiasm was noted and while he was studying at Leningrad State University he was promised a posting. His main early job was as an intelligence officer in the German Democratic Republic. Operating there during the years of Gorbachëv's rule, he was filled with dismay. For Putin, *perestroika's* principal effect was to dissolve a great state, economy and society. But he was also pragmatic and on returning to Leningrad joined the administrative team of mayor Anatoli Sobchak who was seeking to make political and economic reforms work well for the city. Putin was skilled at adapting to circumstances. His organizational talent attracted attention and in 1996 he was promoted to the Presidential Administration in the capital. Soon he was appointed head of the Federal Security Service, and in August 1999 this man whose name was barely known to most Russian citizens became their Prime Minister.[1]

The 'oligarch' Berezovski had boasted to the press that it was he who had put Putin in power. He thought that his commercial interests would be protected in return. He could not have been more wrong. Soon after assuming the presidency Putin called the business elite into the Kremlin and issued a direct warning. Unlike Yeltsin, he would not tolerate their interference in politics. Most of the audience took him seriously but a few individuals chanced their luck. When Berezovski continued to brag and bluster it was made plain to him that his days of pomp were over. Police investigations were started into his alleged frauds. He fled to the United Kingdom in 2001 where he received political asylum and, wrapping himself in a coat of democratic principles and clean capitalism, publicized his accusations against Putin. Next to feel Putin's wrath was Vladimir Gusinski. He too had multiple interests in the economy. And he had political ambitions: his NTV television channel regularly poked fun at Putin through the *Kukly* satirical puppet show.[2] But his business career had had its murky side and a police investigation was started. Gusinski was briefly arrested. He too fled the country in summer 2001, finding refuge in Israel and Spain.

Putin urged that the achievements of Russia after the October 1917 Revolution should be given their due; and he re-introduced the melody – if not the words – of the USSR state hymn.[3] Most Russians welcomed the restoration of a stirring piece of music they associated with victory in the Second World War. They wanted to be proud again about being Russian; and surveys revealed that the proportion of citizens feeling associated more with the USSR than with Russia was going down only slowly.[4] The popular response was favourable. His opinion-poll rating fell drastically only once. This was when he reacted stiffly to an explosion in the nuclear submarine *Kursk* in August 2000. All on board perished. Putin was widely criticized for declining to interrupt his holiday and display personal sympathy. He learned from this setback and tried to avoid falling out of step with national sensibilities. He was tested again in September 2004 when Chechen terrorists occupied a school in Beslan, a town in North Osetiya, and took captive a thousand tiny pupils, their minders and their teachers.[5] Putin was televised supervising the handling of the siege until Russian security forces re-took the buildings. Although the operation was accompanied by many deaths it was not the Russian president who incurred the blame.

He consolidated his position by filling the offices of state with individuals who had ties to the Federal Security Service or other coercive agencies. They ruthlessly enforced governmental decrees. State power was their shibboleth. It is true that newspapers, books and posters continued to criticize or ridicule him. Yet television was the medium with the deepest popular impact, and the humbling of Berezovski and Gusinski had the effect desired by the Kremlin as TV programme editors exercised caution in what they transmitted about the central authorities.

The president was not an enemy of the big business corporations, only of businessmen who got politically too big for their boots. All the remaining 'oligarchs' understood this except the hot-blooded Mikhail Khodorkovski who continued to finance political parties and liberal causes hostile to Putin. As one of the wealthiest men on the planet and owner of the oil company Yukos, Khodorkovski had got used to doing things his own way. He declared his wish to encourage a more pluralist form of politics and a less corrupt environment for commerce in Russia. His newspapers regularly criticized the presidential administration and the government; he also subsidized opposition parties in the Duma. When he refused to desist he was put under investigation for fraud. Prosecutors brought him to court and charged him with tax evasion. A huge bill was delivered to the company. Facing bankruptcy, Khodorkovski was obliged to sell off his Yukos assets at a knockdown price to Rosneft, and in May 2005 he was sentenced to eight years imprisonment in Chita province in eastern Siberia. Rosneft was a private company under tight governmental supervision. Its acquisition of Yukos was the decisive signal that Russia's political economy had changed since Yeltsin's presidency.

The implications for foreign businesses in the country were discouraging. The government's declared priority in the early 2000s had been to attract the maximum of Western capital into the Russian economy. The world's biggest energy companies queued up to buy up rights of extraction in areas of Russia where great profits seemed guaranteed in the near future. Royal Dutch Shell and BP signed early deals. Their investors rubbed their hands with satisfaction as Russia appeared committed to having an internationally open economy.

Both companies soon suffered disappointment when official investigators were sent into their Sakhalin facilities. Infringements of environmental legislation were quickly diagnosed. One by one, American and European energy corporations were compelled to renegotiate their contracts and accept poorer deals or face the loss of all their holdings in the Russian Federation. They all gave way, and Gazprom, Rosneft and other native conglomerates exploited a commercial advantage. Personnel moved flexibly between them and the various ministries in Moscow. Russia was becoming a bastion of state capitalism. The State Duma in March 2008 rationalized the process by passing a bill to restrict foreign investment in forty-two 'strategic' sectors of the economy (which included petrochemicals, nuclear power, armaments, fisheries, airspace and the media). Russia was no longer up for sale to the highest external bidder.

There was no thought of dismantling capitalism. Cabinets during Putin's presidency always included not only former intelligence officers but also liberal economic reformers. Among such liberals was Mikhail Kasyanov, who was Putin's prime minister from May 2000 to February 2004. Kasyanov tried to impose a framework of commercial law – and indeed there was a degree of enhanced protection for small businesses to register and operate even though the local elites remained as corrupt as ever. Improvement was also detectable in the workings of the courts, but only in cases lacking a political dimension.[6] Yet Putin and Kasyanov did not get everything their own way. They worked long and hard for a new Land Code and yet the Duma frustrated them by rejecting the proposal for the privatization of territory outside the urban outskirts. President and Prime Minister were annoyed that farms in the countryside remained outside the jurisdiction of the reform. The Federal Assembly was equally averse to the call for Gazprom to be broken up so that the pieces would compete with each other. Nor did it sanction the demand for electricity and other utilities to be sold at higher prices to Russian domestic consumers.[7]

Putin also ran into difficulties when he attempted to put pressure on the leaders of the various republics and provinces of the Russian Federation. Soon after being elected, he withdrew their right to sit automatically in the Council of the Federation where they could affect the passage of legislation; he awarded himself the power to sack any one of them. He also divided the whole country into seven super-regions and appointed his own plenipotentiary to each super-region with the mission to ensure compliance with central laws and Presidential decrees. Putin's initiatives were greeted with barely a murmur of objection from local leaders.[8] Yet little changed in reality. The sheer complexity of political and economic processes in every republic and province defeated the attempt at abrupt disciplinary action; Putin was more successful in intimidating the media than in securing obedience from the lower levels of the state hierarchy. But one thing he did achieve was a halting of criticism of the government. Mintimer Shaimiev of Tatarstan, who had been a thorn in Yeltsin's flesh, became a garland around Putin's shoulders. In 2004 Putin forced through a measure allowing the presidency not only to remove regional governors but also to appoint new ones without reference to the local electorate.

Formal central prerogatives were one thing, provincial reality was often entirely another. The new governors, being obliged to ensure stability of administration, needed the co-operation of local politicians and businessmen. A strategy of give-and-take worked better in practice than peremptory orders.[9] The old Russian obstacles to achieving an effective political hierarchy persisted, and the Kremlin found itself increasing its fiscal subsidies to the regions.

Putin had formed a party, Unity, in September 1999 to enforce the government's authority. Unity's main function was not to discuss his policies but to agree to them in the Duma. But the party failed to achieve a majority in the Duma election of December 1999. The President in May 2001 engineered a coalition with three other parties called United Russia. Like Yeltsin, Putin refrained from becoming a party member and justified this by saying that the President ought to stand outside the fray of public dispute. In December 2003 the Duma elections left United Russia a little short of an absolute majority. But other Duma deputies quickly came over to Putin's side and the Kremlin at last broke free of the restrictions in the parliament which had plagued Yeltsin. Presidential authority was strengthened as party discipline increased.[10] Indeed Putin needed to veto only one bill produced by the legislature from 2002 onwards. He removed the Communist Party of Russia from the chairmanship of several Duma committees. After 2003, indeed, United Russia supplied the leaders of all such committees. The State Duma and the Council of the Federation had become pliant instruments of presidential rule.

Putin's election for a second presidential term in March 2004 hardly required him to conduct a campaign. This had not stopped him from organizing fawning support from the media. Zyuganov, veteran of presidential contests in 1996 and 2000, said he had had enough and allowed Nikolai Kharitonov, who was not even a communist party member, to take his place. Zhirinovski took a similar decision: not even the chance of months in the political limelight induced him to take part. The liberals were in disarray. Irina Khakamada put herself forward on their behalf but did not succeed in uniting them. Russian TV took little notice of anyone but Putin, who asked to be judged on his record and appealed for patriotic unity. The election was a foregone conclusion: he would have needed to fall under the wheels of a Moscow trolley bus to lose against his rivals. This time Putin took seventy-one per cent of the votes in the first round, again rendering a second unnecessary.

He had been given credit for bringing order and stability to the country. In truth the economic resurgence had little to do with his performance as a leader. Since mid-1999, before he was even prime minister, there had been a steady rise in oil and gas prices on global markets. By the end of 2007 the Russian economy was the world's tenth biggest in gross domestic product, having expanded at an annual rate of seven per cent since Putin's rise to the presidency.[11] This had the effect of widening prosperity in Russia. Real incomes more than doubled in the same period. The size of the middle class purportedly grew to a fifth of the population by 2008. Other estimates put it at a tenth. What was undeniable was that people with a stake in the market economy had grown in number. From stall-holders to owners of small manufacturing or retail companies the proliferation was rapid and constant. Employment in all sectors of the economy had increased. Neglected regions were at last beginning to experience some improvement.

Yet capitalism in Russian remained a wild phenomenon. In industries big and small the executive and judicial authorities turned a blind eye to the infringement of health and safety rules. Mining and chemical enterprises were the tip of a dangerous iceberg for the workforce. But strikes were few and demonstrations were fewer. Political repression and manipulation played a part in procuring this situation, but anyhow the wish of most Russians was to live comfortably. There had been many improvements since the mid-1980s. Citizens of the Russian Federation had freedoms not witnessed since the fall of the Imperial monarchy. They also had a degree of privacy impossible in the USSR. They could enjoy their sense of nationhood without fear of official disapproval. Yet it rankled with them that blatant social inequalities remained. The conspicuous wealth of the few contrasted with the harsh austerities afflicting the many. Unfairness abounded. Administrative processes were still prone to arbitrary rule. Police and judges were venal. Russians went on grumbling and had much to grumble about. In order to cope with existence they turned to the traditions of mutual assistance which had for centuries helped them through the worst times. But they did not take to the streets. The last thing twenty-first-century Russians wanted was a revolution.

In the early years of his presidency Putin had confined his assertiveness to domestic politics. Recognizing that Russian power would remain restricted until the economy could be regenerated, he stressed his commitment to a 'multipolar' world. This was a tactful way of expressing dislike of the USA's dominance as the single superpower. In practice, there was not much he could do to turn Russia into one of the globe's great poles. Like Yeltsin, Putin tried to make up for this by holding frequent meetings with his leaders of other countries. Each get-together was managed superbly by his media experts and Putin, fit and increasingly confident, contrasted sharply with his decrepit predecessor. But substantial results were few.

Putin rushed to offer condolence and support to the USA after 11 September 2001 when Islamist terrorists flew aeroplanes into New

York's World Trade Centre. The destruction of the twin towers and the massive loss of human lives provoked the Americans into a furious reaction involving a military campaign in Afghanistan to eliminate the Al-Qaida organization. American President George W. Bush proclaimed a 'war on terror'. Waiving Russia's conventional claim to exclusive influence in the former Soviet republics of central Asia, Putin made no protest about the Americans using air bases in Kyrgyzstan to attack Al-Qaida in Afghanistan. He also made little fuss when, in December 2001, Bush unilaterally announced his intention to withdraw from the anti-ballistic missiles treaty signed by Washington and Moscow in 1972. Russian diplomatic stock was rising in Washington, and Putin for a while was treated as a worthy partner in international relations. Bush had claimed in midsummer 2001: 'I looked the man in the eye. I was able to get a sense of his soul.' Putin acquired Western indulgence for the continuing military campaign in Chechnya. The fact that international Islamist groups had sent men, arms and money to the Chechen rebels allowed him to represent Russia as having been fighting at the front line against terrorism worldwide.

Washington ceased rewarding Putin for his assistance once the war in Afghanistan had ended in spring 2002. Although he was left alone to do what he wanted in Chechnya he was not encouraged to reassert Russian power outside the borders of the Federation. He continued to devote diplomatic efforts to the forging of closer links with the European Union and indeed with NATO. But the reality of Russia's global weakness was there for all to see.

This situation turned in his favour as the revenues from oil and gas exports started to fill Russian state coffers; and Putin, thinking he had nothing to lose, adopted an assertive manner in reaction to American initiatives in international relations. The USA led an invasion of Iraq, a strong trading partner of the Russian Federation, between March and May 2003 in complete disregard of the Kremlin's objections and concerns. The Americans also announced a willingness to prepare the way for Georgia and Ukraine to join NATO. They interfered in the politics of Uzbekistan. They cheered the 'Orange Revolution' in Kiev when, in December 2004, the anti-

Moscow candidate Viktor Yushchenko won the presidential election despite serial attempts to defraud him of his victory. In 2006 they requested Poland and the Czech Republic, freshly incorporated in NATO, to allow them to install an anti-ballistic missile 'shield' on their territory. President George W. Bush insisted that the enemy he had in mind was Iran; but Russian politicians regarded it as one militant initiative too many against the interests of Russia's security. In each instance Putin made public his criticisms, abandoning any worry of a worsening of the relationship with the USA – and his truculence found favour with Russians, who applauded him for restoring their country to a seat at the table of the world's great powers.

Western politicians continually called on the Kremlin to show greater co-operativeness. They pleaded for NATO's good intentions to be accepted. Putin barked it out at a dinner for Prime Minister Blair: 'This is ridiculous. I am a Russian. I cannot agree with the Americans on everything. My public won't let me for a start. I would not survive for two years if I did that. We often have different interests.'[12] As proof of his determination, in July 2007, Putin suspended Russia's adherence to the Conventional Forces in Europe treaty signed by the Soviet leadership in 1990. His attitude went down well with Russians regardless of political orientation. Disputes among parties were shunted to marginal matters of foreign policy as opinion rallied to Putin.

The broad ruling group, however, never felt completely secure in power, and it was ruthless in enforcing its grip on public debate. Investigative journalists who highlighted official corruption or challenged the government's account of the war in Chechnya exposed themselves to personal danger. In October 2006 Anna Politkovskaya was murdered outside her Moscow apartment. She was the most prominent of the critical reporters targeted in this manner, but there were several others. Her newspaper, *Novaya gazeta*, was subjected to repeated acts of persecution. Vladimir Slivyak exposed the widespread negligence in the civil nuclear industry in the Russian far north; he was treated as a traitor and subjected to continual harassment. In the United Kingdom, where Boris Berezovski stepped up his barrage of accusations against the Russian authorities, Alexander Litvinenko – one of his associates – was poisoned with a lethal dose of polonium-210. Outspoken rival politicians were intimidated. A gang of unidentified thugs had crushed the fingers of Yabloko leader Grigori Yavlinski's pianist son in Yeltsin's time. The dangers of opposition persisted under Putin. Garry Kasparov was temporarily thrown into gaol merely for campaigning for justice and civil rights. The FSB was given licence to act outside the law in defence of the whole state order. Putin himself professed ignorance of the specific cases. What is more, he showed little sympathy for the victims and did next to nothing to rectify the general situation. Russia sank deeper and deeper into a pit of authoritarian rule backed by criminality.

Putin in his second term moved ever further down the road towards a centralization of power. From December 2004 the leaders of the Russian Federation's republics, instead of being elected, were to be selected by the president and their names were to be submitted to the legislative bodies of their localities for approval or rejection. Several of the smaller of the non-Russian republics in the Federation, moreover, were abolished. The authority of 'the centre' was ceaselessly confirmed.

In April 2005 Putin also took a grip of the country's thousands of civil associations from charities to recreational groups, making it compulsory for them to acquire official registration and subjecting them to central supervision through a Public Chamber he himself appointed. Foreign agencies were treated with some suspicion and difficulties were placed in the way of the British Council, the BBC Russian Service and other bodies. Religious denominations too were put under pressure. Although the Russian Orthodox Church was granted privileges, in return it was required to show eager loyalty to the secular authorities. Putin, himself a professed Christian, interfered in personnel appointments in other faiths. Berel Lazar, a Hasid, was his first choice as Chief Rabbi in 2000. Universities were vigorously patrolled. Textbooks were vetted; approved authors had to moderate any criticism of Stalin. A youth movement, *Nashi* ('Our Ones'), was founded to divert adolescents towards patriotic ideals. Its organizations were employed to harass the British ambassador after a worsening of Russo–UK relations in 2006. Lip-service was paid to enhancing social freedom. The reality was that the Kremlin distrusted collective endeavours by citizens unless there could be confidence that respect for the government, its leaders and its policies would be maintained.

Putin and his fellow rulers over several years combined electoral abuse, legislative licence, violent repression and media control to sustain an authoritarian regime. His projects on terrorism, on political extremism and public demonstrations were smoothly passed by the Federal Assembly. The loose wording of the laws was designed to make it easier for government and security agencies to curtail open dissent. Putin also succeeded, after years of trying, to scrap the remnants of the communist system of social security and replace it with monetary payments that gave a lesser guarantee of assistance in times of personal emergency.[13] Yet he could not permanently ignore the popular grievances recorded in sample surveys. In 2005 he announced four 'national programmes' for urgent reform in housing, social welfare, agriculture and health care. The central and local elites had neglected such sectors since the fall of communism since they themselves could easily pay privately for what they needed. Most families, though, experienced dreadful under-provision. They lived in cramped accommodation. They could ill afford the weekly grocery bill. If they fell sick, they had to pay bribes to state-employed doctors for treatment.

His public image was assiduously manicured by his spokesmen, and it elicited a positive response from most Russians. The female pop duo Singing Together had a hit with 'I Want A Man Like Putin'; his sober lifestyle commended itself especially to young women. When he appeared on radio for a question-and-answer programme, middle-aged listeners rang him up to express their heartfelt thanks. Male adults appreciated his relish for macho sports like judo. He also posed for a photo holding a tiger cub which an unknown friend had given him on his birthday. TV stations, all owned by his supporters, joined in the praise. The photographers accompanied him on a tour of eastern Siberia in August 2007 when he took Prince Albert II of Monaco out fishing – and pictures appeared of him stripped to the waist in the bright sunlight. Requests came through from the public for the Constitution to be amended so that he could stand again for a presidential third term. For a while he seemed to toy with the idea. The loyal sections of the media gave the impression that Russia, having found its saviour, should not allow him to stand down from the paramount office.

Outside of politics, Russians also began to do better on the international stage. Official sport recovered. Yeltsin had always supported tennis and the proliferation of private clubs produced a grand slam champion, Marat Safin. Female players thrust themselves forward in 2006–2007. Russian football became a serious force in European competitions. At the Beijing Olympics in August 2008 the country came third in the medals table. In December of the same year Xenia Sikhinova won the Miss World contest in South Africa.

The Duma elections in December 2007 produced 315 seats for United Russia. This was a remarkable endorsement of Putin's period of rule. But he resisted the temptation to alter the Constitution and pondered whom to recommend as his successor. It was thought that his choice might fall on Viktor Zubkov, whom he appointed Prime Minister in September 2007. Like Putin, Zubkov hailed from St Petersburg, and the two of them had worked together for a long time. In the end Putin plumped for Dmitri Medvedev. At the time Medvedev was serving as First Deputy Prime Minister; he was also in charge of the 'national programmes' announced by Putin to improve health care, housing, agriculture and education. He was not a complete unknown but as yet lacked a clear profile in the eyes of most Russians. Continuity would be preserved by a secret deal whereby Putin would be asked to serve as the new Prime Minister. The usual dirty tricks were played. Liberal-minded politicians were ruled out of the contest on spurious technical grounds. These included ex-premier Mikhail Kasyanov. Even the former chess world champion Garry Kasparov was banned. Tired veterans Zyuganov and Zhirinovski were allowed to stand but they received little airtime on television. In stark contrast, Medvedev's every public appearance was filmed and the Kremlin's mastership of 'political technology' secured the desired result in March 2008.

Medvedev was an appropriate selection for Putin to make. A fellow Leningrader, Medvedev had proved his allegiance as a political client over many years. He was bright in intellect and gentle in appearance. If Putin strutted around like a judo master, Medvedev had the aura of a retired member of a 1990s boy band. What attracted the rest of the world was Medvedev's readiness to emphasize Russia's need for the rule of law. But his appointment of Putin as Prime Minister made it clear that change, if it was going to happen, would occur only very gradually.

Russian assertiveness in international relations kept rising. The 'foreign policy concept' adopted in July 2008 took pleasure in the recent strengthening of state power and economic well-being in Russia. Foreign minister Sergei Lavrov suggested that the period of the West's global dominance was over, and Medvedev's team were determined to roll back the recent inroads made by NATO. A suitable opportunity cropped up in August 2008 when President Mikhail Saakashvili of Georgia sent troops into the rebellious republic of South Osetiya. Georgia had already announced its intention to apply for NATO membership. Russian presidents since the break-up of the Soviet Union had regarded the 'near abroad' as a zone where American influence was not welcome. Saakashvili's campaign met with a furious response. The tank units of the Russian Army thrust their way over the mountains down into Georgia, smashing all military resistance and ruining strategic economic infrastructure. Medvedev, while announcing that armed occupation would be only temporary, proceeded to give official recognition to the independence of both South Osetiya and Abkhazia.

The Russian Army carried out a crude operation that attracted opprobium in the rest of the world. It was reported – and never convincingly denied – that Putin told French President Nicolas Sarkozy that he intended to follow the example of what the Americans had done to Saddam Hussein and to 'hang up Saakashvili by the balls'. Sarkozy allegedly asked: 'Yes, but do you want to end up like Bush?' Putin admitted: 'Ah, you've got a point there.'[14] Russia's people in any case felt positive about the Russian campaign. The rulers and the ruled sensed that proof had finally been given that the country would need to be taken seriously even by the Americans. First Putin and then Medvedev demanded that the US should stop using NATO as a means to pursue a unilateralist foreign and security policy around the globe. Medvedev claimed that the difficult stage of rebuilding the Russian state and economy was over. Russia was again a great power. It demanded respect for international law in relations among states. It required to be treated on an equal basis by the countries of NATO. It depicted itself as having its own distinct civilization, and the values and power of the West were declared as being on the decline.

The bludgeoning of Georgia removed lingering doubts in Poland and the Czech Republic about accepting the American proposal to establish installations against long-range ballistic missiles on their territory. Russia caused fear without gaining friends or admirers. It also worried potential investors. Despite its petrochemical riches, it needed help in modernizing its drilling and refining facilities – and the Russian government's bullying of foreign companies was scarcely going to hasten this process. The harassment of Berezovski, Gusinski and Khodorkovski had the effect of inducing other rich businessmen to try and decant their fortunes to London. Putin and Medvedev inadvertently pushed economic talent westwards. The departure of Berezovski and other 'oligarchs' was regretted by few citizens but the atmosphere of Russian big business was not improved. The Kremlin and the petrochemical industrial sector were locked in an intimate embrace. Occasional information trickled out about the wealth of ministers. Public office became a ticket to vast wealth. Liberal political opposition to the Kremlin became demoralized. Yavlinski stepped down from the Yabloko leadership in June 2008. The Union of Right Forces gave up independent activity in November, amalgamating itself with other such parties into the new Right Cause party and campaigning for democracy, the rule of law and free markets; but the fact that Medvedev endorsed its foundation indicated how little a challenge to him it represented.[15]

Moscow's meddling in the post-1991 territorial settlement in the former USSR was on the increase. Medvedev pointed out that this was no different in principle from what the Americans had done with Kosovo (which formally declared its independence from Serbia in February 2008). Russia strengthened its ties with Venezuela and Cuba as if searching to help the enemies of successive American presidents in the New World. A dispute with Ukraine about payment for Russian gas led to a suspension of supplies to several other European countries in January 2009 until the Ukrainian government agreed to terms. In November 2008, furthermore, Medvedev had announced the intention to install missile-launching facilities in the west of the Russian Federation in reaction to President Bush's initiative in Poland and the Czech Republic. By January 2009, after Barack Obama's inauguration as US President, things were calming down, and Medvedev suggested the need to resume negotiations. Russians aimed to bargain from a position of pride and strength. Tacitly they regarded most of the former Soviet Union as falling inside their sphere of legitimate influence and aimed to secure agreement from the Americans to keep their noses out of the region.

The Russian rulers vigorously pursued the national economic interest in international relations. They – or Gazprom and Rosneft – sold their energy resources to Europe. The existing pipelines favoured the maintaining of this commercial connection. The Chinese were known to be slow payers; the Europeans had a record of prompt settling of charges. Medvedev, moreover, was just as aware as Putin that Russia stood in need of foreign capital and technology. The boom in state revenues from gas and oil was disrupted in mid-2008 when world prices dipped; and the forecasts of Russian extraction of its energy resources anyway suggested that output was going to fall. Manufacturing, agriculture and transport remained in an outdated condition. Moscow and a few great cities flourished while the rest of the country awaited 'modernization'. Public education stood in great need of adequate financing and rapid reform. The decline in the birth rate among ethnic Russians continued. What is more, eastern Siberia underwent depopulation as the state withdrew its subsidy for residence there. Although the incidence of poverty across the country declined during Putin's presidential terms it still affected one in seven households in mid-2008.[16] Russia took 131st place in a world ranking of countries according to how 'peaceful' they were. Quite apart from the violence in the north Caucasus, Russian crime, political repression and military expenditure were high and getting higher.[17] Drug abuse, moreover, went on rising. Acute concern grew about Russia's demography as measured in rates of mortality, births and ill-health.

A vast task of transformation lay ahead. The Kremlin elite was aware of its responsibilities to the nation and spoke often about them. Putin and Medvedev settled for a mixture of politics and economics which appeared to have worked elsewhere. Vigorous control over elections and policy-making was imposed. Big business was made to understand that its freedom to make money could and would be revoked if ever its leaders fell out of line with the government's wishes. At the same time the Kremlin held back from censoring the Internet or closing down bookstores. Private dissent was tolerated so long as it stayed inside the apartments of the dissenters or was limited to a few eccentrics selling poorly produced pamphlets on street corners – this was more than what was allowed in China, Singapore or Indonesia.

The Russian economy after 1991 was immensely sensitive to shockwaves emitted by the global economy. When the global 'credit crunch' occurred in summer 2008 the Russian stock exchange had to suspend its operations several times before the end of the year. The decrease in oil and gas revenues in the same months aggravated problems. The budget had been written on the assumption that Russian energy products would continue to command high prices on foreign markets. There was a return to the difficulties of the 1990s with salary and pension arrears, job uncertainty and inflation. The Russian boom had failed to last a full decade. Closures of businesses became an epidemic. Even the mightiest Russian company, Gazprom, experienced an eighty per cent collapse in its share prices in the second half of the year. Many of the most successful entrepreneurs had accumulated their wealth by raising huge loans from foreign banks, and as the value of commodities fell on world markets they faced difficulty in servicing their debts. The solution for them was to sell off assets to the state. Once-mighty oligarchs felt the bruises of a deep recession and started to lose their grip on the country's natural resources. The loans-for-shares débâcle of 1996 was repeated in reverse: this time it was the business elite going cap in hand to the government. The fragility of Russia's decade-long economic upsurge was revealed.

Medvedev feared that the recession might lead to social unrest, and he warned political opponents against trying to exploit the situation. The security forces were held at the ready. Although they could maintain order on the streets there were worries amidst the political elites that this was not permanently guaranteeable. At the end of January 2009 a large protest demonstration was organized on the Pacific periphery of the Russian Federation, in Vladivostok, against the policies of the government. Security forces were put in readiness to deal with angry demonstrators in other cities. Placards were held high: 'Down with capitalist slavery!' and 'Bring back the right to work!' Communist party organizers were not the only militants. Putin's rating in the opinion polls dipped for the first time since the *Kursk* disaster. Suddenly the political order appeared less than completely stable. The Kremlin leaders had always been nervous about popular opinion. This was one of the reasons why they took so much care to emasculate the electoral process. For years the containment of popular grievances had been effective. But when the material improvements made since the turn of the millennium were put under threat the patience of millions of Russians wore thin. The question arose: would the people continue to remain silent?

Afterword

Russia's achievements since 1991 have not been unimpressive. Parliamentary and presidential elections have been held; they have been rough-and-ready processes but the fact that they took place at all has set precedents which it will be hard for Russian rulers to repudiate. Competition among political parties has continued. Social groups have continued to give voice to their aspirations and grievances. A market economy has been established. The heavy hand of the state military-industrial establishment has been weakened. Entrepreneurship has been fostered. The press has enjoyed much freedom. Police agencies invade the privacy of citizens to a lesser extent than at any time for decades, and Russian armed forces have rarely crossed the country's international frontiers in anger. Economic recovery and development have got under way. Russia was a humbled vestige of its old self through to the end of the twentieth century. In the present millennium it is a great power again. Flattened Russia stands tall.

Gorbachëv did the groundwork and put up the scaffolding when reconstructing the USSR. Then Yeltsin built up the new Russian edifice. Russia ceased to be a serious threat to global peace. It is a great power possessing and brandishing nuclear weapons but is no longer a superpower which endangers the rest of the world. Eastern Europe, so long under the USSR's heel, is not menaced by reconquest. Even in the event of a return to power by the communist party it is hard to imagine that a Marxist-Leninist dictatorship would be re-created.

Not everything gave reason for cheer, and in some respects the situation was worse under Yeltsin and his successors than under Gorbachëv. In 1993 Yeltsin reintroduced violence to political struggle in Moscow; and in 1994 and 1999 he ordered the attacks on Chechnya. It is far from clear that Yeltsin and his group would have stood down if he had lost the election of 1996. Subsequent presidential elections have been conducted with gross unfairness. Enormous power is concentrated in the Russian presidency and it has not been exercised with restraint. Democratic and legal procedures have been treated with contempt by politicians in Moscow and the provinces. Public debates have been strident and unbecoming. Administration has been conducted on an arbitrary basis. The judiciary has lost much of its short-lived semi-autonomy. Criminality is rife. Ordinary citizens have little opportunity to defend themselves against the threats of the rich and powerful. Impoverishment remains widespread. Programmes of social and material welfare have been neglected and the economy has yet to surmount the effects of de-industrialization and environmental pollution.

There is also much apathy about current politics, and active membership of parties remains low. Russians agree more about what they dislike than about what they like. The price they are paying is that they have a diminishing impact on the government and other state agencies even at elections.

The burden of the past lies heavily upon Russia, but it is a burden which is not solely the product of the assumption of power by Lenin and his fellow revolutionaries. Under the tsars, the Russian Empire faced many problems; approval of the state's purposes was largely absent from society. The gap in economic productivity was widening between Russia and other capitalist powers. Military security posed acute difficulties; administrative and educational co-ordination remained frail. Political parties in the State Duma had little impact on public life. Furthermore, the traditional propertied classes made little effort to engender a sense of civic community among the poorer members of society. And several non-Russian nations had a sharp sense of national resentment. The Russian Empire was a restless, unintegrated society.

Nicholas II, the last tsar, had put himself in double jeopardy.

He had seriously annoyed the emergent elements of a civil society: the political parties, professional associations and trade unions. At the same time he stopped trying to suppress them entirely. The result was that there was constant challenge to the tsarist regime. The social and economic transformation before the First World War merely added to the problems. Those groups in society which had suffered from poverty were understandably hostile to the authorities. Other groups had enjoyed improvement in their material conditions; but several of these constituted a danger since they felt frustrated by the nature of the political order. It was in this situation that the Great War broke out and pulled down the remaining stays of the regime. The consequence was the February Revolution of 1917 in circumstances of economic collapse, administrative dislocation and military difficulty. Vent was given to a surge of local efforts at popular self-rule; and workers, peasants and military conscripts across the empire asserted their demands without impediment.

These same circumstances made political liberalism, conservatism and fascism unlikely to succeed for a number of years ahead: some kind of socialist government was by far the likeliest outcome after the Romanov monarchy's removal. It was not inevitable that the most extreme variant of socialism – Bolshevism – should take power. What was scarcely avoidable was that once the Bolsheviks made their revolution, they would not be able to survive without making their policies even more violent and regimentative than they already were. Lenin's party had much too little durable support to remain in government without resort to terror. This in turn placed limits on its ability to solve those many problems identified by nearly all the tsarist regime's enemies as needing to be solved. The Bolsheviks aspired to economic competitiveness, political integration, inter-ethnic co-operation, social tranquillity, administrative efficiency, cultural dynamism and universal education. The means they employed inevitably vitiated their declared ends.

After 1917 they groped towards the invention of a new kind of order in state and society, an order described in this book as the Soviet compound. This was not a planned experiment. Nor did

Bolshevik leaders expect to achieve what they did; on the contrary, they gave out their utopian prognosis of a world-wide community of humanity emancipated from all trammels of state authority. Instead they strongly increased state authority. They should have and could have known better; but the plain fact is that they did not. Their policies quickly led to the one-party state, ideological autocracy, legal nihilism, ultra-centralist administration and the minimizing of private economic ownership. Assembled by Lenin, the Soviet compound underwent drastic remodelling by Stalin; and without Stalin's intervention it might not have lasted as long as it did. But Stalinism itself induced strains which were not entirely relieved by the adjustments made after his death in 1953. In their various ways Khrushchëv, Brezhnev and Gorbachëv tried to make the compound workable. In the end Gorbachëv opted for reforms so radical that the resultant instabilities brought about the dissolution of the compound and an end to the Soviet Union.

But why did the compound survive so long? The ample use of force was certainly a crucial factor, and fear of the communist state was a powerful deterrent to opposition. But force by itself would not have worked for several decades. Another reason was the creation of a graduated system of rewards and indulgences which bought off much of the discontent that had accumulated under the tsars. The promotees to administrative office were the system's main beneficiaries; and there was just enough benefit available to others to keep them from actions of rebelliousness. Rewards were a great stabilizer. But even the combination of force and remuneration was not enough to make this a durable system. There also had to be a recurrent agitation of the compound's ingredients. Expulsions from the party; quotas for industrial production; inter-province rivalry; systematic denunciation from below: these were among the techniques developed to keep the compound from internal degradation. They achieved the purpose of acting as solvents of the tendency of the stabilizers to become the dominant ingredients in the compound.

Soviet communism had several advantages in consolidating itself. Firstly it worked with the grain of many popular traditions; in particular it used the existing inclinations towards collective welfare and social revenge. Thus it was enabled to strengthen the existing state forms of repression, state economic intervention and disrespect for due legal process. At the same time it promised to deliver material prosperity and military security where the tsars had failed. To this extent the communist order found favourable conditions in Russia in the early part of the twentieth century.

Moreover, Soviet communism had achievements to its name – and these achievements were indispensable to ensuring its survival. Communism deepened and widened educational progress. It propagated respect for high culture, especially in literature; it subsidized the performing arts; it increased the official commitment to science. It broadened access to sport and leisure activities. It eradicated the worst excesses of popular culture, especially the obscurantist and violent features of life in the Russian countryside. It built towns. It defeated Europe's most vicious right-wing military power, Nazi Germany. In subsequent decades, at last, it succeeded in providing nearly all its citizens with at least a minimal safety-net of food, shelter, clothing, health care and employment. It offered a peaceful, predictable framework of people to live their lives.

There were other achievements of a more objectionable quality which allowed the communists to perpetuate their regime. The USSR made itself into the epicentre of the world communist movement. It also became a military superpower. It not only imposed its authority throughout the outlying regions of the lands of the tsars but also acquired a vast new dominion in Eastern Europe. This inner and outer empire was not formally acknowledged as such; but the popular pride in its acquisition was a stimulus to the belief that Soviet communism was part of the normal world order.

The costs of Soviet rule greatly outweighed the advantages. The state of Lenin and Stalin brutalized politics in Russia for decades. It is true that the communists made many economic and social gains beyond those of Nicholas II's government; but they also reinforced certain features of tsarism which they had vowed to eradicate. National enmities intensified. Political alienation deepened and social respect for law decreased. As the dictatorship broke up society into the tiniest segments, those civil associations that obstructed the central state's will were crushed. The outcome was a mass of intimidated citizens who took little interest in their neighbours' welfare. Selfishness became more endemic even than under capitalism. What is more, as the state came close to devouring the rest of society, the state itself became less effective at fostering co-operation with its own policies. In short, it failed to integrate society while managing to prevent society from effecting its own integration.

Even as a mode for achieving industrialization and military security it was ultimately a failure. Stalin's economic encasement made it unfeasible to attempt further basic 'modernization' without dismantling the Soviet order. His institutions acquired rigid interests and repressive capacity. His rule scared the wits out of managers, scientists and writers, and the freedom of thought vital for a self-renewing industrial society was absent. There was also a lack of those market mechanisms which reduce costs. State-directed economic growth was extremely wasteful. The control organs that were established to eliminate wastefulness became merely yet another drain on the country's resources. Worse still, they made a bureaucratic, authoritarian state order still more bureaucratic and authoritarian. With such an economic and administrative framework it was unavoidable that Stalin's successors, in their quest to maintain the USSR's status as a superpower, diverted a massive proportion of the budget to armaments.

The cramping of public criticism meant that the state's objectives were attained at an even greater environmental cost than elsewhere in the advanced industrial world. Only the huge size of the USSR prevented Soviet rulers from bringing about a general natural calamity which even the dimmest of them would have had to recognize as such.

Gorbachëv was the first Soviet leader to face up to the interconnected difficulties of political intimidation, economic inhibition, militarist organization and environmental pollution – and he failed to resolve the difficulties before he was overwhelmed. The fundamental problem for any gradualist reformer in politics and the economy was that the Soviet compound had eradicated most of the social groups and associations whose co-operation might have facilitated success. By the 1980s, reform had to come from above in the first instance and could be implemented only by a small circle of reformers. A further problem was that radical reform dissolved the linkages of the Soviet compound. Decomposition was inherent in the entire project of change. Those organizations based on politics, religion or nationality which had previously been cowed had no objective interest in conserving the status quo. Gorbachëv's eventual decision to eliminate the one-party state, ideological autocracy, arbitrary rule, ultra-centralist administration and a predominantly state-owned economy was bound to release such organizations into conflict with his government. The only wonder is that he did not see this from the beginning.

As collapse approached it was unsurprising that many beneficiaries of the Soviet compound should seek to make the best of a bad job. They quietly abandoned communist ideology. They engaged in private business. They became more and more openly corrupt. As they flourished locally in both political and material respects they flaunted their disobedience of the Kremlin. Having started by opposing reform, they ended by exploiting it to their advantage.

This happened in many other communist countries which rejected communism in 1989–1991. But de-communization was more difficult in the former USSR than elsewhere. Soviet political and economic interest groups had been consolidated not merely since the Second World War, as in Eastern Europe, but since the establishment of the communist regime through the October Revolution of 1917. Consequently, not only in Russia but also in Ukraine and Uzbekistan there were long-established groups of officials who had plenty of experience and cunning to see off any new opposition. And whereas communism was imported by the Red Army to Eastern Europe, it had been invented by revolutionaries in the former Russian Empire. In revolting against communism, the peoples of Eastern Europe were struggling against foreign domination. In the Soviet Union, communism was a native product. Indeed Lenin retained a remarkable popularity in opinion polls in Russia even after 1991. No wonder that the banner of anti-communism attracted few active followers there.

The question of Russian nationhood aggravated the dilemmas of reform. Before the First World War there had been a fitful privileging of the Russians over the other nations of the empire. This was eliminated under Lenin but resumed under Stalin and prolonged with modifications under successive communist rulers. Nevertheless Russians were confused by the contradictory messages they received. What they had thought of as peculiar to them before 1917 – especially their Orthodox Christianity and their peasant customs – was rejected by the official communist authorities; and Stalin's highly selective version of Russianness was virtually his own invention. Thus Russian national identity under tsars and commissars was cross-cut by an imperial identity. At least until the mid-1960s, moreover, the various alternative versions of Russianness were banned from public discussion – and even through to the late 1980s, debates had to steer clear of overt hostility to Marxism-Leninism. Russians emerged from the communist years with a vaguer sense of their identity than most other peoples of the former USSR.

The Russian Federation received an unenviable legacy from the USSR. The creation of an integrated civic culture had hardly begun. The emergent market economy evoked more popular suspicion than enthusiasm. The constitutional and legal framework was frail. Russians had not had a lengthy opportunity to decide what it was to be Russian. All former empires have been afflicted by this problem. The Russian case was acute because even the borders of the new Russian state are not uncontroversial. Russia's basic territory was never defined during the Russian Empire and was redrawn several times in the Soviet period. And by 1991 twenty-five million ethnic Russians lived in adjacent, newly independent states.

Hopes for democracy and the rule of law were disappointed. Rulers from Yeltsin onwards used a range of dirty methods to exercise their power. The new capitalism brought a windfall of profits to the few, leaving the many – tens of millions of them – to fend for themselves. Reform of police, armed forces and judiciary was not seriously attempted. Multi-party competition was hemmed in by restrictions. Brutal military campaigns were started against Chechen rebels. The President and the rest of the executive exerted dominance over parliament. Elections to high central office were marked by egregious skulduggery. The abuses were not peculiar to the Kremlin. Local politicians and business barons made a mockery of popular choice outside Moscow. The campaign against terrorism was made into a pretext for interfering with civil liberties. Dissent in the media attracted punitive sanctions. Political assassinations were not uncommon. Russia in the twenty-first century became an authoritarian state which has yet to find a settled purpose for itself in its region and in the world.

Must the forecast be pessimistic? Not entirely. The very political passivity that was earlier mentioned as a problem is also an asset. Few Russians have gathered on the streets in support of demagogues of the far right or the far left. Most citizens are tired of turmoil. Even after the disintegration of the USSR, furthermore, Russia was left with a cornucopia of human and natural resources at its disposal. Russia has gas, oil and gold in superabundance. It lacks hardly any essential minerals or metals; it has huge forests and waterways. Its people have an impressive degree of organization, patience and education. Russia has learned from experience about the defects of the alternatives to peaceful, gradual change: it has recent experience of civil war, world war, dictatorship and ideological intolerance.

Yet the preconditions for even a cautious optimism have yet to be met. Time, imagination and will-power will be required if progress is to be made. Russia in the twentieth century was full of surprises. It gave rise to a wholly new way of ordering political, economic and social affairs. Dozens of states adopted the Soviet compound as their model. Russia was the wonder and the horror of the entire world. That single country produced Lenin, Khrushchëv and Gorbachëv; it also brought forth Shostakovich, Akhmatova, Kapitsa, Sakharov and Pavlov. Its ordinary people, from the piteous inmates of the Gulag to the proud Red Army conscript-victors over Hitler, became symbols of momentous episodes in the history of our times. Russia over the past hundred years has endured extraordinary vicissitudes.

It became and then ceased to be a superpower. It was once a largely agrarian and illiterate empire and is now literate, industrial and bereft of its borderland dominions. Russia has not stopped changing. There is no reason to assume that its record in astounding itself, its neighbours and the world has come to an end.

Notes

Short titles are used in the notes. Full references will be found in the bibliography. The following abbreviations are used in notes and bibliography:

GARF	Gosudarstvennyi arkhiv Rossiiskoi Federatsii
IA	*Istoricheskii arkhiv*
ITsKKPSS	*Izvestiya Tsentral'nogo Komiteta Kommunisticheskoi Partii Sovetskogo Soyuza*
OA	Osobyi arkhiv
PSS	V. I. Lenin, *Polnoe sobranie sochinenii*
RTsKhIDNI	Rossiiskii Tsentr dlya Khraneniya i Issledovaniya Dokumentov Noveishei Istorii
SEER	*Slavonic and East European Review*
SVI	*Shestoi s"ezd RSDRP(b). Avgust 1917 goda. Protokoly*
SVIII	*Vos'moi s"ezd RKP(b). Mart 1919 goda. Protokoly*
SX	*Desyatyi s"ezd RKP(b). Mart 1921 g. Stenograficheskii otchët*
SXVII	*Semnadtsatyi s"ezd VKP(b). 26 yanvarya – 10 fevralya 1934 goda. Stenograficheskii otchët*
SXVIII	*Vosemnadtsatyi s"ezd. 10–21 marta 1939 goda. Stenograficheskii otchët*
SXX	*Dvadtsatyi s"ezd Kommunisticheskoi Partii Sovetskogo Soyuza. 14–25 fevralya 1956 goda. Stenograficheskii otchët*
SXXII	*Dvadtsat' vtoroi s"ezd Kommunisticheskoi Partii Sovetskogo Soyuza. 17–31 oktyabrya 1961 goda. Stenograficheskii otchët*
SXXIV	*Dvadtsat' chetvërtyi s"ezd Kommunisticheskoi Partii*

	Sovetskogo Soyuza. 30 marta – 9 aprelya 1971 goda. Stenograficheskii otchët
SXXVII	*Dvadtsat' sed'moi s"ezd Kommunisticheskoi Partii Sovetskogo Soyuza. 25 fevralya – 6 marta 1986 goda. Stenograficheskii otchët*
TP	*The Trotsky Papers, 1917–1922*
VIKPSS	*Voprosy istorii Kommunisticheskoi Partii Sovetskogo Soyuza*

Introduction

1 The last serious such endeavour was M. S. Gorbachëv, *Perestroika. New Thinking for Our Country and the World.*

2 Otto Bauer, *Bolschewismus oder Sozialdemokratie?* (Vienna, 1920).

3 K. Kautsky, *The Dictatorship of the Proletariat*; Yu. Martov, *Mirovoi bol'shevizm*; B. Russell, *The Practice and Theory of Bolshevism*; T. Dan, *The Origins of Bolshevism.*

4 L. D. Trotsky, *The Revolution Betrayed.*

5 I. A. Il'in, *O soprotivlenii zlu siloyu*; A. I. Solzhenitsyn, *Letter to the Soviet Leaders* and *Kak nam obustroit' Rossiyu?*

6 N. Berdyaev, *The Russian Idea.* Ideas of a not dissimilar nature can be found in B. Kerblay, *Modern Soviet Society* and S. White, *Political Culture and Soviet Politics.*

7 R. Fülöp-Miller, *The Mind and Face of Bolshevism: An Examination of Cultural Life in Soviet Russia.*

8 N. S. Trubetskoi, *K probleme russkogo samosoznaniya: sobranie statei.*

9 N. Ustryalov, *Pod znakom revolyutsii.* A recent work stressing the imperial and ethnic dimensions of the USSR is H. Carrère d'Encausse, *Decline of an Empire.*

10 L. N. Gumilëv, *V poiskakh vymyshlennogo tsarstva* and *Ritmy Evrazii.*

11 E. H. Carr, *The Bolshevik Revolution*; B. Moore Jr, *The Social Origins of Dictatorship and Democracy.*

12 R. Neumann, *Behemoth*; M. Fainsod, *How Russia is Ruled*; L. Schapiro, *The Communist Party of the Soviet Union* and *Totalitarianism.*

13 M. Djilas, *The New Class: An Analysis of the Communist System*; M. Voslensky, *Nomenklatura: The Anatomy of the Soviet Ruling Class.*

14 D. Bell, *The End of Ideology.*

15 See I. Kershaw, *The Nazi Dictatorship*, pp. 34–46.

16 D. Granick, *Management of the Industrial Firm in the USSR, A Study in Soviet Economic Planning*; J. Berliner, *Factory and Manager in the USSR*. The journal *Soviet Studies* regularly carried accounts of political, economic and social life below the level of the Kremlin.
17 R. Suny, *The Baku Commune.*
18 R. Service, *The Bolshevik Party in Revolution.*
19 D. Koenker, *Moscow Workers*; S. A. Smith, *Red Petrograd.*
20 F. Benvenuti, *The Bolsheviks and the Red Army*; O. Figes, *Peasant Russia, Civil War*; R. Stites, *Revolutionary Dreams: Utopian Vision and Experimental Life in the Russian Revolution.*
21 R. W. Davies, *The Soviet Economy in Turmoil*; M. Lewin, *The Making of the Soviet System.*
22 F. Benvenuti, *Fuoco sui Sabotatori!*; D. Filtzer, *Soviet Workers and Stalinist Industrialization*; L. Siegelbaum. *Stakhanovism and the Politics of Productivity in the USSR, 1935–1941.*
23 V. Buldakov, *Krasnaya smuta.*
24 S. Fitzpatrick, *The Russian Revolution.*
25 S. Kotkin, *Magnetic Mountain: Stalinism as a Civilization.*
26 M. Lewin, *Lenin's Last Struggle*; S. F. Cohen, *Bukharin and the Russian Revolution*; R. W. Davies, *The Socialist Offensive.*
27 J. Hough, *The Soviet Prefects*; J. Hough, *The Soviet Union and Social Science Theory*; H. G. Skilling and F. Griffiths, *Interest Groups in Soviet Politics.* See also J. Hough's 1979 revisions of the original edition of Merle Fainsod, *How Russia is Ruled.*
28 M. Lewin, *The Gorbachev Phenomenon.*
29 T. H. Rigby, *The Changing Soviet System* and *Political Elites in the USSR: Central Leaders and Local Cadres from Lenin to Gorbachev.*
30 A. Brown, 'Political Power and the Soviet State', in N. Harding (ed.), *The State in Socialist Society.*
31 M. Malia, *Russia Under Western Eyes*; R. Pipes, *Russia Under the Bolshevik Regime.*
32 R. Conquest, *Power and Policy in the USSR*; M. Fainsod, *Smolensk Under Soviet Rule.*
33 A. Brown, *The Gorbachëv Factor.*
34 G. A. Hosking, *A History of the Soviet Union.*

1 And Russia? (1900–1914)

1 T. von Laue, *Serge Witte and the Industrialisation of Russia.*
2 O. Crisp, *Studies in the Russian Economy before 1914*, p. 154.
3 Ibid., pp. 34–5.
4 S. M. Dubrovskii, *Sel'skoe khozyaistvo i krest'yanstvo Rossii v period imperializma*, p. 225.
5 T. Shanin, *The Awkward Class*, ch. 2.
6 This figure does not include Russian-ruled Poland: A. Gershenkron, 'Agrarian Policies and Industrialisation', p. 730.
7 A. G. Rashin, *Naselenie Rossii za 100 let*, pp. 297–9.
8 M. Perrie and R. W. Davies, 'The Social Context', p. 40.
9 A. G. Rashin, *Formirovanie rabochego klassa Rossii*, p. 171.
10 R. Kaiser, *The Geography of Nationalism in Russia and the Soviet Union*, p. 53.
11 J. M. Hartley, *Alexander I*, p. 118.
12 H. Rogger, *National Consciousness in Eighteenth-Century Russia*, ch. 1.
13 B. Eklof, *Russian Peasant Schools*, pp. 243–4.
14 O. Figes, *A People's Tragedy*, p. 196.
15 Kaiser, *The Geography of Nationalism*, table 2:10.
16 Ibid., table 2:8.
17 H. Seton-Watson, *The Russian Empire, 1801–1917.*
18 A. Ascher, *The Russian Revolution of 1905*, p. 163.
19 S. M. Dubrovskii, *Stolypinskaya agrarnaya reforma*, pp. 572, 583, 586.
20 G. A. Hosking, *The Russian Constitutional Experiment*, ch. 2.
21 C. Ferenczi, 'Freedom of the Press, 1905–1914', pp. 198, 211.
22 R. Service, *Lenin: A Political Life*, vol. 1, p. 135.
23 Figes, *A People's Tragedy*, pp. 1–17.
24 V. S. Dyakin *et al.*, *Krizis samoderzhaviya v Rossii, 1895–1917*, p. 448.
25 R. McKean, *St Petersburg Between the Revolutions*, ch. 10.
26 P. Waldron, 'States of Emergency', p. 4.

2 The Fall of the Romanovs (1914–1917)

1 D. Lieven, *Russia and the Origins of the First World War*, pp. 67–9.
2 D. Lieven, *Nicholas II: Emperor of all the Russias*, pp. 200–205.
3 N. Stone, *The Eastern Front*, p. 66.

4 P. V. Volobuev, *Ekonomicheskaya politika Vremennogo Pravitel'stva*, ch. 1.

5 R. Pearson, *The Russian Moderates and the Crisis of Tsarism*, p. 117.

6 S. G. Wheatcroft, 'The Balance of Grain Production and Utilisation in Russia before and during the Revolution', pp. 3–5.

7 R. W. Davies, 'Industry', p. 135.

8 I. I. Mints, *Istoriya Velikogo Oktyabrya*, vol. 1, p. 325.

9 Volobuev, *Ekonomicheskaya politika*, p. 365.

10 A. L. Sidorov, *Istoricheskie predposylki Velikoi oktyabr'skoi sotsialisticheskoi revolyutsii*, pp. 31–2.

11 R. McKean, *St Petersburg Between the Revolutions*, pp. 380–85.

12 Stone, *The Eastern Front*, pp. 240, 247.

13 Pearson, *The Russian Moderates*, pp. 125–6.

14 P. Gatrell, 'The First World War and War Communism', p. 218.

15 Ibid.

16 A. M. Anfimov, introduction to *Krest'anskoe dvizhenie*, pp. 14–18.

17 S. A. Smith, *Red Petrograd. Revolution in the Factories*, p. 46.

18 W. G. Rosenberg, *Liberals in the Russian Revolution*, p. 57.

19 Their dominance was such that the first cabinet was not referred to as the First Coalition.

20 A. H. Wildman, *The End of the Russian Imperial Army*, vol. 1, pp. 186–8.

21 L. Lande, 'Some Statistics of the Unification Congress', p. 389; O. H. Radkey, *The Agrarian Foes of Communism*, p. 236.

22 Z. Galili, *The Menshevik Leaders in the Russian Revolution*, pp. 269–73.

23 See M. Perrie, 'The Peasants', pp. 22–3.

24 Rosenberg, *Liberals*, p. 174.

25 Smith, *Red Petrograd*, p. 55.

26 Ibid., pp. 145–9.

27 V. I. Kostrikin, 'Krest'yanskoe dvizhenie nakanune Oktyabrya', p. 24.

28 Smith, *Red Petrograd*, pp. 169–70.

29 J. Channon, 'The Landowners', p. 124.

30 H. White, 'The Provisional Government and the Problem of Power in the Provinces'.

31 J. Reshetar, *The Ukrainian Revolution*; A. F. Upton, *The Finnish Revolution*; R. G. Suny, *The Baku Commune. Class and Nationality in the Russian Revolution*.

32 S. F. Jones, 'The Non-Russian Nationalities', pp. 55–6.

PART ONE

3 Conflicts and Crises (1917)

1 It ought to be added that they did not intend to scrap such nationally-based units as already existed. Finland was the prime example.
2 I. Getzler, 'Soviets as Agents of Democratisation', pp. 7–30.
3 R. Service, *Lenin*, vol. 2, pp. 154–5.
4 PSS, vol. 31, pp. 113–16.
5 Service, *Lenin*, vol. 2, pp. 156–60.
6 R. Service, *The Bolshevik Party in Revolution*, p. 54.
7 Ibid., p. 43.
8 Ibid., pp. 46, 53.
9 PSS, vol. 31, p. 267.
10 W. G. Rosenberg, *Liberals in the Russian Revolution*, p. 174.
11 A. Rabinowitch, *Prelude to Revolution*, ch. 5.
12 R. A. Wade, *The Russian Search for Peace*, p. 111.
13 P. V. Volobuev, *Ekonomicheskaya politika*, p. 379.
14 Ibid., p. 385.
15 T. Kitanina, *Voina, khleb i revolyutsiya*, p. 344.
16 D. Lieven, *Nicholas II*, p. 238.
17 J. S. Curtiss, *The Russian Church and the Soviet State*, p. 38.
18 A. Rabinowitch, *The Bolsheviks Come to Power in Petrograd*, p. 126.
19 H. White, 'The Urban Middle Classes', pp. 78–9.
20 P. V. Volobuev, *Proletariat i burzhuaziya*, p. 219.
21 PSS, vol. 34, p. 389.
22 A. V. Shestakov, *Ocherki po sel'skomu khozyaistvu*, p. 142.
23 M. Perrie, 'The Peasants', p. 17.
24 S. A. Smith, 'Workers' Control: February–October 1917', pp. 22–3.
25 A. H. Wildman, *The End of the Russian Imperial Army*, vol. 1, ch. 9.
26 Z. Galili, *The Menshevik Leaders in the Russian Revolution*, pp. 387–91.
27 Ibid., pp. 387–9.
28 'Iz rechi tov. Bukharina na vechere vospominanii 1921 g.', *Proletarskaya revolyutsiya*, no.10 (1921), p. 319.
29 Service, *Lenin*, vol. 2, pp. 251–7.
30 Ibid., pp. 273–4.

31 I. Getzler, *Martov: A Political Biography of a Russian Social-Democrat*, pp. 155–6.
32 R. G. Suny, *The Baku Commune*, ch. 3.

4 The October Revolution (1917–1918)

1 PSS, vol. 33, pp. 1–120.
2 R. Service, *Lenin*, vol. 2, pp. 220–24.
3 *Pravda*, 29 October 1917.
4 I. Getzler, *Martov*, p. 162; A. Rabinowitch, *The Bolsheviks*, p. 292.
5 T. H. Rigby, *Lenin's Government*, p. 27.
6 L. Trotsky, *My Life. An Attempt at Autobiography*, p. 355.
7 *Resheniya partii i pravitel'stva po khozyaistvennym voprosam*, vol. 1, pp. 11–12.
8 Ibid., pp. 12–14.
9 Ibid., pp. 15–16.
10 Service, *Lenin*, vol. 2, pp. 270–71.
11 PSS, vol. 35, pp. 51–2.
12 G. Leggett, *The Cheka. Lenin's Secret Police*, p. 17.
13 Service, *Lenin*, vol. 2, pp. 285–6.
14 *Dekrety Sovetskoi vlasti*, vol. 1, p. 40.
15 N. Valentinov, *Vstrechi s Leninym*, pp. 40–41.
16 Service, *Lenin*, vol. 2, p. 185.
17 Ibid., vol. 1, p. 186.
18 PSS, vol. 49, p. 340.
19 This figure is based upon the Central Committee full members; it also takes into account the redating of Stalin's birth.
20 Service, *Lenin*, vol. 2, pp. 10–11.
21 SVI, p. 41: report by I. T. Smilga.
22 Service, *Lenin*, vol. 2, pp. 184–5.
23 Ibid., vol. 3, p. 135.
24 O. Figes, *Peasant Russia, Civil War*, pp. 63–4.
25 J. H. L. Keep, *The Russian Revolution. A Study in Mass Mobilisation*, chs 26, 27.
26 W. Mosse, 'Revolution in Saratov', p. 57.
27 L. D. Trotskii, *O Lenine. Materialy dlya biografii*, pp. 91–2.
28 PSS, vol. 31, pp. 64–5, 197, 250.
29 O. H. Radkey, *Russia Goes to the Polls*, pp. 18–19.

30 Service, *Lenin*, vol. 2, pp. 295–6.
31 *Protokoly Tsentral'nogo Komiteta RSDRP(b)*, p. 168; PSS, vol. 35, pp. 243–52.
32 Trotskii, *O Lenine*, p. 81; *Protokoly Tsentral'nogo Komiteta*, pp. 168–9.
33 C. Duval, 'Yakov Sverdlov', pp. 226–7.
34 *Protokoly Tsentral'nogo Komiteta*, p. 213.
35 B. Pearce, *How Haig Saved Lenin*, pp. 7–8.
36 S. G. Wheatcroft, 'The Balance of Grain Production and Utilisation', pp. 7, 15–17.
37 A. Nove, *An Economic History of the USSR*, ch. 3.
38 S. Malle, *The Economic Organisation of 'War Communism'*, pp. 33, 55.
39 The word used for 'Russian' was *Rossiiskaya*, which (unlike *Russkaya*) did not imply a national orientation to ethnic Russians.

5 New World, Old World

1 O. H. Radkey, *Russia Goes to the Polls*, pp. 16, 18–19.
2 R. Service, 'The Industrial Workers', pp. 159–60.
3 R. Service, *Lenin*, vol. 2, pp. 245–6.
4 Ibid., pp. 239–40.
5 S. F. Jones, 'The Non-Russian Nationalities', pp. 46–7.
6 T. Swietochowski, *Russian Azerbaijan*, pp. 138–9.
7 *Dekrety Sovetskoi vlasti*, vol. 1, p. 40.
8 PSS, vol. 35, pp. 221–3.
9 This was its name until the 1930s, when the order of the words 'socialist' and 'soviet' was reversed and the name therefore became Russian Soviet Federal Socialist Republic.
10 M. Perrie, 'The Peasants', p. 30.
11 D. Atkinson, *The End of the Russian Land Commune*, pp. 181–2, 209.
12 O. Figes, *Peasant Russia*, pp. 207–8.
13 M. McAuley, *Bread and Justice. State and Society in Petrograd*, pp. 270–71.
14 S. A. Smith, 'Workers' Control', p. 23.
15 J. Channon, 'The Landowners', p. 157.
16 F. Lorimer, *The Population of the Soviet Union. History and Prospects*, p. 87.
17 *Izvestiya*, 19 July 1918.

18 Figes, *Peasant Russia*, pp. 138–44.

19 T. Shanin, *The Awkward Class*, p. 174; V. P. Danilov, *Rural Russia under the New Regime*, pp. 211–14.

20 R. Service, *The Bolshevik Party*, p. 77.

21 S. F. Cohen, *Bukharin and the Russian Revolution*, p. 73.

22 P. Kenez, *The First Propaganda State*, pp. 129–31.

23 SVIII, pp. 390–410.

24 *Izvestiya*, 2 August 1918.

25 G. E. Zinoviev, *N. Lenin. Vladimir Il'ich Lenini.*

26 V. Brovkin, *The Mensheviks after October*.

27 Yu. G. Fel'shtinskii, *Bol'sheviki i levye esery*, pp. 145–9.

28 He did not mention the Bolsheviks by name; but his meaning was sufficiently clear.

29 A. Pyman, *The Life of Alexander Blok*, vol. 2, p. 281.

30 C. Read, *Culture and Power in Revolutionary Russia*, chs 2, 3.

31 PSS, vol. 38, p. 437.

32 PSS, vol. 36, pp. 296–300.

33 E. H. Carr, *The Bolshevik Revolution*, vol. 2, pp. 88–9.

34 PSS, vol. 35, p. 311.

35 D. Orlovsky, 'State Building in the Civil War Era', p. 202.

36 V. Brovkin, *The Mensheviks*, p. 181.

37 PSS, vol. 33, p. 74.

6 Civil Wars (1918–1921)

1 PSS, vol. 36, p. 172.

2 PSS, vol. 50, p. 186.

3 B. Pearce, *How Haig Saved Lenin*, p. 65

4 ITsKKPSS, no. 4 (1984), pp. 143–4.

5 V. Fic, *The Bolsheviks and the Czechoslovak Legion*, pp. 20–21, 26–7, 80–91.

6 Yu. G. Fel'shtinskii, *Bol'sheviki i levye esery*, pp. 214–15.

7 L. Trotsky, *My Life*, p. 324.

8 PSS, vol. 50, p. 178.

9 RTsKhIDNI, f. 17, op. 2, d. 1, item 5; GARF, f. R-130, op. 2, d. 1 (3), item 4 and d. 2 (2). See also Yu. Buranov and V. Khrustalëv, *Gibel' imperatorskogo doma*, p. 261 and R. Service, *Lenin*, vol. 3, pp. 37–8.

10 S. Lyandres, 'The 1918 Attempt on the Life of Lenin', pp. 437–41.

11 PSS, vol. 37, pp. 244–5, 250.
12 Quoted in *Komsomol'skaya pravda*, 12 February 1992.
13 Ibid.
14 G. Leggett, *The Cheka*, p. 114.
15 See note 12.
16 Leggett, *The Cheka*, pp. 464–7.
17 R. Conquest, *The Great Terror. A Reassessment*, p. 310.
18 Service, *Lenin*, vol. 3, p. 53.
19 E. H. Carr, *The Bolshevik Revolution*, vol. 2, pp. 52–3.
20 SVIII, p. 354.
21 A. Nove, *An Economic History*, p. 62.
22 R. W. Davies, *The Development of the Soviet Budgetary System*, pp. 9, 31.
23 Nove, *An Economic History*, p. 94.
24 D. Orlovsky, 'The City in Danger', p. 74.
25 Service, *Lenin*, vol. 3, p. 42.
26 T. H. Rigby, *Communist Party Membership*, pp. 52–3.
27 R. Service, 'From Polyarchy to Hegemony', pp. 86–7.
28 R. Service, *The Bolshevik Party*, pp. 96–9, 106–9.
29 See note 27.
30 F. Benvenuti, *The Bolsheviks and the Red Army*, pp. 92–108.
31 Carr, *The Bolshevik Revolution*, pp. 110–11.
32 R. G. Suny, *The Making of the Georgian Nation*, p. 202.
33 See for example GARF, f. 1318, op. 1, ed. khr. 4 (Collegium meeting from 25 August 1919 onwards).
34 R. Pipes, *The Formation of the Soviet Union*, pp. 164–6.
35 Ibid., p. 174.
36 SVIII, p. 425.
37 RTsKhIDNI, f. 17, op. 3, d. 9.
38 Service, *Lenin*, vol. 3, p. 191.
39 P. Kenez, 'The Ideology of the White Movement', pp. 78–83.
40 TP, vol. 2, p. 278.
41 J. Channon, 'Siberia in Revolution and Civil War', ch. 9.
42 W. G. Rosenberg, *Liberals in the Russian Revolution*, p. 340.
43 E. Mawdsley, *The Russian Civil War*, pp. 63, 182–4.
44 S. White, *Britain and the Bolshevik Revolution*, ch. 1.
45 Service, *The Bolshevik Party*, pp. 147–8.
46 S. M. Klyatskin, *Na zashite Oktyabrya*, pp. 396, 463.
47 V. P. Danilov, 'Dinamika naseleniya SSSR', p. 246.
48 J. Aves, *Workers Against Lenin*, ch. 4.

49 Leggett, *The Cheka*, p. 329.
50 O. Figes, *Peasant Russia*, p. 195, 304.
51 Document quoted in *Izvestiya*, 27 April 1992, p. 3.
52 SX, pp. 349–50.
53 PSS, vol. 42, pp. 134, 156–9.
54 PSS, vol. 42, p. 179; RTsKhIDNI, f. 17, op. 2, d. 49, item 1.

7 The New Economic Policy (1921–1928)

1 A. Nove, *An Economic History*, p. 94.
2 R. Service, *Lenin*, vol. 3, p. 169.
3 RTsKhIDNI, f. 17, op. 3, d. 131, item 1.
4 This can be gauged from the written questions passed up to Lenin at the Congress: RTsKhIDNI, f. 5, op. 2, d. 7, pp. 1–88.
5 See ibid., f. 46, op. 1, d. 2.
6 N. Valentinov, *Novaya ekonomicheskaya politika i krizis partii*, pp. 30–31.
7 RTsKhIDNI, f. 17, op. 3, d. 155, item 11.
8 *Krest'yanskoe vosstanie v Tambovskoi*, doc. 266.
9 PSS, vol. 45, pp. 189–90.
10 Stalin referred to it contemptuously as national 'liberalism': ITsKKPSS, no. 9 (1989), p. 199.
11 Service, *Lenin*, vol. 3, pp. 190–95.
12 Originally Lenin wanted to call it the Union of Soviet Republics of Europe and Asia: PSS, vol. 45, pp. 211–12; but, after much haggling with Stalin, there was agreement on the Union of Soviet Socialist Republics.
13 RTsKhIDNI, f. 17, op. 3, d. 291, item 2; I. K. Gamburg *et al.*, *M. V. Frunze. Zhizn' i deyatel'nost'*, pp. 292, 294.
14 SX, pp. 213–14.
15 Ibid.
16 See for example GARF, f. 1318, op. 1, ed. khr. 1 (Narkomnats collegium, 8 March 1919).
17 The Muslim rebels in central Asia, the *basmachi*, were never completely suppressed in the 1920s; but their ability to disrupt the Soviet administrative order was small.
18 G. Hewitt, 'Aspects of Language in Georgia (Georgian and Abkhaz)', p. 132.
19 *Izvestiya*, 1 January 1923.

20 S. Kharmandaryan, *Lenin i stanovlenie zakavkazskoi federatsii*, chs 2–3.
21 G. A. Galoyan and K. S. Khudaverdyan (eds), *Nagornyi Karabakh*, pp. 24, 32–3.
22 Report in *Nezavisimaya gazeta*, 12 May 1991.
23 ITsKKPSS, no. 9 (1990), p. 212.
24 V. Kozlov, *The Peoples of the Soviet Union.*
25 ITsKKPSS, no. 4 (1990), p. 194 (Politburo minute).
26 Ibid., pp. 194, 197.
27 A. Luukanen, *The Party of Unbelief*, p. 183.
28 *Smolensk Party Archives*, WKP6, 9 January 1920.
29 RTsKhIDNI, f. 17, op. 3, d. 187, item 2.
30 A. Blyum, *Za kulisami 'Ministerstva Pravdy'*, p. 79.
31 PSS, vol. 45, p. 13.
32 *Vserossiiskaya konferentsiya RKP (bol'shevikov)*, bulletin 3, pp. 80, 82.
33 Bolshevik-edited satirical magazines were allowed to mock only those phenomena which incurred the party's disapproval.
34 T. H. Rigby, *Communist Party Membership*, p. 52.
35 E. H. Carr and R. W. Davies, *Foundations of a Planned Economy*, vol. 1, p. 545.
36 R. Service, *The Bolshevik Party* , pp. 168–9.
37 L. Gordon and E. Klopov, *Chto eto bylo?*, pp. 92–3.
38 R. Stites, *Revolutionary Dreams*, chs 3, 4.
39 Nevertheless it should be noted that fifty-eight per cent of newspaper copies were sold in Moscow and Leningrad in 1925: R. Stites, *Russian Popular Culture*, p. 42.
40 S. Fitzpatrick, 'Sex and Revolution: an Examination of Literacy and Statistical Data on the Mores of Soviet Students in the 1920s', p. 121.
41 M. Dewar, *Labour Policy in the USSR*, p. 144.
42 Carr and Davies, *Foundations of a Planned Economy*, vol. 1, pp. 460, 605.
43 P. Juviler, *Revolutionary Law and Order*, ch. 2.
44 A. M. Ball, *Russia's Last Capitalists*, pp. 39–40.
45 PSS, vol. 44, p. 397.
46 C. Ward, *Russia's Cotton Workers*, pp. 113–16.
47 W. Chase, *Workers, Society and the Soviet State*, pp. 220–24.
48 D. Thorniley, *The Rise and Fall of the Soviet Rural Communist Party*, p. 17.
49 R. Taylor, *The Politics of the Soviet Cinema*, p. 65.
50 E. A. Rees, *State Control in Soviet Russia*, pp. 87–92.

51 T. H. Rigby, 'The Origins of the Nomenklatura System', pp. 84–5.
52 T. H. Rigby, 'Early provincial cliques and the rise of Stalin'.

8 Leninism and its Discontents

1 R. Service, *Lenin*, vol. 3, pp. 291–4.
2 A. Mikoyan, *Vospominaniya i mysli o Lenine*, p. 195.
3 Service, *Lenin*, vol. 3, p. 257.
4 ITsKKPSS, no. 4 (1991), pp. 187–8.
5 PSS, vol. 54, p. 327.
6 PSS, vol. 45, pp. 344–5.
7 Service, *Lenin*, vol. 3, p. 297.
8 PSS, vol. 45, pp. 329–30.
9 This distinction was pointed out to me by Geoffrey Hosking.
10 The series of the *Leninskii sbornik* continued through to the years of Gorbachëv.
11 J. D. Biggart, 'Bukharin's Theory of Cultural Revolution', pp. 146–58.
12 A. Nove, *An Economic History*, p. 194.
13 R. Service, *The Bolshevik Party*, p. 198.
14 I. V. Stalin, *Sochineniya*, vol. 6, pp. 69–188.
15 R. Medvedev, *Let History Judge*, pp. 509–10.
16 J. Erickson, *The Soviet High Command. A Military-Political History*, ch. 9.
17 A. C. Sutton, *Western Technology and Soviet Economic Development*, p. 11.
18 M. J. Dohan's calculation in R. W. Davies, *From Tsarism to the NEP*, p. 331.
19 R. B. Day, *Leon Trotsky and the Politics of Economic Isolation*, ch. 3.
20 E. H. Carr and R. W. Davies, *Socialism in One Country*, vol. 1, pp. 508–9.
21 On the difficulties of the available statistics see R. W. Davies, 'Changing Economic Systems: An Overview', p. 9.
22 S. G. Wheatcroft, R. W. Davies and J. Cooper, 'Soviet Industrialisation Reconsidered', *Economic History Review*, no. 2 (1986), p. 270.
23 R. W. Davies, *The Socialist Offensive*, p. 8.
24 E. H. Carr and R. W. Davies, *Foundations of a Planned Economy*, vol. 1, part 1, pp. 287, 298.
25 Davies, *The Socialist Offensive*, p. 36.

PART TWO

9 The First Five-Year Plan (1928–1932)

1 J. Hughes, *Stalin, Siberia and the Crisis of the New Economic Policy*, p. 139.
2 E. H. Carr and R. W. Davies, *Foundations of a Planned Economy*, vol. 2, p. 75.
3 A. Larina, *This I Cannot Forget*, p. 251.
4 Y. Taniuchi, 'Decision-making on the Urals-Siberian Method', pp. 79–85.
5 K. Bailes, *Technology and Society under Lenin and Stalin*; N. Lampert, *The Technical Intelligentsia and the Soviet State*.
6 R. W. Davies, *The Soviet Economy in Turmoil*, pp. 68, 126, 180.
7 C. Merridale, *Moscow Politics and the Rise of Stalin*, p. 53.
8 Quoted in D. A. Volkogonov, *Stalin: Triumf i tragediya*, vol. 1, part 2, p. 52.
9 *Pravda*, 5 February 1931.
10 R. Lewis, 'Foreign Economic Relations', p. 208.
11 A. C. Sutton, *Western Technology and Soviet Economic Development*, pp. 362–73.
12 Carr and Davies, *Foundations of a Planned Economy*, vol. 3, part 1, p. 233.
13 O. V. Khlevnyuk, 'Prinuditel'nyi trud v ekonomike SSSR', p. 75.
14 V. P. Danilov, *Pravda*, 16 September 1988.
15 A. Romano, 'Peasant-Bolshevik Conflicts Inside the Red Army', pp. 114–15.
16 M. Lewin, *Russian Peasants and Soviet Power*, p. 391.
17 S. G. Wheatcroft, 'More Light on the Scale of Repression', p. 366.
18 *Stalinskoe Politbyuro v 30-e gody.*, pp. 114–15.
19 R. W. Davies in *The Economic Transformation*, table 19.
20 R. Munting, *The Economic Development of the USSR*, p. 93.
21 R. W. Davies in *The Economic Transformation*, table 22.
22 Ibid., p. 152.
23 Ibid., p. 36 and table 31.
24 *Istoriya SSSR*, no. 3 (1989), p. 44.
25 S. Fitzpatrick, *Stalin's Peasants*, p. 65.
26 Yu. A. Moshkov, *Zernovaya problema*, p. 136; J. Barber and R. W. Davies, 'Employment and Industrial Labour', p. 103.

27 S. Fitzpatrick, 'Stalin and the Making of a New Elite'.
28 T. H. Rigby, *Communist Party Membership*, pp. 52–3.
29 A. K. Sokolov, *Lektsii po Sovetskoi istorii*, p. 130.
30 R. W. Davies, 'Industry', p. 145.
31 R. MacNeal, *Stalin: Man and Ruler*, p. 218.
32 RTsKhIDNI, f. 44, op. 1, d. 5, pp. 20–21; PSS, vol. 41, p. 458.
33 A. di Biagio, *Le origini dell'isolazionismo*, pp. 33–48.
34 O. V. Khlevnyuk, *Stalin i Ordzhonikidze*, pp. 22–9.
35 P. Broué, 'Trotsky et le bloc des oppositions de 1932'.
36 Cited in O. V. Khlevnyuk, 'The Objectives of the Great Terror', p. 159.

10 Fortresses under Storm: Culture, Religion, Nation

1 L. Gordon and E. Klopov, *Chto eto bylo?*, p. 92.
2 *Narodnoe khozyaistvo za 70 let*, p. 528.
3 Gordon and Klopov, *Chto eto bylo?*, p. 87.
4 Ibid., p. 89.
5 *Narodnoe khozyaistvo za 70 let*, p. 569.
6 S. Kotkin, *Magnetic Mountain: Stalinism as Civilisation*.
7 I. V. Stalin, *Sochineniya*, vol. 14, p. 89.
8 E. A. Osokina, *Ierarkhiya potrebleniya*, p. 116.
9 A. Nove, *An Economic History*, pp. 224–5; R. W. Davies in *The Economic Transformation*, p. 17.
10 O. V. Khlevnyuk, *Stalin i Ordzhonikidze*, pp. 35–7.
11 Nove, *Economic History*, pp. 178, 180.
12 O. V. Khlevnyuk, *1937-y: Stalin, NKVD i sovetskoe obshchestvo*, p. 27.
13 Stalin, *Sochineniya*, vol. 13, p. 211.
14 Khlevnyuk, *1937-y*, pp. 28–9.
15 E. Radzinsky, *Stalin*, pp. 279–86.
16 R. Medvedev, *Sem'ya tirana*, p. 4.
17 R. Medvedev, *Let History Judge*, p. 224.
18 D. A. Volkogonov, *Moskovskie novosti*, no. 38 (18 September 1988), p. 16.
19 B. Souvarine, *Stalin*, p. 485.
20 P. N. Pospelov, 'Pyatdesyat let KPSS', pp. 21–2.
21 B. A. Starkov, *Dela i lyudi stalinskogo vremeni*, p. 89.
22 Even after the late 1960s, moreover, there was a recurrence of widespread

popular enthusiasm, especially under Gorbachëv in the second half of the 1980s.

23 R. Stites, *Russian Popular Culture*, p. 97.

24 Ibid., p. 82.

25 S. Fitzpatrick, *Stalin's Peasants*, p. 218.

26 B. Nahaylo and V. Svoboda, *Soviet Disunion*, p. 66.

27 *Akademicheskoe delo 1929–1931*, p. xlviii.

28 Starkov, *Dela i lyudi*, p. 36.

29 K. Simonov, *Glazami*, p. 37.

30 M. Ellman, 'On Sources: A Note', p. 914.

31 R. Conquest, *Harvest of Sorrow*, pp. 323–8.

32 R. Kaiser, *The Geography of Nationalism*, p. 116.

33 D. Pospielovsky, *The Russian Church under the Soviet Regime*, vol. 1, p. 175.

34 Ibid., pp. 173–4.

35 I. Antinova and I. Merkert, *Moskva-Berlin, 1900–1950*, p. 514.

36 S. Bruk and V. Kabuzan, 'Dinamika chislennosti', pp. 3–21.

37 The contributions of S. Crisp (p. 38), S. Akiner (p. 107) and G. Hewitt (p. 143) in M. Kirkwood, *Language Planning in the Soviet Union*.

38 M. Friedberg, *Russian Classics in Soviet Jackets*, pp. 32–56.

11 Terror upon Terror (1934–1938)

1 E. Bacon, *The Gulag at War*, p. 10.

2 This argument is put by Bacon in *The Gulag at War*.

3 This argument is put by O. V. Khlevnyuk, 'The Objectives of the Great Terror', p. 173: the author draws especially on V. M. Molotov's statement in F. Chuev, *Sto sorok besed s Molotovym*, pp. 390–91, 416.

4 F. Benvenuti, 'A Stalinist Victim of Stalinism', pp. 141–2.

5 See Kaganovich's speech on 17 January 1934: *IV Moskovskaya oblastnaya*, pp. 49–50.

6 SXVII, p. 537.

7 T. H. Rigby, *Communist Party Membership*, p. 204.

8 SXVII, pp. 34, 36.

9 SXVII, pp. 353, 566.

10 SXVII, p. 46 (Eikhe); p. 600 (Shiryatov).

11 SXVII, pp. 380–413, 439–41. At the time Mikoyan was only a candidate member of the Politburo.

12 SXVII, pp. 64, 91, 147.
13 SXVII, p. 354.
14 SXVII, pp. 435, 649.
15 SXVII, p. 259.
16 O. V. Khlevnyuk, *1937-y*, p. 36.
17 R. Conquest, *The Great Terror: A Reassessment*, p. 33.
18 SXVII, p. 245.
19 O. V. Khlevnyuk, *Politbyuro. Mekhanizmy politicheskoi vlasti*, pp. 112–13.
20 F. Benvenuti, 'Kirov nella politica sovietica'.
21 O. V. Khlevnyuk, *1937-y*, p. 42.
22 Ibid., p. 49; D. Shearer, 'Social Disorder, Mass Repression, and the NKVD during the 1930s'.
23 G. T. Rittersporn, *Simplifications staliniennes*, p. 27.
24 F. Benvenuti and S. Pons, *Il Sistema di Potere dello Stalinismo*, p. 105.
25 ITsKKPSS, no. 9 (1989), p. 39.
26 E. A. Rees, 'Stalin, the Politburo and Rail Transport Policy', p. 124.
27 F. Benvenuti, *Fuoco sui Sabotatori!*, ch. 2; and D. Filtzer, *Soviet Workers and Stalinist Industrialisation*, ch. 4; E. A. Rees, *Stalinism and Soviet Rail Transport*, pp. 123–7.
28 E. Zaleski, *Stalinist Planning for Economic Growth*, pp. 243–8.
29 P. Broué, *Trotsky*, pp. 709–12.
30 ITsKKPSS, no. 8 (1989), p. 100.
31 S. G. Wheatcroft and R. W. Davies, 'Agriculture', table 19.
32 Khlevnyuk, *1937-y*, pp. 132–6.
33 Rees, 'Stalin, the Politburo and Rail Transport Policy', p. 106.
34 Khlevnyuk, *1937-y*, p. 77.
35 Ibid., p. 114.
36 Ibid.
37 Rittersporn, *Simplifications staliniennes*, p. 144.
38 Document quoted by O. V. Khlevnyuk, 'The Objectives of the Great Terror', p. 166.
39 J. Erickson, *The Soviet High Command*, pp. 296–8, 402–3; S. Pons, *Stalin e la Guerra Inevitabile*, pp. 152–3.
40 *Rodina*, no. 3 (1994), pp. 74–5.
41 *Moskovskie novosti*, no. 15, 10 April 1989.
42 Quoted in B. A. Starkov, *Dela i lyudi*, pp. 127–8.
43 *Trud*, 4 June 1992.
44 *Izvestiya*, 10 June 1992.

45 See note 43.
46 *Pravda*, 19 January 1938.
47 *Moskovskie novosti*, 21 June 1992, p. 19.
48 See note 46.
49 *Otechestvennye arkhivy*, no. 2 (1992), pp. 28–9.
50 S. G. Wheatcroft and R. W. Davies, 'Population', p. 77.
51 Such was the case with the deposition made by Red Army Commander-in-Chief Mikhail Tukhachevski before he was dragged off to the firing-squad.
52 K. Simonov, *Glazami*, p. 299.
53 Conquest, *The Great Terror: A Reassessment*, p. 334.
54 R. W. Davies, 'Forced Labour Under Stalin', p. 67.
55 G. Gill, *The Origins of the Stalinist Political System*, p. 279.
56 *Tak eto bylo. Natsional'ny repressii v SSSR*, vol. 1, p. 44, 50, 86, 96.
57 Stalin's marginal notes as cited by O. Volobuev and S. Kuleshov, *Ochishchenie*, p. 146.
58 *Moskovskie novosti*, no. 32, 7 August 1988.
59 R. C. Tucker, *Stalin in Power. The Revolution from Above*, pp. 482–3.
60 B. A. Viktorov, 'Geroi iz 37-go', *Komsomol'skaya pravda*, 21 August 1988.
61 *Trud*, 4 June 1992.
62 Ibid.
63 Simonov, *Glazami*, p. 315.
64 V. F. Nekrasov (ed.), *Beria: konets kar'ery*, p. 317.
65 Khlevnyuk, *1937-y*, pp. 221–2.
66 R. W. Davies, 'Industry', table 31.
67 N. Khrushchev, *Khrushchev Remembers*, p. 273.
68 Simonov, *Glazami*, p. 58.
69 Rees, 'Stalin, the Politburo and Rail Transport Policy', pp. 107, 111.
70 SVIII, pp. 143–4, 229.

12 Coping with Big Brothers

1 O. V. Khlevnyuk, *1937-y: Stalin, NKVD i sovetskoe obshchestvo*, pp. 232–33.
2 Computed from data in G. Gill, *The Origins of the Stalinist Political System*, p. 416.

3 N. S. Timasheff, *The Great Retreat*, pp. 223, 309.
4 F. Benvenuti and S. Pons, *Il Sistema*, p. 187.
5 See *Istoriya Vsesoyuznoi Kommunisticheskoi Partii*, ch. 12.
6 I. V. Stalin, *Sochineniya*, vol. 14, pp. 142, 152.
7 Ibid., p. 144.
8 Ibid., p. 179.
9 Ibid., pp. 164–5.
10 *Neizvestnaya Rossiya*, no. 2, pp. 279–81.
11 S. and B. Webb, *Soviet Communism: A New Civilisation?*, pp. 432–46.
12 Ibid., p. 152.
13 SXVIII, p. 36.
14 SXVIII, p. 26.
15 T. H. Rigby, 'Was Stalin a Disloyal Patron?', p. 132.
16 N. S. Khrushchev, *The Glasnost Tapes*, p. 38.
17 K. Simonov, *Glazami*, pp. 378–9.
18 P. Juviler, *Revolutionary Law and Order*, ch. 3.
19 *Rodina*, no. 3 (1994), p. 79.
20 D. Filtzer, *Soviet Workers and Stalinist Industrialisation*, ch. 8.
21 N. Jasny, *The Socialized Agriculture of the Soviet Union*, pp. 341–2.
22 R. Conquest, *Industrial Workers in the USSR*, pp. 103–5.
23 Jasny, *The Socialized Agriculture*, p. 342.
24 See note 20.
25 I owe this metaphor to Katherine Braithwaite's intervention in a lecture I was giving.
26 D. Hoffmann, *Peasant Metropolis*.
27 Timasheff, *The Great Retreat*, pp. 197, 200–202.
28 F. Chuev (ed.), *Tak govoril Kaganovich*, p. 59.
29 *Pravda*, no. 179, 1 July 1937 and following copies: no doubt Stalin also wanted to avoid being held personally responsible for the Great Terror if it went wrong and he was brought to account for it.
30 R. O. G. Urch, *The Rabbit King of Siberia* , chs 13, 19.
31 M. Gor'kii, L. Averbakh and S. Firin (eds), *Belomorsko–Baltiiskii Kanal imeni Stalina*.
32 R. Stites, *Russian Popular Culture*, pp. 72–6.
33 A. Bergson, *The Real National Income of Soviet Russia since 1928*, p. 251.
34 A. S. Shinkarchuk, *Obshchestvennoe mnenie*, p. 37.
35 Ibid., pp. 46–7.
36 Stalin, *Sochineniya*, vol. 14, p. 238.

37 S. Fitzpatrick, *Stalin's Peasants*, pp. 289–96.
38 Yu. A. Polyakov, V. B. Zhiromskaya and I. N. Kiselëv, 'Polveka molchaniya', p. 69.
39 J. D. Barber and R. W. Davies, 'Employment and Industrial Labour', p. 103.
40 M. Harrison, 'National Income' in *The Economic Transformation*, p. 53.
41 *Neizvestnaya Rossiya*, no. 2, pp. 272–9. On the complexities of social attitudes in the 1930s see S. Davies, *Public Opinion in Stalin's Russia*.
42 A. Inkeles and R. M. Bauer, *The Soviet Citizen. Daily Life in a Totalitarian Society*, pp. 234–6.
43 Quoted in Khlevnyuk, *1937-y*, p. 88–9; and D. A. Volkogonov, *Stalin*, vol. 1, part 2, p. 58.

13 The Second World War (1939–1945)

1 A. di Biagio, *Le Origini dell'isolazionismo Sovietico*, ch. 1.
2 J. Haslam, *The Soviet Union and the Struggle for Collective Security*, pp. 121, 125, 156–7; R. C. Nation, *Black Earth, Red Star*, pp. 101–2; S. Pons, *Stalin e la Guerra Inevitabile*, pp. 122–3.
3 I am grateful to Silvio Pons for clarifying issues of Soviet foreign policy in the late 1930s.
4 J. Barber and M. Harrison, *The Soviet Home Front*, p. 17.
5 J. Erickson, *The Soviet High Command*, pp. 576, 582.
6 Haslam, *The Soviet Union and the Struggle*, p. 225.
7 Pons, *Stalin e la Guerra Inevitabile*, pp. 273–5.
8 R. MacNeal, *Stalin*, p. 221.
9 N. S. Khrushchev, *The Glasnost Tapes*, p. 46.
10 V. N. Zemtsov, 'Prinuditel'nye migratsii iz Pribaltiki', p. 4; K. Sword, *Deportation and Exile. Poles in the Soviet Union*, pp. 6–7, 13–14.
11 L. Rotundo, 'Stalin and the Outbreak of War in 1941', p. 291.
12 Khrushchev, *The Glasnost Tapes*, p. 50.
13 J. Erickson, *The Road to Stalingrad*, pp. 576, 582.
14 K. Simonov, *Glazami*, pp. 258–9.
15 See the materials in G. A. Bordyugov (ed.), *Gotovil li Stalin nastupatel'nuyu voinu protiv Gitlera?*; V. N. Kiselev, 'Upryamye fakty nachala voiny', p. 78; V. D. Danilov, 'Gotovil li general'nyi shtab Krasno' Armii uprezhdayushchii udar po Germanii?', p. 88

16 IA, no. 2 (1995), p. 30.
17 *Znamya*, no. 6 (1990), p. 165.
18 Erickson, *The Road to Stalingrad*, ch. 3.
19 Yu. A. Gor'kov, *Kreml'. Stavka. Genshtab*, pp. 79–80.
20 D. A. Volkogonov, *Stalin*, vol. 2, part 2, p. 191.
21 V. Kumanëv, 'Iz vospominaniyakh o voennykh godakh', pp. 68–75.
22 J. Barber and M. Harrison, *The Soviet Home Front*, p. 41.
23 Ibid., p. 50.
24 Gor'kov, *Kreml'. Stavka. Genshtab*, p. 155.
25 I. V. Stalin, *Sochineniya*, vol. 15, p. 1.
26 See K. Simonov's record of an interview with Konev, *Glazami*, p. 360.
27 G. Rittersporn, *Simplifications staliniennes*, p. 248.
28 *Neizvestnaya Rossiya*, vol. 2, pp. 63–5.
29 Simonov, *Glazami*, p. 389.
30 Khrushchev, *The Glasnost Tapes*, p. 65.
31 M. Harrison, 'The Second World War', pp. 250–52.
32 J. Erickson, *The Road to Berlin*, p. 533.

14 CODA: Suffering and Struggle (1941–1945)

1 H. Hunter and J. M. Szyrmer, *Faulty Foundations. Soviet Economic Policies*.
2 W. Moskoff, *The Bread of Affliction*, p. 146.
3 S. G. Wheatcroft and R. W. Davies, 'Agriculture', p. 126.
4 N. F. Bugai, *L. P. Beriya – I. Stalinu: 'Soglasno Vashemu ukazaniyu'*, p. 56 ff.
5 A. Avtorkhanov, 'The Chechens and the Ingush during the Soviet Period', p. 47.
6 I. Fleischhauer, 'The Ethnic Germans under Nazi Rule', p. 96.
7 C. Andreyev, *Vlasov and the Russian Liberation Movement*, pp. 199–200.
8 E. Bacon, *The Gulag at War*, pp. 78, 148.
9 N. S. Patolichev, *Ispytanie na zrelost'*, pp. 79, 88, 137, 282.
10 *Skrytaya pravda voiny: 1941 god*, p. 260.
11 Moskoff, *The Bread of Affliction*, p. 180.
12 *Skrytaya pravda voiny*, p. 342.
13 Ibid., p. 364.
14 Bacon, *The Gulag*, p. 24.

15 V. Kravchenko, *I Chose Freedom*, pp. 405–6.
16 *Soprotivlenie v Gulage. Vospominaniya. Pis'ma. Dokumenty*, p. 132.
17 J. Rossi, *Spravochnik po GULagu*, vol. 1, p. 40.
18 F. Benvenuti and S. Pons, *Il Sistema*, pp. 252–3.
19 *Krasnaya zvezda*, 21 June 1989.
20 P. J. S. Duncan, 'Orthodoxy and Russian Nationalism in the USSR', p. 315.
21 P. J. S. Duncan, 'Russian Messianism: a Historical and Political Analysis', p. 316–17.
22 *Pravda*, 21 April 1942.
23 It must be added that the RSFSR did not escape German occupation: about thirty million Soviet citizens had lived in parts of the RSFSR that fell into the hands of the Wehrmacht by the end of 1941: see N. I. Kondakova and V. N. Main, *Intelligentsiya Rossii*, p. 91.
24 Ye. S. Senyavskaya, *1941–1945: Frontovoe Pokolenie*, p. 105.
25 Ibid., pp. 83, 104.
26 Ibid., pp. 108–9.
27 Ibid., pp. 108–9, 170.
28 J. D. Barber and M. Harrison, *The Soviet Home Front*, p. 148.
29 M. Harrison, 'Soviet Production and Employment in World War Two', p. 22.
30 Yu. V. Arutunyan, *Sovetskoe krest'yanstvo*, pp. 360–66.
31 OA, Cherkess Autonomous Region file: location unrecorded, p. 117.
32 S. G. Wheatcroft and R. W. Davies, 'Population', p. 78.
33 In fact Stalin's scorched-earth policy for the retreating Red Army in 1941 limited the benefit for the German economy.
34 S. Kudryashëv, 'Collaboration on the Eastern Front', pp. 15, 17.
35 A. Dallin, *German Rule in Russia*, p. 477.
36 File on Gulyai-Pole in OA, unrecorded file number, p. 266.
37 *Skrytaya pravda voiny*, pp. 266–8.
38 Kudryashëv, 'Collaboration', p. 44.
39 Dallin, *German Rule in Russia*, p. 209.
40 Senyavskaya, *1941–1945*, p. 141.
41 R. MacNeal, *Stalin*, pp. 248–50.
42 G. Bordyugov and A. Afanas'ev, 'Ukradënnaya Pobeda'; S. Fitzpatrick, *Stalin's Peasants*, pp. 293–4.
43 Senyavskaya, *1941–1945*, p. 79.

PART THREE

15 The Hammers of Peace (1945–1953)

1 S. G. Wheatcroft and R. W. Davies, 'Population', p. 78.
2 M. V. Filimoshin, 'Poteri grazhdanskogo naseleniya', p. 124.
3 R. Kaiser, *The Geography of Nationalism*, p. 118.
4 This was so sensitive a topic that Nikita Khrushchëv revealed it to the Central Committee many years later, in July 1953, only in the strictest confidence: see R. Service, 'The Road to the Twentieth Party Congress', p. 237.
5 OA, Cherkessian Autonomous Province file, p. 117.
6 P. Levi, *The Truce*.
7 This had been true also at the end of the First Five-Year Plan: another 'triumph' marred for him by the attendant menace to his regime.
8 E. Yu. Zubkova, *Obshchestvo i reformy*, p. 72.
9 An exception was Andrei Sakharov; but even he, after graduating in 1942, became an armaments factory engineer for the rest of the war.
10 Zubkova, *Obshchestvo i reformy*, pp. 39–40.
11 V. P. Popov, *Krest'yanstvo i gosudarstvo*, pp. 261–80.
12 Zubkova, *Obshchestvo i reformy*, p. 41.
13 See the account of A. S. Belyakov's recollections of A. A. Zhdanov's description of a meeting of central political leaders: G. Arbatov, *Svidetel'stvo sovremennika*, p. 377.
14 Zubkova, *Obshchestvo i reformy*, p. 52.
15 Ibid., p. 43.
16 *Pravda*, 25 May 1945.
17 V. N. Zemskov, 'Prinuditel'nye migratsii iz Pribaltiki', pp. 13–14.
18 Ibid., p. 5.
19 J. Rossi, *Spravochnik po GULagu*, vol. 1, p. 53.
20 E. Bacon, *The Gulag*, pp. 93–4.
21 Calculated from ibid., p. 24.
22 D. Holloway, *Stalin and the Bomb*, p. 193.
23 W. Hahn, *Postwar Soviet Politics*, pp. 98–101.
24 F. Benvenuti and S. Pons, *Il Sistema*, pp. 282–8.
25 T. Dunmore, *Soviet Politics, 1945–1953*, chs 3, 4.
26 A. Nove, *An Economic History*, p. 290.
27 T. Dunmore, *The Stalinist Command Economy*, ch. 5.

28 Nove, *Economic History*, p. 293.
29 A. Nove, 'Industry', p. 62.
30 Holloway, *Stalin and the Bomb*, p. 216.
31 Nove, *Economic History*, p. 293.
32 Ibid., p. 305.
33 A. McAuley, *Economic Welfare in the Soviet Union*, pp. 33–4; and A. McAuley, 'Social Policy' in *Khrushchev and Khrushchevism*, p. 141.
34 McAuley, *Economic Welfare*, pp. 33–4; M. B. Smith, 'Individual Forms of Ownership in the Urban Housing Fund of the USSR, 1944–64', pp. 304–5.
35 M. Djilas, *Conversations with Stalin*, p. 133.
36 A. Agosti, *Togliatti*, p. 275.
37 A. Polonsky (ed.), *The Great Powers and the Polish Question*, p. 246.
38 *The Cominform. Minutes of the Three Conferences, 1947/1948/1949*, pp. 50, 178, 428, 450.
39 Ibid., p. 390.
40 F. Fejtö, *Histoire des démocraties populaires*, pp. 279–80.
41 S. Goncharov, J. W. Lewis and X. Litai, *Stalin, Mao and the Korean War*, ch. 4 ff.

16 The Despot and his Masks

1 K. Simonov, *Glazami*, p. 357.
2 *Kommunist*, no. 7 (1989), p. 68.
3 R. Richardson, *The Long Shadow. Inside Stalin's Family*, p. 44.
4 N. S. Khrushchev, *The Glasnost Tapes*, p. 66.
5 *I. V. Stalin. Kratkaya biografiya*, p. 5.
6 I. V. Stalin, *Sochineniya*, vol. 15, p. 204.
7 R. Stites, *Russian Popular Culture*, p. 119.
8 Khrushchev, *The Glasnost Tapes*, p. 92.
9 A. Adzhubei, *Te desyat' let*, p. 62.
10 D. Deletant, 'Language Policy and Linguistic Trends in Soviet Moldavia', pp. 196–7.
11 It must be added that the titular nationalities of some Soviet republics also behaved imperialistically towards their own national minorities. For example, Abkhaz and Ossetian were eliminated from the schools in Georgia.
12 In the 1930s, Shamil had stopped being treated as a positive anti-colonial rebel, but still not yet as a thoroughly reactionary figure.
13 D. Holloway, *Stalin and the Bomb*, pp. 207–8.

14 Ibid., p. 211.
15 *Marksizm i voprosy yazykoznaniya* in Stalin, *Sochineniya*, vol. 16, p. 159.
16 *Moskovskie novosti*, no. 32, 7 August 1988.
17 *Kniga o vkusnoi i zdorovoi pishche*, frontispiece.
18 V. Dunham, *In Stalin's Time. Middleclass Values in Soviet Fiction*.
19 B. Kerblay, *Modern Soviet Society*, p. 207.
20 I. V. Stalin, *Ekonomicheskie problemy sotsializma v SSSR*, p. 100.
21 Stalin, *Sochineniya*, vol. 16, pp. 115–19.
22 L. Opënkin, 'I. V. Stalin: poslednii prognoz budushchego', p. 113.
23 Stalin, *Ekonomicheskie problemy*, pp. 1–3.
24 Ibid., pp. 35–40.
25 The statue was completed and unveiled only in 1954.
26 Simonov, *Glazami*, p. 214.
27 Ibid., p. 210.
28 Ibid., p. 211.
29 E. Radzinsky, *Stalin*, pp. 549–58.
30 R. W. Davies, 'Forced Labour Under Stalin: The Archive Revelations', p. 67.
31 *Soprotivlenie v Gulage*, p. 209.

17 'De-Stalinization' (1953–1961)

1 See R. Service, 'The Road to the Twentieth Party Congress', pp. 234–8.
2 K. Simonov, *Glazami*, p. 242.
3 ITsKKPSS, no. 1 (1990), pp. 188–9.
4 *Soprotivlenie v Gulage*, p. 209.
5 F. Burlatskii, *Vozhdi i sovetniki*, p. 28. The word used by Khrushchëv was *opora*.
6 D. Holloway, *Stalin and the Bomb*, p. 317.
7 A. Nove, *An Economic History*, p. 334.
8 N. Barsukov, 'Kak sozdavalsya "zakrytyi doklad" Khrushchëva', p. 11.
9 Vlad. Naumov, 'Utverdit' dokladchikom tovarishcha Khrushchëva', p. 34.
10 See note 8.
11 ITsKKPSS, no. 3 (1989), p. 153; N. Khrushchev, *The Glasnost Tapes*, p. 44.

12 See W. J. Tompson, *Khrushchev: A Political Life*, pp. 57–61.

13 This translation is more accurate than the more usual one, 'cult of personality', since it was Stalin's entire role as an individual and not simply his personality that was the object of the cult.

14 N. Bethell, *Gomulka. His Poland and his Communism*, p. 210.

15 W. Lomax, *Hungary, 1956*.

16 IA, no. 2 (1994), pp. 60–61 (Molotov's self-criticism).

17 SXXII, vol. 2, p. 588.

18 R. Medvedev, *Khrushchev: The Years in Power*, p. 74.

19 IA, no. 3 (1993), p. 9.

20 T. H. Rigby, *Communist Party Membership*, p. 52.

21 S. Pons, 'La politica organizzativa nell'apparato del PCUS', pp. 200–204.

22 G. Breslauer, *Khrushchev and Brezhnev as Leaders*, p. 66.

23 Ibid., p. 86.

24 Ibid., p. 95.

25 Burlatskii, *Vozhdi i sovetniki*, p. 64.

26 A. Adzhubei, *Te desyat' let*, p. 150.

27 *Ustav Kommunisticheskoi Partii Sovetskogo Soyuza*, section three, clause 25.

28 Nove, *Economic History*, p. 336.

29 *Narodnoe khozyaistvo SSSR v 1960 godu*, pp. 441, 465, 467.

30 N. Yegorychev, 'Posle XX s"ezda', VIKPSS, no. 5 (1991), pp. 98–9.

31 R. Service, *Lenin*, vol. 3, p. 200.

32 A. di Biagio, 'La teoria dell'inevitabilità della guerra', p. 73.

33 M. Beschloss, *Kennedy vs. Khrushchev*, pp. 328–31.

18 Hopes Unsettled (1961–1964)

1 R. Stites, *Russian Popular Culture*, p. 146.

2 A. Nove, *An Economic History*, p. 353.

3 D. Filtzer, 'Labour', p. 133.

4 D. Filtzer, *Soviet Workers and De-Stalinization*, p. 103.

5 A. McAuley, 'Social Policy', p. 146.

6 P. H. Solomon, *Soviet Criminologists and Criminal Policy*, chs 3, 4.

7 I am grateful to Jovan Howe for pointing out to me the importance of the amalgamation policy on rural traditions and conditions.

8 Filtzer, 'Labour', p. 122.

9 N. Barsukov (ed.), 'N. S. Khrushchëv o proekte tret'ei programmy KPSS', pp. 1–8.
10 F. Burlatskii, *Vozhdi i sovetniki*, p. 124.
11 SXXII, vol. 3, p. 119.
12 The Soviet Constitution of 1936 defined the USSR as 'a state of the workers and peasants'.
13 SXXII, vol. 3, p. 303.
14 Ibid., p. 335.
15 V. E. Yesipov, 'Povsednevnost' ekonomiki Rossii', p. 112.
16 IA, no. 3 (1993), pp. 117, 130–34.
17 Burlatskii, *Vozhdi i sovetniki*, p. 143.
18 V. Kozlov, *The Peoples of the Soviet Union*, pp. 37, 94–5.
19 IA, no. 1 (1992), pp. 48–9.
20 Kozlov, *The Peoples of the Soviet Union*, pp. 37, 94–5.
21 Ibid., p. 194.
22 J. Anderson, *Religion, State and Politics in the Soviet Union and Successor States*, p. 55.
23 B. Kerblay, *Modern Soviet Society*, p. 282.
24 Anderson, *Religion, State and Politics*, pp. 61–2.
25 Burlatskii, *Vozhdi i sovetniki*, p. 122.
26 R. Garthoff, *Soviet Strategy in the Nuclear Age*, p. 57.
27 N. S. Khrushchev, *The Glasnost Tapes*, p. 63.
28 N. S. Khrushchev, *Khrushchev Remembers*, p. 419.
29 Khrushchev, *The Glasnost Tapes*, p. 177.
30 Nove, *Economic History*, p. 363.

19 Stabilization (1964–1970)

1 S. N. Khrushchev, *Khrushchev on Khrushchev*, ch. 2.
2 *Neizvestnaya Rossiya*, no. 1, p. 287 for the notes taken by A. N. Shelepin.
3 IA, no. 1 (1993), pp. 6–7.
4 Ibid., pp. 7–15.
5 F. Burlatskii, *Vozhdi i sovetniki*, p. 213; G. Arbatov, *Svidetel'stvo sovremennika*, p. 118; *Neizvestnaya Rossiya*, vol. 1, p. 286.
6 Burlatskii, *Vozhdi i sovetniki*, p. 220.
7 L. Alekseeva, *Inakomyslie v SSSR*, pp. 201–6.
8 See R. Medvedev, *Lichnost i epokha. Politicheskii portret L. I. Brezhneva*, p. 279.

9 Burlatskii, *Vozhdi i sovetniki*, p. 285.
10 VIKPSS, no. 4 (1991), p. 100.
11 Burlatskii, *Vozhdi i sovetniki*, p. 299.
12 See Arbatov, *Svidetel'stvo sovremennika*, p. 120 for some hearsay evidence.
13 D. B. Diamond, L. W. Bettis and R. E. Ramsson, 'Agricultural Production', p. 145.
14 M. Weitzman, 'Industrial Production', p. 180.
15 R. Pikhoya, 'Chekhoslovakia, 1968', pp. 11, 14, 17.
16 Alekseeva, *Inakomyslie*, pp. 213–14.
17 P. J. S. Duncan, *The Soviet Union and India*, ch. 2.
18 B. Nahaylo and V. Swoboda, *The Soviet Disunion*, pp. 150–51.
19 Ibid., pp. 188–9.
20 Medvedev, *Lichnost' i epokha*, p. 140.

PART FOUR

20 'Developed Socialism' (1970–1982)

1 *Moskovskie novosti*, no. 10 (1990).
2 A. Nove, 'Agriculture', p. 171.
3 Ibid., p. 170.
4 M. S. Gorbachëv, *Zhizn' i reformy*, vol. 1, pp. 195–7.
5 K. Wädekin, 'Agriculture', p. 119.
6 Vladimir Medvedev, *Chelovek za spinoi*, pp. 144, 149.
7 Ye. Chazov, *Zdorov'e i vlast'*, pp. 120–22.
8 R. Hill and P. Frank, *The Soviet Communist Party*, p. 150.
9 R. Medvedev, *Lichnost' i epokha*, pp. 182–4.
10 A. B. Evans, *Soviet Marxism-Leninism*, pp. 105–6.
11 SXXIV, vol. 1, p. 55.
12 *Konstitutsiya SSSR*, p. 1.
13 S. Whitefield, *Industrial Power and the Soviet State*, ch. 3.
14 A. Nove, *An Economic History*, p. 377.
15 M. Matthews, *Class and Society in Soviet Russia*, p. 89.
16 *Narodnoe khozyaistvo v 1980 g.*, p. 406.
17 S. Hedlund, *Crisis in Soviet Agriculture*, p. 173.
18 N. Grant, *Soviet Education*, p. 116.
19 J. Miller, 'The Communist Party: Trends and Problems', p. 6.
20 M. Galeotti, *Afghanistan. The Soviet Union's Last War*, pp. 10–12.

21 Privilege and Alienation

1 Z. Medvedev, *A Question of Madness.*

2 A. D. Sakharov, *Progress, Co-Existence and Intellectual Freedom.*

3 R. Medvedev, *On Socialist Democracy.*

4 A. I. Solzhenitsyn, *Letter to the Soviet Leaders.*

5 G. Hosking, *Beyond Socialist Realism. Soviet Fiction since Ivan Denisovich*, ch. 3.

6 M. Friedberg, *Russian Classics in Soviet Jackets*, pp. 170–76.

7 I witnessed this in 1974 in the Leningrad Library of the Academy of Sciences.

8 See R. Hill and P. Frank, *The Soviet Communist Party*, p. 36.

9 *Narodnoe khozyaistvo v 1990 g.*, p. 188.

10 M. Matthews, *Class and Society in Soviet Russia*, pp. 81–9.

11 S. White, *Political Culture and Soviet Politics*, p. 133.

12 I have yet to see a copy of this decree, but was informed about it in the Moscow bookshop (now a private video-shop: o tempora, o mores!) on Bogdan Khmelnitsii Street in 1989.

13 D. Lane, *The End of Inequality?*, pp. 104–6.

14 Calculated from V. Kozlov, *The Peoples of the Soviet Union*, pp. 94, 206.

15 I am grateful to Archie Brown for elucidating the Yakovlev affair.

16 *Moskovskie novosti*, nos. 8–9 (1990).

17 Hill and Frank, *The Soviet Communist Party*, p. 63.

18 W. E. Butler, 'Techniques of Law Reform in the Soviet Union', p. 210.

19 See D. Volkogonov, *Lenin: politicheskii portret*, vol. 2, pp. 399–401.

20 R. Medvedev, *Lichnost' i epokha*, pp. 298, 300.

22 Towards Reform (1982–1985)

1 M. S. Gorbachëv, *Zhizn' i reformy*, vol. 1, p. 148.

2 R. Medvedev, *Gensek s Lubyanki*, p. 13.

3 F. Burlatskii, *Vozhdi i sovetniki*, p. 35.

4 G. Arbatov, *Svidetel'stvo sovremennika*, p. 139.

5 Gorbachëv, *Zhizn' i reformy*, vol. 1, p. 189.

6 R. Medvedev, *Gensek*, p. 132.

7 I. S. Klemashev, Andropov's doctor, records this in *Fenomen Andropova*, p. 20.

8 Yu. V. Andropov, 'Uchenie Karla Marksa i nekotorye voprosy sotsialisticheskogo stroitel'stva', *Kommunist*, no. 3 (1983).
9 *Pravda*, 1 February 1983.
10 N. Ryzhkov, *Perestroika: istoriya predatel'stv*, pp. 37, 41. For a general account see A. Brown, *The Gorbachev Factor*, pp. 64–5.
11 Ryzhkov, *Perestroika*, p. 61. Gorbachëv says that Politburo candidate member V. I. Dolgikh, too, was involved in the leadership of the research team: *Zhizn' i reformy*, vol. 1, p. 233.
12 Ryzhkov, *Perestroika*, p. 47.
13 See R. Medvedev's account in *Gensek*, pp. 93.
14 T. Zaslavskaya, 'The Novosibirsk Report', p. 88–108.
15 Arbatov, *Svidetel'stvo sovremennika*, p. 322.
16 See M. Walker, *The Cold War*, p. 276.
17 A. Vol'skii, *Literaturnaya gazeta*, 4 July 1990. The episode is still rather obscure: Gorbachëv claims not to have known about it until after Chernenko's selection as General Secretary, *Zhizn' i reformy*, vol. 1, p. 245. See also Brown, *The Gorbachev Factor*, pp. 67–9.
18 R. Medvedev, *Gensek*, pp. 219–22.
19 See R. Sakwa, *Gorbachev and his Reforms*, p. 11.
20 *Narodnoe khozyaistvo v 1983 g.*, p. 129; *Narodnoe khozyaistvo v 1984 g.*, p. 229.
21 A. S. Chernyaev, *Shest' let s Gorbachëvym*, pp. 12–13.
22 Ryzhkov, *Perestroika*, pp. 37, 61.
23 *Istochnik*, no. 0 [*sic*] (1993), pp. 68–72.
24 It was widely reported that Gromyko said that Gorbachëv had a 'handsome smile but an iron bite': see A. Roxburgh, *The Second Russian Revolution*, p. 207. But Gromyko's quip does not appear in any text of his speech so far published.
25 Brown, *The Gorbachev Factor*, pp. 121–6.
26 Gorbachëv, *Zhizn' i reformy*, vol. 1, p. 38.
27 Ibid., p. 74.
28 G. Shakhnazarov, *Tsena svobody*, p. 339.
29 *L'Unità*, 9 April 1985.
30 M. Gorbačov and Z. Mlynář, *Reformátoři Nebývají Šťastni*, p. 39. I am grateful to Kieran Williams for alerting me to the existence of this book and for helping me with the Czech language.
31 Gorbachëv, *Zhizn' i reformy*, vol. 1, p. 210.
32 Gorbačov and Mlynář, *Reformátoři*, p. 39.
33 Gorbachëv, *Zhizn' i reformy* , vol. 1, pp. 165, 169.

34 Ibid., p. 236.
35 Ibid., p. 265: 'Tak dal'she zhit' nel'zya'.
36 I am grateful to Archie Brown for pointing out the significance of the location of the conversation.
37 *Istochnik*, no. 0 [*sic*] (1993), p. 74.
38 E. Shevardnadze, *Moi vybor*, p. 79.
39 Please note that these figures relate to full members of the Politburo.
40 Brown, *The Gorbachev Factor*, p. 77.
41 Gorbachëv, *Zhizn' i reformy*, vol. 1, p. 210.
42 Ryzhkov, *Perestroika*, p. 92.
43 Gorbachëv, *Izbrannye rechi i stat'i*, vol. 2, p. 212.
44 Party Programme: SXXVII, vol. 1, p. 555.
45 T. Colton, *The Dilemma of Reform in the Soviet Union*, p. 91.
46 Gorbačov and Mlynář, *Reformátoři*, p. 69.
47 Walker, *The Cold War*, p. 273.
48 See note 46.
49 Chernyaev, *Shest' let s Gorbachëvym*, p. 57.
50 Ibid., p. 121.
51 SXXVII, vol. 2, p. 32.
52 Z. Medvedev, *Nuclear Disaster in the Urals*.
53 Gorbachëv, *Zhizn' i reformy*, vol. 1, p. 304.

23 Glasnost and Perestroika (1986–1988)

1 J. Graffy, 'The Literary Press', pp. 107–36.
2 A. D. Sakharov, *Memoirs*, p. 615.
3 In Russian, therefore, *razvivayushchiisya sotsializm* replaced *razvitoi sotsializm*: R. Service, 'Gorbachev's Reforms: The Future in the Past', p. 279.
4 Ibid., p. 278.
5 Ibid., pp. 277–8, 283–4.
6 A. Smith, *Russia and the World Economy*, pp. 104–6.
7 *Materialy plenuma Tsentral'nogo Komiteta KPSS*.
8 *Pravda*, 26 June 1987.
9 Gorbachëv has suggested that the illness may have been the result of Yeltsin deliberately harming himself with a pair of scissors: *Zhizn' i reformy*, vol. 1, p. 374.
10 M. S. Gorbachev, *Perestroika. New Thinking for Our Country and the World*, pp. 38–41.

11 Ibid., p. 161.
12 Wisely he agreed to drop the long-winded slogan, 'socialism in the process of self-development', which he had introduced at the January 1987 Central Committee plenum: see Vadim Medvedev, *V komande Gorbachëva*, p. 67.
13 A. Brown, *The Gorbachev Factor*, pp. 33–4.
14 SXXVII, vol. 1, p. 590.
15 G. Shakhnazarov, *Tsena svobody*, p. 339; R. Gorbachëva, *Ya nadeyus'*, p. 23.
16 R. Kaiser, *The Geography of Nationalism*, p. 176.
17 M. S. Gorbachëv, *Gody trudnykh reshenii, 1985–1992*, p. 106.
18 A. S. Chernyaev, *Shest' let*, p. 183.
19 Shakhnazarov, *Tsena svobody*, p. 341.
20 *Devyatnadsataya vsesoyuznaya konferentsiya KPSS*, vol. 1, p. 58.
21 Ibid., vol. 2, pp. 82–8.
22 Ibid., p. 186.
23 M. Gorbačov and Z. Mlynář, *Reformátoři Nebývají Šťastni*, p. 69.
24 E. Pryce-Jones, *The War That Never Was*, p. 307.
25 Gorbachëv, *Izbrannye stat'i i rechi*, vol. 4, p. 278.
26 Ibid., vol. 7, pp. 150–75.

24 Imploding Imperium (1989)

1 M. S. Gorbachëv, *Zhizn' i reformy*, vol. 1, p. 334.
2 A. Smith, 'Foreign Trade', p. 138.
3 P. Hanson, 'The Economy', p. 99.
4 G. Schröder, 'Soviet consumption in the 1980s', p. 97.
5 G. Shakhnazarov, *Tsena svobody*, p. 216.
6 Schröder, 'Soviet consumption in the 1980s', p. 93.
7 S. White, *After Gorbachev*, p. 127.
8 E. C. Cook, 'Agriculture's role in the Soviet economic crisis', p. 197.
9 A. Brown, *The Gorbachev Factor*, p. 144.
10 J. Channon, 'The privatisation of Russian Agriculture'.
11 D. Filtzer, *Soviet Workers and the Collapse of Perestroika*, pp. 94–101.
12 N. Ryzhkov, *Perestroika*, p. 297.
13 Ibid., p. 301.
14 White, *After Gorbachev*, p. 52.
15 Ibid., pp. 52–3.

16 *Pravda*, 28 May 1989.
17 Brown, *The Gorbachev Factor*, pp. 264–7.
18 G. A. Hosking, P. J. S. Duncan and J. Aves, *The Road to Post-Communism*, pp. 19–20, 76–7.
19 Brown, *The Gorbachev Factor*, p. 6.
20 V. A. Tishkov, 'Assembleya natsii ili soyuznyi parlament?', pp. 3–18; M. Buttino, 'La fine dell'Unione Sovietica', pp. 11–13.
21 Ryzhkov, *Perestroika*, pp. 90–92.
22 See the note by Brown, *The Gorbachev Factor*, p. 321.
23 A. S. Chernyaev, *Shest' let*, p. 251.

25 Hail and Farewell (1990–1991)

1 A. S. Chernyaev, *Shest' let*, p. 319.
2 Ibid., p. 356.
3 I owe this point to Peter Duncan.
4 *Pravda*, 5 February 1990.
5 ITsKKPSS, no. 4 (1990), p. 61.
6 Chernyaev, *Shest' let*, p. 278.
7 L. Sukhanov, *Tri Goda s Yeltsinym*, pp. 119–20.
8 *Narodnoe khozyaistvo v 1990 g.*, p. 348.
9 *Pravda*, 14 December 1989.
10 See G. A. Hosking, P. J. S. Duncan and J. Aves, *The Road to Post-Communism*, pp. 45–6.
11 Chernyaev, *Shest' let*, p. 442; Vadim Medvedev, *V komande Gorbachëva*, p. 185.
12 *Soyuz mozhno bylo sokhranit'*, p. 111.
13 A. Smith, *Russia and the World Economy*, pp. 118–19.
14 V. Stepankov and Ye. Lisov, *Kremlëvskii zagovor*, p. 79.
15 *Sovetskaya Rossiya*, 23 July 1991.
16 There was a masculine undertone to the appeal, which was addressed specifically to 'Brothers': see ibid. Even Stalin had made his appeal to 'Brothers *and* Sisters' in 1941.
17 Significantly, Judaism went unmentioned.
18 Stepankov and Lisov, *Kremlëvskii zagovor*, p. 14; M. S. Gorbachev, *The August Coup*, p. 23.
19 *Smert' zagovora. Belaya kniga*, pp. 5–7.
20 B. Yeltsin, *The View from the Kremlin*, p. 58.

21 Stepankov and Lisov, *Kremlëvskii zagovor*, p. 152.
22 Ibid., p. 165.
23 Ibid., pp. 180, 184.
24 Ibid., p. 209.
25 Ibid.
26 *Izvestiya*, 6 September 1991.
27 B. Yeltsin, *Against the Grain. An Autobiography*, p. 15.
28 Ibid., p. 22.
29 Ibid., pp. 96–7.
30 Ibid., pp. 55–6.
31 Yeltsin, *The View from the Kremlin*, p. 192.
32 G. Shakhnazarov, *Tsena svobody*, p. 297.
33 *Izvestiya*, 19 October 1991.
34 *Pravda*, 27 November 1991.
35 Yeltsin, *The View from the Kremlin*, p. 116.
36 M. S. Gorbachëv, *Dekabr'-91. Moya pozitsiya*, pp. 119–20.

26 Power and the Market (1992–1993)

1 A. Aslund, *How Russia Became a Market Economy*, p. 188.
2 R. Service, 'Boris Yeltsin: Politics and Rhetoric'.
3 Ibid.
4 Ibid.
5 V. Bakatin, *Izbavlenie ot KGB*, p. 199.
6 Reported by J. Lloyd, *Financial Times*, 19 December 1991.
7 Interview with E. A. Ryazanov, Moscow Channel One TV: 16 November 1994. I am grateful to Lindsey Hughes for bringing this to my notice.
8 R. Service, 'Boris El'cin: continuità e mutamento di un rivoluzionario democratico', pp. 41–54.
9 V. A. Mau, *Ekonomika i vlast'*, p. 92.
10 Ibid., pp. 47–8.
11 Aslund, *How Russia Became a Market Economy*, pp. 235–6, 251, 256.
12 R. Sakwa, *Russian Politics and Society*, p. 57.
13 Aslund, *How Russia Became a Market Economy*, p. 141.
14 Ye. Gaidar, *Gosudarstvo i evolyutsiya*, p. 164.
15 Aslund, *How Russia Became a Market Economy*, p. 278.
16 J. Channon, *Agrarian Reforms in Russia, 1992–1995*, p. 4.

17 Aslund, *How Russia Became a Market Economy*, p. 278.
18 Ibid., p. 184.
19 R. Kaiser, *The Geography of Nationalism*, p. 161.
20 J. Lester, *Modern Tsars and Princes. The Struggle for Hegemony in Russia*, pp. 65–7.
21 *Rossiiskaya gazeta*, 3 April 1992, pp. 1–2.
22 B. Yeltsin, *The View from the Kremlin*, p. 236.
23 *Programma partii Liberal'no-demokraticheskoi partii*, p. 1.
24 *Rossiiskaya gazeta*, 6 May 1993.
25 Yeltsin, *The View from the Kremlin*, p. 244.
26 B. Clarke, *An Empire's New Clothes*, pp. 234, 240.
27 Aslund, *How Russia Became a Market Economy*, p. 198.
28 This is admitted by Yeltsin in *The View from the Kremlin*, p. 255.
29 Ibid., p. 278.
30 Aslund, *How Russia Became a Market Economy*, p. 284.
31 Ibid., p. 273.
32 Ibid., p. 278.

27 The Lowering of Expectations (1994–1999)

1 R. Service, *Russia: Experiment with a People*, pp. 113–14.
2 *NG-Stsenarii*, January 2000.
3 A. Korzhakov, *Boris Yel'tsin: ot rassveta do zakata*, pp. 210–12.
4 R. Service, *Russia: Experiment with a People*, pp. 183–5.
5 B. Yeltsin, *Midnight Diaries*, p. 25.
6 A. Lieven, *Chechnya. Tombstone of Russian Power*, p. 176.
7 P. Chaisty, *Legislative Politics and Economic Power*, p. 101.
8 *Ibid.*, p. 120.
9 Lieven, *Chechnya*, pp. 58–60.
10 *Sotsial'noe polozhenie i uroven' zhizni naseleniya Rossii*, pp. 138–9 and 305. See also J. Eatwell et al., *Transformation and Integration: Shaping the Future of Central and Eastern Europe*, pp. 73 and 76.
11 C. Freeland, *Sale of the Century*, pp. 166–8.
12 G. Zyuganov, *Rossiya i sovremennyi mir*, pp. 17–18.
13 O. Kryshtanovskaya and S. White, 'From Soviet *Nomenklatura* to Russian Elite'.
14 L. M. Drobizheva, *Asimmetrichnaya federatsiya*, p. 17.
15 R. Service, *Russia: Experiment with a People*, p. 85.

16 B. Granville and P. Oppenheimer, *Russia's Post-Communist Economy*, p. 19.
17 R. Service, *Russia: Experiment with a People*, p. 317.
18 J. Channon, *Agrarian Reforms in Russia, 1992–1995*, pp. 1–5.
19 R. Service, *Russia: Experiment with a People*, chapter 16.
20 '8200': song from *Kostroma, Mon Amour.*
21 R. Marsh, *Literature, History and Identity in Post-Soviet Russia, 1991–2006*, pp. 548–9.
22 R. Service, *Russia: Experiment with a People*, pp. 283–5.
23 B. Yeltsin, *Midnight Diaries*, 386–7.

28 And Russia? (From 2000)

1 See the details in N. Gevorkyan, N. Timakova and A. Kolesnikov, *Ot pervogo litsa. Peregovory s Vladimirom Putinym.*
2 *Moskovskie novosti*, 2 June 2000.
3 R. Service, *Russia: Experiment with a People*, pp. 211–12.
4 S. Whitefield, 'Culture, Experience and State Identity: A Survey-Based Analysis of Russians, 1995–2003', p. 132.
5 T. Phillips, *Beslan: The Tragedy of School No. 1*, pp. 3–8.
6 P. Gustafson, 'Putin and the Judiciary', RESC advanced research seminar, St Antony's College, 12 November 2007.
7 P. Chaisty, *Legislative Politics and Economic Power in Russia*, p. 125.
8 R. Service, *Russia: Experiment with a People*, pp. 273–4.
9 E. Chebankova, 'Putin's Struggle for Federalism: Structures, Operation and the Commitment Problem', pp. 295–7.
10 P. Chaisty, *Legislative Politics and Economic Power in Russia*, p. 69.
11 *RIA-Novosti* 1 May 2008.
12 A. Campbell, *The Blair Years. Extracts from the Alistair Campbell Diaries*, p. 694.
13 P. Chaisty, *Government and Opposition*, no. 3, pp. 446 and 449.
14 V. Jauvert, 'Histoire secrète d'un revirement: Sarko le Russe', *Nouvel Observateur*, 13 November 2008.
15 *RIA-Novosti*, 16 November 2008.
16 *Kommersant*, 15 May 2008.
17 May 2008: www.visionofhumanity.org/gpi/results/rankings.php.

Bibliography

Russian history is graced by many works absent from the Bibliography, which – I want to stress – includes only those documents, books and articles which are cited in the chapters.

Archives

Gosudarstvennyi arkhiv Rossiiskoi Federatsii (GARF): Moscow
Hoover Institution Archives (HIA): Stanford, CA
Osobyi arkhiv (OA): Moscow
Rossiiskii Tsentr dlya Khraneniya i Issledovaniya Dokumentov Noveishei Istorii (RTsKhIDNI): Moscow
Smolensk Party Archives (on microfilm): Birmingham

Documentary Collections

Akademicheskoe delo 1929–1931. Delo po obvineniyu akademika S. F. Platonova (eds V. P. Leonov et al: St Petersburg, 1993)
Bol'shevistskoe rukovodsto. Perepiska, 1912–1927 (eds A. V. Kvashonkin, O. V. Khlevnyuk, L. P. Kosheleva and L. A. Rogovaya: Moscow, 1996)
The Cominform. Minutes of the Three Conferences, 1947/1948/1949 (ed. G. Procacci *et al.*: Milan, 1994)
Dekrety Sovetskoi vlasti, vol. 1 (Moscow, 1957)
Desyatyi s"ezd RKP(b). Mart 1929g. Stenograficheskii otchët (SX: Moscow, 1963)
Devyatnadsataya vsesoyuznaya konferentsiya Kommunisticheskoi Partii Sovetskogo Soyuza (Moscow, 1988)

Dvadtsat' chetvërtyi s"ezd Kommunisticheskoi Partii Sovetskogo Soyuza. 30 marta – 9 aprelya 1917 goda. Stenograficheskii otchët (SXXIV: Moscow, 1971)

Dvadtsat' sed'moi s"ezd Kommunisticheskoi Partii Sovetskogo Soyuza. 25 fevralya – 6 marta 1986 goda. Stenograficheskii otchët (SXXVII: Moscow, 1986)

Dvadtsat' vtoroi s"ezd Kommunisticheskoi Partii Sovetskogo Soyuza. 1–31 oktyabrya 1961. Stenograficheskii otchët (SXXII: Moscow. 1962)

Dvadtsatyi s"ezd Kommunisticheskoi Partii Sovetskogo Soyuza. 14–25 fevralya 1956 goda. Stenograficheskii otchët (SXX: Moscow, 1956)

J. A. Getty and O. V. Naumov, *The Road to Terror: Stalin and the Self-Destruction of the Bolsheviks, 1932–1939* (London, 2001)

M. S. Gorbachëv, *Gody trudnykh reshenii, 1985–1992* (Moscow, 1993)

M. S. Gorbachëv, *Izbrannye rechi i stat'i*, vol. 1 ff. (Moscow, 1987–)

'Iz rechi tov. Bukharina na vechere vospominanii 1921g.', *Proletarskaya revolyutsiya*, no. 10 (1921)

Kak lomali NEP. Stenogrammy plenumov TsK VKP(b), 1928–1929, vols 1–5 (eds V. P. Danilov, O. V. Khlevnyuk, A. Yu. Vatlin *et al.*: Moscow, 2000)

Konstitutsiya Rossiiskoi Federatsii (Moscow, 1993)

Konstitutsiya SSSR (Moscow, 1977)

Krest'yanskoe vosstanie v Tambovskoi gubernii v 1919–1921gg. 'Antonovshchina' (eds V. P. Danilov and T. Shanin: Moscow, 1994)

V. I. Lenin, *Leninskii sbornik, vols 1–50* (Moscow, 1924–85)

V. I. Lenin, *Polnoe sobranie sochinenii, vols 1–55* (PSS: 5th edn: Moscow, 1958–65)

Materialy plenuma Tsentral'nogo Komiteta KPSS (27–28 yanvarya 1987) (Moscow, 1987)

IV Moskovskaya oblastnaya i III gorodskaya konferentsii Vsesoyuznoi kommunisticheskoi partii (b). Stenograficheskii otchët (Moscow, 1934)

Neizvestnaya Rossiya, vols 1 ff (ed. V. I. Kozlov: Moscow, 1992–)

Obshchestvo i vlast'. 1930-e gody. Povestvovanie v dokumentakh (eds. A. K. Sokolov, S. V. Zhuravlëv, L. P. Kosheleva, L. A. Rogovaya and V. B. Tel'pukhovskii: Moscow, 1998)

Perepiska TsK RSDRP(b) s mestnymi partiinymi organizatsiyami. Sbornik dokumentov, vol. 2 (Moscow, 1957)

Pis'ma I. V. Stalina V. M. Molotovu, 1925–1936 g.g. Sbornik dokumentov (Moscow, 1993)

Prezidium TsK KPSS, 1954–1964. Chernovye protokol'nye zapisi zasedanii: stenogrammy, vol. 1 (ed. A. A. Fursenko: Moscow, 2004)

Programma partii Liberal'no-demokraticheskoi partii. (Partiya Zhirinovskogo) (Moscow, 1993)

Protokoly Tsentral'nogo Komiteta RSDRP(b) (Moscow, 1958)

Resheniya partii i pravitel'stva po khozyaistvennym voprosam, vol. 1: 1917–1918 (Moscow, 1967)

Semnadtsatyi s"ezd VKP(b): 26 yanvarya – 10 fevralya 1934 goda. Stenograficheskii otchët (SXVII: Moscow, 1934)

Shestoi s"ezd RSDRP(b). Avgust 1917 goda. Protokoly (SVI: Moscow, 1958)

Skrytaya Pravda voiny: 1941 god (eds P. N. Knyshevskii *et al.*: Moscow, 1992)

Smert' zagovora. Belaya kniga (eds Yu. Kazarin and B. Yakovlev: Moscow, 1992)

Soprotivlenie v Gulage. Vospominaniya. Pis'ma. Dokumenty (Moscow, 1992)

Sovetskoe rukovodstvo. Perepiska, 1928–1941 (eds A. V. Kvashonkin, L. P. Kosheleva, L. A. Rogovaya and O. V. Khlevnyuk: Moscow, 1999)

Soyuz mozhno bylo sokhranit'. Belaya kniga. Dokumenty i fakty o politike M. S. Gorbachëva po reformirovaniyu i sokhraneniyu mnogonatsional'nogo gosudarstva (eds A. B. Veber, V. T. Loginov, G. S. Ostroumov and A. S. Chernyaev: Moscow 1995)

I. V. Stalin, *Sochineniya*, vols 1–12 (Moscow, 1946)

I. V. Stalin, *Sochineniya*, vols 13–15 (ed. R. H. MacNeal: Stanford, CA, 1967)

Stalin i Kaganovich. Perepiska. 1931–1936 gg. (eds O. V. Khlevnyuk, R. W. Davies, E. A. Rees, L. A. Rogovaya: Moscow, 2001)

Stalinskoe Politbyuro v 30-e gody. Sbornik dokumentov (eds O. V. Khlevnyuk, A. V. Kvashonkin, L. P. Kosheleva and L. A. Rogovaya: Moscow, 1995)

Stenogrammy zasedanii Politbyuro TsK RKP(b)-VKP(b), 1923–1938 gg., v trëkh tomakh (eds K. M. Anderson, A. Yu. Vatlin, P. Gregory, A. K. Sorokin, R. Sousa and O. V. Khlevnyuk: Rosspen, Moscow, 2007)

V. Stepankov and Ye. Lisov, *Kremlëvskii zagovor* (Moscow, 1992)

Tak eto bylo. Natsional'nye repressii v SSSR, 1919–1952 gody (ed. S. Alieva: Moscow, 1993)

The Trotsky Papers, 1917–1922 (TP: ed. J. Meijer: The Hague, 1964–1971)

Ustav Kommunisticheskoi Partii Sovetskogo Soyuza (Moscow, 1961)

Vos'moi s"ezd RKP(b). Mart 1919 goda. Protokoly (SVIII: Moscow, 1959)

Vosemnadtsatyi s"ezd. 10–21 marta 1939 goda. Stenograficheskii otchët (SXVIII: Moscow, 1939)

Vserossiiskaya konferentsiya RKP (bol'shevikov). 4–7 avgusta 1922. g. Byulleten' (Moscow, 1922)

Diaries, Memoirs and Single Works by Participants

A. Adzhubei, *Te desyat' let* (Moscow, 1989)

Yu. V. Andropov, 'Uchenie Karla Marksa i nekotorye voprosy sotsialisticheskogo stroitel'stva', *Kommunist*, no. 3 (1983)

G. Arbatov, *Svidetel'stvo sovremennika, Zatyanuvsheesya vyzdorovlenie (1953–1985 gg.)* (Moscow, 1991)

V. Bakatin, *Izbavlenie ot KGB* (Moscow 1992)

O. Bauer, *Bolschewismus oder Sozialdemokratie?* (Vienna, 1920)

V. Bukovskii, *Moskovskii protsess* (Moscow, 1996)

F. Burlatskii, *Vozhdi i sovetniki. O Khrushchëve, Andropove i ne tol'ko o nikh . . .* (Moscow 1990)

A. Campbell, *The Blair Years. Extracts from the Alistair Campbell Diaries* (eds A. Campbell and R. Stott: London, 2007)

Ye. Chazov, *Zdorov'e i vlast'* (Moscow, 1992)

A. S. Chernyaev, *Shest' let Gorbachëvym. Po dnevnikovym zapisyam* (Moscow, 1992)

F. Chuev (ed.) *Sto sorok besed s Molotovym. Iz dnevnikov F. Chueva* (Moscow, 1991)

F. Chuev (ed.), *Tak govoril Kaganovich. Ispoved' stalinskogo apostola* (Moscow, 1992)

T. Dan, *The Origins of Bolshevism* (translation: London, 1964)

M. Djilas, *Conversations with Stalin* (London, 1962)

Ye. Gaidar, *Gosudarstvo i evolyutsiya* (Moscow, 1995)

N. Gevorkyan, N. Timakova and A. Kolesnikov, *Ot pervogo litsa. Peregovory s Vladimirom Putinym* (Moscow, 2000)

M. S. Gorbachev, *The August Coup. The Truth and the Lessons* (London, 1991)

M. S. Gorbachëv, *Dekabr'-91. Moya pozitsiya* (Moscow, 1992)

M. S. Gorbachev, *Perestroika. New Thinking for Our Country and the World* (London, 1987)

M. S. Gorbachëv *Zhizn' i reformy*, vols 1–2 (Moscow, 1995)

R. Gorbachëva, *Ya nadeyus'* (Moscow, 1991)

M. Gorbačov and Z. Mlynář, *Reformátoři Nebývají Šťastni* (Prague, 1995)
M. Gor'kii, L. Averbakh and S. Firin (eds), *Belomorsko-Baltiiskii Kanal imeni Stalina, Istoriya stroitel'stva* (Moscow, 1934)
L. N. Gumilëv, *Ritmy Evrazii* (Moscow, 1993)
L. N. Gumilëv, *V poiskakh vymyshlennogo tsarstva* (Moscow, 1970)
I. A. Il'in, *O soprotivlenii zlu siloyu* (Berlin, 1925)
K. Kautsky, *The Dictatorship of the Proletariat* (translated by H. J. Stenning: Manchester, 1919)
N. Khrushchev, *Khrushchev Remembers* (London, 1971)
N. Khrushchev, *Khrushchev Remembers. The Glasnost Tapes* (New York, 1990)
S. N. Khrushchev, *Khrushchev on Khrushchev* (London, 1990)
I. S. Klemashev, *Fenomen Andropova, Vospominaniya i razmyshleniya lechashchego vracha* (Moscow, 1992)
A. Korzhakov, *Boris Yel'tsin: ot rassveta do zakata* (Moscow, 1997)
V. Kravchenko, *I Chose Freedom: The Personal and Political Life of a Soviet* Official (London, 1947)
A. Larina, *This I Cannot Forget* (London, 1994)
Yu. Martov, *Mirovoi bol'shevizm* (Berlin, 1923)
R. Medvedev, *On Socialist Democracy* (London, 1975)
Vadim Medvedev, *V komande Gorbachëva. Vzglyad izvnutri* (Moscow, 1994)
Vladimir Medvedev, *Chelovek za spinoi* (Moscow, 1994)
Z. Medvedev, *A Question of Madness* (London, 1975)
A. Mikoyan, *Vospominaniya i mysli o Lenine* (Moscow, 1970)
N. S. Patolichev, *Ispytanie na zrelost'* (Moscow, 1977)
B. Russell, *The Practice and Theory of Bolshevism* (London, 1920)
N. Ryzhkov, *Perestroika: istoriya predatel'stv* (Moscow, 1992)
A. D. Sakharov, *Memoirs* (London, 1990)
A. D. Sakharov, *Progress, Co-Existence and Intellectual Freedom* (London, 1968)
G. Seniga, *Una bagaglia che scotta* (Milan, 1970)
G. Shakhnazarov, *Tsena svobody. Reformatsiya Gorbachëva, glazami ego pomoshchnika* (Moscow, 1993)
E. Shevardnadze, *Moi vybor. V zashchitu demokratii i svobody* (Moscow, 1991)
K. Simonov, *Glazami cheloveka moego pokoleniya* (Moscow, 1990)
A. I. Solzhenitsyn, *Kak nam obustroit' Rossiyu? Neposil'nye soobrazheniya* (Paris, 1990)

A. I. Solzhenitsyn, *Letter to the Soviet Leaders* (London, 1974)
I. V. Stalin, *Ekonomicheskie problemy sotsializma v SSSR* (Moscow, 1952)
L. Sukhanov, *Tri Goda s Yeltsinym. Zapiski pervogo pomoshchnika* (Riga, 1992)
L. Trotsky, *My Life. An Attempt at Autobiography* (London, 1975)
L. D. Trotskii, *O Lenine. Materialy dlya biografii* (Moscow, 1924)
L. D. Trotsky, *The Revolution Betrayed: What is the Soviet Union and Where is it Going?* (London, 1937)
N. S. Trubetskoi, *K probleme russkogo samosoznaniya: sobranie statei* (Paris, 1927)
N. Ustryalov, *Pod znakom revolyutsii* (2nd revd edn: Harbin: China, 1920)
N. Valentinov, *Novaya ekonomicheskaya politika i krizis partii* (California, 1971)
N. Valentinov, *Vstrechi s Leninym* (New York, 1962)
A. Vol'skii, *Literaturnaya gazeta* (4 July 1990)
N. Yegorychev, 'Posle XX s"ezda', VIKPSS, no. 5 (1991)
B. Yeltsin, *Against the Grain. An Autobiography* (London, 1990)
B. Yeltsin, *Midnight Diaries* (London, 2000)
B. Yeltsin, *The View from the Kremlin* (London, 1994)
T. Zaslavskaya, 'The Novosibirsk Report', *Survey*, no. 28/1 (1984)
V. Zhirinovskii, *Poslednii brosok na yug* (Moscow, 1993)
G. E. Zinov'ev, *N. Lenin, Vladimir Il'ich Lenin. Ocherki zhizni i deyatel'nosti* (Petrograd, 1918)
G. Zyuganov, *Rossiya i sovremennyi mir* (Moscow, 1995)
G. Zyuganov, *Veryu v Rossiyu* (Moscow, 1995)

Periodicals

Argomenty i fakty (Moscow)
Arkheologicheskii ezhegodnik (Moscow)
Centre for Transition Economies Briefing (London)
Current Legal Problems (London)
East European Markets (Financial Times) (London)
Economic History Review (Kendal)
Europe/Asia Studies (London)
Financial Times (London)
Forschungen zur osteuropäischen Geschichte (Berlin)
Istochnik (Moscow)

Istoricheskii arkhiv (IA: Moscow)
Istoriya SSSR (Moscow)
Izvestiya (Moscow)
Izvestiya Tsentral'nogo Komiteta Kommunisticheskoi Partii Sovetskogo Soyuza (ITsKKPSS: Moscow)
Journal of Communist Studies (London)
Journal of Modern History (Chicago)
Kapital (Moscow)
Kommersant (Moscow)
Kommunist (Moscow)
Komsomol'skaya Pravda (Moscow)
Krasnaya zvezda (Moscow)
Literaturnaya gazeta (Moscow)
L'Unità (Rome)
Moskovskie novosti (Moscow)
New Left Review (London)
Nezavisimaya gazeta (London)
NG-Stsenarii (Moscow)
Novaya i noveishaya istoriya (Moscow)
Ogonëk (Moscow)
Otechestvennye arkhivy (Moscow)
Politicheskoe obrazovanie (Moscow)
Pravda (Moscow)
Revolutionary Russia (London)
RIA-Novosti (Moscow)
Rodina (Moscow)
Rossiiskaya gazeta (Moscow)
Rossiiskie vesti (Moscow)
Russia and the Successor States Briefing Service (London)
Saratovskie izvestiya (Saratov)
Sbornik (Leeds)
Segodnya (Moscow)
Slavic Review (Columbus, Ohio)
Slavonic and East European Review (SEER: London)
Sotsiologicheskie issledovaniya (Moscow)
Sovetskaya etnografiya (Moscow)
Sovetskaya Rossiya (Moscow)
Soviet Studies (Glasgow)
Svobodnaya mysl' (Moscow)

Trud (Moscow)
Voprosy istorii (Moscow)
Voprosy istorii Kommunisticheskoi Partii Sovetskogo Soyuza (*VIKPSS*: Moscow)
Znamya (Moscow)

Secondary Accounts

A. Agosti, *Togliatti* (Turin, 1996)

L. Alekseeva, *Inakomyslie v SSSR* (Paris, 1984)

G. Alexopoulos, *Stalin's Outcasts: Aliens, Citizens, and the Soviet State, 1926–1936* (Ithaca, NY, 2003)

J. Anderson, *Religion, State and Politics in the Soviet Union and Successor States* (Cambridge, 1994)

C. Andreyev, *Vlasov and the Russian Liberation Movement: Soviet Reality and Émigré Theories* (Cambridge, 1987)

A. M. Anfimov (ed.), *Krest'yanskoe dvizhenie v 1914–1917 gg. Sbornik dokumentov* (Moscow, 1965)

A. M. Anfimov, *Rossiiskaya derevnya v gody pervoi mirovoi voiny* (Moscow, 1962)

I. Antonova and I. Merkert (eds), *Moskva-Berlin, 1900–1950* (Moscow, 1996)

A. Applebaum, *Gulag* (London, 2003)

L. Aron, *Boris Yeltsin: A Revolutionary Life* (London, 2000)

Yu. V. Arutunyan, *Sovetskoe krest'yanstvo v gody Velikoi Otechestevennoi voiny* (Moscow, 1970)

A. Ascher, *The Russian Revolution of 1905. Russia in Disarray* (Stanford, CA, 1988)

S. Ashwin, *Russian Workers. The Anatomy of Patience* (Manchester, 1999)

A. Aslund, *How Russia Became a Market Economy* (London, 1995)

D. Atkinson, *The End of the Russian Land Commune, 1905–1930* (Stanford, CA, 1983)

J. Aves, *Workers Against Lenin: Labour Protest and the Bolshevik Dictatorship* (London, 1996)

A. Avtorkhanov, 'The Chechens and the Ingush during the Soviet Period' in M. Brozup (ed.), *The North Caucasus Barrier. The Russian Advance towards the Muslim World* (London, 1992)

J. Baberowski, *Der Feind ist überall. Stalinismus im Kaukasus* (Munich, 2003)

J. Baberowski, *Der Rote Terror. Die Geschichte des Stalinismus* (Munich, 2004)

E. Bacon, *The Gulag at War* (London, 1994)

S. Badcock, *Politics and the People in Revolutionary Russia: A Provincial History* (Cambridge, 2007)

K. Bailes, *Technology and Society Under Lenin and Stalin. Origins of the Soviet Technical Intelligentsia, 1917–1941* (Princeton, NJ, 1978)

A. M. Ball, *Russia's Last Capitalists, 1921–1929* (Berkeley, CA, 1987)

J. D. Barber and R. W. Davies, 'Employment and Industrial Labour' in R. W. Davies *et al.* (eds), *The Economic Transformation of the Soviet Union*

J. D. Barber and M. Harrison, *The Soviet Home Front, 1941–1945* (London, 1991)

A. M. Barker (ed.), *Consuming Russia: Popular Culture, Sex and Society Since Gorbachev* (Durham, NC, (1999)

A. Barnes, *Owning Russia: The Struggle over Factories, Farms and Power* (London, 2006)

N. Barsukov, 'Kak sozdavalsya "zakrytyi doklad" Khrushchëv', *Literaturnaya gazeta* (21 February 1996)

N. Barsukov, 'N. S. Khrushchëv o proekte tret'ei programmy KPSS', VIKPSS, no. 8 (1991)

Yu. M. Baturin, A. L. Il'in, V. F. Kadatskii, V. V. Kostikov, M. A. Krasnov, A. Ya. Lifshits, K. V. Nikiforov, L. G. Pikhoya and G. A. Satarov, *Epokha Yel'tsina: ocherki politicheskoi istorii* (Moscow, 2001)

M. Beissinger, *Nationalist Mobilization and the Collapse of the Soviet State* (Cambridge, 2002)

D. Bell, *The End of Ideology: On the Exhaustion of Political Ideas in the Fifties* (New York, 1962)

C. Bellamy, *Absolute War* (London, 2008)

F. Benvenuti, *I bolscevichi e l'Armata rossa, 1918–1922* (Naples, 1983)

F. Benvenuti, *The Bolsheviks and the Red Army* (Cambridge, 1988)

F. Benvenuti, *Fuoco sui sabotatori! Stachanovismo e organizzazione industriale in URSS, 1934–1938* (Rome 1989)

F. Benvenuti, 'Kirov nella politica sovietica', *Annali dell'Istituto Italiano per gli Studi Storici*, no. iv (Naples, 1979)

F. Benvenuti, 'A Stalinist Victim of Stalinism: "Sergo" Ordzhonikidze' in J. Cooper *et al.* (eds), *Soviet History, 1917–1953*

F. Benvenuti, *La Russia dopo l'URSS. Da 1985 a oggi* (Rome, 2007)

F. Benvenuti and S. Pons, *Il sistema di potere dello stalinismo. Partito e stato in URSS*, 1933–1953 (Milan, 1988)

N. Berdyaev, *The Russian Idea* (London, 1947)

A. Bergson, *The Real National Income of Soviet Russia since 1928* (Cambridge, 1961)

A. Bergson and H. S. Levine (eds), *The Soviet Economy: Towards the Year 2000* (London, 1983)

J. Berliner, *Factory and Manager in the USSR* (Cambridge, MA, 1957)

M. Beschloss, *Kennedy vs. Khrushchev. The Crisis Years, 1960–1963* (London, 1991)

N. Bethell, *Gomulka. His Poland and his Communism* (London, 1972)

F. Bettanin, *La Fabbrica del Mito. Storia e Politica nell'URSS Staliniana* (Naples, 1996)

A. di Biagio, 'La teoria dell'inevitabilità della guerra' in F. Gori (ed.), *Il XX Congresso del PCUS*

A. di Biagio, *Le origini dell'isolazionismo. L'Unione Sovietica del 1988 al 1928* (Milan, 1990)

J. D. Biggart, 'Bukharin's Theory of Cultural Revolution' in A. Kemp-Welch (ed.), *The Ideas of Nikolai Bukharin* (Oxford, 1992)

A. Blyum, *Za kulisami 'Ministerstva Pravdy'. Tainaya istoriya sovetskoi tsenzury, 1917–1929* (St Petersburg, 1994)

G. A. Bordyugov (ed.), *Gotovil li Stalin nastupatel'nuyu voinu protiv Gitlera*? (Moscow, 1995)

G. Breslauer, *Gorbachev and Yeltsin as Leaders* (Cambridge, 2002)

G. Breslauer, *Khrushchev and Brezhnev as Leaders. Building Authority in Soviet Politics* (London, 1982)

P. Broué, *Trotsky* (Paris, 1988)

P. Broué, 'Trotsky et le bloc des oppositions de 1932', *Cahiers Léon Trotsky*, no. 5 (1980)

V. Brovkin, *Behind the Front Lines of the Civil War. Political Parties and Social Movements, 1988–1922* (Princeton, NJ, 1994)

V. Brovkin, *The Mensheviks after October. Socialist Oppositions and the Rise of the Bolshevik Dictatorship* (Ithaca, NY, 1987)

D. P. Brower, 'The City in Danger' in D. P. Koenker et al. (eds), *Party, State and Society in the Russian Civil War*

A. Brown (ed.), *The Demise of Marxism-Leninism in Russia* (London, 2004)

A. Brown, *The Gorbachev Factor* (Oxford, 1996)

A. Brown, 'Perestroika and the End of the Cold War', *Cold War History*, no. 1 (2007)

A. Brown, 'Political Power and the Soviet State', in N. Harding (ed.), *The State in Socialist Society* (Macmillan, 1984)

A. Brown, *Seven Years that Changed the World: Perestroika in Perspective* (Oxford, 2007)

A. Brown, 'Transnational Influences in the Transition from Communism', *Post-Soviet Affairs*, no. 2, (2000)

A. Brown (ed.), *Contemporary Russian Politics: A Reader* (Oxford 2001)

A. Brown and M. Kaser (eds), *Soviet Policy for the 1980s* (London, 1982)

A. Brown and L. Shevtsova (eds), *Gorbachev, Yeltsin and Putin. Political Leadership in Russian's Transition* (Washington, DC, 2001)

K. Brown, *A Biography of No Place. From Ethnic Borderland to Soviet Heartland* (Cambridge, MA, 2004)

Y. M. Brudny, *Reinventing Russia. Russian Nationalism and the Soviet State, 1953–1991* (Cambridge, MA, 1999)

S. Bruk and V. Kabuzan, 'Dinamika, chislennost' i rasseleniya russkikh posle Velikoi Oktyabr'skoi sotsialisticheskoi revolyutsii', *Sovetskaya etnografiya*, no. 5 (1982)

N. F. Bugai, *L. P. Beriya – I. V. Stalinu: 'Soglasno Vashemu ukazaniyu'* (Moscow, 1995)

V. Buldakov, *Krasnaya smuta. Priroda i posledstviya revolyutsionnogo nasiliya* (Moscow, 1995)

V. Buldakov, *Quo Vadis? Krizisy v Rossii – puti pereosmysleniya* (Moscow, 2006)

V. Bunce, 'The Political Economy of the Brezhnev Era: the Rise and Fall of Corporatism', *British Journal of Political Science*, no. 2 (1983)

Yu. Buranov and V. Khrustalëv, *Gibel' imperatorskogo doma, 1917–1919gg.* (Moscow, 1992)

W. E. Butler, 'Techniques of Law Reform in the Soviet Union', *Current Legal Problems* (1978)

M. Buttino, 'La fine dell'Unione Sovietica: la Russia, i russi e il russo', *Europa/Europe*, no. 2 (1992)

E. H. Carr, *The Bolshevik Revolution, 1917–1923*, vols 1–3 (London, 1950, 1952 and 1966)

E. H. Carr and R. W. Davies, Foundations of a Planned Economy, 1926–1929 (London, 1969)

E. H. Carr and R. W. Davies, *Socialism in One Country, 1924–1926* (London, 1958)

H. Carrère d'Encausse, *Decline of an Empire. The Soviet Socialist Republics in Revolt* (New York, 1981)

P. Chaisty, 'The Legislative Effects of Presidential Partisan Powers in Post-Communist Russia', *Government and Opposition*, no. 3 (2008)

P. Chaisty, *Legislative Politics and Economic Power in Russia* (London, 2006)

P. Chaisty, 'Legislative Politics in Russia' in A. Brown (ed.), *Contemporary Russian Politics*

P. Chaisty, 'Party Cohesion and Policy-Making in Russia', *Party Politics*, no. 3 (2005)

L. Chamberlain, *The Philosophy Steamer: Lenin and the Exile of the Intelligentsia* (London, 2006)

J. Channon, *Agrarian Policy in 1994* (London, 1995)

J. Channon, *Agrarian Reforms in Russia, 1992–1995* (London, 1995)

J. Channon, 'The Landowners' in R. Service (ed.), *Society and Politics in the Russian Revolution*

J. Channon, 'The Privatisation of Russian Agriculture', *Russia and the Successor States Briefing Service*, vol. 1, no. 5 (1993)

J. Channon, 'Siberia in Revolution and Civil War, 1917–1921' in A. Wood (ed.), *The History of Siberia from Russian Conquest to Revolution* (London, 1991)

W. Chase, *Workers, Society and the Soviet State: Labour and Life in Moscow, 1918–1929* (Urbana, 1987)

E. Chebankova, 'Putin's Struggle for Federalism: Structures, Operation and the Commitment Problem', *Europe-Asia Studies*, no. 2 (2007)

B. Clarke, *An Empire's New Clothes. The End of Russia's Liberal Dream* (London, 1995)

S. F. Cohen, *Bukharin and the Russian Revolution. A Political Biography, 1888–1938* (London, 1974)

T. Colton, The Dilemma of Reform in the Soviet Union (2nd edn: New York, 1986)

T. Colton, *Yeltsin: A Life* (London: 2008)

R. Conquest, *The Great Terror. A Reassessment* (London, 2008)

R. Conquest, *Harvest of Sorrow. Soviet Collectivisation and the Terror-Famine* (London, 1986)

R. Conquest, *Industrial Workers in the USSR* (London, 1967)

R. Conquest, *Power and Policy in the USSR* (London, 1961)

E. C. Cook, 'Agriculture's Role in the Soviet Economic Crisis' in M.

Ellmann and V. Kontorovich (eds), *The Disintegration of the Soviet Economic System*

J. Cooper, M. Perrie and E. A. Rees (eds), *Soviet History, 1917–1953* (London, 1995)

M. Cox, *Rethinking the Soviet Collapse: Sovietology, the Death of Communism and the New Russia* (London, 1998)

O. Crisp, *Studies in the Russian Economy before 1914* (London, 1976)

O. Crisp and L. Edmondson (eds), *Civil Rights in Imperial Russia* (Oxford, 1989)

J. S. Curtiss, *The Russian Church and the Soviet State, 1917–1950* (London, 1965)

A. Dallin, *German Rule in Russia, 1941–1945: A Study of Occupation Policies* (2nd edn: London, 1981)

V. D. Danilov, 'Gotovil li general'nyi shtab Krasnoi Armii uprezhdayushchii udar po Germanii?' in G. A. Bordyugov (ed.), *Gotovil li Stalin nastupatel'nuyu voinu protiv Gitlera*

V. P. Danilov, 'Dinamika naseleniya SSSR za 1917–1929 gg', *Arkheograficheskii ezhegodnik: 1968*

V. P. Danilov, *Rural Russia Under the New Regime* (London, 1988)

V. P. Danilov and T. Shanin (eds), *Krest'yanskoe vosstanie v Tambovskoi gubernii v 1919–1921 gg. 'Antonovshchina'* (Moscow, 1994)

R. W. Davies, 'Changing Economic Systems: An Overview' in R. W. Davies *et al.* (eds), *The Economic Transformation of the Soviet Union*

R. W. Davies, *The Development of the Soviet Budgetary System* (Cambridge, 1958)

R. W. Davies, 'Forced Labour Under Stalin: the Archive Revelations', *New Left Review*, no. 214 (1995)

R. W. Davies (ed.), *From Tsarism to the New Economic Policy* (London, 1990)

R. W. Davies, 'Industry' in R. W. Davies *et al.* (eds), *The Economic Transformation of the Soviet Union*

R. W. Davies, *The Socialist Offensive* (London, 1980)

R. W. Davies, *The Soviet Economy in Turmoil, 1929–1930* (London, 1989)

R. W. Davies, M. Harrison and S. G. Wheatcroft (eds), *The Economic Transformation of the Soviet Union, 1913–1945* (Cambridge, 1994)

R. W. Davies and S. Wheatcroft, *The Years of Hunger: Soviet Agriculture, 1931–1933* (London, 2004)

S. Davies, *Public Opinion in Stalin's Russia: Terror, Propaganda and Dissent, 1934–1941* (Cambridge, 1997)

R. B. Day, *Leon Trotsky and the Politics of Economic Isolation* (Cambridge, 1973)

D. Deletant, 'Language Policy and Linguistic Trends in Soviet Moldavia' in M. Kirkwood (ed.), *Language Planning in the Soviet Union*

M. Dewar, *Labour Policy in the USSR, 1917–1924* (London, 1956)

D. B. Diamond, L. W. Bettis and R. E. Ramsson, 'Agricultural Production' in A. Bergson and H. S. Levine (eds), *The Soviet Economy: Towards the Year 2000*

S. M. Dixon, 'The Russian Orthodox Church in Imperial Russia 1721–1917', in M. Angold (ed.), *The Cambridge History of Christianity*, vol. 5: *Eastern Christianity* (Cambridge, 2006)

M. Djilas, *The New Class: An Analysis of the Communist System* (London, 1957)

S. M. Dubrovskii, *Sel'skoe khozyaistvo i krest'yanstvo Rossii v period imperializma* (Moscow, 1963)

S. M. Dubrovskii, *Stolypinskaya agrarnaya reforma. Iz istorii sel'skogo khozyaistva i krest'yanstva Rossii v nachale XX veka* (Moscow, 1963)

L. M. Drobizheva, *Asimmetrichnaya federatsiya: vzglyad iz tsentra, respublik i oblastei* (Moscow, 1998)

P. J. S. Duncan, 'Orthodoxy and Russian Nationalism in the USSR, 1917–1988' in G. A. Hosking (ed.), *Church, Nation and State in Russia and Ukraine* (London, 1991)

P. J. S. Duncan, 'Russian Messianism: a Historical and Political Analysis' (Ph.D. dissertation, University of Glasgow, 1989)

P. J. S. Duncan, *The Soviet Union and India* (London, 1989)

V. Dunham, *In Stalin's Time. Middleclass Values in Soviet Fiction* (Cambridge, 1976)

J. B. Dunlop, 'Russia: Confronting a Loss of Empire, 1987–1991', *Political Science Quarterly*, no. 4 (1993)

J. Dunlop, *The Rise of Russia and the Fall of the Soviet Empire* (Princeton, NJ, 1993)

T. Dunmore, *Soviet Politics, 1945–1953* (London, 1984)

T. Dunmore, *The Stalinist Command Economy* (London, 1980)

C. Duval, 'Yakov Sverdlov: Founder of the Bolshevik Party Machine' in R. C. Elwood (ed.), *Reconsiderations on the Russian Revolution* (Berkeley, CA, 1976)

V. S. Dyakin *et al.*, *Krizis samoderzhaviya v Rossii, 1895–1917* (Leningrad, 1984)

J. Eatwell, M. Ellman, M. Karlsson, D. M. Nuti and J. Shapiro, *Transforma-*

tion and Integration. Shaping the Future of Central and Eastern Europe (London, 1995)

B. Eklof, *Russian Peasant Schools: Officialdom, Village Culture and Popular Pedagogy, 1861–1914* (Berkeley, CA, 1986)

J. Ellis, *The Russian Orthodox Church: Triumphalism and Defensiveness* (London, 1996)

M. Ellman, 'On Sources: A Note', *Soviet Studies*, no. 2 (1992)

M. Ellman, 'The Soviet Famine of 1932–33 Revisited', *Europe-Asia Studies*, no. 6 (2007)

M. Ellman, 'Soviet Repression Statistics: Some Comments', *Europe-Asia Studies*, no. 7 (2002)

M. Ellman and V. Kontorovich, *The Disintegration of the Soviet Economic System* (London, 1992)

L. Engelstein, *The Keys to Happiness: Sex and the Search for Modernity in Fin-de-siècle Russia* (2nd edn.: Ithaca, NY, 1996)

R. D. English, *Russia and the Idea of the West: Gorbachev, Intellectuals, and the End of the Cold War* (New York, 2000)

J. Erickson, *The Road to Berlin* (London, 1983)

J. Erickson, *The Road to Stalingrad* (London, 1975)

J. Erickson, *The Soviet High Command. A Military-Political History, 1918–1940* (London, 1962)

A. B. Evans, *Soviet Marxism-Leninism. The Decline of an Ideology* (Westport, CT, 1993)

G. Evans and S. Whitefield, 'The Evolution of Left and Right in Post-Soviet Russia', *Europe-Asia Studies*, no. 6 (1998)

M. Fainsod, *How Russia in Ruled* (Cambridge, MA, 1953)

M. Fainsod, *Smolensk Under Soviet Rule* (London, 1958)

F. Fejtö, *Histoire des démocraties populaires. L'Ère de Staline, 1945–1950* (Paris, 1952)

Yu. G. Fel'shtinskii, *Bol'sheviki i levye esery. Oktyabr' 1917-iyul' 1918. Na puti k odnopartiinoi diktature* (Paris, 1985)

C. Ferenzci, 'Freedom of the Press, 1905–1914' in O. Crisp and L. Edmondson (eds), *Civil Rights in Imperial Russia*

V. Fic, *The Bolsheviks and the Czechoslovak Legion. The Origin of their Armed Conflict, March to May 1918* (New York, 1978)

O. Figes, *Peasant Russia, Civil War* (Oxford, 1988)

O. Figes, *A People's Tragedy. The Russian Revolution, 1891–1924* (London, 1996)

O. Figes, *The Whisperers: Private Life in Stalin's Russia* (London, 2007)

O. Figes and B. Kolonitskii, *Interpreting the Russian Revolution: The Language and Symbols of 1917* (London, 1999)

M. V. Filimoshin, 'Poteri grazhdanskogo naseleniya' in R. B. Evdokimov (ed.), *Lyudskie poteri SSSR v Velikoi Otechestvennoi voine* (Moscow, 1995)

D. Filtzer, 'Labour' in M. McCauley (ed.), *Khrushchev and Khrushchevism*

D. Filtzer, *Soviet Workers and De-Stalinization. The Consolidation of the Modern System of Soviet Production Relations, 1953–1964* (Cambridge, 1992)

D. Filtzer, *Soviet Workers and Stalinist Industrialisation. The Formation of Modern Soviet Production Relations, 1928–1941* (New York, 1986)

D. Filtzer, *Soviet Workers and the Collapse of Perestroika* (Cambridge, 1994)

S. M. Fish, *Democracy Derailed in Russia: The Failure of Open Politics* (Cambridge, 2005)

S. Fitzpatrick, *The Russian Revolution* (Oxford, 1982)

S. Fitzpatrick, 'Sex and Revolution: an Examination of Literacy and Statistical Data on the Mores of Soviet Students in the 1920s', *Journal of Modern History* (June 1978)

S. Fitzpatrick, 'Stalin and the Making of a New Elite, 1928–1939', *Slavic Review*, no. 3 (1979)

S. Fitzpatrick, *Stalin's Peasants. Resistance and Survival in the Russian Village after Collectivisation* (Oxford, 1994)

S. Fitzpatrick, A. Rabinowitch and R. Stites (eds), *Russia in the Era of NEP: Explorations in Soviet Society and Culture* (Bloomington, IN, 1991)

I. Fleischhauer, 'The Ethnic Germans under Nazi Rule' in I. Fleischhauer and B. Pinkus, *The Soviet Germans: Past and Present* (London, 1986)

C. Freeland, *Sale of the Century. The Inside Story of the Second Russian Revolution* (London, 2000)

M. Friedberg, *Russian Classics in Soviet Jackets* (New York, 1962)

T. Friedgut, *Iuzovka and Revolution*, vol. 2, *Politics and Revolution in Russia's Donbass* (Princeton, NJ, 1994)

W. C. Fuller, Jr., *The Foe Within, Fantasies of Treason and the End of Imperial Russia* (Ithaca, NY, 2006)

R. Fülöp-Miller. *The Mind and Face of Bolshevism: An Examination of Cultural Life in Soviet Russia* (tr. F. S. Flint and D. F. Tait: London, 1927)

M. Galeotti, *Afghanistan. The Soviet Union's Last War* (London, 1995)

I. Galfin, *Terror in My Soul: Communist Autobiographies on Trial* (Cambridge, 2003)

Z. Galili, *The Menshevik Leaders in the Russian Revolution. Social Realities and Political Strategies* (Princeton, NJ, 1989)

G. A. Galoyan and K. S. Khudaverdyan (eds), *Nagornyi Karabakh. Istoricheskaya spravka* (Yerevan, 1988)

I. K. Gamburg *et al., M. V. Frunze. Zhizn' i deyatel'nost'* (Moscow, 1962)

R. Garthoff, *Soviet Strategy in the Nuclear Age* (New York, 1962)

P. Gatrell, 'The First World War and War Communism, 1914–1920' in R. W. Davies *et al.* (eds), *The Economic Transformation of the Soviet Union*

P. Gatrell, *Russia's First World War: A Social and Economic History* (London, 2005)

P. Gatrell, *A Whole Nation Walking. Refugees in Russia During World War I* (Bloomington, IN, 1999)

R. Gellately, *Lenin, Stalin and Hitler: The Age of Social Catastrophe* (London, 2007)

A. Gerschenkron, 'Agrarian Policies and Industrialisation: Russia, 1861–1917', *The Cambridge History of Europe*, vol. 6, part 2 (Cambridge, 1966)

J. A. Getty, *Origins of the Great Purges: The Soviet Communist Party Reconsidered, 1933–1939* (Cambridge, 1985)

I. Getzler, *Kronstadt, 1917–1921: The Fate of a Soviet Democracy* (Cambridge, 1983)

I. Getzler, *Martov: A Political Biography of a Russian Social-Democrat* (London, 1967)

I. Getzler, 'Soviets as Agents of Democratisation' in E. R. Frankel, J. Frankel and B. Knei-Paz (eds), *Revolution in Russia: Reassessments of 1917* (Cambridge, 1992)

G. Gill, *The Origins of the Stalinist Political System* (Cambridge, 1990)

G. V. Golosov, *Political Parties in the Regions of Russia: Democracy Unclaimed* (Boulder, CO, 2003)

S. N. Goncharov, J. W. Lewis and X. Litai, *Stalin, Mao and the Korean War* (Stanford, CA, 1993)

L. Gordon and E. Klopov, *Chto et bylo. Razmyshleniya o predposylkakh i itogakh togo, chto sluchilos' s nami v 30–40e gody* (Moscow, 1989)

F. Gori (ed.), *Il XX Congresso del PCUS* (Milan, 1988)

Yu. A. Gor'kov, *Kreml'. Stavka. Genshtab* (Moscow, 1995)

Y. Gorlicki and O. Khlevnyuk, *Cold Peace: Stalin and the Soviet Ruling Circle* (Oxford, 2004)

A. Gorsuch, *Flappers and Foxtrotters: Soviet Youth in the Roaring Twenties* (Pittsburgh, PA, 1994)

J. Graffy, 'The Literary Press' in J. Graffy and G. A. Hosking (eds), *Culture and the Media in the USSR Today* (London, 1989)

D. Granick, *Management of the Industrial Firm in the USSR, A Study in Soviet Economic Planning* (New York, 1954)

N. Grant, *Soviet Education* (4th edn: London 1979)

B. Granville and P. Oppenheimer (eds), *Russia's Post-Communist Economy* (Oxford, 2001)

B. Granville and J. Schapiro, 'K chemu vedët zhëstkaya denezhnaya politika?', *Kapital* (29 November 1995)

A. Graziosi, *The Great Soviet Peasant War: Bolsheviks and Peasants, 1917–1933* (Cambridge, MA, 1996)

P. Gregory, *Before Command: The Russian Economy from Emancipation to Stalin* (Princeton, NJ, 1994)

P. R. Gregory, *Terror by Quota: State Security from Lenin to Stalin (an Archival Study)* (New Haven, CT, 2009)

P. Gregory and N. Naimark (eds), *The Lost Politburo Transcripts: From Collective Rule to Stalin's Dictatorship* (Hoover Institution/Yale University Press, 2008)

B. Grushin, *Chetyre zhizni Rossii v zerkale oprosov obshchestvennogo mneniya*, vol. I, *Zhizn' I-ya. Epokha Khrushchëva* (Moscow, 2001)

P. Gustafson, 'Putin and the Judiciary', RESC advanced research seminar, St Antony's College, 12 November 2007

W. Hahn, *Postwar Soviet Politics. The Fall of Zhdanov and the Defeat of Moderation, 1946–53* (Ithaca, NY, 1982)

L. Halligan and B. Mozdoukov, 'A Guide to Russia's Parliamentary Elections', *Centre for Transition Economies Briefing* (London, 1996)

P. Hanson, 'The Economy' in M. McCauley (ed.), *The Soviet Union under Gorbachev*

M. Harrison, 'National Income' in R. W. Davies *et al.* (eds), *The Economic Transformation of the Soviet Union*

M. Harrison, 'The Second World War' in R. W. Davies *et al.* (eds), *The Economic Transformation of the Soviet Union*

M. Harrison, 'Soviet Production and Employment in World War Two: A 1993 Update', *SIPS* (University of Birmingham), no. 35 (1993)

J. M. Hartley, *Alexander I* (London, 1994)

J. Haslam, *Soviet Foreign Policy, 1930–1933: The Impact of the Depression* (London, 1983)

J. Haslam, *The Soviet Union and the Politics of Nuclear Weapons in Europe, 1969–87: The Problem of the SS-20* (London, 1989)

J. Haslam, *The Soviet Union and the Struggle for Collective Security in Europe, 1933–39* (London, 1984)

S. Hedlund, *Crisis in Soviet Agriculture* (London, 1984)

J. W. Heinzen, *Inventing a Soviet Countryside: State Power and the Transformation of Rural Russia* (Pittsburg, PA, 2004)

J. Hellbeck, *Revolution on My Mind: Writing a Diary Under Stalin* (Cambridge, MA, 2006)

R. K. Herrmann and R. N. Lebow (eds), *Ending the Cold War: Interpretations, Causation, and the Study of International Relations* (New York, 2004)

G. Hewitt, 'Aspects of Language in Georgia (Georgian and Abkhaz)' in M. Kirkwood (ed.), *Language Planning in the Soviet Union*

R. Hill and P. Frank, *The Soviet Communist Party* (London, 1981)

D. Hoffmann, *Peasant Metropolis. Migration to Moscow and the Politics of Social Identity, 1929–1941* (Ithaca, NY, 1994)

D. Hoffmann, *Stalinist Values: The Cultural Norms of Stalinist Modernity* (London, 2003)

D. Holloway, *Stalin and the Bomb. The Soviet Union and Atomic Energy* (New Haven, CT, 1994)

P. Holquist, *Making War, Forging Revolution: Russia's Continuum of Crisis, 1914–1921* (London, 2002)

G. Hosking, *Beyond Socialist Realism. Soviet Fiction since Ivan Denisovich* (London, 1980)

G. A. Hosking, (ed.), *Church, Nation and State in Russia and Ukraine* (London, 1991)

G. A. Hosking, *A History of the Soviet Union* (London, 1985)

G. A. Hosking, *Rulers and Victims: The Russians in the Soviet Union* (London, 2006)

G. A. Hosking, *Russia and the Russians: A History* (London, 2001)

G. A. Hosking, *Russia: People and Empire, 1552–1917* (London, 1997)

G. A. Hosking, *The Russian Constitutional Experiment. Government and Duma, 1907–1914* (Cambridge, 1973)

G. A. Hosking, P. J. S. Duncan and J. Aves, *The Road to Post-Communism. Independent Political Movements in the Soviet Union, 1985–1991* (London, 1992)

G. Hosking and R. Service (eds), *Reinterpreting Russia* (London, 1999)

G. Hosking and R. Service (eds), *Russian Nationalism Past and Present* (London, 1998)

J. Hough and M. Fainsod, *How Russia is Governed* (revd edn: Cambridge, MA, 1979)

J. Hough and M. Fainsod, *How Russia is Ruled* (Cambridge, MA, 1979)

J. Hough, *The Soviet Prefects: the Local Party Organs in Industrial Decision-Making* (Cambridge, MA, 1969)

J. Hough, *The Soviet Union and Social Science Theory* (Cambridge, MA, 1977)

J. Hughes, *Stalin, Siberia and the Crisis of the New Economic Policy* (Cambridge, 1991)

C. Humphrey, *Marx Went Away – But Karl Stayed Behind* (Ann Arbor, MI, 1998)

H. Hunter and J. M. Szyrmer, *Faulty Foundations. Soviet Economic Policies, 1928–1940* (Cambridge, 1994)

E. Huskey, *Presidential Power in Russia* (London, 1999)

M. Ilic (ed.), *Stalin's Terror Revisited* (London, 2006)

A. Inkeles and R. M. Bauer, *The Soviet Citizens. Daily Life in a Totalitarian Society* (Cambridge, MA, 1959)

Istoriya Vsesoyuznoi Kommunisticheskoi Partii: Kratkii Kurs (ed. Commission of the Central Committee: Moscow, 1938)

H. F. Jahn, *Patriotic Culture in Russia during World War I* (Ithaca, NY, 1995)

N. Jasny, *The Socialized Agriculture of the Soviet Union. Plans and Performance* (Stanford, CA, 1949)

P. Jones, *The Dilemmas of Destalinisation: A Social and Cultural History of Reform in the Khrushchev Era* (London, 2006)

S. F. Jones, 'The Non-Russian Nationalities' in R. Service (ed.), *Society and Politics in the Russian Revolution*

S. F. Jones, *Socialism in Georgian Colors: The European Road to Democracy, 1883–1917* (Cambridge, MA, 2005)

K. Jowitt, *New World Disorder: the Leninist Extinction* (Berkeley, CA, 1992)

P. Juviler, *Revolutionary Law and Order. Politics and Change in the USSR* (New York, 1976)

J. Kahn, *Federalism, Democratization, and the Rule of Law in Russia* (Oxford, 2002)

R. Kaiser, *The Geography of Nationalism in Russia and the Soviet Union* (Princeton, NJ, 1994)

J. Kampfner, *Inside Yeltsin's Russia* (London, 1994)

A. Kappeler, *Russland als Vielvölkerreich: Enstehung, Geschichte*, Zerfall (Munich, 1992)

S. Karsch, *Die bolschewistische Machtergreifung im Gouvernment Voronež, (1917–1919)* (Stuttgart, 2006)

J. H. L. Keep, *The Russian Revolution. A Study in Mass Mobilisation* (London, 1976)

C. Kelly, *Children's World: Growing up in Russia 1800–1991* (London, 2007)

C. Kelly, *Comrade Pavlik: The Rise and Fall of a Soviet Boy Hero* (London, 2005)

C. Kelly, *Refining Russia. Advice Literature, Polite Culture and Gender from Catherine to Yeltsin* (Oxford, 2001)

D. R. Kelley (ed.), *Soviet Politics in the Brezhnev Era* (New York, 1980)

A. Kemp-Welch (ed.), *The Ideas of Nikolai Bukharin* (Oxford, 1992)

P. Kenez, *The First Propaganda State. Soviet Methods of Mass Mobilisation, 1917–1929* (Cambridge, 1987)

P. Kenez, 'The Ideology of the White Movement', *Soviet Studies*, no. 2 (1980)

B. Kerblay, *Modern Soviet Society* (London, 1983)

I. Kershaw, *The Nazi Dictatorship. Problems and Perspectives of Interpretation* (4th edn: Oxford, 2000)

S. Kharmandaryan, *Lenin i stanovlenie zakavkazskoi federatsii, 1931–1923* (Yerevan, 1969)

O. V. Khlevnyuk, *1937-y: Stalin, NKVD i sovetskoe obshchestvo* (Moscow, 1992)

O. V. Khlevnyuk, 'The Objectives of the Great Terror, 1937–1938' in J. Cooper *et al.* (eds), *Soviet History, 1917–1953*

O. V. Khlevnyuk, *Politbyuro. Mekhanizmy politicheskoi vlasti v 1930-e gody* (London, 1996)

O. V. Khlevnyuk, 'Prinuditel'nyi trud v ekonomike SSSR', *Svobodnaya mysl'*, no. 13 (1992)

O. V. Khlevnyuk, *Stalin i Ordzhonikidze. Konflikty v Politbyuro vo 30-e gody* (Moscow, 1993)

M. Kirkwood (ed.), *Language Planning in the Soviet Union* (London, 1989)

V. N. Kiselëv, 'Upryamye fakty nachala voiny' in G. A. Bordyugov (ed.), *Gotovil li Stalin nastupatel'nuyu voinu protiv Gitlera?*

T. Kitanina, *Voina, khleb i revolyutsiya* (Moscow, 1985)

J. Klier, 'The Pogrom Paradigm in Russian History' in J. Klier and S. Lambroza (eds), *Pogroms: Anti-Jewish Violence in Modern Russian History*

J. Klier and S. Lambroza (eds), *Pogroms: Anti-Jewish Violence in Modern Russian History* (Cambridge, 1992)

S. M. Klyatskin, *Na zashchite Oktyabrya. Organizatsiya regulyarnoi armii i militsionnoe stroitel'stvo v Sovetskoi respublike, 1917–1920* (Moscow, 1965)

D. Koenker, *Moscow Workers and the 1917 Revolution* (Princeton, NJ, 1981)

D. P. Koenker, W. G. Rosenberg and R. G. Suny, *Party, State and Society in the Russian Civil War: Explorations in Social History* (Bloomington, IN, 1988)

B. Kolonitskii, *Simvoly vlasti i bor'ba za vlast': k izucheniyu politicheskoi kul'tury rossiiskoi revolyutsii 1917 goda* (St Petersburg, 2001)

N. I. Kondakova and V. N. Main, *Intelligentsiya Rossii 1941–1945 gg.* (Moscow, 1995)

V. I. Kostrikin, 'Krest'yanskoe dvizhenie nakanune Oktyabrya' in I. M. Volkov *et al.* (eds), *Oktyabr' i sovetskoe krest'yanstvo, 1917–1927 gg.* (Moscow, 1977)

S. Kotkin, *Armageddon Averted: The Soviet Collapse 1970–2000* (Oxford, 2001)

S. Kotkin, *Magnetic Mountain: Stalinism as Civilisation* (Berkeley, CA, 1995)

V. Kozlov, *The Peoples of the Soviet Union* (London, 1988)

O. Kryshtanovskaya and S. White, 'From Soviet *Nomenklatura* to Russian Élite', *Europe/Asia Studies*, no. 5 (1996)

S. Kudryashëv, 'Collaboration on the Eastern Front', *SIPS* (unpublished paper, University of Birmingham, 1993)

V. Kumanëv, 'Iz vospominaniyakh o voennykh godakh', *Politicheskoe obrazovanie*, no. 9 (1988)

S. Lambroza, 'The Pogroms of 1903–1906' in J. Klier and S. Lambroza (eds), *Pogroms: Anti-Jewish Violence in Modern Russian History*

N. Lampert, *The Technical Intelligentsia and the Soviet State. A Study of Soviet Managers and Technicians, 1928–1935* (London, 1979)

N. Lampert, *Whistleblowing in the Soviet Union. Complaints and Abuses under State Socialism* London, 1985)

L. Lande, 'Some Statistics of the Unification Congress' in L. H. Haimson, *The Mensheviks from the Revolution of 1917 to the Second World War* (Chicago, 1974)

D. Lane, *The End of Inequality? Class, Status and Power under State Socialism* (London, 1971)

I. Lauchlan, *Russian Hide-and-Seek: The Tsarist Secret Police in St Petersburg, 1906–1914* (Helsinki, 2002)

T. von Laue, *Serge Witte and the Industrialisation of Russia* (New York, 1963)

A. Ledeneva, *Russia's Economy of Favours: Blat, Networking and Informal Exchange* (Cambridge, 1998)

G. Leggett, *The Cheka, Lenin's Secret Police. The All-Russian Extraordinary Commission for Combating Counter-Revolution and Sabotage December 1917 to February 1922* (Oxford, 1981)

J. Lester, *Modern Tsars and Princes. The Struggle for Hegemony in Russia* (London, 1995)

P. Levi, *The Truce* (London, 1987)

M. Lewin, *The Gorbachev Phenomenon* (London, 1988)

M. Lewin, *Lenin's Last Struggle* (London, 1969)

M. Lewin, *The Making of the Soviet System* (London, 1985)

M. Lewin, *Russian Peasants and Soviet Power. A Study of Collectivisation* (London, 1968)

R. Lewis, 'Foreign Economic Relations' in R. W. Davies *et al.* (eds), *The Economic Transformation of the Soviet Union*

A. Lieven, *Chechnya, Tombstone of Russian Power* (London, 1998)

D. Lieven, *Empire. The Russian Empire and Its Rivals* (London 2000)

D. Lieven, *Nicholas II: Emperor of all the Russias* (London, 1993)

D. Lieven, *Russia and the Origins of the First World War* (London, 1983)

J. J. Linz and A. Stepan, *Problems of Democratic Transition and Consolidation: Southern Europe, South America, and Post-Communist Europe* (Baltimore, 1996)

B. Lo, *Axis of Convenience: Moscow, Beijing and the New Geopolitics* (Washington, DC, 2008)

E. Lohr, *Nationalizing the Russian Empire: The Campaign Against Enemy Aliens during World War I* (Cambridge, MA, 2003)

W. Lomax, *Hungary, 1956* (London, 1976)

G. Lonergan, 'Resistance, Support and the Changing Dynamics of the Village in Kolchakia in the Russian Civil War', *Revolutionary Russia*, no. 1 (2008)

F. Lorimer, *The Population of the Soviet Union, History and Prospects* (Geneva, 1946)

S. Lovell, *The Russian Reading Revolution: Print Culture in the Soviet and Post-Soviet Eras* (London, 2000)

A. Luukanen, *The Party of Unbelief. The Religious Policy of the Bolshevik Party, 1917–1929* (Helsinki, 1994)

S. Lyandres, 'The 1918 Attempt on the Life of Lenin: A New Look at the Evidence', *Slavic Review*, no. 3 (1980)

R. Lyne, 'Russia, the West and the Arc of Mistrust: From the Megaphone to the Microphone?', *Russia in Global Affairs*, no. 4 (2008)

A. McAuley, *Economic Welfare in the Soviet Union* (Madison, WI, 1979)

A. McAuley, 'Social Policy' in M. McCauley (ed.), *Khrushchev and Khrushchevism*

M. McAuley, *Bread and Justice. State and Society in Petrograd, 1917–1922* (Oxford, 1991)

M. McCauley (ed.), *Khrushchev and Khrushchevism* (London, 1987)

M. McCauley (ed.), *The Soviet Union under Gorbachev* (London, 1987)

R. McKean, *St Petersburg Between the Revolutions: Workers and Revolutionaries, June 1907-February 1917* (New Haven, CT, 1990)

R. MacNeal, *Stalin: Man and Ruler* (London, 1988)

M. Malia, 'Revolution Fulfilled: How the Revisionists are still trying to take the ideology out of Stalinism', *Times Literary Supplement*, 15 June 2001

M. Malia, *Russia under Western Eyes, From the Bronze Horseman to the Lenin Mausoleum* (Cambridge, MA, 1999)

M. Malia, *The Soviet Tragedy : A History of Socialism in Russia, 1917–1991* (New York, 1994)

S. Malle, *The Economic Organisation of 'War Communism', 1918–1921* (1985)

R. Marsh (ed.), *Women and Russian Culture: Projections and Self-Perceptions* (New York, 1998)

R. Marsh, *Literature, History and Identity in Post-Soviet Russia, 1991–2006* (Bern, 2007)

T. Martin, *The Affirmative Action Empire, Nations and Nationalism in the Soviet Union, 1923–1939* (Ithaca, NY, 2001)

M. Matthews, *Class and Society in Soviet Russia* (London, 1982)

M. Matthews, *Privilege in the Soviet Union* (London, 1978)

V. A. Mau, *Ekonomika i vlast'. Politicheskaya istoriya ekonomicheskoi reformy v Rossii, 1985–1994* (Moscow, 1995)

E. Mawdsley, *The Russian Civil War* (London, 1987)

M. McFaul, *Russia's Unfinished Revolution: Political Change from Gorbachev to Putin* (Ithaca, 2001)

R. Medvedev *Gensek s Lubyanki* ((Moscow, 1993)

R. Medvedev, *Khrushchev: The Years in Power* (Oxford, 1977)

R. Medvedev, *Let History Judge. The Origins and Consequences of Stalinism* (London, 1971)

R. Medvedev, *Lichnost' i epokha. Politicheskii portret L. I. Brezhneva* (Moscow, 1991)

R. Medvedev, *Sem'ya Tirana* (Nizhni Novgorod, 1993)

Z. Medvedev, Nuclear Disaster in the Urals (London, 1979)

M. Melancon, *The Lena Goldfields Massacre and the Crisis of the Late Tsarist State* (Austin, TX, 2006)

N. Melvin, *Russians Beyond Russia: The Politics of National Identity* (London, 1995)

S. Merl, *Der Agarmarkt und die Neue Ökonomische Politik. Die Anfänge staatlicher Lenkung der Landwirtschaft in der Sowjetunion, 1925–1928* ((Munich/Vienna, 1981)

C. Merridale, *Ivan's War: Life and Death in the Red Army* (London, 2006)

C. Merridale, *Moscow Politics and the Rise of Stalin* (London, 1990)

C. Merridale, *Night of Stone. Death and Memory in Russia* (London, 2000)

E. Mickiewicz, *Changing Channels and the Struggle for Power in Russia* (Oxford, 1997)

J. Miller, 'The Communist Party: Trends and Problems' in A. Brown and M. Kaser (eds), *Soviet Policy for the 1980s*

I. I. Mints, *Istoriya Velikogo Oktyabrya*, vol. I: *Sverzhenie samoderzhaviya* (Moscow, 1952)

O. P. Molchanova *et al.*, *Kniga o vkusnoi i zdorovoi pishche* (Moscow, 1952)

S. S. Montefiore, *Stalin: The Court of the Red Tsar* (London, 2003)

D. Moon, *The Russian Peasantry, 1600–1930: The World the Peasants Made* (London, 1999)

B. Moore, *The Social Origins of Dictatorship and Democracy: Lord and Peasant in the Making of the Modern World* (London, 1967)

B. Moraski, *Elections by Design: Parties and Patronage in Russia's Regions* (DeKalb, IL, 2006)

Yu. A. Moshkov, *Zernovaya problema v gody sploshnoi kollektivizatsii* (Moscow, 1966)

W. Moskoff, *The Bread of Affliction. The Food Supply in the USSR During World War II* (Cambridge, 1990)

W. Mosse, 'Revolution in Saratov (October-November 1917)', *SEER*, October 1981

A. J. Motyl, *Thinking Theoretically about Soviet Nationalities: History and Comparison in the Study of the USSR* (New York, 1992)

R. Munting, *The Economic Development of the USSR* (London, 1982)

B. Nahaylo and V. Swoboda, *Soviet Disunion. A History of the Nationalities Problem in the USSR* (London, 1990)

N. Naimark, *Fires of Hatred: Ethnic Cleansing in Twentieth-Century Europe* (Cambridge, MA, 2001)

Narodnoe khozyaistvo SSSR v 1960 godu. Statisticheskii ezhegodnik (Moscow, 1961)

Narodnoe khozyaistvo v 1980 g. (Moscow, 1981)

Narodnoe khozyaistvo v 1983 g. (Moscow, 1984)

Narodnoe khozyaistvo v 1984 g. (Moscow, 1985)

Narodnoe khozyaistvo v 1990 g. (Moscow, 1991)

Narodnoe khozyaistvo v 1980 g. (Moscow, 1981)

Narodnoe khozyaistvo za 70 let (Moscow, 1987)

R. C. Nation, *Black Earth, Red Star. A History of Soviet Security Policy, 1917–1991* (London, 1992)

V. Naumov, *'Utverdit' dokladchikom tovarishcha Khrushchëva'*, *Moskovskie novosti*, no. 5 (4–11 February 1996)

V. F. Nekrasov (ed.), *Beria: konets kar'ery* (Moscow, 1991)

F. Neumann, *Behemoth: the Structure and Practice of National Socialism* (London, 1967)

A. Nove, 'Agriculture' in A. Brown and M. Kaser (eds), *Soviet Policy for the 1980s* (London, 1982)

A. Nove, *An Economic History of the USSR* (London, 1969)

A. Nove, 'Industry' in M. McCauley (ed.), *Khrushchev and Khrushchevism*

L. Opënkin, 'I. V. Stalin: poslednii prognoz budushchego', *VIKPSS*, no. 7 (1990)

D. T. Orlovsky, 'State Building in the Civil War Era' in D. P. Koenker *et al.* (eds), *Party, State and Society*

E. A. Osokina, *Ierakhiya potrebleniya. O zhizni lyudei v usloviyakh stalinskogo snabzheniya, 1928–1935* (Moscow, 1993)

B. Pearce, *How Haig Saved Lenin* (London, 1987)

R. Pearson, *The Russian Moderates and the Crisis of Tsarism, 1914–1917* (London, 1977)

S. P. Peregudov, N. Yu. Lapina and I. S. Semenenko, *Gruppy interesov i rossiiskoe gosudarstvo* (Moscow, 1999)

N. G. O. Pereira, *White Siberia: The Politics of Civil War* (Montreal, 1996)

D. Peris, 'The 1929 Congress of the Godless', *Soviet Studies*, no. 4 (1991)

M. Perrie, 'The Peasants' in R. Service (ed.), *Society and Politics in the Russian Revolution*

M. Perrie and R. W. Davies, 'The Social Context' in R. W. Davies (ed.), *From Tsarism to the New Economic Policy*

T. Phillips, *Beslan: The Tragedy of School No. 1* (London, 2007)

R. Pikhoya, 'Chekhoslovakiya, 1968. Vzglyad iz Moskvy po dokumentam TsK KPSS', *Novaya i noveishaya istoriya*, no. 6 (1994)

R. Pikhoya, *Sovetskii Soyuz: istoriya vlasti, 1945–1991* (Moscow, 2000)

R. Pipes, *The Formation of the Soviet Union. Communism and Nationalism, 1917–1923* (Cambridge, MA, 1964)

R. Pipes, *Russia Under the Bolshevik Regime, 1919–1924* (London, 1995)

S. Pirani, *The Russian Revolution in Retreat, 1920–24: Soviet Workers and the New Communist Elite* (London, 2008)

A. Polonsky (ed.), *The Great Powers and the Polish Question, 1941–1945: a Documentary Study in Cold War Origins* (London, 1976)

Yu. A. Polyakov, V. B. Zhiromskaya and I. N. Kiselëv, 'Polveka molchaniya (Vsesoyuznaya perepis' naseleniya 1937 g)', *Sotsiologicheskie Issledovaniya*, no. 7 (1990)

S. Pons, *Berlinguer e la fine del comunismo* (Torino, 2006)

S. Pons, 'La politica organizzativa nell'apparato del PCUS' in F. Gori (ed.), *Il XX Congresso del PCUS*

S. Pons, *Stalin e la guerra Inevitabile* (Turin, 1995)

V. P. Popov, *Krest'yanstvo i Gosudarstvo (1945–1953)* (Paris, 1992)

P. N. Pospelov, 'Pyatdesyat let Kommunisticheskoi partii Sovetskogo Soyuza', *Voprosy Istorii*, no. 11 (1953)

D. Pospielovsky, *The Russian Church under the Soviet Regime, 1917–1982*, vol. I (New York, 1984)

A. Pravda (ed.), *Leading Russia: Putin in Perspective* (Oxford, 2005)

D. Priestland, *Stalinism and the Politics of Mobilization: Ideas, Power and Terror in Inter-War Russia* (Oxford, 2007)

E. Pryce-Jones, *The War That Never Was. The Fall of the Soviet Empire 1985–1991* (London, 1995)

A. Pyman, *The Life of Alexander Blok*, vol. 2: *The Release of Harmony, 1908–1921* (Oxford, 1980)

A. Rabinowitch, *The Bolsheviks Come to Power in Petrograd* (London, 1976)

A. Rabinowitch, *The Bolsheviks in Power: The First Year of Soviet Rule in Petrograd* (Bloomington, IN, 2007)

A. Rabinowitch, *Prelude to Revolution. The Petrograd Bolsheviks and the July 1917 Uprising* (New York, 1968)

O. H. Radkey, *The Agrarian Foes of Communism. Promise and Default of the Russian Socialist-Revolutionaries* (New York, 1958)

O. H. Radkey, *Russia Goes to the Polls: the Election to the Russian Constituent Assembly, 1917* (2nd edn: Ithaca, NY, 1989)

E. Radzinsky, Stalin (London, 1996)

D. J. Raleigh, Experiencing Russia's Civil War: Politics, Society and Revolutionary Culture in Saratov, 1917–1922 (Princeton, NJ, 2002)

A. G. Rashin, *Formirovanie rabochego klassa Rossii: istoriko-ekonomicheskie ocherki* (Moscow, 1958)

A. G. Rashin, *Naselenie Rossii za 100 let (1811–1913gg.): statisticheskie ocherki* (Moscow, 1958)

C. Read, *Culture and Power in Revolutionary Russia* (London, 1990)

P. Reddaway and D. Glinski, *The Tragedy of Russia's Reforms: Market Bolshevism Against Democracy* (Washington, DC, 2001)

E. A. Rees, *Political Thought from Machiavelli to Stalin: Revolutionary Machiavellism* (London, 2004)

E. A. Rees (ed.), *Centre–Local Relations in the Stalinist State, 1928–1941* (London, 2002)

E. A. Rees (ed.), *Decision-Making in the Stalinist Command Economy, 1932–37* (London, 1997)

E. A. Rees (ed.), *The Nature of Stalin's Dictatorship : The Politburo 1924–1953* (London, 2004)

E. A. Rees, 'Stalin, the Politburo and Rail Transport Policy' in J. Cooper *et al.* (eds), *Soviet History, 1917–1953*

E. A. Rees, *Stalinism and Soviet Rail Transport, 1928–1941* (London, 1995)

E. A. Rees, *State Control in Soviet Russia* (London, 1987)

T. M. Remington, *Politics in Russia* (2nd edn: London, 2001)

B. Renz, 'Putin's militocracy? An Alternative Interpretation of Siloviki in Contemporary Russian Politics', *Europe-Asia Studies*, no. 6 (2006)

J. Reshetar, *The Ukrainian Revolution, 1917–1920* (Princeton, NJ, 1952)

R. Richardson, *The Long Shadow. Inside Stalin's Family* (London, 1993)

T. H. Rigby, *The Changing Soviet System* (London, 1990)

T. H. Rigby, *Communist Party Membership in the USSR, 1917–1967* (Princeton, NJ, 1968)

T. H. Rigby, 'Early Provincial Cliques and the Rise of Stalin', *Soviet Studies*, no. 1 (1981)

T. H. Rigby, *Lenin's Government. Sovnarkom, 1917–1922* (Cambridge, 1979)

T. H. Rigby, 'The Origins of the Nomenklatura System' in his *Political Elites in the USSR*

T. H. Rigby, *Political Elites in the USSR: Central Leaders and Local Cadres from Lenin to Gorbachev* (London, 1990)

T. H. Rigby, 'Was Stalin a Disloyal Patron?' in his *Political Elites in the USSR*

G. T. Rittersporn, *Simplifications staliniennes et complications soviétiques: tensions socials et conflits en URSS, 1933–1953* (Paris, 1988)

N. Robinson, *Ideology and the Collapse of the Soviet System: A Critical History of Soviet Ideological Discourse* (Aldershot, 1995)

H. Rogger, *National Consciousness in Eighteenth-Century Russia* (Cambridge, MA, 1960)

A. Romano, 'Peasant-Bolshevik. Conflicts Inside the Red Army on the Eve of Dekulakization (1928–1929)', *Forschungen zur osteuropäischen Geschichte*, no. 52 (1996)

W. G. Rosenberg, *Liberals in the Russian Revolution: the Constitutional Democratic Party, 1917–1921* (Princeton, NJ, 1974)

J. Rossi, *Spravochnik po Gulagu*, vols 1–2 (2nd revd edn.: Moscow, 1992)

J. Rossman, *Worker Resistance Under Stalin: Class and Revolution on the Shop Floor* (Cambridge, MA, 2005)

L. Rotundo, 'Stalin and the Outbreak of War in 1941', *Journal of Contemporary History*, vol. 24 (1989)

A. Roxburgh, *The Second Russian Revolution* (London, 1991)

P. Rutland, *The Politics of Economic Stagnation in the Soviet Union: The Role of Local Party Organs in Economic Management* (Oxford, 1993)

R. Sakwa, *Gorbachev and his Reforms, 1985–1990* (London, 1990)

R. Sakwa, *Russian Politics and Society* (London, 1993)

J. Sanborn, *Drafting the Russian Nation: Military Conscription, Total War and Mass Politics, 1905–1925* (DeKalb, IL, 2003)

L. Schapiro, *The Communist Party of the Soviet Union* (London, 1960)

L. Schapiro, *Totalitarianism* (London, 1972)

G. Schröder, 'Soviet consumption in the 1980s: a tale of woe' in M. Ellman and V. Kontorovich, *The Disintegration of the Soviet Economic System*

J. C. T. Schull, 'What is Ideology? Theoretical Problems and Lessons from Soviet-type Societies', *Political Studies*, no. 4 (1992)

Ye. S. Senyavskaya, *1941–1945: Frontovoe Pokolenie. Istorikopsikhologicheskoe issledovanie* (Moscow, 1995)

R. Service, *The Bolshevik Party in Revolution: A Study in Organisational Change* (London, 1979)

R. Service, 'Boris El'cin: continuità e mutamento di un rivoluzionario democratico', *Europa/Europe*, no. 2 (1992)

R. Service, 'Boris Yeltsin: Politics and Rhetoric, 1991–1992': research paper delivered in St Antony's College, Oxford, 9 March 1992

R. Service, *Comrades. Communism: A World History* (London, 2007)
R. Service, 'From Polyarchy to Hegemony', *Sbornik*, no. 10 (1984)
R. Service, 'Gorbachev's Reforms: The Future in the Past', *Journal of Communist Studies*, no. 3 (September 1987)
R. Service, 'The Industrial Workers', in R. Service (ed.), *Society and Politics in the Russian Revolution*
R. Service, 'Joseph Stalin: The Making of a Stalinist', in J. Channon (ed.), *Politics, Society and Stalinism in the USSR* (London, 1998)
R. Service, *Lenin: A Biography* (London, 2000)
R. Service, *Lenin: A Political Life*, vol. 1: *The Strengths of Contradictions* (London, 1985); vol. 2: *Worlds in Collision* (London, 1991); vol. 3: *The Iron Ring* (London, 1995)
R. Service, 'The Road to the Twentieth Party Congress', *Soviet Studies*, no. 2 (1981)
R. Service, *Russia: Experiment with a People: From 1991 to the Present* (London, 2002)
R. Service (ed.), *Society and Politics in the Russian Revolution* (London, 1992)
R. Service, *Stalin: A Biography* (London, 2004)
H. Seton-Watson, *The Russian Empire, 1801–1917* (Oxford, 1967)
T. Shanin, *The Awkward Class. Political Sociology of Peasantry in a Developing Society: Russia, 1910–1925* (Oxford, 1972)
D. Shearer, 'Crime and Social Disorder in Stalin's Russia: A Reassessment of the Great Retreat and the Origins of Mass Repression', *Cahiers du Monde Russe*, no. 1/2 (1998)
D. Shearer, *Industry, State and Society in Stalin's Russia, 1926–1934* (Ithaca, NY, 1996)
D. Shearer, 'Social Disorder, Mass Repression, and the NKVD During the 1930s', *Cahiers du Monde Russe*, no. 3/4 (2001)
A. V. Shestakov, *Ocherki po sel'skomu khozyaistvu i krest'yanskomu dvizheniyu v gody voiny i pered Oktyabrëm 1917g.* (Leningrad, 1927)
V. Shevzov, *Russian Orthodoxy on the Eve of Revolution* (Oxford, 2003)
S. A. Shinkarchuk, *Obshchestvennoe mnenie v Sovetskoi Rossii v 30-gody* (St Petersburg, 1995)
A. L. Sidorov, *Istoricheskie predposylki Velikoi oktyabr'skoi sotsialisticheskoi revolyutsii* (Moscow, 1970)
L. H. Siegelbaum, *Cars for Comrades: The Life of the Soviet Automobile* (Ithaca, NY, 2008)
L. H. Siegelbaum, *Soviet State and Society between Revolutions, 1917–1929* (Cambridge, 1992)

L. Siegelbaum. *Stakhanovism and the Politics of Productivity in the USSR, 1935–1941* (Cambridge, 1988)

H. G. Skilling and F. Griffiths (eds), *Interest Groups in Soviet Politics* (London, 1971)

Y. Slezkine, *Arctic Mirrors: Russia and the Small Peoples of the North* (Ithaca, NY, 1994)

Y. Slezkine, *The Jewish Century* (Princeton, NJ, 2004)

J. D. Smele, *Civil War in Siberia: The Anti-Bolshevik Government of Admiral Kolchak, 1918–1920* (Cambridge, 1996)

A. Smith, 'Foreign Trade' in M. McCauley (ed.), *The Soviet Union under Gorbachev*

A. Smith, *Russia and the World Economy. Problems of Integration* (London, 1995)

J. Smith, *The Bolsheviks and the National Question, 1917–23* (London, 1999)

M. B. Smith, 'Individual Forms of Ownership in the Urban Housing Fund of the USSR, 1944–64', *Slavonic and East European Review*, no. 2 (2008)

S. A. Smith, *Red Petrograd. Revolution in the Factories, 1917–1918* (Cambridge, 1983)

S. A. Smith, 'Workers' Control: February-October 1917' in *The Blackwell Encyclopedia of the Russian Revolution* (ed. H. Shukman: Oxford, 1988)

A. K. Sokolov, *Lektsii po Sovetskoi Istorii, 1917–1940* (Moscow, 1995)

S. Solnick, *Stealing the State: Control and Collapse in Soviet Institutions* (Cambridge, MA, 1998)

P. H. Solomon, *Soviet Criminologists and Criminal Policy* (New York, 1978)

S. Solomon (ed.), *Pluralism in the Soviet Union: Essays in Honour of H. Gordon Skilling* (London, 1983)

Sotsial'noe polozhenie i uroven' zhizni naseleniya Rossii. Offitsial'noe izdanie (Moscow, 2000)

B. Souvarine, *Stalin* ((London, 1940)

I. V. Stalin. Kratkaya biografiya (2nd edn: Moscow, 1947)

B. A. Starkov, *Dela i lyudi stalinskogo vremeni* (St Petersburg, 1995)

B. A. Starkov (ed), *Rossiiskaya povsednevnost' 1921–1941 gg: novye podkhody* (St Petersburg, 1995)

M. Steinberg, 'The Language of Popular Revolution' in M. Steinberg, *Voices of Revolution, 1917* (London 2001)

A. Stepan, 'Russian Federalism in Comparative Perspective', *Post-Soviet Affairs*, no. 2 (2000)

R. Stites, *Revolutionary Dreams. Utopian Vision and Experimental Life in the Russian Revolution* (New York, 1989)

R. Stites, *Russian Popular Culture: Entertainment and Society Since 1900* (Cambridge, 1992)

N. Stone, *The Eastern Front* (London, 1975)

K. Stoner-Weiss, *Local Heroes: The Political Economy of Russian Regional Governance* (Princeton, NJ, 1997)

K. Stoner-Weiss, *Resisting the State: Reform and Retrenchment in Post-Soviet Russia* (Cambridge, 2006)

R. G. Suny, *The Baku Commune, Class and Nationality in the Russian Revolution, 1917–1918* (Princeton, NJ, 1972)

R. G. Suny (ed.), *The Cambridge History of Russia* (Cambridge, 2007)

R. G. Suny, *The Making of the Georgian Nation* (2nd edn: Bloomington, IN, 1994)

A. C. Sutton, *Western Technology and Soviet Economic Development, 1917–1945* (Stanford, CA, 1968)

A. C. Sutton, *Western Technology and Soviet Economic Development, 1930–1945* (Stanford, CA, 1973)

G. Swain, *Russia's Civil War* (Stroud, 2000)

T. Swietochowski, *Russian Azerbaijan, 1905–1920. The Shaping of a National Identity in a Muslim Community* (Cambridge, 1985)

K. Sword, *Deportation and Exile. Poles in the Soviet Union, 1939–1948* (London, 1994)

Y. Taniuchi, 'Decision-Making on the Urals-Siberian Method' in J. Cooper *et al.* (eds), *Soviet History, 1917–1953*

W. Taubman, *Khrushchev: The Man and His Era* (London, 2003)

R. Taylor, *The Politics of the Soviet Cinema, 1917–1929* (Cambridge, 1979)

D. Thorniley, *The Rise and Fall of the Soviet Rural Communist Party, 1927–1939* (London, 1988)

N. S. Timasheff, *The Great Retreat. The Growth and Decline of Communism in Russia* (New York, 1946)

V. A. Tishkov, 'Assembleya natsii ili soyuznyi parlament?', *Sovetskaya etnografiya*, no. 3 (1990)

W. J. Tompson, *Khrushchev: A Political Life* (London, 1995)

R. C. Tucker, *Stalin in Power, The Revolution from Above, 1928–1941* (London, 1990)

A. F. Upton, *The Finnish Revolution, 1917–1918* (Minneapolis, MN, 1980)

M. Urban, *The Rebirth of Politics in Russia* (New York, 1997)

R. O. G. Urch, *The Rabbit King of Siberia* (London, 1939)

B. A. Viktorov, 'Geroi iz 37-go', *Komsomol'skaya Pravda* (21 August 1988)

L. Viola, *Peasant Rebels under Stalin: Collectivization and the Culture of Peasant Resistance* (New York, 1996)

D. A. Volkogonov, *Lenin: politicheskii portret*, vols 1–2 (Moscow, 1994)

D. A. Volkogonov, *Stalin: Trimf i tragediya*, vols 1–2 (Moscow, 1989)

O. Volobuev and S. Kuleshov, *Ochishchenie. Istoriya i perestroika. Publitsisticheskie zametki* (Moscow, 1989)

P. V. Volobuev, *Ekonomicheskaya politika Vremennogo pravitel'stva* (Moscow, 1962)

M. Voslensky, *Nomenklatura: The Anatomy of the Soviet Ruling Class* (London, 1984)

R. A. Wade, *The Russian Search for Peace, February–October 1917* (Stanford, CA, 1969)

K. Wädekin, 'Agriculture' in M. McCauley (ed.), *The Soviet Union under Gorbachev*

P. Waldron, *Between Two Revolutions: Stolypin and the Politics of Renewal in Russia* (London, 1997)

P. Waldron, *Governing Tsarist Russia* (London, 2007)

P. Waldron, 'States of Emergency: Autocracy and Extraordinary Legislation, 1881–1917', *Revolutionary Russia*, no. 1 (1995)

M. Walker, *The Cold War* (London, 1994)

R. Walker, 'Marxism-Leninism as Discourse: The Politics of the Empty Signifier and the Double Bind', *British Journal of Political Science*, no. 2 (1989)

C. Ward, *Russia's Cotton Workers and the New Economic Policy. Shop-Floor Culture and State Policy, 1921–1929* (Cambridge, 1990)

S. and B. Webb, *Soviet Communism: A New Civilisation?* (London, 1935)

A. Weiner, '*Déjà Vu* All Over Again: Prague Spring, Rumanian Summer and Soviet Autumn on the Soviet Western Frontier', *Contemporary European History*, no. 2 (2006)

A. Weiner, 'The Empires Pay a Visit: Gulag Returnees, East European Rebellions and Soviet Frontier Politics', *Journal of Modern History* (June 2006)

A. Weiner, *Making Sense of War: The Second World War and the Fate of the Bolshevik Revolution* (New Haven, CT, 2002)

M. Weitzman, 'Industrial Production' in A. Bergson and H. S. Levine (eds), *The Soviet Economy: Towards the Year 2000*

S. G. Wheatcroft, 'The Balance of Grain Production and Utilisation in

Russia before and during the Revolution' (unpublished research paper, University of Birmingham, 1982)

S. G. Wheatcroft, 'More Light on the Scale of Repression and Excess Mortality in the Soviet Union in the 1930s', *Soviet Studies*, no. 2 (1990)

S. G. Wheatcroft and R. W. Davies, 'Agriculture' in R. W. Davies *et al.* (eds), *The Economic Transformation of the Soviet Union*

S. G. Wheatcroft and R. W. Davies, 'Population' in R. W. Davies *et al.* (eds), *The Economic Transformation of the Soviet Union*

S. G. Wheatcroft, R. W. Davies and J. Cooper, 'Soviet Industrialisation Reconsidered: Some Preliminary Considerations about Economic Developments between 1926 and 1941', *Economic History Review*, no. 2 (1986)

A. White, *Democratisation in Russia under Gorbachev, 1985–1991: The Birth of a Voluntary Sector* (London, 1999)

H. White, 'The Provisional Government and the Problem of Power in the Provinces, March to October 1917' (Oxford conference paper, January 1982)

H. White, 'The Urban Middle Class' in R. Service (ed.), *Society and Politics in the Russian Revolution*

S. White, *After Gorbachev* (Cambridge, 1993)

S. White, *Britain and the Bolshevik Revolution, A Study in the Politics of Diplomacy, 1920–1924* (London, 1979)

S. White, *Political Culture and Soviet Politics* (London, 1979)

S. White, R. Rose and I. McAllister, *How Russia Votes* (London, 1997)

S. Whitefield, 'Culture, Experience and State Identity: A Survey-Based Analysis of Russians, 1995–2003' in S. Whitefield (ed.), *Political Culture and Post-Communism*

S. Whitefield, *Industrial Power and the Soviet State* (Oxford, 1993)

S. Whitefield, 'Political Cleavages and Post-Communist Politics', *Annual Review of Political Science*, no. 5 (2002)

S. Whitefield (ed.), *Political Culture and Post-Communism* (London, 2005)

S. Whitefield, 'Social Responses to Reform in Russia' in D. Lane (ed.), *Russia in Transition* (London, 1995)

A. Wilson, *Virtual Politics: Faking Democracy in the Post-Soviet World* (London, 2005)

R. Wortman, *Scenarios of Power: Myth and Ceremony in Russian Monarchy*, vol. 2, *From Alexander II to the Abdication of Nicholas II* (Princeton, NJ, 2000)

A. H. Wildman, *The End of The Russian Imperial Army*, vol. 1: *The Old Army and the Soldiers' Revolt, March–April 1917* (Princeton, NJ, 1980)

M. Wyman, *Public Opinion in Post-Communist Russia* (London, 1997)

V. E. Yesipov, 'Povsednevnost' ekonomiki i Rossii' in B. A. Starkov (ed.), *Rosssiiskaya povsednevnost' 1921–1944 gg.: novye podkhody*

E. Zaleski, *Stalinist Planning for Economic Growth, 1933–1952* (London, 1980)

V. N. Zemskov, 'Prinuditel'nye migratsii iz Pribaltiki v 1940–1950 gg', *Otechestvennye arkhivy*, no. 1 (1993)

E. Yu. Zubkova, *Obshchestvo i reformy, 1945–1964* (Moscow, 1993)

Index

HISTORY

[illegible]

ead more

PENGUIN HISTORY

THE WHISPERERS: PRIVATE LIFE IN STALIN'S RUSSIA
ORLANDO FIGES

The Russian language has two words for a 'whisperer' …
Shepchushchii: somebody who whispers out of fear of being overheard
And *sheptun*: a person who informs or whispers behind people's backs

They derive from the Stalin years, when one wrong word could have you incarcerated, exiled or killed … and a whole society was made of whisperers.

Orlando Figes' moving and powerful book illuminates as never before the hidden histories of the ordinary people who lived under Stalin's tyranny.

Drawing on hundreds of private family archives concealed in secret drawers and under mattresses in homes across Russia, and on countless interviews with survivors, Orlando Figes recreates the maze in which people found themselves: a world of terrible moral choices and compromises, where an unwitting wrong turn could either destroy a family or, perversely, later save it. Yet where, amid all this, love, creativity and family resilience somehow managed to defy the state's values – and humanity survived.

'One of the most unforgettable books I have ever read … a celebration of family love in an epoch of hellish cruelty … now in this book these righteous heroes have their rightful memorial' Simon Sebag Montefiore, *Mail on Sunday*

'This is a heart-rending book … its importance cannot be overestimated' Antony Beevor, *The Times*

PENGUIN HISTORY

RUSSIA'S WAR
RICHARD OVERY

In the course of human history, there has probably never been a more terrible place than Eastern Europe between 1941 and 1945.

Estimates of Soviet military and civilian deaths in the period now stand at more than 25 million. In *Russia's War*, Richard Overy re-creates the Soviet Union's apocalyptic struggle against Germany from the point of view of the troops and of the ordinary people.

'Everything is deftly handled – from the German-Soviet pact to the Yalta Conference, from Babi-Yar to the Katyn massacre – without holding up the sweeping narrative…It is the best concise account in English of the war on Soviet soil' Orlando Figes, *The Times*

'Overy is a first-class military historian … He writes concisely and says what he means to say… Now, we have an authoritative British account that understands both sides, without illusions' Norman Stone, *Spectator*

'A dramatic and exciting tale … His set-piece descriptions of such visions of Hell as Stalingrad, the 900 day siege of Leningrad and the crucial battle of Kursk are as fascinating as they are horrifying' Alan Judd, *Sunday Times*

'Excellent … Overy tackles this huge, complex and multi-faceted story with the vital gifts of clarity and brevity' Antony Beevor, *Literary Review*

PENGUIN HISTORY

GULAG: A HISTORY ANNE APPLEBAUM

'Important and moving … a terrifying and unforgettable story' Antony Beevor

'Terrifying, searing … one of the great untold stories of the twentieth century … a triumph' Richard Overy, *Sunday Telegraph*

'A magisterial study that brings to life the hell of Russia's Gulags … it moves as much as it shocks' Simon Sebag Montefiore, *Daily Telegraph*

THE COMING OF THE THIRD REICH RICHARD J. EVANS

'Monumental … gripping … the definitive account for our time' Andrew Roberts, *Daily Telegraph*

'Impressive … perceptive … humane … the most comprehensive history in any language of the disastrous epoch of the Third Reich' Ian Kershaw, author of *Hitler*

NATASHA'S DANCE: A CULTURAL HISTORY OF RUSSIA
ORLANDO FIGES

'Awe-inspiring … *Natasha's Dance* has all the qualities of an epic tragedy' Frances Welsh, *Mail on Sunday*

Orlando Figes's enthralling, richly evocative history has been heralded as a literary masterpiece on Russia, the lives of those who have shaped its culture, and the enduring spirit of a people.

EMPIRE: HOW BRITAIN MADE THE MODERN WORLD
NIALL FERGUSON

'The most brilliant British historian of his generation … Ferguson examines the roles of "pirates, planters, missionaries, mandarins, bankers and bankrupts" in the creation of history's largest empire … he writes with splendid panache … and a seemingly effortless, debonair wit' Andrew Roberts, *The Times*

'Thrilling … an extraordinary story' *Daily Mail*

read more 

PENGUIN HISTORY

FATEFUL CHOICES
IAN KERSHAW

'Powerfully argued ... important ... this book actually alters our perspective of the Second World War' Andrew Roberts

In 1940 the world was on a knife-edge.

The hurricane of events that marked the opening of the Second World War meant that anything could happen. For the aggressors there was no limit to their ambitions; for their victims a new Dark Age beckoned. Over the coming months their fates would be determined. In Fateful Choices Ian Kershaw re-creates the ten critical decisions taken between May 1940, when Britain chose not to surrender, and December 1941, when Hitler decided to destroy Europe's Jews, showing how these choices would recast the entire course of history.

'A compelling re-examination of the conflict … Kershaw displays here those same qualities of scholarly rigour, careful argument and sound judgement that he brought to bear so successfully in his life of Hitler' Richard Overy

'How fortunate that it is Ian Kershaw bringing his immense knowledge and clarity of thought to the task … brilliantly explained … an immensely wise book' Anthony Beevor